The Immigration Crisis

The Immigration Crisis

Nativism, Armed Vigilantism, and the Rise of a Countervailing Movement

ARMANDO NAVARRO

ALTAMIRA
PRESS

A Division of
ROWMAN & LITTLEFIELD PUBLISHERS, INC.
Lanham • Boulder • New York • Plymouth, UK

AʟᴛᴀMɪʀᴀ Pʀᴇss
A division of Rowman & Littlefield Publishers, Inc.
A wholly owned subsidary of The Rowman & Littlefield Publishing Group, Inc.
4501 Forbes Boulevard, Suite 200
Lanham, MD 20706
www.altamirapress.com

Estover Road
Plymouth PL6 7PY
United Kingdom

British Library Cataloguing in Publication Information Available

Library of Congress Cataloguing-in-Publication Data

Navarro, Armando, 1941–
  The immigration crisis : nativism, armed vigilantism, and the rise of a countervailing
movement / Armando Navarro.
     p. cm.
  ISBN-13: 978-0-7591-1208-7 (cloth : alk. paper)
  ISBN-10: 0-7591-1208-8 (cloth : alk. paper)
  ISBN-13: 978-0-7591-1209-4 (pbk. : alk. paper)
  ISBN-10: 0-7591-1209-6 (pbk. : alk. paper)
  ISBN-13: 978-0-7591-1236-0 (electronic)
  ISBN-10: 0-7591-1236-3 (electronic)
  1. United States—Emigration and immigration. 2. United States—Emigration and
immigration—History. 3. United States—Emigration and immigration—Government
policy. 4. Social movements—United States. 5. Nativism. 6. Vigilantes—United States.
I. Title.

  JV6465.N38 2009
  304.8'73072—dc22   2008020732

⊗™ The paper used in this publication meets the minimum requirements of American
National Standard for Information Sciences—Permanence of Paper for Printed Library
Materials, ANSI/NISO Z39.48-1992.

Gracias Maria Anna por tu apoyo y tu acompañamiento en la lucha de nuestro pueblo y especialmente por tu cariño.

Contents

Preface

As the twenty-first century began, the United States (U.S.) was entangled in a political imbroglio over the issue of immigration, which this book will address, as indicated in its main title, *The Immigration Crisis*. It is important to note that my work builds on the plenitude of many fine works on the subject of immigration. The central thrust of my book is rooted in the history of this nation-state's "immigration experience." From the time of the first settlement in the English colony of Jamestown in 1607 to the present, immigration is the one policy issue that has been an integral and driving force of the country's political and economic history. Maldwyn Allen Jones in his major work *American Immigration* wrote, "Immigration, which was America's historic *raison d'etre*, has been the most persistent and the most pervasive influence in her development. The whole history of the United States during . . . four centuries has been molded by successive waves of immigrants who responded to the lure of the New World and whose labors, together with those of their descendents, have transformed and almost empty continent into the world's most powerful nation."[1]

Echoing Jones's words, historian Oscar Handlin wrote in his work *The Uprooted: The Epic Story of the Great Migration That Made the American People*, "Once I thought to write a history of immigrants in America. Then I discovered that the immigrants were American history." [2] His powerful words pervade not only the country's "immigration experience," but also the country's historical folklore, which is predicated on a notion of inclusion. It exemplifies the truism that with the exception of the native peoples who were the continent's first migrants and today comprise a mere one percent of the country's population, 99 percent of the country's population are descendants of immigrants. In book after book, he maintains that the U.S. is a composite of all the peoples of the world. In this classic work he also argues that because immigrants were socio-economically at the bottom, their presence allowed existent native-born groups upward mobility. Therefore, their absence reduced opportunities for mobility for nonimmigrant groups. Quite prophetically, he also prognosticated that migrants from Latin America would replace those from Europe.

Another scholar, Thomas Muller, in his important work *Immigrants and the American City*, captured important questions about the immigration debate. He reminds his readers that the country's immigration experience from its very genesis has been wrought with inherent tensions and conflicting perceptions of immigrants. He wrote, "For centuries, nations receiving immigrants have experienced a fundamental tension. On one hand, governments and business interests generally welcome [immigrants] for the economic benefits they can generate. On the other hand, a large influx of foreigners can be highly disruptive, weakening a nation's sense of cohesiveness." [3] He concedes and aptly demonstrates that immigrants have been a vital force in creating the economic and social vitality of the country's "gateway cities." He also, however, acknowledges that they unleashed political and socioeconomic conditions, such as nativist-inspired immigration restriction laws and middle-class flight to the suburbs that contributed to their deterioration as urban centers after the 1920s.

Several other scholars have written excellent works that have also examined the country's immigration experience. J. Hector St. John Crevecoeur, himself an immigrant from France, in his memorable account *Letters from an American Farmer*, wrote from a Eurocentric perspective, "What then is the American, this new man? He is either a European, or the descendent of a European, hence that strange mixture of blood, which you will find in no other country."[4] Carl Wittke, in his book *We Who Built America: The Saga of the Immigrant*, like Crevecoeur and Handlin, postulates and adulates that the U.S.'s unique mix of peoples were northern European. He diminishes, however, the importance of the southern and central Europeans. Worst, he barely mentions Asians, Mexicanos, Latinos, Blacks, or native peoples in the building of the U.S., negating the significance of their contributions. John Bodnar's *The Transplanted: A History of Immigrants in Urban America* challenged several of Handlin's assumptions and claimed that Handlin's conclusions were not free from Eurocentric biases. Like others, he rooted the U.S. immigration experience to Europe, specifically to that of England. Again, people of color were not treated historically with importance.

The most recent work on the history of the U.S. immigration experience is the voluminous 721-page work by Paul Spickard, entitled *Almost All Aliens: Immigration, Race, and Colonialism in American History and Identity*. His work builds on two generations of scholars, historians of immigration and more particularly of ethnic studies. His historiographical approach incorporates race, ethnicity, and colonialism to the study of the immigration experience. It breaks away from what he calls the European-dominated "Ellis Island paradigm," which embraces the assimilation model, not because it is wrong, but because it obscures rather than clarifies the whole of immigration experience. He strives to be inclusive, to look at the whole of the immigration experiences of other peoples, such as people of color. He goes beyond the idea of merely explaining how immigrants adapted culturally to the white Anglo-Saxon Protestant (WASP) ethos. Using a periodization approach, he examines comprehensively the historical narrative of the immigration experience from the early 1600s to 2004. In his epilogue he explores some of the events that further impacted it up to 2006, such as the great "migrant mobilizations."

Since the 1980s several works have been produced that are profoundly nativist, xenophobic, anti-immigrant, and even racist in their content and arguments. One such influential work was Peter Brimelow's *Alien Nation: Common Sense about America's Immigration Disaster*. In this work the author wages a major attack on immigration. From his perspective, the country is facing an immigration disaster that began with the passage of the Immigration Act of 1965, which rebuked the hegemony of European immigration and shifted it to México, Latin America, and Asia. He zealously embraced a "Eurocentric" posture predicated on the WASP ethos that is hypercritical of the so-called racial/ethnic transformation that had turned the U.S. into a multicultural, multiethnic, and multilingual "Alien Nation." He denigrates the new immigrants for being different ethnically from the old and argues that they are an economic burden on U.S. taxpayers and that they lower the country's standard of living. George J. Borjas's book *Heaven's Door* is another extremist nativist polemic attack from an economic perspective. He analyzes immigrants' skills, national origins, welfare use, economic mobility, and impact on the labor market, and the rise of de facto ethnic segregation. Otis L. Graham Jr., who wrote *Unguarded Gates: A History of America's Immigration Crisis*, examines the historical immigration experience from the 1880s to the impact of 9/11 in 2001. He looks at the pressures immigration has brought, the policy debates and choices, and how immigration is changing the country and warns of its myriad of consequences.

Between 2002 and 2007 with the escalation of the immigration crisis a number of "ultrazealot nativist" rhetorical works were published. Not only were they anti-immigrant, but they were specifically virulently anti-Méxicano and Latino. The common thread that binds them is that immigration is perceived in the context of a deliberate invasion of the U.S. from México. The most prolific writer is Patrick Buchanan, an extremist populist nativist journalist/television commentator and former presidential candidate, whose nativist works include: *The Death of the West* (2002), *State of Emergency* (2006), and his latest, *Day of Reckoning* (2007). All three works resonate with an ominous impending message of the "decline of western civilization, especially that of the U.S.," which in great part he attributes to undocumented immigration. His nativist rhetoric panders to the fears of U.S. Whites with his xenophobic arguments that Whites are under siege by the invasion of migrants from México and Latin America. He calls it the "re-Conquista," which denotes the demographic takeover by Mexicans of the Southwest. Another salient argument of his is that the preceding is exacerbated by White women's low birthrates, versus that of Latinas, who have the highest. In his three works he alleges polemically that white-oriented cultural hegemony is under attack and warns that the country is becoming increasingly a multicultural society. Finally, he makes the ominous prediction that such an egregious trend, if not reversed, will result in the country's "balkanization" (breakup). His prescription to stop the preceding impending disaster is severe border security and enforcement measures, passage of restrictionist laws, and a concerted push for assimilation of the country's immigrants and migrants.

A premiere political scientist from Harvard, Samuel Huntington, in his work *Who Are We?* (2004), buttressed many of Buchanan's arguments. He too threateningly warned his readers about the egregious impact of Mexicano- and Latino-dominated immigration to the U.S. He argues that culturally it is a threat to the hegemony of what he calls the "creed" or WASP ethos. If not halted, he contends, it threatens to transform the U.S. into a "culturally bi-furcated Anglo-Hispanic nation with two national languages."[5] Another scholar, Victor Davis Hanson, in his nativist work *Mexifornia*, like Buchanan and Huntington, buttresses the argument of the re-Conquista. He applies it, however, to California and argues about its "re-Mexicanization." He warns that if this demographic phenomenon is unchecked, it could alter the southwest and the country as a whole. He attributes it to the U.S.'s hemorrhaging borders. He too alleges that the country's cultural failure is in not assimilating the migrant masses from the south.

Journalists and activists too weigh in on the anti-immigrant debate. Journalist Jon E. Dougherty, in his book *Illegals* (2004), argues about the imminent threat presented by the invasion from México and Latin America. Using 9/11 as a buttress, he warns of the looming terrorist threat coming through the porous border. Nativist activist Jim Gilchrist coauthored the book *Minutemen* (2006) with nativist scholar Jerome R. Corsi. The nativist militia called the Minuteman Project rose in 2005 in the desert of South Arizona and then went nationwide. The authors explain that the Minuteman Project, as a patriots' militia, are a re-action to the country's failed immigration policies that have put the country's sovereignty in jeopardy due to México's and Latin America's invasion of the U.S. Journalist Daniel Sheehy, in his book *Fighting Immigration Anarchy* (2006), re-inforces and expands on many of the same nativist arguments made by Dougherty. His work, however, examines some of the white nativist efforts, such as the militias, being initiated to stop the invasion and expose the government's so-called reckless, ineffective, and failed immigration policies.

No review of the literature on immigration would be complete, if mention was not made of the number of other scholars mainly Mexicano/Latinos who have from their historical vantage point written on some aspect of the "Mexicano migration experience." Juan Ramon Garcia's *Operation Wetback* (1980) provides an in-depth study of the mass deportation of Méxicano undocumented workers during Operation Wetback in the mid-1950s. Francisco E. Balderrama and Raymond Rodriguez's *Decade of Betrayal* (1995) is a comprehensive study on the Depression's repatriation and deportation of Mexicanos from the U.S. back to México. David Gutierrez's *Walls and Mirrors* (1995) traces the history of Mexican migration linked to issues of identity and citizenship from 1848 to the 1970s. His epilogue provides a cursory analysis through the 1980s and early 1990s. Oscar Martinez's three works, *Troublesome Border* (1988; revised edition 2006), *Border People* (1994), and *Mexican-Origin People in the United States* (2001), all focus on various aspects of the history of the border and immigration. Louis De Sapio and Rodolfo O. de la Garza, in their book *Making Americans, Remaking America* (1998), present a historical overview of immigration and the public policy and legal debates that have accompanied it. An excellent overview of the more current aspect of the immigration crisis is Justin Akers Chacon and Mike Davis's *No One Is Illegal* (2006). They examine the politics and activities of ultranativist militia forces and their violence along the cactus curtain along with the reaction of pro-migrant rights groups and activists. Last but not least, is historian Rodolfo Acuña's new book, *Corridors of Migration* (2007), that explores the history of Mexican workers and their families from seventeenth-century Chihuahua to twentieth-century Arizona and California. He traces their roots of labor activism vis-à-vis mining and agricultural strikes through to their experiences when migrating to the U.S.

The Study's Historical Immigration Focus

This work, *The Immigration Crisis: Nativism, Armed Vigilantism, and the Rise of a Countervailing Mass Movement* provides an in-depth political historical analysis of the U.S.'s "immigration experience" from the arrival of the first human beings from Asia to the Western Hemisphere some 30,000 years ago to the present immigration crisis in 2007. In addition, it concurrently explores the Mexicano migration experience from México to Aztlán and the U.S. as a whole. As of 2008, no other work on the topic of the country's immigration political history is as current, comprehensive, and controversial as is this study. It is current because its epilogue examines the status of the immigration crisis as of the first three months of 2008. Its comprehensiveness is further based upon a rather complete picture of the U.S. immigration experience from the inclusion of the migration of native peoples to the continent, Spanish colonialism and immigration, Northern European immigration, African migration to the English colonies,

Asian and southern/central European immigration, and lastly, from a historical perspective, the impact of México's history in the creation of the migrant exodus to the U.S.

Moreover, the historical journey of both the U.S. immigrant experience and Mexicano migration to Aztlán and the U.S. is recorded and directed by the book's organization, which uses periodization as a method. Several historical cycles or stages are developed to explain and analyze them both. The historical circumstances, events, laws, ideas, leaders, and organizations that have shaped each cycle are also examined. A unique aspect of my work is that because it is the most current, none of the most recently published above cited works cover such topics as the rise of armed rancher vigilantes, nativist militias, the Minuteman Project, hate groups, and the anti-immigration organizations that emerged or were active especially from 1999 to 2007; nor the statistical Mexicano/Latino demographic profile from 1848 to 2007; nor the Mexicano and Latino pro-migrant rights response to the aforementioned; nor the rise and decline of the unprecedented Movimiento Pro-Migrante's "great migrant mobilizations" of 2006 through 2007. Furthermore, few works provide the scope of analysis or detail of the various federal immigration laws passed or even attempted from 1790 to the failed Senate immigration reform effort of 2007. In particular, also studied is what I call the "nativist legislative surge" of 2004 through 2007 that produced at the federal, state, and local levels a plethora of anti-immigrant laws, initiatives, and ordinances.

Adding to its scholarliness are the innumerable topics examined that have been researched at length, using a combination of primary and secondary sources. In reference to the former, numerous documents, letters, minutes, personal notes, press releases, and reports were used. A number are in my possession in my private archives. As to the latter, innumerable works, journal articles, and newspaper and magazine articles are cited. Methodologically, for chapters 6 through 13, I employed "participant-observation" as a method. In some instances, I participated in leadership and observer roles in several of the immigration events or issues examined. I mention this, because my role as an advocate for immigrant/migrant rights has not prevented me from seeking to be as objective as I possibly can in order to maintain high scholarly standards. It is also important to note that this work is written in a style that seeks clarity and is readable by most people. This means that I have sought to avoid the use of complex esoteric language or terms that all too often pervade scholarly works.

It is important to note that I have a forty-year history of organizing and activism, which began when I was an undergraduate student at Chaffey College in 1968, during the heyday of the Chicano movement that continued incessantly through my undergraduate and graduate years of study and my professional years as a scholar and organizer-activist to the present. Among the many change issues that I have dealt with is immigration. Since 1977, it has been a major focus of my many organizing efforts and activism. Since 2000, as founder and coordinator of National Alliance for Human Rights, a network of activists, community leaders, and organizations committed to the advancement of human rights, social justice, and empowerment of Mexicanos and Latinos, it has been my main preoccupation. My myriad of organizing experiences as an advocate for immigration change adds to the strength of the work's analysis.

I do acknowledge some ideological biases across the board. I am critical of capitalism's capacity to create a prosperous and democratic society. I put my politics on the table and I do not pull any punches. As a political scientist, I speak with integrity, conviction, and equally important, from a knowledge base and experience perspective few academicians have. Embracing an "organic intellectual" role, I have sought to accompany my people, Mexicanos and Latinos, in their often tumultuous, conflictive, and difficult struggles for social change and self-determination. This is reflected in my writings that include with this work, five books, several articles, reports, change-oriented strategic plans, and countless speeches that I have given, paper presentations, and several delegations that I have led to México, Cuba, Central America, and, in 2008, Venezuela.

What makes this work different is its conceptual framework. What will be undoubtedly considered by some as polemical and ideologically normative is actually an etiological explanation of the country's immigration crisis. My work does not excuse or hide what is propelling it. With some exceptions of progressive scholars and activists, too many who today write about immigration do it from a rather myopic or micro neoliberal-biased policy perspective that focuses on its symptoms rather than its main source, the economic system. Driven by years of research coupled with my organizing activism on the subject, my perspective on the matter is more holistic and macro-oriented. It lucidly asserts that the U.S. immigration crisis at its core is a product of two interrelated phenomena, the first macro-oriented, the second micro, which are:

1. At the macro level, the "immigration crisis" is a result of the "economic crisis," which itself is a product of the myriad of egregious contradictions (for example, push and pull forces) inherent ideologically to the globalization of capital and capitalism, as reflected in neoliberal economies globally, but particularly those of the U.S., México, and Latin America.

2. At the micro level, the "immigration crisis" is being exacerbated by the Latino "demographic transformation" endemic to the United States, characterized by the "re-Mexicanization of Aztlán" and the Latinoization and "browning" that in great part are driven by the migrant exodus from México, Central America,

and the rest of Latin America in that order, which, in turn, has engendered a resurgent ultranativist zealotry.

Overview of Book Chapters

The book is organized into an introductory chapter followed by thirteen chapters and an epilogue. The introductory chapter, entitled "The Immigration Crisis," provides the theoretical foundation for the rest of the study. It examines the "globalization of capital," in short, capitalism as being at the heart of the immigration crisis. It makes the argument that the very nature of global capitalism has created a worldwide economic crisis because of its capital accumulation, transnational corporations' voracious appetite for profit via a dependency and addiction to cheap labor (human capital), and control of markets and resources. The U.S., México, and Latin America are inextricably linked and are immersed in their own immigration crises, which are characterized by a number of "systemically" produced "push and pull" factors. Lastly, it analyzes the "Latino demographic transformation" from the perspective that it has further exacerbated the economy-driven immigration crisis by threatening to relegate Whites to a new minority status throughout Aztlán and inevitably the nation, which has fostered a nationwide nativist resurgent reaction.

Chapter 1, "Exodus to the New World and the U.S. Immigration Experience," examines the continent's immigration history from the first migration to Mesoamerica from Asia in 30,000 BC to the rise and decline of the Olmec, Maya, Toltec, and Aztec, and Incan civilizations. Various themes are looked at that include the arrival of the Spanish and Portuguese to the so-called New World, especially Spanish colonialism and its expansion to Aztlán; the rise of México as an independent nation; and the historical episodes that led to the loss of Aztlán and its occupation in 1848 by the U.S. The primary focus, however, of this chapter is the study of the northern European exodus, starting with the genesis of the U.S.'s "immigration experience" at Jamestown in 1607 and the WASP ethos that ensued, which impacted culturally the various immigration stages of the 1600s and 1700s. In addition, the rise of the First Wave (1840–1860), Second Wave (1880s–1920s), the passage of nativist restrictionist laws (1875–1924), and the immigration lull that pervaded the Depression are also studied.

Chapters 2 to 5 focus on the migrant exodus mainly from México and Latin America into the U.S. from 1876 to 1999. Specifically, chapter 2, "U.S. Occupation of Aztlan and Rise of México's Migrant Exodus," explores historical forces, from the conclusion of the so-called U.S. war on México (1846–1848); the relegation of Mexicanos to an "occupied and colonized" status; México's precarious political history (1849–1875); the rise of the Porfiriato (1876–1910); the Mexican Revolution (1910–1920); the violent aftermath (1920–1929); and the migrant exodus (1900–1940) and its implications, which "jump-started" the Mexicano reoccupation of Aztlán. Finally, a demographic analysis of the migrant exodus from 1900 to 1940 and the effects of the Great Depression, meaning the repatriation and deportation of Mexicanos, are also dealt with.

Chapter 3, "Era of the Bracero Programs and Resurgent Nativisim (1942–1964)," looks at World War II's impact on Mexicanos, their contributions, and the paradoxical issues they confronted; the guest worker-oriented Bracero Program of 1942 to 1964; the post-WWII revitalization of the migrant exodus; the passage of restrictionist immigration policies and laws; the nativist-inspired events, such as Operation Wetback; and the demographic aspects of the re-Mexicanization of Aztlán are explored.

Chapter 4, "Re-Mexicanization of Aztlán and Immigration Reform Intensify (1965–1989)," examines the rise of the country's third great wave of immigration; the growth of the migrant exodus; the intensification of the re-Mexicanization of Aztlán and rise of the Latinoization or "browning" of the country; the resurgence of nativist politics and laws, for example, Simpson-Mazzoli and IRCA; and the Mexicano response to nativist politics and immigration reform.

Chapter 5, "Decade of Growing Nationism, Xenophobia and Militarization of the Cactus Curtain (1990–1999)," looks at the continued demographic growth of the migrant exodus and its impact on the re-Mexicanization of Aztlán and Latinoization of the U.S.; the "nativist political war" against undocumented migration; the passage of anti-immigrant initiatives in California, for example, Propositions 187, 209, and 227; México's economic crisis; impact of the passage of NAFTA; militarization of the Cactus Curtain; and Mexicano/Latino resistance to resurgent nativism.

Chapters 6, 7, and 8 are related in that all three deal with aspects of the rise of armed rancher vigilantes and nativist militias, the Minuteman Project (MP), and innumerable nativist hate groups that were active from 1999 to 2007. Chapter 6, "Arizona's Nationist Armed Rander Vigilantes and Militias (1999–2004)" studies the demographics of the period, circumstances, events, personalities, and the rise and activities of the armed rancher vigilantes and nativist militias in southern Arizona from 1999 to 2004. Chapter 7, "Minuteman Project and The Nativist Anti-Migrant Movement (2005–2007)," explores its genesis and formation, and presents a profile of its leadership, organization, beliefs, resources, border activities, and growth into the National Anti-Immigrant Movement (NAMM). The circumstances that have and are contributing to its "self-destruction" are also dealt with. Chapter 8, "Militias, Anti-Immigrant Hate Groups and Nativism on the Rise (2005–2007)" looks at the escalation of the migrant exodus and Latino demographic transformation; myriad of old and new nativist organizations, militias, and hate groups; and nativist intellectuals and media that are active in the anti-immigrant political arena.

Chapters 9 and 10, using a case study format, explore the various aspects of the Mexicano and Latino response, particularly that of the National Alliance for Human Rights (NAHR), to the armed rancher vigilantism, nativist militias, immigration raids, and Minuteman Project from 2000 to 2007. Chapter 9, "Mexicanos Respond to the Rancher Vigilante and Militia Crisis (2000–2005)" as a case study examines NAHR's several rancher vigilante and antimilitia organizing responses and activities via the sending of a number of delegations from California to southern Arizona, the border area, and México. Chapter 10, "NAHR's Struggle Against Raids and Minuteman Project (2004–2005)" documents the countervailing tactics and activities initiated by NAHR against border patrol raids in Southern California during 2004 and its response and countervailing organizing activities against the Minuteman Project in 2005.

The book's last three chapters are also interrelated. Chapter 11, "The Restrictionist Nativist Legislative Surge (2004–2007)" investigates the politics, plethora of proposed and passed laws, initiatives, and ordinances that characterized the "nativist legislative surge" at all levels of government, that is, local, state, and federal. Chapter 12, "Rise of the Cantervailing Movimiento Pro-Migrante (2006)," written in a quasi–case study format, explores the circumstances and climate of change that contributed to its dynamic rise in 2006, which includes, from a social movement theoretical perspective, an analysis of the forces that impacted its rise as a mass movement. It provides an extensive look at the plethora of marches, coalitions, personalities, and events that impelled its "mobilization contagion." Lastly, chapter 13, "Decline of MPM and its Mobilizations (2006–2007)" looks at the manifold factors, especially the rise and pervasiveness of a climate of fear, other conditions, and forces that contributed to its precipitous decline. The various failed mobilizations that were held and the events and efforts that ensued designed to revitalize it are examined.

Lastly, the epilogue, entitled "The Immigration Crisis: What Now?" summarizes my conclusions and analysis on the current status of the "immigration crisis." It delves into the impact of the globalization of capital into its present and future implications to the United States and that of México, Central America, and the rest of Latin America. The future demographic implications are studied as well as the question of what needs to be done to solve or at least mitigate its egregious multiple effects.

Acknowledgments

It is important to acknowledge the excellent feedback I received from a number of contemporary scholars, which contributed to improving the quality and analysis of this work. My appreciation goes to historian Carlos Cortez, historian Mario Garcia, historian Ignacio Garcia, and political scientist Jose Angel Gutierrez, who reviewed for publication purposes two of my chapters. To them I say graciously, gracias.

More particularly, I want to acknowledge the work of Maria Anna Gonzales, my partner and companion of several years, who has accompanied me in my many struggles for social change and has assisted in the editing of my several published previous works. Her meticulous editing of this manuscript dramatically improved its readability and more importantly helped ensure that the essence of my thought was put forth in a manner that could be easily read and understood, especially by those who will be charged as change agents in the future.

Introduction:
The Immigration Crisis

The "immigration crisis" that today plagues the United States (U.S.) is inextricably connected to the "globalization of capital." México, the rest of Latin America, and the developed and underdeveloped countries of the world are all also impacted by it. It is the globalization of capital that has induced the "economic crises" that permeate most of the world's 192 nation-states, particularly those that ideologically embrace neoliberalism. Its historical roots are deep in the colonial mercantilist history of Great Britain, the rise of the U.S. as a sovereign nation-state in 1776 and the subsequent rapid worldwide expansion of its "industrial revolution" in the nineteenth century, the monopoly of capital in the twentieth century, and by the twenty-first century the globalization phenomenon. Today it is characterized by the migration of millions of undocumented workers from their respective underdeveloped or developing countries to First World countries. They cross the borders of foreign nation-states in their quest to ameliorate their economic, social, and even political status. Thus, in the case of the U.S., today's immigration crisis denotes a prevalent and pervasive fear, particularly among some of the country's white population, that the U.S. is in serious danger of being overwhelmed, if not overrun by migrants from Mexico and the rest of Latin America.

A New World Capital Order: Globalization of Capital

Throughout this work it will be argued that the present immigration crisis is the result of the economic workings of a new world capital order, more specifically, that it is the acuteness of the globalization of capital that has produced the current economic crises. Global economic and social interactions have been an integral part of humanity's development. Trade routes between different parts of the world have existed for thousands of years.[1] Karl Marx and Friedrich Engels wrote about nineteenth-century capitalism that "the bourgeoisie has through its exploitation of the world–market given a cosmopolitan character to production and consumption, we have intercourse in every direction, universal interdependency of nations."[2] Andrew L. Barlow writes that "in the course of the last 500 years, capitalism has organized most of the world's nation-states into the market system, either by enslaving people, transforming them into wage labor, or establishing trade relationships with them."[3]

Globalization marks an entirely new epoch in the world's economic history. Its genesis goes back to European feudalism when it began its outward expansion, which began with the first epoch (1492–1775), the discovery of the so-called New World (i.e., western hemisphere) by the Spanish and English, among other colonial powers. This was during the rise of "mercantilist capitalism," or primitive accumulation. The second epoch (1776–1900) of "industrial capitalism" was a result of the age of revolution (for example, the American Revolution of 1776 and French Revolution of 1789), the forging of the nation-state, Adam Smith's *Wealth of Nations* (the capitalist bible), and the industrial revolution, especially both in England and the U.S. The third epoch (1900–1990s) started during the early part of the twentieth century and gave rise to "monopoly capitalism," which was characterized by imperialism, financial-industrial corporations, intensified world wars among imperialist powers, the rise of the socialist alternative, and the Cold War that ensued. Today in the twenty-first century, the fourth epoch (1990s–2008) of capitalism is referred to as "globalization," highlighted technologically by the microchip, computer, information age, collapse of the Soviet Union, and capital hegemony of Pax Americana.[4]

The term "globalization" came in vogue in both popular and academic circles during the 1980s. In its early context, according to Andrew L. Barlow, it specifically "referred to the increasing capacity of people to rapidly (or instantly) interact with one another anywhere on the planet, to share and analyze information gathered globally, and to take a global perspective as a point of reference in their daily affairs." Because of technological advances, he explains, in science, transportation, and telecommunications, they have affected broadly the interactions of human beings.[5] Scholars differ in its definition and explanations, however, in this work it is used to denote the globalization of capital. Nikos Papastergiad provides an excellent compendium from this perspective of what globalization is: "Globalization has been predominantly associated with the flexible and spatially extended forms of production, the rapid mobility of capital, information and goods, the denationalizing of capital, the deterritorialization of culture, the interpenetration of local communities by global networks, and the dispersal of socio-economic power beyond the Euro-American axis."[6]

Globalization further denotes internationalization, interdependence, and the interconnectedness of functions of capital production and formation; control of markets and resources; spread of communication technology; and the blurring of nation-state boundaries. As a global economic and labor phenomenon, it has facilitated the increased flow of goods, services, people, and ideas through traditional as well as new channels.[7] Globalization of capital recognizes no border and respects no flag and is driven by the acquisition of high profits from low wages.[8] Its salient characteristic, writes John Rapley, is that "globalization is drawing all the world's countries into a single global economy,"[9] which is capitalist.

Some would argue that global capitalism has dialectically assumed the form of "predatory capitalism" or "vulture capitalism," unencumbered by few, if any, controls. The former as explained by Naomi Klein in her recent book, *The Shock Doctrine* refers to the rapid fire corporate re-engineering of societies as a result of "shock." According to Norman D. Livergood, the latter refers to where "capitalism becomes a tyranny in which the moneyed class loots the nation, while the working class suffers from lower wages, higher prices, decreased constitutional liberties, and chronic unemployment."[10] Globalization of capital has become synonymous with the principle of the "free-market system," which is adhered to by the majority of the nation-states of the world that are characterized by devastated and impoverished economies.

Capitalist globalization justifies the continued domination of capital, which at a global scale or scope denotes the ownership of the global "means production and distribution" by transnational capital. Today it has integrated capital and markets and is impelled by the transnationalization of "production" and of capital ownership, which has led to the rise of an international plutocratic bourgeoisie that sits at the zenith of the new world order.[11] At the core of their macro global strategy is capital mobility—the ability to move capital around the world.[12] Globally, capital's hegemony is maintained by its control of international financial institutions, such as the World Bank, World Trade Organization (WTO), International Monetary Fund (IMF), Group of Eight (G8), and a myriad of free trade agreements, for example, the General Agreement on Tariffs and Trade (GATT) and the North American Free Trade Agreement (NAFTA). Paradoxically, while capital is free to transcend borders, NAFTA, for example, explicitly bars free immigration.[13] They form what can be described as a supranational policy arena. Jeremy Brecher and Tim Costello explain their policy impact:

> The policies adopted by these international institutions allowed corporations to lower their costs in several ways. They reduced consumer, environmental, health, labor, and other standards. They

reduced taxes. They facilitated the move to lower wage areas and the threat of such movement. And they encouraged the expansion of markets and the "economies of scale provided by larger-scale production."[14]

The transnational bourgeoisie exercises its class power through two mechanisms. One is the transnational or multinational corporations that are an intrinsic part of global networks that increasingly defy the power and authority of the nation-state and thrive on capital accumulation, in short, insatiable corporate greed. Two, the hegemony of capital allows them to inordinately influence, manipulate, or control nation-states, which are transformed into transmission belts and filtering devices that act to advance the global agenda of capital and create the propitious economic and political conditions for global capital accumulation.[15] Motivated by the voracious drive for profits, their corporate agenda includes monetarism, deregulation, and supply-side economics, in short, promotion of neoliberalism. Their adherence to disaster capitalism, as described by Naomi Klein, translates to laissez-faire (no government intervention) markets of unfettered free trade and "shock doctrine" practices that create public disorientation, which in turn produce policies for privatization, economic deregulation, reduced taxes, and in some cases extremely severe political repression.[16] "The instrumental capacity of the nation-state," writes Manuel Castells, "is decisively undermined by globalization of core economic activities, by globalization of media and electronic communication and by globalization of crime."[17]

The nexus between globalization of capital and immigration is inextricable. Reverend Jessie Jackson, in a speech delivered on May 1, 2006, said about the tie between the two, "Today's mass immigration movement is being driven by globalization of capital—capital that no knows no borders. And a government policy that exports capital, jobs and whole industries in search of the greatest profits and lowest possible wages."[18] Accumulation of capital relies on its voracious quest for a labor pool of exploitable cheap labor. Predicated on a "supply and demand" labor principle, when within a given nation-state the demand for cheap labor cannot be satisfied, the labor shortage is filled by immigrant labor. Governments will also often align with capital and will promote immigration covertly and/or overtly. Their calculation of economic expediency is based upon labor demands by capital. Nation-states' role then is to regulate the flow of labor, thereby controlling the workers themselves. In its most basic form, capitalism, whether in the U.S., México, Latin America, or globally, needs immigration, for it provides it with cheap human capital that it can exploit and make its profit.

Global Migration

The immigration crisis must be understood in the context of a global migratory process resulting from the globalization of capital. The concept of migration is complex and is related to a number of factors and interactions that delineate a process entailing the departure of numbers of people from one space, in this case their native country, to some other space or foreign country in search of better life chances. As an integral part of the immigration process, it simply denotes a movement of people from one place to another. When migration crosses an international frontier it is referred to as "emigration" and "immigration." The former simply means leaving one country while the latter refers to entering another.[19] Nikos Papastergiadis writes that "migration, in its endless motion, surrounds and pervades almost all aspects of contemporary society. . . . the modern world is in a state of flux and turbulence. It is a system in which the circulation of people, resources and information follows multiple paths."[20] As a process migration is not unique to modern times; rather, it is as old as is the history of humanity.

The migration that occurred from Asia to the Western Hemisphere some 30,000 years ago illustrates the longevity of the migratory process. Various theories have developed that explain the migratory process: (1) neoclassical economic; (2) historical-structural; (3) migration systems; and (4) transnational.[21] All four theories derive from the consequences of globalization, but seek to explain different aspects or linkages of it. The neoclassical economic theory has its antecedents in the earliest systematic theory on migration that emerged during the late nineteenth century. It is largely based on statistical laws of migration developed by geographer E. G. Ravenstein. Today it is kept alive by theorists who emphasize tendencies of people to move from densely to sparsely populated areas or from low- to high-income areas or link migrations to fluctuations in the business cycle. As an approach it posits the view that migration is a product of "push and pull" forces. The former are forces or factors that impel people to leave their areas of origin, versus the latter, which are the factors that attract migrants to certain receiving countries. Its unit of analysis derives from the premise that the decision to migrate is an individual decision based upon a cost-benefit analysis and the central concept is that migrants are human capital.[22]

The historical-structural theory of international migration emerged during the 1970s. It has its roots in Marxist political economy and world systems theory. It posits the argument that the unequal distribution of economic and political power in the world is what propels international migration. Migration is perceived as a result of uneven capitalist development that exploits the resources of impoverished countries. In addition, the migratory process mobilizes cheap labor, massively recruits it for capital, and links domination of the core economies of capitalism to those of their underdeveloped periphery.[23]

Migration systems theory attempts to include a wide range of disciplines and seeks a broader perspective that includes various dimensions of the migratory process. Using a more interdisciplinary approach, it argues that migratory movements generally arise from the existence of former links between the sending and receiving countries. The former links could be a result of colonization, political influence, trade, investment, or cultural/familial ties. The basic principle is that the migratory process is a result of interacting macro- and microstructures. The former refers to large-scale institutional factors (i.e., the political economy, interstate relationships, laws, structures, and practices of sending and receiving states to control migration), while the latter includes informal social networks (i.e., family and personal relationships, community ties, etc.), practices, and beliefs of migrants. The two levels are linked or intertwined by a number of intermediate mechanisms, which are referred to as mesostructures, that include certain individuals, groups, or institutions that may take on a mediating role between migrants and political and/or economic institutions.[24]

Transnational theory developed in the 1990s has sought to develop linkages between societies built as a result of migration. With its emphasis on "transnationalism" and "transnational communities" it links the effect of globalization to that of rapid improvement in technologies of transport and communication, which facilitate maintaining close linkages with their areas of origin and circulatory or repeated mobility, in which people migrate regularly between several places where they have economic, social, or cultural linkages. The emphasis is on the building of transnational community, which can transcend and impact the nation-state.

Throughout this work the argument is made that at the core of the country's immigration crisis are the economic crises that are inherent and endemic to the globalization of capital. Intrinsic to it is the aftereffect of its global migratory crisis, which has affected millions of people leaving their native country and migrating to another. The above four examined theories seek to explain this phenomena. For purposes of analysis, this work takes on an eclectic perspective in that it creates a fusion of all four theoretical approaches. It leads with the historical-structural theory that argues that migration at a macro level is the result of uneven capitalist development that produces unequal distribution of wealth and power. But it borrows from neoclassical economic theory that argues that migration is a product of an admixture of "push and pull" factors. The revision is that both are symptomatic of the inherent contradictions that plague capitalism and the unit of analysis becomes systemic, which in turn drives the individual to migrate. The decision to migrate is also influenced by neoclassical economic theory, which is impacted by concurrent interacting macro- and microstructures. Lastly, once a migrant arrives at his or her new space, then transnational theory kicks in, to where his or her linkages are transnational and circulatory.

At the crux and core of the U.S.'s immigration crisis is the migrant exodus, a "transnational" migratory process phenomenon from México, Central America, and the rest of Latin America to the U.S. First, it is a product of the history of the southwest or what is called in this work, Aztlán.[25] For Mexicanos in particular, they did not cross the border, the border crossed them. The historical fact is that prior to the imperialist U.S. War on México (1846–1848), Aztlán was México. México was "forced" to cede some million square miles of its sovereign territory. So for the millions of Mexicanos who migrated from México to the U.S. since the genesis of the migrant exodus in the late 1890s to the present, most do not consider themselves to be in a foreign country. For others, it is perceived as occupied México.[26] Second, from a historical-structural theoretical perspective, the migrant exodus is a product of the economic crisis precipitated by capitalism's systemic inherent contradictions. Third, integrating neoclassical economic theory, it is manifested and impelled by multifarious "push" factors, such as poverty, unemployment, low wages, chronic inequality, a plethora of social problems, political repression, and unmet rising expectations. On the "pull" side from a U.S. perspective, it is primarily a result of the U.S.'s capitalist economy's dependence on and insatiable addiction to flexible, cheap labor for maximization of capital accumulation. Other pull factors include available and accessible transportation systems, migrant family reunification, and especially México and Latin America's geographical proximity to the U.S. Fourth, the preceding three pull factors are illustrative of transnational theory's emphasis on the development of linkages between societies built as a result of the rapid improvement in technologies of transport and communication.

Today's U.S. immigration crisis is fed by the incessant influx of the migrant exodus that has brought millions of Mexicanos, Central Americans, and others from Latin America to the U.S. The term "exodus" is used especially for the impoverished Mexicano migrants in the context that they see their departure from México to the U.S., especially Aztlán, as migrating to an economic promised land of opportunity. Most migrants who make the perilous journey north arrive in the U.S. confused by the lure of the country's immigration experience myth being the incarnate of economic opportunity, freedom, and hope. After all, they believe that for all of its contradictions and problems, the U.S. is the ideal country to begin their quest for a new economic life. Its genesis was the result of México's Porfiriato during the late 1890s. Today the migrant exodus acts as a demographic stimulus force to the re-Mexicanization of Aztlán and the Latinoization or "browning" of the U.S.

Globalization Purveyor of Poverty and Inequality

Today the interconnectedness of the globalization of capitalism has wrought an international economic crisis of unparalleled proportions. The planet in the twenty-first century is plagued by wretched poverty, chronic inequality, and a myriad of severe and egregious social problems, especially global warming, which threatens the survival of the planet. Its manifold contradictions, in particular the preceding, are manifested in the economies of Africa, Asia, Latin America, the Middle East, and other areas of the underdeveloped regions of the world. The developed countries of the First World are not exempt, especially the U.S., from poverty. Today much of the world's population is concentrated in the world's poor countries. Currently some 1.2 billion people live in countries classified by the United Nations as developed; whereas, some 5.5 billion people live in developing and underdeveloped countries. An alarming statistic is that some 35 percent of the latter's population suffer from serious hunger. In some impoverished countries such as in sub-Saharan Africa, the figure climbs to 60 percent.[27] According to Anup Shah, "poverty is the state for the majority of the world's people and nations." In a report entitled "Causes of Poverty," Shah states that half of the world's population, nearly three billion people, live on less than $2 a day (all currency is in U.S. dollars). One billion children or one in two children of the world live in acute poverty. Six hundred and forty million persons live without adequate shelter, 400 million have no access to safe water, 270 million have no access to health care, and 10.6 million died in 2003 before they reached the age of five, which translates to roughly 29,000 children per day. World hunger is increasing in the underdeveloped countries.[28]

While the world globalizes, inequality rapidly increases. The gap between the "haves and have-nots" is widening dramatically in most countries of the world. At the nation-state level, wealth has become concentrated among the G8 and Western industrialized nations, along with several Asian countries. The World Institute for Development Economics Research of the United Nations University produced a study that revealed that worldwide 1 percent of adults in 2000 owned 40 percent of the global assets and that the richest 10 percent of adults accounted for 85 percent of the world's total wealth. The disparity of wealth became quite evident in that the bottom half of the world adult population owned a mere 1 percent of global wealth. The great wealth amassed by some First World countries has been at the expense of Third World countries. Income inequality is greater in the United States than in any of the developed countries. Despite its superpower status, the U.S. is not the world's richest nation. With a GDP (the amount of national income generated per capita) of $44,000 it is third with Luxembourg as the leader with $78, 000; second is Norway with $52, 000.[29]

The economic plight of U.S. workers worsens by the year as a result of offshoring or outsourcing of jobs. Both concepts denote a subcontracting process to a third-party company outside of the U.S. The rationale of such a process is to lower a transnational company's production costs, and maximize use of labor, capital, technology, and resources. William F. Jasper writes, "Out sourcing is merely a reflection of globalization . . . a contemporary illustration of Adam Smith's classical trade principle of 'comparative advantage.'"[30] The exodus of U.S. jobs to the Third World is ultimately motivated by maximization of profits by lowering a firm's costs, especially its labor costs. While U.S. workers make from $15 to $25 or more per hour, exploited foreign workers are paid as low as $0.50 to $1 per hour. México's minimum wage alone is a little over $4 per day.

According to a Hewitt Associates study of personnel executives of 500 companies conducted in 2004, about 45 percent of those surveyed had overseas operations, and 71 percent of the remaining firms planned to outsource jobs in 2005. It reported that the percentage of jobs leaving the U.S. was expected to double by 2008. Transnational corporations favored the following countries for outsourcing: India (60 percent), China (36 percent), México (32 percent), Canada (15 percent), and Ireland (14 percent). Alan S. Blinder, former vice chairman of the Federal Reserve, shocked the outsourcing debate by prognosticating that the number of potential offshore U.S. jobs was somewhere around 42 to 56 million, approximately 30 to 40 percent of all U.S. jobs. Ominously, he further estimated that between 22 to 29 percent of all U.S. jobs would be potentially offshorable within a decade or two.[31] The jobs most frequently outsourced include: information technology (67 percent), followed by customer relations (49 percent), manufacturing (42 percent), and supply chain (41 percent) with an average of 13 percent of jobs expected. Outsourcing of jobs is a by-product of the economic crisis of the globalization of capital, which has created the displacement of domestic workers, unemployment, and nativism directed at migrants and immigrants.

Capitalism's impelled economic crisis has fostered a "global immigration crisis," especially for those advanced economies that during the Cold War were designated the First World, which in the twenty-first century includes the U.S., Europe, Japan, Russia, and the People's Republic of China. Europe is one such region of the world that today is confronted by its own immigration crisis, so severe that ethnic/racial tensions in Germany, France, Great Britain, Italy, and Spain, among others, at times, have turned violent in the past few years. If unabated, the nativist-inspired ethnic/racial conflict and polarization threatens the respective countries' stability, progress, and future. Immigration from the underdeveloped countries of the Third World, mainly North Africa, the Middle East, and Asia, are changing Europe's ethnic makeup.

Suffering from acute labor shortages, European countries such as Germany, Great Britain, France, Italy, and Spain have become dependent on and addicted to the importation of exploitable cheap immigrant labor to sustain their economic growth. These countries have compromised and put in jeopardy from their vantage point their white hegemony by allowing other ethnic/racial groups to immigrate for the sake of meeting their capitalist economies' demand for labor. Globalization of capital and its nexus with immigration have created political, economic, social, and cultural consequences with serious public policy ramifications.[32]

While Europe's population is shrinking many Second and Third World[33] countries of Africa, the Middle East, and Asia are experiencing population explosions. Wave after wave from the Islamic nations of North Africa and the Arab Middle East and Africa's sub-Sahara nations have pounded the shores of Europe's countries, altering their ostensibly all-white ethnic hegemonic societies.[34] In 1999, 500,000 undocumented immigrants emigrated to the European Union alone, a ten-fold increase since 1993.[35] Great Britain in 2000 took in a total of 185,000 immigrants.[36] In Germany, with a population of some 80 million, some 7 million are immigrants, with a great number of them coming from Turkey.[37] New shades of black and brown have developed in the past few years that have fostered a rise of anti-immigrant xenophobia and nativism. Increasingly, in several countries of the European Union, violence and open conflict, such as that which occurred in November 2007 in France, exacerbated their immigration crisis. The result is the existence of a powder-keg situation, which stems from the interdependency of European welfare capitalism and immigration.

Without access to immigrant low-wage labor, the crisis of global capitalism would become further exacerbated. The fact is that in 2007 developing and underdeveloped capitalist economies, characterized by an immensity of poverty, unemployment, low wages, pervasive inequality, and a myriad of social problems, have helped sustain the First World's economic development and growth. The latter, however, face a developmental dilemma due to their labor shortage brought about by a serious collapse of birth rates, which has translated to having a shortage of workers. Patrick Buchanan, in his book *Decline of the West*, in an ominous note wrote,

> While world population had doubled to six billion in forty years, the European peoples had stopped reproducing. Their populations had begun to stagnate and, in many countries, had already begun to fall. Muslim Albania was, by 2000, maintaining a birthrate sufficient to keep it alive indefinitely. Europe had begun to die. . . . In 2000, the total population of Europe, from Iceland to Russia, was 728 million. At present birthrates, however, without new immigration her population will crash to 600 million by 2050 . . . The average birth rate of a European woman has fallen to 1.4 children, with 2.1 needed just to replace existing population . . . If the present birthrates hold, Europe's population will decline to 207 million by the end of the twentieth-first century, less than 30 percent of today's . . . Today, in seventeen European countries, there are more burials than births, more coffins than cradles.[38]

In 2006 and 2007 numerous sectors of the economy, especially agriculture reported labor shortages with losses of millions of dollars due to many crops unpicked that were rotting in the fields. Out of desperation, in one instance in Colorado, prison inmates were used in attempts to pick the crops. While nativists intransigently refuse to accept such a reality, the fact is migrant labor allows the country's business sector to make huge profits. The dictum "one person's exploitation and misery is another person's profit and prosperity" is another truism in capitalist societies. As long as the U.S. economy is driven by the "pull" of an insatiable dependency and addiction to cheap labor from the "push" of México and Latin America's migrant exodus, the immigration crisis will continue unabated.

México and Latin America in Crisis

From México to Argentina the economic crisis precipitated by the globalization of capital is evident in the pervasiveness of immense poverty and chronic inequality. In particular, México and Central America are the main contributors to the migrant exodus. Nearly a million migrants every year journey north in their quest to extricate themselves from the desperation and egregiousness of their impoverished existence. Yet the reality of their situation is that their migration north or migrant exodus is the result of their individual countries' capitalist economy's failure and inability to create economic opportunities (specifically jobs with a living wage), distribute the wealth of their countries in an equitable manner, or resolve the myriad of social problems they face, for example, crime, violence, drug trafficking, and so forth.

Their economies have become dependent on the export of human capital. México's nearly $1.2 trillion capitalist economy in 2007 makes it the twelfth largest of the world and second largest of Latin America. With a population of 110 million it is one of the leading developing Second World economies. Rich in minerals and oil and rapidly developing, México should be the Japan of Latin America, an integral economic leader of the First World, but is not. Since the 1980s, its capitalist free market-driven economy has been in an acute economic crisis. While its gross domestic product (GDP) has surpassed the one trillion mark, according to the *Comision Economica para America Latina y el Caribe* (CEPAL), 48 percent of its people are poor.[44] This translates to almost 53 million Mexicanos living under the ominous specter of poverty and almost 9 percent or 14 million living under egregious extreme poverty.

In reference to the latter, some improvement occurred from 2000 to 2007. According to the World Bank, "Extreme poverty fell from 24.2 percent of the population in 2000 to 20.3 percent in 2002." This meant that 3.1 million

Méxicanos had extricated themselves from "extreme poverty," living on less than $1 per day. Those living in so-called "moderate poverty," or on about US$10 per day, fell from 53.7 percent to 51.7 percent, according to the report "Poverty in México."[47] Extreme poverty was most severe in the rural areas of México, where 65 percent of the population lived on less than $1 a day. Furthermore, México's indigenous population that made up 20 percent of those who lived in extreme poverty represented 10 percent of México's then 105 million people (2004 population estimate).[48]

México's shift from a "mixed economy" to a "capital market economy" during the 1980s has been an utter failure. The result has been that metaphorically México's greatest export to the U.S. has been "human capital." The Pew Hispanic Center reported in 2005 that annually some 500,000 Mexicanos migrated successfully to the U.S. México's National Council for Evaluation of Social Development Policy in 2007 reported that poverty levels in México varied significantly, reaching the highest level in the southeast. Mexican officials reported that the southern state of Chiapas with a poverty rate of 75.7 percent was México's poorest, while the northern border state of Baja California had the lowest at 9.2 percent. The poorest states after Chiapas were Guerrero, Oaxaca, and Tabasco; all three are in the south and have poverty rates of at least 59 percent. Even in the least impoverished states, the poverty rates are high, such as in Baja California Sur and the northeastern state of Nuevo Leon, with respective poverty rates of 27.5 percent and 23.5 percent; México City placed third with 31.8 percent.[49]

In another report released by México's National Population Council in 2007, it estimated that 220,000 Mexicanos aged fifteen to twenty-four left the country each year from 2000 to 2005. They comprised about 38 percent of the total number of migrants who headed north to the U.S. It was reported that people in this age bracket, comprising 19 percent of México's population, were twice as likely to migrate as the rest of the populace. According to Cesar Garces, head of the council, 47 percent of México's youth live in poverty and only 70 percent of México's fifteen-year-olds, 50 percent of its seventeen-year-olds, and 29 percent of its twenty-year-olds were still in school.[50]

Failure of México's neoliberal approach is further illustrated by its persistent systemic problem of inequality. In 2000 México's concentration of wealth was the second world's highest. In fact, México's so-called representative democracy more aptly was a "plutocracy." Clearly illustrating that México was far from becoming a nation-state of economic equality, in 2000, 44.3 percent of the country's income was concentrated in the hands of only 10 percent of México's population, a figure that dropped to 41.3 percent in 2002.[51] In 2007 México had twelve billionaires that owned 31.6 percent compared to Brazil's seven who owned 14.8 percent of the country's wealth.[52] As of July 2007, México's Carlos

Slim Helu surpassed U.S. multibillionaire Bill Gates as the world's richest man with a net worth of $67.8 billion.[53] To put it in perspective, Slim's total wealth is equivalent to slightly less than 7 percent of México's total production of goods and services. Gates's total worth of $59 billion merely represents a little less than 0.5 percent of the U.S.'s GDP. Slim is a benefactor of President Carlos Salinas de Gortari, who privatized many of México's government-owned industries. In 1990, Salinas sold Slim the national phone company, Telmex. As a result, Slim owns 90 percent of México's landline phone service and controls almost 75 percent of the cell phone market. Similarly, several of México's other billionaires made their fortunes by the federal government's privatization of state-owned companies during the 1990s.[54]

While México's capitalist economy produced a "super plutocratic-bourgeoisie" or oligarchy with financial empires comprised of monopolies or oligopolies, its poor masses suffered from "systemic" unemployment, dire underemployment, and in some cases less-than-subsistence wages. México's recorded unemployment in 2006 was estimated at 3.2 percent, a relatively low, underinflated government statistic, yet its underemployment was 25 percent. Even more tragic for México's workers and *campesinos* was México's minimum wage, which was $4.63 per day. In December 2006, the Calderon administration increased the minimum wage by 3.9 percent, still less than $5 per day.[55] The prices of México's food and other consumer necessities are similar to those prices in the U.S. The fact is, since the 1990s, some 11 million impoverished Mexicanos migrated to the U.S.

Further contributing to México's capitalist crisis is the utter failure of the North American Free Trade Agreement (NAFTA). President Carlos Salinas de Gortari's PRI government for all intents and purposes resurrected the Cientificos' positivist capitalist policies of the Porfiriato. His neoliberal economic policies subordinated México's economy to the egregious vices of global capitalism; even worse, it transformed México into an "economic dependency" of the U.S. On December 17, 1992, Mexican President Salinas, U.S. President George Bush, and Canadian Prime Minister Brian Mulroney signed NAFTA, which ensured free trade among the three nations by putting forth a reduction of tariffs.[56] It went into effect a year later, on January 1, 1994, and was greeted with repudiation by an armed uprising of the Zapatista Army of National Liberation (EZLN). NAFTA's impact was such that according to historian Lynn V. Foster, "under Salinas, modernization ignored the basic needs of the citizenry and polarized Mexican society into the wealthy few and the increasingly poor masses."[57] From 1994 to 2007 the fact is that México's economy grew sluggishly. It failed to produce the jobs that were promised; all the while, its working-age population swelled. Yet with a constancy of failure, PRI President Ernesto Zedillo (1994–2000), PAN President Vicente Fox (2000–2006), and PAN President

Felipe Calderon[58] (2006–2012) religiously embraced its draconian impoverishment policies. Beyond NAFTA's failures, the Mexican economy in 2007 was suffering flagging competitiveness. Mexican manufacturers had to compete head on with China, which made it difficult for them to compete because of their low labor costs and production volumes. This was hampering México's efforts to preserve its share of U.S. and global markets.[59]

México's economy is thwarted by the myriad of contradictions endemic to capitalism. The aforementioned analysis barely touches upon why México's neoliberal economy is a major "push" culprit of the U.S.'s immigration crisis. Today México's economy suffers from insufficient job creation, low growth rates, and dependence on the U.S. economy. In order to meet the employment demands of the economy, some 1.3 million new jobs must be produced annually. This does not account for the estimated 27 million underemployed and unemployed and millions who migrated to the U.S. President Calderon campaigned as the "candidate of jobs," and while he claimed that up to October 15, 2007, his administration was responsible for the creation of 825,000 new jobs during its first year in power, few put much credibility to such claims. More than 40 percent of Mexicanos between the ages of fifteen and twenty-four were unemployed.[60]

As to the economy's GDP since 2004, México has had an anemic track record: 2004, 4.2 percent; 2005, 2.8 percent; 2006, 4.8 percent; and 2007, 2.9 percent. Economists predicted a best-case scenario of 3.5 percent for 2008.[61] México's economy is perilously dependent on the U.S. economy. Ninety percent of México's exports and 70 percent of its imports go to and come from the U.S. Also, 65 percent of its foreign direct investment comes from U.S. investors. Nearly a third of México's commercial bank assets are owned by U.S. financial institutions.[62] In 2007, México received some $25 billion in remittances from Mexicanos working in the U.S., providing it with the second highest major source of foreign exchange.

In 2007 President Calderon declared war on the cartels in response to what can be described as the "Colombiaization" of México's politics. He assigned 24,000 Mexican troops and police to eradicate the cartel threat. Areas of México, especially along the border, by early 2008 were pervaded by violence and ongoing conflict. Meanwhile, discontent was rampant among the impoverished populace as was demonstrated in 2006 in Oaxaca with the rise of insurgencies. Andres Manuel Lopez Obrador, late in 2007, was in the midst of unleashing a fury of mobilizations over the issue of the privatization of PEMEX and México's crisis was becoming increasingly precarious. An unstable México surely dramatically intensifies the influx to the U.S. of the migrant exodus. The migrant exodus acts as México's "safety valve," which when opened, allows it to export hundreds of thousands of people annually to the U.S. The result has been that since

World War II, it has given México a semblance of political, social, and economic stability. To close it would expedite the probability of social upheaval, a second Mexican Revolution.

Central/Latin America in Crises

While México is the major source of the migrant exodus, Central America and the rest of Latin America also contribute to it. The same and in some cases worse "push factors" impel it. While most of its economies can be described as Third World, their impoverished economies that are in crisis have contributed to the growth of the migrant exodus. Hundreds of thousands of its poor since the 1980s have migrated to the U.S. It suffices to say that in comparison to México, Central America as a region is largely underdeveloped and overshadowed by the colossus of the north, México. After years of political and economic turmoil, since 2004 or so there has been some socioeconomic improvement. As a region, Central America's GDP has consistently grown from 4.1 percent in 2004 to 5.8 in 2007.[63]

As a region it was not exempt from the "capitalist crises" that pervade its economies, resulting in its own "migratory crisis." Yearly, especially from Guatemala and El Salvador, thousands of workers confronted by poverty, unemployment, and a syndrome of social problems migrate north to the U.S., a journey made more perilous by the difficult obstacles that they have to overcome by their migration through a dangerous México. As a region, the poverty level in 1999 was 50 percent and by 2005 decreased slightly to 48 percent.[64] In Guatemala, in 2004 some 21.5 percent of its population lived in extreme poverty, meaning on an income of less than $1 per day. Also, 48 percent of its children suffered from chronic malnutrition. Nicaragua in 2006 suffered from 14.9 percent extreme poverty.[65] Like México, some of its capitalist economies were dependent on remittances. In 2007 some $7 billion was sent home by migrants in the U.S.[66] Wealth has been concentrated in the hands of the few and income has not been distributed.

Latin America as a region was not free from the egregious effects of the globalization of capital and its impelled economic crisis. According to the United Nation's Economic Report of 2005 to 2006 some 194 million people or 36.5 percent were considered poor. About 71 million lived in what can be considered extreme poverty in 2006, defined as those households with incomes insufficient to provide food for all its family members.[67] On the issue of inequality, Latin America continued to suffer as one of the regions of the world with the greatest inequality. In 2003 the richest one-tenth of Latin America's population earned 48 percent of the total income, while the poorest tenth earned only 1.6 percent.

As a region, since 1959 an "anti-globalization of capital" trend began with the start of the Cuban Revolution led by Fidel Castro that repudiated capitalism and embraced Marxism, to today's socialist-driven Venezuelan Bolivarian Revolution led by Hugo Chavez, to other left-oriented socialist governments of Rafael Correa in Ecuador, Evo Morales of Bolivia, and Daniel Ortega of Nicaragua that have opted to "alter-globalization" through pan-Latin American cooperation in trade negotiations with the rest of the world. Left-of-center governments in 2007 also governed in Brazil, Argentina, Chile, and Uruguay; México's Manuel Andres Lopez Obrador won the presidency in 2006, but lost it to vote fraud. Colombia and Peru signed free trade agreements (FTAs) with the U.S. and in 2007 were waiting on ratification by the U.S. Congress.[68] In 2007 the antiglobalization of capital trend in Latin America was represented by a broad turn away from the proglobalization "shock therapy" economics that dominated the 1990s. As long as the aforementioned examined conditions exist in México and Latin America as a whole, the U.S. immigration crisis will continue.

The U.S.'s Latino Demographic Transformation

While the primary causation of the immigration crisis is the aforementioned, a symptomatic aftereffect is the U.S.'s rapidly changing demographics. It is being fueled by the new demographic reality of the re-Mexicanization of Aztlán and Latinoization or "browning" of the country. The Mexicano population alone has grown from 80,000 in 1848 to some 250,000 in 1900 to over 30 million in 2007. Overall the Latino population grew from 7 million in 1970, 14 million in 1980, 22 million in 1990, 35 million in 2000,[69] to over 47 million in 2008. Today with a population of some 302 million, Latinos comprise about 15.3 percent of the country's population. Throughout Aztlán, the demographic shift is dramatic: Latinos in 2007 comprised some 36 percent of California's total population, 36 percent of Texas's, 44 percent of New México's, 26 percent of Nevada's, 26 percent of Arizona's, 20 percent of Colorado's, and 11 percent of Utah's population. In innumerable counties and cities, Latinos make up the new majority or will in a matter of a few years. They are undergoing the demographic "browning" conversion process. As will be examined in the epilogue, within a matter of a few years the majority population of the Aztlán will be Mexicano/Latino—they will make up the region's new majority. Furthermore, by the beginning of the 22nd Century, if present demographic trends continue to prevail, Latinos will constitute the country's new majority.

This demographic new reality has given the economy-impelled immigration crisis a further impetus that has been further exacerbated by the intervention and mobilization of powerful nativist-driven forces. It has fostered a cause-and-effect impact that explains the rise of rancher vigilantes, nativist militias, new hate groups, anti-immigrant legislation at all levels of federal, state, and local governments, and an anti-immigrant political climate that has fostered a climate of fear and terror among undocumented migrants and immigrants nationwide.

Thus, the immigration crisis, which is the focus of study of this work at the macro level is a result of the economic crisis that permeates the globalization of capital. At the micro level (within the U.S.) however, it is a product of the overall Latino demographic transformation that is impacting the country.

CHAPTER 1

Exodus to the New World and the U.S. Immigration Experience (30,000 BC–1930s)

Immigration to the western hemisphere began some 30,000 years ago. Asians were the first immigrants to the continent. After thousands of years of migration south to what today is México and Central and South America, advanced Amerindian civilizations emerged. However, by the sixteenth century the European immigration exodus began with the arrival of the Spanish and Portuguese as colonizers. Not be outdone, England joined in the empire building in 1607 via immigration to the so-called New World. Immigration to what today is the United States (U.S.) was dominated from 1607 to the 1880s by England and northern Europe. Starting in the 1840s, however, the country experienced two major immigration waves: from 1840 to the 1860s from northern Europe; from the 1870s to the early 1920s, the immigrants came from southern and central Europe. Regardless of the countries that contributed to the European exodus to the U.S., it was England's culture, language, and heritage that induced the White Anglo-Saxon Protestant (WASP) ethos. It was this WASP mindset that permeated much of the country's immigration experience and gave way periodically to the rise of virulent anti-immigrant nativism, which was reflected in the various immigration laws that Congress passed from 1790 to the late 1930s.

This chapter provides a historical compendium of immigration patterns into the western hemisphere from Asia and from Spain and Portugal. However, the primary focus is on the U.S. immigration experience from 1607 to the 1930s, namely from Northern Europe to what today is the U.S.

Western Hemisphere's First Immigrants

Emigrants from Asia were the first inhabitants of the western hemisphere arriving sometime during 30,000 BC. These first migrants crossed the frozen Bering

1

Strait into the continent and so began the exodus into the Western Hemisphere. The peoples of the Americas, the Amerindians, were the "first" migrants to the Western Hemisphere.[1] This is an important anthropological and historical fact in that the Mexicano migrant experience in Aztlán is inextricably linked to that of the continent's Amerindian experience.[2] Anthropologists and others contend, based on comparative studies of DNA, that the first peoples in the "Americas" (Western Hemisphere) were related genetically to the peoples of Central Asia, such as the Chinese and the Mongolians. Their arrival to *las Americas* (the Western Hemisphere), according to radiocarbon dating, occurred some 35,000 to 50,000 years ago.[3] This occurred during the Pleistocene, or late Ice Age, when the ocean levels dropped significantly to some 300 feet, converting the Bering Strait into a thousand-mile-wide bridge connecting what is today Russia with Alaska.

These first migrants constituted the first "diaspora" into the Americas, which after thousands of years of incessant nomadic migration they inhabited an area from Alaska to Argentina's *Tierra del Fuego*. They kept coming until about 12,000 BC, when because of global warming, the land bridge resubmerged, isolating the new migrants on their newly found continent. Anthropologists estimate that around 14,000 BC these first migrants established settlements along the Pacific Coast of what today is Canada and the U.S. By 11,000 BC they had settled in México. This has been proven based on the discovery of the earliest known skeletal remains in the Americas, which were the remains of a twenty-four-year-old woman whose skull was found near present-day México City, and that were radiocarbon-dated to 11,000 BC.[4]

Anthropologist Diego Vigil notes that the first migration into the Americas "brought hordes of people whose descendents . . . established themselves throughout North and South America. They were the original Americans."[5] As nomadic hunting-plant and fruit-gathering societies, they were engaged in an incessant search for game, edible plants and fruits, water, and warmer climates. The earliest recorded settlements in what today is the U.S. occurred around 12,500 BC. Anthropologists argue that this was part of the Paleolithic stage (35,000 to 8000 BC) of human development and that the early migrants up to 5000 BC were preagricultural and nomadic.

After thousands of years, some of the continent's first inhabitants migrated and settled in Mesoamerica[6] where they built great civilizations that rivaled and surpassed those of Europe. These civilizations were products of various developmental stages or periods: Archaic (5200 BC–1500 BC); Formative (1500 BC–250 AD); Classic (250–950 AD); and the Militarist or Post-Classic (950–1519 AD).[7] In Mesoamerica great civilizations emerged that rivaled those of Greece, Egypt, and Rome. During the Formative period the Olmeca (emerged 1500 BC and declined around 600 BC) became known as the "mother culture" of all of México's civilizations. The Maya followed (emerging around 200 BC and declining around 850 AD) and because of their advanced civilization have been depicted as the "Greeks" of Mesoamerica. During 900 to 1519 AD, the rise of the Toltecs and Aztecs, or Chichimecas as they were referred to, were warrior-based societies that created empires that enveloped today's central and southern México into much of Central America. The Aztec empire in particular could well be described as the Roman Empire of Mesoamerica.[8]

The Amerindian migration farther south on the continent produced the advanced Inca civilization in the Andes.[9] In South America during the Classic period, a number of Andean civilizations emerged. Building upon their achievements, the Incas emerged as the most advanced Amerindian empire in the twelfth century during the Militarist period. In 1438 they expanded from a city-state, Cuzco, and forged an advanced and powerful empire by 1526 that stretched from present-day Peru to parts of Chile, Argentina, Bolivia, Ecuador, and Colombia.

But immigration into the continent changed dramatically as a result of the arrival of the Spanish in 1492 with the discovery of what they called the New World by Christopher Columbus. The Spaniards became the second immigrant group to reach the shores of the western hemisphere and the first from Europe. With the arrival of Spain's conquistadores who were driven by the pursuit of "gold, glory, and God," Europe's colonization of the Americas commenced. What ensued by the sixteenth century was a dramatic and violent invasion of the great Amerindian civilizations. In Mesoamerica Hernan Cortes's expedition/invasion of México in 1519 led to the downfall of the powerful Aztec empire and the colonization of Mesoamerica.[10] In South America, the Spanish colonial military machine under the leadership of Francisco Pizarro invaded the Incas in 1532 and by 1572 defeated them, allowing Spain to expand its colonial empire to much of South America. Under the leadership of Pedro Alvaro Cabral, the Portuguese in 1500 laid claim to what today is Brazil and would become the third immigrant group and the second from Europe to populate the so-called New World.

Both Spain and Portugal during the mid-1500s began the importation of black slaves from Africa as their main source of forced labor. Blacks became the Western Hemisphere's fourth group of immigrants. They were involuntary immigrants brought to satisfy their labor demands. Spain relied on the exploitive, oppressive, and cruel *encomienda* system,[11] which was a form of quasislavery practiced against the conquered Amerindian. This forced labor, coupled with exposing them to smallpox, measles, chicken pox, and diphtheria, by 1600 had decimated the Amerindian population relied on.[12] It is estimated that in 1519 Mexico's native population numbered some 25 million. By 1650, however, primarily because of the prevalence of a famine of sorts (smallpox), it decreased to 250, 000. Therefore, the conquerors relied on the importation of Black slaves from Africa as their main source of forced labor. Black slavery flourished: from

1551 to 1600 Spain imported 62,500 slaves and from 1601 to 1700 the number increased to 292,500. The Portuguese in Brazil during 1551 to 1600 brought 50,000 slaves and throughout the seventeenth century the figure increased dramatically to 560,000.[13]

The Spanish Colonization of Aztlán

During the sixteenth century Spain accelerated its colonization of México and Latin America, which included as a region the Caribbean, Central America, and much of South America. During this time, several exploring expeditions, such as those of Ponce de Leon (1513), Panfilo de Narvaez (1527), Francisco Vasquez de Coronado (1539), and Hernando de Soto (1542), were initiated geographically in parts of what today is the U.S., especially Aztlán.[14] In 1565 Spanish admiral Pedro Menendez de Aviles founded St. Augustine in what is today Florida, consequently making it the first Spanish settlement. The next was in 1598, with Juan Oñate's expedition and settlement of San Gabriel de los Españoles in what today is Nuevo México. The former occurred forty-two years and the latter nine years before the English settlement of Jamestown. From 1598 to 1821, Spain expanded its colonial settlements to what are today the states of Texas, Arizona, and California. Emigration from Spain and migration from México impelled Spain's colonization into Aztlán. In 1810 under the leadership of a priest, Miguel Hidalgo y Costilla, México declared its independence. After eleven hard-fought and bloody years, México became independent in 1821. Concomitantly, what ensued throughout most of the rest of the Spanish-colonized Western Hemisphere was the spread of wars for independence from Spain, which with the exception of Cuba, succeeded.

For the next twenty-five years, the southwest or Aztlán was an integral part of México. It was during these precarious years that it found itself underpopulated, leading it to make the fatal mistake of allowing immigration into Texas from the U.S. Whites along with their slaves swore allegiance to México and agreed not to practice slavery. Demographically, by 1830, Whites overwhelmed the minority Mexicano population, which comprised no more than 5,000. Moreover, México was now the target and would fall victim to the U.S.'s expansionist plan of "manifest destiny." Simply translated, it was an imperialist belief that the U.S. was ordained by God Almighty to expand its borders, export its institutions, and propagate the WASP ethos-oriented culture westward to the Pacific Ocean. In 1836, with the support of the U.S., the majority of the White immigrant settlers successfully revolted against México and for the next nine years became the Texas Republic.

U.S.-inspired imperialism once again overtly surfaced with the "U.S. War against México" (1846–1848). With the election of expansionist James Polk and the annexation of Texas in 1845 the historical stage was set for war with México. U.S. forces in 1846 invaded México and the Southwest. After nearly two years of war, México was defeated and was compelled to sign the infamous Treaty of Guadalupe Hidalgo, which surrendered to the U.S. all the Southwest (some one million square miles of territory) for a mere $15 million (in U.S. currency).[15]

The significance of the aforementioned events to the present "immigration crisis" is that the first migrants that came from Asia thousands of years ago became the first to settle the Western Hemisphere. Secondly, Spaniards became the second immigrant group to settle on the continent. Spain's colonization of México, paraphrasing the words of Mexican philosopher Jose Vasconcelos, resulted in the miscegenation of the Spanish and Amerindian, thus a new race was born, *la raza Cosmica*. The Mexicano migrant that today is depicted by nativists as an "illegal alien" is in fact a person who has roots deeply planted in history of the Western Hemisphere. This clearly refutes the nativist argument that Mexicanos are foreigners to Aztlán. Today's Mexicanos are 60 percent mestizo; 30 percent Amerindian; and 10 percent Caucasian/other.

Genesis of the Northern European Exodus

The U.S. immigration experience had its roots in England.[16] During the late sixteenth century and well into the seventeenth century, England as an emerging colonial power experienced major changes in its mode of production. The feudal system was giving way to mercantilist policies, meaning it was being replaced with incipient industrialization, that is, the technological changes that occurred would by the eighteenth century usher in the rise of capitalism. This was accompanied by a myriad of demographic, religious, social, and political antagonisms that pervaded England and northern Europe, and which consequently uprooted farmers, artisans, craftsman, and merchants. Poverty, unemployment, and lack of economic mobility were pervasive. Historians Dexter Perkins and Glyndon G. Van Deusen explain that "unrest in the English middle and lower classes, the result of economic and religious difficulties, and a widespread belief England was overpopulated made circumstances propitious, and English merchant capitalists began to move."[17]

Colonization offered a way for England to relieve both problems.[18] England by the sixteenth century experienced major population growth after a century of decline during the Dark Ages. The Protestant Reformation fostered a multiplicity of sects. Religious persecution ensued that created a quest for religious freedom, which the New World English colonies offered. Socially, there was increasing unrest and growing conflict among the sectors of the middle class and poor alike over the preceding situations. Killer diseases ravaged towns and natural disasters hit, especially England during the early 1600s. And politically some, such as the Pilgrims and Puritans, sought the freedom and opportunity to create God's kingdom in the New World.[19]

The U.S.'s immigration experience began with England's colonization of the so-called New World during the late sixteenth century. Spain and Portugal were already well established as colonial powers, with Spain controlling from today's southwest to South America's Argentina. They were extracting gold and silver, had built universities, had numerous printing presses, and had brought in thousands of immigrants. The Portuguese also had begun to colonize Brazil and were exporting dyewood from it. Likewise, the French had already established a presence in Canada and were flourishing in the fur trade. Hence, England as a colonial power in the Western Hemisphere was a latecomer. Like Spain, via its colonies, it sought to bring new wealth and greater power to England's monarchs. As an emerging expansionist colonial power, England claimed the eastern coast of what today is the U.S., after a voyage sponsored by Sir Walter Raleigh in 1584. The English in 1587 attempted unsuccessfully to colonize present-day North Carolina. Some 110 men, women, and children settled in Roanoke Island. Mysteriously a year later when a supply ship returned, all the settlers had disappeared.

The immigration experience of the U.S. started with three colonial events: (1) the settlement of Jamestown in 1607; (2) the landing of the Pilgrims at Plymouth Rock in 1620; and (3) the arrival in New England by the Puritans in 1630. The actual start of the U.S.'s "immigration experience" began on May 14, 1607, with the establishment of Jamestown, located in what today is the state of Virginia. The settlement was financed by the Virginia Company, a joint-stock company whose investors, known as "adventurers," invested what would be $3,000 in today's dollar currency. Their motivation was based on the notion that there existed a river on the Atlantic coast of today's United States that reached the Pacific Ocean, which would provide a shortcut to Asia. In addition, it was reported that gold and diamonds were plentiful in this new land.[20] On December 20, 1606, some 144 immigrants, including crews, set sail on three ships, the *Susan Constant, Godspeed,* and *Discovery,* from London to the Chesapeake Bay. Most were an extension of England's upper class, were Anglican in faith, loyal to King James I, and their chief occupation was farming.[21] They were not paupers. Some were sons of noble families, others from lesser nobility, and still others were middle class.[22]

On April 26, 1606, they arrived at Cape Henry. There the ship's commanders opened a sealed box that included a secret document delineating instructions on how to start a colony. The document specified the creation of a seven-person ruling council, responsible for the governance of the colony. One of the seven was John Smith, who during the voyage got into some problems with the voyage's leadership.[23] He was accused of plotting an insurrection and was confined below deck. He was sentenced to death once on shore. However, by the end of the voyage, his life was spared and he later became a hero. The three ships sailed into the Chesapeake Bay, picked an island and fortified it, and named it after their king, James. Thus, Jamestown was established as the first English settlement in what is now the U.S. Its settlers would be the avant-garde of the "White exodus" from northern Europe that originated in England.

The next fifteen years proved to be extremely difficult, full of trials and tribulations for the settlers. Attacks by Powhatan, chief of a confederacy of two dozen tribes and 200 villages, spread throughout much what today is Virginia. During the ensuing years, Powhatan would tolerate the intrusion and at times even assisted the often-hungry White settlers. Smith and Chief Powhatan developed a personal relationship after Powhatan's daughter Pocahontas saved Smith from being beheaded, which contributed to the settlement's survival.[24] After experiencing a conflict-ridden history, Smith returned to England in 1609, never again to return to the colonies. Jamestown suffered from incompetent leadership. Its leaders were always fighting and because of their gentry background most refused to do physical work.

Many of the early settlers died of diseases or starvation or were killed. In 1610 one of several dreadful incidents occurred when a ship carrying the deputy governor Thomas Gates arrived in Jamestown and found survivors in horrific conditions. According to Lewis Ford, "Powhatan had told his subjects to withhold corn. Food dwindled to nothing that winter and disease broke out. The famished ate horses and dogs, then cats and rats, and finally the leather off their boots. One man resorted to cannibalism. He killed, salted, and ate his wife. Of the 500 colonists alive when Smith left in the fall, barely 60 lasted into spring."[25] In 1612 John Rolfe, who two years later married Pocahontas, imported seeds of tobacco and by 1619, it became a flourishing, lucrative crop for export, which saved the ailing Jamestown and turned it into a prosperous settlement.

The colonizing experience of Jamestown proved to be costly. Of the 7,500 settlers who came to Jamestown from 1607 to 1624, fewer than 1,100 were found to be alive in 1625, which meant that only one in six survived the ordeal.[26] In the words of Richard Brookhiser, "Jamestown left four centuries of myth . . . a record of spite, want and death, to say nothing of the long range problems, from racism to lung cancer, of which the colonists were not aware."[27]

The Pilgrims' landing on Cape Cod in 1620 was the second event that helped shape the country's immigration experience. As a religious Protestant congregation the Pilgrims held irreconcilable antithetical views with those of the Church of England. Originally they had broken away from the Church of England because they felt that it had not gone far enough to implement the changes of the Protestant Reformation. Committed to living a life based upon the Bible, historians have described them as separatists for not accepting the Church of England's authority. As a result of religious harassment and persecution, in 1608 they left England for the Netherlands. By 1617, however, as a congregation they became discouraged over economic realities. Because of the influence of Dutch culture, imminence of war with Spain, and their inability to secure civil autonomy, they voted to emigrate to the English colonies.

They returned to England and on September 16, 1620, about 102 passengers boarded the *Mayflower* and made their historic voyage to the New World. After a sixty-five-day journey, on November 19 they arrived to what today is New England, near Cape Cod, and anchored in what today is known as Provincetown Harbor. It was during this time that they drafted the Mayflower Compact.[28] Knowing they did not have a patent from the London Company, a brief contract was drafted. It promised cooperation among the settlers for the general good of the colony; they promised all due submission and obedience. The compact was ratified by majority rule and the colony's first governor, John Carver, who was chosen.[29] This was the second successful English settlement of the so-called New World in what is today New England (that is, made up of today's states of Massachusetts, Connecticut, New Hampshire, Rhode Island, Vermont, and Maine). The term "Pilgrim" was first used by William Bradford, who would be the colony's second governor for more than thirty years, to describe the Pilgrim separatists.[30]

The original Pilgrims' settlement was established upon the ruins of an abandoned native people's village whose population had died as a result of a smallpox plague introduced by either English or French traders. Lewis Lord writes, "When the pilgrims landed on Cape Cod in 1620, they beheld an astonishing sight. Waiting for them was an empty Indian village, Patuxet and abandoned cornfields. Bones of residents lay scattered about. All of that resulted from an epidemic."[31] Immediately each settler was allocated a plot of land to build his dwelling. By March 1621, however, only forty-seven colonists had survived the diseases that they had contracted on the *Mayflower*. In spite of the devastating hardships endured, they went on to build a successful and rather prosperous colony. The Massachusetts Bay Company was reorganized in 1691 and a new charter was issued as the Province of Massachusetts Bay. From a historical perspective, the Pilgrims were the first immigrant refugees to settle in the new colonies that came chiefly because of religious persecution and not because of economic gain.[32]

The third event of the U.S.'s immigration experience was the arrival of the Puritans to the colonies in 1630. Like the Pilgrims, they too were fleeing from religious persecution. They shared some of the Pilgrims' religious beliefs, yet in comparison, they were not as radical. In England they had clashed with the religious practices of the Church of England, the king, and the aristocracy. They left England voluntarily with full consent of the English authorities, and were not victims of religious persecution. They decided to immigrate to the New World because of their quest to establish a new model of religious and governmental community based upon their own religious principles. Filled with religious zealotry, they believed they were to be the "redemption of Europe."[33] L. Edward Purcell writes, "They felt they were on an 'errand in the wilderness,' believed that they had a mission, as Winthrop wrote in a famous description, to build 'a city upon a hill, the eyes of all peoples are upon us.'"[34] Therefore, they could be described as being religious, and to a degree, social reformers.

Many of the leaders who organized the first voyage were prosperous in England. They formed their own joint-stock company and brought the company's charter with them, which became the basis for their government in the New World. They named their colony Massachusetts and established Boston as their chief settlement.[35] By 1643, the colony of Massachusetts Bay had 16,000 settlers.[36] In the ensuing years they prospered and formed new colonies in other parts of New England.

WASP Hegemony

From the onset of the colony's immigration experience, the hegemony of the WASP ethos was established. From its incipience, England's language, culture, heritage, institutions, religion, political culture, and so forth, were firmly implanted in the colonies. While the term WASP does not have a precise definition and contemporarily speaking has various connotations, throughout this work it is used to describe those Caucasians with historical roots in England and northern Europe. It is important to note that the English are descended from Germanic peoples who settled in the British Isles between the fifth century and the Norman conquest. Furthermore, 98 percent of those who emigrated in the seventeenth century were Protestant.[37] The nexus to England proved to be the cultural foundation and identity upon which the colonial immigration experience from 1607 to 1776 was built. Purcell points out the omnipresent impact of English immigration to the colonies:

> In an important sense, the settlement of the southern colonies and New England by English immigrants of the 1600s and 1700s established the basic context of American society. English was the

dominant language in America; English legal and governmental forms were the norm; and culture was for two centuries copied after English literature, drama, and art. . . . the British immigrants gave us the first model of what Americans thought society should be.[38]

From the incipience of the English colonial experience to 1776, these years were dominated and driven by the WASP ethos, which became the basis for the country's political and cultural national identity. Samuel Huntington, among others, describes it as the American Creed. He writes:

> The Creed . . . was the product of the distinct Anglo-Protestant culture of the founding settlers of America in the seventeenth and eighteenth centuries. Key elements of that culture included the English language; Christianity; religious commitment; English concepts of the rule of law, the responsibility of rulers, and the rights of individuals; and dissenting protest values of individualism, the work ethic, and the belief that humans have the ability and the duty to try to create heaven on earth, a "city on a hill."[39]

The WASP ethos was heavily influenced by English culture, history, and heritage, and religiously influenced by Protestantism, especially Calvinism, with its set of beliefs grounded in predestination, hard work, thriftiness, and acquisition of wealth to ensure salvation. Out of the WASP ethos, the genesis of liberal capitalism originated, as argued by Max Weber in his classic, *The Protestant Ethic and the Spirit of Capitalism*. Thus, during the U.S.'s colonial era, the WASP ethos became an integral and impelling force of the country's immigration experience.

Genesis of the Northern European Exodus (1607–1700)

The northern European exodus was begun and nurtured by the English exodus. Ninety percent of all immigrants came from England. According to estimates, between 1630 and 1700 some 155,000 English immigrated to the colonies.[40] The English colonies grew and expanded. This occurred in New England and in what became known as the middle colonies, that is, New York, New Jersey, Maryland, Pennsylvania, and Delaware. In 1626 the Dutch bought the island of Manhattan from the native peoples for a larcenous $24. By 1664 it was settled by the English and New York was founded. Swedish settlements that were established in 1628, which ultimately became New Jersey, were later taken over by the Dutch, and later by the English. Maryland, which became a refuge for English Catholics, was settled in 1634 by them. Quaker William Penn founded Pennsylvania, which became a refuge for Quakers, in 1681. During the early 1700s, Delaware broke off from Pennsylvania.[41] There were other ethnic groups, such as the Irish and Welsh, that settled in Pennsylvania. By the turn of the century significant numbers were emigrating from Germany, Scotland, and Ireland.[42]

Feeding immigration to the colonies was indentured servitude. Driven by poverty, political unrest, and religious persecution, thousands of poor Whites, under the aegis of mercantilism, immigrated to the southern colonies as indentured servants. Some historians describe indentured servants as a motley group of convicts, vagrants, and paupers. While in England, they were recruited with promises of land and quick riches once they completed their contracted time.[43] In exchange for passage mainly to Virginia and Maryland, they contracted to work for free, and temporarily gave up most of their economic and legal rights under conditions of contract (called an indenture), which was for between four to seven years. Most were young and homeless males between the ages of fifteen and twenty-four. Prior to the 1660s, most indentured servants had emigrated from England and by 1700 totaled some 100,000. They formed the economic and demographic backbone of the English southern colonies.

In reality, these colonists or indentured servants were tantamount to slaves, since they had little or no rights. According to historian Howard Zinn, "indentured servants were bought and sold like slaves."[44] Their motivation, according to Maldwyn Allen Jones, was a combination of "piety and profit," whereas Tomas Muller said it was solely "monetary."[45] Because of the harsh working conditions and prevalence of disease as many as 40 percent of the White indentured servants died. As masters sought to maximize quick profits, they extracted the maximum amount of work. Whippings and beatings were common and servant women were raped. They could not marry without permission and if they did they were subject to being separated from their families.[46] The great difference between indentured servants and slaves was that the former at the end of their contract were free. On the other hand, slaves were simply considered White property in perpetuity.

For the native people of the newly formed English colonies, English immigration proved to be devastatingly harmful. The repressive, oppressive, and exploitive aspects of mercantilism that pushed much of the English immigration impelled the decimation of the native people's population. For the native peoples, the European exodus was their "holocaust," manifested by ethnic cleansing, genocide, and extermination. In 1500 the estimated population of native peoples in what today is the U.S. was around 18 million. Their depopulation began in 1607 and lasted well into the 1890s.[47] Those who managed to survive were relegated to reservations, victims of internal colonialism.[48] At the start of the northern European exodus the native people's population in what constitutes today the U.S. was estimated to be as high as 10 million; during the next 200 years it was down to 1 million.

Initially, Powhatan did not perceive the English settlers as a threat; after all, native people populated them by 500 to one. As long as their numbers were small, he thought that they would either die or leave. But to his surprise, they kept on coming and by the time he realized their intentions were to invade and possess his lands it was too late. There were repeated armed clashes and John Smith did much to pacify the growing conflicts until he left in 1609. The marriage of Pocahontas to John Rolfe in 1614 also contributed to a precarious peace. When she died in 1618 the "married peace" ended. Powahtan too had died and had been replaced by his brother, Chief Opechancanough, who had decided that the English had encroached enough. On Good Friday of March 1622, his warriors attacked and massacred 347 settlers. In retaliation, the English settlers initiated a campaign to eradicate them. What ensued, writes Lewis Lord, were "armies of Englishmen [who] torched Indian villages and cornfields and killed hundreds of men, women, and children. The eradication campaign would continue off and on for decades. By the century's end, only a few hundred Indians remained in a region once inhabited by tens of thousands."[49]

The aforementioned was exemplified in New England in 1637, when after years of both native peoples and English settlers living in relative peace, settlers began to press for more territory into the Connecticut Valley. This warfare was more violent and brutal than that had occurred in Virginia. In what became known as the Pequot War, the so-called God-fearing Christians annihilated much of the Pequot tribe. Those who were not hacked, shot, or burned to death were sold as slaves. After forty years of fighting a struggle of armed resistance, a confederation of tribes, led by a leader known to the English as King Philip, retaliated and nearly decimated the outlying English Puritan settlements before being defeated by the superior force of the Puritans. In 1676, White settlers in Virginia reacted to the increasing native people's threat with Bacon's Rebellion. Conflict developed between Nathaniel Bacon and Virginia governor William Berkeley over the issue of strategy: Bacon wanted to slaughter the native peoples, while Berkeley wanted to build more forts and promote trade with them. The White settlers around Jamestown were divided and drawn into an armed conflict in which Jamestown was destroyed. The rebellion ended with the death of Bacon in 1676 from dysentery.[50]

Throughout the seventeenth century the native peoples' active armed resistance was no match for the European settlers' superior European technology, military organization, and strategy. These White settlers who allegedly were devout Christians adhered to a brutal and inhumane modus operandi against native peoples that incorporated an admixture of ethnic cleansing, genocide, and slavery. By the end of the seventeenth century, the preceding scenario was repeated over and over again, until the native peoples no longer presented a threat or an impediment to the settlers' westward expansion.

The White immigrant relationship with Black involuntary immigrants[51] was no better, since they were victims of slavery.[52] The arrival of the first Blacks to the colonies occurred in 1619 when the Dutch ship *White Lion*, a privateer ship, brought thirty Blacks (i.e., seventeen females and thirteen males) to Jamestown where they were sold to settlers as slaves. Among those sold were second- and third-generation Christians who bore Spanish names, such as Antonio, Maria, Isabell, and Francisco. According to Jamestown's census taken in 1625, they were given English names and surnames: Antonio became Anthony and Maria became Mary and both were given the surname of Johnson, and so on.[53] While most Blacks were in reality slaves, from 1620 to 1662 they were treated as "servants," since slavery did not legally exist either in England or in the colonies. Howard Zinn explains that "they were viewed as being different from white servants, were treated differently, and in fact were slaves."[54] As servants they were given the opportunity to buy their freedom.

But all this began to change in 1662 in the Virginia colony. As the Black population increased it became the labor force of elite White settlers. Moreover, White settler attitudes toward Blacks began to change and so did the laws. Orlando Patterson writes that "the children of all slave women were declared slaves in perpetuity. Five years later, Christianity ceased to be an obstacle to enslavement, and by 1669 a master could legitimately kill his slave while inflicting punishment."[55] Slavery also included native peoples. The difference between indentured servitude and slavery was more sharply defined. By 1691 Jamestown outlawed the freeing of slaves unless the slaveholder transported them out of the colony. In 1705 the Virginia legislature with the passage of the "Virginia State Law" made slavery legal.[56] The law forbade Black slaves from raising their own crops and raising cattle to purchase their freedom. Also, some of the free Blacks who were descended from those who arrived in 1620 were stripped of many of their rights. In less than a century, the Christian English southern colonies institutionalized slavery.

By the latter part of the seventeenth century, the supply of White indentured servants decreased as slavery became more lucrative for southern plantation owners. White slave masters in desperate need of exploitable labor turned to Africa and slavery as their main source of labor supply. As a result, slavery expanded quickly in the southern colonies due to the dependency of their cotton and tobacco economies to slave labor. By the thousands Blacks were forcibly removed from their villages in Africa (i.e., especially from today's Angola) and brought involuntarily to the colonies as slaves for labor-related purposes. For White slave owners, Black slavery became synonymous with "Black gold." Slave owners, who comprised one-fifth of the total English population, under the mercantilist system made huge profits from the exploitation of African labor. Also, the other four-fifths of the colonies' population benefited from the economic by-products of slavery: cheaper prices for food, tobacco, and cotton. The slave population or Black involuntary immigrant population during the seventeenth century numbered 20,500.[57]

White Christian immigrant slave masters of various faiths had no problems reconciling their religious beliefs with "mercantilism,"[58] and its economic by-product, greed, which was inherent to slavery. Adding to the irony was the belief of White supremacy, which was predicated on the notion that Blacks and native peoples were biologically inferior to White Europeans. This attitude gave impetus to the WASP ethos, which has permeated the country's political culture ever since.

Second Stage to the Northern European Exodus (1701–1783)

The northern European exodus from 1701 to 1783 intensified. By 1700 the colonies' population had increased to 250,000 and sixty years later it is estimated that it had increased to 1,695,000 inhabitants. Of these 1,385,000 were White and 310,000 were Black.[59] The demand for labor translated into an increase in birth rates, which contributed to the colonies' population growth. Beyond England, many continued to come as indentured servants, this time from Germany and other parts of northern Europe. As to the English, Maldwyn Allen Jones writes, "The practice of using the . . . colonies as a dumping-ground for undesirables continued into the eighteenth century, and was brought to an end only by the Revolution." It is estimated that England sent some 50,000 felons to the colonies, most of them sent to Virginia and Maryland.[60] By 1775 more than 350,000 indentured servants had been imported to the colonies.[61]

During this second stage, the northern European exodus became ethnically more diversified. Emigration from England to the colonies continued to be dominant, but at a slower rate. Some 250,000 Scotch-Irish—the largest single group—emigrated from Ireland to the colonies prior to 1776. They themselves were descendants of Scottish Presbyterians that had migrated to Ireland during the sixteenth century. Initially, most settled in Pennsylvania, but others migrated to southern colonies. From northern Europe, immigration to the colonies included Dutch, Swedes, French Huguenots, Germans, and Jews. The Dutch settled in what today is New York and became the main rivals to English immigration, followed by the Swedes who settled in Delaware. The French Huguenots, who were Protestants and had been expelled from France, began to arrive during the 1680s and first settled in Massachusetts, and later settled also in New York and Charleston. German immigrants settled in Pennsylvania and North Carolina. By 1760 they numbered some 170,000.[62] European Jews arrived at New Amsterdam in 1654 and by 1776 numbered between 2,000 and 3,000. By 1775 the colonies' population had reached some 2.8 million people, with the English and African slaves forming the largest part of the population.[63]

The eight-year (1775–1783) struggle for independence from England did not alter the ethnic makeup of the colonies. It began as a political conflict or dispute between two power elites: one ruling from England, the other from the colonies, which the latter won. On the issue of independence, immigrants of British ethnicity split; most non-English immigrants supported the struggle for independence. At the end of the conflict, thousands of English loyalists re-emigrated to Canada or Great Britain. Despite ethnic and cultural differences, the conflict brought most of these groups together. The thirteen colonies' population in 1775 numbered some 2.5 million. Its ethnic mix was predominantly English, Scottish, and Scotch-Irish—in that order—followed by German, Dutch, Huguenots, and Jews. From a religious perspective, it was overwhelmingly Protestant. During the conflict, the British halted all immigration to the colonies.[64] It was not until years after the Revolution that immigration gradually began to again increase.

For a time, the Pennsylvania Germans' loyalty came into doubt, especially because of the British use of German mercenaries, known as Hessians. Prior to 1776, the German immigrant was the target of the WASP ethos. As a people, the German immigrants demonstrated a strong propensity for seeking to retain their language and culture by establishing their own schools, and having their own literature and newspapers. Some Anglophiles, including Benjamin Franklin, were driven by a pronounced fear of the "Germanization" of Pennsylvania. During the war for independence, while some sided with the colonists, many Germans remained neutral, preferring not to get involved.[65] In response to this fear, a number of "charity schools" were established, that had as their cardinal purpose to anglicize, meaning assimilate, the German children. Even after independence, German immigrants were subjected to the rise of anti-German xenophobia and nativism.

By the end of the second stage, the number of non-White immigrants both increased and decreased. The decrease and depopulation of the native peoples accelerated under the aegis of the new republic of the U.S. On the other hand, the Black slave population increased substantially. Black slavery flourished primarily in the slave-based agricultural cotton and tobacco plantation economies of southern colonies. By 1710, there were more Blacks than Whites in what today is South Carolina. Between 1713 and 1765, approximately 350,000 Europeans and Africans settled in the colonies; about 40 percent were Black slaves.[66] It was during the eighteenth century that the slave trade reached its peak. By 1776 the Black population reached some 500,000; nine-tenths of them were found in the southern colonies. Their numbers continued to increase in the southern plantations until 1807, when the U.S. government officially, in Article 1, Section 9 of the Constitution, put an end to the slave trade.[67] It also allowed Congress to levy a head tax of up to $10 per slave.[68]

U.S. Immigration Experience (1783–1830s)

From 1783 to the 1830s, the U.S. as a new nation-state continued to rely on emigration from northern Europe for its capitalist development. While in 1776 the country's founding fathers promulgated the Declaration of Independence, Adam Smith, in his *Wealth of Nations*, put forth new economic policies that repudiated mercantilism and promoted capitalism. The state became Smith's unregulated "invisible hand" of market completion (e.g., laissez-faire economics), and the insatiable pursuit of unfettered profit replaced mercantilism.

According to the first census taken, the country's population, in 1790 reached a high of 3,929,214: 49 percent were English; 18 percent were African; 15 percent were Scottish-Irish, Scottish, or Irish; 7 percent were German; 3 percent were Dutch; and 2 percent were French.[69] By 1800 the native people's population dwindled to 600,000; fifty years later, it reached a low of 250,000.[70] English colonization was worse than that of the Spanish in Latin America. Spaniards moderated their brutality by being less racist and marrying native women; while the English colonial experience conversely, because of their racism, and anti-miscegenation sought the native peoples' extermination.

From 1774 to the early 1820s, the northern European exodus slowed to a trickle. Europe's wars and conflicts, particularly the Napoleonic Wars,[71] during the previous twenty-five years had put a brake on massive immigration. The British government restricted emigration into the U.S., until the 1820s. Although no records were kept until 1820, it is estimated that the immigration did not exceed 10,000 per year. Total immigration to the U.S. between 1783 and 1815 came to about 250,000.[72] From 1790 to 1820s high birth rates accounted for virtually all of the country's population growth.

For the U.S.'s first thirty years, no general consensus existed among its governing White elites on the issue of unlimited immigration from Europe. While the White tide of immigration remained low for years; the federal government generally adhered to an "open door" immigration perspective, especially as it related to Europe. President George Washington was generally supportive of immigration. He spoke of a United States that welcomed not only the opulent and respected stranger but also the oppressed and persecuted of all nations and religions. In his correspondence on the matter, he expressed a tolerant attitude toward immigrants. He expressed, however, the need to attract immigrants with capital and professional and skilled workers from Europe and said, especially for the latter, financial assistance should be provided as an inducement. However, he expressed some reservation or concern on immigration: he believed that immigrants should not be concentrated in one region, for it would make difficult their assimilation.[73]

Most of the country's other notable governing elites likewise were supportive of an "open border" immigration perspective. Thomas Jefferson favored immigration as a stimulus for economic development. Unlike other elites, he favored immigration from southern Europe, those from the Mediterranean basin. Moreover, he expressed some anxiety about immigrants coming from countries ruled by absolute monarchs. He believed that they would have a difficult time in adapting to the country's representative democracy. Yet Jefferson was not an immigration restrictionist. Others like James Madison were also supportive. He believed there were a myriad of benefits for the young country in attracting immigrants, particularly from Europe.[74] Alexander Hamilton likewise favored the continuation of the European exodus. This open border view was never addressed in the Constitution. The country needed to populate the thirteen states and the new lands it was acquiring during the turn of the nineteenth century. At the crux of this openness, was the WASP ethos that became increasingly pervaded by a sense of "manifest destiny" for economic, military, and political reasons. As to the Constitution itself, historian Charles Beard wrote in his work, *An Economic Interpretation of the Constitution*, paraphrased by Howard Zinn, "The rich must, in their own interest, either control the government directly or control the laws by which government operates."[75]

Congress, however, was empowered to deal with naturalization and the rights of the foreign born—two issues closely tied to immigration. Congress in 1790 passed the first naturalization laws, which allowed all "free White persons" to become citizens after being in the U.S. for only two years. The obvious intention, according to Roger Daniels, "was to bar the naturalization of Blacks and indentured servants."[76] A Black at this time as a slave was considered three-fifths of a human being. Europe's political volatility, especially the French Revolution, produced some resistance to the country's open border policy. The sense of immigration tolerance that preceded the 1790s began to give way to a growing nativist sentiment. In 1794, Congress passed a statute derived from the English poor laws that sought to return immigrant paupers to their country of origin. Political chasms occurred among the governing elites over the French Revolution, and growing political and economic differences induced the rise of the country's two-party system. Because of the expense of transatlantic removal, this law of immigrant deportation never went into effect.[77]

With the Federalists in control, Congress passed a second naturalization statute that increased the waiting period for eligibility for citizenship from two to five years. It also proposed unsuccessfully a tax of $20 (an incredibly large sum of money for the time) on certificates of naturalization. The Federalist Congress, however, did succeed in passing a new naturalization law that set the waiting period for citizenship to fourteen years.[78]

The most notorious Federalist attack on immigrants came in 1798 with the passage of the Alien and Sedition Acts. With concern over going to war with France and the presence of French sympathizers in the country, four acts were passed: (1) the Alien Enemies Act; (2) the Alien Friends Act; (3) the Naturalization Act; and (4) the Sedition Act. The Alien Enemies Act, which was never used, enabled the president to deport foreign residents if their home countries were at war with the U.S. (this act remains still in effect today). The Alien Friends Act allowed the president to deport foreigners who were considered "dangerous to the peace and safety of the U.S." (but this lapsed after two years). The Naturalization Act extended the required time for citizenship from five years to fourteen years (it was repealed by Republicans in 1802). The Sedition Act made it a crime to publish "false, scandalous, and malicious writing" against the government or its officials (this act expired in 1801).[79] The Federalists sought to silence foreign-born journalists and pamphleteers who were hypercritical of the government. The penalty was five years in prison or a $5,000 fine. It was during this time that "alien menace" entered the country's political lexicon.[80]

It was not until 1819 that Congress passed its first statute that directly dealt with immigration, which began the practice of the U.S. maintaining statistics on the numbers of immigrants that entered the country. Captains of ships were required to maintain records of immigrants that entered the U.S. Also, as a provision dealing with import duties, every vessel that entered a U.S. port had to deliver a list of its passengers to the collector of customs for said district. According to Roger Daniels, "No other immigrant statutes were enacted until after the Civil War."[81]

With the return of a prolonged period of relative peace in Europe and the U.S. economy in need of labor, European exodus to the U.S. again increased during the next twenty years. During the 1830s alone, some 600,000 immigrants arrived, more than doubling the number in the quarter century after 1790.[82] Between the years 1820 and 1830 some 143,000 immigrants arrived to the country, chiefly from Ireland (50,424), Great Britain (25,079), France (8,497), and Germany (6,761). During the next decade, 1830 to 1840, a major increase occurred: the total number was 599,125. The numerical sequence, however, changed slightly: Ireland (207,381); Germany (152,484); Great Britain (75,810); and France, (45,575). By the end of the 1830s, the northern European exodus had intensified dramatically.

First Great Immigration Wave (1840–1860s)

What happened between 1840 and 1860 was unprecedented and was appropriately called the First Great Immigration Wave. During the 1840s the northern European exodus intensified. The number jumped to 1.7 million and to a high of 2.6 million during the 1850s.[83] By 1860 the country's population swelled to some 30 million. During its thirty-year duration, a total of 6,626,289 immigrants to the U.S. from Europe. Germany was the biggest contributor with 2,173,761; followed by Ireland, 2,130,116; Great Britain, 1,297,914; Canada/Newfoundland, 153,878; and lastly, France with 153,620.[84] The influx of immigrants was such that in 1850 it exceeded the country's native population. The native peoples' population by 1850 had been reduced to about 250,000.[85]

The First Great Immigration Wave (hereafter described as the First Wave) was a product of a myriad of "pull" and "push" factors. L. Edward Purcell writes that "elements must be in place at both ends for immigration to occur: elements in the old land must push immigrants to uproot themselves and leave home; other elements in the new land must look so attractive that immigrants are pulled to a new place. During 1815 to 1860, both sorts of incentives were at work."[86] On the pull side, with the U.S capitalist economy in the midst of the industrial revolution, the demand for cheap labor heightened, especially for unskilled labor. Immigrants were also attracted to the U.S. because of "rising expectations." Economic opportunities, abundant land, and the great demand for cheap labor helped nourish the U.S.'s fledgling liberal, capitalist-driven "industrial revolution." Individual states and private companies advertised and actively recruited in Europe for immigrants to come to the U.S. Easier access to cheap transportation also contributed to the pulling of immigrants from Europe.

On the "push side," northern and western European countries during these years experienced a population explosion. Such was the impact that some of the economies could not accommodate the demand for job creation. This was in great part ascribable to the manifold ill effects of industrialization, that is, displacement of workers, low wages, and bad working conditions, which consequently created impoverished masses. Because of political struggles and conflicts (i.e., the political revolutions of 1830 and 1848) which fostered political repression, thousands were pushed into being part of the resurgent European exodus to the U.S. By 1855, Castle Garden on Manhattan Island was the primary receiving point for immigrants from Europe.

Economic dislocation became so exacerbated in some European countries that people were on the verge of starving, as was the case in Ireland's potato famine. Given the choice of either emigrating or starving, the "push" factor, the potato famine (1847–1851), between 1847 and 1854 helped about 1.2 million Irish, who were Roman Catholic, choose to come to the U.S.[87] During the 1840s alone, the Irish provided the largest influx numbering some 780,219. They constituted 45.5 percent of the country's total immigration. As a result, during the potato famine, a million died and Ireland's population was reduced by over 2 million in ten years.[88] The northern European exodus dramatically increased during the 1850s to some 951,667 and diminished to 435,778 by the 1860s. The Irish constituted respectively 35.2 percent of the country's total immigration during the 1850s and in the 1860s, 18.8 percent.

Germany was the second largest contributor of immigration into the U.S. during the First Wave with a total of 2,173,761. During the 1840s, Germany was the second largest contributor with 434,626, comprising 24.4 percent of the decade's immigration, many of whom were Jewish. Germany was the largest contributor to the exodus with 951,667 during the 1850s and 787,468 in the 1860s. During the former decade, Germans made up 36.6 percent of the total immigration into the U.S., while in the latter decade, they comprised 34 percent. Like Ireland, the German exodus was in great part pushed by poverty created by poor harvests. Political unrest due to the failed revolution of 1848 was another push factor that spurred many to emigrate.

Great Britain was the third largest immigrant contributor with a total of 1,297,914 for the thirty-year period. From the 1840s to 1850s, during the next decade, it ranked second with 606,896. English immigrants constituted 26.2 percent of the total immigration into the U.S. Canada and Newfoundland were the third largest contributors with 153,878. Comprising a mere 6.6 percent of the country's total immigration, their exodus into the U.S. occurred during the 1860s. During the Civil War, Abraham Lincoln's administration created "a period of good will toward immigrants unparalleled in American history." Thomas Muller explains,

> The increased demand for industrial labor during the conflict prompted President Lincoln and the Congress to promote and financially assist immigrants for the first time–and only–time at the federal level. The brisk economic growth that followed Appomattox tempered opposition to European immigration for a generation.[89]

Nativism, the fear of foreigners, was imbedded in the country's immigration experience, yet it was the northern European exodus from Ireland and Germany during the 1840s and 1850s that fostered an unprecedented anti-immigrant reaction. The WASP hostility toward these new immigrants was largely induced by three concerns: (1) they were competing for jobs, resulting in the displacement of domestic workers; (2) they were willing to work for lower wages, creating lowering wages; and (3) at the crux of their attacks, was that they were Roman Catholic. As Thomas Muller explains, the Irish immigrant was the main target of the nativist attacks:

> The astonishing growth of American Catholicism revived the fears of popery that had been so widespread in America in colonial days. . . . The characteristic feature of protestant nativism was rather its constantly expressed fear that the Catholic influx threatened American institutions. The Catholic Church, because of its authoritarian organization and its close connection with despotic monarchies of Europe, was regarded by many Americans as the inveterate enemy of political liberty, and there were not a few who believed in the existence of a far reaching popish plot to subvert free government in the young republic.[90]

Some nativists resorted to the use of violence with their bellicose attacks on Irish immigrants. While there was evident hatred of the Germans, some of whom were Jewish, it was the Irish that received the brunt of the nativist attacks. Several episodes of riots and conflict directed at Irish immigrants occurred, particularly in the country's northeast region. During these years some Catholic religious houses were targeted. The Ursuline Convent at Charlestown, Massachusetts in 1834 was burned down by nativists. Convents and monasteries were depicted publicly as dens of iniquity and vice.[91] By the mid-1840s a four-day riot occurred between Catholics and Protestants over the use of Bibles in Philadelphia schools that was finally quelled by the use of military force.[92]

The Irish were recruited into the U.S. military with promises of citizenship. The U.S. War on México during 1846 to 1848 produced contradictory experiences for the Irish immigrants, as they were forced to participate when U.S. forces invaded México and burned and desecrated Catholic churches, raped nuns, and beat priests. Some could not take it, so they deserted and joined the ranks of the Méxican army and formed the famous "Saint Patrick's" battalion.[93] Tragically those who were not killed in battle were captured and shot as traitors.

During the early 1850s, nativism reached its height with the formation of the Order of the Star Spangled Banner and the formation of the American Party. Historians Dexter Perkins and Glyndon G. Van Deusen describe them as an "anti-Catholic movement that received impetus from the flood of immigrants in the early 1850s."[94] The former were labeled the "Know-Nothings" because members were sworn to secrecy and when asked questions responded by saying, "I know nothing." Taking as their slogan "Americans should rule America," they alleged "illegal" voting by immigrants. They also attributed the country's rising crime and disorder in the urban areas to immigrants. The Know-Nothings' anti-Catholic posture was directed specifically at the Irish, who were perceived because of their faith to be part of a conspiracy concocted by the Vatican to undermine the WASP-oriented U.S. As a third party, the American Party became a vehicle for abolitionists. Its culturally and politically nationalist posture was conflicting: anti-immigration and antislavery.[95] Hypercritical of the Know-Nothings,

Abraham Lincoln wrote, "When the Know-Nothings get control, it will read all men are created equal, except Negroes, and foreigners and Catholics."[96]

Hundreds of thousands joined and supported the American Party. During the 1854 congressional elections, the American Party scored significant political gains: five were elected to the Senate and seventy-five to the House of Representatives.[97] Its platform was imbued with acrimonious anti-immigrant/anti-Catholic rhetoric. One such stance called for an extension of the period of naturalization from five years to twenty-one years.[98] By 1856, as quickly as the American Party rose, it collapsed due to sectional tensions. Forced to choose between nativism and abolition, its leadership made the strategic error of choosing the former. At its convention, when a proslavery platform was adopted, the majority of its northern delegates walked out.[99] A mass departure of its northern states supporters went over to the new Republican Party.

Nativism by the 1850s was deeply ingrained in the country's immigration experience and during the ensuing years, it was nurtured by the country's changing ethnic/racial makeup. With the discovery of gold in California in 1848, thousands of Chinese immigrants were "pulled" and settled primarily in California. They were tolerated as long as they stayed away from the mining fields. Chinese immigrants developed laundries, ran restaurants, and worked in the fishing industry. Later, during the 1860s and 1870s, they worked in the construction of the Union Pacific Railroad. During the period of 1851 to 1860 some 41,397 emigrated, and from 1861 to 1870, the figure was higher: 64,301. With their population increasing and the competition for jobs, by the end of the 1860s anti-Chinese sentiment increased.[100]

The Civil War (1861–1865), temporarily put a brake both on anti-immigrant nativism and the northern European exodus of the First Wave into the country. The violent and destructive Civil War was not conducive to attracting immigrants. Without the demand (pull) for cheap labor, emigration from Europe decreased to a trickle. But with the end to the Civil War and the North victorious, the country's capitalist economy was again in need of repair, so the demand for cheap labor created a pull for increased immigration.

Second Great Wave of Immigration (1870–1920s)

During the next fifty years, the U.S. experienced an unprecedented immigration wave that surpassed the former one. Some 26 million people immigrated to the U.S. from 1870 to the 1920s, exceeding the country's national population of 1850.[101] This swell of humanity was ascribable to a combination of "push and pull" factors. The salient immigration "push" factors were demographic, economic, and political in nature. They included an astonishing surge in European population growth; an increase in rural poverty and unemployment; and civil wars, political instability, and political repression. On the "pull" side was the U.S.'s insatiable demand for cheap labor in the industrial and agricultural sectors of its capitalist economy, along with the immigrants' access to reasonably priced transportation via steamship lines.

During the first twenty years (1870–1890) of the Second Great Wave the majority of immigration to the U.S., as had been the case during the previous decade, was fed primarily by the countries of Germany, Great Britain, and Ireland. Total immigration into the U.S. during the 1870s was 2,812,191. Germany was number one with 718,182 (25.8 percent); Great Britain was number two with 548,043 (19.5 percent); and Ireland was third with 436,871 (15.5 percent). Canada and Newfoundland were fourth with 383,640 (13.6 percent). During the 1880s a total of 5,246,613 emigrated from Europe to the U.S. Germany again was the largest contributor with 1,452,613 (27.7 percent) followed by Great Britain with 807,357 (15.4 percent); Ireland with 655,482 (12.5 percent); and Norway-Sweden with 568,362 (10.8 percent).[102]

A dramatic change occurred during the years between 1890 and the 1920s: the Second Great Wave shifted from northern Europe to southern/central/eastern Europe. While the influx of immigrants to the U.S. from northern Europe decreased, it still continued. The new influx of immigrants were not Protestant in faith, but Roman or Orthodox Catholic and Jewish. Immigrants also came from other parts of Asia, the Americas, and Africa. Most of these new immigrants did not settle in one particular region; they settled in various parts of the country. This diversity was the beginning of the country's ethnic/racial transition to becoming a multicultural, multiethnic/racial, multilingual society. It was during this wave that the Statue of Liberty was given to the U.S. by France and erected in New York harbor on Ellis Island[103] in 1892, which became the country's main processing immigration center.

Between 1890 and 1920 some 18,188,761 immigrants settled in the U.S. The combined totals of German, English, and Canadian immigrants numbered, respectively, in the 1890s, 3,687,564; in the 1900s, 8,765,386; and in the 1910s, 5,735,811.[104] The number of immigrants from southern/eastern Europe became dominant: from Italy, 651,893 (24.5 percent); followed by Austria-Hungary, 592,707 (16.1 percent); and Russia, 505,290 (13.7 percent). During the 1900s the Second Wave reached its apogee with a total of 8,765,386 immigrants. This time the four countries to dominate the White exodus were Austria-Hungary, 2,145,266 (24.5 percent); Italy, 2,045,877 (23.3 percent); Russia, 1,597,306 (18.2 percent); and Great Britain, 525,950 (6 percent).[105]

The predominantly European exodus subsided almost by a third during the 1910s. The foreign-born population comprised some 13 to 15 percent of the country's population.[106] A total of 5,735,811 persons emigrated from southern, central, and eastern Europe to the U.S. Italy regained its number-one position with 1,109,524 (19.3 percent); Russia was second with 921,201 (16.1 percent);[107] Austria-Hungary was third with 896,342 (15.6 percent); and Canada and Newfoundland were fourth with 742,185 (12.9 percent).[108]

Emigration from China and Japan contributed as well to the Second Wave's changing ethnic and racial diversity. During the 1870s, Chinese continued to emigrate and there were some emigrants from Japan.[109] From 1849 to 1882, some 105,000 Chinese immigrated to the U.S., 70 percent of whom lived in California. A mere 3 percent lived in all the territory east of Denver and males outnumbered females by more than twenty to one.[110] By 1880, some 300,000 Chinese had emigrated, mostly from the region of Canton, of which some 90 percent again settled in California.[111] In 1870 there were only fifty-six Japanese immigrants in the country. However, by 1890 they exceeded 24,000 and by 1910 their number grew to 72,000 and reached a high of 111,000 in 1920.[112]

Rise of Nativist Restrictionist Immigration Laws (1875–1924)

As a reaction to the arrival of non-northern European immigrants, nativism intensified during the Second Wave. These new immigrants were poor and could barely make ends meet and lived in overcrowded and unheated houses, damp cellars, and even shacks that were crime ridden. Moreover, they were accused by nativists of taking jobs away from domestic workers and driving wages down. Overshadowing the preceding was the nativist fear predicated on the WASP ethos that the country would not be able to assimilate them due to their diversity of cultures, languages, and even religions.

In response, from 1875 to 1924, the U.S. government moved aggressively to centralize legal/governmental control over immigration via the passage of restrictionist laws. Prior to 1875 there were few fixed policies for regulating immigration, which meant the federal government practiced "unrestricted" immigration. The few restrictions that did exist were initiated by state or local governments. The latter in some instances charged an immigration tax as a way to generate revenues, but it was not intended to restrict immigration. The federal government began, however, to adopt gradually policies that set limits, included restrictions, and centralized administration of immigration.[113]

Immigration historians described the Chinese immigrants as sojourners— immigrants whose intention was not to settle permanently, who ultimately intended to return to their native lands. Roger Daniels says that Chinese immigrants considered themselves "guests." Nativists shifted their attacks from the Irish Catholics to the Chinese, who by the 1870s were depicted as the "yellow peril." By far they were the worst received of all the immigrant groups. Chinese were treated differently from all other nationalities. They were discriminated against, segregated, physically attacked, lynched, and were victims of "ethnic cleansing." Their story is one of the unhappiest of this country's immigration experience.[114] Even though they contributed substantially to economic development of the southwest, that is, the construction and completion of the Transcontinental Railroad in 1869, they were never accepted by native and immigrant Whites.

The federal government's efforts to restrict their entry into the U.S. began in the 1860s. In 1862, Congress passed legislation barring U.S. vessels from transporting Chinese immigrants. Nativists driven by xenophobia alleged that Chinese immigrants were an economic liability and resorted to extreme forms of propagating racism and fear. A front-page article in the *New York Tribune*, a vivid example of yellow journalism, warned of the threat of an invasion of the U.S by an Asian army of immigrants. The attacks on Chinese increased during the 1870s. Their race, language, culture, and religion were looked upon as being incompatible with the country's dominant WASP ethos.

Congress became more proactive in passing immigration control legislation. In 1870, the Federal Naturalization Act was passed by Congress, which dated back to 1790 and had limited naturalization only to Whites and free Blacks. It meant that Chinese immigrants were barred from citizenship and were not welcome in the U.S. Five years later, Congress passed the Page Act. It excluded criminals, prostitutes, and contracted labor from China, Japan, and other Asian countries that had forcibly been brought into the country. With its passage, Congress began to regulate immigration by targeting specific types that were considered "undesirable." Its contract labor provision vis-à-vis Asia was the first policy to restrict Chinese immigration. It prohibited the importing of any subject from China, Japan, or any other Oriental country without their consent and treated it as a felony.[115] In 1875, the U.S. Supreme Court ruled that immigration was a federal responsibility, not a state or local one.[116]

With the passage of the Page Act, Congress authorized in 1876 a joint congressional committee, composed of Democrats and Republicans, to investigate Chinese immigration. The Chinese bashing became evident in the platforms of both parties in 1876. It was the Republicans, however, that were at the avantgarde of the zealous nativist attacks on Chinese. The joint committee congressional report released in 1876 "demonized" Chinese immigrants. It warned that the Pacific Coast of the U.S. was becoming "Mongolian" and insisted that the Chinese as a race did not have sufficient brain capacity for self-government. In addition, it exhorted President Rutherford B. Hayes to modify the Burlingame Treaty and for Congress to legislate against "Asiatic immigration." President Hayes responded with a veto message, but indicated interest in stemming Chinese immigration.[117]

By the early 1880s the federal government moved assertively to bring immigration under its control. The political efficacy of nativists became apparent with the renegotiation and passage of the Burlingame Treaty in 1881. Under its provisions, the U.S. had the right to unilaterally "regulate, limit, or suspend" the "coming or residence" of Chinese laborers. Chinese, however, who were teachers, students, or merchants, and Chinese laborers were allowed to go and come of their own free will and accord.[118] Nativist politicians in the West continued to nefariously warn about the threats posed by Chinese labor: White workers were being displaced, Chinese worked for lower wages, and millions of Chinese threatened to invade the U.S. with their incompatible culture and religion. Leslie V. Tischauser writes, "This 'yellow peril' threatened the existence of Christian civilization because, as every white American knew, the Chinese were racially and culturally inferior to people of European heritage."[119]

The next year, Congress approved by a wide margin the infamous Chinese Exclusion Act of 1882, which became its most racist discriminatory statute ever passed. It was the first attempt by the federal government to limit immigration by race and nationality. It suspended further Chinese immigration to the U.S. for ten years, forbade the naturalization of Chinese, and placed other restrictions on them.[120] It had a class bias since it did not prohibit "elite" Chinese from emigrating. The effects of the law were immediate and dramatic. Prior to its enactment, some 12,000 Chinese entered the country in 1881 and 40,000 in 1882. After its enactment, the influx dropped to a trickle: 8,031 in 1883 and a mere 23 by 1885.[121] Because of the constancy of nativist pressure, it was amended and extended until 1943 when it was officially rescinded.

Congress also passed the Immigration Act of 1882, which gave the secretary of the treasury responsibility for its administration, but enforcement was left up to state boards or persons. As a generally restrictionist law, it excluded "any convict, lunatic, idiot, or person unable to take care of himself or herself without becoming a public charge." A tax was also levied on newly arrived immigrants. In 1885, Congress passed the Foran Act, which prohibited the entry of contract laborers. It made it unlawful for individuals or businesses to import foreign workers. Also, foreign-born convict laborers were to be sent back to the country they came from.[122] With nativist proclivities, organized labor, particularly the Knights of Labor, organized for its passage.

The country was experiencing two depressions during the 1880s and 1890s, and concurrently nativism flourished. Nativist politicians worked the legislative process, while others resorted to organization to influence it. One such nativist influential interest group was the American Protective Association (APA). Formed in 1887, it became the strongest secret anti-Catholic society. Unlike the Know-Nothings, the APA was not successful in translating its hatred of Catholics into electoral gains. Ironically, at a time when the tide of nativism was rising, the Statue of Liberty was dedicated in October of 1886. The growing anti-immigrant mood was not in sync with sentiment expressed in the famous poem "The New Colossus," written by Emma Lazarus, inscribed on the statue's base.

> "Give me your tired, your poor
> Your huddled masses yearning to breathe free,
> The wretched refuse of your teeming shore,
> Send these, the homeless, tempest-tost to me.
> I lift my lamp beside the golden door!"[123]

In 1891 Congress passed legislation that created the position of superintendent of immigration, which in 1895 was changed to commissioner-general of immigration. In addition, legislation was passed in 1891 that excluded the insane, paupers, polygamists, and persons with contagious diseases from entering the U.S. A Bureau of Immigration was established within the Department of the Treasury. Supported by labor, the Geary Act of 1892 extended the Chinese Exclusion Act for another ten years. That same year, Ellis Island in New York Harbor opened its facilities and became the focal point for immigration processing from Europe; some 8,000 immigrants per day were processed. The foreign-born and their children comprised 34 percent of the total White population in 1880. By the end of the 1890s, one-fifth of the country's workforce was foreign born and by 1910, it had increased to 40 percent. The receptacle of immigration became the great industrial urban centers, which moved the country toward urbanization.[124]

The unbridled nativism present in the 1890s was manifested by Senator Henry Cabot Lodge's legislation that proposed the use of literacy tests to screen immigrants. Congress passed such legislation in 1896, but it was vetoed by President Grover Cleveland. The APA reached its high point of influence in 1895, but declined due to internal schisms. Another nativist group came up, the Immigration Restriction League, which for the next twenty-five years spearheaded the anti-immigrant restrictionist efforts. Most unions by the 1890s joined the pronativist anti-immigrant crusade. Samuel Gompers of the American Federation of Labor (AFL) argued that the new immigrants crowded into any available employment as unskilled workers, and that they worked for starvation wages, which undermined labor standards that affected the growth of unions. In 1896, with the country in the midst of a depression, Democrats, Republicans, and Populists were adamant about effectuating immigration reform that was more restrictive. Newspapers and magazines also contributed to the anti-immigrant political climate.[125]

During the early 1900s, the country's nativist posture further intensified. As a result of the industrial expansion of the country's capitalist economy, social critic Henry George observed, "poverty and progress" seemed to go hand in hand.[126] The country's chronic inequality, meaning the gap between the rich and the poor, was more apparent in the cities, which were heavily inhabited by immigrants. Nativists pejoratively perceived cities as cauldrons of pauperism, crime, sin, lust, corruption, and drunkenness. Politically, they saw them as easy prey for the cities' corrupt bosses who led political machines. These and other circumstances produced a major push for restrictionist anti-immigrant legislation. Congress in 1903 passed legislation that sought to prevent the immigration of anarchists, professional beggars, and epileptics. It also mandated that immigrants who became a public charge for more than two years were subject to deportation. Again in 1907, Congress passed legislation prohibiting the immigration of persons who were imbeciles, feebleminded, had physical or mental defects, children under sixteen unaccompanied by their parents, and women who came for immoral (prostitution) purposes.[127]

Another immigrant group from Asia came under severe nativist attack during the early 1900s—the Japanese. Emigration from Japan had increased significantly in the 1890s. Many Japanese had migrated to Hawaii as agricultural workers. With the annexation of Hawaii by the U.S. in 1898, Japanese immigration shifted to the West Coast mainland, especially California. By the early 1900s, Japanese dominated certain aspects of California's agricultural labor sector. By the end of the decade, they numbered some 75,000 and most resided on the West Coast with over half living in California. In California, the state legislature passed a number of nativist anti-Japanese resolutions. What is more, violent anti-Japanese riots occurred in San Francisco. The anti-Japanese nativist attacks intensified to where Congress entertained the passage of the Japanese Exclusion Act. It never developed legislative traction due to president Theodore Roosevelt's opposition based on his concern that it would create bad relations with Japan. Unlike China, which was weak militarily in the 1880s and not able to contest the severity of the Chinese Exclusion Act, by the early 1900s, Japan had emerged as a major military power in Asia with the defeat of Russia (1904–1905).

Roosevelt instead resorted to diplomacy and negotiations and in 1907 produced what became known as the "Gentleman's Agreements." They were "executive agreements" or informal agreements between the two governments. Since they were not treaties, they did not require approval by the Senate. The provisions of said agreements provided that the U.S. would not pass discriminatory legislation against Japanese. The U.S. government would also initiate steps to stop state governments from discriminating against Japanese. Japan also agreed to stop the issuance of passports to laborers bound for the U.S. Both countries also agreed that the parents, wives, and children of those Japanese in the U.S would be eligible for passports. As a result of this last provision, in the ensuing sixteen years, some 20,000 Japanese came to the U.S.[128] Japanese immigration to the U.S. continued, but at a declining rate: 83,000 during 1911 to 1920; 33,000 during 1921 to 1930; and 3,000 during 1931 to 1940.[129] The decline momentarily deintensified the nativism directed at Japanese.

From 1909 to 1917 nativist restrictionists mounted their "Americanization" crusade. Culturally, this meant that nativists accentuated adherence to the WASP ethos. Driven by the ethnic/racial diversity of the new immigrants, nativists pushed for its adoption. They sought to strip immigrants from their so-called "alien cultures and languages," advocated the need for them to become assimilated and thus become "Americanized." According to Roger Daniels, most nativists adhered to the "melting pot" approach, which saw immigrant culture as something to be boiled away, as impurities are boiled away in making steel. This concept of assimilation was given further credence in 1908 by the European playwright Israel Zangwell and his Broadway hit, *The Melting Pot*. One of the play's characters explained, "The real American is only the Crucible, I tell you— he will be the fusion of all races, the coming of superman." Yet most of those who espoused it in most cases propounded the concurrent belief that immigrant cultures had nothing to contribute to American society,[130] which in reality meant a melting into a society dominated by the WASP ethos.

By the early 1900s, politicians in Congress perceived the country to be in the midst of an immigration crisis. Congress established in 1907 the Dillingham Commission. According to Thomas Muller, "Various studies were sponsored to demonstrate the criminality of these new arrivals. The most exhaustive was by the Dillingham Commission."[131] Headed by Senator William Dillingham of Vermont, its cardinal mission was to examine immigration and develop a comprehensive immigration policy. After three years of study, the Commission in 1911 released its conclusions in forty-one volumes. Its findings buttressed the views of those who embraced the "Americanization" of the immigrant. It compared the "old" (northern European) versus the "new" (southern/eastern European) immigrants. The former were described as being usually Protestant, except for the Irish and some Germans that were Catholic or Jewish; boasted a high literacy rate; and fit relatively easily into the country's Anglo-Saxon Protestant-dominated society. Whereas, it concluded that the latter had altered the U.S. immigrant mainstream by coming from southern/eastern Europe; were predominantly of Catholic, Orthodox, or Jewish faiths and "were inferior in education, ability, and genetic make-up to most of those who had come previously."[132] It alleged that the new immigrants were exploiting their new country and were contributing little to it.[133] In order to restrict immigration, it also proposed the use of literacy tests and the establishment of national quotas.

Influenced by the Dillingham Commission's report recommendations, Congress aggressively moved to pass restrictionist legislation. The first to be passed by Congress was the Immigration Act of 1917. For some twenty years, the use of literacy tests to restrict immigration had been defeated by presidential vetoes, but with its passage it became law. It stipulated that all future adult immigrants would have to be literate, but in a case of family immigration, if the husband was literate the wife did not need to be. All immigrants sixteen years of age or older had to demonstrate the ability to read a forty-word passage in their native language. One of its provisions, however, established an "Asian Barred Zone," which barred laborer emigration from Asia, except from China, Japan, and the Philippines. Besides hardening previous restrictions, it banned illiterates and certain persons of radical persuasions, immoral persons, chronic alcoholics, stowaways, vagrants, and persons who had suffered attacks of insanity.[134]

Again the U.S. capitalist economy's demand for cheap labor and Europe's dire economic and political straits brought millions of immigrants from Europe to the U.S.'s shores. Yet, during the ensuing four years, the Immigration Act of 1917 failed to restrict or curb the tidal wave of immigration to the U.S. As a result, the Americanization crusade, with its nationalist proclivities, grew. This was evident in the country's cities and towns where nativists sought to rename so-called foreign-sounding streets by giving them U.S. or English names. What ensued was further calls for more restrictionist immigration reform.

Both California and Oregon passed anti-immigrant legislation that the courts declared unconstitutional. California, for example, passed a law that ordered every male adult who was undocumented to register and pay a special poll tax of $10. The Ku Klux Klan (KKK) grew in numbers and advocated strict limits on immigration. Henry Ford's newspaper, the *Dearborn Independent*, initiated a massive anti-Jewish campaign and exhorted its readers to support immigration restriction. Various labor unions, including the AFL, accelerated their campaigns to limit the influx of cheap labor. The country's two major parties' platforms contained planks for effective limits on immigration.[135] By 1921, the U.S. experienced a depression, which caused unemployment, especially of veterans. It contributed to the growing Americanization crusade. As in previous economic hard times, immigrants were accused of taking jobs from domestic workers, depressing wages, and lowering the people's quality of life.

With the country's political climate at a nativist fever pitch, Congress passed the Immigration Act of 1921, also known as Quota Law of 1921. Primarily directed toward curbing the influx of immigration from southern/eastern Europe, it placed limits on the number of immigrants that could be admitted. It also predicated admissions on a system of national quotas, which restricted the number of any nationality entering the U.S. to 3 percent of the foreign-born persons of that nationality who were residents of the country in 1910. An annual immigration ceiling of 350,000 was established. Influenced by the Dillingham Commission report, it produced totals of 200,000 for northern and western Europe, whereas for southern and eastern Europe the quota was 155,000. Also, it specifically singled out nationalities and assigned quotas to them.

Yet its passage did not halt the influx of immigration into the U.S. In 1921 the total number of immigrants admitted was 800,000, but in 1922 it decreased to 310,000. During the ensuing two years, however, the country experienced a surge in immigration: in 1923 it increased to 523,000; and in 1924 to 707,000.[136] The increases occurred at a time when the country was in the midst of an economic recession, which helped fuel the resurgent nativism. Not satisfied with the effects of the Quota Law of 1921, the Americanization crusade next sought to push for even more restrictionist legislation.

Three years later, Congress passed the Immigration Act of 1924, which was called the Johnson-Reed Act. By far, this act was the most restrictionist legislation ever passed by Congress. With Democrats badly divided on immigration, the Republicans pushed hard to amend the Quota Law of 1921, which had been extended for two additional years. Republicans believed it had not sufficiently reduced emigration from southern and eastern Europe. After three years of acrimonious debate, Republicans in 1924 changed the baseline of the quota system. The division of quotas among Europeans countries was to reflect the national origins of the country's population as recorded in 1890. What occurred was that the Quota Law of 1921 was amended to where the total number of immigrants allowed for the next five years was pushed back from the year 1910 to 1890, which favored northern Europeans. The percentage was lowered from 3 to 2 percent, which meant the total number was limited to 165,000 per year. Another provision applied the racial criteria of the 1790 Act, which cut off completely the tiny quota that had existed for immigrants from Asia. Because of the growing dependency in Aztlán on Mexican labor, the Republicans set no numerical limitation on the Western Hemisphere.[137]

Signed into law by president Calvin Coolidge in May 1924, the Johnson-Reed Act[138] was a restrictive and bigoted piece of legislation. In highly discriminatory fashion, it sought to reverse the influx of immigration from central and southern Europe. It favored immigration from northern Europe, which meant that its paramount objective was to dramatically increase the quotas for Great Britain, Scandinavia, and Germany and substantially reduce those deemed "undesirable," such as the Italians, Greeks, Slavs, and Jews, among others.[139] Thus, with its quota system, once again immigration from Northern Europe was favored and that of southern and central Europe was further restricted.

That same year, Congress passed the Labor Appropriations Act of 1924. Essentially, it established the U.S. Border Patrol to enforce the law's provisions. As a pseudofederal police immigration enforcement agency, its cardinal function was to patrol both the Mexican and Canadian borders. Congress appropriated $1,000,000 in March 1924 and a staff of some 450 men who began patrolling, particularly México's border, on horseback.[140] By 1928 its numbers grew to 747 men. In explaining its role, Lawrence A. Cardoso states that when formed, it did not "ever consider the apprehension of would-be illegal Mexican immigrants to be their primary function . . . most of their efforts went toward the enforcement of customs and prohibition laws."[141] In explaining the impact of the restrictionist immigration laws passed, Roger Daniels states, "The real tragedy is not that the United States restricted immigration, but that it did so in a blatantly racist way that perpetuated old injustices and created new ones, which endured for decades."[142]

By the mid-1920s, nativists became embroiled in a political tug of war with the country's capital business interests over the issue of labor. While the former as capitalists defended the pragmatism of immigration as a requisite source of cheap labor for the country's economic development, nativists unequivocally disagreed. Congressman Albert Johnson publicized a State Department report that stated the U.S. was about to be swamped by abnormally twisted and unassimilable Jews, who were "filthy, un-Americans, and often dangerous in their habits."[143] Others politically argued on the need to protect the country's homogeneity, meaning its historic ethnic Anglo-Saxon/Nordic roots. Otis L. Graham wrote that 34 scholars including eugenicists from Yale, Harvard, and Princeton, lobbied Congress to pass national-origin legislation, in order to protect the country's basic homogeneity, without which they propounded "no civilization can have its best development."[144] Even President Calvin Coolidge in his message to Congress in December 1923 said, "America must be kept American."[145] Another scholar, Roger Daniels, writes that years earlier, Vice President Coolidge had published an article entitled "Whose Country Is This?" In it he defended the theory of Nordic superiority and argued against the intermarriage of Nordics to other ethnic groups that produced deteriorated offspring.[146]

By the end of the Second Wave of immigration, native peoples constituted about 250,000 of the nation's population. By the turn of the twentieth century, they numbered a mere 200,000.[147] From being the initial owners of the land, they found themselves tragic victims of brutal genocide, as occurred at the Wounded Knee massacre in 1890 where scores of men, women, and children were butchered by the U.S. Army. They were subjected to a violent imposed internal colonialism characterized by reservations that bred racism, poverty, powerlessness, and marginalization. Native peoples were the country's forgotten and totally disenfranchised. As an example, in 1884, the U.S. Supreme Court in *Elk v. Wilkins* ruled that the Fourteenth Amendment's guarantee of citizenship to all persons born in the United States did not apply to the country's native peoples. It was not until 1924, however, that Congress passed the Indian Citizenship Act, which conferred citizenship on all native peoples.[148]

No longer slaves as a result of president Abraham Lincoln's Emancipation Proclamation promulgated in 1863, the Black population grew significantly. At the turn of the century, according to the U.S. Census Bureau, they numbered some 8.9 million. By the end of the Second Wave, they had increased to 11.6 million. Although legally free in theory, in practice they were victims of a deleterious segregation built on pronounced racism, bigotry, prejudice, and internal colonialism. Although in the 1870s they briefly experienced the taste of political representation, it was short-lived with the passage of Jim Crow laws. A blatant example was the racist U.S. Supreme Court decision, *Plessy v. Ferguson*, of 1896, which sanctioned legally the practice of the "separate but equal" doctrine. Blacks were relegated to living under the virulent specter of de jure segregation. "Racism," writes S. J. Makielski, "seemed to have gained the status of virtual respectability in the United States."[149]

Yet during the Second Wave, Blacks were not immune to or exempt from the cancerous xenophobic vices of nativism. Some Blacks felt threatened, especially economically, by the mass arrival of millions of European and Asian immigrants. For Blacks, the negative economic consequences of immigration were real, especially in the northern cities and parts of the South, where they allegedly lost jobs and were displaced by the newly arrived immigrants, who because of desperation were willing to work for lower wages in substandard working conditions. This bred deep-rooted hostilities toward immigrants among some Blacks. A number of Black leaders and organizations adopted a form of "Black nativism," such as that of Booker T. Washington, who in 1895 delivered a blistering attack on immigrants before an audience of White business leaders at the Atlanta Exposition:

> To those of the white race who look to the incoming of those of foreign birth and strange tongue and habit for the prosperity of the South, were I permitted I would repeat what I say to my own race, "Cast down your bucket where you are." Cast it down among the eight million of Negroes whose habits you know . . . among these people, who have, without strikes and labor wars, tilled your fields, cleared your forests, built your railroads and cities.[150]

Nativists pitted Blacks against immigrants by pandering to their fears. The idea that immigrants were taking their jobs and therefore impeding their progress was accentuated.

Lull in U.S. Immigration

The years from 1925 to 1941 in the context of immigration history were different from the Second Great Wave. Immigration to the U.S. slowed down considerably. With the economic recession of the early 1920s having passed, the U.S.

from 1924 to 1929 experienced only a modest increase in immigration. In great part it was a product of the migrant exodus from México, which entailed the migration of hundreds of thousands, which by 1930 numbered 1.5 million. The Congress continued its debate on a method to determine a permanent quota system. In the 1920s a total of some 4,107,209 persons immigrated to the U.S. The number of immigrants from Canada and Newfoundland was the highest, 924,515; followed by Italians, 455,315; and Germans, 412,202. Most of the preceding immigration, however, occurred during the decade's first four years. Migration from México was actually second numbering 459,287.[151]

The consequences of the Johnson-Reed Act of 1924 were dramatic. European immigration decreased over 800,000 to less than 150,000 by the end of the decade. Under the interim quotas recorded immigration to the U.S. from 1925 to 1929 averaged 300,000 annually. This was sharply down from the 600,000 in each of the decade's first four years. From 1924 to 1930, fewer than 90,000 Italians and 50,000 Poles entered the country. Immigration from northern Europe, which when aggregated totaled 62 percent of quota immigration, again dominated.[152]

Although its full provisions did not go into effect until 1929, during the preceding five years, much debate over its provisions occurred and amendments were made. In 1927 the annual immigration ceiling was reduced to 150,000 and the quota was revised to 2 percent of each of the nationality's representation in the 1920 census. Two years later, it was revised and Congress sought a decrease in immigration. The annual immigration ceiling of 150,000 was made permanent for countries outside the Western Hemisphere.[153] Within this limit, quotas were apportioned to northeast and southeast Europe roughly in the proportion of five to one. The effects of the WASP ethos were apparent. The national origins system doubled the British quota and drastically reduced those of Germany, Scandinavia, and the Irish Free State.[154]

The stock market crash of 1929 ushered in the Great Depression. The U.S. and much of the world were detrimentally economically impacted. Even though immigration to the U.S. was not halted, during the Depression's ten-year period (1930–1940), it hit a historical low of 68,693.[155] Literally, with millions of unemployed workers in the country coupled with millions worldwide, the U.S.'s economy, unable to provide jobs for its native workers, was in no position to provide jobs for immigrants of other countries. The consequences were so severe that during four consecutive years—1932 to 1935—more persons left the country than entered, something that had not occurred since the exodus of the Loyalists to England during the Revolutionary War. The following table (1.1) provides a statistical profile of immigration and emigration for the decade of the 1930s.

According to the table, during the 1930s, the U.S. experienced a total "input" of 528,431 immigrants; whereas for emigration "output" the figure was 459,738—a net gain in immigration of a mere 68,693.

Table 1.1.   Immigration and Emigration United States, 1931-1940

Year	Immigration	Emigration	Net
1931	97,139	61,882	35,257
1932	35,576	103,295	−67,719
1933	23,068	80,081	−57,013
1934	29,470	39,771	−10,301
1935	34,956	38,834	−3,878
1936	36,329	35,817	512
1937	50,244	26,736	23,508
1938	67,895	25,210	42,685
1939	82,998	26,651	56,347
1940	70,756	21,461	49,295
Total	528,431	459,738	68,693

Source: U.S. Department of Commerce, Historical Statistics for the United States, Series C 88-144, Washington: GPO, 1957

The economic dislocations created by the Great Depression served to enhance the federal government's "clamp-down" on immigration. President Herbert Hoover was elected in 1928 on a Republican Party platform that accentuated further immigration restriction. According to L. Edward Purcell, "Not only did the Depression make [the United States] less attractive to many potential immigrants, but the Hoover Administration intentionally used the phrase 'likely to become a public charge,' a section of the 1917 literacy test immigration act to effectively bar many who might otherwise have come."[156] Congress strictly enforced the quotas and curtailed immigration even further: it denied cases involving family reunification. Even children facing extreme hardships, even death in their home countries, were denied entry on grounds that they would contribute to unemployment. Yet wealthy elites from Europe who sought to emigrate were largely allowed entry.[157] The election of Democrat Franklin D. Roosevelt in 1932 did not alter or foster any great immigration reform. Nativism prospered during the years of the Great Depression. The Americanization crusade that included the KKK of the 1920s continued into the 1930s nurtured by a growing eugenics movement.

Thus, the 1930s was the U.S.'s worst decade or period of immigration. But with Europe by 1939 enveloped in World War II, the U.S. began to prepare for a new chapter in the history of the country's immigration experience.

CHAPTER 2

U.S. Occupation of Aztlán and Rise of México's Migrant Exodus (1848–1940)

As a result of México's military defeat in 1848 by the United States (U.S.) it lost Aztlán, which encompassed some million square miles of territory. For those Mexicanos who remained on this side of the new boundary, the loss translated to their land becoming occupied and as a people they were relegated to an internal colonial status that was characterized by exploitation, oppression, and powerlessness. For the next fifty years or so the Mexicano population in Aztlán remained small. However at the same time, México experienced the rise of the "Porfiriato," named after México's President Porfirio Díaz, that fostered the antecedents to the Mexican Revolution. Their impact was such that during the zenith of the Second Wave of immigration to the U.S. it gave rise to the migrant exodus, which in turn precipitated the re-Mexicanization of Aztlán. In greater numbers than before they began to repopulate Aztlán. With the Depression crisis of the 1930s plaguing the country, Mexicanos came under nativist attack and were subjected to massive repatriations and deportations to México.

The chapter examines the impact of the U.S. occupation of Aztlán, México's migrant exodus to the U.S., and the manifold historical forces that impacted its genesis.

The Mexicano Occupied/Colonized Experience

AZTLÁN'S EARLY DEMOGRAPHIC PROFILE

Mexicanos in the U.S. at the beginning of the occupation of Aztlán in 1848 were ostensibly numerically insignificant. Prior to the U.S. War on México in 1846, as a region it was so underpopulated that it was difficult, if not impossible to conduct a census. According to Carey McWilliams in his classic *North from México*, when the "Treaty of Guadalupe Hidalgo was signed in 1848, approximately 75,000 Spanish-Speaking people [Mexicanos] were living in the Southwest: around 7,500 in California; a thousand or so in Arizona; 60,000 in New México; and perhaps 5,000 in Texas."[1] Yet historian Oscar Martinez argues that the Mexican population by 1850 was much higher than McWilliams' estimates. He explains that while no accurate figures exist, his figures run somewhere between 86,000 and 116,000. Much of the Mexican population was concentrated in New Mexico. Its population was between 62,000 and 77,000; California's was 9,100 to 14,300; Texas, 13,900 to 23,200; and Arizona 1,000 to 1,600.[2]

Right after the U.S. War on México there was no massive exodus of Mexicanos from Aztlán to México. Under the Treaty of Guadalupe Hidalgo's Article VIII, Méxicanos had one year to decide if they were going to stay in the new U.S. territory or return to México: only two thousand or so decided to return to México. Post 1848, with the exception of New México where they for decades would continue to be in the majority, Mexicanos were relegated to an insignificant population status. With the discovery of gold in California at Sutter's Mill in 1848 some 200,000 immigrants poured into California, reducing dramatically the proportion of the Mexican population.[3] Regardless of which figures are used, border scholars concur that the country's Mexicano population around 1850 and for the next fifty years was small and that Whites constituted overwhelmingly the majority of Aztlán's population.

David Gutierrez, extrapolating from U.S. and Mexican census sources, writes that in California by "1880 the number of U.S. residents born in México was probably no more than 68,000. By 1890 the Mexican born population had increased moderately to approximately 78,000." While there was an increase by 1893 "ethnic Mexicans had become a tiny fraction of the total population of the region that had once been their domain."[4] In Los Angeles, a city where Mexicanos in 1850 comprised 82 percent of the population, by 1880 they had dwindled to only 20 percent. In Santa Barbara where Mexicanos in 1860 comprised 70 percent of the population, by 1870 that number had dropped to 50 percent, and by 1880 it had dropped to 27 percent. The border city of San Diego reflected the same population pattern. Its numbers dropped from 28 percent in 1860 to only 8 percent ten years later.[5] Thus, by the 1890s, the Mexicano population remained small.

AZTLÁN'S COLONIAL EXPERIENCE BEGINS

In the country's immigration history there has been no other ethnic/racial group, with the exception of Blacks and native peoples, who were victims of internal colonialism. Sociologist Robert Blauner defines it as "the establishment of domination over a geographically external political unit, most often inhabited by people of a different race and culture, where domination is political and economic and the colony exists."[6] In his classic first edition, *Occupied America: Chicano's Struggle toward Liberation*, historian Rodolfo Acuña buttresses this argument:

> [The] conquest of the southwest created a colonial situation in the traditional sense—with the Mexican land and population being controlled by an imperialistic United States. Further, I contend that this colonization—with variations—is still with us today. Thus, I refer to the colony, initially in the traditional definition of the term, and later as an internal colony. . . . The parallel is between Chicano's experience in the United States and the colonization of the other third world peoples too similar to dismiss.[7]

Internal colonialism differs from traditional colonialism in that the latter entails control of the majority by a minority of outsiders, whereas in the former the colonized conversely comprise a minority and the colonizer a majority. Therefore, internal colonialism does not entail the subordination of a foreign land, but instead the acquisition of contiguous territory. While a traditional colony has some legal and formal status an internal colony does not; at best, it has an informal status and existence.[8]

Unlike other minorities that came to the U.S., Mexicanos, Blacks, and native people fit the model of internal colonialism. Why? Because all three groups' historical and political experiences coincide with Blauner's four salient characteristics inherent to internal colonialism: (1) forced entry; (2) destruction of culture; (3) external administration; and (4) racism. He argues that Mexicanos, Blacks, and native people suffered from "forced entry," meaning force was used to control them. Unlike other immigrants, their entry into U.S. society was involuntary: no election was held. Secondly, the U.S. internal colonial experience was characterized by a deliberate attempt to destroy their culture, language, and heritage, while implanting a form of "cultural imperialism" and domination via their compelled adherence to the White Anglo-Saxon Protestant (WASP) ethos. Third, all three groups were relegated to a politically marginalized and powerless status controlled by White external administrators and their colonial lackeys. Lastly, all three groups became victims of a virulent racism predicated on White supremacy; specifically, Mexicanos were cast ethnocentrically as inferior.[9]

Beyond the aforementioned four factors there is one more that is integral to internal colonialism—economic superexploitation. In all these cases, the U.S. as a colonial power was driven by the exploitive nature of liberal capitalism with its insatiable greed for profit, cheap labor, control of resources, and markets. Mexicanos became subjects of economic exploitation and subordination, which in turn fostered impoverishment. Moreover, they were robbed of their land and their land's resources were exploited and stripped of their wealth. Their labor was used to promote the agricultural and industrial capitalist development of the U.S. As migrants they became an integral part of the overall supply of cheap and exploitable labor. As a colonized people, Mexicanos were ethnically/racially segregated, which meant they were separated from Whites and targets of discrimination. The end result was a plethora of segregated, impoverished, and exploited mini-colonies within the U.S. that became known as enclaves or *barrios*. Regardless of the Treaty of Guadalupe Hidalgo with its variegated provisions formally extending the full protection of the U.S. Constitution, the decades that ensued relegated the Mexicano to a conquered, occupied, and internal colonial status.

Historians have documented how Mexicanos, as a people, during these years became strangers in their own land. After 1848, Mexicanos quickly were relegated to what historian David Gutierrez explains was "an inferior, caste-like status in the region's evolving social system."[10] Another historian, Manuel G. Gonzales, in arguing the overt neglect Mexicanos experienced during these years wrote, "Still another reason for the neglect of this period was the abject condition of the Mexican population in the Southwest before 1900. Small and powerless they were despised and oppressed by mainstream society. It is a sad and depressing story, but one that needs to be told nonetheless."[11]

The violence propagated by "forced entry" became evident in a plethora of historically recorded incidents. While some Mexicanos resisted the occupation, such as Joaquin Murrieta, Juan Flores, and Tiburcio Vasquez in California; Juan Cheno Cortina in Texas; and Las Gorras Blancas in New México, they and other forms of resistance were suppressed, often ruthlessly, by way of brute force.[12] The Texas Rangers in particular were known for their racist treatment of Mexicanos. They were the apprehenders, the judge, and often the executioner all in one. Violations of Méxicanos' civil and human rights were commonplace. Violence became the medium by which the White controlled and governed.

White politicians assumed the power and governance over Mexicanos. The *barrios* (enclaves) and *colonias* (unincorporated neighborhoods) were administered externally. In California, cities such as Los Angeles and Santa Barbara that during the first twenty years of the occupation had some Mexicano local and state representation by the 1880s had none. Lacking a population base, victimized by gerrymandering, escalating racism being directed at them, and a deliberate effort by White politicians to keep them out of the political arena were some of the reasons why Mexicanos by the 1890s were virtually excluded from politics.[13]

The same political scenario developed in Texas and Arizona. In Texas, Mexicano political participation was ostensibly limited to a few cities, for example,

San Antonio, and Laredo, which was where powerful White-controlled "political machines" directed by political bosses dictated the local political agenda. New México was the exception due to the Mexicanos' majority status and the effectiveness of Mexicano elites in cutting their deals with White elites who belonged to the "Santa Fe Ring."

Those Mexicanos with land grants given to them by either Spain or México, prior to 1836 and 1848 owned all of Aztlán, yet by the late 1870s had lost most of it a result of racist laws, chicanery, and confiscation. Mexicanos throughout Aztlán became landless and impoverished. One such piece of legislation was the Federal Act of 1851, which with its racist provisions deprived Mexicanos of their land.

It was during these years that Mexicano labor and know-how were used to work the mines, ranches, railroads, and farms. The barrios were impoverished and provided easy access to cheap and exploitable labor. Mexicanos were subjected to exploitative practices such as a duel wage system, which meant a higher wage for Whites for performing the same job. Segregation in the barrios fostered Mexicano businesses. Yet, Whites controlled much of the economy including the land surrounding the *barrios* and *colonias*.

Mexicanos were labeled as "greasers," inferring that they were inferior to Whites. They were not exempt from the nativist-driven WASP ethos, which sought to destroy the solvency of the Mexicano's culture, heritage, and Spanish language. Consequently, in seeking the "Whiteization" of Aztlán, internal colonialism instituted de jure segregation as a result of the *Plessy v. Ferguson* Supreme Court decision of 1896, which approved the "separate but equal" doctrine. Regardless of its legal status, segregation meant Mexicanos attended separate and inferior schools, were forced to live separately from Whites, and were socially ostracized by Whites. Paradoxically, segregation did much to foster a sense of "we," a common identity and community that aided in the preservation of their Mexicano culture, heritage, and language. In defense, Mexicanos started forming their own mutual benefit self-help organizations.

In spite of the prevalence of racism and White ethnocentrism, numerous cities throughout Aztlán managed to keep their Spanish/Mexican names, such as, in California, Los Angeles, San Francisco, San Diego, San Jose, Santa Barbara; in the state of Texas, San Antonio, Laredo, and El Paso; in New Mexico, there was Santa Fe and Albuquerque; in Arizona, Tucson; and in Colorado, Pueblo. With the gradual population increases that occurred by the 1890s new *barrios* and *colonias* were formed throughout Aztlán. This occupation and relegation to internal colonialism is in part what is contributing to today's immigration crisis. In other words, the first fifty years of the occupation set the historical foundation or paradigm for the ensuing decades.

Historical Antecedents
to the Re-Mexicanization

MÉXICO'S MID-CENTURY PRECARIOUS HISTORY

The re-Mexicanization of Aztlán was the product of a myriad of "push and pull" forces. The argument is made that the border crossed Mexicanos—Mexicanos did not cross the border. Implicit in this argument is that the region of Aztlán post-1848 with the signing of the Treaty of Guadalupe Hidalgo became occupied México. The re-Mexicanization of Aztlán would have never occurred if it had not been for a number of historical antecedents that ultimately produced the migrant exodus.

México's political history from 1848 to 1876 was characterized by incessant political chaos and instability, and the U.S. War against México only added to this situation. The intransigent political tug of war between Conservatives, who were chiefly monarchists, and Liberals, who adhered to a republican form of government, continued to weaken México on all fronts. Debilitated militarily and politically, and economically in shambles, México in 1853 bowed to U.S. diplomatic and military coercion and signed the Gadsden Treaty, which caused it to cede another chunk of Aztlán (i.e., the southern part of today's state of Arizona) for the sum of $10 million. In 1855 the Liberals by means of the "Revolution of Ayutla" succeeded in chasing México's infamous "real estate broker," General Santa Anna, and the Conservatives out of power. At a Liberal convention, the Plan de Ayutla was promulgated on March 1, 1854. Its liberal principles included a commitment to free and honest elections, free public education, the separation of church and state, and a return to a federal republic as delineated in México's 1824 Constitution.[14]

During the next three years, with Juan Alvarez elected as president and Zapotec Amerindian Benito Juarez as his minister of justice, the Liberals promulgated the Constitution of 1857 which incorporated various reforms of the Plan de Ayutla and subsequent reforms, such as the Ley Juarez[15] and the Ley Lerdo.[16] Both of these laws sought to curb the power of the military and the Catholic Church. The Conservatives rejected these reforms by initiating an internal war against the Liberals that once again plunged México into a morass of political conflict and instability. The War of the Reform (1857–1861), as it became known by historians, again pitted militarily the Liberals against the Conservatives. Civil war would wrack the country for the next three years. Under the able leadership of Benito Juarez the Liberals defeated the Conservatives by 1861 and adopted the Liberal Constitution of 1857.

In October of 1861, México again would be the victim of imperialism when Spain, France, and Great Britain met in London and agreed to a tripartite military mission to México, to remedy México's failure to make payment on its foreign debts. Spain was the first to land some 4,000 military personnel at Veracruz in December 1861, which were shortly thereafter joined by a contingent from Britain and France. As a result of differences as to the purpose of the three-power occupation, Spanish and British forces withdrew from Veracruz in 1862. However, Napoleon III, supported by México's conservatives, ordered the French military to remain as part of a scheme to take control of México and to build a new French empire in Latin America. With the arrival of additional French armed forces and the U.S. unable to invoke the Monroe Doctrine due to its own civil war, the French forces sought the occupation of México. The French were temporarily routed on May 5 at Puebla by the ill-equipped Mexican forces under the able leadership of General Ignacio Zaragoza and General Porfirio Díaz. From 1862 to 1867, Juarez's forces assembled into guerrilla units, and struggled to remove the French from México and to also defeat the Conservative forces. During this time México was ruled by Austrian Duke Ferdinand Maximilian. With the end of the U.S. Civil War and pressured by the U.S. and Prussian militarism in Europe, France pulled its forces out of México, abandoning Maximilian and the Conservatives. By 1867 without the military support of the French, the Conservative armies were defeated; and Maximilian was captured and executed along with a few other Conservative generals.[17]

In 1867 Juarez was elected president and the liberal political forces moved México into the U.S. political and economic orbit, embracing liberal capitalism. A semblance of stability and change returned to México. Juarez served as president until his death in 1872. Sebastian Lerdo de Tejada was designated as Juarez's replacement. He ran for and was elected president in 1873 and México again for a brief time enjoyed some political stability and change.

PORFIRIATO (1876–1910)

The *Porfiriato* became the salient historical antecedent to the genesis of the re-Mexicanization of Aztlán. It all began when General Porfirio Díaz, who had lost the presidential election of 1873 to Tejada in March of 1876, promulgated the Plan de Tuxtepec and led a successful revolt against Tejada.[18] For the next thirty-four years, Díaz ruled México with an iron hand through the effective use of his ruthless *rurales* (his personal rural police force made up of mostly former criminals)[19] and the military. Díaz fostered relative peace, stability, and political order in México. He surrounded himself with a group of positivists, the *Científicos*, who were technocratic social Darwinists that sought to transform México into a modern nation using scientific principles. Positivist José Ives Limontour, in an address to the National Science Conference in 1901, said, "The weak, the unprepared, those who lack the necessary tools to triumph in the evolutionary process, must perish and leave the field to the strongest."[20]

The positivists further believed that México's native people were inferior because nature willed it. They believed that the future and development of México rested on transforming it from a largely Amerindian and *mestizo* country to a White majority, one oriented by European values and customs.[21] According to James D. Cockcroft, "Justo Sierra, Diaz's Minister of Education, encouraged the 'Canonization'—including more U.S. and European immigration—to develop the nation's culture and economy." He mandated the teaching of English.[22] Relations with the Catholic Church at times were precarious and contradictory. Catholic Church properties were at times confiscated and distributed among the oligarchy. At other times, the Catholic Church was allowed to buy new property.

Much of México's means of production and distribution was controlled by foreign capital. During the Porfiriato, México was relegated to being an "economic colony" of foreign capital. Capitalist development occurred with the influx of numerous foreign companies from the U.S., Great Britain, Germany, and France, among others. They were allowed by Díaz to rapaciously exploit México's rich mineral and oil resources at the expense of its downtrodden masses. They controlled rural lands and dominated mining, railroads, utilities, industry, and commerce. The result was a pronounced disparity of wealth among the millions of Mexicanos who lived in impoverished, squalored, and repressive conditions. Left landless, according to Matt S. Meier and Feliciano Ribera, "many former small land owners were forced into peonage. While debt peonage among day laborers increased rapidly, domestic and foreign investors prospered as never before."[23] While the poor became poorer and farmers were left without farms, Díaz and his plutocratic positivist elites became richer and controlled much of the farmland.[24] Frank R. Brandenburg explains, "A pseudo-aristocratic society prevailed in which the rich, the foreigner, and the select politician denigrated the lower classes. The middle-class professional and intellectual was little better off unless they worked for a foreign concern, where they also felt shackled by a superiority-conscious employer."[25]

In an effort to offset U.S. hegemony or possible further annexation of Mexican territory, Díaz sought diversification of foreign enterprises and capital. John Ross writes that "the axiom Poor México, so close to the United States and so far from God may be the Dictator's most lasting contribution to Mexican nationalist thought."[26] México by 1910 had become known as "the mother of foreigners and the stepmother of Mexicanos."[27] México's economic reality during the Porfiriato was that most of México's natural resources were owned by foreign capitalist powers. By 1910 the U.S.'s investment reached a total of $640 million.[28] Brandenburg provides a specific profile of the aforementioned:

> Americans seized the cement industry. The French monopolized large department stores. The Germans controlled the hardware business. The Spanish took over the foodstores and, together with the French, controlled the textile industry. The Canadians, aided by Americans and Englishmen, concentrated on electric power, trolley lines, and water companies. The Belgians, Americans, and English invested heavily in the railroads. And what ultimately shook the roots of revolutionary ideology was the American and British exploitation of minerals, especially oil.[29]

In reference to the railroads, they became the vehicles with which Díaz opened Mexican resources to global capital exploitation. When Díaz took power in 1876 there were only 200 miles of track; by the time he went into exile in 1910 there were 12,000 miles, most of which ran from the south to the north toward the U.S. The railroad served a number of functions: (1) economically it facilitated export and import of goods; (2) for internal security purposes, it allowed Díaz to deploy troops rapidly and squelch any resistance to his regime; (3) it facilitated the travel of migrants from central to northern México; and (4) it made possible the economic development of various industries in northern México, which in turn began a demand for migrant labor.

The Díaz legacy was blood and brutality and loss of political freedoms by the masses.[30] Díaz's despotic regime, however, from 1900 to 1910 encountered growing political resistance and discontent. Opposition to the Porfiriato increased under the Liberals; while they were fragmented and forced to operate underground, this did not stop the discontent from surfacing. Initially, the Liberals' ideological program was to put into effect the provisions of the Mexican Constitution of 1857. They included the following: Díaz would honor his commitment not to run again, military conscription would be abolished, freedom of the press would be restored, there would be increased budget outlays for education and school construction, the anticlerical provisions of the Constitution of 1857 would be enforced, land reforms would be enacted, and the wealthy oligarchy would be deprived of its influence.[31]

During these years, the following two "antagonisms"[32] played substantial roles in starting the Mexican Revolution: (1) Ricardo and Enrique Flores Magon; and (2) Francisco Madero. Under the leadership of the former, the Mexican Liberal Party was formed. Ideologically, some Liberals during the early 1900s shifted to an anarchist or syndicalist's ideological posture that espoused the total destruction of the Porfiriato and the formation of a worker-state. Ricardo and his brother Enrique were jailed in 1901 and upon their release in

1903 went into exile in the U.S. From the U.S. the Magon bothers and other exiles continued their revolutionary struggle to topple the Díaz regime. Using the newspaper *Regeneración* and an alliance with the anarchist Industrial Workers of the World (IWW) they by 1906 formed El Partido Liberal Mexicano (PLM—the Mexican Liberal Party).

From St. Louis, Missouri, PLM promulgated its revolutionary social change manifesto in 1906, which included a call for the general distribution of land by breaking up the large haciendas. For the industrial workers, PLM proposed a minimum wage and maximum hour legislation, an end to child labor, the outlawing of company stores, and payment of wages in cash, not chits. Moreover, it demanded the closing of Catholic schools and replacing them with lay institutions.[33] Between 1908 and 1910, galvanized by the *Regeneracion*, some 5,000 liberal clubs formed in México.[34] Up to 1910, Ricardo Magon and the PLM played a significant role in engendering a "climate of change" for revolution in México.

The "second antagonism" that helped cause the Mexican Revolution was Francisico Madero's arrest on charges of sedition. Liberal Madero, a wealthy *haciendero* from Coahuila who had studied in the U.S., broke away from the Magonistas due to their adherence to violence. As a leader he inspired many to rebel against the Porfiriato. Feeling confident and secure, when interviewed in March 1908 by U.S. journalist James Creelman, Díaz boasted of the political maturity that México had achieved under his leadership; however, he made the mistake of stating that the presidential elections of 1910 would be unencumbered. Inspired by the Creelman interview, Madero wrote a politically innocuous treatise entitled *The Presidential Succession of 1910* in which he mildly proposed that if Díaz ran for reelection, the people should be free to elect their own vice president. As a result, liberals had rising political expectations and pressured Madero into running against Díaz. They formed the Anti-Reelectionist Party and their motto became "effective suffrage and no-reelection."[35]

At the macro level of capitalist economics, México's economy showed some development; at the micro level the overwhelming majority of the people lived in wretched poverty, dire oppression, and egregious exploitation. México's society was acutely stratified—rich against poor. It was a pyramid of oligarchic elite families at the top and at the bottom was the broad base of impoverished workers and peons. As explained by Hector Aguilar Camín and Lorenzo Meyer, "The pyramid of the monopoly reproduced itself, and both large cities and small towns saw their avenues of upward mobility being closed, as well as the deterioration of the most basic forms of local life."[36] Ninety-two percent of the rural families owned no land. Malnutrition was rampant and infant mortality exceeded 25 percent.[37] In México City's slums, the life expectancy of the poor was twenty-four years, and 50 percent of all babies did not survive the first year. In the rural areas, 80 percent of the population was tied to agricultural production, although less than 3 percent of Mexicans owned land. Rural wages by 1910 were depressed to where México's peons were paid 35 centavos a day.[38]

The worldwide depression of 1907 created economic havoc for the Porfiriato. In the words of John Ross, "henequen prices plummeted; copper prices collapsed; and the textile market disintegrated."[39] Labor unrest plagued the Díaz regime. The Cananea Strike of 1906 produced a violent outburst. Díaz officials gave permission to Arizona Rangers and volunteers to cross into México in order to assist 2,000 Mexican troops in ruthlessly squelching the strike. Scores of Mexicano workers were killed. In 1907, during another clash in Veracruz, 6,000 striking textile workers were beaten and gunned down by Díaz's *rurales*. For the next three years, civil unrest intensified and discontent grew, fostering a political climate of change propitious for revolutionary change.

The Mexican Revolution

CATALYST FOR THE MIGRANT EXODUS

The Mexican Revolution of 1910 was the greatest historical force to influence the demographic re-Mexicanization of Aztlán. The Mexican Revolution was the twentieth century's first major social revolution. Like all social revolutions, it was a product of innumerable historical antagonisms. From 1910 to 1920 the winds of violent revolutionary change blanketed México. *Caudillos* (strong regional leaders) relentlessly struggled for power and control. It brought massive destruction and the death of some one to two million people. It was the twentieth century's bloodiest social revolution. As a result, hundreds of thousands of Mexicanos migrated to the U.S. Prior to its examination, however, a terse case study of the Mexican Revolution is provided, which is indispensable to understanding its rise.

Diáz felt unfazed by the Madero electoral challenge. In June 1910 Madero won his party's nomination. Propounding liberal reforms, his campaign had been successful in galvanizing support among the masses. Threatened by Madero's surge in popularity, Díaz had him arrested and incarcerated on false charges of sedition. Madero escaped from prison, fled México, and went into exile in El Paso, Texas. Meanwhile, in the fraudulent election of 1910, Diáz won reelection. On October 25, 1910, Madero and his supporters promulgated the *Plan de San Luis Potosi*, an antimilitaristic plan that promised a return to the provisions of México's Constitution of 1857. Strategically, it called for an internal war against the Díaz regime and for the uprising to start on November 20. As planned, Madero crossed into México on the date designated and minor insurrections broke out in some dozen states. However, lacking coordination, the insurrections were initially effectively put down by the *federales* (federal troops). A dejected Madero returned to Texas to regroup his forces.[40]

In February of 1911 Madero reentered México to lead the revolution against Díaz. By this time, an "insurrection contagion" pervaded much of México. In northern México, near Chihuahua and Coahuila, Doroteo Arango (a former bandit who became known as Pancho Villa) and Pascual Orosco joined the struggle against Díaz. In the south, Emiliano Zapata and Juan Andreu Almazán joined the insurrection in support of Madero's cause. In northern Baja California, the Magonistas as well joined the struggle to depose Díaz. Meanwhile, in Coahuila, Madero's home state, Venustiano Carranza also organized revolutionary forces against Díaz.[41] On May 10, 1911, Ciudad Juarez fell and shortly thereafter on May 25, 1911, Díaz, fearing for his life, capitulated to Madero's Ejercito Libertador (Liberation Army). Díaz's thirty-five year dynasty came to an end. That May, at the age of eighty-one, he was forced into exile. He settled in Paris, where he lived another four years until he died a bitter and broken man.[42] As his ship departed from Veracruz, he had made the following warning, "The wild beasts have been loosed. Now let us see who can cage them."[43] Díaz's prophetic words came true.

With the successful overthrow of the Porfiriato and the rise to power of Madero, the second phase of the Mexican Revolution began. Instead of taking power immediately at the height of his popularity, Madero allowed Díaz's former minister of foreign relations, Francisco León, to become interim president until elections were held in October 1911.[44] In November, the interim president turned over the reins of power to Madero in the midst of growing instability and counterrevolutionary activity. Madero, who became known as the "Apostle of Democracy," proved inept at governing México. Politically, he was an idealist who was naïve in the art of revolutionary governance. He made blunder after blunder; for instance, he kept intact Díaz's military apparatus and bureaucracy. Lieuwen argues that "it is generally futile for a ruler to attempt to control, by gentle tactics, a praetorian army."[45] One of the Mexican Revolution's most prominent intellectuals, Luis Cabrera, in a journal article expands on this theme:

> This revolution had as its portent the political insurrection of Madero. But Madero saw no more than the political side of the Méxican situation. He professed that a change of government was sufficient to bring about a change in the general conditions of the country. Madero compromised with the Díaz regime, acquiesced in taking charge of the government, and ruled the country with the same laws, the same procedures, and even with the same men, with which General Díaz had ruled. The logical consequence was that Madero had to fail, because he had nor destroyed the old nor attempted to build a new regime.[46]

Equally as bad, Madero failed to control the bellicose revolutionary *caudillos*. Madero's *federales* faced the Magonista invasion of northern Baja California. By the time Madero took power on November 1911, Emiliano Zapata had openly broken with him over the issue of land reform and had promulgated the famous *Plan de Ayala* that same year, under the slogan of "*tierra y libertad*" (land and liberty). Beyond these uprisings, Madero faced two others: Orozco in Chihuahua, and Felix Díaz (nephew of the exiled dictator) in Veracruz.

Madero's downfall came in February 1913, after the "tragic ten days" when General Victoriano Huerta sought to subdue the insurrectionist forces of Felix Díaz, who were protected inside an old military garrison in México City known as the Cuidadela. William Johnson described the "tragic ten days" as part of a plot between Huerta and Díaz to reap the spoils once Madero was overthrown. He wrote, "As a battle it was spurious, fraudulent, a grand deception."[47] After ten brutal days, Huerta in collaboration with U.S. Ambassador Henry Lane Wilson engineered a coup d'etat against Madero. This lead to his arrest and execution as well as that of his brother Gustavo, Vice President Jóse María Pino Suarez, Chihuahua Governor Abraham González, and a few other lesser-rank officials.[48]

The third phase of the Mexican Revolution began with Huerta's dictatorship, which was supported by U.S. Ambassador Wilson. Huerta, however, was doomed from the start, unable to control the tigers (*caudillos* and *caciques*) that rose up against his illegitimate authority. During his brief tenure as dictator of México, Huerta faced the combined revolutionary armies of Villa, Zapata, Carranza, and the Magonistas, among others. What's more, Huerta engaged in an exchange of insults with President Wilson over the U.S. naval blockade of Mexican ports, that is, Tampico and Veracruz, which was supposed to curb the flow of arms from Germany. War between the U.S. and México was averted through the diplomatic intervention of Argentina, Brazil, and Chile.[49]

Huerta's *federales* (federal troops) proved to be no match for the combined might of the revolutionary armies. On March 26, 1913, Carranza promulgated the *Plan de Guadalupe*, which called for the overthrow of the Huerta regime and recognition of himself as *primer jefe* (first chief) of the Constitutionalist Army. The plan called for the occupation of México City by Constitutionalist forces. Carranza became interim president and called for general elections of federal officials. In addition, state provisional governors recognized by the *primer jefe* were to call elections for selecting state officials.[50] The armed struggle to overthrow Huerta allowed Carranza's Constitutionalist Army, if for a brief time only, to unite most of the tigers under a unified command, except Zapata.

The armed struggle against Huerta took eighteen months. On July 15, 1914, he fled México to Europe with a generous part of the Mexican treasury. A few months later, he returned to El Paso, Texas, to organize a rebellion against Carranza, and was arrested for violating the U.S.'s Neutrality Act. He was jailed at Fort Bliss, and cirrhosis of the liver claimed his life on January 15, 1916.[51] On August 14, 1914, Carranza's Constitutionalist army of 40,000 descended on México City. By early August, the *federales* surrendered unconditionally with the signing of the Treaty of Teoloyucan.[52]

The fourth phase of the Mexican Revolution began that August of 1914 with Carranza's rise to power as de facto president of México. He placed command of his Constitutionalist Army under the leadership of General Alvaro Obregón. With the ousting of Huerta, the power struggles intensified between Villa and Zapata on one side and Carranza on the other. After a series of confrontations, both camps agreed to meet in the neutral city of Aguascalientes on October 10, 1914. The so-called Aguascalientes Convention concluded on November 10, 1914, but produced only greater polarization. After the Carrancista delegates walked out, the Villa/Zapata delegates held Carranza in contempt. In addition, they adopted the main articles of the Plan de Ayala; disavowed Carranza as the interim president of México; appointed Villa as chief of the Division del Norte; and named Eulalio Gutiérrez, a *caudillo* from San Luis Potosi, as interim president.[53] The lines were drawn and *caudillos* and *caciques* from throughout México chose sides. In a show of power, Villa and Zapata's armies marched into México City in December 1914, but in early January 1915 they vacated the capital and soon after it was reoccupied by Obregón's forces.

The Mexican Revolution reached its Zenith in 1915. Internecine warfare engulfed much of the country, especially the central part. Obregón's tactical adroitness became evident in the battles the Constitutional Army won against Villa and Zapata's armies. Camín and Meyer argue that essentially four major battles won by Obregón's forces turned the military tide: "the two Celaya battles in April, the battle for positions in Trinidad during the month of May, and the Battle of Aguascalientes at the beginning of June." Because of food shortages, the latter battle forced Obregón to launch a sudden offensive that caught the Villista lines off guard.[54] By early August, after control of México City had changed hands several times, Constitutionalist forces under the command of General Pablo González retook México City. By October 1915, Carranza had the upper hand militarily and politically. The decisive defeat of Villa's Division del Norte occurred at the battle of Agua Prieta, near the Sonora/Arizona border, by the Constitutionalist Army under the command of General Plutarco Elías Calles.[55]

By 1916, Villa's forces were on the defensive, and in retaliation over the recognition of Carranza by the U.S., Villa attacked Columbus, New Mexico, causing seventeen U.S. casualties. In response President Wilson ordered General John J. Pershing to organize a military expedition into México to capture Villa. The Pershing Punitive Expedition, as it became known, was comprised of some 10,000 U.S. soldiers. It was a military fiasco for the U.S. Villa eluded capture and inflicted casualties on Pershing's forces. The effort only made Villa a greater folk hero in México.[56] Relations between the two countries further deteriorated with the interception of the Zimmerman note by the U.S. Telegraphed by German Foreign Minister Arthur Zimmerman to his ambassador to México, to be delivered if and when war between the U.S. and Germany became inevitable, it read: "We make México an offer of alliance on the basis of make war together, make peace together. We guarantee generous financial support (To be conveyed through a Japanese conduit) and the understanding that México is to recoup its lost territories."[57] Earlier in 1915, the *Plan de San Diego*, which called for an armed insurrection in Aztlán by Mexicanos, was intercepted and squelched by Texas Rangers and U.S Army in Texas.[58]

The fifth phase of the Mexican Revolution began on September 19, 1916, with Carranza's call for a constitutional convention in Querétaro. During the previous months, Obregón's forces continued their effective military offensive against the debilitated Villa and Zapata forces. The convention produced México's present Constitution. The 221 delegates in attendance were introduced to Carranza's moderate social reform program. By January 1917, after holding a number of sessions at Querétero, the socialist delegates, some of whom were military, such as Generals Francisco Mujica and Heriberto Jara, opposed several of Carranza's recommendations and pursued their own. Most of the military delegates were representatives of General Obregón. [59]

Under the leadership of Francisco J. Mujica, the delegates introduced several important articles to the new constitution. It embraced many of the liberal tenets of the 1857 Constitution. However, as explained by Robert E. Quirk, "In the Constitution of 1917 the basic principles of the Flores Magonistas and of Villa and Zapata won a political victory denied to them by Carranzas's forces in the battlefield."[60] The uniqueness of the Constitution of 1917 was its eclectic mix of socialist, nationalist, and liberal capitalist ideas. This was illustrated by the approval of several new articles: Article 3 prohibited the Catholic Church from participating in elementary public education; Article 27 provided the basis for agrarian reform and for nationalization of México's natural resources; Article 33 opened the door for the Mexican president to expel foreign companies and personnel from the land; Article 123 gave workers the right to collective bargaining, allowed for hours and wages legislation, and provided for the protection of women and children in industry; and Article 130 was a catch-all of restrictions directed at the Catholic Church, which prohibited and/or curtailed many of its activities.[61]

The years between 1917 and 1920 presented the sixth phase of the Mexican Revolution. Turmoil and political instability plagued México so Carranza reluctantly accepted the new constitution, but did little to enforce it. Few changes were implemented during the remaining years of Carranza's administration, which is what contributed to the existent discontent among the masses. Villa and

Zapata continued their guerrilla activities against the Carranza regime. The Zapatista insurgency was squelched by the *federales* with the assassination of Zapata. He was assassinated due to his betrayal by Colonel Pablo González, who allegedly agreed to provide him with a load of ammunition. Zapata was asked to come to the hacienda of Chinameca on April 10, 1919. Surrounded, the *federales* riddled him with bullets after first saluting him.[62]

Zapata's fate became Carranza's as well. By 1919, México was economically on the brink of collapse. Carranza refused to support Obregón politically and attempted to curb his power during the 1920 presidential election by fronting his own candidate, Ignacio Bonilla. With his life in jeopardy, Obregón consolidated his control over the military and in April 1920, his generals and supporters forged the Plan of Agua Prieta, which disavowed the Carranza regime. With the loss of military support, Carranza reorganized his forces and loaded up the treasury onto a twenty-one-car train bound for Veracruz.[63] Pursued by Obregón's forces, however, Carranza abandoned the train and took refuge in the indigenous village of Tlaxcalantongo. On May 21, 1920, he was assassinated while he slept by forces loyal to General Manuel Paez.[64]

POST–MEXICAN REVOLUTION YEARS

From 1920 to 1929, México was marked by political instability and counterrevolutionary struggles. This chronic instability continued to impel the migrant exodus and fueled the re-Mexicanization of Aztlán. Adolfo de la Huerta served as interim president until the election of General Obregón in 1920. Obregón governed México from 1921 to 1924 and implemented a number of reforms, especially in public education. Obregón in 1920 convinced Pancho Villa to retire from his revolutionary activities, offering him amnesty and a lucrative package of material incentives. Three years later, Villa was assassinated in an ambush. From 1921 to 1923, Obregón successfully crushed several conspiracies. The most serious was the three-month rebellion (1923–1924) led by General de la Huerta that nearly toppled his government. The revolt cost 100 million pesos and some 7,000 lives.[65]

In 1924, Obregón turned over the presidency to General Plutarco Elías Calles, who served as México's president until 1928. Calles focused particularly on implementing the anticlerical provisions of the Constitution of 1917. The government confiscated church properties, abolished religious instruction in public school, and deported and expelled foreign priests. As a result, México experienced another unsuccessful armed rebellion, this time from rightist and clerical fanatics[66] who called themselves *Cristeros*. From 1926 to 1929, the *Cristero* Rebellion involved some 25,000 insurgents. Their battle cry was *"Viva Cristo*

Rey!" (long live Christ the king) and fostered once again an armed struggle and unrest throughout the states of Jalisco, Michoacán, Durango, Guerrero, Colima, Nayarit, and Zacatecas. The Cristeros were militarily no match for Calles's *federales*. When the rebellion ended in 1929, some 90,000 people had been killed.[67] It ended after lengthy negotiations brokered by U.S. Ambassador Dwight Morrow. Catholic Church officials agreed to register priests as demanded by Calles. In return, Calles allowed religious classes to be taught within the churches. He succeeded in neutralizing the political influence of the Catholic Church.

In 1928, while campaigning for the presidency for a second term, Obregón was assassinated by a religious fanatic. After 1929, Calles maintained his political control behind the scenes by fronting a number of presidential puppets, for example, Emilio Portes Gil, Pascual Ortiz Rubio, and Abelardo Rodriguez.[68] It was not until 1934 with the election of General Lazaro Cárdenas that the spirit of the Mexican Revolution became institutionalized. It was facilitated in 1929 by the formation of the one-party dictatorship—Partido Nacional Revolucionario (National Revolutionary Party).

Migrant Exodus

RETURN TO THE PROMISED LAND (AZTLÁN)

While the migrant exodus had its genesis around the mid-1890s, it was during the Mexican Revolution (1910–1920) and its aftermath (1921–1929) that over a million Mexicanos left México and migrated to the U.S. It served as a "safety valve" or "outlet" for México's regimes during these turbulent years. On the "pull" side was the U.S. capitalist economy with its insatiable hunger and dependency on cheap labor. Capitalist development called for labor in a number of sectors, such as industry, agricultural, mining, railroad, manufacturing, and service.[69] The restrictive changes in the country's immigration laws, that is, the 1917, 1921, and 1924 Immigration Acts, which were explained in the previous chapter, impeded immigration from southern and central Europe. These conditions acted as a "pull" factor, since it precipitated a growing "demand" for Mexicano labor. Mario Garcia describes the historical impact of the migrant exodus: "At no other time in Chicano history [had] Mexican immigrants and refugees so totally dominated the Spanish-speaking Mexican condition in the Southwest and elsewhere."[70]

Much of the literature on migration to the U.S. from México concurs that the migrant exodus, or as some other scholars have labeled it, the "Great Migration," started in the late 1890s. It was impelled in three major phases: (1) the Genesis Wave (1890–1910); the Mexican Revolution Wave (1910–1920); and the Post-Mexican Revolution Wave (1921–1929).[71] México during these years lost about 10 percent of its population to the U.S.[72]

In the first migrant phase (1890s–1909), the first wave of the migrant exodus was the result of an "open door policy" that existed between both countries. During this phase no real or well-defined border existed between the U.S. and México. The border metaphorically was a "cactus curtain" that was characterized by the circular migration of people on both sides. Julian Samora explains that "people moved back and forth across the border without much interruption, with Mexicans supplying the labor for the region."[73] Another scholar, Leo Grebler, writes:

> This was still our period of our "open door" immigration policy, modified only by some qualitative restrictions and a small "head tax." Admission to the United States was arranged at the border station, and no visa was required . . . Shepherds, cowboys and farmworkers crossed the border in all directions as if there was no boundary.[74]

Throughout the 1880s and 1890s, the Porfiriato stimulated the economic development of the northern states of México. New industries and mining and agricultural enterprises were established that created a demand for labor. The expansion of the railroads north toward the U.S. increasingly provided workers with accessible transportation and job opportunities. For unskilled agricultural workers, the demand for their labor created opportunities for higher wages and better working conditions, which meant almost four times their agricultural wage of 12¢ a day. Expanding capitalist enterprises in northern México relied on labor-recruiting agents to draw workers from central México. Mexicano workers made their way to México's northern states, driven by rising expectations of better wages, opportunities, and working conditions. This internal situation of Mexican migration to México's northern states during the Porfiriato contributed to the first phase of the migrant exodus.[75]

Further contributing to the migrant exodus was México's population explosion. Due to the Porfiriato's imposed peace and improvements in health care, México's population between 1875 and 1910 increased by nearly 50 percent, which added some 6 million people to an already subsistence economy. México's population by 1910 had increased to 15,160,000.[76]

The rapid expansion of the U.S. capitalist economy in the agricultural, mining, transportation, and manufacturing sectors in Aztlán fostered an insatiable demand for a source of cheap labor.[77] It was not until the turn of the century, however, as explained by Lawrence A. Cardoso, that "large numbers of Mexicanos crossed the border . . . because of strong economic inducements in the southwestern United States."[78]

By the end of the first phase in 1910, the agribusiness, railroads, and mining sectors of the U.S. economy had become increasingly dependent on Mexicano migrant labor. The reasons are several. One, the overwhelming majority of European immigrants came into the country through New York and they were primarily absorbed into the industrial economies of the Northeast and Midwest. In comparison to European and Asian immigrants, Mexicano migrants were readily more available. They did not have to travel thousands of miles to secure employment. Two, Asians, by this time, for racist reasons as demonstrated by the passage of the Chinese Exclusion Act of 1882 and the Japanese Gentleman's Agreement of 1907, were no longer sought. Three, White capital interests did not perceive Mexicanos as any kind of threat to their political, economic, social, and cultural interests. Four, Mexicano migrants were said to possess a "homing pigeon instinct," meaning that they would work for a few months in the U.S. and then return to México. Their migrant pattern was not to settle permanently, but to work in the U.S. for only short periods of time. Five, the demand for Mexicano migrant labor was also based upon a lower wage paid to them, which increased capital profits. It was commonplace for Mexicanos to be victimized by a "double wage system"—Whites, including immigrants from Europe, were paid a higher wage, sometimes double that of Mexicanos, even though they performed the same labor. By this time, a number of U.S. employers were heavily engaged in labor recruitment efforts in México. And six, a capitalist White racist mentality that stereotyped Mexicano migrants as being tractable, obedient, hard working, and quick to learn under proper supervision was prevalent.[79]

It was during this first phase that the re-Mexicanization of Aztlán as a demographic phenomenon began. It is important to note that no records on immigration were kept between the years 1886 and 1893; consequently, figures were largely based on estimates. Referencing that prior to the 1890s, Aztlán's population was relatively small, David Weber writes, "The Mexican born population of the United States increased rapidly from 1870 on, more than doubling by 1900 when some 103,000 Mexican born were recorded as living in the United States."[80] James D. Cockcroft explains that in 1880 the number of Mexicano migrants born in México living in the U.S. was no more than 68,000 and by 1890 the figure increased slightly to 78,000; by 1900, it increased to 103,393.[81] Carey McWilliams contends for example, that Texas in 1900 had a Méxicano migrant population of 71,062; Arizona, 14,171; California, 8,086; and New Mexico, 6,649.[82] The bulk of these migrants settled in the borderlands.

The U.S.'s population by 1900 reached nearly 100 million and Mexicanos constituted a mere 0.5 percent.[83] This translated to a figure somewhere between 381,000 and 562,000 with almost all of them located in Aztlán. Economist Victor S. Clark in a report submitted to the U.S. Department of Labor in 1908 noted that an increasing number of Mexicanos were living outside of Aztlán, which notes the beginning of the Mexicanos' diaspora, meaning the scattering of the Mexicano migrant population. The report also acknowledged that the number of Mexicanos migrating to the U.S. was about 60,000 per year.[84]

In the second migrant phase (1910–1919), the Mexican Revolution of 1910 "pushed" Mexicanos by the hundreds of thousands out of their country into the U.S.[85] The U.S.'s capitalist economy demand for cheap labor from México continued to grow. This coupled with the existent open border acted as a powerful "pull" catalytic agent that accelerated the re-Mexicanization of Aztlán via an intensifying migrant exodus.[86] At the start of the Mexican Revolution, the total number of Mexicanos born in the U.S. was 221,915.[87] An additional 173,663 Mexicanos migrated from México into the U.S., which meant that for the years 1910 to 1914 the number was 82,588, and for the next four years it increased to 91,075.[88]

During this second phase, the passage of the Immigration Act of 1917, which had a literacy requirement to slow down the influx of immigration from southern and central Europe, contributed to the labor shortage. Also, with the beginning of World War I, the shortage of domestic workers was used as an argument by U.S. employers to pressure the federal government to "open" the country's southern border with México. This was illustrated by the fact that Mexicanos and Filipinos were exempt from the provisions of the Immigration Act of 1917.

That year the first Bracero (guest worker) Program between the U.S. and México was established. Under the guise of the Temporary Admissions Program of 1917, U.S. farmers and others were allowed to recruit seasonal labor from México. In 1917 some 18,000 workers were admitted and in 1920 the number increased to 52,000. The program was in effect until 1921, which during its four-year duration allowed a total of 80,000 Mexicanos to work in agriculture, railroads, and in the mines.[89] Many of the migrant workers did not return to México. In addition, the number of undocumented workers that came into the U.S. during this period reached some 100,000.[90] With the country hit hard by an economic recession in 1921, coupled with the Mexican government's growing dissatisfaction over the bad treatment of its *braceros* by some racist farmers, it allowed the program to end that year.

In the third migrant phase (1920–1929), the total number of Mexicanos born in the U.S. by 1920 dramatically increased to 486,418. Texas enjoyed the highest increase from 125,016 in 1910 to 251,827 ten years later, followed by California, which went from 33,694 to 88,771.[91] In Texas, the Mexicano-born population in the Lower Rio Grande Valley by 1920 had more than doubled.[92] Colorado, however, had the highest percentage of growth: it went from 2,602 in 1910 to 11,037 in 1920. Arizona also showed a substantial increase, growing from 29,987 to 61,580.[93] During the next nine years Aztlán experienced a migration from México of some 487,775. Between 1920 and 1924 alone, some 249,248 Mexicanos migrated to the U.S.[94] The volume and magnitude of the migrant exodus provided the matrix for most present-day Mexican communities, except in New México, which attracted few migrants during this phase.[95]

During the brief U.S. depression of 1921 to 1922, the first repatriation of thousands of Mexicanos to México occurred. To aid in the return of citizens, México spent some $2.5 million for food and transportation. Meier and Ribera explain that "this large sum indicates heavy repatriation during this period."[96] As to the lessons of the 1921 depression, Cardoso writes, "Many braceros that toiled in the United States became helpless in times of economic crises. Their value was only in times of prosperity; in periods of retrenchment it was minimal. Ethnocentrism and the needs of employers and United States citizens at large dictated that Mexicans lost their jobs first."[97]

México's incessant internal conflicts and violent politics continued to push migrants north to the U.S. Two such events were: (1) the unsuccessful revolt of 1923 led by General de la Huerta; and (2) the Cristero Rebellion of 1926 to 1929. During these years, the earlier migration patterns shifted to a more pronounced Mexicano diaspora. Mexicanos in greater numbers migrated and settled in other states beyond Aztlán, particularly in the Midwest region of the country and even into the Northwest. As a result, new *barrios* and *colonias* were formed in both the rural and urban areas of Aztlán and the rest of the country as well.

During the 1920s a reduction of immigration from southern and central Europe occurred as a result of the passage of the 1921 and the 1924 Immigration Acts,[98] which relied on the use of a head tax, literacy requirements, quotas, and prohibition of contract workers.[99] The two immigration acts did not affect the migrant exodus. In fact, México and the rest of Latin America were largely exceptions to the rule. According to Joan Moore and Harry Pachon, "Entry was increased or decreased by changes in law enforcement rather than by changing a policy."[100] Growers and railroad magnates in particular sought to prevent any quota restrictions against Mexicano migrant workers, because their labor was in such demand.[101] The huge Mexicano migrant influx created during these three phases substantially impacted the re-Mexicanization of Aztlán.

Impact of the Migrant Exodus

DEMOGRAPHIC PROFILE

The three phases of the migrant exodus symbolized one of the twentieth century's greatest mass movements of humanity. This was evidenced by the dramatic population growth of Mexicanos in the U.S. According to the U.S. Census, the total Mexicano population in the U.S. in 1930 reached 1,422,533.[102] This meant that some 10 percent of México's entire population lived in the U.S.[103] According to Francisco Balderrama and Raymond Rodríguez, "Research indicates that in all probability more than one million Mexicans entered the United States before the advent of the Great Depression."[104] On a state by state basis, the 1930 census also revealed that the Mexicano population in Texas was 683,681; California, 368,013; Arizona, 114,173; Colorado, 57,676; and New México, 59,340. Inaccuracies, however, permeated the 1930 census process.[105] For example, New México's population of 59,340 was dramatically undercounted; this was corroborated by a local report on school population that concluded that New México's "Spanish" population was actually 202,709.[106]

The third phase of the immigrant exodus showed a net increase of 152,599 over the total of the earlier period. The Mexicano population increased from 486,418 in 1920 to 639,017 in 1930. California outpaced Texas, the numbers increased from 88,771 in 1920 to 191,346 in 1930. Yet, in total numbers, Texas still had the largest Mexicano population in the country; from 251,827 in 1920 to 262,672 in 1930. During the ten-year period there were some states that lost some of their Mexico-born population. Arizona went from 61,580 in 1920 to a low of 47,855. New México experienced a decline as well from 20,272 in 1920 to 15,983 in 1930.[107]

In 1930 only 10 percent of the Mexican-origin population in the U.S. lived outside Aztlán. Illinois had a Mexicano population of 28,906; Kansas, 19,150; Michigan, 13,336; Indiana, 9,642; Oklahoma, 7,354; Wyoming, 7,174; Nebraska, 6,321; Missouri, 4,989; Iowa, 4,295; Ohio, 4,037; and Utah, 4,012.[108] During this same decade the Mexicano population also became increasingly urbanized. According to Rodolfo Acuña, "The move to cities by Mexicans was significant; by 1930, 51 percent of the Mexican population was urban (as was 56 percent of the population at large)."[109] The significance of this thirty-year period is that 94 percent of the foreign-born Mexican population in the U.S. arrived after 1900, whereas some 62 percent arrived after 1915.[110] Indicative of the rapid slowdown of the migrant exodus after 1930 was that only 38,980 Mexicanos migrated legally into the U.S. The following year, it decreased to only 11,915. Between 1931 and 1941, the number fluctuated between a high of 2,627 in 1932 to a low of 1,232 in 1935.[111]

The migrant exodus's demographic impact was felt in numerous cities and locales throughout Aztlán and the Midwest. The first three decades of the twentieth century witnessed the migration of some 728,000 documented immigrants and thousands of undocumented ones into the U.S.[112] Gomez-Quiñonez explains that "increased migration, combined with the rapidly expanding economy of the Southwest, led to the expansion of large urban concentrations of Mexicans in the Southwest's major cities."[113] Numerous *barrios* developed within many of the urban areas.

The population of south Texas at the turn of the century was 79,934. By 1920 it was recorded at 159,822, and by 1930, it reached 322,845. During this same period, Mexicans in the Winter Garden area grew from 8,401 to 36,816.[114] By the 1920s, Juan Gonzales writes, "The Rio Grande Valley was as segregated as apartheid South Africa."[115] Montejano explains that "in the new era of commercial agriculture, South Tejas remained basically Mexican."[116] South Texas cities such as Corpus Christi, Laredo, and Brownsville were major recipients of the influx of new migrants. Outside of south Texas, migrants settled in cities like Austin, Houston, Dallas, and Lubbock. The city of Houston, for example, went from a few hundred Mexicanos in 1900 to over 15,000 by 1930.[117] El Paso and San Antonio also experienced growth but it was El Paso that served as the major distribution point for Mexicano migrants, in some months processing more than 5,000.

In California the city of Los Angeles experienced a Mexicano population explosion. It increased from 5,600 in 1910 to 97,000 in 1930.[118] Other California cities were affected by the migrant exodus, but to a lesser degree: Santa Barbara, San Diego, San Francisco, San Jose, Fresno, Brawley, El Centro, Calipatria, and Calexico, among others. In the Midwest, Chicago's recorded number of Mexicanos went from 4,000 to nearly 20,000 between 1920 and 1930. Almost 70 percent of the Mexicano population in Illinois lived in Chicago. In Wisconsin, some 60 percent of the Mexicanos lived in Milwaukee.[119] The Mexicano population in Detroit in 1926 was 5,000 and two years later it increased to 15,000.[120] Some Méxicano migrants also settled in western states such as Nevada, Utah, Wyoming, Oregon, and Washington.[121] Even Alaska experienced Mexicano migration.

Implications of the Migrant Exodus

During the twentieth century's first twenty-four years the migrant exodus flourished due to the open border that existed between México and the U.S. Few restrictions existed before the establishment of the U.S. Border Patrol in 1924. It was well understood and accepted by economic, political, and immigration interests and by U.S. officials along the Cactus Curtain (U.S.-México) border that cheap labor was crucial to the success of their large-scale capitalistic enterprises.[122] Mexicanos were the new coveted source for cheap labor, particularly by farmers and ranchers. An important aspect of the migrant exodus was "recurrent migration," which meant that some migrant workers would work in the U.S. for a certain period of time and then would return to México. The majority of them, however, settled permanently in the U.S.

The migrants' class and occupational composition was diverse. It included workers, peasants, professionals, merchants, intellectuals, former soldiers, and political refugees. More specifically, however, according Del Castillo and de León:

> For the most part, the large percentage of immigrants who came north during the early twentieth century descended from the ranks of the lower class. Some 80 percent to 90 percent of them had experience in nothing other than agricultural work or unskilled occupations. The rest were clerks, craftsmen, and other types of skilled workers. The latter groups encompassed elites escaping the wrath of compesinos or revolutionary armies bent on retaliation for past injustices and oppression.[123]

They were lured, especially into Texas, by the prospect of jobs from México's border states: Tamaulipas and Nuevo León. Those who came from Guanajuato, Michoacán, Jalisco, and San Luis Potosí migrated mostly to California, although some went to states in the Midwest region of the U.S.[124] The vast majority found work mainly in the expanding agricultural, mining, and railroad construction and maintenance sectors. According to Gonzales, they also "found work as laborers on construction sites, public works systems, service and food establishments, lumbering camps, and ranches."[125]

The heavy influx stimulated a nativist resurgence, this time against the Mexicano migrants. Nativists publicly attacked and condemned the influx of Mexican migrants and demanded a halt to their migration. By the 1920s, Mexicano migrants were the main labor force in California's agricultural sector. In a xenophobic reaction Samuel Bryan, a professor at Stanford University, stated:

> "The evils to the community at large, which their presence in large number almost invariably brings, may more than overbalance their desired qualities. Their low standards of living and of morals, their Illiteracy, their utter lack of proper political interest, the retarding effect of their employment upon the wage scale of the more progressive races, and finally their tendencies to colonize in urban centers, with evil results, combine to stamp them as a rather undesirable class of residents."[126]

It was during the 1920s, the third wave, that nativists accelerated their vitriolic attacks. During the debate of the Immigration Acts of 1921 and 1924, nativist groups sought to include Mexicanos in their quota provision. Organized labor alleged that Mexicano migrants were taking jobs from domestic workers, were depressing wages, and were degrading working conditions. Some, with their inflammatory racist rhetoric, alleged that Mexicanos could not be assimilated because of their biological "mixture." Even politicians like Congressman John Box of Texas warned of the threat Mexicanos posed to the U.S. by describing them as illiterate, unclean, and peons, and warned of possible mongrelization.[127] In the end, southwestern corporations and growers and their need for cheap labor proved successful in lobbying Congress to their advantage.[128] Yet the nativists did prevail in influencing Congress to establish the U.S. Border Patrol in 1924 with an appropriation of $1 million and the hiring of 450 men to patrol both the 2,000-mile long U.S./México and 4,000-mile long U.S./Canadian borders.

From 1926 to 1928, nativists once again sought unsuccessfully to limit Mexicano migration by including México in the Immigration Act of 1924 quota system. Understanding the significant contributions made by Mexicano workers, once again, powerful White rancher and grower interests lobbied Congress to defeat the nativist efforts. Among them was Fred H. Bixby, a prominent southwesterner who owned some 100,000 acres in California and 250,000 acres in Arizona. In justifying the need for Mexicano migrant labor, he said, "We have no Chinamen, we have no Japs. The Hindu is worthless, the Filipino is nothing, and the white man will not do the work."[129]

The Great Depression

MEXICANO REPATRIATION AND DEPORTATIONS

The Great Depression of 1929 unleashed unemployment, economic dislocations, and an intensification of nativism directed specifically at Mexicano migrants. As a result, the surge of the migrant exodus during the 1930s slowed down to a trickle. Its impact was so acute that during the 1930s only 27,000 Mexicanos entered the U.S. on permanent visas. The share of Mexicanos in total immigration into the country was less then 4 percent compared to 11 percent during the previous decade.[130] The deleterious impact of the Depression on migration from México was illustrated in its first five years: in 1929, 40,154 migrants; in 1930, 11,915; in 1931, 2,627; in 1932, 1,674; and in 1933, 1,514.[131] From 1929 to 1941, Mexicanos were repatriated and deported in what can be described as a reverse migrant exodus.[132]

The Depression years marked the first time in the country's immigration experience that the federal government sponsored and supported the mass expulsion of immigrants, in this case Mexicano migrants. What occurred was tantamount to ethnic cleansing. The repatriations and deportations[133] sought to rid the country of as many Mexicanos as possible. Initially, the repatriation was directed at all immigrants, but according to Camille Guerin-Gonzales, in a matter of months Mexicanos were singled out.[134] Government at all levels and nativists overtly proposed, "Mexicanos go home! You are not needed any longer!"

Since World War I and into the 1920s, the U.S. enjoyed great economic prosperity, which was interrupted in 1921 by a brief depression. It was in 1929, with the stock market crash,[135] that the U.S. began to feel the horrendous impact of the financial downturn. Mario Barrera explains. "The economic dislocations of the Depression are well known: a substantial drop in the level of economic activity, dramatic declines in wage rates in industry and agriculture, and decline in the length of the average workweek."[136] With masses of workers unemployed, the federal government was compelled to develop social welfare programs designed to meet the urgent needs of the millions of impoverished people. The number of unemployed increased from 4 million in 1930 to more than 13 million in 1933, which translated to 25 percent of the U.S. labor force. Wages dropped from 35¢ an hour to 14¢ and 15¢, and in some instances down to 10¢, and weekly wages of $1.50 were commonplace throughout the Southwest.[137] The economic crisis worsened even further with the accelerated mechanization of agriculture, which displaced many workers, particularly Mexicanos.[138]

For Mexicanos the effects of the Great Depression were devastating, for it brought further economic misery[139] and increased nativist racist attacks. Many could not get jobs while others were fired to make room for non-Mexicanos such as Whites escaping the poverty of the Dust Bowl in Kansas and Oklahoma.[140] Their internal colonial status was exacerbated by massive layoffs, unemployment, worsening poverty, and loss of homes. Francisco E. Balderrama writes, "Many families not only lacked food but also shelter because they were unable to pay rent or mortgages."[141] Many of them found themselves on the rolls of the welfare agencies.

Increasingly Mexicanos were singled out as "scapegoats" for the serious socioeconomic ills that the country faced.[142] The Great Depression served to reinforce the already existing racism and discrimination, especially in the workplace. Few Mexicano workers applied for work since the perception was the jobs were reserved for Whites.[143] The Great Depression produced what Balderrama and Rodríguez describe as the "Decade of Betrayal," which was evident by the federal government's call for deportations and repatriation drives.[144] Both were norms of a "ethnic cleansing," meaning the depopulation of Mexicans. New restrictions on immigration to the U.S. were also adopted not through legislation, but instead through federal administrative regulations.[145] Deportation was a formal procedure conducted by the Immigration and Naturalization Services to remove a person from the country on the grounds that he or she was illegally residing in the U.S. in violation of the country's immigration laws.[146] During this time there were some twenty-six reasons for deportation—from being in the country illegally to advocating the overthrow of the U.S. government.[147] Deportation proceedings were based on: (1) formal deportation hearings under warrant proceedings; and (2) voluntary departures without warrant proceedings. The former was discouraged because of hearing and transportation costs, which resulted in the latter being more commonly used. The repatriation process denoted a voluntary process of immigrants returning to their respective native countries. It offered advantages to both the government and undocumented worker. The government saved money by paying for his or her transportation to the border, and in turn, the undocumented migrant was able to enter the U.S illegally once again. Most chose the option of "voluntary deportation."[148]

During the early 1930s, the federal government carried on highly publicized "deportation roundups" in numerous large cities both in the Southwest and Midwest. The deportations and threats of deportations, coupled with nativist hostile attacks, convinced thousands of Mexicanos, especially from Texas, to voluntarily return to México. While deportation drives began on more of a regional basis in 1929, by 1931 they had spread nationally. From 1929 to 1935, the U.S. government utilized both formal deportation and voluntary departure to deport some 80,000 Mexicanos to México.[149] From 1930 to 1939, Mexicanos comprised 46.3 percent of all the people deported and yet they only constituted 1 percent of the country's population.[150]

The massive deportations conducted engendered a "climate of fear" among Mexicanos throughout Aztlán. No other ethnic/racial group in the country suffered such a humiliating and racist experience. Carried out under the auspices of the Department of Labor's Bureau of Immigration, most of the deportation roundups resembled full-fledged paramilitary operations. Although conducted in several cities throughout Aztlán, southern California was the focal point of the deportation frenzy. One of the most famous roundups occurred at La Placita in Los Angeles on February 26, 1931. Some 400 Mexicanos were herded together like animals in spite of protests from México's vice consul to Los Angeles.[151] Mexicanos as a targeted and persecuted ethnic group, like the Jews in Germany, became the locus of nativist attacks. For Mexicanos, the Bureau of Immigration, Border Patrol, and local law enforcement agencies were this country's Storm Troopers.

Mexicanos came under a "state of siege" not only by government agencies, but by so-called reputable White nativist organizations and unions. Patriotic organizations such as the Veterans of Foreign Wars and the American Legion and the American Federation of Labor spearheaded many of the anti-Mexicano and anti-migrant attacks. They were joined by a plethora of newspapers (e.g., *Chicago Tribune*) and magazines (e.g., *Saturday Evening Post*) that fanned the racist fires against the Mexicanos and other so-called aliens.[152] They all alleged that Mexicanos were taking jobs away from White workers. Few non-Mexicanos came to their aid or spoke out against the nativist attacks. The state of siege revealed that Mexicanos had few allies or friends. Numerous foreign consulates did come to the defense of the migrant in the major cities that contained numbers of Mexicanos.[153]

Repatriation drives were far more effective than deportations in returning migrants to México. The heaviest years of repatriation occurred from 1929 to 1932 with 1931 being by far the highest. The number of those repatriated during this three year period was as follows: 1929, 79,419; 1930, 70,127; 1931, 138,519; and 1932, 77,453. In 1931 alone, during the month of November some 20,756 Mexicanos were repatriated. From 1933 to 1937, the numbers dramatically declined. In 1933, the total number of repatriations was 33,574; 1934, 23,943; 1935, 15,368; 1936, 11,599; and 1937, 8,037.[154] Thus, between 1929 and 1937 nearly 500,000 Mexicanos were repatriated and deported from Aztlán to México, many of them with their U.S.-born children.[155]

With the introduction of President Roosevelt's New Deal in 1933, Mexicanos started to shy away from voluntary repatriation. Mexicanos who were not U.S. citizens were not eligible to work on Works Progress Administration (WPA) projects.[156] Some of those repatriated had children who were born in the U.S., which made them U.S. citizens. To them, México, not the U.S., was a foreign land.[157] Some Mexicanos did return to México voluntarily without any assistance. Still others were encouraged to repatriate by local welfare bureaus and private charitable organizations that sponsored city or county repatriation drives. Indigence, not citizenship, was the criteria used to ascertain which Mexicanos were subject to repatriation.[158] The methods of persuasion for voluntary repatriation included inducements of free food, clothing, medical aid, and free transportation to the border and into México as well. This meant that counties paid for rail transportation to México's border.

From the border to the interior of México, the Mexican government provided free rail passage. Balderrama and Rodriguez explain that "trains with hundreds, sometimes over a thousand, repatriates aboard regularly left collection centers such as Detroit, Chicago, St. Louis, Denver, Phoenix, Oklahoma City, and Los Angeles."[159] Once in México, the Mexican government set up new *colonias* and some of the returnees were given land and assistance. By 1940, the U.S. economy began to improve and the Mexicano population in 1940, because of increased migration from México after 1938 and high birth rates, witnessed a slight increase from that of 1930.

Mexicano Demographic Profile of 1940

The Mexicano population in the U.S. was still relatively small in 1940. According to the U.S. Census Bureau the country's total Mexicano population was 1,624,733. Some historians allege that due to a major undercount, the actual figure was much higher, more like 2,125,000.[160] The urbanization of the Mexicano continued with some 60 percent living in the cities.[161] Cities offered greater employment opportunities and generally better-quality education, even though the schools were segregated.[162] David Gutierrez points out that the 1940 census showed there were 377,000 resident undocumented Mexicanos in the U.S., and nearly 700,000 Mexicanos born in the U.S. had at least one parent born in México.[163]

The data suggested that as the economy began to improve and demand for labor rose by the late 1930s, many of those who had been repatriated or deported began to return to the U.S. From 1930 to 1940, only about 20,000 Mexicanos immigrated to the U.S. legally and the federal government adamantly discouraged illegal entrance into the U.S.[164]

Mexicano population growth was the result of slight improvements in the U.S. economy due to President Roosevelt's New Deal policies and the start of World War II in Europe in 1939. Labor shortages began to occur both in factories (e.g., packinghouses, foundries, canneries, and the like) and fruit and vegetable fields, particularly in the Midwest. This served to strengthen the migrant stream, which included migrant workers from states like Texas who would work for a few months as seasonal worker, then return to their respective states; others, however, stayed.[165] High birth rates among Mexicanos also contributed to the population increase. Prior to World War II, only 10 percent lived outside Aztlán. With Europe enveloped in World War II and Japan threatening war in the South Pacific, the U.S. economy by 1941 once again showed signs of a demand for cheap labor, which in turn after World War II reaccelerated the migrant exodus.

CHAPTER 3

Era of the Bracero Program and Resurgent Nativism (1942–1964)

After suffering a "forced reverse migration" during the Depression years, the migrant exodus from México to the United States (U.S.) was revived from 1942 through 1964. With this revival also came the re-Mexicanization of Aztlán. Integral to World War II (WWII) was the Mexicano's role in filling the country's chronic labor demand for workers, particularly in Aztlán's agricultural sector. In 1942 the U.S. and México signed a bilateral agreement, the Bracero Program (BP), which produced a twenty-two-year guest worker program. For México, it acted as a "safety valve," a political and economic stabilizer. For the U.S., it was a "labor drug" that fed its addiction to México's migrant labor market. As the U.S.'s post-WWII capitalist Cold War addiction grew so did the migrant exodus, and consequently so did the country's Mexicano population. As was the case in the past, nativists once again began their attacks in the 1950s with "Operation Wetback."

This chapter provides a political historical analysis of the events from WWII to 1964 that shaped the era of the Bracero Program and resurgent nativism directed at Mexicanos.

Mexicano World War II Experience

MIGRANT EXODUS IS REVIVED

With the bombing of Pearl Harbor by the Japanese on December 7, 1941, the U.S. became engaged in WWII against Japan, Germany, and Italy. The Great Depression came to an end by 1942, in great part, as a result of WWII and the New Deal's economic policies.[1] The national propaganda called on all "Americans," including Blacks and Mexicanos, to join the war effort to defeat Hitler,

Mussolini, and Emperor Hirohito, whose totalitarian and tyrannical forces sought the annihilation of democracy worldwide. Mexicanos in the U.S., who had just experienced the egregious effects of "ethnic cleansing" during the Depression years, were now being invited back to participate in the U.S.'s so-called war effort to save democracy.

WWII produced a paradox for the Japanese American immigrant. From the onset of the war, fearing a Japanese invasion of the Pacific Coast of the U.S., President Franklin D. Roosevelt (FDR) ordered all designated enemy aliens, for example, German, Japanese, and Italian, to register with the federal government. In one of the most notoriously racist actions taken by a U.S. president, in February 1942 Roosevelt put forth Executive Order 9066, which authorized the War Department to send the aforementioned ethnic groups to internment camps. From nativist media to politicians, the country was sold on the idea that all Japanese were a security risk and needed to be interned. This, however, was not the case with the Germans and Italians. Only a few were interned because they in general were considered to be safe, supposedly because these two immigrant groups had been assimilated. The Japanese, on the other hand, were perceived to be a threat because they had not assimilated. Momentarily, the jingoist nativists shifted their earlier racist attacks on Mexicanos to what they referred to as "Japs."[2]

During WWII some 110,000 Japanese Americans were placed in segregated prisoner of war concentration camps.[3] There were a total of ten internment camps, all located in isolated areas of Aztlán.[4] Two-thirds of those interned were citizens of the U.S. They lost their jobs, properties, and homes; their education was interrupted; and their legal and constitutional rights were violated. They were treated as suspected terrorists and collaborators with Japan. The U.S. Supreme Court in 1944 in *Koramatsu v. United States* ruled that the internment of Japanese was legal and that the federal government had acted properly.[5] Yet in spite of their victimization, some young Japanese joined the army and fought gallantly against Hitler's armies in Italy.

For Chinese immigrants WWII was also imbued with contradictions. After sixty-one years of being in effect, the Chinese Exclusion Act of 1882 was repealed in December 1943. A broad-based committee of some 150 persons lobbied Congress to put an end to the highly discriminatory act. The decision was political and largely driven by wartime strategic circumstances, such as the need to reward the Nationalist Chinese government for its military contributions to the Allies in their struggle to defeat Japan. The final bill that Congress ultimately approved and FDR signed called for: (1) the repeal of all fifteen statutes enacted between 1882 and 1913 that had enforced Chinese exclusion; (2) the Chinese were to be given an annual quota of 105 with a preference of up to 75 percent given to persons born and resident in China; and (3) the nationality acts were amended so that persons of Chinese ancestry were eligible for naturalization on the same terms as other eligible citizens. Some anti-Chinese nativist groups unequivocally opposed the legislation on racial grounds. One such group opposed it on grounds that Chinese were allegedly morally the most debased people on the face of the earth. President Roosevelt countered by signing the legislation, claimed it was a manifestation of the American people's affection and regard for the Chinese people.[6]

The same WWII paradox applied to Blacks and native peoples. Thousands of Blacks who had long been victimized by the deleterious realities of segregation, internal colonization, and blatant racism, nonetheless participated in the war but in segregated units. They fought courageously and died in the defense of a democracy that had enslaved them and, even after their emancipation during the Civil War, denied their rights and segregated them. Native peoples, likewise, although they had historically been victimized by genocidal government policies continued to be relegated to an oppressed, marginalized, and exploitive status via colonial-governed reservations, they too mobilized for the defense of the country.

As for Mexicanos' role in WWII, as was examined in the previous chapter, they were victimized in the 1930s, by way of "ethnic cleansing"; yet, with the start of WWII, they were expected to put aside their nightmarish past and respond to the call by Roosevelt to defend democracy and freedom. Paradoxically, the very virtues the country was supposedly fighting for were being denied to them as a result of their relegation to internal colonial status. They lived under the specter of segregation, poverty, and powerlessness. Nevertheless, Mexicanos put their colonized status aside and responded to the call vigorously, positively, never vacillating. By the hundreds of thousands, Mexicanos came to the defense of the country. In the battlefield they were zealously gallant. Those who did not join the military ranks contributed to the war effort by working in the country's factories and agriculture fields that fed the nation.

During WWII some 375,000 to 500,000 Mexicanos joined the various branches of the U.S. armed forces, especially the Army and Marines.[7] On June 1, 1942, President Avila Camacho exhorted Mexicanos in the U.S. to put lingering animosities aside and support the U.S. war effort. Thousands of undocumented Mexicanos who resided in the U.S. enlisted in the U.S. armed forces. As an incentive for their enlistment, wartime legislation was created that gave them U.S. citizenship in exchange for their service. Relations between the two countries improved to where México declared war on the Axis powers in 1942. It also contributed a fighter squadron, *Esquadron 201*, that fought with distinction in the Pacific theater.

As an ethnic group, Mexicanos distinguished themselves in combat. They garnered proportionately more military honors (e.g. medals of honor) than any other ethnic group. Based on their percentage of the total population, more

Mexicanos served in combat divisions than any other ethnic group. In addition, a high percentage of Mexicanos volunteered for the more hazardous duties, such as the paratroopers and Marines.[8] They fought on every war front—from the jungles of the South Pacific, to the deserts of North Africa, to the invasion of Italy and Europe itself. Raul Morín's book *Among the Valiant* documents the numerous military contributions and the valor displayed by Méxicanos to the war effort. Morín reminds his readers that 25 percent of the U.S. military personnel who were captured and forced to participate in the infamous Bataan Death March in the Philippines were Mexicanos.[9] As Carlos Vélez-Ibañez points out, Mexicanos "over participated in combat units and suffered casualties in inordinate numbers."[10] By the end of the war, seventeen Mexicanos had received the Medal of Honor, of which five were awarded posthumously.[11] Equally important, none faced charges of desertion, mutiny, or treason.[12] Morín explains that some Mexicanos in the armed forces, however, felt a sense of betrayal because of the prevalence of racism back in the U.S. While Mexicanos were dying in the battlefields, at home they continued to be victimized by segregation, poverty, and racism.[13]

During the war a cultural rebellion known as *pachuquismo* (zoot-suiterism), a form of gang subculture, emerged. With its cultural roots in the late 1930s in urban areas such as El Paso, Los Angeles, and Tucson, young Mexicanos in the *barrios* joined gangs that wore faddish tapered suits with large lapels, padded and pointed shoulders, lengthy draped pegged pants, flat-crowned and broad-brimmed hats that included a feather, and a long chain that hung from the belt to the pants pocket. They wore their hair in a long, duck-tailed fashion and got tattooed; especially popular was a cross on their hand. Mexicanas associated with the gangs wore short skirts and blouses, and their hair was combed into a high roll. Gang members spoke a slang called *caló*, which was an admixture of English and Spanish, and were also zealots of swing music or jitterbug. Integral to their subculture was the adherence by some to violence and criminal activity, which ranged from petty harassment to murder.[14]

Two major incidents that involved *pachuco* gangs vividly illustrate the ironies associated with the WWII era.[15] The first incident was the Sleepy Lagoon case,[16] which occurred on August 1, 1942, in Los Angeles, involving Henry Leyva and several other youths from the 38th Street gang. While at a swimming hole called the Sleepy Lagoon, a fight between rival gangs resulted in the death of a young Mexicano teenager. Using the incident as a pretext, on August 10 and 11, the police conducted raids of Mexicano *barrios* around Los Angeles. Some 600 young people were arrested on suspicion of robbery, auto theft, and assault.[17] A total of twenty-four members of the 38th Street gang were indicted for the murder of the rival gang member.[18]

The Sleepy Lagoon trial lasted several months and on January 13, 1943, three of the twenty-four were found guilty of first-degree murder, nine were found guilty of second-degree murder, and five were found guilty of assault. During the trial, so-called experts attributed the gang warfare and bloody killings to their Mexicano ancestry. Particularly, Captain E. Duran Ayres of the Los Angeles Sheriff's Department argued that the Mexicanos' Indian blood predisposed them to a life of delinquency, crime, and wretchedness.[19] On October 4, 1944, after the case received national attention, the District Court of Appeals reversed all the convictions.[20]

During April and May of 1943 altercations occurred between *pachucos* and primarily U.S. sailors in cities such as Los Angeles and Oakland. The altercations were part of the anti-Mexicano *pachuco* crusade initiated by the police and hostile nativist press. After weeks of minor incidents, a blowup occurred in June 1943 in Los Angles when sailors went into East Los Angeles en masse. The sailors beat up, stripped, and cut the hair of suspected *pachucos*, while the police looked the other way. To add insult to injury, after the beatings, the police moved in and further victimized the *pachucos* by having them arrested for disturbing the peace.

For a week, the *Los Angeles Times* and the *Herald Examiner* inflamed and sensationalized the situation to the point that other clashes occurred. Both newspapers condoned the sailors' violent and illegal actions. Rioting also broke out in Pasadena, San Diego, and Long Beach. During the summer of 1943, similar confrontations took place in Chicago, Detroit, and Philadelphia. Nationwide, there was a "state of siege" mentality toward Mexicano *pachucos*. *Time* magazine called the situation "the ugliest brand of mob action since the coolie race riots of the 1870s."[21] After a few weeks of unbridled attacks by largely Navy personnel, as a result of diplomatic pressure exerted by México on the U.S., the Navy canceled overnight passes and instituted strict controls and order was reestablished.

Thus in spite of manifold contradictions Mexicano labor played a pivotal role in the war effort in both the factories and fields, since a shortage of workers existed in both the industrial and agricultural sectors of the economy. Numerous Mexicanos left the rural areas and agricultural work in the pursuit of employment in the urban area's numerous defense factories.

BRACERO PROGRAM

By 1942 facing a desperate worker shortage, the U.S. once again turned to México as a cheap supplier of labor.[22] Between 1940 and 1942, growers petitioned the U.S. government for permission to use foreign labor, and pressured the Roosevelt administration for an open border policy. This allowed growers, as had been the case during WWI, to simply hire individual Mexicanos who crossed the border. México's response to the growing pressure for some sort of informal labor agreement was not enthusiastic. Juan Ramon García writes, "Mexicans still recalled the deportation of their compatriots during the Depression; they were aware of the mistreatment suffered by United States citizens of Mexican descent; and they knew of the long history of cultural conflict between Mexicans and Americans, especially in the state of Texas."[23] In 1942 México conceded; however, not everyone in México was supportive of the idea. Numerous organizations and minor political parties opposed the guest worker program due to their profound sense of Mexicano nationalism.[24]

On August 4, 1942, a labor accord was signed by both the U.S. and México.[25] It was officially called the Mexican Farm Labor Supply Program and informally it became known as the *Bracero*[26] Program.[27] It was modeled after an earlier bilateral accord that was in effect during most of World War I, from 1917 to 1920. Established by executive order, México permitted its nationals to come and work in the U.S. for temporary periods and under stipulated conditions.[28] Though amended several times, as a conduit for Mexicano guest workers, it remained relatively unchanged from 1942 to 1947 when it first expired.[29] Ernesto Galarza provides a summary of the principal provisions of the agreement:

> Mexican workers were not to be used to displace domestic workers but only fill proved shortages. Recruits were to be exempted from military service, and discrimination against them was not to be permitted. The round trip transportation expenses of the worker were guaranteed, as well as living expenses en route. Hiring was to be done on the basis of a written contract between the worker and his employer and the work was to be exclusively in agriculture. *Braceros* were to be free to buy merchandise in places of their own choice. Housing and sanitary conditions were to be adequate. Deductions amounting to 10 percent of the earnings were authorized for deposit in a savings fund payable to the worker on his return to México. Work was guaranteed for three-quarters of the duration of the contract. Wages were to be equal to those prevailing in the area of employment, but in any case not less than 30 cents per hour.[30]

Employers were also required to post a bond for every guest worker and they had to abide by the agreement. Women were excluded because the Mexican government felt that they would be subjected to unacceptable treatment and abuse at the hands of greedy employers and sundry predators.[31] As Acuña points out, "Neither nativist groups, nor organized labor, not even the Communist Party objected to the admission of seasonal agricultural laborers under the terms of the agreement."[32]

It was not until seven months after the executive order was issued that President Roosevelt received congressional approval for BP under the aegis of Public Law 45. Yet it was as early as September 27, 1942, when the first *braceros* arrived in El Paso, Texas, followed by the second grouping two days later in Stockton, California.[33] Records show that from 1942 to 1945, some 167,925 *braceros* worked in the U.S. with the highest number in 1944, which was a total of 62,170.[34] In effect it was a federal subsidy designed to meet the agricultural labor demands[35] of agribusiness, which at the time proved beneficial to both countries. For México it was as a "safety valve"; it alleviated the pressures of high levels of unemployment and poverty.

During its first five-year period, some 220,000 *braceros* participated in the program.[36] In 1942 only 4,203 *braceros* were admitted, with the highest number being 62,170 in 1944, and by 1947, during its last year, the number declined to only 19,632.[37] More than half of the *braceros* contracted to work in the U.S. were employed in California agriculture. In 1945 alone, California growers employed 63 percent of the total *bracero* work force. During the off-season months, from January to April, 90 percent of the *braceros* went to California. As an agricultural workforce, they were used to pick cotton, sugar beets, fruits, and vegetables. In some areas they comprised the bulk of the unskilled labor for these crops.[38]

Beyond California, some 46,972 *braceros* were sent to Washington, Oregon, and Idaho. The remainder worked mostly on southwestern railroads and agribusiness farms. As to the former, in 1941 Southern Pacific Railroad requested permission to bring in workers from México for track maintenance work. The U.S. government took no action until 1943 when some thirty-two railroads requested and secured *braceros* under an agreement that included a minimum wage and a guarantee of 90 percent employment during the six-month contract period. During the program's first five years, according to Meier and Ribera, "About 80,000 Mexican *braceros* worked for railroads, over half of them for two companies, the Southern Pacific and Santa Fe lines."[39] By 1946, however, their use for railroad maintenance terminated due to political pressure generated by the major railway worker's union.[40]

Nativist forces became a major impediment to the BP's implementation in Texas. As a state it did not participate in the wartime BP due to the lack of support from growers and ranchers. They favored an "open border" policy, which was antithetical to the BP's provisions. They argued that for years it had functioned very well for them. In May 1943, the Immigration and Naturalization Services (INS) authorized one-year work permits, which in effect sanctioned an open border. Some 2,000 Mexicanos entered Texas before the border was shut down because of protests by the Mexican government.[41] Finally, during the summer of 1943, Texas growers requested the use of *braceros*. The Mexican government, in spite of their request, refused to issue permits on the grounds of discrimination against Mexicanos in Texas, which México deemed to be brutal and intolerable due to the practice of de jure segregation. According to Nelson Gage Copp, the Mexican weekly *Mañana* wrote, "The Nazis of Texas are not political partners of the Fuhrer of Germany, but indeed they are slaves to the same prejudices."[42]

In an attempt to placate the Mexican government, Texas Governor Coke Stevenson pushed through the so-called Caucasian Race Resolution. It affirmed the rights of all Caucasians to equal treatment in public places of business and amusement. This proved to be a major political mistake since most Whites in Texas did not consider Mexicanos Caucasians.[43] On September 4, 1943, Governor Stevenson established the Good Neighbor Commission of Texas, again in an effort to appease the concerns of the Mexican government. Funded with federal money, it sought to end discrimination against Mexicanos through better understanding, but it was not until October 1947 that México agreed to issue permits to Texas.[44]

Beyond nativist opposition, the BP was plagued by a myriad of shortcomings and was not uniformly implemented. The typical *bracero* was an unmarried male, came from a rural working environment, was barely literate, and spoke little or no English. México's chronic poverty, low wages, and unemployment raised Mexicanos' expectations of improving the quality of their lives and drove many of them to endure numerous hardships. These included harsh working conditions, prejudice, substandard housing, poor quality food, physical mistreatment, undue exposure to pesticides, unjust wage deductions, unreasonable charges for room and board, and low net earnings. The housing issue was slightly improved by late 1943 with the federal government's construction of ninety-five labor camps. A *bracero*'s weekly earnings were at times below the cost of shelter and board. The average annual income did not exceed $500 until the 1950s and it reached a level of $900 by 1960 (all dollar amounts are in U.S. currency).[45]

Under the aegis of Public Law 45, the BP continued after WWII until its formal expiration in 1947.[46] On November 15, 1946, the U.S. State Department notified the Mexican government of its desire to terminate Public Law 45. Growers, who had profited greatly from it, lobbied for its continuation. They argued that the need for agricultural migrant workers had not yet diminished and that they required more time to replenish their former labor sources. In response to pressure by the agricultural industry, in January 1947 legislation was introduced to Congress that called for the BP's extension until the end of June 1948. The bill was amended and passed on April 28, 1947, as Public Law 40. It was extended only until December 31, 1947, was to discontinue in thirty days,[47] and stipulated that the remaining *braceros* had to depart from the U.S. by no later than January 30, 1948.

The years between 1947 and 1951 constituted the BP's second phase. It operated under negotiated administrative agreements with México. With Congress intent on terminating the program in 1947, agricultural employers of *braceros* mounted a concerted campaign that swamped INS offices with petitions. They warned of continued labor shortages and demanded the extend stay of *braceros*. On February 21, 1947, the State Department negotiated a new accord with México that allowed for its continuation. Seven months later, Congress passed Public Law 893, which fostered little debate and no public hearings. One year later, it expired and left the BP to operate outside of any formal congressional oversight or legislation.

During this phase, according to Rodolfo Acuña, "growers were permitted to hire undocumented workers and certify them on the spot." He further notes that "between 1947 and 1949, 142,000 undocumented workers were certified, whereas only 74,600 *braceros* were hired by contract from México."[48] Between 1948 and 1951, a total of 401,845 *braceros* worked in the U.S. The highest number was in 1951 when some 192,000 participated. Since the beginning of the program over 600,000 guest workers had participated.[49]

The Mexican government became dissatisfied with the way the BP was administered because of the reported abuses against *braceros*. An incident occurred on October 1948 in Juarez when the Mexican government denied thousands of frantic workers access to the program. Pressured by Texas growers, the INS opened the floodgates at the border on October 13, 1948, allowing the unregulated entrance of undocumented Mexicanos into the U.S. Three days later, after some 4,000 had crossed, the gates were once again closed. In response to the incident, México annulled the 1948 agreement. In a diplomatic face-saving effort, according to Richard B. Craig, "Washington denied having sanctioned the action and apologized for the entire incident. México accepted the apology, but did not sign another agreement until August 1949."[50] In the words of Juan Ramon Garcia, "The bracero program deteriorated as legislation governing its operation removed much of the previous governmental supervision and placed the contracting of Mexican workers into the hands of private employers, which gave rise to many problems and abuses."[51] The government-to-government contracts that México had insisted on during WWII were replaced by direct grower-*bracero* work agreements.[52] "Between 1947 and 1951," as Meier and Ribera point out, "workers continued to be brought across the border as agribusiness returned to prewar practices. Labor contracting was undertaken directly by agricultural organizations and farmers without any arrangements between the two governments and with extremely limited supervision, México only."[53]

The passage of Public Law 78 by Congress essentially replicated the earlier arrangement. It marked the beginning of the BP's third phase. During the

Korean Conflict, which broke out in 1950 and lasted some three years, power-ful capitalist interests in the agribusiness sector argued that an acute labor short-age existed, which strengthened México's negotiating hand. Conferences were held in México City in January and February of 1951 involving U.S. and Mex-ican delegates at which a migrant labor agreement was reached that extended the BP until July 1, 1951.[54] On February 27, 1951, Senator Allen J. Ellender sub-mitted S984 as an amendment to the Agricultural Act of 1949, which was sought to curb the influx of undocumented workers.[55] After a rancorous con-gressional hearing process, floor debate, conference negotiations, and a myriad of compromises, it passed. It was signed by President Truman on July 13, 1951, as a temporary worker two-year measure, under the aegis of Public Law 78.

The BP's renewal was another indicator of the pronounced labor addiction to and dependency of the U.S. on México's migrant labor. In spite of this, as a result of a growing anti-Mexicano nativism, stricter controls over the importa-tion of Mexican labor were enacted. President Truman that same year appointed the Commission on Migratory Labor, which included Archbishop Robert Lucey of San Antonio, to study the problem.[56]

With the passage of Public Law 78 the U.S. again was the government guar-antor of individual work contracts.[57] It also was responsible for the establishment of reception centers near the border, housing, subsistence, and transportation for contracted laborers. Recruitment and management fell under the auspices of the Department of Labor. The INS was responsible only for the entry and departure aspects of BP,[58] whereas the Mexican government, using a quota system per state, assumed responsibility for the recruitment of workers and for making sure the contract was honored on both sides.[59] Because of the great number of applicants a lottery system for selection was used.

In México processing centers were established in Hermosillo, Chihuahua, and Monterey. Once processed, successful applicants were taken across the bor-der to U.S. recruitment centers and given medical examinations. Employer rep-resentatives then made their selection. After one week, those who were not picked were sent back across the border to fend for themselves. There was no provision for transportation support for their return to their respective village, town, or city. Selected workers signed contracts and were then transported to their work sites. The contractor farmer provided the transportation, housing, and work; the *bracero* was responsible for his health insurance, Mexican social se-curity, and food, and all costs were deducted from his check. Conditions of em-ployment, such as basic living and health needs, and the protection of the worker's civil rights were an integral part of Public Law 78.

With its main base of support coming from a coalition of conservative Re-publicans and southern Democrats, Public Law 78 was extended for two-year in-tervals in 1954, 1956, and again in 1958. By 1958 a serious attempt was made to terminate it, but was defeated. The Eisenhower administration called for a two-year study to be conducted to determine if it should be continued. The number of *braceros* who entered the U.S. increased dramatically, from a low of 187,894 in 1952 to a high of 450,422 in 1957, while the average number between 1955 and 1959 was 400,000 per year. By 1956, there were approximately 193,000 in Texas; 151,000 in California; 30,000 in Arizona; 20,000 in New México; 7,000 each in Colorado and Michigan; and 15,000 elsewhere.[60] From 1952 to 1960, the number who worked in the U.S. reached a total of 3,276,303.

Public Law 78 came up for renewal in 1960 and was the subject of controversy and debate. The 88th Congress in May 1963 voted down a bill to extend it for two more years. However, in December of 1963 it voted to extend it for one more year specifying that it was the final year. After twenty-two years of longevity (1942–1964), a total of 4,921,156 *braceros* had participated in this sanctioned migrant stream. The BP officially expired in December 1964 and the number of *braceros* dropped to 181,738.[61]

The end of the BP was ascribable to the country's changing economic and political climate, and demography. On the economic side, mechanization of agribusiness began to diminish the demand for agricultural labor. Politically, the climate was changing with the rise of the civil rights movement and resurgent nativism. From 1946 to 1964, nationwide numerous civic, labor, and religious organizations protested and pressured Congress for the BP's termination,[62] and various Mexicano civic organizations zealously opposed the BP. Organizations such as the League of United Latin American Citizens (LULAC) and the American G.I. Forum were against it on grounds that the BP and undocumented migration impeded the integration and assimilation of what they described as the "Mexican-American" community. Manuel Gonzales explains that "native-born Mexicans with weak sentimental ties to the Old Country were likely to reject the guest worker program."[63]

Not only middle-class organizations were against the BP but also many of those who lived in the impoverished colonized *barrios*. Conflict was commonplace between *braceros* and *barrio* Mexicanos, who were old migrants or first generation or both. The conflicts at times escalated to beatings, killings, and so on. The most disparaging criticism of the BP came from those who were estranged from their Mexicano roots, such as those that identified as Hispanos from New México. New México Hispano Senator Dennis Chavez up to his death in 1962 was a vociferous critic of the BP.[64] Those Mexicanos, however, who were from the lower class and were first generation adhered more to their Mexicano cultural, historical, and nationalistic roots and therefore were more accepting of the new Mexicano migrants.

A number of unions nationwide pressured for the BP's termination. They alleged that *braceros* thwarted labor organizing efforts, especially of agricultural workers. They argued that the BP lowered the wages of domestic agricultural workers and displaced them, worsened working conditions, and was used by growers to break strikes. Unions, such as the National Farm Workers Union (NFWU), founded by Ernesto Galarza in 1947, and its successor, the National Agricultural Workers Union (NAWU), the Agricultural Workers Organizing Committee (AWOC), and Cesar Chavez's National Farm Worker Association (NFWA) argued against it.[65]

Several religious groups also opposed the BP chiefly on humanitarian grounds. The California Migrant Ministry, National Council of Churches of Christ in America, and National Catholic Welfare Council,[66] among others, spoke out against a myriad of *bracero* abuses: terrible working and housing conditions, meager pay and absence of benefits, prevalence of discrimination, and racist attacks.

Nonetheless, the country's capitalist addiction to and dependency on Mexicano migrant labor generated once again a facsimile of the BP's guest worker program that was enacted in 1965 under the aegis of Section H-2 of the McCarran-Walter Act. The Lyndon Baines Johnson administration allowed 20,000 temporary workers to be brought in from México.[67] In response to the globalization of capital the Border Industrialization Program was established. The program allowed U.S. industries (*maquiladoras*) to set up business on México's side of the U.S.–México border and for them to hire thousands of workers at low wages. It also allowed for the importing of finished manufactured goods from México into the U.S. duty-free.[68]

REVITALIZATION OF THE MIGRANT EXODUS

Demographically, the growing Mexicano population by 1960 increased to some 4 million. The issue of the re-Mexicanization of Aztlán began to slowly take traction. For some White nativists, there were simply too many Mexicanos coming from México to Aztlán. From 1942 to 1964 the BP revitalized both the migrant exodus and, demographically, the re-Mexicanization of Aztlán. About 2 million documented and undocumented Mexicanos migrated from México and settled in the sprawling *barrios* of the U.S.[69]

As a "pull" factor the BP proved to be as powerful as the "push" factor of the Mexican Revolution.[70] "The bracero program acted as a magnet," writes Mario Barrera, "drawing Mexican workers into northern México. When many were not accepted as *braceros*, they crossed the border anyway."[71] From 1946 to 1955, a steady flow of undocumented migrants crossed into the U.S., which paralleled the number of *braceros*.[72] The BP itself proved to be a product of "push" and "pull" factors. México's pervasive poverty, unemployment, underemployment, internal migrations from the rural to the urban areas, and burgeoning population growth acted as "push" factors.[73] Also, acting as a "push" factor was the country's improved transportation system, which facilitated mass migration from the interior to the border. In 1940 all-weather roads covered a mere 2,000 miles. However, by 1950 they had increased to 15,000 miles and there were also 15,000 miles of railroad lines.[74]

Capital-intensive crop farming in northern México "pulled" large numbers of workers from central México to the northern and border areas of the Cactus Curtain. The cardinal "pull" factor, however, was the U.S.'s need for cheap labor, which was the result of a rapidly expanding economy. Between 1945 and 1955 alone some 7,500,000 acres of newly irrigated farmland came into production in seven southwestern states.[75] Demand for farm worker labor skyrocketed during harvest time. In the U.S. the absence of legal penalties, insufficient border control, a heavily populated Mexicano Southwest, the presence of border and trans-border recruiters, and widespread lack of concern, at least until 1951, contributed to the growing migrant exodus. The impact was so great that Ciudad Juarez's population increased from 48,881 in 1940 to 121,903 in 1950.[76]

Once the undocumented migrants reached the U.S.–México border, the motivation for crossing into the U.S. to make U.S. dollars became the driving incentive. Their impact on the U.S. workforce, especially throughout Aztlán, was such that during the postwar years, they began replacing Mexicanos born in the U.S., particularly in Texas. Many of the returning Mexicano veterans, who originally lived in the rural areas and worked in the fields, moved instead to the urban areas. Agribusiness demand for cheap labor was increasingly filled by Mexicano undocumented migrants. Not all migrated to rural areas to do agricultural-related work; instead, some migrated to the urban areas and worked in service, light manufacturing, and construction-related jobs.

Even though the BP provided agribusiness with thousands of contracted temporary guest workers, their hunger for exploitable labor could not be satisfied. Mexicano migrants became undocumented, according to John Chavez, "when the *bracero* program failed to accept them or because they wished to avoid the bureaucratic difficulties involved." He further explains that "they were hired by employers who were unable to obtain *braceros* or who wished to avoid the minimum wage and other restrictions imposed under the program."[77] Undocumented migrants were usually hired for wages substantially lower than the modest levels that agribusiness established for *braceros*.[78] Unlike *braceros*, they did not have to secure a permit; nor did employers have to abide by contractual agreements. In differentiating between *braceros* and undocumented migrants, Julian Samora writes there was "no need for contracts, minimum wage, health benefits, housing, transportation, etc. Since the workers are illegal aliens, they have few rights before the law and can be dismissed at a moment's notice."[79] Undocumented migrants resided in the *barrios* and some married Chicanas (Mexicanas born in the U.S.), had families, and remained in the U.S.

Undocumented migrants were now called "wetbacks" or in Spanish, *mojados* or *alambristas*. The former referred to those who allegedly swam across the Rio Grande between Brownsville and El Paso. The irony was that most "wetbacks" did not swim or wade across the river—they walked across.[80] An *alambrista* was a migrant who crossed the border illegally by presumably climbing over or cutting through a fence.[81] The smuggling of undocumented migrants became a lucrative business. There was the "coyote" that arranged the undocumented migrant's crossing, which all too often was a perilous journey. The undocumented were also forced to do business with the guides called *polleros*, who provided transportation and/or counterfeit papers.[82] Their fees could vary from $100 to $300, which included transportation costs.[83]

Braceros and undocumented migrants often worked side by side. After WWII, growers colluded with the INS, meaning that those undocumented workers rounded up by the Border Patrol would be brought back into the U.S. legally contracted when the growers experienced a shortage of workers. It was a process called "drying out" the "wetbacks."[84] Rodolfo Acuña explains:

> Collusion between the Immigration and Naturalization Service (INS) and the growers was a fact. For instance, the INS rarely rounded up undocumented workers during harvest time, and it instructed its agents to withhold searches and deportations until after the picking season. A rule of thumb was that when sufficient numbers of *braceros* or domestic labor worked cheaply enough, agents enforced the laws; when a labor shortage occurred, they opened the doors, regardless of international or moral law.[85]

In spite of agreements between both governments to curb the influx of undocumented migrants, between 1946 and 1951 this practice was common. A recession in 1949, however, stimulated an accord ratified in August 1949 that emphasized the suppression of illegal entry; consequently, INS initiated massive roundups of undocumented workers.[86] Growers who were caught hiring undocumented workers were denied access to *braceros*. In 1949, 87,220 undocumented workers were legalized as *braceros*, and an estimated 60,000 were legalized in 1950.

By 1951, U.S. Border Patrol efforts to control undocumented migration from México into the U.S. had failed. Between the years 1940 and 1950, some 800,000 undocumented migrants were apprehended.[87] During the WWII era, from 1943 to 1945, some 98,480 undocumented workers were reported to have crossed into the U.S. During 1950, the number of *braceros* was 67,500, compared to 458,215 undocumented.[88] The Border Patrol was not successful neither in curbing the migrant exodus or the growing diaspora. Its failure to halt the migrant exodus was evident: the total apprehensions of undocumented between 1946 and 1951 reached 1,690,580.[89] In 1953, for every migrant worker contracted legally, four undocumented workers were apprehended—some 875,000, with around 30,000 working in the industrial and trade sectors.[90]

The McCarthy Era: The Resurgence of Nativism

The Cold War's "red scare" politics of McCarthyism led to nativist and xenophobic reactions. The Cold War was not a battle of armies, but instead of ideologies. It pitted the Marxist Soviet Union and its Eastern Bloc against the liberal capitalist U.S. and its allies in Europe. It was a relentless struggle for world hegemony between these two diametrically opposed ideological blocs and superpowers. McCarthyism took the fears of the Cold War to an extreme: it was an inquisition that accused many individuals and organizations of being Communist sympathizers or fronts.

Even prior to WWII, the U.S. was leery of so-called Communist subversion and in 1940 passed the Smith Act. This act made it a criminal offense to advocate the violent overthrow of the U.S. government or to organize or be a member of any organization or group devoted to such an end. Numerous left-oriented organizations and leaders came under scrutiny. Federal Bureau of Investigation (FBI) Director J. Edgar Hoover played on the growing paranoia by postulating that the "free world" was in a do-or-die struggle against Communism. Numerous politicians, such as Richard Nixon, Pat McCarran, and Joseph McCarthy, pandered to the ideological fears of the people, which were exacerbated by the country's propaganda machinery.[91] The "red scare" politics were also buttressed by world events, such as the Berlin Crisis (1948), the success of the Maoist Revolution in China (1949), the Korean Conflict (1950–1953), and the Soviet Union's transformation into a nuclear superpower by the early 1950s.

Senator Joseph McCarthy used the investigative hearings to accuse numerous individuals and groups that he suspected of being Communist or Communist sympathizers. The McCarthy era produced a reactionary political climate predicated on fear, repression, and witch hunts. As Juan Ramon Garcia notes, "the times were not conducive to protest and resistance."[92] The country's political culture was such that dissension or criticism of the system were suspect and perceived as being part of Communist infiltration and activity.

Reflective of the right-wing political climate was the passage of restrictive laws. The Internal Security Act of 1950 and the McCarran-Walter Act of 1952 provided the mechanism for political control of naturalized citizens and in the words of Rodolfo Acuña, "laid the foundation for a police state."[93] David G. Gutierrez notes that "the Internal Security Act was passed as a means for prosecuting anyone who had ever been even nominally affiliated with a Communist, Socialist, or other organizations deemed subversive."[94] Its architect was Senator Pat McCarran from Nevada, who saw himself as the chief guardian in Washington of maintaining the country's racial (White) purity. He opposed admitting more foreigners into the country on grounds that it threatened national security.

In 1950, Senator McCarran introduced the McCarran Act to the Senate, which sought to tighten immigration laws and exclude subversive elements. By 1952 the legislation had a coauthor, Congressman Francis Walter of Pennsylvania. Designated as the Immigration and Naturalization Act or more commonly called the McCarran-Walter Act (MWA), it passed Congress over President Harry S. Truman's veto[95] who had argued that it created a group of second-class citizens. Truman specifically opposed the provision that naturalized citizens should have their citizenship revoked and that they would be subject to deportation on political grounds.[96] As a statute the national origins quota system was extended and comprehensively brought together with some modifications of previously enacted laws governing immigration and naturalization. One such modification was that it eliminated the racist and egregious provision of the Naturalization Law of 1790, which precluded non-Whites from becoming citizens, voting, and running for public office. In reference to this highly discriminatory law, Oscar J. Martinez comments:

> The law reinforced the common views that since Mexicans, including those born in the United States, were essentially of the Indian race, they could not be recognized as U.S. citizens. That interpretation allowed many local officials to classify Mexican Americans as nonwhite and to exclude them from voting or running for office. The law also helped to legitimize segregation and dispossession of property. All these practices violated the Treaty of Guadalupe Hidalgo, which implicitly recognized Mexicans as whites and explicitly granted them citizenship rights and protection under the U.S. Constitution.[97]

Other provisions of the McCarran-Walter Act included: (1) the codification of previous immigration acts related to national origins; (2) the establishment of a complicated procedure for the admission of Asians; (3) the inclusion of a long list of grounds by which undocumented workers identified as "aliens" could be deported or excluded; (4) the inclusion of conditions under which naturalized citizens could be denaturalized; and (5) the granting of power to the INS to interrogate undocumented workers suspected of being illegally in the country; to search boats, trains, cars, trucks, or planes; to enter and search private lands within twenty-five miles of the border; and to arrest so-called illegals and those suspected of committing felonies.[98]

Moreover, under Title I of the MWA a Subversive Activities Control Board was established to investigate suspected subversion. Title II was equally as harmful in that it authorized the construction of several camps to intern suspected subversives without a trial or hearing if either the president or Congress called for a "national emergency." Two years after its passage, some six camps were built.[99] Some Mexicano community leaders considered to be as subversives were deported and denaturalized. Organizations came under scrutiny and were subject to investigation as well. Passage of the MWA served to reveal the fears and biases of the country's governing leadership by defining very specifically the parameters of who was or was not eligible for citizenship. With few exceptions most Mexicano middle-class organizations supported its passage and progressive ones rejected it. The passage of MWA helped pave the way for Operation Wetback.[100]

Operation Wetback: A Nativist Crusade

The McCarthy fear-driven politics contributed to the resurgence of nativism directed at the migrant exodus. The President's Commission on Migratory Labor released a report in 1951 that sounded an alarm over the rise of undocumented migration, warning ominously that "the magnitude of the wetback traffic has reached entirely new levels in the past 7 years. . . . In its newly achieved proportions, it is virtually an invasion." It went on to say that "the wetback traffic has reached such proportions in volume and in consequent chaos, it should not be neglected any longer."[101] Growers and their allies in Congress attacked the report as being biased by union sympathies and reformist in nature. It acted as a catalyst for mobilizing anti-immigrant nativist sentiments among the White populace and opened a Pandora's box of xenophobia.

Upon the report's release, the *New York Times* ran a five-part series on undocumented migration, blaming southwestern growers for bringing them into the country, then treating them as peons who depressed wages and contributed to crime. The series served to further politicize and bring other media onto the nativist bandwagon. Radio stations reacted by pandering to Whites' fears and incertitude. A *New York Times* service broadcast from Los Angeles alleged that undocumented migration from México had reached such overwhelming proportions that INS officers had admitted candidly that there was nothing to stop the whole nation of México from moving into the U.S. It stressed that 10 percent of México's population was already in the U.S.[102] Nativist-driven media depicted undocumented migrants as dangerous "aliens" who posed a security threat to the country.

Further adding to the media frenzy against undocumented migrants was the release of another report prepared by the American G.I. Forum in collaboration with several labor unions that same year (1953), entitled "What Price Wetbacks?" Written in vitriolic language, much like that of reactionary-right politicians like McCarthy and McCarran, it concluded that the "wetback problem" was the fundamental problem facing Mexican Americans (Mexicanos born in the U.S.) in the Southwest. The report ardently supported the Border Patrol's efforts to curb undocumented migration, calling for additional resources and facilities and the passage of stronger restrictionist immigration laws.[103] The American G.I. Forum took the position that both were major obstacles for Mexican Americans in their struggle to achieve their civil rights and economic objectives.[104] For Mexicano undocumented migrants, they had met the nativist enemy and paradoxically, the enemy included their own.

With the U.S. plagued by an economic recession in 1953, widespread alarm grew about the "wetback invasion." Nativist activists and politicians recommended to Congress that the U.S. Army be utilized to "stem the tide."[105] In Washington politicians were under tremendous pressure, especially by labor unions, to do something about the influx of undocumented workers. With the appointment of retired Lieutenant General Joseph M. Swing as INS commissioner by newly elected President Eisenhower, the stage was set for Operation Wetback. Swing's background, says Rodolfo Acuña, was that of "professional longtime Mexican hater." Swing had been a classmate of President Eisenhower at West Point in 1911, and had participated in General Pershing's punitive expedition against Pancho Villa in 1916.[106] With Swing's appointment, the INS became more assertive in its tactical efforts to deport undocumented migrants and adhered to a quasi-military posture. Commissioner Swing, in his efforts to halt the so-called invasion, requested $10 million to build a 150-mile fence along the U.S.–México border and set a quota for those to be deported from each target area. In 1953 alone, the INS deported some 886,000 Mexicanos.[107] Of those, 20,174 were airlifted into México from Spokane, Chicago, Kansas City, St. Louis, and other cities.[108] Named by Commissioner Swing, Operation Wetback was not officially launched until June 1, 1954.

In June 1954, U.S. Attorney General Herbert Brownell, Jr., ordered a massive deportation drive that put Operation Wetback into full speed. He cited the possible illegal entrance of political subversives into the U.S. as the rationale for launching the drive.[109] California was the first target and then Texas, and within weeks it was extended throughout Aztlán and several Midwest cities.[110] During the ensuing months, *barrios* were under a "state of siege." Undocumented migrants lived under the constant fear of deportation both at their residences and workplaces. The civil liberties and human rights of deportees were often callously ignored. Simply looking Mexicano often sufficed as a reason for official scrutiny and apprehension. Without appropriate legal documentation on hand, suspected undocumented migrants ran the risk of arrest and deportation. Treatment of deportees at times was marked by the use of intimidation, harshness, and contempt.[111]

Supported by a high-profile media campaign, Border Patrol agents conducted military type sweeps of *barrios* and workplaces, deporting thousands of undocumented migrants annually. In 1954 the number of undocumented migrants apprehended dramatically increased to 1,089,000, but in 1955, with the economy beginning to improve, the number decreased to 254,000. Ironically, even though the country was no longer in a recession and the demand for cheap labor was again rising, the number in 1956 decreased even further to 88,000. During the next three years, the numbers continued to decrease: in 1957, 60,000; in 1958, 53,000; and in 1959, 45,000.[112] In 1960 the number increased to 71,000, but decreased in 1964 to 43,844; in 1965 there was another slight increase, bringing the number to 55,349.[113] The total apprehended during the official two-year (1954–1955) duration of Operation Wetback was 1,343,000.

The above figures suggest that the highest number of apprehensions and deportations occurred during the country's years of economic recession, while the lowest number occurred during those years that the economy was stable and relatively healthy. This reveals that during times of economic recession the country experiences a resurgence of nativism. In reference to their INS processing, some went through formal hearings; the great majority, however, were merely sent across the border. In some cases, with the cooperation of the Mexican government, they were sent to points designated near their homes in México.[114]

INS Commissioner Swing officially announced the termination of Operation Wetback in 1955, calling it a great success. Juan Ramon Garcia notes, "Operation Wetback marked the end of the wetback decade. However, it did not mark the end of the illegal. The mass deportation of undocumented workers was only a temporary stopgap measure, designed to quell critics and assuage an aroused public. For the moment, employers had to content themselves with contracting *braceros*."[115] Because of its large scale and quasi-military thrust and rough treatment of the undocumented migrants, it became one of the most traumatic experiences endured by Mexicanos in their dealings with the federal government.[116] No *barrio* or *colonia* in Aztlán remained untouched; neither did those in the regions of the Northwest and Midwest. In short, it became a deliberate attemt by the federal government to "ethnic cleanse" Mexicano undocumented migrante.

Paradoxically, while the growers sought access to a cheap source of labor and spoke out against Operation Wetback, the overwhelming number of middle-class Mexicano organizations, such as LULAC and the American G.I. Forum, supported it. One of the few organizations to ardently speak out against it was La Asociacíon Nacional México Americana.[117] Unlike most other Mexicano organizations that were middle class, its leadership and membership were working-class based and were committed to protecting the interests and rights of undocumented migrants.

Re-Mexicanization of Aztlán Intensifies

During the 1950s and early 1960s, due to the BP and unremitting migrant exodus, the re-Mexicanization of Aztlán was heightened. Due to México's serious economic problems and a U.S. economy that desperately needed undocumented migrants, many *braceros* returned to the U.S. and established residence in *barrios* throughout Aztlán, the Midwest, and Northwest. Regardless of all the inequities Mexicanos faced in the U.S., socioeconomically they felt that they were better off in the U.S. than living under the impoverished conditions of México.

The Mexicano population increase was also ascribable to high birth rates. Above all other ethnic or racial groups in the U.S., Mexicanos had the largest families. Joan W. Moore noted that no other category of people in the U.S. except Native Americans matched their typical family size of 4.8 persons. Whites in Aztlán averaged 3.4 persons per family in 1960, and the non-Whites in the same region, 4.5 persons.[118] Mexicanos living in the rural areas had larger families than those living in urban areas.[119] The median age of the entire Mexicano population was 19.6 in 1960, a full ten years lower than that of Whites and four years lower than that of non-Whites. Some 40 percent of the Mexicano population was younger than fifteen years of age, whereas for Whites only about 30 percent were under fifteen years of age.[120]

According to the U.S. Census, the country's population in 1950 was 150,216,110. The Spanish-surname population, as it was designated, in Aztlán was 2,289,550, which by 1960 increased to 3,464,999; and nationwide, was almost 4 million. Although the majority of the Mexicano population was native-born in 1950, by 1960, the number of foreign-born had increased significantly.

California experienced the most dramatic population shift. In 1950 its Spanish-surname population was 760,453 but by 1960 it had increased to 1,426,538. California had the largest concentration of Mexicanos of any state followed by Texas, which had a population in 1950 of 1,033,768 and by 1960 it had increased to 1,417,810. New México's Spanish-surname population went from 248,880 in 1950 to 269,122 in 1960, while Arizona's went from 128,318 in 1950 to 194,356 in 1960, and finally, Colorado's went from 118,131 in 1950 to 157,173 in 1960.[121]

Overall U.S. Legal Immigration

During the years 1940 to 1960, overall immigration into the U.S. increased. Census Bureau statistics reveal that during the 1940s a total of 1,035,039 legal immigrants arrived. Of the total, the largest legal immigrant group came from Germany, numbering 226,578, followed by Canada and Newfoundland with 171,718, the United Kingdom with 139,306, and México with 60,569. Mexicanos made up 5.9 percent of the country's legal immigration, whereas White immigrants from northern European countries made up 52 percent. Germans constituted the largest immigrant group, with 21.6 percent. A major increase in legal immigration occurred during the 1950s. A total of some 2,515,479 legal immigrants came to the U.S. Of that total, 477,765 came from Germany, 377,952 from Canada 299,811 from México, and 202,824 from the United Kingdom. Germany and Canada combined comprised a total of 34 percent of the legal immigrant population, while México increased to 11.9 percent and the United Kingdom's share decreased to 8.1 percent.

By the 1960s, the total number of legal immigrants increased dramatically to 3,321,677. This time, México was the number-one contributor with 453,937, followed by Canada with 413,310, Italy with 214,111, and the United Kingdom with 213,822.[122] For Mexicanos, legal immigration via permanent visas began to accelerate by the early 1950s. An appreciable increase in immigration occurred; Mexicano immigration went from 6,372 in 1951 to 65,000 in 1956. During the decade, nearly 299,811 were recorded, which meant that during the second half of the 1950s, some 15 percent of the total legal immigration into the U.S. was Mexicano. The increased volume did not reflect a relaxation of the law or its administration, but merely indicated the changes introduced by the McCarran-Walter Act of 1952. The number of Mexicanos decreased in 1960 to 32,684, by 1963 increased to 55,291, and by 1964, because of new administrative restrictions, again decreased to 32,967.[123] Thus, by the mid-1960s with the termination of the BP, a resurgence of the migrant exodus occurred; thus butressing the re-Mexicanization of Aztlán.

CHAPTER 4

Re-Mexicanization of Aztlán and Immigration Reform Intensify (1965–1989)

The expiration of the Bracero Program (BP) in 1964 did not slow down the re-Mexicanization of Aztlán. In fact, the migrant exodus from México into the United States (U.S.) during the next twenty-four years of its third phase intensified. México's impoverished economy and the U.S. economy's continued addiction to and dependency on Mexican migrant labor strengthened the growing economic interdependence between the two countries. Not only did the Mexicano population in Aztlán significantly increase, but the country as a whole experienced a new demographic phenomenon—its Latinoization or "browning." Nativists again became alarmed over the incessant influx of the migrants (undocumented) and now adding to their trouble was fear over the rise of a radical ideological posture that emphasized self-determination. Irrendentia[1] was the code adhered to by some activist leaders, scholars, and organizations within the Chicano movement. Nativist forces on the other hand during these years responded by intensifying efforts to have restrictionist immigration reform passed, and they heightened their xenophobic attacks on Mexicanos.

This chapter examines the changing demographics that characterized the incipience of the re-Mexicanization of Aztlán, occurred during the third phase, the nativism and politics of immigration reform, and the impact that the Chicano movement (CM) had on the migrant exodus.

Restrictionist Immigration Reform Measures

RISE OF THE THIRD GREAT WAVE

The re-Mexicanization of Aztlán got a major injection with the passage of the Hart-Celler Act of 1965, also known as the Immigration and Nationality Act of

1965. It profoundly impacted the ethnic composition of the immigrant population during that time and would continue to do so to date. Unlike the First Wave of immigration, which came chiefly from northern Europe, and the Second Wave, which came largely from southern and central Europe, the Third Wave deprived mainly from Latin America and Asia. México, however, was the main supplier of migrant labor from Latin America to the U.S. As a result, there was an unprecedented increase in legal and undocumented migration.

The Hart-Celler Act was a product of a dynamic era, the 1960s, that was imbued with a spirit of change as illustrated by the rise of the civil rights movement, the New Left, and the anti-Vietnam War movement, which produced a propitious political climate for the politics of immigration reform. Up to this time, the McCarran-Walter Act of 1952, remained the country's foundation of immigration law, which subsequently was amended several times. Since the passage of the Quota Acts of 1921 and 1924, especially the latter with its reliance on the "quota system," they had been considered by some as unjust since they operated on a strict per-country system.[2] After World War II, the country came under increasing strain due to the myriad issues related to refugees, displaced people, and the Cold War.

By the 1950s the country's political culture was such that it began to change. Racial attitudes were becoming more tolerant; consequently, in some liberal political circles, the quota system was viewed as being "anachronistic" and in need of major change.[3] Massachusetts Senator John Fitzgerald Kennedy in 1958 in his book *A Nation of Immigrants* called for immigration reform. He argued that the nation had prospered because of immigrants' positive contributions to society. When elected president in 1960, he asked Congress to eliminate what he considered an iniquitous quota system and sought to change the eugenics-driven notion that non-European immigration was undesirable. Immigration reform would have been a major policy focus in his 1964 State of the Union message[4]; however, he was assassinated in 1963.

Vice President Lyndon Baines Johnson became the country's new president and assumed the mantle of leadership for not only civil rights but also immigration reform. Driven by his call for a "Great Society" and pressured by the civil rights movement, President Johnson pressured Congress to pass his desegregation legislation, the Civil Rights Act of 1964 and the Voting Rights Act of 1965. Their passage gave impetus to Johnson's immigration reform legislative agenda, which sought to advance the struggle for racial equality. President Johnson and the Democrat-controlled Congress changed the course of immigration history.

In 1965 Congress passed the Hart-Celler Act, also known as the Immigration Act of 1965, as an amendment to the McCarran-Walter Act of 1952. President Johnson, on October 3, 1965, at Ellis Island with the Statue of Liberty in the background, signed it, making it one of the country's most important immigration laws ever passed.[5] Its impact altered the makeup of the country's immigration flow. The new law eliminated the national origin quotas and substituted upper limits on total immigration with a system of graded family and occupational preferences determining who would be allowed to fill the overall quotas.[6] It also abolished the national origins quota system created in the Quota Acts of 1921 and 1924, which discriminated against all immigrants that were not from the northern or western parts of Europe. In its place, the law enacted a preferential system with specified ceilings and an overall immigration maximum of 290,000 immigrants per year. The 1965 law set a ceiling of 170,000 visas a year from Europe, with a limit of no more than 20,000 visas per country based on a preference system. The Western Hemisphere's ceiling was originally set at 120,000 visas with no specific national limit and was on a first-come first-serve basis rather than preferences. In 1976 it was limited to 20,000 visas per country. In 1978 the law's immigration ceiling was increased to 290,000 and the preference categories were extended to include the Western and Eastern Hemispheres.[7]

Moreover, Congress established two categories of immigrants that would be welcomed: (1) under the guise of "family reunification," family members of U.S. citizens and permanent residents; and (2) persons of special skills, occupations, or training. Under the former, the law gave priority to family members that included spouses, children, parents of citizens, and permanent residents. The latter included scientists, professionals, artists, and skilled and unskilled workers in occupations where a labor shortage existed.[8] The available visas were granted as follows: 74 percent went to nonimmediate relatives of people already in the U.S.; 20 percent went to those with special skills; and 6 percent went to refugees defined as those fleeing from the tyranny of Communist countries.[9]

Re-Mexicanization of Aztlán Intensifies

1970 U.S. CENSUS

During the twenty-five years of the Third Great Wave the re-Mexicanization of Aztlán intensified. Nationwide, the country experienced a demographic Latinoization or "browning." México's population in 1970 was estimated to be at around 48,000,000. During the period between 1970 and 1980, the Mexicano and Latino population in the U.S. increased dramatically. The Census Bureau in 1970 reported that the U.S. population had increased to 203,211,926 and that the Latino[10] population, which included Mexicanos, had grown to 9,072,602.[11] Due to the criteria used to count Mexicanos, there was most likely an undercount. It was estimated that the number of persons who identified themselves as being of Mexican origin was 4,532,000, which by 1973 increased to between 6 and 7 million.[12] Regardless, even by the most conservative figures, Mexicanos were the fastest growing ethnic group in Aztlán. In a single decade they increased by some 32 percent. They comprised 15 percent of the Southwest's 36 million inhabitants. Some 90 percent lived in Aztlán, and 50 percent of that number lived in California and 36 percent in Texas. This meant that no more than 10 percent of Mexicanos lived outside Aztlán. Their combined population in New México, Arizona, and Colorado was 16 percent. At the national level, only 15 percent of Mexicanos lived in rural areas; in California 90 percent were city-based.[13]

It was estimated by the U.S. Census that during the 1970s the Latino population was undercounted by some 27 percent. The Census also reported that Latinos were a largely urbanized population, meaning that some 87 percent of Latinos lived in metropolitan areas, compared to 74 percent of the total U.S. population.[14] One of the most telling findings was the Latino population's comparatively low median age. For Latinos, it was twenty-two years of age compared to thirty years for the total U.S. population. Next to Puerto Ricans, Mexicanos had the lowest median age of twenty-one years.[15] Next to migration from México and Latin America, high birth rates also contributed significantly to the Latinos' population growth.

1980 U.S. CENSUS: THE "BROWNING" ACCELERATES

Once again, the 1980 census revealed that the Mexicano and Latino population increases were dramatic. The U.S. was undergoing a major demographic transformation, which was chiefly due to the migrant exodus. Both the re-Mexicanization of Aztlán and "browning" or Latinoization of the U.S. continued to intensify. It was during the 1980 Census count that the U.S. Bureau of the Census used "Hispanic" as its designated term to count peoples that came from or had their ethnic origins in Latin America, Spain, or Portugal.

Based upon a method of self-identification, it allowed persons with Spanish surnames to use a number of identifiers, which included Mexican American, Mexicano, Chicano, Puerto Rican, Cuban, Central and South American, and other Spanish origin. On the question of race, Hispanics were asked by the U.S. Census to identify themselves by race as either Black or White; however, 40 percent who identified as Hispanics chose "other." There were some 3,113,867 people who chose to classify themselves as other Hispanics rather than Mexican, Puerto Rican, or Cuban origin. Of these, 8 percent resided in Colorado and New México.[16]

Hispanics were identified as the country's second-largest and fastest-growing national minority group. According to the U.S. Census, the Latino[17] population in 1980 was estimated to be 14.6 million, which translated to about 6.5 percent of the country's total population of 226,545,805.[18] It experienced an increase of 61 percent between 1970 and 1980, compared to a mere increase of 8 percent for Whites. Blacks, who formed the country's largest nonwhite population, numbered some 27 million and were nearly 12 percent of the population. The average annual population growth rate for Latinos during the 1970s was 8 percent. By 1983, the country's Latino population had increased to an estimated 16.9 million. Of the preceding total, almost 60 percent or 8.7 million were Mexicanos; 15 percent or 2 million were Puerto Rican; about 5 percent were of Cuban origin; and the remaining 3 million were from Spain or other countries in Latin America.[19] The Puerto Ricans increased by 41 percent and Cubans by 47 percent.[20]

Throughout Aztlán, Latinos were the largest ethnic minority. Mexicanos, however, constituted by far the largest Latino subgroup, numbering some 7,227,339, compared to Aztlán's total regional population of 44,808,166. Mexico's population in 1980 increased to 67,000,000 people. The Mexicano population growth was particularly evident within Aztlán's numerous cities, *barrios*, and *colonias*. In the Midwest, it numbered some 820,218, compared to 344,305 in the South, and 87,776 in the Northeast.[21] The regional distribution was 82.7 percent for Aztlán, 9.4 percent for the Midwest, 3 percent for West, and 1 percent for the Northeast.[22] While most of the Puertoriqueño population was concentrated in New York, Cubanos were heavily located in Florida, due to a major exodus after the Cuban Revolution in 1959 and an acceleration occurred during the 1980s.

The Latino population was concentrated primarily in ten states. The largest was in California (4,544,331), followed by Texas (2,985,824), New York (1,659,000), Florida (858,000), Illinois (636,000), New Jersey (492,000), New México (477,000), Arizona (441,000), Colorado (340,000), and Michigan (162,000).[23] California and Texas had the highest number of Latinos in the country; one half of the Latino population lived in those two states. During this decade there was a noticeable population shift occurred from Texas and Arizona to California and later to the Midwest. This was illustrated by the fact that in 1980 Illinois had more Mexicanos than did the traditional states of Arizona, New Mexico, and Colorado.[24]

Contributing to the dramatic Mexicano and overall Latino population growth were high birth rates and immigration. Simply put, as ethnic groups, they had more recorded births than other ethnic group. In 1980 the Latino birth rate was 23.5 live births per 1,000 of the total population, compared to 14.2 for Whites and 22.9 for Blacks. Of all the Latino subgroups, Mexicanas had the highest number of live births, 26.6 per 1,000, and the lowest number was Cubanas, with an overall birth rate of 9.6 per 1,000.[25] Yet, while high birth rates were a major factor, it was immigration, especially via the escalation of the migrant exodus, that was the paramount contributor.

Migrant Exodus Escalates

Immigration (both documented and undocumented) was the major contributor to the intensification of the migrant exodus. The passage of the Hart-Celler Act in 1965 became the catalyst for the Latino demographic transformation.[26] By the end of the 1970s, immigration from Europe was reduced to a trickle, opening the floodgates from the Third World into the U.S., especially Latin America and Asia. When it went into effect in 1968, it eliminated the bias toward Europe that many in Congress had considered racist. There was, however, as L. Edward Purcell explains, a temporary burst of immigration from Europe that occurred after 1965 as family members joined those already in the U.S.[27]

According to Peter C. Meilaender, "although its supporters had claimed that it would neither radically increase the amount nor alter the composition of American immigration, these predictions proved to be false. Beginning in the late 1960s, the number of immigrants to the U.S., especially from Latin America and Asia, grew rapidly and by the late 1980s, it reached a level not seen since the turn of the century."[28] Some 1,123,492 emigrated from Europe. During the subsequent two decades the figures diminished: 1970s, 800,368, and 1980s, 761,550. In comparison, from Latin America, including México and the Caribbean, the numbers significantly increased: from 1961 to 1970, 1,193,645; from 1971 to 1980, 1,618,884; and from 1981 to 1990, 3,111,760.[29] Legal immigration from Europe thus shrank from 113,000 in 1965 to an average of 65,000 a year by the late 1970s.[30]

From 1971 to 1980 legal immigration reached a high of 4,493,314, and from 1981 to 1990 it crested at 7,338,062.[31] By the 1980s, immigrants from Latin American and Asia comprised some 79 percent of all legal immigrants. The figures for regional origins of the immigration population for 1981 to 1990 illustrate the dramatic turnaround: 35 percent had emigrated from Asia, 18 percent from North America, 16 percent from the Caribbean island nations, 7 percent from South America, 3 percent from Central America, 2 percent from Africa, and 1 percent from other countries.[32] From 1965 to 1990 the overwhelming majority of legal immigrants came from Latin America, especially México, and Asia.

From 1945 to the late 1980s, there was a strong and steady increase in Mexican legal migration to the U.S., which was a powerful stimulus toward the re-Mexicanization of Aztlán. It continued to be the result of México's inability to provide meaningful jobs and economic opportunities for its impoverished masses. Poverty, unemployment, low wages, inequality, acute social problems, and workers' rising expectations were push factors that continued to drive the migrant exodus. Héctor Aguilar Camín and Lorenzo Meyer argue that the 1980s were plagued by an economic crisis in México that produced severe features of inequality. They explain that:

> A total of 22.3 million Mexicans—46 of every 100—lacked the minimal standards of welfare in nutrition, education, health, and employment. In contrast, only 14.8 million Mexicans—30 of every 100—showed levels of marginalization. . . . 35 of every 100 families had incomes below the minimum wage (scarcely above $100 per month) and 19 million persons were undernourished—13 million of them in rural areas.[33]

Research conducted in 1987 concluded that nearly 60 percent of México's population was poor. México's acute socioeconomic crisis was further exacerbated by the devaluation of the peso during 1986 and 1987. Similar scenarios had occurred in 1976 and again in 1982. México's economic crisis also contributed significantly to increases in its people's legal immigration to the U.S. Starting from 1940 to 1990 a total of 3,110,474 Mexicanos legally migrated to the U.S., which translated to 16.6 percent of all legal immigration for the fifty-year period. From 1961 to 1970, the figure was 453,937; from 1971 to 1980, it increased to 640,294; and from 1981 to 1990, a gigantic increase occurred, to 1,655,843.[34] In comparison to previous decades, legal migration from México to the U.S. during the 1980s reached an unprecedented high of 22.6 percent.

Before the passage of the Hart-Celler Act, it was almost impossible for Asians to emigrate to the U.S., due to there being only a few national quotas open for Chinese. After World War II (WWII) a quota of only 100 Filipinos were allowed annually to emigrate. The 1960 census reported the country's Asian population as being very small. It increased significantly, due to the Hart-Celler Act's "family preference" or "family reunification" section of its provision. Many Asian immigrants perfected what some called a "chain system" or "pyramid immigration." Both meant that one person would emigrate, then would use the "family preference" to bring in close relatives, who in turn invoked the family preference, and so on.[35] The following totals are for legal immigration from 1961 to 1990 for the divergent Asian nations: China, 792,526; India, 442,109; Japan, 136,848; Korea, 657,151; the Philippines, 1,002,127; and Vietnam, 457,942.

The Hart-Celler Act provided a specific formula for the admittance of 17,400 refugees only from Communist countries or the Middle East.[36] Political and military circumstances produced a plethora of refugees. President Jimmy

Carter (1977–1981) via executive order created additional refugee slots by putting them in parole. After the Vietnam War, from 1975 to 1979 some 200,000 Vietnamese refugees came to the U.S.,[37] and by the 1980s that number increased to 400,000. A few thousand more also came as refugees from Laos, Cambodia, and Thailand.

Congress, in response to the growing refugee problem, passed the Refugee Act of 1980. It established a system designed to handle refugees as a class separate from other immigrants. The politics of the Cold War were evident in its various provisions. One such provision defined refugees as those who fled a country because of persecution for reasons of race, religion, nationality, or political opinion. In consultation with Congress, another provision was that the president was authorized to establish an annual ceiling as to the number of refugees that would be admitted. The law also gave the president discretion to admit any group into the country on an emergency basis.[38] The new law set the refugee quota at 50,000 and reduced the numbers to be admitted as immigrants to 20,000, which, combined with the figure of 270,000 stipulated by revisions made to the Hart-Celler Act of 1965, created an annual immigration total of 320,000.[39]

One such example of how U.S. foreign policy politically used and applied the Hart-Celler Act was in the case of Cuba. In order to better understand the uniqueness of Cuban emigration, it is important to understand its intertwined history with the U.S. As a result of the Spanish-American War of 1898, with Spain militarily defeated, from 1898 until 1958, Cuba was a U.S. protectorate. During those years, the U.S. practiced an "open door" migration policy with Cuba. Cubans traveled back and forth between the two countries without many constraints.[40] In spite of this liberal arrangement, the Cuban population in the U.S. prior to 1960 was small. Most of it was concentrated around the Key West, Florida, area. In 1930 Cubans numbered a mere 19,000; but by 1960 their numbers had increased to 79,000 as a result of the Cuban Revolution.[41] Immigration from Cuba to the U.S. prior to Fidel Castro's rise to power in 1959 had been a trickle, but after 1959 became a flood.

Cold War politics also affected Cuban immigration to the U.S. Immigration became a weapon in the U.S.'s arsenal for attaining world hegemony against its rival the Soviet Union. The rise to power of Fidel Castro, his proclamation that he was a Marxist-Leninist in 1961, the Bay of Pigs debacle of 1961, and the Cuban Missile Crisis of 1962, as well as other events, helped propel a Cuban exodus of refugees. Both President Kennedy and President Johnson sought to embarrass Fidel Castro and his Marxist regime by allowing thousands of Cubans to emigrate to the U.S. during the years 1960 through 1962; thus setting off the first wave of Cuban emigration to the U.S.

In January 1961 the Kennedy administration established the Cuban Refugee Program, which along with parallel efforts by various local and religious organizations provided Cubans with assistance upon arrival. The assistance included securing housing, jobs, schools, and other forms of aid, such as assistance for their departure from Cuba. Whereas other immigrants or migrants from México were prohibited, for propaganda reasons the U.S. government welcomed Cubans as political refugees allegedly because they had fled from the so-called tyrannical rule of Castro's Marxist dictatorship. They were first admitted provisionally, which meant that they were given a temporary refugee visa. No ceiling to their numbers was established.

By 1966 Cubanos' legal status in the U.S. was normalized with Congress's passage of the Cuban Refugee Adjustment Act.[42] In effect, it acted both as a "push" and "pull" factor that from 1966 to 1973 stimulated the second wave of Cuban emigration to the U.S. For those Cubanos who did not support the Cuban Revolution and wanted to flee the island, it was a "push" factor, while for the U.S., because of its ideological and propagandistic value, it was a "pull" factor. Arriving Cubans were granted a special immigration status.

The Cuban Revolution was benevolent toward Bautista's "oligarchy" and their families, which consequently acted as a major "push" factor for Cuban immigration to the U.S. during 1959 to 1960. Instead of having massive executions and incarcerations of Cuba's bourgeoisie who had been supportive of the U.S.-backed dictator Fulgencio Batista, as a humanitarian gesture most were allowed to leave the island. Cuba's Marxist-socialist posture also "pushed" business and professional elites to immigrate to the U.S. From 1966 to 1973, some 273,000 Cubans were airlifted from Cuba to the U.S. Overall, from 1959 to 1973 some 677,000 Cubans entered the U.S. and during the years 1960 to 1980 the number increased to 800,000.[43] The "brain drain" that occurred forced the Cuban government in 1973 to clamp down on the airlift exodus.

In 1980 Cuban emigration to the U.S. resumed when some 10,000 Cubans stormed the Peruvian embassy and sought political asylum. The Cuban government resolved the crisis by allowing some 125,000 Cubans, most of them poor, to leave from the Cuban port of Mariel. Considered by U.S. officials to be refugees, the *Marielitos*, as they were labeled, settled mainly in Miami, Florida, forging the third wave of Cuban emigration.[44] During the peak of the crisis some 3,000 Cuban refugees a day were intercepted by the U.S. Coast Guard. Reports alleged that the Cuban government had purposely sent criminals and inmates from mental institutions on boats to the U.S. It fostered such a groundswell of domestic pressure that the U.S. government put a halt on the Cuban exodus's "Mariel boatlift." A negotiated agreement was reached by both governments and the Cuban exodus crisis ended, but no long-term solution was reached.[45]

In 1984 a bilateral immigration agreement was concluded between the two countries that set the maximum number of Cuban immigrants permitted into the U.S. at 20,000 annually via the normal visa process handled by the U.S. Interest Section in Havana. In return, Cuba agreed to accept the Mariel refugees who were housed in U.S. prisons. The agreement went into effect in 1986. Fearing deportation, some of the imprisoned *Marielitos* rioted; nevertheless, hundreds were subsequently deported to Cuba. During the ensuing four years, the number of visas granted by the U.S. Interest Section rarely numbered over 2,500.[46] Cuban emigration to the U.S. from 1959 to the late 1980s numbered close to 1 million.[47]

U.S. foreign policy also impacted the Hart-Celler Act of 1965 in several Latin American countries. Although not considered by U.S. officials as refugees, those emigrating to the U.S. from Latin America were categorized as immigrants. In reality they were "economic" refugees who did not meet the criteria of being categorized as political refugees. Driven by "push" factors of chronic poverty, unemployment, low wages, inequality, and political instability, Haiti from the early 1970s to the 1980s experienced an acute undocumented immigration exodus to the U.S. During the 1970s alone, some 60,000 Haitians came to the U.S. Many died at sea and those who did make it to land were not received with the same attention and/or support by the federal government officials as were the Cuban refugees. Simply put, they did not represent the same ideological propaganda value as did the Cubanos, and secondly, there was the race factor—most Haitians were Black, which did not set well among White nativists.

With the Sandinistas in power in 1979, Nicaragua experienced revolutionary change. Both El Salvador and Guatemala were embroiled in civil wars and Honduras was threatened with an insurgency during the 1980s. Concerned with the Cold War ramifications of Marxist-inspired revolutionary governments taking control in Central America, the U.S. reacted by initiating indirect military intervention: armed the Contras (U.S.-supported insurgents) against the Sandinistas, trained and equipped the Salvadorian military, established military bases in Honduras, and trained and equipped the Honduran army. As a region, Central America was plagued by not only "push" factors such as poverty, unemployment, and social problems, but it also was beset by acute political repression and instability during the 1980s.

The increase in migrant exodus from Latin America exacerbated the rising nativist hysteria against Mexicanos and Latinos in general. The U.S.'s capitalist economy "pulled" thousands of desperate undocumented workers every year into the country. It was estimated that in 1975 some 4 to 12 million had migrated north to the U.S. A year later the estimate was modified to 6 to 8 million, and by 1978, the new INS commissioner, Leonel Castillo, projected the figure to be between 3 and 6 million.[48]

Indicative of the migrant exodus's huge undocumented influx were the number of Mexicanos apprehended crossing the U.S.–México border. The number in 1969 was 202,000, but under "Operation Clean Sweep" the U.S. Border Patrol in 1971 arrested some 348,178 undocumented migrants. The next year, the numbers increased to 430,213 and in 1973 it jumped to 609,573. But by 1979, the figure escalated to 989,000, and yet in 1981 there was a slight decrease to 831,000.[49] Overall, from 1971 to 1980, the Immigration and Naturalization Service (INS) reported the formal removal at 240,217 undocumented migrants, and voluntary departures at 7,246,812, for a total of 7,487,029. During 1981 to 1990, those formally removed numbered 232,830 and those that left voluntarily at 9,961,812 for a total of 10,194,642.[50] As immigration sweeps intensified, U.S. corporate and business interests proposed the reintroduction of the BP, which necessitated the annual importation of some 300,000 *braceros* from México. It was not enacted due to México's Echevarria administration, which broke off negotiations on the matter.

From 1965 to 1990 the foreign-born population in the U.S. from Latin America increased substantially. In 1960 Latinos comprised a mere 9 percent, but in 1970 the figure increased to 19 percent. By 1980, the number escalated to a high of 33 percent and by 1990 it increased to an unprecedented 44 percent of the total.[51] These figures fueled the right-wing activists and politicians, who then pandered to the fears of the public. They alleged that the security of the country was threatened. During the initial phase of the Third Great Wave, México's biggest export into the U.S. was its people. This impacted dramatically and altered the country's demographic ethnic/racial profile.

Resurgence of a Nativist Politics: Restrictionist Legislation

During the initial years of the Third Great Wave, in response to the re-Mexicanization of Aztlán and the Latinoization or "browning" of the U.S., nativists, impelled by a growing fear, sought the passage of restrictionist immigration legislation to curb the heavy influx of legal and undocumented migration from México and Latin America. As early as 1971 in California, nativists succeeded in passing the Dixon Arnett Act, which fined employers who hired undocumented workers; however, it was later declared unconstitutional. At the federal level, in 1972, Congressman Peter Rodino (D) from New Jersey introduced legislation that made it a felony to knowingly employ undocumented workers, with penalties that ranged from warnings to jail terms for repeated offenders. Senator Edward Kennedy also introduced a similar bill, which included amnesty for those undocumented workers who had been in the country for at least three years. Lacking support, it was killed in committee.[52]

During the 1970s INS abuses of undocumented workers became increasingly commonplace. One such case occurred in October 1971 when U.S. Border Patrolman Kenneth Cook raped an undocumented Mexicana and threatened to harm her children.[53] A second major case of abuse was the Hanigan case that occurred in Arizona in 1976. George Hanigan and his two sons were arrested for kidnapping three undocumented workers who had been looking for work. In brutal fashion, they stripped, stabbed, and burned them with hot pokers, and then dragged them into the Arizona desert. They further terrorized them by conducting a mock hanging of one of them and another was shot with a shotgun. The undocumented men managed to escape and reported the incident to Mexican authorities. A local judge, a friend of the Hanigan family, refused to issue arrest warrants. Finally, arrested and charged, the Hanigan case demonstrated the outright racism against Mexicanos: an all-White jury acquitted them. Activists from both the U.S. and México pressured U.S. Attorney General Griffin Bell to file suit. The case went to a federal grand jury, which in 1979 indicted the Hanigans for violating the Hobbs Act that involved interference in interstate commerce. An all-White jury deadlocked in the first trial; however, in 1981, at the second trial, although the father had died by then, the jury found the brothers guilty and they were jailed.[54]

By 1975 the anti-immigrant hysteria picked up momentum. In particular, undocumented Mexicanos were stereotyped and denigrated by nativists as being criminals or bandits. As Rodolfo Acuña writes, "the country had come full circle since the nineteenth century when the Mexican was stereotyped as a bandit. . . . In the 1970s, Mexicans again became bandits, blamed for stealing jobs." He further explains that "they were made outlaws in order to criminalize them, to justify paying them less and hounding them like the bandits of old, while at the same time demonstrating the pseudo-need to appropriate more funds to the INS."[55] The media too fed into the frenzy by frequently reporting with a "sensationalist" thrust on the growing anti-immigrant hysteria.

As early as 1975, reacting to the influx of immigrants, some U.S. scholars and policy makers raised issues of national security. Funded by the National Endowment for the Humanities, Arthur F. Corwin sent a letter to then Secretary of State Henry Kissinger in which he demanded that action be taken to halt the incessant immigration from Latin America. He argued that the U.S. had become a "welfare reservation" and if it continued, the Southwest would become a "Quebec." In addition, he requested that President Gerald Ford militarize and seal the border and that Congress appropriate $1 billion for the INS to hire 50,000 new Border Patrol agents and that an electric fence be constructed. México's press secured a copy of Corwin's letter and reacted by blasting and discrediting him.[56] While the Ford administration did not heed Corwin's recommendations, his opinion was indicative of the vitriolic nativism directed at Mexicanos.

President Jimmy Carter was elected in 1976 and during his four-year presidency became engaged in the growing immigration debate. His administration in 1977 asked Congress to draft a new restrictionist immigration law, which would impose sanctions on those employers who knowingly hired undocumented workers. In addition, his administration encouraged Congress to draft a bill that would grant amnesty to those undocumented workers already in the U.S and would strengthen the Border Patrol. These three provisions became the foundation of immigration reform legislation introduced in the 1980s.[57] The Carter Plan, as it became known, generated much debate, but failed to create legislation. Lisa Magaña explains why: "It failed because critics of immigration legislation claimed that it was not supported by factual analysis and that other alternatives to curb illegal immigration had not been adequately examined."[58]

In 1976 the country's growing nativist political climate directed at Mexicanos became apparent with the passage of the Western Hemisphere Act. Introduced by Congressman Joshua Eilberg (D) of Pennsylvania, it extended the preference system. It lowered the number of legal immigrants who entered the U.S. from any one Latin American country from 40,000 to 20,000. This was particularly a slap at México, the only Latin American country to send 40,000 annually. A backlog of 173,000 visa requests from México existed in 1980, which served to further encourage undocumented migration.[59]

In 1978, CIA Director Stansfield Turner depicted the migrant exodus as the single most serious threat to the security of the U.S. He equated the influx of Mexicano migrants as a greater threat than that of the Soviet Union. He warned of the possibilities and dangers of the emergence of a Quebec-like separatist movement within Aztlán. Republican Senator Alan Simpson echoed Turner's call by alleging that the migrant exodus presented an ominous threat to the country's national unity and stability. Arthur F. Corwin as well that year in an essay cowritten with John M. McCain reminded the country that it was aiding the militancy of the so-called Chicano. They argued that "Chicano nationalism, sprouting in barrios across the country [United States], and reinforced by mass immigration, works for the political re-conquest of the Southwest by the Mexican race, that is, *la raza*, and the spiritual restoration of the mythical Aztlán, or the original homeland of the Aztecs."[60]

By 1978 the nativist pressure on Congress had intensified to where a sixteen-member Select Commission on Immigration and Refugee Policy was formed and headed by Reverend Theodore Hesburgh, president of Notre Dame University. The commission conducted seven public meetings and twelve regional hearings and sponsored a major report, "U.S. Immigration Policy and the National Interest," which was released in March 1981.[61] Its policy recommendations included employer sanctions, an amnesty program, expansion of the Border Patrol, and a guest worker program that would recruit temporary seasonal workers to fill labor shortages.[62] It also proposed that the annual ceiling of 270,000 set by the

Hart-Celler Act of 1965 be raised to 350,000. With the exception of employer sanctions, there was a spirit of general consensus among commission members. With nativists voicing warnings of a pending "balkanization" of the U.S. if restrictionist legislation was not passed, the report provided the justification for more stringent enforcement of immigration laws and more rigid border enforcement. One year later, the Simpson-Mazzoli legislation was proposed.[63]

Simpson-Mazzoli Legislation

For nearly a decade, Congress tried unsuccessfully to craft immigration policy to deal with what nativists considered to be tantamount to a so-called immigrant invasion specifically from Mexico. The Census Bureau by 1982 estimated that there were between 3.5 and 6 million undocumented workers in the U.S. Open paranoia pervaded the nativist politic, which increasingly became desperate, xenophobic, and racist. Nativist politicians in Congress were concerned about by the growing migrant exodus and its demographic impact and were equally troubled by the bad publicity the Cuban Marielito crisis had fostered. Moreover, nativists in general argued that undocumented workers were taking jobs away from domestic workers, depressing wages, were carriers of AIDS, and that they overloaded the welfare, education, and health care service systems. The general message was that they were a burden on the taxpayer, which was the nativist's justification for their push for restrictionist legislation.

The nativist manipulation of general public opinion moved the country's political climate in the direction of being increasingly anti-immigrant and susceptible to calls for new restrictive immigration policy. It was alleged that undocumented migrants by definition because of their so-called illegal entry into the country had broken the country's laws and were criminals. Others like columnist Carl Rowan instilled fear by claiming that migrants from México were an integral part of a clandestine movement to return Aztlán to México. In an article in 1981 he wrote that "the United States is a nation without meaningful control of its borders. So many Mexicans are crossing U.S. borders illegally that Mexicans are reclaiming Texas, California, and other territories they have long claimed the Gringos stole from them."[64] Republican Senator Alan Simpson of Wyoming also claimed that immigrants were not willing to assimilate into U.S. culture[65]; likewise, the president's select commission's report warned that "if language and cultural separation rise above a certain level, the unity and political stability of our nation will—in time—be seriously eroded."[66]

Reflecting the aforementioned nativism, in 1981 Republican Senator Alan Simpson from Wyoming and Representative Romano Mazzoli, Democrat from Kentucky, introduced legislation in 1982 that became known as the Simpson-

Mazzoli Immigration Reform Bill, which specifically called for employer sanctions, amnesty for some immigrants, and a special guest worker program for agricultural workers. In both the Senate and the House, vociferous and at times acrimonious debate occurred throughout 1982. Amendment after amendment was introduced on its various provisions. Senator S. I. Hayakawa, for example, sought unsuccessfully to attach an "English as the official language" provision to the legislation. Consensus was difficult to achieve among the divergent special interests that were politically battling the legislative matter.

In particular, the employer sanctions provision was opposed by most probusiness, Latino, and minority rights groups on grounds that it was discriminatory. Organized labor was divided: Cesar Chavez's United Farm Workers (UFW) supported it initially. The American Federation of Labor and Congress of Industrial Organizations (AFL-CIO) was apprehensive of its H-2 program, but in the end supported it. Church groups and those critical of U.S. policy toward Central America, were concerned about the possible deportation of thousands of Central American refugees who had fled to the U.S., opposed it.[67] Opposition mainly to employer sanctions derailed its passage. Speaker Thomas O'Neill was not enthusiastic about immigration reform and deliberately postponed acting on the Simpson-Mazzoli legislation until the last minutes of the 97th session. Gimple and Edwards, in their extensive examination of the matter, wrote:

> Sensing that time was running out for the members to deal with the legislation before the holidays, Mazzoli (D-KY) made the decision to pull the bill from the floor and re-introduce it in the 98th Congress. . . . So it was a coalition of Hispanic members and Republicans, who were hostile to employer sanctions for different reasons that ultimately defeated the attempt to pass this bill.[68]

It failed in large part due to the pressure exerted by the Congressional Hispanic Caucus led by Representative Edward Roybal (D-CA) and Representative Robert Garcia (D-NY). They had launched an effective and well-organized political campaign against a bill that they considered to be inimical to the civil rights of their constituencies.[69]

During the 98th Congress the Simpson-Mazzoli legislation was reintroduced. The specter of an escalating immigration crisis pervaded Congress, therefore facilitating its reintroduction. In 1983 alone, over 1,250,000 undocumented workers were apprehended and deported by the INS, double the number from the prior decade.[70] The provisions on amnesty, employer sanctions, and the guest worker program, among others, remained substantially the same as the 1982 version. Introduced by Senator Jesse Helms, however, was one heinous amendment that would permit states to deny public education to the children of undocumented parents, in spite of a U.S. Supreme Court ruling, *Phyler v. Doe*, in 1982, which stipulated that states do not have the right to deny undocumented parents access to public education for their children. Although defeated on a 34 to 60 Senate vote due to the vigorous opposition by both Senators Edward Kennedy and Alan Simpson, the Helms Amendment garnered support from some southern Democrats, such as Senators Sam Nunn and Lloyd Bentsen. In the end, the few amendments offered for Senate debate were soundly defeated in roll calls.[71]

The Senate proved to be more united and supportive of the Simpson-Mazzoli legislation than was the House. In the House the amnesty and employer provisions were the most controversial. Various committee chairs were unable to achieve consensus on even the basics of the bill, not to mention the number of amendments that would be permitted. The existent divisions among House representatives and the 1984 presidential primaries further exacerbated the political impasse. Representative Roybal again played an important antinativist leadership role in the legislative process. Although defeated on a 120 to 304 vote, he introduced an amendment to eliminate from the bill's language "employer sanctions." House Speaker O' Neill reacted to these events by blocking consideration of the legislation until after the presidential primaries.

After a bitter session and several amendments debated, the House passed its version of Simpson-Mazzoli by a razor-thin majority, 216 to 211. In the end, however, on a House-raised issue of reimbursement to states, and with the presidential election only three weeks away, the conference committee was unable to reconcile the House and Senate versions and therefore a stalemate occurred. Congress adjourned and the Simpson-Mazzoli measure died for a second time.[72]

Immigration and Reform Control Act (IRCA) of 1986

After nearly five years of debate, the 99th Congress in 1986 reintroduced the Simpson-Mazzoli legislation under a new rubric, the Immigration Reform and Control Act (IRCA). The contentious conflicts that had permeated the congressional and White House debate over the Simpson-Mazzoli measure in previous years surfaced again. President Ronald Reagan contributed to the anti-immigrant hysteria and fear when he said that the country was being flooded by what he called "feet people" from Central America. By 1986, nativist estimates of the number of undocumented workers in the U.S. ranged from 2 to 8 million.[73] In nativist fashion, President Reagan in 1984 remarked, "We have lost control over our own borders," which was a sentiment widely shared.[74] However, by 1986 the

Reagan administration's position on IRCA had changed. Its probusiness and free market philosophy put it on the side of those who favored unlimited immigration as a valued source of cheap labor.[75] Yet, there were policy differences within the Reagan administration. The Department of Justice adhered to a stringent "law and order" posture that favored greater control over the U.S.–México border. Yet in the end, the Reagan administration quieted those criticisms of IRCA and formally supported it.[76]

In spite of contentious debate, Congress in November 1986 enacted IRCA. Both chambers approved the conference report: the Senate easily passed it by a 63 to 24 vote; and the House also passed it, by a vote of 238 to 173. An analysis of selected floor votes illustrates that voting was sharply divided between Democrats and Republicans. Suggestive of the preceding was the passage of the conference report: only 70 percent of the Democrats voted for it, whereas 38 percent of Republicans supported it.[77] Its passage was considered by many, then and afterward, as one of the most important pieces of immigration reform to be adopted.

The three provisions that caused the greatest debate and contention were amnesty, employer sanctions, and the farm-worker guest worker program. For nativist conservatives in particular, amnesty was unlawful because it rewarded those that, from their perspective, had broken the law. When it came to employer sanctions, it was opposed by liberals, most moderates, the Congressional Hispanic Caucus, civil rights groups, and business interests for the potential discriminatory effects. Lastly, the farm-worker guest worker provision went through an amendment process and a compromise was reached that changed the required time farm workers had to reside in the country from sixty days to ninety days.

IRCA's diverse provisions and passage was based on the assumption that it was going to reduce substantially the levels of undocumented immigration. Under IRCA the annual immigration ceiling was increased to 540,000 and border enforcement was also accentuated. At the heart of IRCA were the following three major provisions:

1. *Amnesty*: Under this provision those undocumented workers able to prove continuous residence in the U.S. since January 1, 1982, qualified for legalization or amnesty. The law provided temporary-resident status to eligible residents and they were on track to become permanent residents.
2. *Employer sanctions*: Stiff sanctions, that is, fines, were introduced for employers who knowingly employed undocumented workers. Employers were prohibited from hiring undocumented workers and were required to verify workers' eligibility for employment and could be fined up to $10,000 for violations.
3. *Farm-worker provisions*: In order to placate the capitalist agribusiness interests, IRCA provided three related farm-worker provisions. The first was the Special

Agricultural Worker (SWA) program, which permitted legal residence, followed by the possibility for citizenship, for those who could prove that they had worked in the agricultural sector for at least ninety days between 1980 and 1985. The second was the Replenishment Agricultural Worker (RAW) program, which allowed new immigrant workers to enter the U.S. between 1990 and 1993—after working three consecutive seasons they would be eligible for permanent residence. The third was the H-2A program, which allowed seasonal workers to be brought in to work temporarily when a labor shortage existed that farmers could not fill. Thus, in the absence of suitable U.S. employees, agricultural employers could hire temporary workers, provided that minimum wage, housing, and working conditions were met.

Integral to the amnesty provision was the allocation of $1 billion per year for four years under the State Legislation Impact Assistance Grant for classes in English, U.S. history, and government, which were mandatory for IRCA amnesty applicants.[78] This was requisite for the transition into becoming a naturalized citizen.

Because of its amnesty provision, some 2.7 million migrants were legalized and became permanent residents. Yet, conservatively, over 2 million were left out because they did not qualify for its legalization provisions. As to border enforcement and control during the ensuing years, IRCA's provisions failed to halt the migrant exodus. The influx of undocumented workers continued to increase. In 1988, during the first fiscal year after IRCA went into effect, INS reported 1,008,145 apprehensions. Of the total number, 949,722 or 94.2 percent were of Mexicano nationality.[79]

IRCA's employer sanctions failed since few employers were fined or incarcerated. A contributing factor to its failure was that counterfeit immigration document production kicked in big time. Documents on the black market became readily available, seriously impeding INS efforts to enforce immigration sanctions. It did succeed, however, in fostering higher levels of employment discrimination against Mexicanos and Latinos. One of the unintended positive aspects of IRCA was that it strengthened migratory networks via the legalization process and induced the naturalization of some 2 million.[80]

Mexicano/Latino Immigration Response: Rise of the Chicano Movement

The rise of the Chicano[81] movement (CM) during 1966 to 1974 contributed to the intensification of nativism against Mexicanos. The progressive and cultural nationalist leaders and the organizations they led, such as Reies Lopez Tijerina's Alianza Federal de Mercedes, Corky Gonzales's Crusade for Justice, Jose Angel Gutierrez's Mexican American Youth Organization (MAYO), and David Sanchez's Brown Berets, rekindled fear among some White nativists. Labor leader Cesar Chavez and the UFW, which in reality were both moderately reformist in their politics, were also singled out as radical forces.[82]

This fear was exacerbated by what was perceived as the CM's adherence to Chicanismo, a quasi-ideology predicated on cultural nationalism that categorically rejected assimilation and embraced the concept of self-determination—the idea of creating Aztlán, a separate and sovereign Chicano nation within the territories of occupied México. The unprecedented renaissance of cultural nationalism induced a neomilitancy that produced a contagion of marches, for example, the east L.A. walkouts of 1968, the National Chicano Moratorium antiwar march of August 29, 1970, boycotts (that is, Cesar Chavez's UFW Delano strike of 1966–1970), and other direct action mobilizations.

Chicanos during this dynamic epoch of change adhered to a new form of militancy and protest that in turn fed the resurgence of anti-Mexicano nativism. A myriad of manifestos and plans promulgated by Chicano activists rejected the Mexicano's internal colonialist status and were also hypercritical of the White liberal capitalist U.S. Nativists responded with great concern to the *"Plan Espiritual de Aztlán."* Promulgated in 1969 at the Chicano Youth Liberation Conference convoked by Gonzalez's Crusade for Justice, it embraced Chicanismo and self-determination predicated on the creation of a separate Chicano nation— Aztlán. Adding to their concerns was the *"Plan de Santa Barbara,"* drafted at a student/community conference at the University of California, Santa Barbara, that called for major reform in higher education for Chicanos and the creation of a new student umbrella organization, *El Movimiento Estudiantil Chicanos de Aztlán* (MEChA). MEChA became a major concern for nativists because of its cultural nationalist ideological orientation, which embraced the Plan Espiritual de Aztlán and the call for Aztlán.

Increasingly, White nativists began to react to the dramatic growth of the Mexicano population, which in many parts of Aztlán was growing so rapidly that it threatened White hegemony and ultimately their control and power. This situation was particularly evident with the rise of the Raza Unida Party during the early 1970s, which as a Chicano third party, under the leadership of both Jose Angel Gutierrez and Rodolfo Corky Gonzales, rebuked the dictatorship of the two-party system and called for the ideals of self-determination and empowerment. The rise of Marxist organizations that were proimmigrant and had roots in México like CASA-HGT (Centro de Accion Social Autonoma-Hermandad General de Trabajadores, led by Bert Corona), among others, contributed to the growing radicalization of the Mexicano *barrios* throughout Aztlán and beyond.

The demise of the CM by 1974 did not alter the rise of anti-Méxicano nativism. A social movement, the CM was induced in great part because of the presence of several exogenous factors, for example, civil rights, the New Left, anti-Vietnam War actions, Black Power, President Johnson's war on poverty, and foreign movements, and endogenous antagonisms, for example, growing Méxicano population, socioeconomic changes, rise of Chicano leaders, and so forth, that pervaded the mid-1960s. In the radicalized political climate of the 1960s, the CM flourished. By 1974, however, with most of the above mentioned exogenous movements gone, especially the Vietnam antiwar movement, the country's climate of change transitioned into a new political epoch (i.e., the Viva Yo Hispanc Generation) that was increasingly conservative, materialist, and rejected the militant politics of the preceding years.

Chicano activism continued, yet it was at a less militant and/or protesting level. The "Viva Yo" Hispanic generation gained prominence with its accommodation, integrationist, and system maintenance politics, but regardless, it too did not stop the growing anti-Mexicano nativist politics. Increasingly, throughout the late 1970s and 1980s, Mexicanos and Latinos were targeted by nativists. They injected into their anti-immigrant posture an unprecedented growing sense of fear, desperation, and heightened racism, particularly directed toward Mexicanos. At the crux of it was first the Mexicano/Latino "demographic transformation," second, the historical fact that Aztlán had been an integral part of México, and third, as a region, Aztlán shared a contiguous 2,000-mile-long porous border; and fourth, that these three salient factors combined contributed to growing political circumstances that could threaten the country's White hegemony, security, and ultimately its sovereignty.

Chicano/Latino Immigration Response (1968–1989)

As the country's immigration debate grew, Chicano activists by the 1970s gradually began to prioritize the issue of immigration. At the forefront was Bert Corona, a longtime activist, labor organizer, and leader of many causes, who as a visionary propounded the view that immigration was going to be for Mexicanos for years to the new issue policy battleground. Corona's CASA-HGT through up to 1978 remained the premiere migrant rights advocacy organization in the country.

By the early 1970s, however, another pro-migrant rights group was formed, the Committee on Chicano Rights (CCR). Led by Herman Baca and based in

National City, California, CCR well into the early 1980s was at the forefront of the emerging pro-migrant rights struggle. According to Baca:

> From 1970 to 1976, the issue of immigration grew from an anthill to a Mount Everest issue. The Committee on Chicano Rights, as an advocacy group, became increasingly involved in immigration related issues. This was because of our proximity to the U.S./México border. The issue of immigration itself caused a lot of fear among our people. We saw the undocumented as part of our Chicano community problem. For us, the San Diego border area was the Vietnam of the Southwest.[83]

Most activists between 1970 and 1974 were wrapped up in building the Raza Unida Party (RUP) or were dealing with education and police brutality. By the mid-1970s, Chicano activists began to direct their activism in defense of the undocumented workers. Immigration reform and calls for amnesty became more frequent. In great part the shift was ascribable to the growing resistance against the resurgent and overt nativism directed at Mexicanos. Chicano activists, such as Corona and Baca, among others, effectively at the state level opposed the Dixon Arnett bill and at the federal level, the Rodino and Kennedy bills, which died in committee.

The National Chicano Forum was held in May 1976 in Salt Lake City, Utah, under my leadership and that of poet Abelardo Delgado. Some 600 activists met to discuss the strategic revitalization of the moribund CM, and the issue of immigration. Plagued by contentious ideological wrangling and conflicts that led to unbridgeable chasms, no major plan of action came out of the forum.[84]

It was not until May 5, 1977, in Ontario, California, that mobilization on the evolving immigration crisis began at a summit which this author facilitated. It was attended by some forty-five activist leaders and scholars from throughout Aztlán. There was consensus on the need to respond to the increasing deportations and to the proposed immigration policy by the Carter administration. A few days after the summit, RUP leader Jose Angel Gutierrez was asked to make a "call for action" on behalf of RUP leaders in Texas for a conference on immigration. On May 23 he sent a letter to numerous activists throughout the country,[85] which read, "The Carter Administration is designing a new immigration policy. We are the main targets. The phobia mongers insist our people, because of our numbers, birth rate, geographic spread and undocumented status threaten the very underpinnings of this society."[86]

As a result, two major immigration related events were held during the latter part of 1977: (1) the National Chicano and Latino Immigration Conference; and (2) the Mobilization March along the California San Ysidro/Tijuana border. The former was hosted by RUP in Texas on October 28–30, in San Antonio.

Some 1,500 activists from throughout the country attended the largest conference ever held by Chicanos on immigration. The agenda specified the formulation of a strategic response to the Carter administration's immigration plan, which included employer sanctions, more stringent border enforcement, giving the U.S. Border Patrol expanded police powers, and extending amnesty to undocumented workers who were already residents of the U.S.[87] During the course of the debate, however, participants representing a plethora of organizations from divergent ideological persuasions came into conflict.

A repeat of the scenario that took place at the National Chicano Forum held in 1976 in Salt Lake City occurred. Conflict and ideological schisms plagued the conference, which were started by the Socialist Workers Party (SWP) that was at odds with the Maoist-oriented August 29th movement, the Marxist-Leninist CASA-HGT, and other Chicano cultural nationalists who were aligned with Gutierrez's archrival, Rodolfo "Corky" Gonzales. Opposition to the left-supported resolutions was heightened by the Mexican American moderate organizations: the League of United Latin American Citizens (LULAC), the Mexican American Legal Defense and Education Fund (MALDEF), the National Council of La Raza, and the American G.I. Forum.[88] Despite rancorous debate, a ten-point plan calling for unconditional amnesty for all undocumented workers was endorsed and the call for nationwide protests was made.[89]

While the National Chicano and Latino Immigration Conference was being held in San Antonio, Chicano activists, led by Herman Baca's CCR, organized a mobilization march along the San Ysidro/Tijuana Cactus Curtain. Two major factors contributed to holding the march: (1) a boycott of the National Chicano and Latino Immigration Conference; and (2) the visit of KKK leader David Duke to the San Ysidro/Tijuana border. Baca called for a boycott of the San Antonio conference due to the SWP's participation.

Baca released an open declaration condemning the SWP "for not respecting the right of Chicanos to pursue their own struggle for self-determination."[90] A few weeks prior to the border march, KKK leader Duke toured the San Ysidro/Tijuana border with the collaboration of the U.S. Border Patrol. Organized as a media event, Duke announced that KKK members were scheduled to patrol the border. His media blitz dramatized the so-called invasion of the U.S. by Mexicano undocumented workers. The anti-KKK march was supported by numerous other Chicano activists and leaders, including Corky Gonzales, Bert Corona, Abe Tapia, Raul Ruiz, and this author, among others. Some 4,000 Chicano activists participated in the border mobilization march, which demonstrated the growing commitment of Mexicano activists to the issue of immigration reform.

The national conference and the San Ysidro march sparked increased activism. For the next two years activists and various organizations from California, such as CCR, CASA-HGT, National Institute for Community Development (NICD), which this author founded and led, and Raga Unida Party, forged an immigration advocacy coalition. Several meetings organized by NICO were held throughout southern California for purposes of advocating for immigrant rights and immigration reform. Without resources and divided over strategy, the coalition disintegrated by 1979. Each group, with the exception of CASA-HGT, which had folded in 1978, continued to be active in the immigration arena of politics. In some instances they coalesced on immigration-related issues.

From 1977 to 1981, CCR held three more marches along the San Ysidro/Tijuana border. In 1981 it protested the proposed Simpson-Mazzoli legislation and held its last major mobilization march. When interviewed Baca explained why he decided against holding other such marches: "When we were marching along the border I saw and heard some Border Patrolman mocking the march. It was then that I decided to never return or repeat such a march in a non-violent fashion."[91]

From 1977 to 1980, NICD and its sister mass-based organization, Congreso para Pueblos Unidos (Congress for United Communities or CPU), and (by 1983) the Institute for Social Justice (ISJ) held numerous direct action mobilizations in southern California on immigration-related issues.[92] In one particular case, U.S. Border Patrol agents in 1977 went into Our Lady of Guadalupe Catholic church in Ontario, California, and apprehended several undocumented migrants. Under the aegis of NICO, press conferences, letters of protest, meetings with Border Patrol officials, and finally a meeting with INS Commissioner Leonel Castillo ended the Border Patrol's gestapo-like tactics at least for a time in the San Bernardino/Riverside counties.

During the early 1980s, Mexicanos and Latinos responded to the growing immigration crisis, in particular the Simpson-Mazzoli legislation. Immigration fostered political divisions among the country's divergent ethnic/racial communities and organizations. Most Mexicano and Latino moderate advocacy organizations, for example, LULAC, NCLR, and others, supported the notion of immigration reform predicated on having a strong provision on legalization. On other provisions, however, such as employer sanctions, guest worker programs, and border enforcement, divisions set in.

These differences became evident during the 1984 legislative battle over its approval. The American G.I. Forum initially supported the idea of immigration restriction and increased support for the Border Patrol, but by 1984 supported amnesty. CCR adamantly supported amnesty while it strongly opposed employer sanctions and border enforcement provisions. CPU and its new sister organization, ISJ, which replaced the NICD as CPU's organizing entity, held numerous demonstrations and forums in support of the legalization provision. MALDEF supported the call for major immigration reform, but opposed the Simpson-Mazzoli bill. LULAC took the position of calling for a boycott of the

National Democratic Party Convention unless the delegates voted to oppose it. Concerned about undocumented workers being used as strike breakers, the UFW supported Simpson-Mazzoli's employer sanctions and border enforcement provisions. With CASA-HGT defunct, Bert Corona, with his revitalized HMN (Hermandad Mexicana Nacional) organized as well against its passage as did the Mexican American Political Association (MAPA). By 1984 national organizations, such as the NCLR, LULAC, and MALDEF, closed ranks and formed the "Latino lobby" in their struggle to defeat the Simpson-Mazzoli bill. Within the House of Representatives, the Congressional Hispanic Caucus led by California Representative Edward Roybal played a pivotal legislative role in the efforts to defeat it.

Just before the Democratic National Convention, three summit meetings were held to produce a strategic plan of action to defeat Simpson-Mazzoli. Facilitated by Danny Villanueva, KMEX television station general manger, and Vilma Martinez, MALDEF general counsel, the meetings were held in Washington, D.C., Denver, Colorado, and Los Angeles, California. The Los Angeles summit was attended by some forty Mexicano/Latino leaders that included Mario Obledo, Henry Cisneros, Tony Bonilla, and others, including myself. A two-prong strategy was formulated that called for picketing the Democratic Party Convention and for a nationwide concerted lobbying effort to pressure Democratic presidential candidate Walter Mondale to oppose it, which he did.[93] Its defeat was in great part due to the concerted efforts of scores of organizations, politicians, and activists who organized against its passage.

After two years of wrangling, Simpson-Mazzoli was reintroduced and approved in 1986 under a new name, the Immigration Reform Control Act (IRCA). One reason why it passed this time was the "absence" of effective organizing by Mexicano and Latino organizations, politicians, and activists. The opposition to IRCA never equaled the efforts of 1984. The level of leadership and organization in opposition had declined in 1986 and divisions set in. Some of the organizations that opposed it in 1984 supported it in 1986. Corona and the HMN and One-Stop Immigration in California, among others, supported it. At the crux of why it passed was the continued increase of the migrant exodus, which intensified the call for immigration reform. Erroneously, both President Reagan and Congress believed that IRCA would greatly reduce or put a halt to the migrant exodus.

With IRCA's passage, a transition occurred within Mexicano and Latino proimmigrant forces.[94] During the next three years, numerous activists and promigrant rights groups transitioned from being advocates to becoming service providers. Almost overnight a plethora of immigration service agencies surfaced throughout Aztlán's barrios. The $1 billion per year for classroom instruction of English, U.S. history, and government or civics was made available in grants by the federal government to numerous nonprofit agencies. By 1989 some 2.96 million people had applied for amnesty, of which 70 percent were Mexicanos.

IRCA became effective in diminishing the Mexicano and Latino community's capacity to advocate, since grant recipients were prohibited from attacking or fighting the hand that was feeding them, that is, the federal government.[95] The number of Mexicano/Latino organizations, especially at the local level, doing organizing and advocacy work on behalf of undocumented migrants, was greatly reduced. As for the migrant exodus, while there was a decrease in the number apprehended during IRCA's first two years, by 1988 the numbers had returned to what they were during the pre-IRCA years.

Nativist IRCA adversaries lost the political war against IRCA in 1986, yet they won the battle of "English only" in California. While no federal law existed making English the country's official language, California by a three to one margin passed Proposition 63, entitled "English Is the Official Language." The state made English its official language. Nativists spent some $1 million, including some $500,000 from U.S. English, the largest and most influential group in the English-only movement. The momentum it created led to the introduction of six similar bills at the federal level in 1987. Previous to its passage, five other states had approved similar English-only measures.[96]

For a time, U.S. English, led by Linda Chavez, a young Mexican Republican from New México, claimed a membership of over 400,000. It engaged in fund raising via mass mailings to advance its English-only cause, garnering some $6 million annually. Chavez argued zealously that Mexicanos and Latinos should embrace English and assimilate in order to prevent the "Quebecization" of the U.S. In 1988, Chavez resigned in protest over a memo written by its founder, John Tanton, which stated that Mexicanos and Latinos were uneducable, that they were corrupting the morality of U.S. public life, and that because of their reproductive power they would soon overwhelm the country's White population. As a result of the memo being made public, U.S. English lost membership and notable supporters like Walter Cronkite quit.[97]

Nativist "immigrant bashing" activities flourished after IRCA's passage. Abuses and attacks on immigrants continued to escalate. In response to numerous INS abuses that occurred during the 1980s, by 1988 they were recorded by the American Friends Committee headed by Roberto Martinez out of San Diego. He publicly revealed that between May 1988 and May 1989, 814 complaints were reported. A sizable number involved immigrants that were going through the amnesty process. The U.S. Border Patrol blamed the war on drugs as a pretext for the misconduct of its agents.[98]

In 1988 ISJ, under this author's leadership, handled the famous "Victorville Five" case in which five undocumented Mexicano migrants were beaten by San Bernardino County sheriff's officers. What made this case unique was that it attracted national and international media attention since the beatings were captured on video by a neighbor. For weeks, vigils, community town hall meetings, and marches were held in the high desert area of San Bernardino County. A civil suit in federal court was won two years later by attorneys Steve Yagman and Carlos Juarez, and the five were awarded some $600,000.[99]

As the 1980s came to a close, nativist forces did not let up in their attacks on immigrants, particularly Mexicanos. The paranoia that fed the nativist politics of the early 1980s continued. Democrat Richard Lamm, governor of Colorado, coauthored a book, *The Immigration Time Bomb*, in which he argued that the U.S. should curtail immigration from Latin America because it negatively impacted the country's economy, corrupted U.S. culture, and fragmented the country. Tom Metzger, who resided in San Diego County, reorganized the Ku Klux Klan and called it the White Aryan Resistance. He organized rallies and other events and anti-immigrant hate literature was distributed warning Mexicanos to leave the U.S. or face the consequences. The insinuation was that violence would be used. In explaining the precariousness of the Cactus Curtain, Richard Griswold and Arnold Deleon stated that "in the 1980s the U.S.-Mexican border region became the most dangerous terrain in America, as every year hundreds of undocumented immigrants were robbed, beaten, raped, and killed as they tried to cross."

CHAPTER 5

Decade of Growing Nativism, Xenophobia, and Militarization of the Cactus Curtain (1990–1999)

The passage of the Immigration Reform and Control Act (IRCA) failed to halt the migrant exodus or stop the re-Mexicanization of Aztlán and Latinoization or "browning" of the United States (U.S.). During the decade of the 1990s, the Latino demographic transformation continued to surge. México continued to be plagued by crippling economic and political problems coupled with the U.S.'s continued dependency on Mexican undocumented migrant labor. The country's nativist forces, for example, activists, anti-immigrant organizations, and politicians, responded to the migrant exodus in a dramatic fashion. They successfully pushed for the militarization of the U.S.–México border. In addition, the nativist forces intensified their xenophobic attacks on immigrants and initiated an anti-immigration political war. California was their main battlefield and their main weapon was the passage of xenophobia-inspired initiatives. Mexicanos in California, in particular, under a state of siege by nativist forces, responded with direct actions.

This chapter examines the 1990's as the decade of growing nativism, xenophobia, and militarization of the Cactus Curtain (U.S–Mexico border) that was given impetus by Aztlán's demographic re-Mexicanization.

The Latino Demographic Transformation Accelerates

1990 U.S. CENSUS

The 1990 U.S. Census revealed the growth of both the re-Mexicanization of Aztlán and the Latinoization or "browning" of the U.S.[1] Overall, the Latino population was officially designated as the country's fastest-growing ethnic minority and second-largest minority group. It significantly increased to 22,354,059, a 53 percent increase between 1980 and 1990.[2] Latinos comprised 9 percent of the total U.S. population of 248,709,873.[3] Overall, the Mexicano population in the U.S. increased at a rate of 54.4 percent, whereas the total U.S. population grew by a mere 9.8 percent. One in eleven persons in the country was Latino. In comparison, Blacks numbered 29.9 million, Asians/Pacific Islanders 7.2 million, and Native Americans 1.9 million. Of the various Latino subgroups, Mexicanos increased by nearly 4.8 million. Approximately 84 percent of the growth occurred in Aztlán as a region and comprised 5.4 percent of the country's total population, which translated to 13.5 million in 1990.[4] In comparison to the other subgroups, Mexicanos comprised 62.6 percent of the total Latino population, Central and South Americans 13.8 percent, Puerto Ricans 11.1 percent, Cubans 4.6 percent, and other Latinos 7.6 percent.[5] The percentage of Mexicanos by 1995 had increased to some 64 percent of the Latino population.[6]

The great majority of Latinos continued to live in urban areas, 91.8 percent compared to 72.8 percent for non-Hispanics. The percentage for Mexicanos was 90.5, compared to 95.2 for Puerto Ricans, 95.7 for Cubans, and 97 for Central and South Americans. Latinos again proved to be younger than other U.S. residents, with a median age of 26.2 compared to 33.8 for non-Hispanics. Of all the Hispanic subgroups, Mexicanos were the youngest with a median age of 24.3 years, compared to 26.7 for Puerto Ricans, 27.9 for Central and South Americans, and 39.3 for Cubans.[7] Third, at the regional level, Aztlán had the largest concentration of Mexicanos, numbering 11,237,325,[8] followed by the Midwest with 1,153,296, the West with 477,618, the South with 452,703, and the Northeast with 174,996.[9] At the state level, approximately three-fourths or 74 percent were concentrated in California and Texas. With the former having a population of 6,118,996 and the latter a population of 3,890,820, three of every four Mexicanos lived in these two states, followed by Illinois, 623,688; Arizona, 616,195; New México, 328,836; Colorado, 282,478; Florida, 161,499; Washington, 155,864; Michigan, 138,312; and New York, 93,244.[10] The Mexicano population, with the exception of Chicago, was largely concentrated in the following ten cities, all located in Aztlán: Los Angeles, California, 936,507; San Antonio, Texas, 478,409; Houston, Texas, 358,503; Chicago, Illinois, 352.560; El Paso, Texas, 338,844; San Diego, California, 194,400; Dallas, Texas, 185,096; Phoenix, Arizona, 176,139; San Jose, California, 173,803; and Santa Ana, California, 173,776.[11]

The demographic effects of the re-Mexicanization of Aztlán were particularly apparent in smaller cities in south Texas, California, and Arizona. A partial list of small cities with Mexicano populations of over 85 percent included the following: Socorro, Texas, 93 percent; Calexico, California, 92.9 percent; Eagle Pass, Texas, 91.9 percent; Coachella, California, 91.6 percent; Laredo, Texas, 89.3 percent; Nogales, Arizona, 87.7 percent; East Los Angeles, California, 87.5 percent; Mercedes, Texas, 86.8 percent; Robstown, Texas, 85.7 percent; and Calexico, California, 92.9 percent.[12] In California, the city of Los Angeles was 40 percent Latino and other municipalities were even higher: Maywood, 93 percent; Huntington Park, 92 percent; Bell Gardens, 88 percent; Irwindale, 86 percent; and San Fernando, 83 percent. The Mexicano population in the city of Long Beach doubled to 101,419. In Orange County, Anaheim grew by 122 percent and Santa Ana by 111 percent.[13]

From 1950 through 1990 some 2 million Mexicanos migrated legally to the U.S., more than the total immigrants from any other country in the world.[14] Despite more stringent enforcement of immigration laws and the militarization of the U.S.–México border, the migrant exodus was not impeded. During the previous years, undocumented Mexicano migration increased significantly. In 1979 it totaled 989,000; in 1989, 831,000; and in 1996, 1.6 million.[15] In 1996 INS (Immigration and Naturalization Services) estimated that out of a total of 5 million undocumented immigrants, Mexicanos comprised 2.7 million.[16] By 1999 the number apprehended throughout Aztlán topped 1.5 million, slightly more than in 1998 and 20 percent higher than during the first year of Operation Gatekeeper.[17] INS reported that in 1999 the undocumented population reached some 5.5 million, a figure increasing annually by 275,000. About 40 percent of the country's undocumented population resided in California.[18] With an increased budget of $3.9 billion (all dollar amounts are in U.S. currency), INS added some 1,600 additional Border Patrol agents and immigration inspectors, which further increased the militarization of the border.[19]

Contributing to the migrant exodus from México was legal migration. Between 1961 and 1990, 18 percent of all legal immigration came from México, 30 percent from Latin America, 31 percent from Asia, and 18 percent from Europe. Between 1981 and 1996, some 3.3 million Mexicanos entered the U.S. legally.[20] By the late-1990s, legal immigration into the U.S. totaled some 800,000. By 1998, the figure for México increased to 20 percent.[21] The Mexicano population increased in the border states of California, Arizona, New México, and Texas. According David E. Lorey, "by 1990, the border's Mexican-origin population was 16.8 percent of the total population in Arizona, 20.6 percent in California, 21.7 percent in New México, and 22.9 percent in Texas." He goes on to cite that "in 1990, 14.2 percent of Arizonans, 20 percent of Californians, 22.1 percent of Texans, and 27.9 percent of New Mexicans spoke Spanish at home."[22]

Overall, the immigrant and migrant population constituted about one in ten U.S residents, the highest number since 1930. México, by far, had the largest percentage with 18 percent.[23] From 1980 to 1999, the Latino foreign-born population increased to nearly 10 million, a percentage increase of about 240 percent. In 1990 the proportion of the country's foreign-born population from Latin America made up 44 percent.[24] By 1996, the Latino population had increased at a rate of 900,000 a year, a net immigration of 350,000.[25]

A third factor contributing to the Latino demographic transformation was high birth rates. The Census Bureau reported the rates for the overall population in 1990 showed a birth rate of 67.0 per 1000 women ages fifteen through forty-four. The birth rate for White women was 65.2, for Black women 74.8, for Asians/Pacific Islanders 58.1, and for Latinas 93.2.[26] Latino familes in 1980 included one more person than did the average White family. Mexicano families were the largest with 4.07 persons, followed by Puerto Ricans with 3.67, Cubans with 3.58 persons, and then others of Spanish origin with 3.37.[27] A pattern change became apparent among Latinas when they increased their level of education and economic standing—birth rates decreased.

The "White and Black exodus" was a fourth factor that contributed to the Latino demographic transformation, especially in California. In 1995 the U.S. Census reported on out-of-state migration. California had a net migration outflow of 138,000 in 1990 through 1991, for a 0.5 percent decline. That rate nearly tripled in 1995 by a loss of 426,000, representing a 1.4 percent decline. The Los Angeles-Anaheim-Riverside metropolitan area, in particular, showed the highest decline: for every person who came into the region, three left, resulting in a net loss of 351,000 people.[28] Blacks in Southern California were moving out of traditionally Black areas, such as Watts, Compton, and South Central Los Angeles, and resettling in Pasadena, Rialto, San Bernardino, and Moreno Valley. Others joined Whites in the out-of-state migration to other states in Aztlán, the Midwest, and the South.

Nativists' Legislative Political War

NATIVISTS RESPOND TO THE MIGRANT EXODUS

In response to the re-Mexicanization of Aztlán and the Latinoization and "browning" of the U.S., immigration restrictionists and nativists joined ranks in pushing for changes to the existent immigration laws as well as the passage of new immigration legislation. During the 1990s, nativist activists, politicians, and scholars, troubled by increasing alarm over the growing Mexicano and Latino population declared legislative political war against the migrant exodus. Increasingly, at all levels, nativists resorted tactically to a xenophobic politics predicated on "immigrant bashing" and "scapegoating." They contended that the undocumented migrants and immigrants were a socioeconomic burden on the economy and taxpayers, and were ultimately a disaster for the country. During the 1990s, numerous nativist groups and leaders escalated their attacks by pandering to the growing fears of Whites over the issue of immigration.[29] Nationwide, the Federation for American Immigration Reform (FAIR), which was especially vocal in California, and Voices of Citizens Together accelerated their nativist lobbying and organizing efforts.

Politicians and scholars joined in the growing nativist/anti-immigrant crusade. As early as 1985, Governor Richard D. Lamm and Gary Imhoff, in their book *The Immigration Time Bomb: The Fragmenting of America*, in zealous nativist language warned the country, "Today, immigration to the United States is massive, and it is out of control . . . And efforts to cope with the breakdown of immigration law or to moderate the high levels of legal immigration are stymied in Congress by an unlikely coalition of the far right and the far left, fueled by a coalition of big business and Hispanic pressure groups." Throughout the book the authors make arguments as to why the U.S. must control its southern border with México and limit legal immigration.[30] Ten years later, scholar Peter Brimelow, in his book *Alien Nation*, described immigration as a "disaster." He contended that the new immigrants were different than those who had come before. In a disparaging way, he describes them as being less educated, unskilled, not inclined to assimilate into the Anglo-Saxon culture, more prone to criminal activity, and an alleged major burden on the economy. The flood of immigration, he alleged, threatened to turn the country into an "alien nation."[31]

The growing nativist politic became even more evident during the 1990s when Congress initiated the passing of restrictionist immigration legislation. With the passage of IRCA in 1986, Congress's concern homed in on undocumented migration. But in 1990, the 102nd Congress shifted its cardinal concern to legal immigration. After much debate in both the House and the Senate and a number of amendments, Congress passed the landmark[32] Immigration Act of 1990.[33] According to Roger Daniels, it "was the last statute in the twentieth century to attempt a general overhaul and it [had] a generic relationship with the 1921, 1924, 1952, and 1965 acts."[34]

Its provisions fostered a major revision of the McCarran-Walter Act of 1952. Congress raised the number of immigrants to be admitted and set a cap. It set the annual ceiling level of legal admissions to 700,000 for 1992 through 1994, which after 1995 would drop down to 675,000 under a flexible cap. Of the said figure, 480,000 were family-sponsored, 140,000 employment-based, and 55,000 diversity-based via lottery visas. Inherent to it was a class bias, which provided an incentive to rich immigrants: 10,000 permanent resident visas were offered to those that agreed to invest at least $1 million in U.S. urban areas or $500,000 in rural areas.[35] It also expanded employment-related immigration by authorizing

131,000 "H" category temporary work visas in four new categories: O, P, Q, and R. It further provided a "temporary protected status," which enabled the country's attorney general to exempt from deportation undocumented nationals of countries that were plagued by violent conflagrations or natural disasters.[36]

In the end, according to Carolyn Wong, "the Immigration Act of 1990 augmented legal immigration levels by more than 30 percent, and did that with bipartisan support." Democratic Congressman Edward Roybal once again played a pivotal leadership role in the defeat of an amendment introduced by Republican Senator Alan Simpson. The amendment included a driver's license pilot program to be implemented in three states, which would produce a fraud-proof driver's license to be used for employment verification.[37] Beyond securing bipartisan support, it received strong coalitional support from labor, Latino, Asian, and church groups.[38] With the passage of the Immigration Act of 1990 Congress did not deliberate again on immigration reform until 1995, during President Clinton's first term.[39]

The Immigration Act of 1990 also established a Commission on Immigration Reform (CIR), comprised of nine members chosen from the public at large. Republican President George Bush appointed as the original chairperson of CIR Cardinal Bernard Law of Boston.[40] In 1993, however, Democratic President Bill Clinton appointed former Congresswoman Barbara Jordan from Texas as CIR's new chair. Because of Jordan's assertive and effective leadership, CIR became known as the "Jordan Commission." Its cardinal purpose was to formulate new procedures designed to curb both legal and undocumented immigration and to prepare a report by 1994.[41] The assumption of the CIR report was that border enforcement efforts had largely failed in deterring unlawful immigration.

Two CIR reports were issued, one in 1994 and the second in 1995. CIR's first report released identified "undocumented immigration" as the pressing public policy action issue. One recommendation was to establish a computerized registry of Social Security numbers for verification of work eligibility. It argued that such a verification system would eliminate the "job magnet" that "pulled" a lot of undocumented immigrants and migrants. IRCA's employer sanctions were considered flawed by CIR due to the widespread use of fraudulent documents. It was proposed that business and INS authorities work together to come up with a system to verify the validation of a Social Security number and those who had been issued a card.

CIR also recognized that IRCA border enforcement of the U.S.–México border was in need of change. It recommended the expansion of the size of the U.S. Border Patrol; use of improved technology, that is, field sensors, nighttime infrared scopes; erection of more fences at U.S.–México border; more vehicles and equipment; and denying public benefit services to both undocumented migrants and legal or documented migrants. In the case of the latter, the individuals would be eligible within five years of their entry into the U.S. In preparing the report, Jordan and other CIR participants held a number of House subcommittee hearings.[42]

In its second interim report, CIR focused on "legal immigration." While generally supportive of the current three-part framework of family-based, employment-based, and refugee immigration, it asserted that the current immigration system had to undergo major reform in order to ensure that admissions continued to serve the country's national best interests. Changes in its three-part framework were recommended: (1) nuclear family-based immigration limited to 400,000 visas; (2) skill-based immigration limited to some 100,000 visas; and (3) refugees limited to 50,000 visas. It also recommended yearly cuts on immigration levels to 550,000 a year and set refugee admissions under the overall ceiling.

Because of existent backlogs of visa applications, CIR proposed the prioritized admission of nuclear family members and skilled workers. In order to eliminate the backlog's long waiting period, CIR also proposed to eliminate the nonnuclear family preference categories. The intent was to grant visa allotments estimated at 150,000 each year to the more immediate family members. This would expedite the reunification of families and reduce the visa backlog to zero by 2002, and legal immigration to the U.S. would be about 700,000 persons.[43]

In 1995 Congress, supported by the Clinton administration, revised the Cuban Adjustment Act of 1966, which became known as the U.S.'s "wet feet, dry feet" policy. The influx of Cuban "boat people" went from a few hundred in 1989 to a few thousand in 1993. Cuba's severe economic crisis, ascribable to the loss of economic assistance by the collapse of the Soviet Union in 1991, escalated the post-Mariel immigration. Some 40,000 Cubanos were intercepted by the U.S Coast Guard and U.S. Border Patrol.[44] Fearing a larger exodus, the Clinton administration adopted a "wet feet, dry feet" policy, which allowed the U.S. Coast Guard to summarily return to Cuba or send to a third country Cuban boat people caught in the ocean. Those who made it successfully to U.S. soil (i.e., dry feet) qualified to remain in the U.S. They would qualify for permanent residence, be eligible for U.S. citizenship, and be given economic assistance. A salient provision of the policy was that the U.S. would admit no more than 20,000 from Cuba annually via the use of a visa lottery program to select those who would be eligible to emigrate to the U.S. The issue of the 33,000 Cuban boat people that had been apprehended in the high seas by the U.S. and were encamped at Guantanamo was negotiated. Cuba agreed to credit 5,000 per year for the next three years toward the minimum 20,000 allocated annually.[45] By 1995 the Cold War had ended and the Soviet Union no longer existed, yet the Clinton administration continued the economic embargo of Cuba and discriminatorily gave Cuban exiles preferential economic treatment and political refugee status because they had fled so-called Communist Cuba.

México's Economic Crisis: Migrant Exodus Intensifies

While Cubanos were given preferential treatment by the Clinton administration, undocumented Mexicanos and Latinos during the 1990s, were considered and treated as illegal. The intensity of their migrant exodus was evident by the number of apprehensions along the Cactus Curtain, which in 1993 totaled 1,213,000; 1994, 979,000; and 1995, 1,271,000.[46] México's capitalist economic crisis, coupled with Central America's impoverished economies that had been plagued by political instability, violence, repression, and insurgencies in El Salvador, Guatemala, Honduras, and Nicaragua, propelled this growth. The immense poverty that plagued the Caribbean and the rest of Latin America further contributed to this mass exodus or departure from their homelands. The economic "push" factors fed into a "pull" factor, which was the U.S. economy's dependence on cheap labor first from México and then Latin America.

The Mexican Revolution of 1910's promise of massive social change, with the exception of the administration of Lazaro Cardenas (1934–1940), failed. During his six-year governance, Cardenas managed to institute some major changes that included major land and labor reforms, political stability, expropriation of the country's railroads, and nationalization of México's oil in 1938. He is credited with introducing a mixed economy, which was a hybrid or combination of socialism and capitalism. The social change aspects embodied in its Constitution of 1917, which was to catapult it to modernity and development after the Cardenas era of change from 1940 to the 1980s, evolved to where the socialist aspects were purged and was instead dominated by neoliberalism.

Under the aegis of the PRI (Partido Revoluciónario Institucifinàl or Revolutionary Institutional Party), the regimes of Manuel Avila Camacho (1940–1946), Miguel Alemán Valdís (1946–1952), Adolfo Ruiz Cortinas (1952–1958), Adolfo López Mateos (1958–1964), Gustavo Díaz Ordaz (1964–1970), Luis Echeverría (1970–1976), José López Portillo (1976–1982), Miguel de la Madrid (1982–1988), Carlos Salinas de Gortari (1988–1994), and Ernesto Zedillo (1994–2000) failed miserably to produce the requisite economic changes that México needed to end the "push" factors causing the migrant exodus.

While Mateos, Echeverría, and Portillo adhered to México's mixed-economy developmental approach, it was under de la Madrid, Salinas, and Zedillo that México transitioned into a neoliberal free market economy. De la Madrid, constrained by the debt crisis, set a new course in economic policy predicated on capitalism, one that sought to create a more open economy that would enable México's economy to recover from its debt and introduced the "privatization" of many government holdings. His administration withdrew the government from the private sector of the economy by lifting protective tariffs from many products. México joined the international free-trade GATT (General Agreement on Tariffs and Trade) in 1986. De la Madrid negotiated the debt with the International Monetary Fund (IMF), World Bank, and foreign banks that owned a piece of México's debt problem. In renegotiating its debt, he committed 53 percent of the federal budget to repayments, devalued the peso, lifted price controls, cut spending by one-third, and reallocated funds from rural development into export production. Lynn V. Foster writes, "Instituting purer forms of capitalism into the Mexican government, de la Madrid hoped to jump start the Mexican economy. This complete reversal of Mexican post-war economic strategies would become the hallmark of the 1990s."[47]

Carlos Salinas de Gortari, a Harvard-trained economist/technocrat, using a neoliberal free market approach, momentarily stabilized México's economy. While de la Madrid introduced neoliberalism, Salinas institutionalized it with his capitalist free-trade policies. He unequivocally abandoned the few vestiges of México's post-Mexican Revolution mixed economy policies. His administration was zealous in its adherence to and promotion of "privatization." It sold as much as 85 percent or some 400 state-owned enterprises, including the government-owned banks acquired under de la Madrid. PEMEX, the country's state-owned oil company, was spared for nationalist political reasons. Also, for the first time, the Constitution's Article 27 was revised, specifically giving peasants the option of continuing to own the land as part of the *ejido* (collective farm) or to sell it. This was done so that the privatization of *ejidos* would allow wealthy Mexicanos or foreign agribusiness to acquire the land. Inflation was lowered to 8 percent, the budget was balanced, and even a surplus was created. Salinas reduced the onerous debt from 79 percent of the gross domestic product (GDP) to 29 percent. Unions that opposed his free-market policies faced government-imposed restrictions.[48] His administration negotiated the North American Free Trade Agreement (NAFTA), which is subsequently examined.

When Zedillo took office he faced an exacerbation of the Salinas economic crisis. With the Salinas economy collapsing (called the "Crash of 1995"), Zedillo once again devalued the peso. The peso fell to 12 percent of its value and then dropped to 50 percent. As the economic crisis deepened, Zedillo turned to the Clinton administration for a bailout. México received some $28 billion from international lending agencies and $20 billion from the U.S.[49] As a result of the crisis, a million jobs were lost, the costs of consumer loans dramatically increased, and inflation soared to a horrendous 52 percent.[50]

In 1994, PRI presidential candidate Luis Donaldo Colosio was assassinated, which revealed a brutal power struggle at the highest level among the PRI's oligarchic elites. Adding to Salinas's political crisis was the murder of Francisco Ruiz, who was the PRI's second-highest ranking official. President Salinas's brother, Raul Salinas, was charged in 1995 and imprisoned for his murder. Cracks in the PRI's hegemony also appeared with the rise of two insurgencies: in 1994 the Zapatista Army of National Liberation (EZLN) in Chiapas and the Popular Revolutionary Army (EPR) in 1996 in the Pacific region.[51] In explaining the nexus between México's political and economic crises, James D. Cockcroft writes,

> The political crisis had underlying economic causes rooted in the nature of Mexican capitalism. Neoliberalism failed to address these underlying causes, and in fact made matters worse . . . Economically, the crisis [is based on] uneven patterns of capital accumulation because of foreign domination and a weak bourgeoisie's historic reliance on low-paid labor . . . failure to develop either a large, dynamic home market or a vigorous production of capital and intermediate goods; and the consequent lower levels of productivity of Mexican capitalism.[52]

México's continued dependence on foreign capital and the shortcomings of the "import-substitution industrialization" and "stabilization development models" were at the crux of both crises.[53]

PRI President Zedillo in December 1994 inherited an economy on the verge of collapse and had to confront Salinas's corrupt legacy and failed neoliberal economic policies. Zedillo responded to the crisis by initiating a devaluation of the peso, which further exacerbated México's ongoing economic crisis. As the economic crisis deepened, Zedillo turned to the U.S. and the Clinton administration for financial assistance. A bailout of $50 billion was raised from international agencies, with the U.S. providing $20 billion. While the bailout prevented the collapse of the economy, interest rates for loans reached 100 percent—it did not halt the unemployment of some 800,000 Mexicanos during the first six months of 1995.[54]

México's impoverished masses, under Zedillo, suffered an intensification of poverty, unemployment, underemployment, low wages, inequality, and a plethora of social problems, for example, the growth of drug cartels, crime, and violence. In 1995 México's unemployment rate reached some 23 percent, and experts concluded that without the "safety valve" of immigration the rate would have been around 35 percent.[55] In 1997, it was reported that in the rural areas of México and among the indigenous populations 24 million people lived in "extreme poverty." Only 20 percent earned more than the minimum wage, which at 23 pesos was equivalent to $3.[56] The *campesino*'s acute marginalization was evident in the high number of unemployed that in 1997 totaled some 13 million.[57] By 1999 no appreciable progress had been made. Twenty percent of the workforce made the minimum wage of 34.50 pesos or $3.63.[58]

NAFTA Stimulus for Greater Poverty

President Salinas's neoliberal policies produced NAFTA, which from 1994 to 1999 worsened México's ongoing economic crisis. With neoliberal policies increasing discontent, Salinas's technocrats believed that they had not failed, but in fact, needed more time to succeed. They argued that a more "free trade" and "free market" approach was the answer to resolving México's economic crisis. In order to create an unprecedented "economic miracle," they believed that trade barriers needed to be removed, tariffs lowered, and privatization accentuated.[59] This would enable México to extricate itself from the economic morass of being a Third World economy and catapult it into the paragon of First World developed economies. México's economy as a result of NAFTA became more entangled in the monolithic web of "globalization of capital."

NAFTA's roots go back to 1965 with the establishment of the Border Industrialization Program.[60] It redirected México's national efforts at industrialization away from the state and to foreign capital via the creation of *maquiladoras*, foreign-owned assembly plants situated in "free-trade zones" along the U.S.–México border.[61] México's membership in the General Agreement on Tariffs and Trade (GATT) was the antecedent to NAFTA. President Portillo in 1980 refused to join GATT because he felt that it threatened México's sovereignty. President de la Madrid, on the other hand, embraced neoliberal policies, thus having México join GATT with the intent of lowering tariffs. In 1990 President George Bush and México's President Salinas publicly announced their intentions to initiate negotiations on a free-trade agreement that would include the U.S., México, and Canada. For three years, there were negotiations on the specifics of such an agreement, in particular, within the framework of export-driven development and rapid growth of transnational corporations that sought to invest in overseas markets. Neoliberal free-market exponents both in the U.S. and in México argued that its passage would greatly reduce the migrant exodus.

On January 1, 1993 Salinas, Bush, and Canada's Prime Minister Brian Mulroney signed NAFTA. The area became the largest free-trade region in the world with a GNP (gross national product) of almost 5 trillion and a combined population of some 360 million people. It freed up the movement of capital and goods among the three participating countries and provided for the elimination of most tariffs and nontariff barriers. Some were under a short-term schedule, while others were under a long-term schedule. In addition, it also facilitated cross-border investment and included side agreements that sought to improve cooperation between labor and the environment. Supported by the Democratic Clinton administration, Congress approved NAFTA in November 1993 and it went into effect on January 1, 1994, and was scheduled to conclude on January 1, 2008.[62] As to its main objective, according to Oscar Martinez, "NAFTA also removed traditional obstacles to cross-border trade and business, such as extant barriers to foreign investment."[63]

In response to concerns expressed by unions and environmental groups, NAFTA established two commissions and a development bank to deal with issues of worker displacement and pollution problems. NAFTA also precluded the free flow of labor across the three countries' borders.[64] As Justin Ankers Chacon and Mike Davis elucidate, "NAFTA also guaranteed that the Mexican government would not interfere with the operations of foreign corporations, favor domestic over foreign capital, or require 'technology transfers' that would force corporations to share technology with local hosts."[65] For México, NAFTA meant an unequivocal rejection of México's past mixed economic developmental policies. "Hoping to impress global investors with the strength and stability of the peso," according to Lynn Foster, "Salinas over-inflated the peso while holding down wages. To further expand the export-driven economy, he thought low wages were essential." In his push for México's modernization, Salinas ignored the basic needs of the citizenry and polarized Mexican society into the wealthy few and the increasing poor masses.[66]

Many of México's intellectuals warned about the potential loss of México's national sovereignty and its cultural sense of *Méxicanidad*. Small businesses recognized that their survival was in jeopardy. Economists predicted losses of millions of jobs, especially within the first five years of its enactment. In spite of the legacy of the Mexican Revolution and the death of nearly 2 million Mexicanos, with the enactment of NAFTA, President Salinas in essence, historically repressed and re-embraced the economic policies of the *"Porfiriato."*

NAFTA proved to be a disaster for México's impoverished masses. Nonetheless, for México's oligarchic economic elite and transnational corporations, it was an incredibly lucrative agreement. In pushing for it, President Salinas in 1992 abolished a provision within Article 27 of México's constitution that protected small Mexican farmers from unequal competition with U.S. agribusiness. From the onset, NAFTA did not improve the economic lot of México's marginalized masses, but instead served to further exacerbate México's economic crisis; specifically, it further propagated México's poverty syndrome. It created higher unemployment and underemployment, especially among *campesino* farmers.

NAFTA gave México's agriculture industry a life-threatening blow. A country whose history depended greatly on maize (corn), in particular, as a food staple, during the NAFTA decade México began importing corn from the U.S. México's small farmers could not compete with the U.S corn, which was cheaper and substandard, because of U.S. government subsidies. For years, they had been protected by Mexican government price controls and subsidies. NAFTA's implementation resulted in the loss of some 1 million jobs. Social service programs were cut by 10 percent during a time of mounting poverty.

Scores of manufacturing businesses specializing in clothing, toys, leather, and footwear went out of business. México's economy reoriented to being export-driven and bound to and dependent on the U.S. economy. México became the U.S.'s second largest trading partner. Numerous *maquiladoras*, with their subsistence wages, downsized or closed down and left for other Third World countries.[67] While wages varied regionally, in 1997 México's minimum wage was uniformly at $3.50 per day,[68] and even full-time employment meant being poor.

NAFTA proved to be an utter failure in stopping or even reducing the migrant exodus. In fact, it served as a stimulus for the intensification of the migrant exodus. For all the propaganda from neoliberals from both the U.S. and México that NAFTA was going to create jobs in México, strengthen the Mexican economy to produce a larger middle class, and create more economic opportunities for México's growing labor force, the opposite proved to be true. While by 1997 the Zedillo administration succeeded in arresting high inflation to a level of 17 percent and moved the economy toward a positive growth rate of 8.8 percent, two years later 50 percent of all Mexicanos lived in dire poverty.

U.S.–México Border Crisis: Militarization of the Cactus Curtain

NAFTA's failure to stop the migrant exodus into the U.S. enhanced nativists' efforts to militarize the Cactus Curtain. By the early 1990s, instead of receding, it increased. In 1991 the Border Patrol apprehended some 1.13 million undocumented migrants and this figure increased in 1992 to 1.5 million.[69] Likewise, legal immigration increased dramatically from 1988 to 1992. During these four years, some 5.4 million legal immigrants entered the country. Alarmed by the influx, nativists propounded the militarization of the U.S.–México Border. Public opinion polls demonstrated the hostile anti-immigrant political climate. Polls taken in July 1993 and again in January 1995 reflected the anti-immigrant feeling. In each, nearly two-thirds or 65 percent favored decreasing immigration. In the 1993 poll, a small minority, some 7 percent, favored an increase, and in the 1995 poll the figure went down to 6 percent. By 1995 only one-third of the country's population or 31 percent reported a favorable view of immigration levels.[70] At the core of the increased nativist attack was the Latino demographic transformation. Demographically, as previously examined, it was an empirical reality: the Latino population increased from 14.4 million in 1980 to 22.4 million in 1990 and continued being the country's fastest growing population. The ongoing media coverage helped foment a resurgence of xenophobia, nativism, and racism specifically directed at Mexicanos.

Beyond the demographics, certain events occurred in 1992 and 1993 that energized the country's nativist-pervaded White Anglo-Saxon Protestant (WASP) ethos. The Los Angeles Eruption of 1992 was one such event, which saw Latino migrants along with Blacks riot and pillage. A second event was the 1993 terrorist bombing of the World Trade Center. These two events coupled with the country's nativist-permeated political culture significantly contributed to a growing anti-immigrant WASP ethos. By 1993 undocumented migration was often equated to terrorism by nativists. Most polls indicated that the overall population wanted tighter controls over immigration and the U.S.–México border.[71] The porosity of the 4,000 mile-long U.S.–Canadian border was not an issue, only México's 2,000-mile border.

As a consequence, during the early 1990s both the Bush and Clinton administrations initiated efforts that led to the Cactus Curtain's militarization. This occurred within a political climate of economic recession, especially in California, a growing perception of socioeconomic insecurity, and constant images of a border out of control. The militarization began in 1990 with the Bush administration's approval of the construction of an eleven-mile-long fence along the San Ysidro–Tijuana border area as part of its war on drugs. Two years later, the militarization accelerated under the Clinton administration. President Clinton's perception was that during the next ten years immigration would be the most difficult problem that the country would have to confront. Under the heading "Enforce and Improved Border Controls," he articulated the following three goals: "(1) Enhance the enforcement of the laws controlling our borders, and ensure that the human rights of all immigrants are respected; (2) Improve the border patrol and ensure that it is held accountable for its actions; and (3) provide new technology and training in enforcement techniques."[72] Pressured by California Governor Peter Wilson and other Republican governors, Clinton took a more activist posture on border enforcement.[73] Floodlights along a thirteen-mile-stretch were installed and Attorney General Janet Reno also approved accelerated raids and blockades of the San Diego and El Paso border areas.

Clinton's administration implemented four major "border operations," which illustrate the egregious effects of the militarization. The first of these operations was initiated in Texas in 1993, called "Operation Hold the Line." In Texas, Silvestre Reyes, the U.S. Border Patrol chief of the El Paso sector, arbitrarily launched Operation Blockade, subsequently renamed Hold the Line. Its cardinal purpose was to pressure the Mexican government into curbing the migrant exodus. In a well-publicized show of force, Reyes deployed 400 agents and their vehicles along the twenty-mile stretch marking the El Paso–Ciudad Juarez border. Inspections at official ports of entry were intensified. The strategy represented a major shift. Instead of the Border Patrol waiting to apprehend undocumented migrants after they crossed into the U.S., the intent was to stop them before they crossed. On a short term basis, it worked: there was a reduction in apprehensions.

A few weeks later, INS border chief Gustavo de la Viña, heads of San Diego County, and city police departments called for increased federal funding for border enforcement. Governor Pete Wilson joined the political bandwagon and called for a similar operation to be implemented along the Tijuana–San Ysidro border.[74] Pressured by the nativist politicians and activists in California who had produced Proposition 187, the Clinton administration instituted "Operation Gatekeeper."[75] Joseph Nivens further explains that "opportunistic politicians and nativist organizations presented the undocumented migrant not only as a lawbreaker, but more importantly, as a threat to national sovereignty and the American social and economic fabric. Such imagery is rooted in the history of largely race-based anti-immigrant sentiment in California and more generally, the United States."[76] Funded for some $300 million, it was designed to fortify and seal the U.S.–México border between Tijuana and San Ysidro, California.

Operation Gatekeeper became "ground zero" in Clinton's anti-immigrant war.[77] Based upon a "prevention through deterrence" approach, it entailed the construction of a Berlin-type iron curtain, deployment of more U.S. Border Patrol officers, placement of electronic monitoring equipment, utilization of helicopters and ultimately aircraft for surveillance, and the use of U.S. military and National Guard forces in a supportive role in border enforcement. The use of military personnel was justified under the federal government's guise of the "war on drugs." In explaining its impact Wayne Cornelius writes, "Gatekeeper has sought to force crossings into the much less hospitable, mountainous terrain in the eastern portion of San Diego County and into the desert of neighboring Imperial County." He goes on to write that it was to prevent entry of undocumented immigrants by deterring them from leaving their places of origin. It was believed that it would impede their reaching the border and also would prevent them from crossing it; consequently they would return home.[78]

Between 1995 and 1999, the Clinton administration intensified the militarization of the border by implementing two more similar operations[79]: "Operation Safeguard" in 1996 in Nogales, Arizona, and two years later "Operation Rio Grande" in the southern part of the Texas–México border. The administration increased the size of the U.S. Border Patrol by 45 percent between 1993 and 1996. Attorney General Reno was appointed "border czar" of all border enforcement efforts. On September 1996, President Clinton signed the Illegal Immigration Reform and Immigration Act, which, as previously explained, nearly doubled the U.S. Border Patrol by the year 2001, an increase that went from 5,175 officers to nearly 10,000, called for the construction of a triple iron fence along the fourteen-mile Tijuana–San Ysidro border, and increased penalties for undocumented smuggling.[80] Even legal immigration came under heavy scrutiny.

INS in 1998 reported that legal immigration dropped to 637,000, its lowest level in a decade. It reflected a 17 percent drop from 1997 and a 28 percent drop from the year before.[81]

Regardless of the reports by INS, by the end of the 1990s, no evidence existed that supported the effectiveness of the four border militarization operations in halting or reducing the flow of the migrant exodus. Their effectiveness was in question, despite a budget in 1999 that swelled to $3.9 billion. Total border apprehensions increased from 1,212,886 in 1993 to 1,368,707 in 1997, an increase of 12 percent. By the end of the 1998 fiscal year, the number increased to 1,527,000, yet the total number of undocumented migrants in 1999 was estimated at 5.5 million, a figure that increased annually by at least 275,000.[82] While proponents of Operation Gatekeeper claimed success in apprehensions along their particular border sectors, the fact was that the migrant exodus moved east to other areas of the cactus curtain.[83]

By 1999, the migrant exodus shifted to Arizona's dangerous snake- and scorpion-infested desert area as its main entry. The change was evident by the Nogales/Douglas sector Border Patrol report that some 400,000 had been apprehended, while in comparison, California's San Ysidro/Tijuana sector had decreased significantly to less than 200,000. In California's Imperial County sector, in 1998 some ninety-five deaths were recorded that were due to either dehydration in the oppressive summer desert heat, canal drowning, crime, or other causes. It was the highest of any border region of the country. In August 1999, a drop occurred: the number of dead was at sixty-four. In 1995, however, only six perished, 1996 only twelve, and in 1997, only thirty-nine.[84]

The militarization of the Cactus Curtain by 1999 contributed to a volatile climate. Increasingly, undocumented migrants became victims of violent crimes, that is, robbery, rape, assault, and murder along the various border sectors. Some were also victimized by the Border Patrol and U.S. military personnel. One such incident occurred in 1997, when a U.S. Marine, a Mexicano enlisted man, shot and killed eighteen-year old Ezequiel Hernandez, who allegedly was mistaken for a drug trafficker while tending his family's goat herd.[85] After an inquiry, the marine was exonerated. There were also several Border Patrol shootings of migrants that occurred from Texas to California.

Nativist-Inspired Legislation of the 1990s

THE CLINTON ADMINISTRATION'S REFORMS

After five years of no deliberation by Congress on immigration reform and with Republicans winning control of both the House and the Senate in 1994 the political stage was set for restrictionist immigration reform, which in 1995 did resume. The CIR report issued in 1995 became the basis for debate, resulting in five separate immigration reform bills being introduced in Congress that year. Each bill sought to make major changes in the country's existent immigration laws. Two major bills emerged: one in the House, the other in the Senate. The House bill, designated the "Immigration in the National Interest Act," was introduced by Republican Congressman Lamar Smith. In the Senate, Republican Senator Alan Simpson, chair of the immigration subcommittee, introduced his own bill, the "Immigrant Control and Financial Responsibility Act."

Smith's House bill included eight titles: border security, undocumented worker smuggling, removal of undocumented and criminal undocumented workers, employer sanctions and verification, legal immigration reform, eligibility for benefits and sponsorship, facilitation of legal entry, and miscellaneous provisions, including H-1B skilled nonimmigrant visas.[86] Injecting a dosage of nativism, he said, "The nation's legal immigration system [was] broken and it no longer [served] the national interests."[87] It embraced most of CIR's recommendations to combat undocumented immigration, including fines placed on undocumented workers found to be employed. CIR's "diversity" immigrant program would be eliminated. It also sought to restrict access by undocumented workers to most social benefit programs. In addition, it also sought a reduction in legal immigration and limited refugees to no more than 595,000 persons per year by the year 2001. Family reunification would be limited only to the nuclear family. No employment-based visas would be issued to unskilled workers.[88] Eight hearings were held on Smith's proposed legislation and some 100 witnesses testified. Debate often became intensely partisan and acrimonious. Several Democrats, such as Xavier Becerra, Howard Berman, and Mel Watt, opposed it. After being subjected to various amendments, the House voted for Smith's bill, which included the controversial Gallegly Amendment that denied children of undocumented parents admittance to public schools.

In the Senate, Simpson's bill primarily addressed undocumented immigration and adhered to several of CIR's recommendations and proposals made by the Clinton administration. Its provisions included improved employment verification, tougher undocumented smuggling and document fraud penalties, reduction of welfare use by undocumented workers, a border crossing fee, use of closed military bases as detention camps, and stronger border enforcement. Simpson subsequently added a legalization provision that changed the numerical caps on family and employment categories. It also set limits on immigrant numbers from any one country. It sought to lower legal immigration to 540,000 per year, 135,000 lower than the current law allowed. The family category would retain the largest segment, with 450,000 admissions. The employment category would drop from 140,000 to 90,000 slots.[89] After weeks of wrangling over various amendments, the Simpson bill underwent major surgery, eliminating restrictions on legal immigration. By the end of 1995, no major immigration reform had been passed.

In 1996 the country was in the midst of a presidential election and Congress was divided on the issue of immigration reform. With Republicans in control of Congress, serious divisions existed among themselves as well as a major chasm between the House and Senate. Nonetheless, two pieces of legislation were passed by Congress that significantly impacted immigration. The first was the Personal Responsibility, Work Opportunity, and Medicaid Restructuring Act (PRWORA), the second was the Illegal Immigration Reform and Immigrant Responsibility Act (IIRIRA).

As to the former, the Clinton administration showed its conservative colors by seeking to reform the country's welfare system, which also impacted immigration. As a welfare reform bill, PRWORA, passed by Congress in August of 1996, initiated cuts in many social programs and benefits used by immigrants. It denied undocumented immigrants, as well as in some cases legal immigrants, any access to social service programs and benefits. Debra L. Delaet explains that it prohibited undocumented "immigrants and non-immigrants from receiving federal public benefits, with limited exceptions for certain benefits, including emergency medical services, certain emergency disaster relief, public health immunizations and treatment of communicable diseases, housing assistance."[90] With the preceding exceptions, undocumented migrants were prohibited from receiving federal, state, and local benefits. Legal immigrants were no longer eligible for food stamps or Social Security benefits. They were also denied Medicaid and Supplemental Security Income, which is a program for older, blind, and disabled people.[91] Public housing was also denied during the first five years of residence in the U.S.

Under PRWORA's provisions, legal immigrants were also impacted. One of its provisions allowed states to deny legal immigrants cash welfare and other benefits. It increased the responsibility of the immigrant's sponsors by making the affidavit of support legally enforceable, imposing new requirements to more programs and lengthening the deeming period. The eligible income and assets of the immigrant's sponsor were deemed to be part of the immigrant's application for most types of public assistance, and the deeming period was extended for up to ten years.[92] Its policy impact was such that it established restrictions on the eligibility of legal immigrants for means-tested public assistance and denied undocumented migrants access to benefits and services. Even before President Clinton signed it into law, he was vehemently criticized by pro-migrant rights groups and activists. As a welfare reform bill it was considered to be onerous, inhumane, and unjust toward immigrants. Many of the immigrant related provisions were never enforced. The balanced budget agreement concluded in 1997 between the

Republican-controlled Congress and President Clinton repealed most of its measures that were deemed to be draconian against immigrants.[93]

With the passage of PRWORA, Congress and the Clinton administration next passed IIRIRA, border security and enforcement reform legislation. Its paramount purpose was to curb the influx of the migrant exodus. Attached to a 3,000-page appropriation law for fiscal year 1997, after last-minute political maneuvering, a deal was struck in late September 1996 and was passed by Congress. Unlike previous acts that addressed numbers and quotas, IIRIRA was designed toward targeting undocumented border crossing. It increased funding for border control and immigrant apprehension and strengthened the employer sanctions provision of the law.[94] It was broken down into six general provisions with each one containing several other provisions: border enforcement, alien smuggling and document fraud, removal and detention, employer sanctions, benefit eligibility, and miscellaneous.[95]

IIRIRA authorized the Border Patrol, under Title I, to hire 1,000 additional Border Patrol agents and 300 new support staff each year for five years and ordered INS to relocate agents to border areas where undocumented migrant traffic was high. In addition, it authorized $12 million to add two additional fences and for road construction at a fourteen-mile section of the U.S.–México border near San Diego. Other IIRIRA border enforcement provisions included an entry-exit database, establishment of preinspection stations at selected airports, INS promotion of state/local enforcement cooperation, and issuance of tamper-proof border crossing cards. Under Title II, it authorized the use of wiretaps and undercover operations in efforts to enforce laws against undocumented smuggling and document fraud and for increased penalties for these violations. Under Title III, the law provided new grounds for exclusion, including "incitement of terrorist activity" and falsely claiming to be a citizen. It also restricted undocumented migrants from filing class action suits against INS.

Under Title IV, IIRIRA required the U.S. attorney general to develop pilot programs to test various employment verification methods. Work eligibility would be determined only by a Social Security card, green card, U.S. passport, or INS employment authorization card. As to "benefit eligibility," under Title V, it set the minimum household income level for sponsors of immigrants at 125 percent of the poverty level. It also specified that undocumented workers were not eligible for Social Security benefits and required HUD (Department of Housing and Urban Development) to deny them subsidized housing assistance.[96] While Congress and the Clinton administration legislatively sought to curb the incessant flow of the migrant exodus, California passed nativist-inspired propositions.[97]

CALIFORNIA'S NATIVIST PROPOSITIONS

In California, the Clinton administration's militarization of the Cactus Curtain acted as a catalyst for a resurgence of the politics of nativism at the state level. Driven by the belief that the country was in the midst of an "immigration crisis," nativists in California initiated an anti-immigrant political crusade using racist initiatives. Some analysts alleged that it actually began with the passage in 1978 of Proposition 13, which limited property tax in California. Lisa Magaña explains that "because state taxes and resources were reduced, redistribution expenditures, such as education, became more difficult to fund. As a result, immigrants were blamed for the economic downturn in the state."[98] Others attributed it to the rise of the "English-only" movement that during the 1980s held that "multilingualism" eroded the English language and fragmented detrimentally the country's national heritage. In 1982 California U.S. Senator S. I. Hayakawa's call to make English the official language of the U.S. further buttressed the rise of the official English-language movement. In California in 1986 the English-only anti-immigrant movement succeeded in its passage of Proposition 63, the English-only initiative. It passed by a three to one margin, making English the official language in California. By the early 1990s, seventeen states had approved similar legislation.[99]

By the early 1990s, California was caught up in a devastating recession. With the end of the Cold War in 1991, California's defense and aerospace industries were particularly negatively impacted. There was unemployment, there were plant closures, and industries left the state. Some 200,000 defense-related jobs were lost as a result of the recession. The recession strained state government's fiscal capacity to provide services, particularly in education. Increasingly, nativists blamed "immigrants" for California's socioeconomic ills.

During the 1990s the Mexicano and Latino population's growth fed the nativist politic of the fears of *la reconquista* of Aztlán. In particular, California's Latino population had increased to 6,118,996[100] and in various cities it comprised a new majority. Nativists' fears were exacerbated by demographic studies that prognosticated that Whites nationwide by 2050 would constitute a minority and that "people of color" would be a majority.

California became a conflict-ridden battleground from 1993 to 1998. Nativist forces, led by Republican Governor Pete Wilson and a number of right wing politicians, activists, and organizations, accelerated their immigrant-bashing campaign. Their attacks were tantamount to a declaration of political war directed at the state's migrant communities. Thus, their weapon of choice became the initiative process via three propositions.

The first was Proposition 187. By 1993 nativists "scapegoated" migrants by blaming them for California's growing socioeconomic ills. During the

1990s, California had the largest number of foreign-born residents of any state. According to the 1990 U.S. Census, of California's 19.8 million people, approximately 6.5 million were foreign born.[101] Their acrimonious attacks were particularly directed at migrants from México and secondly at Latino immigrants in general. On October 5, 1993, a meeting held to discuss immigration, convoked by Ron Prince and California Republican Assemblyman Richard L. Mountjoy, drew the participation of several nativist leaders: Alan Nelson and Howard Ezell, both former INS officials; Robert Kelly, political consultant; Barbara Kiley, mayor of Yorba Linda; and Barbara Coe, leader of FAIR, among others.

Prince, Coe, and Bill King, a former INS border agent, formed the California Coalition for Immigration Reform. While reportedly eating at a Méxican restaurant, they met and opted to work to place an anti-immigrant initiative on the California ballot for 1994. They selected the name SOS (Save Our State) for their anti-immigrant campaign. At the national level, Nelson and Ezell established Americans Against Illegal Immigration (AAII), an organization that sought to aid in the development of grassroots anti-immigrant groups.[102] Their nativist politic picked up momentum with the support of Governor Wilson, who had a history of having a love/hate relationship with immigration. As a California U.S. senator, he pushed to assure that growers had access to a continuous supply of cheap migrant labor. As California's governor, however, he adopted a more blatantly xenophobic, nativist, and racist politics on immigration. In a xenophobic manner, he alleged that a Mexican invasion of Aztlán was in progress and that the federal government was doing little to stop it.

Spearhead by Governor Wilson, nativist forces succeeded in garnering the requisite signatures to place the SOS initiative, otherwise known as Proposition 187, on the 1994 ballot. In spite of the fact that it was unconstitutional in that it went against the 1982 Supreme Court decision *Ply v. Doe*, which ruled that undocumented children have a right to access to an education and should not be punished because of the undocumented legal status of their parents, Governor Wilson used it to prop his possible bid for the Republican presidential nomination for 1996. It was used to pander to the growing nativism of frustrated White voters and signaled the incipience of a declaration of political war against the country's Mexicano and Latino communities. Its proponents proclaimed that "we" (Whites) must be "saved" from "illegal aliens" (their term) and their "invasion" (migrant exodus). Proposition 187's punitive effects were twofold: (1) It sought to deny public education (from primary to postsecondary levels) to children of undocumented migrant parents, regardless if the children were U.S. citizens; and (2) it sought to deny social services and health care, with the exception of emergency services, to undocumented migrants.

School and social service agency officials were required to verify the legal status of both students and parents. Those that were found to be undocumented would be turned in to the INS and state attorney general. Law enforcement agencies were also required to collaborate with INS and the state attorney feneral in identifying suspected undocumented migrants/immigrants in expediting the deportation of those alleged to be criminals. In addition, it established stiff penalties for those trafficking in the manufacture of counterfeit documents.[103]

California's growing nativist political climate was such that even some Democrats joined the anti-immigrant bandwagon. California U.S. senatorial candidate Dianne Feinstein ran an ad in which she claimed that some 3,000 "illegals" crossed the border each night. While most Democrats opposed Proposition 187, their opposition was halfhearted, perhaps because the majority of the White electorate and some Latinos supported it. In September, a *Los Angeles Times* poll showed that, paradoxically, 52 percent of Latinos supported it.

In the November elections, Proposition 187 passed with 59 percent of the votes cast for it and 41 percent against it.[104] Its passage sent a nativist message: White voters, including some persons of color, expressed their vehement concern and anger, if not their racism, by voting for it in massive numbers. The vote returns showed that two out of three Whites (67 percent) voted for it, nearly half of both African American and Asian American voters also supported it, and only 23 percent of Latinos voted for it.[105] Its passage fostered a catalytic nativist contagion across the country that increased nativist immigrant bashing and scapegoating and signaled an intensification of the anti-immigrant political war against the migrant exodus.

The Mexican American Legal Defense and Education Fund (MALDEF) challenged Proposition 187 in the courts. In 1995, a federal judge struck down the provision of the law that denied public services to undocumented migrants. Nativists in 1996 failed in their attempts to put on the ballot another initiative called Save Our State, which sought to deny citizenship to children born in the U.S. of undocumented migrant parents. After nearly five years of political and legal pressure, Democrat Governor Gray Davis in 1999 abandoned any further court proceedings on the contested Proposition 187 on grounds that it was unconstitutional. The only provision that was maintained was the one that pertained to penalties for the production and use of fraudulent immigration documents.[106] According to Oscar Martinez, "the burial of Proposition 187 marked one of the most significant political victories ever achieved by Latinos/as in the Golden State."[107]

Nativists next pushed Proposition 209. Nativists continued their siege on the immigration issue well into 1996, but also directed their political guns at affirmative action. After nearly thirty years of promoting the principle of "equal opportunity" in employment and contract compliance, affirmative action programs[108] came under fire in California again from ultraright wing nativist forces, which sought their termination. For years, challenges to affirmative action had been commonplace. One such legal challenge resulted in the infamous U.S. Supreme Court decision of 1978, *Regents of the University of California v. Bakke.* In a 5 to 4 decision, based upon the 1964 Civil Rights Act, the U.S. Supreme Court ruled that "race" could not be used as the sole criterion for admission, which struck down alleged quotas or "preferential admissions." However, it did allow race to be taken into consideration as one of the several "plus" factors designed to enhance the diversity of a school's student body.[109] During the post-Bakke years, affirmative action came under increasing attack.

By the 1990s, affirmative action had become a wedge issue. In college admissions, the post-Bakke years showed some improvement for people of color, but improvements were erratic. In professional schools, according to Susan Welch and John Gruhl, "the number of minorities in medical and law schools showed little increase during the decade from 1976 to 1986." They explain that it was "less than 0.5 percent in the case of Black medical students, nearly 1 percent for Hispanics, and close to 3 percent for both in law schools." Yet between 1987 and 1994, Black and Latino college enrollments increased. Latino overall college enrollments increased by over 50 percent, as did the number of bachelor's, master's, and doctorate degrees awarded. The number of doctorates granted increased by some 30 percent. In professional schools, the number of Latinos and Blacks increased by some 50 and 40 percent respectively. While not a panacea, affirmative action programs did make a difference in admissions.[110]

With nativist forces in California savoring their victory in Proposition 187 they next directed their attack on affirmative action. In great part their political motivation was largely driven by their fear that the state's population was rapidly changing to where Whites were on the verge of becoming a minority and people of color, for example, Latinos, Blacks, Asians, and native people were on the verge of constituting its new majority. In essence nativists felt their influence, power, and ultimately their hegemony were in jeopardy. Their weapon of choice was the initiative process. In 1995 the University of California (UC) board of regents, supported by Governor Wilson, an ex-officio member, voted to prohibit affirmative action preferences in admissions, employment, and contracts.[111] Nativists then moved to dismantle affirmative action statewide. They successfully secured the requisite number of signatures to get the initiative officially on the 1996 presidential ballot by playing the "White" race card.

Designated the California Civil Rights Initiative (CCRI), it became known as Proposition 209. The two White scholars who authored it, Glynn Custard and Thomas Wood, argued that affirmative action was tantamount to preferential treatment in employment and contract compliance, which was forbidden on the basis of race, sex, ethnicity, or national origin.[112] Anti-affirmative action zealots alleged that affirmative action discriminated against Whites who were better qualified and was unconstitutional as it applied to California's public institutions.

At the helm of the anti-affirmative action leadership was UC Regent Ward Connerly. Others who supported it included the California Association of Scholars, Republicans, Governor Pete Wilson, and Voices of Citizens Together (VCT). With President Clinton running for reelection, Democrats failed to mount an effective counteroffensive, fearing alienating White voters. Only toward the end of the campaign did the Democratic Party take a more proactive stance against the measure.[113] While it passed by a vote of 54 percent in favor to 46 percent against it, Latinos voted three to one against it.[114]

On a bandwagon, nativist groups, activists, and politicians in 1998 next directed their political guns at bilingual education. Again, using the initiative process, they succeeded in demonstrating their political power within the electoral arena with the passage of the insidiously named English for the Children initiative, or Proposition 227. It qualified in December 1997 for the June 1998 primary.[115] Its main purpose was the eradication of bilingual education in California's schools. As to its specific provisions, it called for students with limited English skills to receive a year of intensive English instruction or "immersion" and then be moved to regular English classes. Few exceptions would be allowed, and educators who violated its provisions could be sued. In addition, it would take effect two months after its passage.[116] It was estimated that out of the 1.4 million students in California who needed help learning English 80 percent were Latino.[117]

Like the two previous racist propositions, 187 and 209, Proposition 227 was a reaction by nativists to the escalating re-"browning" of California. Nativists understood that Whites in California were fast becoming a minority in the state and that Mexicanos and Latinos would be the new majority. They sought to create many legal obstacles to thwart their educational and employment opportunities, which can be argued was part of their xenophobic "colonial" mentality. Even at the federal level, Republican House Speaker Newt Gingrich, motivated by presidential aspirations, launched a well-organized and acrimonious attack on bilingual education in January as part of a seventeen-state tour. In one of his many pronouncements on the issue, Gingrich stated that "the fact is English is the common commercial language of America" and argued for "English immersion."[118]

For Mexicanos in particular, bilingual education, coupled with its once bicultural component, had been a product of the activism fostered by the Chicano movement of the late 1960s and early 1970s. Driven by a pronounced sense of cultural nationalism, Chicanismo, activists sought for Mexicanos and Latinos in the U.S. to become bilingual and bicultural. Yet by the 1990s, the bicultural component had long been dropped and bilingual education had been watered down to where it was merely a transition vehicle from Spanish into English. To nativists, however, as innocuous as it was, they felt that it still presented a threat to their English-only WASP ethos cultural hegemony.

At the leadership helm of Proposition 227 was Silicone Valley millionaire Ron Unz followed by Republican Governor Wilson and Los Angeles Mayor Richard Riordan. Yet a few Republicans, such as candidate for attorney general Dan Lundgren, circumspect about the political damage it would create for Republicans among the growing Latino voters, did not support it. Democrats, as with Propositions 187 and 209, did little to help defeat the measure and at best offered symbolic political support. Finally, a few weeks prior to the election they went against it. The Clinton administration vacillated as well and did not oppose it until late April.[119] In the end Proposition 227 won by a landslide 61 percent. Whites overwhelmingly supported it, Latinos opposed it by a two to one margin: 63 percent voted against it and 37 percent voted in favor, which was still a significant share.[120]

Latino Resistance to Nativist Political War

MEXICANO/LATINO COUNTERATTACK

During the early years of the 1990s, few pro-migrant rights advocacy groups were viably functional and those few that were did not possess the capability to mount an effective countermobilization. One cardinal reason was that some had become social service providers dependent on federal funding. Most of those that did have federal funding, however, were not willing to take on an advocacy posture for fear of jeopardizing their funding. Unfortunately, those groups that were not receiving funding did not have an organized mass power base. Their counterattacks during 1990 to 1993 had been largely ineffectual and defensive. But in late 1993, because of Proposition 187, they heightened their involvement and began counterattacking the nativist forces.

On January 6, 7, and 8, 1994, the National Summit Conference on Immigration was held at the University of California, Riverside, by the newly formed Ernesto Galarza Public Think Tank on Public Policy (EGTTPP) which this author founded and directed. Held at the Riverside Raincross Square Convention Center, some 450 scholars, leaders, politicians, and activists gathered to address the heightened nativist immigrant bashing at both the state and national levels, but particularly Proposition 187. The three-day summit received state, national, and international media coverage. Speakers addressed the summit in a number of panels held on various aspects of Proposition 187 and in general on the intensifying immigration crisis. Former New México Governor Tony Anaya, in the summit keynote address, reminded participants of the many positive contributions immigrants made to their communities. He emphasized that Latinos should use their numbers and purchasing influence to exert their political power on the matter. Former Texas Raza Unida Party leader Jose Angel Gutierrez took issue with Proposition 187 and Governor Wilson's proposal to deny citizenship to children born to undocumented residents in the U.S. despite its being a constitutional right.

Numerous other speakers homed in on the immigration debate. California State Senator Richard Polanco warned summit participants that it was "going to get ugly this year. There's been a lot of political posturing, and its hardening and polarizing our communities."[121]

In this author's keynote address, I reminded summit conference participants that in order to countervail the nativist political war and siege, Latinos needed to get recommitted to the struggle for social justice and human rights, reorganized via the formation of grassroots coalitions, committed to policy change, and remobilized to demonstrate the power of the Mexicano and Latino communities through a bifurcated strategy of electoral politics and massive direct action mobilizations.[122] My speech became the basis for the approbation of the "Plan de Riverside," a strategic plan of action designed to defeat Proposition 187.[123]

In February, at a press conference and rally held in Los Angeles, the plan was formally unveiled. It was released simultaneously at other press conferences held in other cities in California, Texas, New México, and Illinois. At the Los Angeles event, representatives of various pro-migrant groups called for a mobilization against Proposition 187. They argued that if Latinos did not respond, the anti-immigrant hysteria would worsen. Operation Gatekeeper was attacked and so were both Democrat California U.S. Senators Dianne Feinstein and Barbara Boxer for supporting it. They were also chastised for supporting the use of California's National Guard to assist the Border Patrol in its patrol of the border.

In the months that followed several of its direct action measures were put into effect.[124] La Coordinadora, a coalition of organizations under the direction of One Stop Immigration (a local immigration service/advocacy agency from Los Angeles) and under the leadership of Jose Jacques Medina, Felipe Aguirre, Juan Jose Gutierrez, Fabian Nunez, among others, in February held an anti-Proposition 187 march and rally in Los Angeles that drew some 6,000 people. On May 28 it held a second mobilization in Los Angeles, which drew some 18,000 protestors. In September and October in protest against Proposition 187 thousands of high school students in various parts of the state initiated spontaneous one-day massive walkouts, waving Mexicano flags. In the San Fernando Valley alone some 10,000 students walked out from thirty-nine schools.[125]

On October 16 in Los Angeles, La Coordinadora made history by holding the largest march and rally ever in the history of the country's Mexicano political experience. Held downtown at the City Hall, estimates of the size of the crowd ranged from 75,000 to 100,000 people. Many of the marchers carried placards, banners, and Mexican flags, and displayed an ardent Mexicano nationalist fervor. Some moderate Latino *politicos* (politicians) and organizations voiced their concern that such a display of Mexicano nationalism served to alienate and further anger White voters. Undeterred, up to November, several other anti-187 marches and demonstrations were held throughout the state by a number of organizations and coalitions. On the eve of the November election, a concert was held at East Los Angeles City College that was attended by 10,000 "U.S. flag-waving people" protesting Proposition 187.[126] In spite of the mobilizations, Proposition 187 passed overwhelmingly. What ensued was a nativist legislative surge in several states, especially in Arizona, to pass similar initiatives and laws.

The passage of Proposition 187 became the clarion call of nativists and promigrant rights activists alike. On January 13 and 14, 1995, EGTTPP held at the University of California, Riverside, its second national summit conference, entitled "The Immigration Crisis, Proposition 187: A Post Election Policy Analysis on Its Implications." Over 500 activists, academicians, leaders, politicians, and community leaders met to decide what needed to be done to counteract its onerous provisions. The summit engendered an aura that momentarily seemed to rekindle the cultural nationalist (Chicanismo) spirit of the *movimiento*. Several of the Chicano movement's leaders participated: Reies Lopez Tijerina, Jose Angel Gutierrez, Herman Baca, Raul Ruiz, among others, including me, addressed the summit. As with the first, the second EGTTPP summit received wide media national and international coverage. At the summit a plan of action was developed, entitled "Post 187 Strategy for Mobilization." It called for the formation of a national Latino united front and a combination of direct action and electoral mobilizations, including a national march on Washington, D.C., a resource development fund, a revitalization of the student organizations, and the building of a nexus for support internationally, especially with México and Latin America.[127]

The political response of Mexicanos and Latinos in California to CCRI or Proposition 209 was at best lackadaisical. While MALDEF and a few other organizations spoke out against the measure, unlike with Proposition 187, no groundswell occurred to mobilize against it. "Unfortunately," explains Acuña, "the Latino community did not organize marches of any magnitude against proposition 209."[128] While some events, such as rallies, colloquia, and conferences, were held at universities, no major student mobilizations occurred. As usual, most Latino politicians procrastinated and failed to exercise leadership on the issue. With its passage,[129] California enhanced its pacesetter role for the exportation of nativist initiatives.

That same year, Governor Wilson sought to cut off food stamps to some 400,000 legal immigrants and prenatal care to undocumented migrants.[130] In

April 1996 the violent beating of undocumented migrants by Riverside County Sheriff's deputies in California was recorded and televised by a news station, which covered the story via helicopter. Deputies were captured viciously hitting two migrants with their batons, while others ran for cover following a dramatic chase on a Los Angeles freeway. After much pressure by Latino pro-migrant rights groups one of the deputies was fired and another was suspended.[131]

In response to the growing nativist political war, during 1996 Latino pro-migrant rights groups and activists increasingly became more active. At the 1988 Republican National Convention held in San Diego, a coalition of organizations and individuals (IMPACTO 2000–a coalition that this author had founded and led) held a march and rally on August 10 at the San Ysidro–Tijuana border to protest the Republican Party's anti-immigrant politics and to make a call for a new amnesty program. With some 1,000 protestors in attendance, the rally held at the San Geronimo Ranch featured numerous speakers and protest music. The nearly five-mile-long march along the border ended at Border Field Park where, led by La Coordinadora, about 200 people rallied on the Mexican side of the border.[132] Voices of Citizens Together, a nativist group led by Glen Spencer rsponed by organizing a organized counter anti-immigrant demonstration that drew a mere one-hundred protesters along the border.

Other protest groups held demonstrations in downtown San Diego. One such protest was *la Marcha de la Reconquista*, which retraced in reverse the first march organized by the Brown Berets in 1971 that started in Calexico and concluded in Sacramento. Organized by El Movimiento Estudiantil Chicanos de Aztlán (MEChA) students from San Diego, this march started in Sacramento and ended in San Diego with a culminating protest. The San Diego Federation, an umbrella social service-type organization, also held a day-long National Latino Leadership Summit to denounce the politics of scapegoating and call for a Latino voter mobilization for November.[133]

The transient activism that surfaced in 1996 culminated on October 12 with the first Latino National March on Washington, D.C. Organized by La Coordinadora, its purpose was to call for support of immigrant rights and immigration reform. With crowd estimates ranging from 25,000 to 50,000, Latinos from throughout the country gathered for a one-day show of "Latino power." Initially, organizers had predicted several hundred thousands of Latinos would participate. The geographical distance from Mexicano-populated Aztlán, the lack of massive Latino population concentrations in the local to regional areas of Washington, D.C., the admixture of Latino subgroups that lacked a common strategy and purpose, insufficient resources and staff to do the organizing, and the presence of an uninterested White conservative and nativist media were the salient factors that impacted the march's lower numbers.[134]

From 1997 to 1999, Mexicano and Latino pro-migrant rights advocacy efforts were more defensive than offensive in nature. La Coordinadora continued to develop its national immigration network and lobbied for unconditional amnesty. In advancing its *politica sin fronteras* (politics without borders) in February 1997 it negotiated successfully with México's leading political parties, the *El Pacto de Californias*. As an agreement, it called for the improved protection of the undocumented migrants' human and labor rights in the U.S.[135] In March 1997 IMPACTO 2000 held a counterdemonstration against an anti-immigrant border rally held at Howard Lane Park, San Diego, organized in support of the U.S. Border Patrol and Operation Gatekeeper by Spencer's Voices of Citizens Together. With some 200 pro-migrant rights people in attendance, a picket was set up and a protest was held to denounce the border rally. Separated by a police barrier and uniformed police, the two adversarial groups exchanged taunts and racial epithets.[136] Roberto Martinez from the American Friends Committee in San Diego spoke about the numerous documented and undocumented migrant abuses at the hands of the Border Patrol.

Latino resistance in 1998 to Proposition 227 was mediocre at best. Assembly Speaker Antonio Villaraigosa, State Senator Richard Polanco, and Congressman Esteban Torres, among a few others, procrastinated on the measure. They along with the so-called national Latino organizations did little to organize against it. A few weeks prior to the June election they and others came out in opposition to the measure. Again, the counterresponse was largely symbolic opposition, indicative of a Latino community not being well organized enough to protect its interests. MALDEF was the exception, it provided the most visible and vociferous opposition. There were other non-Latino organizations, such as the American Civil Liberties Union (ACLU) and California Teachers Association (CTA) that zealously opposed it. The Latino community as a whole was paradoxically divided on the issue.[137] In April of 1998, just two months prior to the primary election, a *Los Angeles Times* poll taken revealed that some 50 percent of Latino voters supported it and 32 percent opposed it.[138] Even famed teacher hero Jaime Escalante, who had produced top Latino students in math and was depicted in the film "Stand and Deliver," supported the antibilingual initiative.[139]

Latino activism against Proposition 227 intensied during the closing weeks of the June election. Overall, however, the response was too little and too late. The protests were poorly organized and failed to foster massive direct action or an electoral mobilization. In June, in Los Angeles just before the election, some 500 students, mostly from Belmont High School walked out of class for a day to protest what they perceived to be a racist initiative. It was spontaneous, lacked planning and organization. A few students were arrested, but the walkouts failed to create a contagion for other mobilizations.[140] Thus, in the end, Latinos failed to galvanize a sufficient critical electoral mass to defeat the measure.[141]

With its approval by the electorate, a number of civil rights organizations, led largely by MALDEF and ACLU, days after the election, initiated a legal challenge to block its implementation. The suit alleged that the initiative was unconstitutional and violated federal laws guaranteeing equal access to education.[142] California State Board of Education officials announced that requests for exemptions from the law would be denied.[143] That July, a federal judge refused to halt its implementation, which cleared the way for its enactment. Some school districts sought to maintain a semblance of bilingual education via the use of "waivers." Parents were given an option to keep their children in bilingual classes provided they requested a waiver from the school district. The student, however, needed to have some knowledge of English, be at least ten years old, and have special physical, emotional, psychological, and educational needs. By September, some thirty-seven school districts requested waivers and by October the state Board of Education okayed their use.[144] Thus, during the ensuing two years, a semblance of bilingual education was kept alive by some school districts via the use of waivers.

In 1999 newly elected Democratic Governor Gray Davis effectively killed Proposition 187's implementation. Davis agreed not to appeal an earlier court ruling that held that the initiative was unconstitutional, which precluded lawyers on both sides from taking it to the U.S. Supreme Court. The nativists reacted to Davis's decision with anger. Nativist Glenn Spencer, head of Voices of Citizens Together, said, "Davis sold his soul for the Hispanic vote, and now he is paying for it."[145] Governor Davis's action was a major setback to California's nativist forces and a victory for pro-migrant rights proponents. Thus, as they transitioned into the twenty-first century, the nativists' political war against the Migrant Exodus intensified.

CHAPTER 6

Arizona's Nativist Armed Rancher Vigilantes and Militias (1999–2004)

During the first four years of the twenty-first century, both the Mexicano population in Aztlán and Latino population nationwide increased at a much faster pace than anticipated earlier by demographers. Nativists reacted by intensifying their political war against undocumented migration, particularly against first the Mexicano and second the Latino. In unprecedented fashion, from 1999 to 2004, as a region Aztlán, specifically southern Arizona, experienced the rise of nativist armed rancher vigilantes and militias. Xenophobia-based fears of the present and future consequences of the Latino demographic transformation caused them to seek curbing the influx of the migrant exodus by conducting quasi-military border patrols along the Arizona–México border. It was during these five years that nativism directed at Mexicano and Latino migrants became more acute and assertive.

This chapter provides an in-depth examination of the Latino demographic transformation, the rise of Arizona's nativist armed rancher vigilantes, and militias from 1999 to 2004.

The Latino Demographic Transformation

NATIONAL LATINO DEMOGRAPHIC PROFILE

The 2000 U.S. Census data validated the fact that the country during the 1990s had experienced a demographic transformation.[2] This meant that the re-Mexicanization of Aztlán and the Latinoization and "browning" of the country had intensified. The results signaled that the country was increasingly becoming a multiethnic/racial, multicultural, and multilingual society. The data validated

experts' prognostication made ten years earlier that the country's White population within the next fifty years would be relegated to a new minority status and
that people of color would be the new majority. Also revealed was that the effects
of the Latino demographic transformation were evident at all levels: national,
state, and local.

Nationwide, the U.S. Census reported that the U.S. population in 2000
reached 281 million. More revealing, however, was the growth of the Latino[3]
population. It increased to some 35.3 million, a 58 percent increase, from 1990
to 2000. This was about 3 million more than what the Census Bureau had predicted. One out of eight residents of the U.S. was of Latino origin.[4] Latinos comprised 12.5 percent of the country's population, making Blacks still the largest
ethnic/racial minority. They numbered 36.1 million and comprised 12.7 percent of the country's population, followed by Asians at 4 percent and native peoples at 1 percent. The country's White population decreased to 67 percent.[5] A
year later in 2001 Latinos increased to 37.4 million, which represented 13.3
percent of the total and translated to a 4.7 percent increase among Latinos between April 2000 and July 2001.

In 2003 the Census Bureau released adjusted census figures for 2000–2002.
Fueled by the growing migrant exodus, especially from México, and high birth
rates, the Latino population increased to 38.8 million in 2002. The impact of
the migrant exodus was evident in that 40.2 percent of the Latino population
were foreign born.[6] Officially, Latinos became the largest and fastest-growing
ethnic/racial minority group in the country, surpassing Blacks, who in 2002
numbered 36.6 million and grew by a mere 3.1 percent.[7] Analysis of census data
by the Tomas Rivera Policy Institute revealed that Latinos outnumbered Blacks
in twenty-three states.

The Census Bureau released data in 2004 for 2003 that showed that the
Latino population was still the fastest-growing minority. Nationwide the dramatic Latino population increase by 2004 also manifested the growing Latinoization and "browning" of the country's population. While the total U.S. population went from 131.7 million in 1940 to 290.3 million in 2003, the Latino
population increased almost thirty times during that same period, from 1.4 million to 39.9 million. Equally significant was that from 2000 to 2003 the Latino
population grew by 13 percent—almost four times as fast as the nation as a
whole, and fourteen times faster than the White population, which grew by a
mere 0.9 percent.[8] *The Almanac of Latino Politics* reported that by 2004 the
Latinos had increased to 40,459,196.[9] Whites decreased to 68 percent, while
Latinos increased to a high of 14 percent, Blacks experienced a slight increase to
13 percent, Asians stayed about the same at 4 percent, and others remained at
1 percent.[10] In two years, Whites grew by a mere 0.7 percent, compared to a
9.8 percent increase for Latinos. This was nearly four times the rate of the country as a whole and seven times the non-Latino rate, which meant that Latinos ac-

counted for half (i.e., 3.5 million) of the country's total population growth (i.e., 6.9 million).

The effect of the re-Mexicanization became clearly evident in 2000. The U.S. Mexicano population increased by 54 percent and was estimated at 23 million. In ten years, it had increased by some 7.1 million. They constituted the largest subgroup of the country's Latino population. In the West, they constituted 74 percent; Midwest, 71 percent; South, 56 percent; and Northeast, 9 percent.[11] In 2002, Mexicanos comprised 66.9 percent of the total Latino population; 14.3 percent were Central and South American, 8.6 percent were Puerto Rican, 3.7 percent were Cuban, and the remaining 6.5 percent were of other Latino origins. By ancestry or origin, the Latino population was 66.9 percent Mexican, 14.3 percent Central and South American, 8.6 percent Puerto Rican, 3.7 percent Cuban, and 6.5 percent other.[12] For the next 28 years, the Mexicano population in the U.S. was expected to grow by 400,000 to 500,000 due to migration from México.[13] In 2004, it was estimated that the Mexicanos in the U.S. numbered nearly 25 million.

A unique aspect of the Latino demographic transformation was its youthfulness. The U.S. Census Bureau in 2002 reported that 18 percent of the country's children were Latinos, an indicator of future population growth. The U.S. Census in 2002 reported that 34.4 percent of Latinos were under the age of 18, compared to Whites, 22.8 percent. Mexicanos had the highest proportion under the age of 18 (37.1 percent), while Cubans had the lowest (19.6 percent).[14] Overall among Latinos, 14.3 percent were 45 to 64, compared to 25.7 percent for Whites. Also, 5 percent of Latinos were 65 and older, compared to 14 percent of Whites.[15] Whites were an aging population, while Latinos were a more youthful population. Mexicanos had the lowest median age, 24.2 years, compared to Puerto Ricans, 27.3 years; Cubans, 40.7 years; Central Americans, 29.2 years; and South Americans, 33.1 years. By ancestry or origin, the Latino population was 67 percent Mexican, 14 percent Central and South American, 9 percent Puerto Rican, 4 percent Cuban, and 6 percent other.[16]

LATINO STATE POPULATION

The effects of the Latino diaspora were also evident at the state level. By 2004 about 80 percent of Latinos lived in only 10 states by population, including California, the largest, with 12,246,122; followed by Texas, 7,656,151; New York, 3,003,572; Florida, 3,250,768; Illinois, 1,739,870; Arizona, 1,584,217; New Jersey, 1,274,500; New México, 808,693; Colorado, 862,631; and Georgia, 576,113. According to the 2000 census data Latinos constituted the largest minority group in some twenty-one states.[17] States outside of Aztlán with growing Latino populations included Washington, 441,509 (7.5 percent); Oregon,

275,314 (8 percent); Michigan, 323,877 (3.3 percent); and Massachusetts, 428,729 (6.8 percent); and particularly southern states. Lured by jobs in the expanding poultry processing plants and textile mills, Mexicano and Latino migrants, especially undocumented, migrated in large numbers to Alabama, Arkansas, Georgia, South Carolina, North Carolina, and Tennessee.[18] North Carolina experienced a 393.9 percent increase—from 76,000 in 1990 to 379,000 in 2000. Georgia's Latino population grew from 108,022 in 1990 to 435,227 in 2000, a 299.6 percent increase.[19] Latino migrants altered the demographic, cultural, and economic complexion of the South. The result by 2004 was increasing ethnic/racial tensions between the newly arrived mostly Mexicano migrants and Blacks and Whites.[20] The Midwestern states of Iowa, Nebraska, Kansas, and Minnesota were not exempt from the Latinoization contagion. Both legal and undocumented migrants reinvigorated the declining White populations in a number of Midwest towns. Driven by the availability of jobs in meat processing plants, in spite of facing a myriad of tribulations, (e.g., nativism, racism, and poverty) they migrated in their quest of a more prosperous future.[21] As their numbers increased, so did the tensions with nativist Whites.

LOCAL LATINO POPULATION GROWTH

The effects of Latinoization were especially evident at both the county and city levels as well as in their growing density. According to the U.S. Census, Latinos constituted a majority in some fifty counties and of these, thirty-five were in the South, thirty-four in Texas alone and fifteen in the West. Of the latter, New México had nine counties of Mexicano majorities and two each in Arizona, Colorado, and California. Latinos were between 25 percent to less than 50 percent of the population in some 152 counties. Los Angeles County had the largest number of Latinos in the country, numbering over 4.2 million (42 percent). In California, Riverside and San Bernardino Counties had a combined population of 1,248,586; Latinos respectively comprised 36.2 percent and 39.2 percent. These two counties experienced a phenomenal growth rate of 323 percent from 1980 to 2000, making them the sixth-largest Latino region in the country.[22]

The 2000 census also revealed that Latinos were a highly urbanized population. Nearly 46.4 percent lived in a central city within a metropolitan area, while 45.1 percent lived outside of central cities but within a metropolitan area.[23] According to a July 2002 Brookings Institution report, an exodus of Latinos from the cities to the suburbs had begun: 54 percent of the nation's Latinos lived in the suburbs, which represented a 71 percent increase since 1990.[24] The urbanization and suburbanization of the Latino population was evident in their large presence in the country's large cities: Los Angeles, California, 1,719,073 (47 percent); Chicago, Illinois, 753,644 (26 percent); Houston, Texas, 730, 865 (37.4 percent); San Antonio, Texas, 671,394 (58.7 percent); El Paso, Texas, 431,875 (76.6 percent); Dallas, Texas, 422,587 (35.6 percent); Phoenix, Arizona, 449,972 (34.1 percent); and San Jose, California, 269,989 (30.2 percent). People of color, essentially Latinos and Blacks, became the "new minority-majority" in the country's top 100 cities between 1990 and 2000. Latinos and Blacks were respectively 23 percent and 24 percent.[25]

The U.S. Census in 2003 reported that although Miami, Florida, as a city had the highest percentage of foreign born at 61.6 percent, California dominated the nation's top ten ranked cities: Santa Ana, 48.4 percent; Los Angeles, 41.3 percent; Anaheim, 40.3 percent; San Francisco, 36.7 percent; San Jose, 36.5 percent; Long Beach, 30.9 percent; and San Diego, 27.9 percent.[26] The U.S. Census revealed that in a majority of the country's cities, Latinos and Asians were the country's most isolated or most segregated ethnic groups.[27]

The Census Bureau reported that the country's foreign-born population had increased from 31 million in 2000 to 34.2 million in 2004, an increase of over 3 million. They made up nearly 12 percent of the country's total population. This compared to 1920 when the foreign-born population reached its apogee, which at the time was 13.9 million. By regional origin, Latin America represented the largest, comprising 15,668,000 or 44.6 percent; followed by Asia, 8,970,000 or 25.5 percent; then Europe, 4,519,000 or 12.9 percent; other, 5,979,000 or 17 percent.[28] 27.6 percent of the foreign-born population were from México.[29]

As had been the case for previous decades, undocumented migration was the cardinal force in the Latino demographic transformation. The Census Bureau demographic report for 2000 to 2002 revealed that of the nearly 10 percent Latino population increase, 53 percent was attributed to undocumented immigration.[30] The Pew Hispanic Center in 2004 estimated that the number of undocumented migrants that had successfully crossed the Cactus Curtain since 2000 averaged about 500,000 people per year, of which 56 percent came from México.[31] The distribution of Mexicano undocumented migrants by state included 2,000,000 in California; 700,000 in Texas; 540,000 in New York; 350,000 in Florida; 290,000 in Illinois; 135,000 in New Jersey; and 115,000 in Arizona.[32] By 2002 the INS calculated that nationwide there were a total of some 8.7 million undocumented migrants, of which 3.9 million or 44 percent were from México.[33] Even though by 2002 a decrease of 29 percent occurred in the number of undocumented migrants apprehended along or at the border, some 900,000 were caught, which suggested that the migrant exodus was still booming.[34]

During October 2000 to September 2001, of the some 1,064,318 legal migrants that came into the U.S., Mexicanos comprised almost one-fifth of the total, more precisely 206,426, or 19.4 percent. Legal immigration from other

Latin American countries included: El Salvador, 31,272 (2.9 percent); Cuba, 27,703 (2.6 percent); Dominican Republic, 21,313 (2 percent); Nicaragua, 19,986 (1.9 percent); Colombia, 16,730 1.6 percent); and Guatemala, 13,567 (1.3 percent). Over one-quarter or 282,957 (26.6 percent) settled in California.[35]

Beyond immigration, the Latino demographic transformation was also a product of high birth rates. Latinas, particularly Mexicanas, proportionate to their overall national population, in several states had higher birth rates than any other group in the U.S. According to the 2000 U.S. census, at the national level, among women between the ages of 15 to 19, the Latino birth rate was 93.4 per 1,000, compared to 81 for Blacks, and 34 for Whites. The nation's birthrate in 2002 dropped to its lowest level since 1909. The rate fell to 13.9 births per 1,000 women ages 15 to 44, down 1 percent from 2001 and 17 percent from its most recent peak in 1990. The birthrate also fell to its lowest level on record, 43 births per 1,000 among teen women ages 15 to 19.[36] Conversely, this was not the case for Latinas. The U.S. Census Bureau in 2003 reported that 47 percent of the Latino population increase was ascribable to high birth rates.[37] By 2004 the rate for Latinas 15-19 years of age was 82.6 per 1,000, more than double the national rate of 41.1 per 1,000, meaning Latinas had the highest teen birthrate among the major racial/ethnic groups in the U.S. Furthermore, Latina teen birthrates vary substantially from state to state, from 34.9 per 1,000 in Louisiana to 164.3 per 1,000 in North Carolina.[38]

The significance of the aforementioned was that the Latinas were having more children than White women or any other ethnic/racial group. By 2000 White women averaged just 1.8 children, which suggested that Whites were moving toward having a low replacement rate. Conversely, Latinas, especially Latina immigrants, were the major demographic force behind the country's continued population growth. Study after study by 2002 concluded that the immigrant birthrate was at least 40 percent higher than that of the country's native population. This decline in the White population was a demographic trend that also plagued Europe[39] from Great Britain to Russia, which had precipitated an immigration crisis of its own. Increasingly, several of Europe's economies had become dependent on labor from the Third World. Simply stated, this meant that Latina migrants during their lifetime averaged three children as opposed to two for other groups.[40] Latinos also had the largest families of any other ethnic/racial group. The average family size for Latinos was 4.27; Blacks, 3.32; Native Americans, 3.70; Asians, 3.70; and Whites, 2.95.[41]

As the state level, California being an illustration, Latinas dominated birthrate statistics. In a study conducted in 2002 during two consecutive quarters by the UCLA Center for the Study of Latino Health and Culture, under the direction of David Hayes-Bautista, Latinos for the first time accounted for more than 50 percent of California's births.[42] During the first quarter, there were 138,892 births in California, of which 69,672 were Latino. Non-Latino Whites accounted for 31.4 percent of the births for the quarter, while Asians and Pacific Islanders comprised 11.3 percent and Blacks 6.1 percent. During the subsequent quarter, the percentage of Latino births experienced another increase to 50.6 percent, while non-Latino Whites experienced a birthrate decrease to 30.4 percent. Asian and Pacific Islanders percentage increased to 11.7 and Blacks stayed at 6.1 percent.[43] In numerous counties, the percentage of babies born to Latinas was high. Los Angeles had the highest with 63 percent; Riverside, 58 percent; San Bernardino, 55 percent; Ventura, 54 percent; and Orange, 50 percent.[44]

A third major force contributing to the Latino demographic transformation was White and Black flight. As a term, it signifies the voluntary depopulation of a certain ethnic or racial group from a certain geographical space, that is, neighborhood, city, region, or state, and resettlement to some other area. Other contributing factors were the state's economic difficulties, growing social problems, high cost of living (particularly in housing), traffic congestion, and the demographic re-"browning" of the state. As a phenomenon with roots in the past decade, it intensified during the turn of the twenty-first century. Some regions and cities within certain states experienced a decline in the White and Black population. At the crux of this drop was growing Latinoization, especially within Southern California's coastal counties.[45] During the 1990s, the White population in Los Angeles shrunk from 3.6 million to 2.96 million. Southern California's five counties in 2000 lost a total of 840,000 people due to White flight.[46]

Droves of Californians, mostly Whites, left the state and sought to live their golden years in states such as Texas, Washington, Arizona, Nevada, Oregon, or Colorado.[47] Between 1995 and 2000 some 568,000 people migrated out of California to other states, particularly Nevada (199,125), Arizona (186,151), and Texas (182,789).[48] In 2001 it was reported that in 1999 somewhere between 80,000 and 115,000 more people left the state than came into the state. By 2004 some 100,000 more people had moved out of than moved into California.[49] Beyond California, New York and Illinois lost both natives and immigrants to other states, yet they continued to attract large numbers of immigrants.[50] In California numerous cities and counties experienced White and Black flight. Cities where Mexicanos and Latinos were once minorities, such as Bell, Bell Gardens, Huntington Park, Maywood, and South Gate, in 2004 had Mexicano and Latino populations of over 90 percent. Yet thirty-four years earlier Latinos had only comprised around 28 percent.[51] A common practice among these communities, predicated on financial necessities, was the "bunching" of Latino families. Simply put, two or three families or several persons pulled their resources together in order to afford rent or a house payment, which contributed to the Latino community's density and growing concentration. San Bernardino and

Riverside in 2004 were in transition to becoming majority Latino counties by 2015, if not sooner. Statewide there were seventeen counties where minority populations exceeded 50 percent.[52]

Black flight also contributed to the Latinos' increasing concentration. Black flight started during the 1980s, accelerated in the 1990s, and increased significantly in 2000 through 2004. As the Latino population increased in what used to be predominantly Black communities and areas, Blacks moved out to other neighborhoods, communities, and states. Black flight, however, has been much more intrastate migration-oriented, meaning people moved out of one community to another instead of leaving the state. Several cities and areas in Los Angeles County that once had been demographically majority Black some twenty-five years ago, such as Watts, Compton, Inglewood, and South Central Los Angeles, by 2005 had transitioned to Latino majority status.

Thus, the net effect of White and Black flight was that Latinos by 2004 had become more concentrated and segregated. As a result, ethnic/racial tensions between Latinos and Whites and Latinos and Blacks increased. Particularly among White nativists in Arizona, the political war against immigration resorted to armed rancher vigilantism and formation of militias directed specifically at Mexicanos.

The Rise of Anti-Immigrant Vigilantes and Militias

NATIVISM INTENSIFIES

During the years from 1999 to 2004, for some White nativists, the Latino demographic transformation, particularly the re-Mexicanization of Aztlán, was salt on their wounds. Their nativist politics was driven by a pronounced fear that demographically Whites would soon become a minority in Aztlán. It meant the hegemony of their White Anglo-Saxon Protestant (WASP) ethos was seriously in jeopardy. They were cognizant that most undocumented migrants were not interested in assimilating into the WASP ethos of the "melting pot." While some adhered to a "cultural pluralist" or "salad bowl" perspective, predicated on acculturation and a blending of cultures, the majority sought to retain their culture, heritage, and language. Whites were hypercritical of the migrants' refusal to sever the umbilical cord with their mother country, that is, family, relatives, village, city, or state, as demonstrated by their generous remittances of billions of dollars and frequent travels to their home country.

To some nativist zealots the country's "immigration crisis" was tantamount to an invasion of the U.S. by México. Their xenophobic fear of the "re-Conquista" was that there was a deliberate attempt by México to recapture the Southwest, which it had lost to the U.S. in 1848 intensified. Nativists sought to put the brakes on both undocumented and legal migration. Their strategy was twofold: (1) "conventional," which relied on anti-immigrant initiatives, laws, ordinances, electioneering, pressure, lobbying, and manipulation of the media; and (2) "unconventional," which relied on protest, militancy, confrontation, armed vigilantism, and militias. Particularly, militias became organizationally a locus for an extremist nativist response to the immigration crisis.

HISTORICAL PROFILE OF MILITIAS

Militias are part of the U.S. political experience. They are as old as the country itself. Over the years militias have had an ill-defined and at times a controversial existence. To this day, debate and controversy exists over what constitutes a militia, and how they qualify under the protection of the Constitution's Second Amendment—the right to bear arms. Neil A. Hamilton explains that "militias are . . . formal, structured, private organizations of armed citizens that declare themselves militias and engage in paramilitary training sessions or preparedness meetings."[53] Proponents argue that the Constitution defines militias as "the citizenry at large." According to Yale law professor Akhil Amar, when the Second Amendment to the Constitution was drafted, "militia" referred to all citizens capable of bearing arms; consequently, a militia is a voluntary paramilitary organization comprised of citizens, therefore it would seem to qualify. The U.S. Supreme Court, however, in *Presser v. Illinois*, ruled that the right to raise a militia belonged to the states rather than private citizens. Therefore, only states have the power to organize and mobilize a militia in order to defend from both domestic and foreign enemies.[54]

During the seventeenth century, militias were an integral part of the British colonization efforts of the thirteen colonies. They were used by the British to protect the colonies from attack by native peoples or from foreign powers, such as France or Spain. All men sixteen and older were required to become part of a militia. By the eighteenth century, however, while militias continued to operate, the responsibility for defense of the colonies fell to the British Army. In 1775 a militia calling itself the Minutemen in Massachusetts effectively fought the British at Lexington and then at Concord, two famous battles that began the Revolutionary War.[55]

With the U.S. as a nation-state by 1790, the role of militias declined as a result of the federal government's development of a permanent regular standing army. It was not until after the Civil War (1861–1865) that militias reemerged as part of the country's political experience. Some scholars, such as Stan Weber and Daniel G. Rodeheaver contend that the Ku Klux Klan (KKK), formed in the

1860s, was a militia. In response to increasing Black political activism and limited political gains, they explain that the Ku Klux Klan adhered to an antidemocratic, racist, and authoritarian posture. In describing its orientation, they state that "the public legitimacy and support granted to the earliest militias was now almost completely gone due to the violent tactics of the newer ones. For instance, the original Ku Klux Klan used murder, torture, rape, beatings, and arson to drive Black people back into subjugation and to restore White rule and planter control through the Democratic Party."[56] Its terrorist activities were halted in the 1870s because of President Ulysses S. Grant's intervention, which resulted in the suspension of the writ of habeas corpus in nine South Carolina counties, which led to the conviction of some 1,250 Klansman for various offenses and impacted the disbandment of the Klan as a militia. During the 1920s, after World War II, and again in the 1960s, the KKK resurfaced.[57]

From 1945 to the late 1980s, the Cold War between the U.S. and Soviet Union produced a political climate propitious for the rise of militias. Anticommunist zealots, such as Senator Joseph McCarthy, whose relentless anticommunist crusade via his infamous hearings, provided an antecedent for the rise of militias during the 1960s. Fanatical individuals concerned about the threat of communism coupled with the rise of the civil rights movement resorted to the formation of right-wing militias. They differed in orientation, strategy, and politics, yet regardless of their differences, they had a common historical thread— they perceived themselves to be in the tradition of the colonial militia, defenders of the country against foreign and domestic threats.

The militias that formed during this time were essentially two types: (1) constitutionalist; and (2) Christian identity. The "constitutionalist" adhered to the sanctity of the U.S. Constitution, contended that certain groups were conspiring to destroy the U.S., was ethnocentrically White supremacist, and perceived the federal government as the enemy engaged in taking away people's freedoms. Furthermore, they espoused such beliefs as anti-gun control, protection of the Second Amendment to the Constitution (the right to bear arms), property rights, and a government conspiracy of building a new world order. Several prominent conservative groups contributed to their growth: the John Birch Society, tax protestors, the Posse Comitatus, and the Mormon Church. One of several constitutionalist militia types was the Minuteman Project, formed by Robert DePugh. Another was the Posse Comitatus, formed by William Gale and Mike Beach in the late 1960s.

The Christian-identity militia adhered to a line of thought that was both religious and racist. As White Aryan Christians, they believed that they were the true descendants of the biblical tribes of Israel; that Jews were completely unconnected to the early Israelites and were instead descendants of the devil; and lastly, that the world was on the verge of a final apocalyptic struggle between the forces of good and evil, the latter represented by the collectivist "evil" Jewish conspiracy. The California Rangers, formed during the 1960s by William Gale, was one such Christian-identity militia. Another was the Christian Defense League, formed by Richard Butler. During these years, the Christian-identity type of militia was the most common.

Militia activity in the U.S increased significantly during the decade of the 1990s. The militias that emerged were much more difficult to characterize than the Christian identity or constitutionalist. The decade proved to be a time of militia expansion, increasing antigovernment assertiveness, and anger that at times led to violent confrontations. Three such events were Ruby Ridge (1992), Waco (1994), and Oklahoma (1995). The shootout at Ruby Ridge, Idaho, in 1992 was the first major violent confrontation between militia zealots and agents of the U.S. Bureau of Alcohol, Tobacco, and Firearms (BATF). Militia zealot Randy Weaver, an Aryan Nations supporter, was arraigned on weapons charges for allegedly selling two sawed-off shotguns to an informant of the BATF. After failing to appear in court, a bench warrant was issued for his arrest.[58]

On August 21, 1992, FBI agents attempted to arrest Weaver at his mountain cabin retreat. A ten-day siege and shootout ensued that involved the use of helicopters, armored personnel carriers, and scores of FBI and law enforcement agents and officers. Weaver and his friend Kevin Harris surrendered, but not until one marshal, Weaver's wife, and his thirteen-year-old son were killed and Weaver and Harris were wounded. Both Weaver and Harris were tried and acquitted by the jury for the death of the marshal. A subsequent federal investigation concluded that the FBI was guilty of violating the rules of engagement and that Weaver's deceased wife's rights had been violated. After some legal wrangling on a civil suit, the Department of Justice agreed to settle in 1995, awarding Weaver's family $3.1 million.[59] For far-right militias, the Ruby Ridge incident was illustrative of the federal government's use of excessive force and Weaver became a target because of his militant anti-federal government beliefs.

The second major violent confrontation was the Waco incident. On February 28, 1993, some 100 agents of the BATF tried to serve search warrants on David Koresh, leader of the Branch Davidian commune located east of Waco, Texas. BATF's action was the result of their efforts to seize a stockpile of legal and illegal weapons and ammunition stored at the compound in anticipation of Armageddon. The FBI led a fifty-one-day siege, which lasted until April 19, when agents supported by helicopters, armored personnel carriers, and several combat tank-like vehicles broke through the haphazard defenses, used tear gas, and set the compound's buildings on fire. After a ninety-minute gun battle, four agents were killed and twenty were wounded, and six Davidians were also killed. The siege was violent, devastating, and horrific. Richard Abanes writes, "When the billowing black smoke from that fiery episode cleared, cult leader David Koresh and more than eighty of his followers, including two dozen children, were dead."[60]

For the far-right militias, the Waco conflagration became the second symbol of the government's tyrannical excessive use of power. Waco became an instrument of propaganda to further fuel their hatred for the federal government. A video, *Waco: The Big Lie,* was produced that provided footage of the incident. It argued that the attack was part of a federal government evil conspiracy to eradicate militias. Waco served to galvanize the militia movement.[61]

The third major incident, the Oklahoma City bombing, gave further impetus to the growth of the militia movement. On April 19, 1995, the Alfred P. Murrah Federal Building in Oklahoma City, which housed FBI offices, was destroyed because of a militia terrorist bombing. Some 100 people were killed, including children at a day care center. The bomb consisted of slightly less than 5,000 pounds of ammonium nitrate fertilizer and fuel oil placed in a Ryder moving truck parked next to the building. Within days Timothy McVeigh was arrested for the crime and Terry Nichols was indicted for conspiracy to blow up the federal building.

The federal government's investigation revealed that McVeigh, a former soldier, had evolved from conspiracy-antigovernment beliefs to a militant neo-Nazi ideology. While he had attended meetings held by the Michigan Militia and militias in Arizona, he had no formal connection to or involvement with any particular militia. Some observers, however, would disagree. They alleged that since the bombing occurred on April 19, the date of the Waco incident, there was a connection between the two. Others drew similarities to the bombing scenario depicted in *The Turner Diaries*, a novel written by William Pierce, a self-professed neo-Nazi. It depicts the exploits of a militia group that successfully overthrew the U.S. government and at one point blew up a federal building. Ultimately, the militia gains control of the U.S. and Europe, and uses nuclear, biological, and chemical weapons to get rid of all non-Whites.[62]

McVeigh was known to have read, sold, and given copies of *The Turner Diaries*. He was a voracious reader of right-wing literature and a viewer of militia-produced videos.[63] Others propound the view that his motivation for the bombing was to protest the federal government's abuse of power that he and others believed was a manifestation of a prelude to a tyrannical new world order.[64] The reaction to the Oklahoma City bombing by right-wing militias was initially mixed. Some were caught off-guard due to the devastation and loss of human life, especially that of children, so their responses were carefully crafted. Some, on the other hand, were quick to blame the federal government.

From 1995 to 2000, the militia movement in the U.S. grew. A report entitled "Militias: A Growing Danger," released on April 10, 1995, prepared by Kenneth S. Stern in corroboration with Thomas Diaz and Richard Foltan, pushed for congressional hearings on the matter. The report began:

We issue this report . . . with a sense of urgency. [The militia movement] is quickly spreading and has all the ingredients to lead to disaster: an ideological caldron of dissatisfaction, hate, conspiracy and violence brewing a fast growing grassroots movement with documented ties to hate groups. Some people connected with this movement advocate killing government officials. They may attempt such an act.[65]

The report further explained that while the militias had yet to develop a central command structure, as paramilitary entities, they shared a paranoiac, violent ideology and belief that the federal government was evil and conspiring to take away the people's freedom and establish a one-government new world order.[66]

By the turn of the twenty-first century, in some thirty states militias were formed. An Anti-Defamation League (ADL) report released in September of 2004 stated that "the militias are testing the waters in the post-9/11 world to see whether they can continue to operate just below the radar screen of law enforcement and the media." According to ADL national director Abraham H. Foxman, "While less vocal, less public and less visible, the militias are quietly attempting to retool, restructure, and reorganize and are still players on the extremist scene." The report identified six strategic traits common to militias: (1) kept a low profile, while enhancing their coordination; (2) with 9/11 and passage of the Patriot Act, fear of government has increased; (3) paramilitary training and training on use of firearms increased; (4) coordination increased among most militias, especially with armed vigilantes and nativist militias in Arizona; and (5) the rate of militia-related arrests remained constant.[67]

The militia's involvement with immigration contempary can be traced back to the late 1970s when former KKK leader David Duke in 1977 initiated efforts to have the KKK patrol the U.S.–México border in order to curb the migrant exodus. Chicano activists' countervailing mobilization efforts prevented their border patrol efforts from getting off the ground. In the early 1980s, Aryan Nations ambassador at large Louise Beam ran paramilitary operations and activities along the Texas–México border, but never developed into a strong concerted border patrol militia effort. Like in Duke's case, they primarily led symbolic media events. It was Arizona, however, that contributed the most to the rise of nativist armed vigilantes and militias.

ARIZONA'S NATIVIST HISTORY

Arizona's pronounced practice of internal colonialism toward Mexicanos was instilled with a conservative and racist political culture. Its adherence to Republicanism in great part contributed to the rise of vigilantism and the formation of nativist militias. The infamous "Hanigan Case that occurred in 1976, serves as a reminder of just how cruel and savage armed White ranchers can be."[68] During the 1980s, violence, attacks, and vigilantism against Mexicanos sporadically broke out. One such incident occurred in 1981 involving a local rancher, who chained a sixteen-year-old Mexicano migrant by the neck to an outhouse toilet. He was tortured and starved for four days. Another henious incident occurred in 1986 with a White supremacist paramilitary group known as Civilian Material Assistance (CMA), which allegedly had ties to the Contras in Nicaragua. CMA in Cochise County established "sniper nests" from which it could shoot at Méxicano undocumented migrants. That year, CMA members detained and harassed at gunpoint several undocumented migrants. They were held for several hours and finally released to the Border Patrol.[69] Local human rights groups eventually drove CMA out of the state but without the assistance of local law enforcement agencies.[70]

Other incidents were reported by México's Ministry of Foreign Affairs. Between 1988 and 1990 some 117 human rights abuses were recorded, including fifteen deaths. Rodolfo Acuña, in an essay written in 2000 entitled "Murder in Arizona: Its Only the Third World," wrote, "During the 1980s, Border Patrol agents shot dozens of people, killing eleven, and permanently disabling ten."[71] During the 1990s, Arizona experienced a resurgence of militia activity. Contributing to the militia reemergence was Arizona's state constitution with its vague legal stance on the formation of militias. Militia advocates, in defending their status and role, cite Title 26 of the *Arizona Revised Statutes*, sections 121 and 122. Section 121 states that any person between the ages eighteen to forty-five that is not a member of the national or state guard can be a member of an unorganized militia. On the role of the militia, section 122 reads, "The militia is divided into the national guard of Arizona, the state guard when organized, and the unorganized militia." The term "unorganized militia" in paragraph (E) of the same section states: "The unorganized militia consists of members of the militia not members of the national guard or state guard when organized."[72] In other words, by law militias come under the jurisdiction of the state and not federal government. Arizona's relatively liberal gun-control laws that allow persons easy access to sidearms also added to the rise of nativist vigilantes and militias.

The Anti-Defamation League, in 1996, reported that Arizona was home to militias that were comprised of tax resisters, anti-federal government zealots, sovereignty movements, right-to-trial groups, and a few of the religious right. According to Maricopa County Attorney Rick Romley in testimony given before a U.S. Senate Committee investigating militias, there were some twelve militias operating in Arizona. Their organizing efforts were reported in Phoenix, Prescott, Payson, Snowflake, Kingman, Tucson, Mesa, Wickenburg, Pinedale, and Four Corners.[73] Of the twelve, the seven most prominent were Viper Militia, Militia of Arizona Republic (MOAR), Arizona Sons and Daughters of Liberty, Militia of Arizona, Alliance in Militia, Police Against the New World Order, and Militia of Montana (MOM). By 2003 it was estimated that there were 2,000 Arizonians participating in militias. Although difficult to verify, one source alleged that ethnically and racially, 90 percent were White, and some 10 percent were Black, Latino, or other, which did not fit the WASP stereotype of militias.[74] Their pervasive presence in Arizona served to further enhance the rise of rancher vigilantes and nativist militias.

Increasingly, the nationwide conservative and nativist political climate, particularly in California, impacted Arizona's nativist politics. Furthermore, California's passage of racist and xenophobic propositions 187 (1994), 209 (1996), and 227 (1998) added to Arizona's growing anti-immigrant political climate. The intensification of the migrant exodus, Arizona's "history and culture of violence and hate," and the state's burgeoning Mexicano population growth, which according to the 2000 U.S. Census, had increased to 1,295,617 (25.2 percent) of the state's population,[75] were catalytic conditions that encouraged the rise of armed vigilantism and nativist militias in southern Arizona.[76]

MIGRANT EXODUS SHIFTS TO ARIZONA

The migrant exodus shift from California and Texas to Arizona also contributed to the rise of militias. Due to Operation Gatekeeper, the migrant exodus into the U.S. shifted from the San Ysidro–Tijuana border sector eastward to the Mexico–Arizona border sector, especially along the Agua Prieta, Sasabe, Yuma, and Nogales areas. From 1994 to 2004, the shift resulted in undocumented workers having to cross hot, dry, inhospitable, snake and scorpion-infested Arizona deserts.[77]

Prior to 9/11, of the total 9,700 U.S. Border Patrol agents only 331 were assigned to the U.S.–Canadian border. By March 2002, the number had increased to a mere 346. Yet prior to September 11, there were 9,061 agents and by March 2002 the number increased to 9,094. Despite the Bush administration's commitment to bolster security after 9/11, the northern border merely had one border patrol agent for every sixteen miles, compared to one agent for every 1,100 feet on the southern border.[78] Even though Canada's border with the U.S. was by far the most porous and susceptible to entry by terrorists, México was perceived as a greater security threat. Pressured by nativists, for fiscal year 2003 the Bush administration requested funding for an additional 570 agents that supposedly were to be divided evenly between the country's two borders, and also federalized 1,600 National Guard personnel to be that were to be deployed to both borders.[79]

The Public Policy Institute of California in a report in 2002 concluded that the massive enforcement buildup along the Cactus Curtain had not reduced the migrant exodus. Some 400,000 to 500,000 undocumented migrants were successfully migrating into the U.S. annually. Its failure was particularly evident in the devastating loss of human lives. In May 2003, it was reported that since the militarization of the border began in 1994 some 2,300 undocumented migrants had died crossing the border. According to Border Patrol figures from 1998 to February 2002 some 1,234 migrants had died. Broken down by year, in 1998, 261; in 1999, 236; in 2000, 370; and in 2001, 329. At the close of fiscal year 2002 (September 30), the number of undocumented migrants who died crossing the hostile deserts of Arizona was 134, whereas the year before the number was 103, resulting in an increase of 31. The seriousness of the situation was such that the Border Patrol rescued some 1,764 people who were near death, up from the previous year's 1,234.[80]

Rise of Nativist Vigilantes and Militias

Between 1999 and 2004, the southern Arizona–Sonora border was a hotbed of White rancher vigilante[81] and nativist militia activity. As undocumented workers crossed into Arizona's dangerous deserts, they were met with a new threat— armed White ranchers and nativist militias. Both the ranchers and the militias chose to take the law into their own hands by intercepting and impeding the undocumented migrants' entry into the U.S. by apprehending them and then turning them over to the Border Patrol. The Bush administration's ineffectual border enforcement policies contributed to the rise in vigilantism. From the beginning, they perceived themselves as true patriots, defending the country's southern borders with México. With the migrant exodus intensifying, these nativist militants armed themselves and adopted a vigilante *modus operandi* and joined in the "political war" against undocumented migrants.

Increasingly, post-9/11 the country's political climate became more and more jingoistic and nativist. George Bush generated a "fear contagion" via his "war on terror," coupled with the U.S.'s imperialistic "neo-Manifest Destiny" foreign policy of "preventive war doctrine." Bush's U.S. invasion of Afghanistan in 2001, as well as the U.S. invasion of Iraq in 2003, also served to fuel the rise and development of the vigilantes.

As a result emergent armed vigilantes and militias, particularly in Arizona, they sought to pander to the growing fears especially of the country's white populace. In order to make their nativist politics more palatable to a greater number of people, they adopted as part of their xenophobic lexicon such terms as "border enforcement" and "national security." They alleged that the U.S. was in mortal danger of another terrorist attack. This time, however, the undocumented terrorists would enter the country via the "porous" and "penetrable" Cactus Curtain. Border Network in a report amplified on the preceding and on the threat posed by armed vigilantes:

> In a post-September 11th climate and with an Administration that has supported secret detentions of immigrants, military tribunals, and neighbors reporting activities of neighbors, border vigilantes have been attempting to fuel anxieties about terrorism and national security. These groups are broadcasting the message that the U.S. is literally "under siege" by immigrants and that federal law enforcement agencies have failed to protect citizens from this perceived threat. Arizona vigilantes have created a climate of fear and anxiety that further justifies the aggressive and forceful tactics they claim are necessary to "protect" our borders. . . . For these reasons, the vigilantes are able to cast their actions as both mainstream and patriotic, and the real human costs of these activities are left to outsiders.[82]

The existent "Arizona cowboy gunslinger" and "Wild West" mindset, particularly pervasive in Cochise County, also added to the volatility of the political climate that was giving rise of Arizona's armed rancher vigilantism and militia formation. This attitude was further aggravated by a xenophobic, even racist, anti-Mexicano/Latino nativism. The following illustrates their attitude:

> Rather than look at socio-economic and political reasons for migration into the U.S., they instead condemn an entire culture and people. Nor do they differentiate between the U.S. born Latino/as and migrants. They paint with a very large brush, condemning all non-white immigration. These groups are also laden with conspiracy theories, believing that migration from México is guided by the Mexican government to destroy [U.S.] white culture.[83]

Armed rancher vigilantes and militias in southern Arizona aimed their guns at Mexicanos because of their pervasive fear of the re-Conquista (the reconquest). Undocumented migrants from Central America and Latin America likewise were not exempt from the vigilantes and militia's nativist racist politics and wrath.

Contributing to the vigilantes and militia's amplification was the failure and/or inability of local, state, and federal law enforcement agencies to curb their growth. In reaction, pro-migrant rights groups and activists alleged collaboration between them, the U.S. Border Patrol, and local law enforcement agents and officers. They contended that these forces operated without fear, serious opposition, and with impunity from law enforcement. As cited by Border Watch in a report, "On a number of occasions, vigilante leaders have openly challenged the legitimacy of law enforcement agencies, yet much vigilante group membership consists of retired military, INS, and police officers. The result: law enforcement inaction, which becomes tacit approval of vigilantism and anti-immigrant activities."[84] The report also cited that the majority of southern Arizona's vigilante groups were part of a national network of interconnected lobbyists and nonprofit organizations that preached the preservation of White "supremacy" and "hegemony." It also stated that "American identity is and should remain exclusively White, and that their White identity was under siege and had to be defended aggressively."[85]

ARMED RANCHER VIGILANTISM

By 1999 some armed ranchers took it upon themselves to assume the role of border enforcement agents. While several ranchers were involved, Roger Barnett, a former deputy sheriff turned cattleman, and his brothers Bret and Don and ranch employee Roger Abbey, known as the "Barnett Boys" in Cochise County, became the catalytic leadership of the vigilante force. Their early vigilante exploits began in 1996 when Roger Barnett first made a citizen's arrest of undocumented migrants who crossed onto his ranch. However, it was not until 1999 that his efforts increased. On March 20, 1999, Barnett and twenty fellow ranchers formed the Cochise County Concerned Citizens. They released a signed proclamation that warned, "If the government refuses to provide security, then the only recourse is to provide it ourselves."[86]

The locus of their activity emanated from Barnett's Cross Rail Ranch, which consisted of some 22,000 acres outside Douglas (14,000 acres of which were leased state lands) and was contiguous to the Arizona–Sonora border. They responded by conducting armed patrols against what they as ranchers characterized was an "invasion from México." Roger Barnett gained national notoriety because of his armed vigilantism.[87] Armed with M-16s, Colt .45s, and trained dogs, the Barnett Boys from 1999 to 2004 were the avant-garde of armed rancher vigilantism. The "stalking" and "hunting" of undocumented Mexicano/Latino migrants was turned into a sport of sorts. A flyer circulated nationwide in April 2000 solicited volunteers, particularly those of who adhered to a supremacist and xenophobic politic. They exhorted volunteers to vacation at the Barnett ranch and other ranches in order to participate in "hunting" expeditions (armed patrols). Under the guise of "Neighborhood Ranch Watch," the flyer read:

> This vacation is for the winter visitor that wants to help an American
> Rancher keep his land protected while enjoying the great southwest-

ern desert at the same time. No great sailing ships on the desert. Just
the great outdoors and good Ole western individualism spirit of private property and enjoyment of the great outdoors. You are invited to
take part. Come and stay at the ranches and keep trespassers from destroying private property.[88]

The flyer encouraged tourists to come to Cochise County and have "some fun
in the sun." The "hunt" was not for deer, mountain lions, or any other wild
game; it was for undocumented migrants, especially of the Mexicano type.[89] The
flyer explained that volunteers would be working with ranchers under the direction of a sheriff-sponsored program.

In May of 2000, Barnett and his brothers were engaged in several anti-
immigrant armed vigilante incidents that captured the attention of the national
media. On May 3, ABC News reported that Barnett and two women, armed and
with two dogs, apprehended nine Mexicano migrants. Another incident occurred on May 12 that also got wide media attention: two armed persons on
horseback ambushed five Mexicano migrants near the town of Sasabe, México.
One of the migrants, Miguel Palafox Arreguin, was shot in the back. After initially losing consciousness, Palafox, twenty, walked back across the border into
México and secured medical treatment for his wound at a hospital in Caborca,
México. Palafox claimed that he had been shot by two men on horseback who
were vigilante ranchers. Another border shooting occurred on May 21 that allegedly involved armed rancher vigilantes. The Arizona press reported that six
migrants had been shot at some nineteen miles from Sasabe not far from where
Palafox had been shot earlier. One migrant, Guadalupe Sanchez Murrieta, resident of Caborca, was killed and one was wounded in the arm. These violent incidents were part of a pattern of vigilantism that had started in February 1999.[90]

By late May 2000, the Barnett Boys bragged to the press that since February 1999 they had apprehended and turned over to the Border Patrol some 2,000
undocumented migrants. Barnett told the press that just in one week in May,
they had arrested 174. In late May, he told a USA Today reporter that he was
"prepared to kill Mexicans," if need be, to stop the influx.[91] Out of twenty-five
armed encounters that occurred in May 2000, the Barnett Boys were involved in
at least fourteen.[92] By June the armed rancher vigilantism contagion had spread
to other parts of the Cactus Curtain, such as Texas, where another shooting occurred. A Mexicano migrant, Eusebio de Haro, was shot in the groin and left to
bleed to death after he and a companion approached a rancher near Brackettville,
Texas, and pleaded for a drink of water.[93]

Roger Barnett's national call to secure volunteers to come to his ranch to
hunt Mexicans was answered primarily by California-based nativist organizations and leaders. Voices of Citizens Together, led by Glenn Spencer, in May

2000 convoked a meeting in Sierra Vista, Arizona, in support of Barnett and the armed rancher vigilantes. In support of their vigilante activities, Spencer said, "The American People are going to rise to the defense of these ranchers. They are American heroes who are standing up against a wholesale invasion of our nation being orchestrated by México with hostile intent."[94] At the meeting, Spencer laid out his plan to form his own militia, American Border Patrol. The Burnett Boys used it to link their efforts to other nativist leaders and groups.

From 1999 to 2004, the media—from CBS News, CNN, Fox, *Time* magazine, to *USA Today*, to name a few—catapulted Roger Barnett into national notoriety. For some nativists, he became a romanticized vigilante hero who was a relentless patriot determined to protect the country's sovereignty from the so-called illegal invasion. To militant right-wing nationalist nativists both in Arizona and the country as a whole, he became their poster boy. In a plethora of media interviews, he bragged and elucidated about his exploits in apprehending migrants. He portrayed himself as a patriot, a relentless defender of property rights, and a victim of "criminal aliens" who was fighting back.[95]

He has said that the migrants when apprehended were made to sit on the ground and when they "get mouthy with us," at times, he was compelled to become physically aggressive in order to control them.[96] He claimed that he learned his tracking skills from the Border Patrol. Roger Barnett's brother, Don, was also a racist and callous toward undocumented migrants, especially toward those from México. This was corroborated by his own words: "The bottom line is if some Mexican is squatting behind a bush on private property, he gets what's coming to him. They are not all so innocent. There are drug smugglers out there with a lot more firepower than me. I am not a vigilante. I carry a Colt .45, but I keep it in my holster. The day I pull it out is the day I pull the trigger."[97]

Roger Barnett's numerous interviews conducted during 2000 to 2004 revealed an evident xenophobic, nativist, and racist political inclination. His rhetorical emphasis on property rights and adherence to armed vigilantism showed his propensity for developing a constitutionalist-type militia. Like Spencer, he too propounded that the U.S. was being invaded by México and that the federal government was inept in stopping the re-Conquista. In an alarmist jingoistic manner, Barnett claimed that the border was "out of control" and that if necessary in order to stop the invasion, "maybe the troops need to go down and occupy México."[98] He went on to say, "They should send the military down here or tell México to stop it. It's upsetting that a big country like the United States would let a Third World Narco-dictatorship like México run the show."[99] He seemed to relish the possibility of an armed conflict between the U.S. and México. His rhetoric demonstrated a vitriolic disdain, if not hatred, for México and Mexicanos. He and the rest of the Barnett Boys came under scrutiny and attack from the Southern Poverty Law Center, which designated them as a hate group. With their militant emphasis on armed vigilantism and racist White nationalism, a more appropriate term to describe them would be "domestic terrorists."

They developed the financial resources to maintain their high-profile armed vigilantism. Beyond the 22,000-acre ranch, they also owned a large tow truck company and a propane company. Their tow truck company profited from their anti-immigrant activities. The vehicles of undocumented migrants impounded by the Border Patrol in Cochise County, and in most cases, the Barnett Boys were given first dibs on getting the title and then selling the vehicle.[100]

For their notorious vigilante reputation, Roger Barnett, his wife, and his brothers, from 2003 to 2004, were plagued by a number of legal suits. Their boisterous vigilante exploits came back to legally haunt them. A number of civil lawsuits were filed by a number of pro-migrant rights groups as a result of the detention of undocumented migrants. One such incident occurred on January 19, 2003, that involved an undocumented migrant, Jose Rodrigo Quiroz Acosta, and Roger Barnett. After spending several days in the desert, without water and food, Quiroz decided to walk on a paved highway where he flagged down a truck. The truck driven by Roger Barnett stopped and he promptly released his dogs on Quiroz. Quiroz ran but the dogs attacked him. While on the ground, Barnett beat and kicked him. A civil suit against Barnett was filed on July 16, 2004, on charges of battery, false imprisonment, and intentional infliction of emotional distress.[101]

A second incident occurred on October 11, 2003, at a ranch owned by Donald J. Mackenzie, when some thirty undocumented migrant men and women were detained by the Barnett Boys. Mackenzie initially believed that the Barnett Boys were U.S. Border Patrolmen. After questioning them, he realized that they were not. Fearing for his life and the lives of the thirty undocumented migrants he called the Border Patrol. On November 26, 2004, a civil suit was filed by Mackenzie, charging the Barnetts with trespassing and impersonating Border Patrol agents.[102]

A third incident occurred on October 20, 2004, when Ron Morales, his father Arturo, two daughters, and a friend went deer hunting on state land outside Douglas when they were confronted at gunpoint by the Barnett Boys. Roger Barnett alleged that the Morales hunting party had trespassed on his land, which Morales rebutted by showing him a hunting permit. During the course of the incident, Barnett and others pointed their loaded weapons at the entire Morales hunting party, yelling racist expletives. According to the Southern Poverty Law Center (SPLC), Roger, yelling, introduced himself: "My fucking name is Roger Barnett! If you don't get off my property, I'm going shoot you and shoot you and shoot you!" In a civil suit filed by SPLC on November 26, 2004, the Barnett Boys, as a result of the above incident, were accused of assault, battery, false imprisonment, negligence, gross negligence, and intentional infliction of emotional distress.[103]

GLENN SPENCER: AMERICAN BORDER PATROL

Glenn Spencer had an anti-immigrant track record that started in California back in the early 1990s and even as far back as 1987, when he wrote a number of letters to newspaper editors that were hypercritical of the Immigration Reform and Control Act (IRCA). His nativist activism, however, did not really take off until 1990. With a degree in economics from California State University, Northridge, he conducted research on various aspects of the immigration crisis and sought unsuccessfully to form a chapter of the Federation of Immigration Reform (FAIR). Instead he formed his own group in 1992, initially called Valley Citizens Together, later changed to Voices of Citizens Together (VCT). Its motto was "Citizenship/Sovereignty/Law." Spencer claimed that he was a card-carrying member of the Jewish Defense League (JDL).[104] His style of nativist activism differed sharply from the existent anti-immigrant groups. His nativism was directed specifically at Mexicanos, regardless if they were undocumented or not. From 1994 to the late 1990s, supported by Barbara Coe, who in 1994 launched the anti-immigrant California Coalition for Immigration Reform (CCIR), Spencer played an active leadership role in supporting racism-inspired Propositions 187, 209, and 227.

Spencer's rhetoric resonated with a vehement hatred for México and anything that was Mexicano. In a letter sent in May 20, 1996 to the *Los Angeles Times*, for example, Spencer wrote "the Mexican culture is based on deceit. . . . The Mexican Government has threatened the United States with hostilities. How on earth could this two-bit gangster-run country threaten this country with hostilities? Easy—the weapon would be civil war in the United States . . . México, which has been hostile toward the U.S. for 100 years, is invading us with the intent of conquering the American Southwest. There is no question of this." When questioned, he responded that the letter was not racist. "It has nothing to do with race," he said. "It has to do with culture . . . there's no way to pass enough laws to protect yourself from a deceitful culture."[105] Spencer injected into the WASP ethos a strong dosage of racist nativism. He contended that the growing number of Mexicanos threatened to subvert the very essence of Anglo-Saxon-dominated culture, society, and ultimately the political system itself.

His anti-Mexicano posture was embedded in his belief of a "conspiracy theory." It was grounded on his zealous belief in the re-Conquista, which he alleged meant that México in collaboration with Mexicano activists had unleashed an "orchestrated invasion" of Aztlán with the intent of recapturing it. In 1997 when interviewed by a reporter on the subject, he said, "Unless we stop [Mexican immigration], we're going to lose control of our culture and eventually our political culture in the Southwest."[106] His ultranativist posture pandered to the fears of Whites by blending anti-Mexicano bigotry with antigovernment rhetoric. His vehicles were the use of his documentary and video series, "Bonds of Our Union," a website, press releases, myriad media appearances, events, protests, and the hosting of a local radio show. During the late 1990s, he initiated character assassination efforts directed at several Méxicano leaders that included Mario Obledo, Rodolfo Acuña, Art Torres, and many others, including myself. All were depicted as separatists and re-Conquistas whose political agenda was to establish their own sovereign country, Aztlán.

From 1993 to 2002, VCT operated out of Sherman Oaks, California. In 1995 it bought full-page ads in various newspapers, including the *L.A. Times*, denouncing the alleged Mexican invasion of Aztlán. Using the Internet, Spencer established a website called "American Border Patrol" that sought to awaken primarily the White masses to the peril of the re-Conquista. VCT also became engaged in various anti-immigrant demonstrations and efforts. One of its largest protests was held in 1997 along the San Ysidro–Tijuana border where 600 supporters rallied to reaffirm the sovereignty of the U.S., support the U.S. Border Patrol, and to pressure the Clinton administration into constructing a fourteen-mile-long iron fence at Otay Mesa, located east of the port of entry at San Ysidro. In 1999 Spencer's VCT also unsuccessfully sought to launch an initiative to unseat Democratic Governor Gray Davis for killing Proposition 187. The year before, it had been ruled unconstitutional by federal judge Mariana Pfaelzer. While it failed due to insufficient signatures, three years later Governor Davis was thrown out of office.[107]

In 2000 Spencer and Barbara Coe, head of the California Coalition for Immigration Reform (CCIR), and other nativists in California answered the Arizona rancher vigilantes' call for assistance. A meeting was held in Sierra Vista in South Arizona for the purpose of developing a plan of action to deal with the so-called Mexican invasion. Barnett, Barbara Coe, leaders from Concerned Citizens of Cochise County, Arizonans for Immigration Reform, and People for the USA were present. According to *La Reforma* of México, the meeting was also attended by the Arizona 9th District of the Imperial Wizards of the Ku Klux Klan.[108] At that meeting, Coe said, government policies to halt the so-called invasion from México had been an utter failure to where ranchers had been forced to "defend our borders and defend themselves from illegal alien savages who kill their livestock, and slit their watch dog's throats . . . burglarize their homes and threaten the physical safety of their loved ones."[109] Spencer, by now, had a radio program and a website, "American Patrol," to preach his anti-immigrant propaganda. VCT during this time was a zealous defender of the Border Patrol and militarization of the Cactus Curtain, especially Operation Gatekeeper.

The incessant attacks by pro-immigrant rights groups in California coupled with VCT's serious financial problems, caused Spencer in 2002 to move his operation to Cochise County, to a secret location in Sierra Vista, south Arizona.

Spencer told a reporter for the *Los Angeles Times* that VCT was "strapped for cash," yet the sixty-five-year-old nativist told others that he left for different reasons. He openly blamed California's politicians and citizens for not being interested in controlling the state's border with México. "California is a lawless, lost state," Spencer declared, shaking his head sadly as he paced in front of the U.S. flag. "It's a mess. There's nothing I can do for California. It is finished."[110] In September 2002, at a hotel in Sierra Vista, Spencer formally announced that southern Arizona, a simmering cauldron of armed vigilantism, was now his home. Embracing the role of "White exile" from California, he also introduced two entities: American Border Patrol (ABP), a 501(c)(3), nonprofit anti-immigrant group, and Voices of Citizens Together (VCT), his old 501(c)(4), a nonprofit corporation that was to act as ABP's political advocacy entity.[111] ABP was the first nativist militia formed in southern Arizona.

Spencer launched ABP with the support of the Barnett Boys. While the U.S. Border Patrol had no direct relationship with ABP, two former border patrol employees were board members of ABP's corporation: Ron Sanders of Tucson, who once headed the agency's Tucson sector, and Bill King, who lived in Big Bear City and was a former California sector head.[112] While critical of INS's lax border enforcement, Spencer was supportive of the Border Patrol. With the support of the Barnett Boys, Coe, and other nativists nationwide, Spencer regained national notoriety status. He was catapulted into being what Bob Moser describes as "one of the nation's noisiest anti-immigrant rabble-rousers."[113]

Since its formation in 2002, ABP embodied VCT's driven extremist xenophobic and nativist politics and anti-re-Conquista crusade. Spencer in 2002 alleged that INS deliberately failed to stop the invasion. In a television appearance on the Phil Donahue show in November, Spencer said, "If the Border Patrol had done its job, using technology that is available to us, we could stop these people. This is an invasion of the United States." In 2003, he predicted the possibilities of a new "Mexican-American War" and was quoted as saying, "We have on our hands a Mexican border civil war that could happen tomorrow."[114] Pandering to the xenophobic fears of White America, he reminded Whites that "if our government doesn't stop illegal immigration and secure the border, America will become a Third-world nation and México will have achieved the conquest of Aztlán."[115] His overt anti-Mexicano demeanor was evident in an interview with a reporter from *Tucson Weekly*: "Mexican culture is based on deceit." He went on to say that "Chicanos and Mexicanos lie as a means of survival." In an attempt to clarify the statement, he went on to say that "the point was that Mexicans have to cheat and lie because their government is so corrupt."[116]

The Anti-Defamation League, Southern Poverty Law Center, and various Mexicano pro-immigrant rights groups considered Spencer's ABP a hate militia. Their allegations were supported by Spencer's linkages to racist right-wing groups, such as the Council of Conservative Citizens, one of the largest White separatist groups in the country, and the National Alliance.

His racial "paranoiac schizophrenia" became evident in 2003, when (indicative of his nativist-inspired racism) on his website, Spencer called for White flight. He said, "White Americans should get out of California—now, before it is too late to salvage the equity they have in their homes and the value of their businesses."[117] That same year Spencer was involved in a shooting incident. Believing Mexicanos were out to get him, Spencer claimed that he heard a noise at his home, so he grabbed his .357 caliber rifle and started to shoot indiscriminately into the dark. While no one was shot, one of the bullets did hit a neighbor's garage. He was charged with four felonies. He explained to the arresting officer that he had received "death threats" through e-mail and that ABP offices had been recently trashed. In January 2004, he pleaded guilty to one charge of endangering persons with a substantial risk of imminent death, which was reduced to a misdemeanor. He was fined $2,500 and given a year's probation. He also agreed to pay $601.10 in restitution for the damage caused to the garage.[118] When his lease was terminated he was forced to relocate to a ranch near the Arizona–Sonora border in Cochise County where today he lives in a trailer.[119]

Although ABP volunteers were armed, Spencer insisted that they did not hunt down migrants and that ABP was not a militia. He claimed that ABP volunteers known as "hawkeyes" used sophisticated high-tech surveillance and communication equipment to monitor, videotape, and broadcast "border intruders" over the Internet as they crossed into Arizona.[120] The hawkeyes dressed in military-style fatigues and were armed, allegedly to protect them from mountain lions, when they conducted surveillance missions. ABP was committed to the apprehension and detainment of undocumented migrants, which were then turned over to the Border Patrol. As cited in the Border Action Network's report, Spencer in 2003 used "digital video cameras, mobile computers with GPS technology, and aircraft to broadcast on the internet the 'invasion' and conquest of the southwest by Mexicans."[121] Border Hawk airplane drones (small unmanned aerial vehicles that cost $5,000 each) measured five feet in length and two meters in wingspan. They could reach speeds of 65 kilometers per hour, achieve an altitude of 100 meters, and stay up for 90 minutes. ABP used them to detect undocumented migrants and then communicated their locations to the Border Patrol.[122] ABP used them to support several of the Barnett Boys' border patrol efforts. Spencer's sophisticated use of high-tech equipment and his ability to effectively manipulate the media by 2004 meant that ABP represented a greater threat than some of the other vigilante and hate groups in Arizona.

Spencer in March 2003 had a falling out with Chris Simcox, the militia leader of Civilian Homeland Defense, over the use of force and staying within the framework of the law. According to Spencer, he warned Simcox that it was imperative that they obey all laws and avoid the threat of the use of force on the border. He was quoted as saying, "I told Mr. Simcox that I have worked for twelve years on the border problems and I was not interested in having all that work ruined by the irresponsible act of some misguided publicity seekers."[123]

In 2004 ABP circulated petitions across the country in support of pressuring the Bush administration into placing federal troops along the border. While at best only symbolic, ABP was able to collect some 115,000 signatures. The petitions were sent to Secretary of Defense Donald Rumsfeld and in March 2004 ABP held a rally and march near the federal building in Tucson to demand that the U.S. military patrol the border. The ABP protest was held at the same time that President Bush was meeting with México's President Vicente Fox at his Crawford, Texas ranch. That year, ABP also supported "Protect Arizona Now," also known as Proposition 200, which was passed by the Arizona voters. The law required showing proof of citizenship to register to vote, showing a photo ID when voting, and showing proof of eligibility to receive non–federally mandated public benefits.[124] ABP and VCT's militia activities were financially supported nationwide, via their website that solicited donations from divergent anti-immigrant sources. In 2003 it was estimated that ABP financial contributions totaled some $400,000. Moreover, since its formation ABP maintained a working relationship with a number of nativist White supremist groups and militias.

JACK FOOTE: RANCH RESCUE

Perhaps the most bellicose and virulent of the nativist armed vigilante militias active in southern Arizona was Ranch Rescue (RR). It was founded by a coterie of eight nativists in June 2000 and included Texas rancher and Gulf War veteran Jack Foote, who became its national spokesperson.[125] As an armed militia, RR's orientation combined a constitutionalist view with an extreme nativist White nationalist approach. Foote described RR as a volunteer organization "that help[s] private landowners with the repair of private property destroyed by the mass numbers of criminal trespassers and provide[s] volunteer security for these land owners, their homes, and their private property."[126] RR represented a more serious physical threat to undocumented migrants because of its ultraparamilitary orientation, structure, and willingness to use armed force. Its base of operation was in Abilene, Texas. Its volunteers were reserve police officers, sheriff's deputies, former military and border patrol personnel; almost all subscribed to *Soldier of Fortune* magazine. RR first appeared in Cochise County, Arizona, in 2000 when its volunteers were sent by Foote to assist the Barnett Boys and vigilante ranchers in their efforts to protect their private property from the undocumented migrants or drug traffickers. RR organized armed patrols of the border.[127]

RR was an ardent proponent of the Second Amendment to the Constitution, guaranteeing the right to bear arms. Firearms ownership and possession were perceived as being a personal, individual, and God-given right of all citizens.[128] The Anti-Defamation League (ADL) labeled RR as a White supremacist paramilitary hate group with affiliations to the neo-Nazi National Alliance. Like Spencer, Foote also displayed xenophobic and racist attitudes toward Méxicanos. He among others in RR saw the migrant exodus as a full-fledged invasion from México. In order to stop it, like Roger Barnett, Foote advocated a U.S. invasion of México. His xenophobic view of Mexicanos was illustrated in an excerpt from an e-mail he sent to a man identified as Gonzalo:

> You and the vast majority of your fellow dog turds are ignorant, uneducated and desperate for a life in a decent nation because the one you live in is nothing but a pile of dog (excrement), made up of millions of little dog turds like you. You stand around your entire lives, whining about how bad things are in your dog of a nation, waiting for the dog to stick its ass under our fence and (defecate) each one of (you) into our back yards. Just be careful where the dog (defecates), pal, because sooner or later we will be there.[129]

By 2003 RR claimed to have chapters in six states, including Arizona, Texas, California, New México, Illinois, and Washington, and one chapter in South Africa.[130] Numbering some 250 members,[131] RR volunteers dressed in military camouflage fatigues and were heavily armed with 5.56mm assault rifles, .45 caliber pistols, shotguns, and bolt-action sniper rifles.[132] RR was structured as independent chapters. Each chapter was comprised of five- to ten-man teams who were trained to "deter criminal trespassers." RR's paramilitary posture and weaponry was used to intimidate and strike fear into the minds of its adversaries with impunity, especially the undocumented migrants.

In October 2002, RR made Arizona its primary locus for its militia activities. In Cochise County it established a base camp only forty miles from Spencer's "secret headquarters."[133] It launched Operation Hawk, a field mission of armed volunteers who patrolled the Arizona–México border. As explained by Foote, its purpose was to help private landowners repair private property destroyed by what he called "mass numbers of criminal trespassers."[134] The patrol's target was a 10,000-acre ranch owned by Earl Hardy, located near the border hamlet of Lochiel, which was sixty-five miles southeast of Tucson.[135] Some thirty-five RR volunteers participated, including Tim Meyer, a former U.S.

Customs inspector and current "private investigator"; Rusty Rossey, an ex-Marine who was involved with the Contras in Nicaragua and counterinsurgents in Guatemala and ran a sniper range in Alabama; a former Army special-forces soldier; and two former Canadian soldiers. While initially invited to protect a particular targeted area, a thirteen-volunteer "special operations" team led by Rossey was dispatched without being invited to a nearby ranch owned by the Nature Conservancy. After two encounters with marijuana traffickers, the team recovered a total of 279 pounds of marijuana. They called the sheriff to turn over the contraband; however, the process turned into a media spectacle.[136]

RR in 2003 initiated Operation Falcon, which turned into an incident that ultimately fostered its demise. On March 18, at a ranch near Hebbronville south Texas owned by Joe Sutton, two Salvadorans were terrorized and abused by four RR volunteers led by Jack Foote. Migrants traveling on foot through the Sutton Ranch were captured and held at gunpoint by their RR assailants. While detained they were interrogated as if they had been prisoners of war, threatened with death, attacked by an RR dog, and terrorized. During their forced detention, Casey James Nethercott pistol-whipped one of the Salvadorans on the back of the head, while Henry Mark Conner aimed a rifle at both Salvadorans. In a ridiculous gesture, after detaining and mistreating them for an hour or so, the migrants were given cookies, water, a blanket, and were then released.[137]

The RR incident wound up in the courts. The Southern Poverty Law Center (SPLC) and the Mexican American Legal Defense and Educational Fund (MALDEF) filed a civil suit, *Leiva v. Ranch Rescue*, on behalf of the two undocumented workers. The suit's defendants were Jack Foote, Joseph Sutton, Henry Mark Conner, and Casey James Nethercott. The plaintiffs were the two Salvadorans Edwin Alfredo Mancia Gonzales and Fatima Del Socorro Leiva Medina.[138] SPLC lead attorney Ricardo De Anda, in explaining the significance of the suit said, "We feel if we get the landowners to stop cooperating with these Ranch Rescue paramilitary types, they will wilt on the vine."[139] The cardinal objective of the civil suit was to bankrupt RR and vigilante rancher Joe Sutton so that other ranchers would not be willing to work with RR. In March 2004, both Nethercott and Connor were indicted on felony charges of aggravated assault and unlawful restraint. Nethercott was also indicted on the felony charge of unlawful possession of a firearm by a felon. He was arrested in Arizona and turned over to Texas Ranger officials. He unequivocally rebutted the charges and told the press, "They made it up, if I had pistol-whipped these people, they'd have been dead . . . They're making me out to be a racist and a liar, and they're lying."[140] Jack Foote asserted that the incident "never happened" and that the two RR volunteers were victims of the "Texas Taliban," the county sheriff and district attorney of Jim Hogg County.[141]

In 2004 RR's base of operations was a ranch near the Arizona–México border owned by Nethercott called Camp Thunderbird. RR continued to attract volunteers from several White nationalist extremist groups. In January 2004, Dick Wolf, a member of the Kentucky State Militia, met with Foote and then made a trip to Douglas to assess the border problems. Foote in March sought to secure recruits for RR by appearing as a guest on White supremacist Hal Turner's radio show. That same year RR targeted the border activities of México's military. He alleged that the Mexican military was engaged in several incursions into the U.S., particularly RR's Camp Thunderbird. He warned that next time a Mexican soldier set foot on RR's property volunteers would open fire: "Two in the chest and one in the head."[142]

Under increased scrutiny by law enforcement agencies, RR by 2004 began to fall apart. In September the FBI arrested Foote in Sierra Vista, Arizona, on a warrant that charged him with possession of a firearm by a person convicted of domestic violence. According to the U.S. Attorney's office, Foote was convicted of domestic violence in Montana in 1996.[143] Adding to RR's growing troubles, that year it was plagued by serious internal schisms over the Texas SPLC civil suit. A falling out occurred between Foote and Nerthercott over the suit. It resulted in a splintering of RR: Nerthercott formed his own nativist militia, the Arizona Guard, which operated out of his ranch located near the border.[144]

CHRIS SIMCOX: CIVIL HOMELAND DEFENSE

In 2002, in southern Arizona, the Barnett Boys, ABP, and RR were joined by yet another nativist militia, Civil Homeland Defense. It was led and founded by Chris Simcox, a divorced former kindergarten teacher from Los Angeles who migrated to southern Arizona. Devastated by 9/11, he sought to join the Border Patrol, but was turned down. After spending weeks in the desert supposedly tracking smuggling operations, he arrived in Tombstone. He worked as a hired gunslinger in Tombstone's daily orchestrated shootouts for tourists and also as a reporter for the local newspaper, the *Tombstone Tumbleweed*, which he later purchased and became its editor.[145] Inspired by Jack Foote's RR, on October 24, 2002, using the front page of his newspaper, Simcox called for the formation of another armed citizen's militia. The banner read, "ENOUGH IS ENOUGH!" followed by "A PUBLIC CALL TO ARMS! CITIZENS BORDER PATROL MILITIA NOW FORMING!" In smaller print, it read: "JOIN TOGETHER TO PROTECT YOUR COUNTRY IN A TIME OF WAR!" In the newspaper's editorial, he encouraged citizens "to organize, pool supplies and equipment, train responsibly and move out in groups to protect the border."[146] A few days later, he claimed to have received over 1,000 e-mails supporting his cause. His reference to war was not the pending U.S. conflict with Iraq, but instead to the war along the Cactus Curtain, specifically the Arizona–Sonora border.

Simcox's initial response to repel the alleged invasion called for the formation of paramilitary-oriented committees of vigilantes. Their purpose was to patrol the borderlands and apprehend undocumented migrants and return them back to México via the Border Patrol. He studied Arizona's lax laws pertaining to militias and the use of arms, and received some assistance from RR's Jack Foote.[147] After holding several organizing meetings at his office, the decision was made to name the committees of vigilantes Civil Homeland Defense (CHD). Ideologically, it adhered to an extremist White nationalist and nativist posture. His response to the migrant exodus was like that of the Barnett boys, Glenn Spencer, and Jack Foote. He wrote: "A swarm of uncontrolled refugees are fleeing a Marxist structured government." He equated it to an "invasion by México" of Aztlán.[148]

With the formation of CHD, Simcox became an armed vigilante competitor to Roger Barnett and Glenn Spencer. Unlike Spencer and Barnett, however, he did not appear to be connected to any national anti-immigrant or White supremacist groups.[149] His open support for establishing an armed militia coupled with its adherence to the use of force, if necessary, brought increasing media attention to a man who was described by Tombstone's Mayor Dusty Escapule as a "lunatic" who was "going to get somebody killed."[150] The characterization was due to Simcox being quoted in several articles in which he suggested that he might be killed for his actions his willingness to use violence as an "any means necessary" approach to halt the migrant exodus. In a letter to President Bush, Simcox exhorted him to use troops at the border to stop the alleged invasion. He wrote, "Mr. President, use American troops and American technology to protect American citizens . . . or, we will continue to use common sense in our continued efforts to protect the people . . . with restraint . . . but ultimately . . . by any means necessary! Speak up America."[151] He also alleged that the Mexican Army in its patrolling of the Cactus Curtain was supported by Chinese troops and weaponry.[152]

Simcox and a small contingent of CHD volunteers patrolled the border near Douglas to stop "the flood of immigrants funneling through Cochise County."[153] Some of the CHD border armed patrols included volunteers from RR and ABP. In January 2003, National Park Rangers cited Simcox and a companion on misdemeanor charges for conducting a border patrol in Coronado National Memorial Park without a permit. According to the Central America/México Report, "He was charged with carrying a loaded weapon inside a national park, operating without a special permit and interfering with law enforcement function." Simcox was subsequently found guilty of carrying a .45 semiautomatic firearm on federal property and of lying to a park ranger about it.[154] He was fined and his weapon was confiscated.

Simcox's gun incident did not deter CHD's armed vigilante militia activities. In a speech given at an anti-immigration meeting held in Garden Grove, California, by Barbara Coe, Simcox warned the nativist audience to "take heed of our weapons because we're going to defend our borders by any means necessary." He further warned, "There's something very fishy going on at the border. The Mexican Army is driving American vehicles—but carrying Chinese weapons. I have personally seen what I believe to be Chinese troops."[155] In mid-March 2003, Simcox led thirty-four members of CHD in a major patrol of Cochise County's border area with México. He claimed that forty-three undocumented migrants had been apprehended and that they had been turned over to the U.S. Border Patrol.

In March of 2003, a rift developed between Simcox and Glenn Spencer over strategic differences. Spencer took offense to Simcox's publicized bellicose message, which read, "Do not attempt to cross the border illegally; you will be considered an enemy of the state; if aggressors attempt to forcefully enter our country they will be repelled with force if necessary."[156] Spencer alleged that Simcox was attracting "unsavory elements" that were hurting the overall effort to stop the migrant exodus. As a result Spencer openly distanced himself and ABP from Simcox and CHD. During the months of March and April 2003, Simcox reported that his militia had seized some 200 migrants.[157]

By the summer of 2003, Simcox claimed that CHD's membership had increased to some 600 and that he had garnered support from local ranchers, law enforcement, some high-ranking U.S. Border Patrol officials, Congressman Tom Tancredo of Colorado, and the Federation for American Immigration Reform.[158] In October, Simcox reported that CHD's patrols, comprised of about six volunteers or so, conducted during the weekends, had turned over to the U.S. Border Patrol some 1,600 undocumented migrants. He also reported that CHD's patrols of the border would be extended to the Yuma border sector, which were repudiated in the press by local Yuma political and business leaders.[159]

During 2004 the earlier gun charges levied against Simcox affected CHD's organizing. The court convicted him on two federal misdemeanor counts. He was placed on two years' probation and was barred from carrying a gun. Simcox's response to the court's decision was that his arrest had been politically motivated due to his activism. According to press accounts, Simcox perceived the federal government as a possible enemy rather than ally in the struggle to secure the nation's borders.[160] In doing so, early in 2004, Simcox reported to the press that CHD had apprehended and turned over to the U.S. Border Patrol some 2,300 undocumented migrants from twenty-six countries. By late 2004 the decline in CHD's militia activities gave rise to a new nativist militia—the Minuteman Project.

CHAPTER 7

Minuteman Project and Nativist Anti-Migrant Movement (2005–2007)

The rise of armed rancher vigilantism and of nativist militias in Arizona produced the political conditions for the rise in 2005 of the Minuteman Project. At the avant-garde of the militant White nationalist nativist militia was the Minuteman Project. From 2005 to 2007 it experienced phenomenal growth, in great part due to the country's nativist anti-immigrant political climate and a supportive xenophobic-oriented media. Minuteman Project chapters sprang up not only throughout Aztlán but nationwide. As its membership grew so did its resources. From the onset, the Minuteman Project struggled against schisms and fractures so prevalent that by 2007 as a militia it was in decline. Yet MP's political impact was such that it acted as a catalyst to the rise of a nationwide Nativist Anti-Migrant Movement. Nativism against Mexicano and Latino migrants intensified—from Californai to the country's southern and eastern regions.

Using a case study format, this chapter provides an in-depth examination of the rise of the Minuteman Project and Nativist Anti-Migrant Movement. The circumstances, leaders, structure, orientation, events, and activities that shaped their rise are dealt with.

The Minuteman Project

GENESIS OF THE MINUTEMAN PROJECT

After five years of anti-immigrant activities in southern Arizona by armed rancher vigilantes and nativist militias, the political climate in 2005 was ripe for the rise of the Minuteman Project (MP). In explaining its origin, Daniel Sheehy said that James Gilchrist, a retired accountant and Vietnam veteran from Orange County, California, after deliberating for a time on the question of the "illegal alien invasion of America," on October 1, 2004, made a call using the Internet to some two dozen persons, inviting them to join him in a month-long border watch and protest in southern Arizona on April 1, 2005. He explained in his Internet message that the volunteers would converge on the Arizona–México border to aid the U.S. Border Patrol in spotting intruders entering the United States (U.S.) illegally. He alluded to the migrant exodus as a "40 year invasion" that needed to be halted and argued that the U.S.–México border (also referred to as the Cactus Curtain) was out of control and that 5,000 undocumented migrants entered Arizona daily and 10,000 throughout the entire border. He praised the nativist militia efforts of Chris Simcox and his Civil Homeland Defense (CHD). Prior to Gilchrist sending out his Internet communiqué, he had already reached an accord with Simcox, agreeing to work together to develop a nationwide nativist militia movement.[1]

In his call for volunteers, Gilchrist alluded to the U.S. Revolutionary War's Minutemen as a militia and Paul Revere, who gallantly rose from the ranks of the people on a moment's notice to alert them of the approaching British Army. Gilchrist believed the Minutemen to be a patriotic symbol and called the MP volunteers "Warriors of Democracy." The volunteer's job was to do the job the federal government refused to do and protect the U.S. from what he considered to be the "tens of millions of invading illegal aliens who are devouring and plundering our nation."[2] The use of arms for self-defense during the border patrols was accentuated.[3] At a press conference held in late 2004 Gilchrist revealed that the idea for MP was inspired by George Putnam, Chris Simcox, Representative Tom Tancredo, and Barbara Coe, all four zealous anti-immigrant nativists.[4]

From January to March both Gilchrist and Simcox spent time working the media prior to the big April 1 event. They accentuated various themes that justified the call for MP. One was that Arizona's 370-mile long border was the most porous stretch of the U.S.–México 2,000-mile-long border. Two, they propounded that the federal government was impotent in stopping the so-called invasion and in securing the country's southern border with México. Both President Bush and Congress were vehemently attacked for their allegedly failing "open border" immigration policies. Three, Gilchrist when asked by reporters if MP volunteers were taking the law into their own hands, suggesting that they were vigilantes, he responded, "That is an outright bogus statement. We are going down to assist law enforcement."[5] Simcox as well denied that MP volunteers were vigilantes. He argued that they would fan out along the Arizona–Sonora border to observe and report on undocumented migrants to the Border Patrol. Their cardinal objective was to deter so-called "illegals" and "drug smugglers."

Both Gilchrist and Simcox pandered to the fears of the public by alleging the possible entry into the U.S. of Al-Qaida terrorists via the México–U.S. border. Adding to this fear in February 2005 was a statement by James Loy, deputy secretary of the Homeland Security Department, who said, "Several al-Qaida leaders believe operatives can pay their way into the country through México, and also believe illegal entry is more advantageous than legal entry for opera-ʾtional security reasons."[6] Coincidence or not, it served to further heighten the media's interest in the forthcoming April 1 event. Gilchrist and Simcox, among others, met, planned, and worked on the mechanics of the April 1 MP border operation. For Simcox, the publicity helped increase CDH's membership to 400, which had declined in 2004. Simcox was quick to claim victory for MP even before it got underway. He took credit for the Bush administration's decision to send an additional 500 U.S. Border Patrolmen to southern Arizona. Simcox said, "We've already gotten our message out. If the U.S. government doesn't soon deploy National Guard troops on the border, there will soon be Minutemen Projects up everywhere."[7]

In March MP's organizing efforts gained momentum. Both México's President Vicente Fox and U.S. President George Bush reacted with criticism to MP's rise. President Fox used strong, acrid language to criticize MP: "We totally reject the idea of these migrant-hunting groups. We will use the law, international law, and even U.S. law to make sure these groups, which are a minority, will not have the opportunity to progress." On March 23, President George Bush, at a meeting with President Fox and Canadian Prime Minister Paul Martin in Waco, Texas, during a news conference rebuked MP: "I'm against vigilantes in the United States of America. I am for enforcing law in a rational way. That's why you've got a Border Patrol, and they ought to be in charge of enforcing the border."[8]

In late March, the media reported that the violent Central American gang Mara Salvatrucha (MS-13), allegedly with thousands of members in the U.S., planned to "teach the Minuteman vigilantes a lesson they [would] never forget." Around the same time, the Department of Homeland Security announced the arrest of 103 MS-13 members in six U.S. cities.[9] Gilchrist responded to the MS-13 threat: "We're not worried because half of our recruits are retired trained combat soldiers."[10] By the end of March, Simcox reported that some 1,100 volunteers from twenty-nine states had registered to participate in the four-week MP "county-wide block-watch" border enforcement operation.[11] MP volunteers were armed citizens, who were mostly retired policeman and veterans with experience in law enforcement and the use of military tactics and who operated within the law.[12]

The *Los Angeles Times* reported that Gilchrist had said that MP "was a dog and pony show designed to bring in the media and get the message out and it worked."[13] For many in the media, MP was a novelty ostensibly driven by its own nativist inclinations. Nativist Mark Edwards from the 50,000-watt radio station KDWN in Las Vegas, dedicated his daily broadcast to disseminating Gilchrist's MP call for volunteers. Coast to coast, radio stations played a significant role in mobilizing support regionally and nationwide for MP.[14] The media frenzy was enhanced in late March with the announcement by the Mexican government that some 1,000 additional Mexican troops had been sent to the volatile and precarious Arizona–México border, where MP volunteers were to assemble. A number of antivigilante groups, such as the National Alliance for Human Rights (NAHR)[15] and the ACLU (American Civil Liberties Union) publicized that they would be in Arizona: the former to protest and the latter to legally monitor the armed vigilante activities of MP volunteers.

MP PATROLS OF BORDER BEGIN

On April 1 MP went into effect in the targeted San Pedro Valley border area of Cochise County.[16] The border operation began with an orientation session in Tombstone at Schieffelin Hall, attended by some 100 volunteers, far short of the 1,000 publicized prior to April 1. Present were about forty anti-MP protestors who banged pots and pans while Aztec dancers performed to the beat of drums.[17] Congressman Tom Tancredo, Team America Chairman Bay Buchanan, and Gilchrist and Simcox addressed the MP volunteers. Their nativist rhetoric was vociferous and applauded the volunteers' commitment to secure the border. Tancredo said, "I'm proud of every single one of you. You are heroes. You are not vigilantes. You are heroes, with each one of you representing hundreds of thousands of Americans."[18] He underscored that MP volunteers were "a kind of neighborhood watch program to help the Border Patrol spot illegal aliens as they enter our country." He reminded them that already MP had produced results: the federal government had announced in late March the allocation of an additional 500 U.S. Border Patrolmen for Arizona.[19] Attacking the Bush administration, Bay Buchanan said, "You [Bush] have failed. You have failed because you allow drugs and criminals to come across our borders! You have failed America!"[20] Gilchrist and Simcox explained that MP's goal was to foster a national awareness of the "illegal immigration crisis" and that the presence of MP volunteers could halt the migrant exodus in the targeted Douglas area of the Arizona–Sonora border.[21]

While many of the volunteers were armed, Gilchrist portrayed them as patriots with a specific mission to observe and report and not to fight. In calling for a further militarization of the border, Simcox added, "We are showing the government the model for homeland security. If they deployed 10,000 to 15,000 National Guard troops on the border, there would be nowhere else to funnel people."[22] During the next two days, MP-sponsored rallies were held in Naco and Douglas in support of the Border Patrol. A common theme of the speakers at these events was their dissatisfaction with President Bush's alleged "open-borders" policy. MP's activities during the next three weeks would ostensibly be a media charade. Prior to April 1, Gilchrist claimed that 40 percent of the MP volunteers would be minorities. The fact was that, as reported by the Southern Poverty Law Center, nearly all MP volunteers were White.[23]

As the days passed during MP's twenty-one-day border-watch efforts, the numbers of volunteers dwindled. During the first few days there were more reporters, cameramen, photographers, anti-MP protestors, ACLU observers, and costumed gunfight-show actors than there were MP volunteers—around 200 compared to 150; also, over 1,000 press reporters were present. Prior to April 1, Gilchrist and Simcox claimed that some 1,300 persons had volunteered; yet that number never materialized. Reporter Michael Martinez from the *Chicago Tribune* reported a count of only 150 volunteers. *Los Angeles Times* reporter Jennifer Delson's figure was 200. Lacking the anticipated numbers, Gilchrist and Simcox inflated the number to some 450 volunteers that had showed up. Marc Cooper, reporter for the *Los Angeles Weekly*, wrote, "Almost no one wanted to tell the real story once they got out here: The Minutemen were basically a flop." He asserted that no more than 150 MP volunteers had showed up.[24] On April 20, evidently because of insufficient volunteers, MP's border enforcement operation ended prematurely. In reality, MP's border enforcement operation ended as a media hype event. During its brief twenty-day border patrol operation, MP received millions of dollars worth of free coverage by both print and electronic media, especially from cable networks. The MP operation became one of the country's great media shams of recent times.[25]

MP was comprised of what could be described as wannabe militia vigilantes. Volunteers were disproportionately retired, elderly, White males, some armed, who sat in lawn chairs, under an umbrella with flags from their respective states flying, drinking cold beer while listening to radios, and some using binoculars while yet others were using night-vision goggles, all hoping to spot undocumented migrants as they crossed their paths.[26] In the end, the event turned out to be nothing more than media hype; yet, both Gilchrist and Simcox savored the national to international media attention they and MP received. Both boasted about MP's success in reducing the percentage of undocumented migrant apprehensions by 50 percent. MP's volunteers, however, did little to impact the reduction, since it was actually attributable to the Mexican government's successful efforts via the Mexican Army that convinced undocumented migrants not to cross and stay clear of the border during MP's border operation.

RISE OF THE NATIVIST ANTI-MIGRANT MOVEMENT

What Gilchrist and Simcox accomplished with their April border operation was the rise of a nationwide Nativist Anti-Migrant Movement (NAMM). Almost overnight, both were catapulted into national leader prominence by a sensationalist nativist-friendly media. As a coarchitect of MP, Gilchrist had no previous organizational activist leadership record to speak of. Simcox had patrolled the Arizona–México border for some two years in near anonymity. But MP changed all this: their effectiveness in manipulating the media elevated both to near-iconic leadership status.

Comprised of a multiplicity of independent and diverse nativist entities and individuals up to 2007 MP remained precariously the flagship of NAMM. The North American Congress on Latin America (NACLA) ACRI Report entitled "Of Migrants & Minutemen: Inside the Immigration Battle," published in May 2007 examines its complex composition:

> This movement is a complex, decentralized web of think tanks, foundations, political action committees, politicians, media personalities, and grass roots groups. It spans both private and public power, from the white supremacist fringe to the halls of Congress. It not only musters support and helps to foster a general anti-immigrant climate, but it also raises millions of dollars to advance its policy goals (curtailing immigration, deporting the undocumented) in Washington.

NAMM's heterogeneity became evident during the twenty-day operation. David Hothouse from the Southern Poverty Law Center identified two individuals who were self-professed members of the National Alliance, a violent neo-Nazi organization. Both were dressed in full-body camouflage and strapped with semi-automatic pistols. The *Washington Times*, an ultraconservative nativist newspaper, came to MP's rescue in an editorial vehemently critical of President Bush's vigilante assertion.[27]

At the invitation of Congressman Tancredo, Gilchrist and Simcox, accompanied by two dozen or so other MP members on April 27 arrived in Washington, D.C., to meet with ten members of the anti-immigrant congressional Immigration Reform Caucus.[28] Both militia leaders were congratulated on MP's bringing attention to the need to retake control of the U.S.–México border. Tancredo conveyed to Gilchrist and Simcox that is was a "job well done."[29] While in Washington, D.C., Simcox participated in a number of rallies and lobbying activities organized by the Federation for American Immigration Reform (FAIR) under the rubric "Hold Their Feet to the Fire." Simcox commented that MP had just begun: "We were bold enough to stand-up and tell the federal government that it's not securing our borders. But our efforts will continue in the future with a multi-state campaign. There will be no compromise!"[30] Both leaders stressed the importance of building a powerful anti-immigrant national political movement with the capacity to pressure politicians in Washington, D.C.[31]

The cordial partnership and accord between Gilchrist and Simcox that began in October 2004 ended in late April 2005. At the crux of the dissolution were conflicting, power-hungry egos. Both perceived themselves to be "top gun" of the emerging NAMM. As a result, Gilchrist maintained control over MP and incorporated it as Minuteman Project, Inc. in Delaware and designated himself as the only board member.[32] He hired a consultant and initiated a national fundraising campaign. MP's cardinal purpose was to investigate violations of immigration, tax, and employment laws—in short, campaigning against employers who hired undocumented migrants. Under the guise of Operation Spotlight, it was to put together cases against employers who hired undocumented migrants in what Gilchrist called, "the illegal alien slave labor market."[33] As for Simcox, on May 12, via the Civil Defense Corps (CDC) website, he announced a name change: CDC would now be called Minuteman Civil Defense Corps (MCDC). As a nativist militia, its main purpose would continue to be to organize, train, and conduct border surveillance operations.[34]

MP MOVEMENT INITIAL ACTIVITIES

From May through July of 2005, MP and MCDC expanded rapidly. With debate increasing over the immigration crisis, the media continued to cover extensively the emergent national anti-migrant movement, particularly Gilchrist and Simcox. Its rise was propitious, since Congress was considering immigration reform legislation. NAMM's unprecedented momentum was ascribable to the country's growing anti-immigrant political climate. Gilchrist, as the leader of MP on the national level, during the month of May was in great demand by other nativist groups. *Los Angeles Times* staff reporter David Kelly reported that as a consequence of MP patrolling of the Arizona–México border, "Illegal Immigration Fears Have Spread" beyond the country's border states. He added that "the armed volunteers patrolling the Arizona-México border may be the starkest sign of frustration with the nation's immigration laws, but across the country there is a growing populist movement also taking matters into its own hands."[35]

In May 2005 in Garden Grove, California, at a meeting of the California Coalition for Immigration Reform, an altercation occurred between MP supporters and 300 or so migrant rights advocates. With Gilchrist scheduled to be honored, protestors charged that Gilchrist was a racist. Two demonstrators were injured when a slow-moving van driven by MP supporter Hal Netkin drove into the protesting crowd. Only one of the injured required medical treatment. As Netkin was placed in handcuffs and taken away by police, some pro-migrant rights protestors threw rocks. The police swarmed in and declared the protest an

unlawful assembly and ordered the crowd to disperse; six protestors were arrested. Meanwhile, Gilchrist addressed 150 MP supporters assembled inside the
Garden Grove Women's Club. With a sense of pride, he said, "I'm damned
proud to be a vigilante" and reminded his audience that "illegal immigrants will
destroy this country."[36]

Netkin later alleged that his hitting the two protestors with his car was not
deliberate, but was instead an accident. He explained to police that he was trying to escape the protestors when the protestors started hitting his van with placards and other objects. He said that he became frightened and therefore gunned
his car to avoid the protestors.[37] The incident sparked a volley of acrimonious accusations by both sides. Charges were not pressed against him on grounds that
it was "reasonable for [the driver] to be afraid," yet charges were pressed against
the six protestors arrested. Chris Simcox's reaction to the press was that "it's heat-
ing up. I've got a feeling you're going to see some violent civil unrest."[38] The
event was a prelude to a growing militant response by pro-migrant rights activists
against Gilchrist, MP, and its activities.

Indicative of NAMM expansion, on May 27–30 at La Plaza Hotel in Las Vegas, Nevada, a summit of anti-immigrant leaders was held. In attendance were
Gilchrist, Simcox, Congressman Tom Tancredo, Glenn Spencer, Barbara Coe,
and Andy Ramirez, among others.[39] In his address, Gilchrist pandered to his nativist audience by "bashing" Mexicanos: "Every time a Mexican flag is planted on
American soil, it is a declaration of war."[40] The summit's agenda focused on matters pertinent to NAMM's expansion.

While the top NAMM leaders met in Las Vegas, others began to separate
themselves from both MCDC and MP and opted to form their own nativist vigilante groups and militias. In California, MCDC volunteer Nancy Hubbard of
Temecula, California, promulgated Simcox's call to patrol the California–México border in October of 2005.[41] Not wanting to come under the aegis of
MCDC, two other independent nativist entities emerged. Both soon found
themselves, however, at odds and in competition with MCDC. One group was
the Friends of the Border Patrol (FBP), led by Andy Ramirez from Chino, California. Organized in 2004, Ramirez rebuked the armed militia approach, but
adhered to a nonviolent form of vigilantism that sought to patrol the California–México border during the 2005 summer months.[42] In a gesture of support
for Ramirez and a jab directed at Simcox, Glenn Spencer, head of American Border Patrol (ABP) in Arizona supported Ramirez's call for a border vigil in August.

The second group was the Oceanside-based United States Border Patrol
Auxiliary (USBPA), which became known as the California Minutemen. Led by
Jim Chase, a former army officer, its orientation was that of an armed vigilante
nativist militia. In May Chase announced the California Minutemen's patrol of
the eastern part of the San Diego–México border. In comparison to FBP, Chase's

USBPA was a full-fledged militia. It was organized, armed, and adopted a more militant nativist posture. Chase identified USBPA's primary mission as one of ensuring national security, meaning a commitment to preventing terrorists, drug smugglers, and felons from entering the country. He distanced himself and US-BPA from Simcox's MCDC by claiming that USBPA was more humanitarian, which meant that when apprehending undocumented migrants, they were given water, food, and blankets.

In June, Chase reported that USBPA had chapters in several states under the aegis of such names as California Minutemen, Arizona Minutemen, Texas Minutemen, and New México Minutemen. The latter on June 12 began to patrol a portion of the state's border with México, which created a firestorm of protests by a number of pro-migrant rights groups, especially LULAC (League of United Latin American Citizens). New México Governor Bill Richardson also expressed strong opposition to the New México Minutemen's patrol of the New México–México border.[43] Mike Giddy, director of Simcox's New México chapter of MCDC informed the media that efforts were under way to reconcile conflicts between USBPA and MCDC. Simcox on July 11 convoked a meeting of MCDC in Las Cruces, New México, which was attended by only a few dozen people, and was protested by mostly Mexicano/Latino groups and activists who accused Simcox and MCDC of being racist.[44]

Like California and New México, Texas was not immune from the growing fractures within the NAMM. By July there were two active militias: one in the Goliad area, which was affiliated with MCDC; the second was in the Dallas area, the Texas Minutemen. Both claimed territorial patrol rights over various parts of the Texas–México border. The former announced it would patrol the Rio Grande River that stretches from Brownsville to El Paso, while the latter publicized that it would concentrate its patrols along the border area, around El Paso, Fabens, and Fort Hancock, Texas.[45] In utter rejection of the two militias, eleven state senators came out against them as well as various Mexicano/Latino organizations, such as LULAC.

Indicative of NAMM's expansion, MCDC in July announced that it had organized chapters in some twenty-one states. Each chapter's membership ranged from six persons to hundreds. Gary Cole, MP chief of operations, reported in July that chapters had been formed in Texas, New México, California, Utah, Michigan, and Tennessee. Another indicator of its growth was the Department of Homeland Security (DHS) Custom and Border Protection Commissioner Robert C. Bonner who on July 20 openly praised NAMM and said that his initial concerns about vigilantism by citizen patrol groups was eased by the volunteers' conduct. In a visit to the port of Los Angeles, Bonner said, "We welcome the eyes and ears of citizens who help us gain control of our borders, especially when they do so in a peaceful way." He reported that the DHS was working on a process that would permit citizens to volunteer to help the Border Patrol. The next day, however, DHS announced that there were no plans to enlist citizen volunteers to patrol the U.S. borders.[46] Bonner's brief praise of NAMM suggested approval by the Bush administration, but because of growing political opposition DHS reversed itself.

MP CALIFORNIA'S CONFLICTIVE ORGANIZING EFFORTS

On July 16 about two dozen volunteers, some armed, organized by California Minutemen, began their patrol of the "Campo" border area, situated outside of San Diego on the border. For the next three weeks, the region was the locus of conflict between USBPA patrol activities and pro-migrant rights groups, which at times bordered on violence and polarization over the issue of the migrant exodus.[47] Pro-migrant rights coalitions, groups, and activists from San Diego and southern California on a daily basis monitored Chase's USBPA border activities. Scores of protestors came to Campo, held press conferences, denounced the patrols as racist, and picketed USBPA. All this time, Chase's militia volunteers numbered only a handful. Chase, like Gilchrist and Simcox, was able to turn his small border patrol operation into a media event. Pro-migrant rights advocates likewise responded by waging their own political media game. Every day there was an ongoing struggle over who would win the media exposure for the day.

On July 16, Gilchrist, accompanied by Republican State Senator Bill Marrow, during a visit to Chase's group at Campo, was met by a strong contingent of anti-MP protestors. Allegedly, the protestors stormed and damaged the VFW (Veterans of Foreign Wars) Lodge, which was being used by Chase's group as its headquarters for conducting its border watch. The incident ended when the San Diego Sheriff's Department intervened. There were no arrests made, but the incident was used by Gilchrist to put out a national call for MP reinforcements to come to Campo to assist USBPA. In a rather alarmist propagandistic manner he stressed that USBPA volunteers were under siege by "60 belligerent, death-threatening anti-Americans." He further accused this author of orchestrating what he called the "rampage."[48] An aide to Senator Marrow, Mark Belgen, accused this author of kicking him in the shin. He filed a police report and said he was going to call for pressing charges. The charges never materialized—it was a case of mistaken identity since this author was never present.[49]

Chase's USBPA border surveillance activity at Campo lasted until late August. It failed to attract large numbers of volunteers. Conversely, pro-migrant rights groups consistently countervailed its border surveillance activities with large numbers of protestors. Initially, Chase claimed to have some 990 volunteers ready to participate in the hunt of Mexicano undocumented migrants. However, by the end of the three-week patrol only a handful showed up. Its record of interdicting and apprehending undocumented migrants was dismal—only three, two of whom were hitchhiking on the road when Chase picked them up and turned them over to the Border Patrol. There were two shooting incidents reported. In one incident Chase admitted that "rogue" volunteers shot at two undocumented migrants form or near Tecate, México. Another shooting incident occurred near Jacumba, California,[50] but in neither case was anyone reported shot.

During the summer, nationwide MP continued to fracture and divide itself particularly over issues of strategy and tactics. During the summer, Simcox reported that MCDC in October planned to patrol both the Mexican and Canadian borders and anticipated the participation of 7,000 volunteers. Others also made similar pronouncements, but their focus was on the California–México border. Growing internecine conflicts occurred among the competing and uncoordinated groups, with each being hypercritical of the others' operations. The report also alluded to there being three MP groups scheduled to patrol parts of the California–México border: Chase's USBP, Ramirez's FBP, and Simcox's MCDC. The schisms between the three groups by August worsened, especially among the former two. Both Chase and Ramirez cited organizational differences. Ramirez was hypercritical of Chase's use of firearms and of patrolling close to México's border, a potentially dangerous area. In turn, Chase was critical of Ramirez, who was unemployed, and therefore was taking monetary donations and paying himself. Ramirez's FBP differed tactically from Chase's USBPA in that FBP would only operate on private property when conducting its patrols near the border areas of Calexico and Border Field State Park, north of Tijuana. Chase publicized that USBPA patrols would operate near San Diego on the Campo area of the border.[51] A third nativist militia, the Minuteman Corps of California, led by Tim Donnelly of Twin Peaks (allied with Simcox's MCDC), also announced that patrols would be conducted in October near the San Diego–San Ysidro border area.[52]

The Chase and Ramirez patrols of the California border started in September. Chase, suffering from decreasing numbers of volunteers, began his border patrol on September 11, while Ramirez began his patrols on September 16. A number of anti-NAMM groups responded by initiating protests against USBPA's largely media-driven patrols. Perhaps due to the pressure exerted by these groups, Ramirez's FBP patrol of the Calexico and Border Field State Park border proved to be a disaster. After months of informing the media of FBP's planned border surveillance efforts, Ramirez on September 17 canceled the patrols one day after they started as a result of a scuffle with protestors. He explained, "I can't send them out if somebody is going to try to harm them."[53] The fracas took place at the Scottish Rites Center in San Diego after some twenty counterdemonstrators disrupted a training session of FBP volunteers. One of the counterdemonstrators was charged with battery after knocking down one of those attending the training session. Later that Saturday afternoon in Calexico, some 200 anti-FBP demonstrators marched through the streets and rallied at the border where they declared their victory. Adding insult to injury, the hundreds of volunteers that Ramirez had predicted would turn out,[54] turned out to be a mere forty, of which only twenty registered for training to participate in the border watch.[55] In a letter publicly released on September 18, Ramirez provided a summary of what he perceived took place, the assault and battery of several FBP volunteers. He promised to continue FBP's border watch efforts. He closed the letter with a call to "join FBP today and stop the smugglers, secure our borders, and support the US Border Patrol, and our fellow US citizens living along America's borders."[56] During the next two weeks, Ramirez sought to reinitiate a border watch, but failed to draw the needed support.

California Governor Arnold Schwarzenegger in September reiterated his earlier praise of NAMM. In April he praised the efforts of the MP volunteers: "They've done a terrific job. And they cut down the crossing of illegal immigrants by a huge percentage."[57] Again in June, he reinforced his praise for NAMM. He came under severe criticism, however, after saying that the state's border with México should be "closed" and compared the MP volunteers in Arizona to a "neighborhood watch" group. Publicly criticized, he quickly took back what he had said and explained that what he really meant to say was that the border should be "secured" and that the federal government was falling short on the job.[58] In September, when asked by reporters his opinion of MPP, he repeated his earlier support for the group: "It's no different than if you have a neighborhood watch person there that's watching your children at the playground. I don't see it any different." He further explained his position: "Or if I have my personal guards at the house, because I feel like the police [are] not going to be able to take care of the job because they are overwhelmed. It's just that private persons take the responsibility."[59]

During October, Simcox's MCDC initiated its patrols of the U.S.–Canadian border. He reported that some 4,500 volunteers had registered from Michigan to California and that organizing requests had been received from all fifty states.[60] In California, Tim Donnelly, who headed the Minuteman Corps of California reported that fifty volunteers had participated in its border watch operation around the San Diego border area. In Texas, some 500 volunteers signed up with the MCDC's border watch efforts. They targeted the Texas–México border from El Paso to Brownsville.[61] Along New York's Canadian border, MCDC volunteers also conducted a border watch operation. Associated Press reporter Elliot Spagat described the hundreds of volunteers who participated in the more than twenty border watch operations nationally:

Many of the hundreds who make-up the self-appointed civilian patrols monitoring the border to deter smuggling of people and drugs are unemployed or underemployed ex-military men who have long resented Mexicans who come to the United States illegally and, in their view, compete for jobs, crowd hospitals and schools, and threaten English as the nation's dominant language.[62]

Anti-MCDC protestors responded to the border watch by initiating their own form of countersurveillance of the militia group. In Texas, some 200 persons protested in Austin at the capitol and got into a shouting match with some 100 pro-Minutemen supporters. At a prayer vigil held in Brownville against MCDC's border watch operation, ACLU sent observers to monitor it. Civic leaders from along the Texas–México border condemned the border patrols.[63] In El Paso, the city council passed a resolution asking them to stay away.[64] A former president, Kenneth Buelter of Texas's first chapter of the Minutemen Border Patrol warned of possible violence resulting from MCDC's first Texas border watch operation. In a statement to the press, he said, "I dissolved the Minutemen organization because it was not following its own written procedures. If they do not follow these policies, I foresee the potential for problems."[65]

Also in October, Gilchrist's MP chapter organized a "Secure Our Borders" rally at the footsteps of the state capitol building in Sacramento. Attended by some 200 supporters, the main speakers included Jim Gilchrist; Tim Donnelly, leader of the California MP chapter; Lupe Moreno, president of Latino Americans for Immigration Reform; and Frank George, a naturalized Cuban immigrant and spokesperson for the Texas MP. The event drew some 600 counterprotestors, of which three were arrested: one for assaulting a California highway patrol officer, and one for an attack on a city police officer with pepper spray.[66] Conflict also surfaced in Arlington Heights, Illinois, when some 100 volunteers attended the first MP summit in Chicago and hundreds of protestors rallied outside the school meeting site. Among the protestors were self-described anarchists who blocked the entrance to the meeting site. After a scuffle, five were arrested for assaulting police officers.[67]

By December 2005, NAMM had grown nationwide and had contributed significantly to the country's further nativization of its body politic. Much of its growth was ascribable to a White-controlled sympathetic media that gave the various vigilante groups and nativist militias extensive media coverage. Even though few people participated in NAMM activities, the media considered them newsworthy.

NAMM, in particular, significantly impacted politicians in Congress, especially the House of Representatives. The country's WASP ethos, driven by a profound sense of xenophobia, nativism, and racism, reached a high point when the House passed especially restrictionist legislation, HR4437 (House Resolution

4437), which criminalized the status of undocumented immigrants and migrants and further militarized the border.

GILCHRIST RUNS FOR CONGRESS

Gilchrist in the summer of 2005 decided to run in California for the 48th Congressional District. The seat was vacated by Republican Christopher Cox, who was appointed by President Bush to head the Securities and Exchange Commission. A special primary election was scheduled for October 4. If none of the candidates received more than 50 percent of the votes, a runoff would be held on December 6. Gilchrist, who ran as an American Independent Party candidate, was assured a spot on the December 6 ballot, providing no candidate won the primary. He felt that he had a good chance of winning because of his recent national notoriety. He also believed the political timing was propitious for him to enter the electoral arena which would concomitantly advance MP's anti-Mexicano/immigrant agenda. Gilchrist's strongest challenge came from Republican State Senator John Campbell, who had been anointed by the Republican Party to be Cox's replacement.

On August 19 before an enthusiastic crowd of supporters at the Convention Center Ballroom in Ontario Gilchrist made it official and declared his candidacy for the congressional seat. A live broadcast from KFI's Jon and Ken show also kicked off the "California Border Police" initiative that would be on the 2006 ballot. In his address, although he covered other issues, he accentuated that the cornerstone of his campaign was immigration. He said, "I'm here today because, like you, I have grown weary and frustrated with the decades-long refusal of federal, state, and local government to simply enforce U.S. immigration laws."[68] Gilchrist tried to have the title "Minuteman Project founder" included on the ballot. But California's Secretary of State Bruce McPherson ruled against it and consequently the space next to his name was left blank. Gilchrist appealed the decision to the Sacramento County Superior Court, but to no avail: Judge Judy Holzer Hersher upheld the decision.[69] On the Democratic Party ticket was candidate Steve Young, on the Green Party ticket, Bea Tiritilli, and Bruce Cohen was on the ticket for the Libertarian Party.

Throughout his campaign, Gilchrist utilized his national MP exposure and contacts to secure support and contributions. He raised some $600,000 for his campaign. The media again was generous in providing him with visibility. Colorado Congressman Tom Tancredo endorsed Gilchrist and appeared in radio and television ads exhorting voters to vote for him. Gilchrist ran as a citizen activist driven by a campaign on immigration. *Los Angeles Times* reporter Jean O. Pasco wrote, "Gilchrist controlled the debate, focusing almost solely on illegal immigration." One radio spot said that "every vote that Jim Gilchrist receives is a message to President Bush that his guest-worker program-amnesty program is wrong and that it's time to secure our borders now" and spoke out in support of employer sanctions.[70] Republican Campbell, armed with a $1.2 million war chest[71] and supported by the party's machinery, took the offensive. Running in a safe Republican conservative district, his position on immigration reform ostensibly mirrored that of Gilchrist.

In the October primary no candidate garnered the required 50 percent to avoid a runoff election. Gilchrist got 15 percent, while Campbell got 46 percent. In the runoff election held in December, Republican Campbell won with 45 percent (41,450), followed by Democrat Young with 28 percent (25,926), and Independent Gilchrist, who managed to garner 25 percent of the vote (23,237).[72] Gilchrist's strong showing was interpreted by some analysts as an omen of campaigns to come if the immigration crisis continued to be exacerbated. As a result of the campaign Gilchrist managed to secure additional national media visibility which strengthened his national image as an anti-immigrant nativist leader and buttressed the growing NAMM. After the campaign, Gilchrist made it clear that he would consider running for Campbell's seat in 2008 or for some other office, such as the U.S. Senate, lieutenant governor, or even governor. In response to the election results, Gilchrist said, "This is only round one. Even Rocky Balboa didn't win in the first round."[73]

THE LEADERSHIP RISE OF GILCHRIST AND SIMCOX

The country's existent and exacerbating nativist anti-immigrant political climate, coupled with Gilchrist and Simcox's pandering and manipulating of those conditions, were major factors that contributed to their leadership rise. From October of 2004 to April of 2005, the collaboration of the two leaders was one of expediency and mutual exploitation, meaning that in a Machiavellian manner, each sought to use the other in order to achieve an end—*lider maximo* status of the emergent NAMM.

With their split they became leadership competitors. As both leaders competed for media attention and resources, animosities between the two NAMM leaders set in. When asked in May, why the split between the two leaders? Gilchrist responded, "I think he was jealous and it was clear he wanted my segment of the Minutemen campaign to fail."[74] The leadership rivalry between them during the next two years was symptomatic of the leadership schisms and power struggles that pervasively plagued NAMM. Both Simcox and Gilchrist took advantage of their national notoriety to promote not just their respective militias, but particularly themselves.

Gilchrist made himself available to the media for a plethora of interviews, radio, and television appearances. During the next two years or so he participated in some 2,700 interviews.[75] He went on tours to different parts of the country and effectively solicited financial support, membership, and convinced volunteers to form MP chapters. His appearances on television, radio programs, and in newspaper interviews were an intrinsic part of his strategy for building up his nationwide image. Supported by politicians like Congressman Tancredo of Colorado, among others, and anti-immigrant activists such as Barbara Coe and Deborah Courtney, they opened doors to influential nativist political and economic individuals and groups.

In the case of Simcox, he got the attention of the right-wing conservative Diener Consultants. Led by Phillip Sheldon, who was the son of Traditional Values Coalition founder Lou Sheldon, a vociferous antigay crusader who pandered to the far right, Simcox recruited him to direct MCDC's national media and fund-raising efforts. Sheldon's job was to market both organizationally and financially of Simcox and MCDC. According to staff writers Susy Buchanan and David Holthouse of the Southern Poverty Law Center:

> With Simcox's blessing Diener quickly moved several employees into key administrative positions within MCDC and began a slick media and fundraising campaign. Fundraising appeals became aggressive and frequent. A spiffed-up Simcox turned into a cable-news fixture, while full-color ads promoting MCDC and requesting donations began to appear in the conservative *Washington Times*.[76]

Simcox, short on eloquence and with little charisma, depended on his shrewd sense of timing and ability to network with those of like persuasion. His anti-immigrant message resonated well with a number of powerful Republican neoconservative leaders. Other right-wing nativist forces, such as Allan Keyes's Declaration Alliance, aligned themselves with MCDC. The affiliation was irrefutable since on its home page it identified itself as a project of the Declaration Alliance.[77] As MCDC's leader, Simcox sought to position himself politically as the *lider maximo* of NAMM.

MP AND MCDC ORGANIZATIONAL FORMATION

Both MP and MCDC were incorporated as 501(c)(4) nonprofit "pressure groups," which meant that neither had to pay taxes; however, this meant that they could not claim contributions as being tax-exempt, nor could they legally endorse candidates or engage in the electoral arena. Both Gilchrist and Simcox solicited funds by way of political action committees (PACs). Simcox established

Minutemen PAC Inc., while Gilchrist created a campaign fund for his race for Congress in 2005. Incorporated as a pressure groups, neither MP or MCDC functioned as one. Instead both functioned as paramilitary-oriented armed militias.

Neither MP nor MCDC was well organized. Both lacked a pluralistic leadership, were structurally decentralized, and lacked a well-defined state or national hierarchical structure that included a committee infrastructure. Their national boards of directors consisted of a few leaders, which both Simcox and Gilchrist handpicked. Democracy was absent, meaning that there were never elections held where the mass membership voted on who would be in the leadership role of either organization. From the beginning both militias were personality and not organization driven. MCDC, from its retransformation in April from MCD into MCDC, adhered to a loose and flexible structure comprised of a few volunteers that came in at specified times and formed the equivalent of "squads" comprised of ten or so men. Press reports on MCDC border operations suggest that at no time did its border surveillance patrols ever reach forty to fifty volunteers at any one time. MCDC's volunteers' paramilitary demeanor was buttressed by their use of pistols, rifles, binoculars, radios, knives, and at times fatigues.

Membership in MCDC was the relatively simple process of paying a fee of $50. The loyalty of most that joined hinged ostensibly on being anti-immigrant and anti-Mexicano. According to Simcox, by January of 2006, MCDC had forty-one chapters and some 6,000 members nationwide.[78] Three months later he claimed that MCDC's membership had increased to 6,500, but the number of chapters had declined to thirty-one. In September he reported that MCDC's membership had increased to 7,451 volunteer *cazamigrantes*, or migrant hunters, and that some 60,000 people had sent in donations.[79] In early 2007, MCDC, according to Solana Larsen, editor of openDemocracy.net, had at least sixty-two chapters nationwide.[80] By late August, a Minuteman communiqué, was reported that MCDC had 100 local chapters in fifty states.

Gilchrist's MP after the split with Simcox did not resemble a nativist militia. Instead, its cardinal purpose was to influence policy, especially the enforcement of employer sanctions. Its chapters were usually comprised of only a handful of people and resembled much more a militant traditional pressure group. As NAMM evolved and Simcox's MCDC picked up momentum, financial resources, and membership; while Gilchrist's MP shifted tactically from its pressure group influence orientation to its original vigilante militia posture. As a result, some chapters began to organize border surveillance patrols. Gilchrist really never made public MP's number of members or its chapters. By the start of 2007, nonetheless, it was reported that MP had twenty-four chapters in twenty states and some 200,000 paying members.[81] Salient organizational characteristics of MP and MCDC were: (1) up to 2007 neither had developed a grassroots powerbase; and (2) both leaders had little or no control over their respective chapters.[82]

MCDC AND MPP'S IDEOLOGY

Ideologically, both MP and MCDC as nativist militias were xenophobic, nativist, and racist, especially toward Mexicanos. They adhered to a White nationalism that was permeated by the WASP ethos. In their political marketing, both Simcox and Gilchrist claimed to capture the true essence of the patriot struggle of the country's war for independence. As nativist militias, they sought to exemplify that they were comprised of patriots who were ardently committed to the defense of the country's sovereignty from an alleged invasion from México. Both also saw themselves as fulfilling the duty of a U.S. government that had failed to exercise control of the U.S.–México border. Gilchrist, during the twenty-one-day patrol of the Arizona border in April 2005, said, "We have demonstrated that ordinary citizens sitting in lawn chairs not only have the will but the means to secure the border. If our own elected officials will not defend our nation's border, American citizens will."[83] In the book Gilchrist co-authored, *Minutemen*, he warns of the "Trojan Horse" invasion:

> We are allowing an unrestrained flow of illegal immigrants into the United States, anticipating little or no threat to our national security or our standard of living. The fear is that, like the ancient Trojans, we are naively bringing grave danger into our city walls. The illegal immigrants invading our country will quickly destroy the United States as a safe, economically sound nation that abides by the principles of law established by our Founding Fathers. We have allowed into our midst an army of illegal immigrants who will cause our downfall unless we do something about it now.[84]

Simcox ideologically echoed the same nativist rhetoric. As a jingoist, he depicted México as a serious security threat to the U.S., equating the migrant exodus to an invasion, and argued for a full-fledged militarization of the border. Simcox told the press that MCDC would continue to exercise its civic duty by patrolling the border until relieved by the National Guard or the U.S. military.

Both leaders pandered to the fears of the already-inclined nativists, who were mostly Whites. Their xenophobic perceptions and attitudes were based upon their assertion that "brown people" were egregiously changing the ethnic and cultural makeup of the U.S. and threatened its security and survival as a sovereign nation-state. They were driven by a hatred of the undocumented migrants, especially Mexicanos. Neither Gilchrist's MP nor Simcox's MCDC possessed a clear-cut ideology of its own. Yet both were conservative, libertarian, and capitalist, adhering to a laissez-faire free-market economy; both were business oriented, and were zealous and ambitious exploiters of the nativist/racist marketplace. Left activists cataloged both leaders and militias as "fascist" in that they were authoritarian and were an admixture of racism, fear, and extreme White nationalism. What it boiled down to was that both Simcox and Gilchrist were foremost driven by greed, profit, power, and fame rather than their nativist rhetoric and ideas that drove their politics. As nativist militias, both MP and MCDC shared some of the beliefs of other militias, such as Ranch Rescue and ABP. Both adhered to their right to defend private property, their distrust and criticism of the federal government, their right to bear arms, the power of the citizenry over that of the government, and, as White supremacist militias, a pronounced racism directed against Mexicanos and Latinos, in that order.

MCDC AND MP STRATEGIC PROFILE

Both MP and MCDC by 2007 adhered to a paramilitary structure. By April, the nativist politics of Gilchrist and Simcox were so extreme that both could be categorized as "domestic terrorists" in that they instilled fear among migrants. Both leaders relied on the use of "conventional and unconventional" politics. The former entailed the use of lobbying, litigation, press conferences, media events, and pressuring politicians via letters, phone calls, visits, e-mails, and electioneering, while the latter that was much more militant relied on a repertoire of protest tactics, for example, marches, pickets, confrontations, armed military patrols, and ultimately, the use of violence. Tactically, MP had a duel personality: at times it functioned as an armed militia that conducted border surveillance operations; while concurrently, it also functioned as a pressure group that sought to influence immigration policy. Most MP chapters participated with other extremist right-wing nativist groups in protests. In California, MP chapters collaborated with Save Our State (SOS) and participated and organized a number of direct actions (e.g., pickets, rallies) against *jornaleros* (day laborers) at Home Depots and pro-migrant rights marches and rallies. Protests were used as media events to politically nurture the growing nativist anti-immigrant political climate, to enhance their recruitment of new members, and chapter formation. Both MP and MCDC used the Internet as a vehicle for political education, dissemination of information, and mobilization. With the latter, however, neither was successful in demonstrating a "power capability," meaning that neither displayed the capacity to mobilize large numbers of people. Their border patrols typically involved only a handful of volunteers and their protests seldom ever exceeded more than 200 persons. Most protest events ranged from 30 to 100 people. The majority of their activist support was White, retired, and in their late fifties to seventies. There were very few young people who filled their volunteer ranks.

The Nativist Anti-Immigrant Movement

NAMM NATIONWIDE

During 2006 and 2007, both MP and MCDC continued to drive much of the NAMM nationwide. While other nativist vigilante groups and militias had been formed and were active it was MP and MCDC that were in the lead. With the passage of HR4437 in December 2005 and the immigration reform debate in 2006 at full speed in Congress, the country's political climate remained propitious for the NAMM's continued growth. With both political parties divided on the issue of immigration reform, especially on the issue of "amnesty" or legalization, the acrimonious debates resonated with many of the same anti-immigrant arguments made by Gilchrist, Simcox, and other nativist leaders. The ongoing border watches produced few apprehensions of undocumented migrants but they did play well before a hungry sensationalist media, especially demagogues like CNN's Lou Dobbs.

NAMM peaked with the passage of Republican Congressman James Sensenbrenner's HR4437 draconian restrictionist legislation that called for the "criminalization" of the country's 12 million undocumented workers and stronger border enforcement. From April to December 2005 anti-immigrant groups, especially MP, throughout the country held rallies, meetings, and direct action protests, including picketing and demonstrations, all for the purpose of pressuring Congress into passing restrictionist border enforcement-oriented legislation. In February 2006 MP held a protest in Washington, D.C., that was attended by a few hundred people. Gilchrist's message resonated with a call for "revolution." "This is a bloodless revolution. Nobody's getting hurt, but we're changing the way our country thinks and we're changing its immigration policy."[85] In January 2006 the country experienced the rise of the primarily Mexicano and Latino organized *Movimiento Pro-Migrante* (pro-migrant movement) that through May produced a plethora of unprecedented pro-migrant mobilizations that drew literally millions demanding the defeat of HR4437 and legalization.[86] The pro-migrant marches drew hundreds of thousands from New York to Los Angeles, while NAMM counterprotests only drew a few dozen. For example, in California, while the pro-migrant rights groups held in Los Angeles the megamarch that drew nearly 1 million persons on March 25, MP in southern California held a rally in Temecula that was attended by Gilchrist and Assemblyman Ray Hayes, which only drew a crowd of 200.[87]

Gilchrist and Simcox were hypercritical of the massive pro-migrant mobilizations. Gilchrist responded with a threat: "We're not controlling the outcome of Congress and we're livid about it—and so are millions of Americans. I am willing to see my country go into battle if necessary for our sovereignty and to be governed by rule of law."[88] Simcox's response was not as virulent or bellicose: "While the nation watches this [pro-immigrant] spectacle in our streets, the Minutemen will be working night and day on America's borders to uphold the rule of law in the name of liberty—the price for which is eternal vigilance."[89]

Others within NAMM, however, responded with threats of violence. The Southern Poverty Law Center (SPLC) reported that neo-Nazis, hate, and several anti-immigrant extremist groups responded with open calls for violence. This included the use of terrorist tactics, such as the use of truck bombs, machine gun attacks, and assassination of some politicians and activist leaders. Neo-Nazi radio host Hal Turner, in response to the million person Los Angeles pro-migrant mobilization of March 25, 2006, said, "All of you who think there's a peaceful solution to these invaders are wrong. We're going to have to start killing these people." He further stated, "I advocate using extreme violence against illegal aliens. Clean your guns. Have plenty of ammunition. Find out where the largest gathering of illegal aliens will be near you. Go to the area well in advance, scope out several places to position yourself and then do what has to be done." In response, a survey was posted on Turner's website asking how politicians in both the Senate and House could be considering granting amnesty. Many of the responses stated "machine gun them to death," "firebomb their district office as a warning," and lastly, bomb their House and Senate offices.[90]

Members of the California-based anti-immigrant hate group, SOS, led by Joseph Turner, added their voices to the call for blood: "I see people with vans driving by, gunning them down on street corners, and leaving them to feed the buzzards and worms."[91] For some nativist extremist groups within the MP movement, their perception of the massive Mexicano/Latino mobilizations was that a race war was imminent. SPLC concluded its report, citing a statement by the neo-Nazi on Vanguard News Network: "The bad news is many whites will die. It is imperative that you make proper connections NOW and form networks of like-minded armed whites to defend yourselves . . . It will be grand. More exciting than Zombie flicks. If you have a good defense line and lots of ammo the carnage will be orgasmic."[92]

MCDC EXPANDS BORDER PATROLS

MCDC during the rest of 2006 and into 2007 focused much of its organizing activities on working the media, forming chapters, expanding its membership, securing donations, building a border fence, and conducting border surveillance operations. During 2006, MCDC's organizing activities focused on three issues: (1) month-long border patrols; (2) protests against day laborer centers; and (3) a boycott against Miller Brewing Company. In April 2006 MCDC volunteers conducted month-long border patrols in New México, Texas, and California. Likewise, patrols were concomitantly initiated on sections of the U.S.–Canadian border in the states of Washington, New York, and Vermont. They were used to buttress the passage of HR4437 by the Senate or to pass legislation that prioritized border security. Simcox explained, "If the Senate does not pass a border security bill soon, you are going to see our numbers double probably by the end of the summer. People are frustrated and I think this political process of coming to the border and setting up a lawn chair and saying, 'we have the will to do it,' sends a strong message to Washington D.C."[93] MCDC in October 2006 again carried out month-long border patrols of the country's two borders.

In April 2007, MCDC again repeated its border-watch operations along the U.S.–México and Canadian borders. Called "Operation Stand Your Ground," it was billed as involving thousands of volunteers. In reality, however, it produced only a few hundred. In addition due to continued shortages in volunteers, the media frenzy that existed before had largely disappeared. Regardless that the U.S. Border Patrol reported a decline in the number of apprehensions of undocumented workers, Simcox argued that the Arizona–México border, particularly the Sasabe, México, area, was still being overrun by undocumented traffic.[94] That month an outside rally was held at the University of Texas at San Antonio that was organized by the Young Conservatives of Texas. Simcox, who was one of the speakers at the event that drew some 700 persons (the largest NAMM mobilization), was interrupted by protestors with booing, yelling, and bullhorns; ultimately there was a clash with police.[95]

Some MCDC chapters also conducted protests against day laborer centers. The Maryland chapter focused on protesting the hiring of undocumented workers, especially at county-funded day laborer centers. Alan Tonelson, a consultant to the television talk show host Lou Dobbs on the issue said, "Day laborer centers are clearly an example of subsidizing the presence of illegal immigrants in whatever area they're in. It couldn't be more obvious. There is no doubt that as day laborer centers get created, they'll draw a larger illegal immigrant population to that area."[96]

Because of its alleged support of pro-migrant rights groups, MCDC in September 2006 launched a national boycott of the Miller Brewing Company. Al Garza, a leader within MCDC, stated, "We found out that they are very instrumental in financing illegal immigration in different forms." MCDC charged that Miller donated some $30,000 to the pro-immigrant marches earlier that year, a charge Miller denied unequivocally.[97] The *Chicago Tribune* reported on September 6 that MCDC and 9/11 Families for a Secure America had announced a national boycott against Miller Brewing Company. Garza alleged that they were in fact hiring undocumented immigrants. Miller's official statement on the matter was posted on its website. The statement read:

Miller Brewing Company has never supported illegal immigration and we have always supported the full enforcement of current U.S. laws . . . Going forward, Miller will closely review all requests for support from community and charitable organizations to ensure that we are not indirectly funding or associating our name with advocacy efforts on the immigration issue.[98]

The MCDC boycott against Miller Brewing Company failed to develop any traction. It proved to be more symbolic than substantive.

In March 2006, Simcox on the Fox News show *Hannity & Colmes* launched MCDC's campaign to construct a border fence on private ranch properties along the Arizona–México border. The fence resembled an Israeli-style security fence, with a six-foot trench and coils of barbed wire backed with fifteen-foot steel mesh. On the other side of the fence, it called for a "60 to 70 foot" graded road followed by another fifteen-foot fence, and more concertina wire.[99] Video cameras would also be installed. Simcox issued an ultimatum to President Bush demanding that he "declare a state of emergency and deploy the National Guard and military reserves" on April 19, 2006, or by Memorial Day weekend at the latest. He warned that if President Bush did not, "We're going to break ground and we're going to start helping landowners to build a double layer security fence along their properties."[100] His threat, it could be argued, worked since on May 15 President Bush pledged to deploy 6,000 members of the National Guard to assist the U.S. Border Patrol along the U.S.–México border.

In a matter of a few weeks, the MCDC "border fence" project generated thousands of dollars. By May 9 MCDC had received some $175,000 in donations and by May 28, that amount increased to $380,000. Realizing that he had struck gold, several weeks later Simcox announced that MCDC's fundraising goal for a seventy-mile border fence was $55 million. On Memorial Day, "Fence-Gate" was born. In no time, controversy and criticism from a number of sources among NAMM entities became public over the accounting of MCDC's finances. The issue opened questions regarding all the donations collected since April of 2005. Some NAMM leaders such as Glenn Spencer of the American Border Patrol viewed it as a "scam." In an Internet communiqué sent by the Texas Minutemen, part of the MP, Spencer wrote:

> Thousands of Americans have donated hundreds of thousands, if not millions of dollars, to build a fence on the border to stop illegal aliens. One man mortgaged his home and donated $120,000 that otherwise would have gone to Disabled American Citizens. Chris Simcox continues to sell the plan as an Israeli-style fence when in fact the only thing built is a five-strand barbed wire livestock fence that a rancher says won't keep illegals out.

He was also quoted saying, "I have warned from the beginning not to donate money to any such effort until the promoters produce a building permit that includes the specifications as being sold by those promoters."[101] By July several of MCDC's top officers had quit and others threatened to quit over the financial accounting crisis.

They argued that the first section of the fence built omitted trenching and did not match the Israeli-Gaza style fence described earlier by Simcox. Simcox quickly responded to the growing criticisms and questions regarding contributions, volunteers, and timelines. He explained that the costs for the border fence that included barbed wire, concertina wire, and vehicle barriers on the Ladd ranch ran approximately $17,000.[102]

In July, pressured by the escalating Fence-Gate crisis, Simcox released financial records of MCDC's Minuteman PAC, Inc., which he chaired. Registered with the Federal Election Commission and required by law to file periodic financial reports, on July 13 the first of these reports revealed that at this point it had received $214,015 in donations and had disbursed $97,076. The report also indicated only $5,000 had been used for campaign contributions. The greatest portion of Minutemen PAC expenditures, $87,432, was spent on direct-mail fund-raising and advertising.[103]

The conservative *Washington Times* came out with a stinging article entitled "Minutemen Not Watching Over Funds," by Jerry Seper, who wrote, "A growing number of Minutemen Civil Defense Corps leaders and volunteers are questioning the whereabouts of hundreds of thousands, perhaps millions, of dollar donations collected in the past 15 months, challenging the organization's leadership over financial accountability." The donations were funneled through a Virginia-based charity, the Declaration Alliance Foundation, headed by ultra-conservative Alan Keyes. There were also public accusations from volunteers who participated in MCDC's border patrols who alleged that Simcox had never fulfilled his promise to provide financial support for the purchase of equipment and supplies. Seper reported that Simcox during an interview revealed that MCDC had received an estimated $1.6 million in donations collected by Keyes's Declaration Alliance, and that of that amount, $600,000 had been donated specifically for the construction of the border fence. Simcox also reported that some $160,000 had been spent during the last two months on border-watch operations.

Adding to the growing controversy was that the expenses alleged by Simcox could not be independently verified. He never produced a financial statement for September as he had publicly promised. He unequivocally denied the accusations. In an effort to defuse the situation Simcox reported that an auditor had been secured and that a financial audit would be delivered to the Internal Revenue Service by November 15.[104] Adding to his growing financial/political problems was the open declaration by Gilchrist disavowing any business dealings with Simcox or MCDC.

The audit reported that MCDC had spent nearly $450,000 in the last year for volunteers to patrol the U.S.–México border. This was $31,000 more than collected in donations and registration fees. The report also listed expenditures of nearly $285,000, or 63 percent, for program management and operating expenses, such as travel expenditures, salaries, educational materials, and office expenses. Some $145,000 or about 32 percent went for MCDC's fund-raising programs. Only $20,000 or 5 percent was actually spent on field supplies and equipment for the volunteers who did the border watches. The audit concluded that the total amount collected in donations was significantly less than the $1.6 million Simcox had claimed earlier.[105] The report did absolutely nothing to resolve or mitigate the escalating attacks on Simcox.

The "Fence-Gate scandal" continued to be a major headache for Simcox in 2007, since up to May MCDC had built only eleven miles of fence. This continued to fan allegations of fraud directed at Simcox by a number of sources within NAMM. In May a number of prominent anti-immigrant leaders across the country blasted Simcox and accused him of being a charlatan, a sellout, and a traitor to their cause. Coalition for Immigration Reform (CCIR) leader Barbara Coe said, "Simcox doesn't seem to know that his days on the Minuteman gravy train [have] ended."[106] Other former allies openly criticized him, including MP leader Jim Gilchrist, American Border Patrol leader Glenn Spencer, former MCDC field team chief Joe McCutchen, Americans for Mass Deportation founder Liz DeMarco, and SOS group leader Joseph Turner. Spencer in May wrote, "Chris Simcox and the Declaration Alliance are continuing to raise funds to build a border fence to stop illegal aliens that has not been built and cannot be built. If this isn't fraud, we don't know what is."[107] SOS leader Turner said, "Simcox was a nobody until Gilchrist made him a somebody. And this is how he repays Gilchrist."[108] In mid-May 2007 Simcox again refuted the allegations made against him. He conducted a purge of MCDC and rejected a call for a MCDC board meeting on May 19 by disgruntled MCDC leaders who he had perceived had planned the "palace revolt." Simcox fired three national officers peremptorily, one regional leader, and fourteen of MCDC's twenty-seven state leaders.[109] Up to the end of 2007 the "Fence-Gate scandal" continued to plague Simcox and MCDC and was a divisive wedge issue among NAMM leaders and entities.

During the summer months of 2007, MCDC momentarily joined other NAMM groups in the struggle to defeat the Senate's Border Security and Immigration Reform Act of 2007. Their opposition was grounded on a provision that included a guest worker program. In numerous communications sent by MCDC and at press events people were exhorted to call or e-mail senators in mass numbers to not approve it, which proved to be successful in defeating the measure. Overall, MCDC as a nativist militia had lost momentum and its status was precarious at best.

GILCHRIST'S MP ORGANIZING ACTIVITIES

Gilchrist's MP organizing during 2006 and 2007 consisted of dealing with a number of anti-immigrant related activities and conducting border surveillance. During the first four months of 2006, Gilchrist spent a lot of time organizing MP in California. In January 2006, he and his MP volunteers in California protested in Costa Mesa in support of having the local police enforce immigration laws. The City Council voted of 3 to 2 to have forty officers of the Costa Mesa Police Department trained to enforce immigration laws, a function supposedly of the federal government. While Gilchrist was given ample time to speak in favor of said action, pro-migrant rights activists were denied the opportunity to speak. In fact, when the leader of the Tonantzin Collective, Coyotl Tezcalioca, attempted to speak, the mayor had the police forcibly remove him from the city council chambers.[110]

Regarding another local issue, that same month in Laguna Beach, California MP was denied a parade permit that would have allowed it to participate in the city's parade. In response, MP filed a lawsuit that argued that its free-speech rights had been violated. The suit charged that some groups within the parade association adhered to antiwar and pro-immigrant philosophies and ardently opposed MP's politics, philosophy, and activities. Prior to their request, Gilchrist and MP volunteers conducted anti-*jornalero* (day laborer) protests in Laguna Beach. As a result, the organizers of the annual Patriot's Parade refused MP participation on the grounds that they violated the parade's twenty-five-year-old bylaws that excluded "religious or political entries."[111] As it struggled in Laguna Beach, MP in Vista, California, held a San Diego County-wide protest, which sought to discourage employers from hiring undocumented migrants.[112]

A few MP members along with a few members of Joseph Turner's SOS were active in conducting weekend protests at Home Depots on the issue of day laborers in El Cajon, Lake Forrest, Rancho Cucamonga, Laguna Beach, San Bernardino, and Glendale. Regardless that these protests produced small numbers, in most cases they got good media coverage. In March, a protest event attended by some 200 people was held in Temecula in support of Congressman Sensenbrenner's bill. Gilchrist and Assemblyman Ray Haynes addressed the importance of supporting HR4437. Gilchrist characterized the Saturday rally as a wake-up call to Congress and President Bush on the need to secure the country's borders. In his address, Gilchrist said, "We are a nation governed under the rule of law, not the whim of mobs of illegal aliens who just storm across our borders endlessly."[113] In April, MP held a protest outside the Hyatt Regency Hotel in Irvine, where President Bush spoke to Orange County business leaders about his proposals on undocumented immigration.[114] The protest drew no more than fifty supporters, which continued to demonstrate its lack of massive support.

In response to the great Mexicano/Latino pro-migrant mobilizations of 2006, Gilchrist organized a national ten-day tour of thirteen major cities. The MP tour was an effort to regain the limelight after the huge Mexicano/Latino mobilizations of May 1. The kickoff for the caravan was held at Leimert Park in South Central Los Angeles, an area that previously had been populated predominantly by Blacks, but had become in recent years Latino majority. In speech after speech, he pushed for a greater militarization of the border, strengthening of employer sanctions, and membership and chapter formation for MP. Prior to the event MP organizers anticipated some 400 people, yet only a handful of supporters showed up. Stephen Eichler, MP executive director, qualified the small numbers to the press: "Our power is not putting a million people on the street; our power is putting 10 million people at the voting box."[115] There were more members of the media present than MP supporters.

The send-off caravan rally drew a number of anti-MP protestors, which as usual, were significantly larger numbers than the MP volunteers. The protestors chanted "Minutemen Go Home!" through a bullhorn. Gilchrist responded, "Minutemen, stand your ground. Do not fire unless fired upon, and if its war he wants, then let it begin here."[116] In a strategic move to show that MP had support from Blacks, Ted Hayes, a homeless activist from Los Angeles, spoke out on how immigrants were taking jobs away from Blacks. He went on to say, "Illegal invaders are using our hard-earned civil rights as a key to justify their illegal intrusion across our border. . . . If we allow them to take our civil rights—black people, hear me—they will take our heart and soul out of our heritage."[117] He qualified his nativist posture by explaining that he was not against Latinos, but was hypercritical of the economics that forced immigrants to leave their countries and take jobs that paid impoverished wages that benefited the employers who employed them.[118] Another Black leader, Reverend Jesse Lee Peterson, an MP supporter, said, "Illegal immigration has had and is having a devastating effect on the black community." He added that Black Americans "are being put out of jobs, they're put out of their own homes."[119] The MP caravan traveled from Los Angeles to Phoenix, Arizona; Albuquerque, New México; Abilene, Texas; Crawford, Texas; Little Rock, Arkansas; Memphis and Nashville, Tennessee; Montgomery, Alabama; Atlanta, Georgia; Richmond, Virginia, and Washington, D.C. At most of their stops rallies were held and petitions were circulated. Although the crowds were small they managed to get significant media coverage.

In response to the great pro-migrant May 1 march and boycott, Gilchrist, his MP followers, and Hayes countered with a march in downtown Los Angeles in the Broadway Latino commercial area. The route of the march followed that of the March 25 one that drew 1 million. The march was a disaster, for it drew only sixty persons: forty were Whites who belonged to MP and SOS and the other twenty were Black. It failed miserably in its efforts to demonstrate that MP included a White/Black alliance. A few hundred pro-migrant protestors yelled, "Racists go home," and "Why are you here to provoke us?" Police stepped in to separate the two groups and arrested four anti-MP protestors. Gilchrist commented to the press, "We are not surprised by the people's reaction, we simply want to send a message to the local, state and federal governments that it is necessary to secure our borders and then after that we can dialogue on a guest worker program." Ted Hayes told the press, "For my part, my [Black] community has experienced humiliations, beatings, assassinations, everything in the struggle for civil rights, but for what?" As before, he stressed that the new struggle was against the 'undocumented invasion.'[120] Once again MP exposed its inability to mobilize large numbers of people, yet managed to secure extensive media coverage.

During the rest of 2006, MP volunteers in collaboration with SOS continued a number of local protest activities. In July, MP and SOS held another extremely small march in Hollywood, which resulted in four anti-MP protestors being roughed up and arrested by police.[121] Lending support to MP was California Governor Schwarzenegger during a visit to Lynwood. The trip was intended to strengthen his ties with the Mexicano/Latino communities; yet paradoxically, he issued a strong statement of support for NAMM.[122] The next month, MP and SOS, among other nativist organizations, initiated a new round of protests against day laborers in several communities, mainly in southern California. In August, in Temecula about sixty MP supporters, organized by a new nativist group, Citizens for a Secure America (CASA) held a protest rally in an area of Old Town known for day laborer activity.[123] In Maywood some seventy or so MP and SOS supporters protested the city's decision to declare the city a "sanctuary city" for undocumented migrants. Waiting for them, however, at the city hall were some 200 pro-migrant advocates. No one was arrested, but the tensions were extremely high and there were some acts of violence.[124] Four cars belonging to MP volunteers were vandalized. They were keyed, tires were slashed, windows were broken, and they were painted with the expletive "fuck you." Anti-MP protestors jumped the fence, surrounded the post office, and took down the U.S. flag and raised México's flag.[125]

In September, in a similar situation, they protested against National City's decision to become a "sanctuary city." Pro-sanctuary supporters numbered some 400, while MP and SOS protestors were around 100. Police kept the two crowds apart. Both waived placards and flags, with the difference being that MP opponents were waving U.S. and Mexican flags. Neither Mayor Inzunza, who was under fire on a number of alleged charges of corruption, nor other city council members attended the event. An MP protestor was arrested for kicking a San Diego sheriff's deputy, which angered the MP protestors.[126]

At the national level, during the summer months of 2006, MP announced Operation Sovereignty. The eight-week border surveillance effort was to work jointly with the Texas Minutemen and the American Border Patrol. It was timed to run from 9/11 through November 7, which was election day. MP anticipated the participation of some 200 to 300 volunteers patrolling the El Paso sector and 800 to 1,000 patrolling the Laredo sector.[127] Its objectives were to show the commitment of the three militias to secure the border and to encourage the enforcement of U.S. immigration, labor, and tax laws.[128]

Operation Sovereignty was kicked off on September 11 in Laredo with a small rally. Most volunteers were armed; carried binoculars, night vision goggles, and lawn chairs; some had heat and motion sensors; and some wore camouflaged fatigues or khakis and military boots—in short, their image was that of an armed militia. In his address at the rally Gilchrist said, "It's not our job to engage in law enforcement. It's our job as a neighborhood watch to help law enforcement because the U.S. deliberately, by design, deprived them of funding they need to carry out their jobs."[129] Volunteers were reminded that they were to abide by the MP's policy of "observe and report." Anti-MP protestors showed up at the rally, and while there was yelling from both sides, police maintained order. Operation Sovereignty failed to draw the large numbers Gilchrist and others had predicted. Only 200 to 400 volunteers showed, paying their $50 for a background check. Most of their activity was limited to patrolling on private property and/or ranches contiguous to the border around the El Paso and Laredo areas.

Increasing problems, conflict, and trouble seemed to follow Gilchrist. Increasingly he became a target of protests by pro-migrant activists. In October 2006, invited to speak by the Columbia University Republicans, he was rousted by protesting students, forcing him to terminate his speech. Prior to the event he was met by hundreds of protesting students who carried signs with messages, such as "Minute-Klan," "Get the Knell Out of New York," and "The Minutemen Are Not Our America." Upon starting his speech, student leader Karina Garcia, political chair of the Chicano Caucus at Columbia University, interrupted Gilchrist and began to argue with him. Just then two students rushed from behind the stage toward Gilchrist and unrolled a banner that read in Spanish, English, and Arabic, "No One is Illegal." This led to a rush of some two dozen students to the stage. Campus security was overwhelmed; they knocked over the lectern, and Gilchrist fell back, smashing his glasses.

No one was arrested, but the incident made the national news. The student protestors in a released statement explained that "we peacefully occupied the stage and spoke ourselves. Our peaceful protest was violently attacked by members of the college Republicans and their supporters. . . . The Minutemen are not a legitimate voice in the debate on immigration. They are a racist, armed militia who have declared open hunting season on immigrants." Gilchrist's response to the incident was that Columbia University was "a gutter school. The students [were] not being taught how to learn but how to hate . . . It is a shame that we cannot discuss the issues."[130] The issue got media coverage and resonated nationwide.

The year 2007 was a year of decline for Gilchrist, MP, and NAMM. In February 2007, Gilchrist became the target of a "coup" by MP board members Barbara Coe, Marvin Stewart, and Deborah Courtney. In late January, they met and informally decided to fire Gilchrist. Three days later, the three met with Gilchrist and informed him that he was terminated as MP's president. According to *Los Angeles Times* reporter Jennifer Delson, "The story behind the vote to dismiss America's most famous anti-illegal immigrant fighter contains allegations of hubris and missing money, jealousy, backstabbing, and extremism."[131] Just a few months before, Coe had criticized Simcox for fraud. She now accused her close ally of the same charge. Coe accused Gilchrist of not being able to account for some $750,000, which allegedly was missing from MP accounts. The three also publicly accused him of embezzling $13,000 from MP funds to pay for his own legal fees and also of diverting $400,000 in donations to MP for his congressional campaign and to promote his book on MP. They retained control of MP membership lists, office equipment, and stationery, but control of the funds came into dispute. Gilchrist reacted by claiming that MP had been hijacked, denied any wrongdoing, and rejected unequivocally all their charges.[132]

In seeking to solidify their control of MP, the three filed papers with the State of Delaware showing that Stewart was MP's new president and Courtney was the treasurer. The office of Delaware's secretary of state informed them that no one but Gilchrist could legally make such changes. In the legal conflict that ensued this became a point of contention, since when he incorporated MP Gilchrist had listed himself as the only board member. Public documents showed that Gilchrist listed Coe, Stewart, and Courtney merely in an advisory capacity. By late February, Gilchrist went on the legal offensive and filed a lawsuit alleging that they had illegally fired him, misallocated MCDC's funds, and commandeered his website.[133] He also waged a public relations battle, claiming MP had been "hijacked" and seeking to galvanize support from those within NAMM.

In late March, Orange County Superior Court Judge Randell Wilkinson heard the arguments about who should control MP. Gilchrist refused the judge's recommendation to resolve the disagreements through intermediaries and instead sought to secure a temporary restraining order precluding control of MP by the three coup leaders. Gilchrist said he could not deal with people who had betrayed him to the FBI and Internal Revenue Service. "I gave a long leash to people, and they got carried away with power. I really question their motives." Representing the three board members, attorney Jim Lucey said, "We're willing to do whatever it takes to preserve the Minutemen Project. This is all about Jim Gilchrist and his ego."[134]

On March 6, Coe abruptly resigned from the MP board under intense pressure by pro-Gilchrist supporters from within her own nativist entity, California Coalition for Immigration Reform (CCIR).[135] Judge Wilkinson rejected Gilchrist's request that he be granted immediate and sole control of MP. The ruling left MP in a leadership limbo. The judge also placed restrictions on the three mutinying board members: they were prohibited from spending donations and could not use MP stationery with Gilchrist's signature.[136] The judge's writings on the case suggested that MP was headed for receivership. In April Gilchrist petitioned the court to have the lawsuit dropped because it could have led to a judge appointing an independent party to control MP's finances. In late April he incorporated a new organization in place of MP. He named it Jim Gilchrist's Minuteman Project (JGMP). Marvin Stewart, the new MP president, accused Gilchrist of "spinning lies." On the issue of Gilchrist's JGMP, he said, "There is already one and I'm the president."[137] In May, MP was unable to effectively continue in its anti-immigrant/Mexicano organizing. While Congress debated immigration reform, MP and its leader were too embroiled in the "politics of self-destruction" to respond effectively.

Thus by late 2007 both MP and MCDC were beset by the "politics of self-destruction" characterized by deep divisions, scandals, and a diminishing base of support and membership, and dwindling resources. MP was politically neutralized and Gilchrist's new JGMP was politically wobbly and not really operational. It remained for the most part a paper organization led by a desperate egocentric. For Gilchrist, like Simcox, his nativist national leadership status was in decline beset by issues, scandals, and organizational problems. Overall, by 2007 many militias and vigilante groups were in a state of decline.

CHAPTER 8

Militias, Anti-Immigrant Hate Groups, and Nativism on the Rise (2005–2007)

While the Minuteman Project (MP) and Minuteman Civil Defense Corps (MCDC) by 2007 experienced an implosion, the nativist anti-migrant movement (NAMM) from 2005 to 2007 was far from moribund. In fact, during these years, it experienced considerable growth with the participation of other nativist entities. While by the end of 2007, both MP and MCDC were floundering; nevertheless, neither one was completely defunct. The Barnett Boys and nativist militias like American Border Patrol, among others, that operated from 1999 to 2004 in southern Arizona were still functional. Nationwide a myriad of nativist anti-immigrant militias, organizations, and hate groups were also on the rise. As they increased so did NAMM's momentum that was more and more being driven by the pervasive nativist White Anglo-Saxon Protestant (WASP) ethos. Fueling their drive was the dramatic demographic transformation of the United States (U.S.) by way of the re-Mexicanization of Aztlán and its Latinoization and "browning." This "White fear contagion" helped multiply the number of anti-immigrant hate groups forming throughout the country. The myriad of vigilante, militia, and hate groups that impelled NAMM as an extremist nativist movement all agreed on one goal—the country's preservation of White hegemony at whatever the cost.

This chapter examines the incessant Latino demographic transformation and its continued impact on Arizona's rancher vigilantes and other than MP and MCDC militias from 2005–2007. It profiles NAMM's leading anti-immigrant and hate groups, intellectuals, and media commentators, and purports that nativism in 2007 was on the rise.

The Re-Mexicanization Intensifies

LATINO DEMOGRAPHIC TRANSFORMATION

NAMM from 2005 to 2007 was fueled by the re-Mexicanization of Aztlán and the Latinoization and "browning" of the U.S. The results of the U.S. Census adjusted census report for 2005 revealed that Mexicano and Latino demographics had increased significantly. In 2005 the U.S. population was at 296.4 million, and Latinos made up 42.7 million, or 14.4 percent, of the country's total. The country's population from July 1, 2004, to July 1, 2005, grew by some 2.8 million, of which nearly half were Latinos. While minorities increased in population, Whites decreased to 198.4 million and comprised 66.9 percent of the country's population. Latinos remained not only the country's largest ethnic minority, but also the fastest growing. Blacks were the second largest with 39.7 million, followed by Asians with 14.4 million, and native peoples with 4.5 million.

In October 2006 the Census Bureau report verified that the country was becoming increasingly ethnically and racially diverse. Demographically it was significant because the 300 millionth resident of the U.S. was a Mexicana baby, Catalina Meza, born in Los Angeles.[1] The Latino population reached a high of 44.3 million, meaning that it comprised 15 percent of the country's total population and one of every two persons added to the country's population between July 1, 2005, and July 1, 2006, was Latino. During the one-year period, Latinos increased by some 1.4 million.[2] Between July 2005 and July 2006, they experienced a growth rate of 3.4 percent. Asians were second with a growth rate of 3.2 percent, followed by Blacks with 1.3 percent, and Whites with 0.3 percent. One out of three or 100.7 million U.S. residents were "people of color."[3] A year later, the Latino population increased to 46 million and comprised 15.2 percent of the nation's total population. Adding Puerto Rico's 4 million, Latinos in 2007 made up over 50 million.

At the state and local levels, the Census Bureau reported in 2006 that 48 percent of the Latino population lived in California and Texas. In the former state Latinos increased to 13.1 million of the state population or a little over 36 percent, whereas in the latter state Latinos increased to 8.4 million and comprised 36 percent of the total population. New México had the highest percentage of Latinos at 44 percent. Arizona's Latino population increased to 29 percent. Indicative of the ongoing diaspora was that even several Southern and Midwest cities that ten or twenty years before had few if any Latinos, by 2007 had appreciable numbers. Throughout Aztlán numerous cities and counties experienced the browning effects of its re-Mexicanization. In Los Angeles County theLatino population of nearly 5 million made up 50 percent of its total populace. It had the largest Latino population of any county in the U.S.

The catalysts of Latino population growth continued to be undocumented and legal migration. Both accounted for the dramatic growth of the Latino demographic transformation. In 2005 about 12 percent of the U.S. population was foreign born. This was still below the high peak of 1910 when 14.7 percent of the people in the country were foreign born.[4] Hence, the immigration rate was higher during the early 1900s than it was at the close of 2007. In 2006, the Census Bureau reported that the country's undocumented migrant population numbered some 12 million and by 2007 the estimate was closer to 13 million. Some nativist leaders, such as James Gilchrist, head of the Minuteman Project (MP) in 2006 superinflated the preceding figures to 30 million. He alleged that some 10,000 crossed the U.S.–México border every day, which annually totaled some 4 to 5 million.[5] The Census Bureau in 2006 reported that Latinos continued to be the fastest growing ethnic group. Annually, it was estimated by the Pew Hispanic Research Center that undocumented migration from Latin America, including México, to the U.S. numbered 500,000. According to the Migration Policy Institute's figures released in 2007, legal immigration into the U.S. in 2006 increased to 1,266,264, up from 849,807 in 2000 and 1,122,373 in 2005. The highest migrant-sending country in 2006 was México with 173,753, followed by the People's Republic of China with 87,345.

Latino population growth continued to be impacted by high birth rates. The Census Bureau reported that of the Latino population increase of 1.4 million experienced in 2006, some 800,000 was due to natural increase (births minus deaths). The National Center for Health Statistics released their figures, which indicated that the total birth rate by race had risen only for Hispanic women by 2 percent and decreased significantly for non-Hispanic White women by less than 1 percent. High birth rates for Black and Asian women remained unchanged from 2004. According to the report, "births fell 3 percent each for non-Hispanic White and non-Hispanic Black teenagers 15 to 19 years."[6] The Associated Press reported in 2006 that birth rates for Latinas were higher than for Whites and Blacks in the country's southeastern states.[7]

White and Black flight also continued to affect the concentration or density of the Latino population growth. Immigration was changing the demographic face of many cities nationwide. According to Michael Barone in his *Wall Street Journal* article "The Realignment of America" of May 8, 2007, "Americans are now moving out of, not into, coastal California and South Florida, and in very large numbers they're moving out of our largest metro cities." He cites New York, Los Angeles, San Francisco, San Jose, San Diego, Chicago, Miami, and Washington as cities that have experienced White fight and immigrants moving in. Particularly, in southern California, numerous local cities experienced not only White flight, but also Black flight. Thus, the demographic effects of both the "re-Mexicanization of Aztlán" and "Latinoization or Browning" of the United States in great part fed and impelled the nativist politics of Arizona's rancher vigilante, militias, and that of a plethora of anti-immigrant and hate groups.

Arizona's Armed Rancher Vigilantes and Militias

OLD VERSUS NEW MILITIAS

While anti-immigrant activity swelled throughout the country, Arizona and its border sector of the Cactus Curtain (U.S.–México Border) continued to be the locus of rancher vigilante and militia activity. While these groups' level and intensity of anti-immigrant activity reached their zenith in 2005, by 2007 their movement had diminished appreciably. This was evident by the decline of the nativist militia Ranch Rescue. Crippled by the departure of its main leader, Jack Foote, and plagued by internal problems, by 2005 it had faded from the nativist militia political landscape. The lessening of vigilante and militia activity was illustrated by their diminished media coverage and their decreased border surveillance activity.

The Barnett Boys, under a legal siege, battled a number of civil law suits that decreased their vigilante patrol activities. The Ron Morales deer hunting incident that occurred in October 2004 continued to haunt them. Spearheaded by Border Action Group and the Southern Poverty Law Center (SPLC), a civil suit filed in November 2004 by attorney Jesus Romo Vejar asked for $200,000 in damages. Facing charges that included assault, false imprisonment, negligence, and intentional infliction of emotional stress on the Morales family on November 14, 2006, the Barnett Boys went to trial. The trial included emotional as well as intense testimony from all the Morales family including the three children, psychologists, land surveyors, a sheriff's deputy, an Arizona Game and Fish employee, and other bow hunters who had also been physically assaulted and verbally attacked with racist obscenities by Barnett.[8]

On November 22, 2006, an eight-member jury in Cochise County Superior Court issued its verdict in the case of *Ronald Morales et al. vs. Roger Barnett.* Although the jury found Roger Barnett only partially to blame for the incident, he was assessed a total of $210,000 in damages and was directed to pay the principal plaintiffs, the Morales family, $98,750 for the terrorist incident.[9] Speaking after the verdict, Attorney Vejar announced that County Attorney Ed Rheinheimer had told the Morales family that if the jury ruled against Barnett he would consider filing criminal charges. Vejar told the *Bisbee Herald Review,* "It's obvious that the civil jury saw something, and so we're going to take a good look at the jury's findings."[10] Three important aspects of the Morales suit were: (1) as of spring 2007, Rheinheimer had yet to file criminal charges against Barnett[11]; (2) all members of the Morales family were U.S. citizens; and (3) the Morales suit was a major blow against Arizona's armed rancher vigilantism.

In January 2007 Roger Barnett again became the subject of an investigation by the Cochise County Sheriff's Department. Five weeks after the Morales verdict, he got into a heated confrontation with two medics who had tried to provide medical aid to an injured undocumented Mexicano migrant that the Border Patrol had apprehended on Barnett's ranch. The migrant was carrying marijuana in his backpack when he was intercepted by Barnett, who set three dogs on him. In trying to escape the dogs, the migrant fell and injured his knee. Border patrol agents arrived and called paramedics. After the medics picked up the injured migrant, the medics alleged that Barnett flagged them down and demanded to be let into the ambulance to examine the patient's shoes to ascertain if they matched the footprints of the person he had been tracking earlier on his property. The medics refused and Barnett, armed with a pistol, became irate and abusive.[12] Paramedic Robert Vega filed a criminal complaint against him. Barnett accused Vega of "fucking lying" and said the incident described by Vega "never happened."[13] When asked to give his account of what had happened Barnett refused to do so. Two months later, Cochise County Attorney Ed Rheinheimer refused to press criminal charges against Barnett for lack of evidence. For the second time in weeks, Roger Barnett had been legally protected from criminal charges by Rheinheimer.

In 2007, with litigation hanging over their heads, the Barnett Boys decreased their rancher vigilantism. It appeared that after losing the Morales suit and having to pay $98,000, their vigilante activities were more circumspect. This notwithstanding, in 2006 their commitment to vigilante activity was still evident in their claim to the media that since 1999 they had apprehended and turned over to the U.S. Border Patrol nearly 12,000 undocumented migrants.[14]

From 2005 to 2007, Glenn Spencer's American Border Patrol (ABP) was exempt from the "self destructive politics" and decline that had pervaded other nativist militias. From 2002 to 2005, ABP largely refrained from following the modus operandi of other nativist militias of organizing armed surveillance patrols of the Arizona–México border. Instead ABP chose to document border intrusions, through the use of cameras, sensors, "hawkeye" spotters, and (unmanned Ariel Vehicle Systems (UAVS) to identify undocumented migrants crossing into Arizona. ABP outfitted three model airplanes equipped with cameras, which were designed to home in on ground sensors triggered by anyone walking in the designated areas of the desert. Once identified, the intruders were videotaped when possible and reported to the Border Patrol.

ABP continued to strive to be a sophisticated, high-tech militia. It deployed a border patrol comprised of a few volunteers that went into the desert areas equipped with a high-tech camera that provided live color video that was sent live over the Internet.[15] Spencer replaced the UAV model airplanes with a Cessna aircraft to monitor the border. The aircraft, equipped with a high-tech camera and infrared equipment, sent live video over the Internet. ABP, as a militia, instead of having armed militia units, formed a tactical operations unit called TAC-OPS, comprised of highly skilled technicians and pilots.

Up to 2007, ABP evolved into NAMM's air force. Spencer's ABP TAC-OPS unit consistently conducted aerial surveillance patrols. While its base of operations was its secluded 104-acre ranch on the border near Naco, Arizona, its TAC-OPS unit had collaborated with other nativist militias in Arizona and Texas, conducting coordinated land and air border surveillance operations. In 2006 it launched its biggest aerial operation, called Operation BEEF (Border Enforcement Evaluation First). It entailed Spencer piloting ABP's Cessna TU206 airplane from El Paso to San Diego. At an altitude of 500 feet, every inch of the Cactus Curtain was videotaped with high definition cameras. Strategically, Operation BEEF monitored the influx of undocumented migrants that crossed into the U.S. It also monitored the U.S. government's construction of the 700-mile-long border fence mandated by the Secure Fence Act of 2006[16] and the border fence under construction on private properties by Simcox's MCDC.

Between August 13 and September 3, 2007, ABP conducted an aerial survey of 550 miles of border. The areas covered were primarily along the Arizona and California–México border. The ABP survey report was hypercritical of the Department of Homeland Security (DHS), particularly of Secretary Michael Chertoff. He was accused of deceiving the public by promising that by September some 150 miles of fence construction along critical areas of the border would be completed. On September 5, 2007, ABP released its aerial survey and charged that DHS had failed to live up to its promise of the 550-mile border fence.

ABP's main criticism was that DHS had failed to keep its fence construction schedule and that much of what had been constructed was inadequate in halting the influx of the migrant exodus. In particular, they alluded to the 16.5-mile sections that were still under construction. Another related concern was the vehicle barriers. Spencer remarked, "We think the vehicle barriers that they're putting up are pretty ineffective."[17] In October, Spencer exhorted DHS to condemn and level all land contiguous to the border fence and create a "buffer of land." He also reported that ABP was in the process of raising the money to construct a viable border fence to illustrate how they should be built.[18] Apparently, ABP, long critical of Simcox's MCDC Fence-Gate scandal as noted previously, by October 2007 sought to venture into the lucrative marketplace of border fence construction.

In 2007 Spencer's ABP continued to have a high media profile. He periodically made television and radio news program appearances, including on CNN's nativist Lou Dobbs program. Spencer continued to gain support from divergent nativist vigilante/hate groups and other militias, and in particular from Roger Barnett, James Gilchrist, and Congressman Tom Tancredo. The Anti-Defamation League reported that Spencer had attended numerous events organized by supremacists and racists.[19] In 2007 while Gilchrist's MP was being hijacked by a "board coup," Spencer courted and gave support to a new nativist militia, Patriots' Border Alliance.

Spencer utilized ABP's website, www.americanborderpatrol.com, as an effective medium for nativist anti-immigrant/Mexicano propaganda and political education. By late 2007, the ABP website had recorded some 22 million hits. In 2006 and 2007 he used the ABP website to advance the "nativist legislative surge" at all levels, especially at the federal level, where he zealously supported HR4437 and called for the defeat of the Senate's reform legislation. His xenophobic, nativist, and racist politics were illustrated in the potpourri of nativist, anti-immigrant/Mexicano/Latino articles posted daily on his website. Spencer in October 2007 issued a call on the ABP website for financial support in order to maintain it, since due to insufficient funding the website was in danger of closing down.

Throughout 2007 Spencer and ABP came under increasing attack by pro–migrant rights forces and others as well. In February 2007, fearing for his life and reprisals from drug cartels, he put out a call for more support for ABP in order to protect its employees and volunteers. In May shots were fired at the ABP headquarters. Cochise County Sheriff's deputies arrived and took a report, but no one was ever arrested.[20] At the close of 2007, ABP appeared to be solvent and active in propagating its antimigrant and anti-Mexicano message.

RISE OF A NEW NATIVIST MILITIA

Out of the burning ashes of Simcox's MCDC, a new nativist militia was formed in 2007. Several former leaders of MCDC, angry over Simcox's failure to provide an accounting of allegedly hundreds of thousands of dollars, perhaps millions, formed the Patriots' Border Alliance (PBA). The leadership base of PBA was comprised of persons who had been fired by Simcox for allegedly planning his overthrow. These included former MCDC Executive Director Bob Wright; Bill Irwin, former national operations officer; Greg Thompson, former national training coordinator; Stacey O'Connel, former key organizer; and the former MCDC Arizona state chapter director among a few others. Glenn Spencer and ABP from the onset publicly supported its formation.

PBA's major purpose, according to Wright, who became PBA's main leader, was that "PBA is committed to carrying on with the mission of fighting illegal immigration in a form of protest, the form of continued border watch efforts.

This will be our mission, and we will succeed."[21] In an information piece put out by PBA's leadership in July of 2007 he described its role: "A group of American patriots have formed a new alliance to see the borders and ports of the United States secure." It further explained its function as a nativist militia:

> [PBA] was formed for providing information and documentation through civilian border watches, day labor site watches and illegal immigration informational rallies in various locations, illustrating the lack of border security and the effects of illegal immigration on the nation as a whole and critical infrastructure of.[22]

On August 3–5, PBA volunteers conducted their first border surveillance operation at the New México–México border. Two weeks later, it conducted its second, designated as Operation Gatekeeper, around Palominas, Arizona. According to *Herald/Review* reporter Gentry Braswell, "Some 30 of the alliance's weekend-long 'Operation Gatekeeper,' [and] virtually all of the . . . participants told [the] alliance's organizers that they had experience with this kind of civilian patrol by working with similar-minded groups like the Minuteman Civil Defense Corps, the American Border Patrol and the Texas Minuteman."[23] Its policy for the apprehension of undocumented migrants differed from other nativist militias in that volunteers were not to have any direct contact with undocumented migrants. If sighted, volunteers were to report them to the U.S. Border Patrol. PBA kicked off with a marketing blitz in July and August, but after its inaugural patrols, little information was available as to its activities; consequently its status was in question.

Other Nativist Organizations

HATE GROUPS INCREASE

Several nativist organizations, not previously examined, and hate groups, also formed the organizational ranks of NAMM. They were characterized by an ultra extremist nativism that was racist and grounded in white supremacy. Like ABP and PBA their extremist anti-immigrant postures were a rancorous reaction to both the re-Mexicanization of Aztlán and the Latinoization and "browning" of the U.S. During the spring of 2007 the SPLC released a report that warned of the significant increase of 5 percent in the number of anti-immigrant hate groups. In one year the number of hate groups had increased by forty-one—from a total of 803 identified in 2006 to 844 in 2007. SPLC attributed their increase to the issue of undocumented migration, which in the country was being perceived as a pressing issue.[24] Every state in the country had at least one hate group.

The Southwest as a region had a significant number: California, sixty-three; Texas, fifty-five; Colorado, thirteen; Nevada, twelve; Arizona, ten; New México, two; Utah, one; and Nevada, twelve.[25]

The following summary is based on the SLPC's categorization of hate groups. One such hate group was the Ku Klux Klan. Initially formed in the late 1860s, in 2005 to 2007 it showed signs of a revival. Although it lacked a national unitary structure, it was comprised of many divergent and competing hate groups that in 2007 numbered 165 chapters. Integral to their racist agenda was their ardent anti-immigrant posture. A second type of hate group was the "Neo-Nazis" that ideologically adhered to fascist beliefs and also espoused an antimigrant agenda; they numbered 191 chapters. A third type was the "White Nationalists" that espoused either White-supremacist or White-separatist ideologies or both and embraced an antimigrant agenda; they numbered 110 groups. A fourth type was the "skinheads" that accounted for 78 chapters. A fifth type was "Christian identity groups" with 102 chapters, which combined Christian religion with racist and anti-Semitic beliefs. A sixth type of hate group was the "Neo-Confederate groups" that sought to rekindle many of racist principles of the antebellum South and accounted for 102 groups. The seventh type was "General hate groups." With seventy-three chapters, they were subdivided into anti-immigrant, antigay, and anti-Holocaust, racist music, and radical traditionalist Catholic groups. The eighth and final type of hate group was "Black separatist groups." They supported nationalist beliefs grounded with tenets of racially based hatred and accounted for some eighty-eight groups.[26] From the preceding hate groups, 144 were identified as nativist extremist groups, which meant they targeted individual immigrants rather than immigration policies. They were active across thirty-nine states with some 100 or so groups formed since April 2006.[27]

The pervasive growth of hate groups was evident also in the U.S. armed forces. Increasingly nativist and violent, some had specifically infiltrated the army and marines. A SPLC report released in July 2006 stated that neo-Nazis and skinheads had successfully infiltrated the U.S. military and that the number could be in the thousands. The SPLC charge was buttressed by an article in the National Alliance magazine *Resistance* that solicited skinheads to join the army and that they demand to be assigned to the infantry. A former Special Forces officer who advised the racist group explained why. "Light infantry is your branch of choice because the coming race war and ethnic cleansing to follow will be very much an infantryman's war. As street brawlers, you will be useless in the coming race war. As trained infantrymen, you will join the ranks of the Aryan warrior brotherhood."[28]

In May 2007, five members of the Alabama Free Militia were arrested for planning a machine-gun attack on Mexicano migrants that resided in the small town of Remlap just north of Birmingham. Prior to the planned attack, the five men on April 20 conducted a scouting of the town.[29] Jim Cavanaugh, Bureau of Alcohol, Tobacco, Firearms and Explosives (ATF) southeastern U.S. regional director, said in reference to the quantity of munitions and arms, "They had enough to outfit a small army." Although the media played down the attack on Mexicanos, the five arrested faced major federal prison sentences.[30]

PROFILE OF OTHER NATIVIST GROUPS

Beyond MP, MCDC, and the aforementioned hate groups were a number of other anti-immigrant-oriented pressure groups. Some had been functional for years prior to the rise of nativist militias and were an integral part of the rise of NAMM. They have been vital contributors to the WASP ethos and the creation of an anti-immigrant/Mexicano political climate. Some of these groups were national and others region-based, and they were in existence before the rise of the rancher vigilantes and nativist militias. For purposes of analysis, the following profile covers what this author considers to be "extremist moderate" to the most "ultraextremist groups." Both types are extremely nativist in their politics and both are perceived as extremist. While the former profess a more tempered or moderate posture, the latter are not only nativist, but are emphatically racist, openly declared White supremacists and, it could be argued, are also fascist.

Federation for American Immigration Reform (FAIR)

At the national level, FAIR was an "extremist moderate" nativist pressure group within NAMM. Incorporated as a nonprofit, public interest, membership pressure group, FAIR was founded in 1979 by John Tanton. It has been known as the premiere nativist pressure group, since as a zealous protagonist it has consistently advocated for restrictionist-oriented immigration reform legislation. In 2007 it was the largest membership nativist organization with a membership base of some 70,000 and numerous supporters nationwide. As its founder, Tanton acted as the self-appointed czar of nativism and architect of anti-immigration organization development. He was credited for financing and helping establish a nationwide network of several anti-immigrant organizations that include Numbers USA and Project USA.

FAIR reflected the nativist, xenophobic, and racist views of its founder Tanton and its leaders. In a 1997 interview, Tanton said that unless the U.S. borders were sealed, it would be overrun by people "defecating and creating garbage and looking for jobs."[31] FAIR's executive director at the time, Dan Stein, warned that certain immigrant groups were engaged in "competitive breeding" aimed at diminishing "white power."[32] As an organization, FAIR blames immigrants for many of the country's social problems, such as poverty, crime, disease, urban sprawl, health care disparities, and inadequate education.

Buttressing the claim that FAIR is racist, Deepa Fernandez argued that "FAIR has received a large portion of its funding from the overtly racist Pioneer Fund."[33] The Center for a New Community, which tracks and monitors White supremacist groups, has described the Pioneer Fund as "a centerpiece in keeping scientific racism alive via the allocation of grants for pseudo-scientific studies."[34] Although FAIR officials have claimed that it severed its ties to the Pioneer Fund, between 1985 and 1994, according to the Institute for the Study of Academic Racism, FAIR received $1.2 million from the organization, which continues to illustrate its racist underpinnings.

Since its inception, FAIR has been at the forefront of proposing blatantly nativist legislation, such as HR4437, which would have criminalized the status of 12 million undocumented immigrants and constructed an iron wall along the Cactus Curtain. Its national focus has allowed it to be active in Washington, D.C., lobbying Congress for restrictionist immigration, as well as in various states supporting anti-immigration legislation such as Proposition 187 in California in 1994, and more recently, Proposition 200 in 2004 in Arizona. From 2005 to 2007, it played a pivotal role in the promotion of the nativist-driven legislation manifested by the passage of a numerous nativist-oriented local and state initiatives, laws, and local ordinances.

California Coalition for Immigration Reform (CCIR)

CCIR was another rather extremist moderate nativist pressure group of NAMM, founded in 1994 in California by nativist Barbara Coe. Since its formation, Coe has used it as an anti-immigrant vehicle. Its genesis was the result of Coe's promotion and support of Proposition 187, which sought to deny children of undocumented migrant parents access to an education and to social and medical services. She claimed that CCIR's paid membership was around 26,000. Coe as the leader of CCIR developed the reputation of being a racist and xenophobic anti-immigrant advocate who referred to Mexicanos as "savages." Like ABP's Glenn Spencer, she claimed that México was conspiring to retake control of Aztlán. She favored the full militarization of the U.S.–México border, and expressed that "globalist" forces were actively advocating the imposition of a new world order.

From the onset in 1994 to 2007, she was active with ABP leader Spencer and MP leader James Gilchrist, among others, in the building of NAMM. Her nativist leadership stature within nativist anti-immigrant circles grew as a result of her involvement in anti-immigrant activities. In 1999, Coe unsuccessfully worked to organize a recall of California Governor Gray Davis due to his anti-187 efforts that led to it being declared by the courts unconstitutional. She accused him of being a communist and called him Governor Gray "Red" Davis. In the last few years, CCIR has put up anti-immigrant billboards along the Arizona–California border, which for example read: "Welcome to California, the Illegal Immigration State. Don't Let This Happen to Your State."[35] The *Denver Post* reported that she was a member of the racist Council of Conservative Citizens, which has called Blacks "a retrograde species of humanity." From 2005 until February 2007 she and two other MP board members initiated the "Gilchrist coup" and then resigned.

American Immigration Control Foundation (AICF)

Another NAMM extremist moderate nativist entity was AICF. Founded in 1983, AICF was not organized as a pressure group, but was incorporated as a nonpartisan 501(c)(3), nonprofit research and educational organization. Funded essentially by private contributions for many years up to 1998, it was funded by the Pioneer Fund for $190,000. AICF's cardinal purpose was to "educate our fellow citizens on the disastrous effects of uncontrolled immigration"[36] Led by President Robert Goldsborough and spokesperson Phil Kent, AICF functioned more as a think tank, and was a strong national protagonist of nativism via its educational mode that professed a restrictionist immigration posture. Its overt and ardent nativist posture was evident on its website, which alleged that immigrants have "sown the seeds of ethnic strife in America." Especially on the issue of Third World immigration, it adhered to a "policy rooted in humanistic pride and the worship of Mammon [a reference to anti-Christian materialism]."[37]

AICF's five cardinal objectives or tenets underscored its nativist anti-immigrant posture. One, it propounded that the federal government should immediately secure the nation's borders, especially with México, from terrorists, drug smugglers, and undocumented migrants. Two, it believed that all undocumented migrants presently in the country should be deported immediately. Three, it called for increased penalties for those who knowingly transport, recruit, solicit, or hire undocumented workers. Four, it advocated that legal immigration into the country be reduced to numbers that would facilitate their assimilation. And, five, it emphatically opposed all amnesty and guest worker program proposals to immigration reform.

AICF used its resources to develop programs and it utilized the media to educate the public and policy makers on the particulars of its anti-immigration agenda. Its staff testified at congressional hearings; organized conferences and events that highlighted Congressman Tancredo, Gilchrist, and MP, among other nativist leaders; and it published and distributed anti-immigrant materials and books.[38] In recent years, AICF collaborated with FAIR and Numbers USA in a million-dollar billboard campaign that blamed immigrants for many of the country's social problems. In 2007 it was active in pressing for restrictionist immigration reform measures that were pro-border enforcement and anti-amnesty and guest worker programs. AICF, armed with resources and staff, was active fanning the fires of NAMM's nativism.

Numbers USA (NUSA)

As an extremist moderate entity founded by Roy Beck in 1997, NUSA was an immigration-reduction, nonprofit, nonpartisan public policy pressure group, which has as its main purpose to reduce the country's annual immigration to pre-1965 levels but without the "country of origin quotas" placed by the Hart-Celler Act of 1965. It was alleged that NUSA was founded not by Beck in 1997, but in 1996 by FAIR's founder John Tanton and that it is part of FAIR's anti-immigrant network of various groups.[39] Based in Arlington, Virginia, it directed lobbing activities in both the executive and legislative branches of the federal government for immigration reduction.

NUSA defined optimal immigration levels as being no more than 200,000 per year and proposed the elimination of both "chain migration" and "diversity immigrant visa lottery." In addition, it engaged in extensive research on the environmental and financial policy impact of the migrant exodus. As Washington editor of *Social Contract*, Beck put out a quarterly journal that published articles written by White nationalists. In 2007, NUSA, like other of NAMM's entities, engaged in heavy lobbying for more restrictionist immigration reform.

Project USA (PUSA)

Another extremist moderate nativist entity was PUSA, founded in 1999. Like NUSA, it is alleged that it was the creation of FAIR's John Tanton, who provided its initial funding, and it formed an integral part of his network of anti-immigrant organizations. On paper, however, Craig Nelsen was PUSA's executive director and was credited with being its founder. He explained that his motivation for starting the organization was the severe problems associated with overpopulation and immigration.[40] As a restrictionist immigration pressure group, PUSA adhered to a rather nationalist and ultraconservative agenda. It advocated: (1) putting an end to undocumented immigration; (2) reducing legal immigration to traditional sustainable levels; and (3) a "ten-year timeout" on immigration, while the country reassessed its immigration policies from a long-term perspective.

As to PUSA's activities, in 2004 in five states it engaged in the production of radio ads and billboards in support of anti-immigrant challengers to Republican and Democrat incumbents.[41] It put up billboards, including in New York, that show a White boy and the words "Immigration is doubling U.S. population in my lifetime. (Please don't do this to us Congress)," which drew harsh criticism from pro-migrant rights groups. On its website, PUSA warned of the dangers of immigration: "We believe there is a very strong possibility that present policy will lead to a balkanized America of hostile and competing ethnic groups."[42]

Save Our State (SOS)

Founded in 2004 in California by Joseph Turner, SOS as a nonprofit 501(c)(3) corporation because of its militant protest tactics can be categorized as an "ultraextremist nativist" entity. Its purpose was to educate "California's citizens about the disastrous effects of illegal immigration in and creating positive change through aggressive activism and advocacy."[43] Using the Internet to recruit and organize direct actions, SOS according to its web forum in 2007 had some 1,000 members. Organizationally, SOS was loosely structured and personality (e.g., Joseph Turner) leadership driven. It lacked a formal hierarchical structure that lacked chapters, standing committees, and so forth. It was comprised largely of unaffiliated at-large members who functioned as a network rather than an organized pressure group.

Although Turner openly rejected extremist racist or neo-Nazi organizations such as the KKK, its politics, protest activities, and the pronouncements of its leader clearly made it an ultraextremist nativist entity. In October of 2006, for example, what appeared on SOS's Web forum echoed Nazi propaganda. One poster suggested that Latino birth should be reined in with "crop dusters spraying birth control powder" and concluded, "STOP BREEDING LIKE RODENTS! YOU'RE RUINING MY COUNTRY!"[44] In addition, Turner was quoted as saying "just because one believes in white separatism that does make them a racist."[45] SOS demonstrations attracted with regularity neo-Nazi and racist skinheads.

SOS adhered to what Turner alluded to as the "transference of pain." SOS's tactics were aggressive, polarizing, and in your face-oriented.[46] They included conflict by using haranguing name calling, using caustic racist expletives on its opponents to where the conflict bordered on violence. In none of the SOS protests did it demonstrate a capacity to draw large numbers of protestors. In most cases, the protests were relatively small, entailing at most a couple of dozen protestors. Some of its activities were organized collaboratively with MP and CCIR, among others.

The first anti-immigrant action that SOS conducted was in December 2004 when Turner announced a boycott of a Home Depot for funding day labor centers on or near their store locations. From then up to 2007, SOS (particularly in Southern California) continued being active, mostly on weekends, picketing Home Depot stores, and protesting the presence of *jornaleros* (day laborers) and those who hire them. In December 2005 Turner, during a Home Depot protest, was charged with battery after a confrontation with a pro-immigrant protester. His assault reaffirmed the SOS leader's violent propensities. Throughout southern California cities such as Victorville, Santa Clarita, Laguna Beach, Glendale, Burbank, San Bernardino, Rancho Cucamonga, and Maywood experienced SOS protests. In most cases, SOS protests drew a larger number of pro-migrant rights counterprotesters. Although Turner repudiated their participation, counter-demonstrators have alleged that several hate groups, such as neo-Nazis, skin-heads, and the KKK, among other White supremacist groups, have participated in SOS's day labor protests, which by 2007 had become increasingly more volatile and susceptible to violence.

In another action, SOS in 2005 protested billboards that advertised KRCA-TV's Spanish language newscast, which displayed the city of Los Angeles skyline with México City's landmark Angel of Independence in the center.[47] As a result of their pressure the billboards were removed. On May 14, 2005, some forty SOS supporters protested at Baldwin Park in front of a publicly displayed artwork that it found to be racially offensive. The inscription read: "This land was Mexican once, was Indian always, and will be again." Turner demanded unsuccessfully from the city that it remove what he perceived to be seditious language on a city monument. Hundreds of counterprotesters showed up; which led the city of Baldwin Park to mobilize scores of riot police. The protest wound up costing the city of Baldwin Park $40,000 in police security.[48]

SOS's anti-immigrant struggle targeted local governments using the weapon of the initiative. Turner in 2006 in the city of San Bernardino introduced a local initiative entitled "Illegal Immigration Act Ordinance." Its provisions banned renters from renting their properties to undocumented migrants, prevented the city from operating day labor centers, denied business permits to businesses that aided and abetted illegal aliens, empowered police to seize the vehicles of employers who solicited undocumented workers for day labor, and required private centers to ensure that day laborers were legal.[49] The measure failed due to a judge's decision because the initiative did not have enough signatures to place the measure before the voters. Turner's unsuccessful measure, however, had a "multiplier contagion" in that efforts to pass similar initiatives and laws quickly spread to other cities nationwide, such as Hazelton, Pennsylvania; Riverside, New Jersey; and Escondido, California.

In March of 2007, SOS in collaboration with MP organized one of its larger statewide protests of around seventy-five demonstrators against a National Alliance for Human Rights march and rally held in San Bernardino. Later that year, after being soundly defeated for a seat on the school board in San Bernardino, Turner next decided to run for city clerk of San Bernardino. Again, he was soundly defeated. SOS's legacy to nativist politics was its pioneering use of the initiative process at the local level as a medium for ethnic cleansing.

Council of Conservative Citizens (CCC)

As an ultraextremist nativist entity, CCC was more extremist and racist than the aforementioned moderate extremist entities. Out of the racist residue of the White Citizens' Council (WCC) that vehemently struggled against desegregation in the 1950s and 1960s, CCC was founded in Atlanta in 1985 by Gordon Baum.[50] At its zenith, WCC attracted some 1 million members. Its membership included powerful political, business, and media elites, but avoided recruiting overt racists such as the Ku Klux Klan into its ranks. The inconsistency of the preceding is that CCC was built on the membership lists, connections, networks, and contacts of its mother entity, the WCC.[51]

CCC's headquarters were located in St. Louis and it had a paid membership of some 15,000.[52] It chapters were scattered both in the South and in the Northeastern parts of the country. During the last few years it played a pivotal leadership role in the anti-immigration political arena, particularly by supporting racist local ordinances, state laws, and federal restrictionist legislation. In response to the arrival of large numbers of undocumented migrants in the South, it organized a number of anti-immigrant direct actions, rallies, pickets, marches, and so forth in such states as South Carolina and Michigan.

Since its beginning, CCC rigorously supported White separatism and opposed racial/ethnic integration and multiculturalism. With an adherence to White Power, its racist views were underscored in its statement of principles. One of its tenets includes the belief that "American people and government should remain European in their composition and character." A second tenet further underscored its unequivocal "opposition to immigration from non-European and non-Western peoples" as it "threatens to transform our nation into a non-European majority in our lifetime." Another tenet clearly suggested that it is homophobic and that it adheres to a patriarchal view of women.[53]

During its first fifteen years existence, CCC experienced several highs as well as lows. On the high side, in its early years, it enjoyed support from of the South's most powerful politicians at all levels of government. The late Lester Maddox, the segregationist former governor of Georgia was a charter member. Increasingly, in the 1990s, it became engaged at all levels of electoral politics, actively supporting racist politicians. It organized numerous events and rallies in support of the issue of flying the Confederate flag. Several prominent Republican politicians, such as Senator Jesse Helms, Senator Trent Lott, and even former House Majority Leader Democrat Dick Gephardt, addressed CCC functions.

One of CCC's political lows occurred in late 1998, when controversy arose as a result of a report by the *Miami Herald* that alleged that numerous southern politicians had dealings with CCC. According to CCC's own *Citizens Informer* newspaper, it had more than twenty state lawmakers, seventeen of them from Mississippi. During the next five years or so, however, it turned into a political high again. The SPLC and the *Miami Herald* tally reported that some thirty-eight federal, state, and local politicians had appeared in CCC events during 2000 to 2004,[54] most of whom were Republican. In 2005 Alabama's George Wallace, Jr. and a number of distinguished southern politicians attended its national conference.

National Organization for European American Rights (NOFEAR)

Founded in January 2000 by the former grand wizard of the Knights of the Ku Klux Klan David Duke, NOFEAR was the replacement for the former White supremacist organization the National Association for the Advancement of White People (NAAWP). As an ultraextremist nativist group, NOFEAR's racist politics reflected those of its founder, David Duke and that of its media director Bruce Allan "Vince" Breeding (alias Vincent Edwards), a long-time member of the National Alliance. In justifying its formation, Duke declared, "European-Americans must band together as a group the same way African-Americans do." Otherwise, he warned, "the European American people will basically be lost as an entity."[55] NOFEAR's cardinal purpose was to "defend the civil rights of European-Americans."[56] Its orientation was an admixture of anti-Semitic, extremist White nationalist and ultranativist beliefs, which bordered on fascism.

During 2005 to 2007, it claimed it had members in every state and had some sixteen active chapters. While NOFEAR had various interests, immigration was its priority issue and interest of concern. Duke, in his book *My Awakening*, on the issue of immigration wrote:

> More than 95 percent of both legal and illegal immigration into the United States is non-white. Because of the way immigration law is structured, the highest-skilled nations on earth—those of Europe—are allowed only a tiny percentage of immigrants, while the third world nations such as México are dumping their chaff onto American shores at the highest rate in history.[57]

Since NOFEAR's founding, Duke actively both nationally and internationally, especially in Europe, pressed its White supremacist agenda. Within the context of U.S. nativist politics, it collaborated with other extremist groups, like the National Alliance and Council of Conservative Citizens, in a number of anti-immigrant activities.

National Alliance (NA)

Still another ultraextremist nativist organization was the National Alliance (NA), founded in 1967 by Dr. William L. Pierce. He was a former physics professor and authored the controversial book *The Turner Diaries*, a futuristic novel that plots a White revolution in the U.S. Based in Hillsboro, West Virginia, NA was a White nationalist and separatist organization that openly embraced fascist and extremist nativist views. On the latter, in order to rationalize and justify its White separatist position, as issues it used the country's changing demographics due to immigration, especially from Latin America, and also decreasing White birth rates.[58] Membership in NA was contingent upon being a person of purely White or of non-Jewish ancestry. In Las Vegas, NA's nativist posture was evident in a recruitment billboard: "Stop Immigration. Join the National Alliance." In advancing its nativist politics, it enjoyed good relations with ABP's Glenn Spencer, which gives credence to the argument that most right-wing nativist groups network with each other.[59]

Since its formation, NA was plagued by internal infighting and differences that resulted in its splintering. Pierce died in 2002 and was replaced by Erich Gliebe. After his death, what ensued was infighting and schisms. In 2005, Kevin Alfred Strom, the editor of *National Vanguard* magazine and former editor of the magazine *National Socialist World*, in an unsuccessful coup demanded that Gliebe step down as chair of NA. Pressured, Gliebe resigned in 2005 and was replaced by Shaun Walker, who in 2006 was indicted by an grand jury for civil rights violations in Utah. Strom resigned and formed a new group, called the National Vanguard. In January 2007, he was arrested and charged by the federal government for possession of child pornography.[60]

Thus, directly or indirectly, the aforementioned entities' anti-immigrant politics was buttressed by the writings and words of nativist intellectuals and media commentators, and the presence of a xenophobic political climate that pervaded the country.

Nativist Intellectuals and Media

Vigilantes, militias, hate groups, and nativist extremist organizations were not the only vehicles that impelled NAMM. Nativist intellectuals and particularly the electronic and print media also were powerful forces. Their contemporary role in anti-immigration politics is a matter of record. Such scholars as Patrick Buchanan, Samuel Huntington, Victor Davis Hansan, Jerome R. Corsi, Otis L. Graham, Jon E. Dougherty, and Daniel Sheehy[61] contributed through their writings to the NAMM's rise and growth. As intellectuals they all shared one common thread, which was their adherence and espousal of the WASP ethos. However, in most cases their writing echoed the nativist cry for harsher restrictionist immigration reform. They pandered to the growing fears, especially of whites, among others to the immigrant's dramatic population growth and serious threat they posed to the country's WASP ethos.

Buchanan, in his two books *The Death of the West* and *State of Emergency*, in his analysis on the immigration crisis expounded and personified his nativist anti-immigrant proclivities. In both works, he expounds on the re-Conquista, the alleged demographic takeover by Mexicanos of Aztlán. As a prophet of the country's doom, he predicts that the consequences of the Latino demographic transformation will be so severe that they could foster the country's "balkanization," the splitting of the country into smaller nation-states. He argued that Western civilization was in decline and that Whites in both the U.S. and Europe were in peril, threatened by unbridled immigration from Third World countries and low birth rates by White women.

Samuel Huntington, one of the country's premiere political scientists, joined NAMM's nativist intellectual crusade with his book *Who Are We?* He shared many of Buchanan's same nativist views and conclusions. He forcibly argued that the Latino demographic transformation threatened to create a bifurcated Anglo-Hispanic society, with two national languages.[62] If left unchecked, it threatens the cultural hegemony of the WASP ethos that he described as the "American Creed." Like Buchanan, he warned the country of the re-Conquista by Mexicanos and of the country's possible balkanization. Victor Davis Hanson joined the "nativist NANN's intellectual bandwagon" with his book *Mexifornia*. He warned that if the border was not secured the Mexicanization of California was but a prelude of what was to come for the country. Others who were mentioned above examined from a nativist anti-immigrant perspective the history and/or policy implications of the various aspects of the immigration crisis.

The country's print and electronic media almost on a daily basis fomented and ignited the nativist fires fueling the WASP ethos. Scores of television, radio, and print journalists contributed to the people's growing fears inherent to the immigration crisis. CNN's Lou Dobbs transformed himself into television's nativist apostle of anti-immigration, especially directing his rhetorical attacks at migrants from México. He preached a political gospel of xenophobia, nativism, and racism. Through an admixture of populism and nativism coupled with a strong dosage of conservatism his CNN news reporting resonated similar arguments made by Buchanan. There was no objectivity to his reporting on immigration.

His commentaries were alarmist and propagandist, pandered, like that of other nativist militia leaders, to the worst fears, anxieties, and tribulations of Whites in the U.S. In 2006 and 2007, Dobbs came under increasing criticism by pro-migrant advocates and SPLC for his inaccurate and biased reporting.[63] Some protested and demanded to CNN that he be fired, but to no avail.

There were others on television that propagated the WASP ethos and the growing fear of the "brown peril." The list was long and the following are but a few who stood out were MSNBC's Patrick Buchanan and Joe Scarborough; CNN's Glenn Beck; and Fox's Bill O'Reilly. In general, the news and public affairs programs of the major networks, ABC, CBS, NBC, Fox, CNN, and MSNBC, by and large were not exempt from promoting the WASP ethos and its anti-immigrant attitudes. Their reporting on the issue of immigration usually had a bias that accentuated the negatives of the migrant exodus and seldom homed in on the positive contributions migrants made to the country's general welfare. Their reporting primarily focused on the southern border, seldom if ever, on the porous 4,000-mile-long Canadian border. They were more readily disposed to report on anti-immigrant advocacy efforts than on pro-migrant rights groups. As examined previously, the Minutemen Project was largely a creation of sensationalist ratings-driven electronic media.

Radio was a more powerful medium for nativist communication and information dissemination than was television. A plethora of radio stations across the country carried anti-immigrant programming. Numerous talk show hosts sensationalized the myriad of alleged evils and dangers resulting from the migrant exodus and re-Conquista syndrome in order to beef up their ratings and make big profits for the owners of the stations. On a day-to-day basis, nativist if not racist radio talk hosts propagated their hateful and xenophobic racist rhetoric. From the east to the west and from the north to south, radio was a powerful "socialization" agent that reinforced the country's nativist political culture imbued with the WASP ethos. New Jersey's Hal Turner was one of those who used his radio program to threaten immigrants and those who defended them. In 2005, he encouraged listeners to "kill illegal aliens as they cross into the U.S. When the stench of rotting corpses gets bad enough, the rest will stay away."[64] In southern California, another radio program was KFI's Jon and Ken, for years used the airwaves to propagate nativist anti-immigrant opinions. With some exceptions, the radio airwaves largely were slanted toward a nativist perspective in their reporting on the immigration crisis. Those exceptions included National Public Radio and a few stations, such as KPFK in Los Angeles, among a few other progressive ones that formed part of the nationwide Pacifica Radio Network which exposed NAMM's myriad of anti-immigrant myths and politics.

Lastly, newspapers across the country almost on a daily basis reported on the growing immigration crisis from a nativist perspective and served as an effective anti-immigrant socialization agent. They too inculcated the people with fear, apprehension, and hate toward migrants. While they claimed to be impartial and objective, when reporting most stories on the immigration crisis they accentuated the alleged negatives of immigration, such as immigration's alleged detrimental economic impact; U.S. workers losing jobs to undocumented migrants; the cultural implications of undocumented migrants refusing to assimilate; the high crime rate perpetrated by migrants; the alleged egregious social service impact and its burden on U.S. taxpayers; and its demographic impact of Whites becoming the "new minority." Editorial after editorial in 2005 to 2007 promulgated a more restrictionist approach to immigration reform. Magazine articles usually followed as well the same pattern created by the newspapers.

The Omnipresence of the WASP Ethos

Through the combined activities of nativist rancher vigilante groups, militias, hate groups, anti-immigration organizations, intellectuals, television and radio personalities, and newspapers, the country's political culture, permeated by the nativist-driven WASP ethos, acted as powerful socialization agents of anti-immigration, especially toward Mexicanos. In short, an anti-immigrant political climate with deep historical roots continued to permeate U.S. society during 2005 through 2007. Mediums such as books, articles, newspapers, magazines, radio and television reporting, commentaries, and the Internet were invaluable purveyors of the sort of nativism that was moderately extremist to ultraextremist. The historical omnipresence of the WASP ethos has been well documented throughout the various chapters of this book, and more recently, numerous polls taken by a number of news entities during 2005 to 2007 verified its pervasiveness.

The divergent polls conducted underscored that among some Whites a "fear of foreigners" existed, first directed at Mexicanos, second at Latinos, and third at people of color. The increasingly xenophobic, nativist, and racist WASP ethos was particularly evident in people's opinions on issues related to immigration. Its prevalence was buttressed by a *Time* magazine poll taken nationwide and reported in its issue of April 10, 2006. The following includes its major findings: 82 percent said that the U.S. was not doing enough to keep undocumented migrants from entering the country; 32 percent responded that undocumented migration into the U.S. was extremely serious; 36 percent said it was very serious; 51 percent said the U.S. would be better off if it deported undocumented migrants versus 38 percent who said the country would be worse off; 71 percent believed major penalties should be levied against employers who hire undocumented workers; 75 percent believed that undocumented immigrants should have greater restrictions on government services; 51 percent believed that they should not be allowed to attend public schools; 69 percent believed that they should not be allowed to obtain a driver's license; 62 percent favored taking whatever steps necessary at the border (including the use of the military) to cut the flow of migrants entering the country, 56 percent favored the construction of a fence along the border and 55 percent believed undocumented workers were displacing U.S. workers by taking jobs away from U.S. workers.

On the positive side, 78 percent believed undocumented migrants should be allowed to have access to citizenship, if they learned English, had a job, and paid taxes. Also, 72 percent favored allowing undocumented workers to secure temporary U.S. work visas.[65] Poll after poll taken by *USA Today*/Gallup, CNN, NBC/*Wall Street Journal*, and others in 2007[66] generally were in accord with *Times'* findings.

Thus, the presence and growth of nativist oriented rancher vigilantes, militias, anti-immigrant organizations and hate groups buttressed by xenophobic intellectuals, media, and a WASP ethos-permeated political climate precipitated an organized response by Mexicano and other pro-migrant advocates.

CHAPTER 9

Mexicanos' Response to the Rancher Vigilante and Militia Crisis (2000–2005)

Worsening the growing immigration crisis was the expanding rancher vigilante and militia presence during 2000 to 2005. Their presence produced a Mexicano response, which meant engaging and challenging them. Mexicanos rebuked their vigilantism, border surveillance patrols, and virulent xenophobia, nativism, and racism by mounting countervailing actions. It meant that some, in particular Mexicanos, were prepared to respond to the defense of the undocumented migrants should they be abused and/or should their human rights be violated. Pro-migrant rights entities in Arizona came to the defense of the undocumented and challenged at all levels, including in the courts, the nativist militias and vigilantes; however, advocacy efforts were also launched from California by the National Alliance for Human Rights (NAHR), a human rights, social justice, and empowerment network of activists and organizations, which responded aggressively by propounding the creation of a bi-national mobilization coming from both the United States (U.S.) and México.

Using a case study format this chapter documents the Mexicano organizing responses to the rancher vigilantism and militias from 2000 to 2005, particularly of the organizing efforts; however, it primarily focuses on the efforts of the pro-human rights network, NAHR,[1] which I founded and coordinate today.

Mexicano/Latino Response to the Border Crisis

MEXICANOS RESPOND TO THE BARNETT BOYS

Roger Barnett and his two brothers started their armed rancher vigilantism against undocumented immigrants in 1999; however, it was not until May 2000

231

that the first major response from Mexicano activists outside of Arizona occurred.[2] Prior to that a number of Arizona pro-immigrant rights groups, such as the Tucson-based Coalition for Human Rights (CHR) and Border Action Watch, had condemned the Barnetts' armed vigilante antics and racist rhetoric. CHR in particular responded with a letter addressed to U.S. Attorney General Janet Reno, dated April 25, 2000, in which it petitioned her office to intervene in the growing armed vigilante crisis and take action to stop what CHR perceived as illegal actions. The letter in part said, "For the past year, Barnett and others have openly violated state and federal laws, stopping vehicles on public highways, detaining and assaulting immigrants at gunpoint and shooting at immigrants." The letter alleged that abuses by the Barnett Boys had been documented by the local media and underscored attempts to get law enforcement agencies and U.S. Attorney Jose de Jesus Rivera to halt these illegal actions had failed.[3]

During May, Roger Barnett worked the media, increasingly receiving national exposure. He told the media that during the past thirteen months they had detained some 2,000 undocumented migrants, and stated to a *USA Today* reporter that he was "prepared to kill Mexicans"[4] if necessary. His controversial words seemed to resonate well with the media. The League of United Latin American Citizens (LULAC), at the Arizona state level as well as at the national level, responded to Barnett's racist pronouncements by forwarding letters to several state and federal government officials requesting their intervention. In the letters, California LULAC Deputy State Director Jessica Castro alleged that the California Coalition for Immigration Reform's (CCIF) Barbara Coe, Roger Barnett, and Glenn Spencer at the Sierra Vista meeting had discussed the idea of planting land mines along the border. She chastised Coe for her hate-filled remarks that were "incendiary, defamatory, and encouraged acts of violence."[5]

The first organized response by Mexicanos outside of Arizona to the Barnett Boys' vigilantism occurred in late May. Outraged over the growing issue, I spoke by telephone with Isabel Garcia, CHR's principal leader on the matter, who described the situation as extremely serious and stressed the urgency due to the mounting tensions at the border. I asked her if CHR had received support from Mexicano/Latino politicians, activists, or organizations outside of Arizona. She said that besides LULAC, the answer was no. I let her know that I and others were committed to assisting CHR in confronting the armed rancher vigilantism. A few days later, I was invited to speak at a CHR-organized peace vigil on the militarization of the Cactus Curtain in Tucson on June 2. With the assistance of Mary Ann (hereafter to be referred to as Maria Anna) Gonzales, a then research analyst with the University of California Riverside's Ernesto Galarza Public Policy Institute, in less than one week we held a community meeting in Riverside, at which a fact-finding delegation was formed that would travel to Arizona.

As part of the delegation's outreach efforts, at la luncheon held by the National Council of la Raza (NCLR) at the Mission Inn in Riverside on May 25, from the floor I apprised the 200 attendees and in particular NCLR National President Raul Yzaguirre of the increasing and dangerous activities of the armed rancher vigilantes in southern Arizona. I invited Mr. Yzaguirre to attend CHR's vigil, to which he responded that he would. I also asked for his group's intervention since it claimed to be the largest national Hispanic civil rights organization in the country. Unfortunately, when I called him a few days later, at his office in Washington, D.C., to verify his attendance, I was informed by NCLR's Vice President Charles Kamasaki that NCLR would not take on such an issue because it was too controversial and could detrimentally impact its funding. I told him that if Blacks were being hunted like animals every Black leader, from Louis Farrakhan to Jessie Jackson, and a range of organizations from the Black Muslims to the NAACP would be protesting in southern Arizona against the racist armed vigilante Barnett Boys and others of their kind. I failed to convince him.

On May 30 I sent a letter requesting the intervention of the Congressional Hispanic Caucus (CHC) to the attention of the chair, Congresswoman Lucille Roybal-Allard. Copies were also sent to all nineteen caucus members. The letter delineated a five-point request for support: (1) that CHC members attend CHR's peace vigil; (2) that CHC join with others in forming a "united front" against armed rancher vigilantism; (3) that the CHC hold congressional hearings in southern Arizona on the growing vigilante crisis; (4) that CHC pressure the Clinton administration, in particular Attorney General Janet Reno, to investigate the apparent civil rights violations of Mexicano migrants by the armed rancher vigilantes; and (5) that CHC pressure Arizona State Attorney General Janet Napolitano to investigate violation of state laws and charge vigilantes with aggravated assault with a deadly weapon, kidnapping, and false imprisonment.[6]

As preparations were finalized for the fact-finding trip to Arizona, media reports indicated a worsening of the situation along the Arizona–México border. More U.S. Border Patrol agents were assigned to the Tucson/Douglas sector, an increase of some 126 agents for fiscal year 2000. The number of undocumented migrants apprehended in April by the Border Patrol soared. Some 65,213 had been detained and deported, a 37 percent increase over the previous twelve-month period since April of 1999. In Douglas alone the arrests totaled 33,008 and the number of border crossing deaths in the Tucson/Douglas sector increased over the previous year to twenty-nine. On May 29, an undocumented mother was found dead, a victim of dehydration after giving the available water to her two-year-old child, who was found alive next to her corpse.[7] The deadly situation further motivated the efforts of the California fact-finding delegation.

On May 31, a press conference was held at the Zacatecas Restaurant Hall in Riverside at which we announced the delegation's trip to southern Arizona.

México's consul for San Bernardino/Riverside Counties and various organizations that were sending representatives as part of the delegation participated. In the press release I explained the purpose of the delegation's trip to Arizona:

> Latinos in Arizona are not alone in their struggle to bring peace to a border that is a powder keg and to efforts to put an end to the armed vigilantism that is victimizing our Mexicano immigrants at the volatile Arizona/Mexico border. . . . The severity of the crisis that threatens relations between the United States and Mexico and further violence at the border is why the delegation is going to Douglas to meet with the Mexican Consul and Border Patrol, U.S. Attorney, city, and religious officials on a fact finding mission that will produce a report that will be released to the public.[8]

The consul reported that the Mexican government regarded the actions of the armed vigilante ranchers as violations of human rights and also publicly supported the mission of the fact-finding delegation. El Movimiento Estudiantil Chicanos de Aztlán (MEChA) of the University of California, Riverside, leader Gabby Ocon captured our purpose with her emotionally delivered remark, "We're not going to permit our brothers and sisters [to be] treated as animals."[9]

The delegation was composed of thirty representatives of several organizations: La Cordinadora, Comite Pro-Uno, LULAC, the Mexican Political Association (MPA), MEChA, Union del Barrio, Raza Rights Coalition, Inland Empire Latino Lawyers, and American Friends Service Committee. It departed on June 2 and caravanned from Riverside and San Diego to Tucson.[10] On Friday, June 2, the delegation met with officials headed by Chief Patrol Agent David V. Aguilar. The meeting lasted a mere thirty minutes, and on more than one occasion there were allegations made by delegation members of U.S. Border Patrol agents collaborating with Barnett and his fellow rancher armed vigilantes. Aguilar and other Border Patrol officials unequivocally refuted the charges. In a rather supportive manner, Aguilar argued that the Barnett Boys and other ranchers who were apprehending undocumented migrants were not vigilantes. He described them as concerned citizens who were merely exercising their constitutional rights to protect their property and bear arms, especially since Arizona law allows private citizens to carry arms. He also denied allegations of wrongdoing in the shooting of the migrant Palafox by armed rancher vigilantes. Aguilar stated that the shooters were more than likely "Mexican bandits." He explained that Mexican government authorities had conducted an investigation on the shooting and had concluded there was no rancher involvement. He underscored that the real criminals were the *coyotes, los contrabandistas.* Aguilar stressed the humanitarian role of Border Patrol agents and described them as angels of mercy. He claimed that they had rescued scores of migrants and had provided them with water and food.

As the meeting concluded, Aguilar reminded the delegation that the U.S. Border Patrol did not support the armed rancher vigilantes. However, he said to us that they had the right to protect their property.[11] Before exiting the meeting, I told him that the actions of the armed rancher vigilantes were no longer an issue of Arizona alone, that we were prepared to return in support of those protecting the human rights of the undocumented. Before leaving I also told him that the relationship of the U.S. Border Patrol to the armed rancher vigilantes was open to serious scrutiny. The other delegates as well warned that the U.S. Border Patrol should not tolerate and support the rancher vigilantes' "domestic terrorist" activities.[12]

The delegation then traveled to Douglas for two concurrent meetings. Some members of the delegation met with México's Consul Miguel Escobar Valdez in Douglas, while others attended a meeting with community leaders from both Douglas and Bisbee. The purpose of the former meeting was to ascertain from the Consul his perception of the degree of gravity that the armed rancher vigilantes presented. Consul Escobar reported that the situation was precarious, tense, and extremely dangerous. He also reported that México's Foreign Minister Rosario Green had stated at a press conference on the matter that "there are possibilities for bringing charges, from illegal detention to aggravated assault." Escobar confirmed that his office was looking into the possibilities of initiating litigation against suspected vigilante ranchers. He told us that all three of the consulate offices in Arizona were strongly encouraging victims to come forward and file complaints so that charges could be initiated. However, he pointed to the fact that this was extremely difficult since most undocumented migrants were too afraid to come forward. He told us that his office had investigated some twenty-five cases involving armed rancher vigilantes. He also wanted us to note that the Mexican government on México's side of the border had posted police officers known as "Grupo Beta" who were specifically trained to protect migrants from unscrupulous *coyotes y polleros*. When I asked him which Mexicano or Latino organizations or *politicos* had come forward to address this urgent matter, he said none, with the exception of CHR from Arizona. This concerned him gravely, because White anti-immigrant organizations were coming to Douglas.[13]

The community meeting included our delegates and around twenty or so Douglas area pro-migrant rights activists. There was an exchange of information followed by their wanting to know why we had traveled to Douglas. The delegates first conveyed our mission, which was to ascertain the nature of the rancher armed vigilante issue, and second, the delegation's proposed strategy to expand the advocacy efforts nationwide. Professor Rodolfo Acuña reminded the attendees of Dr. Martin Luther King's words: "An injustice anywhere is an injustice everywhere." Douglas advocates weighed in on just how volatile the situation was due to the arrival of outside extremist, racist-type groups that were in support of the vigilantes.[14]

That same day the delegation left Douglas and headed to Tucson to attend the candlelight peace vigil. In Tucson, prior to the event a few of the delegates held a closed session with U.S. Attorney Jose de Jesus Rivera at the Best Western Hotel. He was accompanied by Assistant U.S. Attorney Jan E. Kearney and Vermont R. McKinney, Carol A. Russo, and Ron Wakabayashi from the U.S. Justice Department. There was the usual exchange of information as well as the delegation's specific and pointed questions as to the federal government's role on the issue of Barnett and his armed rancher vigilantes. Rivera proceeded to lecture and somewhat patronize the delegates on to the workings of the U.S. Attorney's Office.[15]

The delegates told Rivera that they had not come from California to be lectured and that they specifically wanted to know what he and his office were doing to curb the Barnett Boys' vigilante activities against undocumented migrants. Rivera alluded to the involvement of his office in the Hannigan case. Professor Acuña corrected him and alluded to the major legal leadership role played in the case by attorneys Isabel Garcia and Jesus Romo.

The meeting with Rivera int sensified when attorney Carlos Juarez, representing the Inland Empire Latino Lawyers Association, pointedly asked Rivera why there had been no legal action taken against Barnett. Rivera responded that his office had been investigating the matter, but that his office "had not been able to find the right legal hook." On the issue of the flyer soliciting recruits to hunt Mexicans, he stated that that issue too was part of his ongoing investigation. Before ending the meeting the delegates urged Rivera to expedite a legal remedy and warned that if the domestic terrorist activities of the armed rancher vigilantes were not halted there could be serious domestic and international consequences.[16]

That evening CHR held a candlelight vigil at Armory Park in Tucson, which was billed as a statewide event. It drew a crowd of 400, which included our fifty-member delegation from California. The crowd was comprised of both Whites and Mexicanos. The low numbers led the delegates to believe that the issue had yet to hit home, therefore not engaging more people to mobilize against it. It was a surprise to many of us that the vigil's cardinal theme did not highlight the rancher vigilante issue; instead it accentuated the militarization of the Cactus Curtain, the ill effects of NAFTA and globalization, and in general the speakers were hypercritical of U.S. economic capitalist policies.

The vigil's program included a number of speakers: Isabel Garcia, CHR; Maria Jimenez, American Friends Service Committee; Paul Gatone, National Lawyers Guild; Professor Rodolfo Acuña, CSU Northridge; and me. While most focused their remarks on the themes previously identified, a few did allude to the growing armed rancher vigilante crisis. Garcia's message accentuated the number of people who had died crossing the Cactus Curtain. She said, "It's unreasonable, it's inhumane, and we have to stop it." Jimenez accused the federal government of using an "out of sight, out of mind" strategy in dealing with said issue. Gatone said, "Letting people run around like cowboys holding people at gunpoint is clearly not the answer." He reminded the ostensibly solemn crowd that "vigilantism, increased militarization, and scapegoating of undocumented migrants were not solutions." Professor Acuña told the crowd that historically Arizona had a rich history of progressive activism that went back to the early 1900s.[17]

In my address I called for the need to mobilize and prioritize the growing armed vigilante menace. I warned that Barnett and his rancher vigilantes were only the beginning of worse things to come. I urged that as Mexicanos we were facing a growing state of siege as demonstrated by the passage in California of several nativist-inspired and -backed propositions, 187, 209, and 227, and I also conveyed the need for us to create a national pro-migrant rights movement. I raised the question as to why at the national level Mexicano/Latino congresspersons, especially those from Arizona such as Congressman Ed Pastor, and national Latino organizations had not taken on the armed rancher vigilante issue. I argued that the siege was due to the demographic transformation, the re-Mexicanization, of Aztlán. Lastly, I committed on the behalf of our delegation, that upon our return to California we would begin to organize against the vigilante ranchers.

On the morning of Saturday June 3, CHR held a strategy meeting at the Clarion Hotel in Tucson. Attended by some fifty persons mostly from Tucson, Douglas, and Bisbee and ten of the remaining delegates from California, presenters reported that Barnett's ranch was 80 percent public land, meaning in reality it was owned by the state and leased to him for almost nothing. Another person reported that vigilantes were apprehending undocumented migrants on public roadways. It was also said that not all the ranchers supported Barnett's vigilantism. Isabel Garcia alluded to the use of litigation and referenced the Hannigan case as an illustration of how the fight could be taken to the courts. At the meeting there was also reference made to the collaboration between U.S. Border Patrol agents and rancher vigilantes.[18]

Others attacked the militarization of the U.S.–México border, specifically Operation Gatekeeper and Operation Safeguard. Ultimately, discussion evolved to blaming the immigration crisis on the globalization of capital via NAFTA and the like. A number of recommendations were approved: (1) that a border summit be held in December; (2) that there be a boycott of Barnett's businesses in Tucson; (3) that there be a concerted challenge of the vigilante rancher's use of public lands; (4) that a call be made for an investigation by the United Nations; (5) that a call be made a call for congressional hearings; (6) that a public education drive be initiated on the dangers of rancher vigilantism; (7) that Interior Secretary Bruce Babbitt pressured on the use of public lands by vigilante ranchers;

(8) that a call be made for a national mobilization/march on Washington, D.C.; and (9) that efforts be initiated to organize at the *barrio* level against the rancher vigilante threat.

Prior to the departure of the ten members of the delegation, a meeting was held with CHR's Mexicano(a) leadership that included Isabel Garcia, Jesus Romero, Lupe Castillo, and Maria Jimenez of American Friends Service Committee. The delegation committed to organizing efforts immediately upon arriving in California. The fact-finding delegation succeeded in garnering media coverage that showed that Mexicanos were not afraid of confronting the vigilantes.

THE BORDER CRISIS IS EXACERBATED

During June and July 2000 the border crisis in southern Arizona worsened. An increased numbers of migrants were found dead in the desert in the Douglas/Tucson corridor. The migrant deaths were a result of dehydration, heat exhaustion, freezing cold, drowning, snake bites and scorpion stings, and so forth. In early June, the *Tucson Citizen* reported that fifteen migrants had died from heat exposure, three more from exposure to the cold, and that a total of thirty-five had died from a variety of other causes. On June 8, it reported the death of a twenty-four-year-old woman who was the seventh migrant to die of exposure within a two-week period. The *Daily Star* reported on that same day that the number of deaths had increased to forty. By July, 230 migrants had perished crossing Arizona's desert. The Tucson and McAllen sectors also showed that there had been an increase in the number of migrant deaths over the previous year. It jumped from twenty deaths in 1999 to fifty-two deaths in 2000. The San Diego sector experienced only a slight increase: from twenty-one deaths in 1999 to twenty-six in 2000. The Yuma sector experienced ten in 1999 and twenty in 2000.[19] In June, for all the nonbelievers, a television crew captured on film the drowning of two migrants in the Rio Grande River in Texas.[20]

The total estimated number of migrant deaths since Operation Gatekeeper went into effect in 1994 to July 2000 was 545. The high number of migrants rescued was indicative of the exacerbating border crisis. The U.S. Border Patrol reported in July that a total of 1,425 migrants had been rescued along the border since October 1999.

The border crisis in southern Arizona was exacerbated even more by the killing of migrants who were crossing the border. While Governor Napolitano condemned the actions of the vigilantes, no measures were initiated to stop their activities. *Time* magazine reported that in June three migrant workers had been killed and seven others wounded on the U.S. side of the border. On July 3 in North San Diego County a young migrant was beaten and dragged and ultimately killed. At the end of July police had yet to determine the victim's identity and they had also not made any arrests.[21] On July 5 again in North San Diego, five Mexicano migrant workers were savagely beaten at the migrant camp located near the nursery where they worked by ten alleged skinhead youths, ages fourteen to seventeen. The victims, all men in their sixties, reported that they had been beaten with metal pipes and fists, shot at with pellet guns, and one was robbed. Three of the victims were shot at close range and required hospitalization. San Diego police treated the attack as a "hate crime" since the attackers used racial slurs and expletives. The city of San Diego posted a $30,000 reward, and on July 17 seven white youth were arrested and an eighth youth was arrested a few days later. In Arizona, the federal government allocated $5 million in emergency relief for border counties in a supposed effort to help defray the costs associated with processing the undocumented migrants by law enforcement agencies and the courts.[22]

RISE OF NAHR

During June and July I initiated efforts in California to organize on the issue of the vigilantes.[23] On June 7, at a meeting held in Riverside there was a debriefing on the delegation's trip to Arizona. Based on the delegation's report and conclusions the fifty persons in attendance agreed to develop a plan of action to deal with the burning issue. Calls were made and messages went out on the Internet, all for the purpose of garnering support for NAHR's organizing activities against Arizona's rancher vigilaties. In addition, Congressman Joe Baca of the 43rd District was contacted for the purpose of requesting that the Congressional Hispanic Caucus (CHS) hold congressional hearings on the vigilante crisis in Douglas. The request for hearings fell on deaf ears. In late June, Congressman Baca informed me that while CHC had discussed our request during their session, they would not take a position because they said that Arizona Congressman Ed Pastor would have to request the hearings first, since the rancher vigilante crisis emanated from the southern part of his state. Baca stated, however, that CHC was prepared to hold a hearing in Washington, D.C., and they were already trying to meet directly with Attorney General Reno to solicit her help.[24]

Congressman Baca on July 7 in a speech delivered to the Inland Empire Hispanic Chamber of Commerce reported that the delegation's trip to southern Arizona had pressured CHC to hold hearings. However, by the end of July it was evident that our request for hearings in Douglas would not come to be. Adding insult to injury, Congresswoman Roybal never responded to my letter sent to her in late May. It became apparent to many of us CHC felt that the issue of the nativist armed rancher vigilantes was just too controversial, particularly for Pastor.

Perhaps he figured that there would be a backlash among White Arizona voters which could hurt him in his re-election efforts. The fact that CHC failed to hold hearings on the vigilante crisis and NCLR's refusal to take a leadership role in addressing the issue accelerated the call I made for a California border summit.

Calls were made to a number of activists and meetings were held for the purpose of garnering support for a border summit and a march along the border on July 29. In three weeks, with the help of an organizing committee, the events were organized. On Friday, July 28, at a press conference held in Riverside, I released the "Delegation's Fact-finding Report on the Vigilante Ranchers." The next day, the Bi-National Border Summit (henceforth referred to as the Summit), solidarity march, and bi-national vigil were held along the border in San Ysidro, California.[25] The Summit was held in the morning from 8:00 a.m. to 1:00 p.m. at Mount Carmel Catholic Church, in San Ysidro, a few miles from the border. The march and vigil were held that afternoon at Border Field State Park, which is contiguous to the México–U.S. border.

The Summit drew some 250 activist organizational, religious, student, academic, political, and community leaders, who came mostly from California, with a few from Arizona and Texas. The Summit's fundamental message was to challenge the threat of the vigilante crisis effectively, by the erection of a powerful mass movement. For purposes of keeping the Summit's agenda on focus, I wrote and presented a plan of action, "El Plan de San Ysidro," which after much debate and a few amendments was approved.[26] Briefly, it called for a human rights advocacy network, not an organization, comprised of groups and activists and that it would be the National Alliance for Human Rights (NAHR). Its mission would be the promotion of human rights, social justice, and political empowerment. Moreover, its basic premise was to be a change-oriented network with the capacity to coordinate and implement the offensive against the vigilantes. Its uniqueness was twofold: (1) it would not displace existent organizations, but would instead convene them when needed on a given issue; and (2) it would act as a "rapid deployment" organizing and advocacy vehicle.

El Plan de San Ysidro included other aspects as well. It called for: (1) the formation of a bi-national border commission, comprised of representatives from both the U.S. and México, that would deal with the plethora of border problems, especially the rancher vigilante issue, and would propose policy recommendations to both the U.S. and Mexican governments for their resolution; (2) lobby Democratic politicians at their national convention for a strong plank against NAFTA, against the militarization of the border, and their repudiation of the nativist armed rancher vigilantes; (3) call for marches and direct actions at the Democratic National Convention scheduled to be held in August in Los Angeles; (4) intensify pressure on CHC to hold congressional hearings on the vigilante issue; (5) secure support from México and other Latin American countries on the rancher vigilante issue and for efforts to protect the human rights of the undocumented migrants from abuses; (6) support La Cordinadora's proposed march for immigrant rights in Washington, D.C., scheduled for October 14; and (7) initiate litigation against Barnett and other rancher vigilantes for civil and human rights abuses and violations.[27]

The culmination of the day's organizing events were the solidarity march and unity vigil. Both events were held at Border Field State Park and drew about 1,000 participants, short of what was anticipated. The turnout was fair, considering the obstacles faced by the organizing committee such as a short organizing time frame (three weeks) and extremely limited resources. One of the key organizers of all three events was Fabian Nuñez, who in 2007 was California Speaker of the Assembly. With colorful placards, Mexican and U.S. flags, a huge banner of Che Guevara, and vociferous protest chants, the marchers traversed along the 4.5 miles of iron fence with a sense of purpose and ardent solidarity.

The vigil was held at the park right along the boundary fence. On both sides of the border the participants prayed and made a myriad of pronouncements against the militarization of the border and rancher vigilantes in Arizona and for the creation of a pro-migrant rights mass movement. On the Mexican side, some fifty people were led by members of La Cordinadora, specifically Jose "Pepe" Jacques Medina, who in 2007 was a congressman in México's Chamber of Deputies.[28] Various speakers addressed the results of the Summit. Both events received wide media coverage on both sides of the border, and even a documentary was done.

Implementation of El Plan

Under my leadership, throughout the rest of 2000, the fledgling NICD sought to implement El Plan de San Ysidro. The first direct action occurred in late August at the Democratic Party Convention held in Los Angeles. In a matter of three weeks we had pulled together a contingent of some 100 Mexicano activists from throughout Southern California were mobilized. Under the leadership of Vicente Rodriguez from San Diego, NAHR distributed some 239 Styrofoam crosses that symbolized up to August of 2000 the total number of migrants who had died crossing the Cactus Curtain. With some 3,000 protestors in attendance, I spoke, focusing specifically on four points: (1) the vigilante crisis and the need to organize against them; (2) the egregious effects of the militarization of the border; (3) the detrimental aspects of NAFTA; and (4) NAHR's mission.

During the ensuing months efforts to implement the particulars of El Plan de San Ysidro became problematic. As usual in movement politics, people who come together at conferences, summits, and meetings make decisions to do "x" number of things; however, the question never fails to arise as to who is actually going to do the work. Being a full-time professor and the chair of the Department of Ethnic Studies at the University of California, Riverside (UCR), and acting as NAHR coordinator, I found myself overextended. Without having the requisite resources of staff, office, and an operating budget, NAHR's development turned into a major challenge for me and the few committed volunteers who maintained it.

Because of the above reasons from 2000 to 2003 not all the particulars of El Plan de San Ysidro were enacted, especially on the issue of the vigilante crisis. Much of the organizational leadership on the issue fell on CHR and Border Watch. NAHR continued to monitor the issue and maintained communication with CHR on the particulars of the rancher vigilante issue. In December 2000, CHR held a regional border conference in Tucson that was attended by some 500. The agenda focused on the growing militarization of the Cactus Curtain border and the issue of the armed rancher vigilantes. NAHR sent two delegates to monitor and participate in the conference. Upon their return, however, they reported that no coordinated plan had been developed.

From 2000 to 2002, NAHR dealt with a number of issues; but its focus was on education reform in particular. Prior to my involvement with the vigilante crisis issue in early May 2000, assisted by Maria Anna Gonzales and an ad-hoc group, a statewide summit, "Latinos and the Education Crisis" was held in Riverside, at a local middle school. Attended by some 300 people from throughout the state, issues of underrepresentation of Chicano/Latino faculty and administrators, undergraduate student retention, graduate school recruitment, and the status of Chicano studies were addressed. From 2000 to 2002 a NAHR task force on education reform was formed which targeted California State University (CSU), San Bernardino. The objective was to create a Department of Chicano Studies. After nearly two years of negotiations and organizing, a few Chicano Studies courses were added to the Ethnic Studies curriculum, a few additional Mexicano faculty members were hired, and a commitment for the creation of a Department of Chicano Studies some time in the future was secured. In 2002 with a vacancy for chancellor at UCR, the NAHR Education Task Force pressured the University of California (UC) board of regents and the governor to appoint a Latino(a) chancellor. The NAHR lobbying effort that included national, state, and local organizations and politicians, resulted in the appointment of the first Latina in the history of California as chancellor of a UC campus—France Cordova.

By 2003, the immigration crisis particularly in southern Arizona had worsened. Rancher vigilantism was on the rise as were the formation of new nativist militias. After contacting various activist leaders and organizations in California, the decision was made for NAHR to intervene and respond to the growing nativist anti-immigrant threat.

NAHR Responds to Growing Militia Threat

NATIVIST MILITIA ACTIVITIES ESCALATE

In 2003 with the rise of militias and increased patrolling of the Arizona–México border, NAHR shifted from education to immigration reform as its primary focus. Due to the armed rancher vigilantism and militias forming and becoming stronger, it was concluded by NAHR activists and groups that Mexicanos and Latinos needed to adopt a much more assertive, if not militant, strategic posture toward these two anti-migrant forces. In Arizona, CHR's leadership however, did not concur with our conclusion. Their organizing approach was to not aggressively confront the anti-immigrant force or to provide the circumstances or events that would give them visibility or credibility by the media. They elected instead to educate the public on their nativist racist agenda and the evils of militarizing the border via NAFTA and neoliberalism.

That same year the number of violent incidents directed by rancher vigilantes and militias against undocumented migrants increased considerably since the reported cycle began in 1999. NAHR took the position that the border situation in southern Arizona had reached a dangerous powder-keg level. It viewed the rancher vigilantes and most nativisit militias as "domestic terrorists" that had directed their attacks against defenseless undocumented migrants. As a result of 9/11, coupled with the U.S. invasion and occupation of Iraq, the country's political climate had become more conservative, if not racist, and increasingly nativist oriented. In a report released in 2001 by the nonpartisan U.S. General Accounting Office, a sheriff of Santa Cruz County commented, "Crimes against illegal aliens have increased because the migrants are forced"—by U.S. border policy—"to attempt entry through the remote areas outside town, where criminal activity is less likely to be detected and more difficult to respond to."[29]

Numerous anti-migrant incidents were documented from along the Arizona–Sonoa border May 2000 to mid-March 2003 that allegedly involved armed vigilantes in the apprehension of migrants.[30] The following incidents involving shootings and violence illustrate the preceding.

- May of 2000: Two ranchers on horseback armed with high-power rifles shot and critically wounded an undocumented migrant who sought to cross near Sasabe, Arizona.
- March 21, 2001: Near the San Pedro River, nine migrants while crossing a ranch were shot at several times by an unnamed assailant who was accompanied by a dog. All nine migrants fled uninjured.
- Year of 2002: Eight migrants were shot execution-style west of Phoenix. No one was apprehended and the suspected perpetrators ran the gamut from armed militias to criminal elements.

- October 16, 2002: A pair of masked gunmen opened fire on twelve migrants who were resting near a cattle pond outside the town of Red Rock (northeast of Tucson in Pinal County), some ninety miles north of Earl Hardy's ranch. Two were killed and nine were allegedly kidnapped. One eyewitness escaped and claimed that the two men were dressed like soldiers. Speculation was that a unit of the Ranch Rescue militia was involved. Nothing was known as to the whereabouts of those allegedly kidnapped.
- November 1, 2002: While walking through the desert some twenty miles southwest of Tucson, a group of migrants was fired upon by masked men.
- January 19, 2003: Migrant Rodrigo Quiroz Acosta was stopped, ruthlessly beaten by an armed rancher vigilante, and was also bitten by one of his dogs. A woman jumped from the rancher's vehicle and attempted to stop the beating of Acosta. In the commotion, Quiroz jumped the barbed wire fence and escaped but was caught by border patrol agents.[31]

NAHR SENDS DELEGATION TO ARIZONA–MÉXICO BORDER

On February 1, 2003, a statewide Latino Leadership Summit was convoked by NAHR in Riverside, California. The 150 participants, representing a number of organizations and communities, adopted a plan of action for mobilization on four issues: (1) Arizona's rancher vigilantes and militias; (2) the U.S.'s Iraq War and occupation; (3) the pending affirmative action crisis; and (4) the California budget cutback crisis. Of the four issues, the former two became NAHR priorities for action and mobilization in 2003. The issue of the vigilantes and militias in Arizona was prioritized. In order to launch a national or bi-national campaign against them, it was decided that another fact-finding delegation would be sent into southern Arizona during May 22–25, 2003. On the U.S. war against Iraq, the decision was made for NAHR to encourage activists and groups to join and support existent antiwar efforts and, if possible, initiate protests against the Bush administration.

On the issue of the rancher vigilante and militias, NAHR in late March made the call via the internet and telephone to selected groups to become part of the bi-national delegation that would travel to southern Arizona and Sonora, México. The delegation headed by this author was comprised of thirty-one delegates that represented various organizations from Illinois, Texas, New México, California, and México.[32] On May 22, 2003, the delegation itinerary included meetings with México's Consul General Ruben Beltrán in Phoenix and Tucson Consul Carlos Flores Visquida.[33] When the delegation's caravan left Riverside it was split in two with one headed toward Phoenix and the other heading to Tucson. Both delegations upon their arrivals to their respective destinations were joined by others from California, Illinois, and México.

The NAHR delegation that met with México's Consul General Beltrán at his office in Phoenix was led by me. Prior to the meeting, a short press conference was held at the consul's office, at which time the delegation explained its mission, which was twofold: (1) demonstrate bi-national solidarity with Arizona's pro-migrant rights groups and activists in their struggle against the "domestic terrorist" threat represented by both vigilantes and militias; and (2) convey a lucid message to them that their violation of undocumented migrants' human rights would not be tolerated and that they would be dealt with accordingly.[34] Consul General Beltrán during the two-hour meeting explained to the delegates the various aspects of the growing "vigilante/militia border crisis," which he broke down into four major areas: (1) geography; (2) organized crime; (3) vigilantism; and (4) enforcement.[35]

On the topic of geography, Consul General Beltrán said Arizona's hostile desert environment was the main factor that contributed to the growing number of migrant deaths. He explained that their dangerous journey north began from the time they departed their village, town, or city, and traveled north to the border area. He said it was a financial hardship for them, for it required an investment of anywhere from $1,000 to $1,500. This meant that most migrants sold everything or borrowed and went into debt. Next was the actual crossing of the border, which in most cases required the hiring of a *coyote* or *pollero* (guide who directs them across the border for a fee). And lastly, Beltrán stated once they made it to the border the biggest challenge was to survive the crossing into the U.S., specifically Arizona's extremely dangerous, hot, and snake- and scorpion-infested desert. The migrants faced exposure, dehydration, starvation, and were subject to becoming targets of criminal activity. He cited some alarming statistics: in 2002 alone some 172 migrants had died crossing the border, whereas, in 2003, from January to May, thirty-five migrants had died, twenty-seven men and eight women. Furthermore, he reported that since 1994 a total of 2,300 migrants had died along the 2,000 mile Cactus Curtain. He identified the counties of Cochise, Pima, and Yuma as having the highest undocumented migrant traffic.[36]

Consul General Beltrán, on the issue of organized crime, said trafficking of human cargo (e.g., migrants) had become a lucrative business. He said that criminal bands or rings were well-organized and emanated from various parts of México, such as Chiapas, Veracruz, and Puebla. He alluded to how drug traffickers were coercing migrants into smuggling drugs into Arizona. Furthermore, that conflict between rival *coyote* gangs for control of the migrant exodus market, including that of migrant children, had increased, especially that of *bajadores*, that is, *coyotes* who forcibly took migrants from other *polleros*. He cited some 150 cases involving violence that had been reported and that 10 percent of Arizona's state's prison inmate population was comprised of Mexicano undocumented migrants.[37]

On the issue of vigilantism he said that of all the border states, Arizona was plagued by the most serious escalation of militia anti-immigrant activity. In a rather diplomatic manner, he was hypercritical of U.S. federal and state government agencies. He said that when militia volunteers or rancher vigilantes committed a crime against migrants these agencies were not that assertive or thorough in conducting their investigations and ultimately in making arrests. Although México's consuls in Arizona had met with them to pressure them into being more proactive in dealing with the issue of vigilantism, little had changed. He qualified the preceding by saying that his office enjoyed a cordial and generally cooperative relationship with Governor Janet Napolitano as well as some members of the state legislature, especially on the issue of the *matricula* (identification card). He stressed that in dealing with the growing vigilante problem there was the need for better coordination among all entities. The consul general also reported that several Mexican government officials had come to Arizona to ascertain various aspects of the state's immigration crisis.[38]

Beltrán said that the unwillingness of migrants who had been victimized by vigilantes or militias to testify and cooperate in the prosecution of the alleged perpetrators was a serious problem for both law enforcement and consul officials. Rather than seek redress for crimes committed against them, most opted to be returned to México as quickly as possible so that they could once again try to cross. Beltrán said they were simply not interested in making civil demands or pressing criminal charges, although they had access to attorneys who needed their testimony.[39]

When asked about the alleged shootings of migrants by armed militias in Maricopa County, Consul General Beltrán said that it was unclear who the actual shooters were. He said that some believed that the killings were a result of organized crime, mainly drug traffickers, and that no arrests had been made. He agreed that armed vigilante ranchers like the Barnett Boys had increased considerably. When asked about the status of the militias, he responded that Chris Simcox's militia activities had momentarily decreased due to charges filed against him for carrying a weapon into a federal park. He then mentioned Glenn Spencer's American Border Patrol (ABP), which he described as an effective agent of electronic vigilantism, referring to the ABP website and its use of airplane drones to conduct border surveillance. Beltrán referred to Spencer's website as "pages of hate" and mentioned that Spencer was quite adept in the workings of the media. He said that armed vigilantism in Arizona had grown because of the existent ultraconservative and anti-immigrant political climate. He explained that militias turned over to the Border Patrol hundreds of apprehended migrants, but did not elaborate on the two's working relationship. During the course of our meeting he made no mention of Ranch Rescue.[40]

When asked if his office had received support from the Latino community, he said that turf battles seemed to get in the way of their being effective. With a sense of disappointment in his tone he said that at times Whites tended to be more supportive of migrant protection efforts than did Mexicanos and Latinos. Furthermore, he went on to say that with the exception of CHR in Tucson, few Mexicano or Latino organizations in Arizona were actively combating the vigilante militias issue or other migrant-related problems. He praised the work of Isabel Garcia and Congressman Raul Grijalva as being representative of a new generation of Mexicano leaders from Tucson that possessed a clearer political vision. He emphasized the need to forge strong pro-migrant coalitions and that consuls could act as facilitators for their formation. He stressed the importance of existent Mexicano leaders and organizations becoming more engaged in trying to resolve the immigration crisis. He spent considerable time pointing out the manifold contributions that Mexicano migrants made to Arizona's economy—some $8.1 billion and some 50,000 jobs. He emphasized that what was needed to halt the migrant exodus was an amnesty agreement. On this point, he challenged us by saying, "*Hay que hacer politica*" (We have to make law).[41]

That same day the other part of the delegation met in Tucson with Mexican Consul Carlos Flores Visquida. This segment of the delegation was headed by Catholic priest Patricio Guillen, executive director of the San Bernardino-based Libreria del Pueblo. The forty-five-minute meeting focused on the various functions of the consulate, especially in the area of protection. Consul Visquida gave a geographical analysis of the counties in southern Arizona that experienced the highest traffic of undocumented migrants, particularly Pima County. He reported that in the Tucson sector, which includes Pima and Pinal counties, in 2002 between January and December a total of 147 migrants had died due to a number of causes, for example, dehydration, exposure, and accidents. He explained that a well-organized network of *coyotes* was responsible for the high numbers of migrant traffic through the Tucson zone. He also informed the delegates that during the last two days, three migrants were found dead in the desert. Consul Visquida commented that 70 percent of those who died did so in the Tahono O'Odham indigenous reservation, which was desert and contiguous to México's border. He stated sadly that because the reservation was considered a sovereign nation, efforts to establish water drops had failed. For the indigenous of the area the militarization and harassment by vigilantes was problematic in that they had historically inhabited both sides of the U.S.–México border. Consul Visquida said the Tucson zone was experiencing the heaviest migrant crossings and that in the Sasabe area alone at least 800 people crossed into the U.S. daily.[42]

Consul Visquida admitted to the presence of armed rancher vigilantes and militias, but qualified it by saying that they were most active in Cochise County.

He alluded to rancher vigilante Roger Barnett and militia leaders Spencer and Simcox, as not being active within the Tucson zone. He also said that although shots allegedly had been fired by vigilantes at migrants, no one had been reported injured or killed. In addition, he acknowledged that human rights violations had ocurred and continued occurring. He alluded to a particular incident the year before the delegates' visit when the bodies of two migrants were found badly decomposed in the trunk of a car. In another case near Tucson, he reported that a migrant was killed when he found himself in the way of a shootout between two warring drug groups.[43] Consul Visquida expressed concern that few groups outside of Tucson had offered to help in dealing with the vigilante and militia crisis. He particularly praised the efforts of CHR and Operación Rescate as two examples of groups that actively supported his office. He suggested that much more input from the community was needed, especially when his office was conducting investigations that involved human rights violations. With the summer heat approaching, he said that he expected many more deaths.[44]

Two members of the delegation attended a CHR meeting that afternoon. The focus of the meeting was the teach-in scheduled for May 31 on the militarization of the Cactus Curtain. After the meeting, the delegation attended CHR's weekly vigil held at *El Tiradito*. The vigil was attended by some thirty persons. Unity songs were interspaced with short presentations on a number of social justice concerns including the militias and immigration. Those members of the delegation who attended the meeting with the consul also participated in the vigil, with Father Guillen speaking.

The delegation's schedule for Friday started with an orientation session provided by CHR leaders on the status of its organizing activities on the border militarization and vigilante and militia crisis. A videotape was shown encapsulating its advocacy activities. Its leadership and membership were comprised of both Mexicanos and Whites. CHR's membership appeared to adhere to a progressive "left" agenda. They reported that vigilante and militia activity had increased significantly. CHR leadership underscored that their strategy was to not confront them directly or to create situations that would give them publicity and stressed the importance of educating the public on the antimigrants' negative values. They also reported that they had been researching their funding sources and that they would be exposing their findings to the public. They acknowledged that CHR did not have the capacity to curb the domestic terrorist activity of these groups and individuals and that a much bigger effort was needed, but insisted that it had to be one that was well coordinated. They cautioned that any strategic move against these players must be predicated on not worsening the existent precarious and volatile situation in southern Arizona.[45] During the orientation various delegate members, including Jose Angel Gutierrez from Texas, were interviewed by print and electronic media.

After the CFR presentations the delegation caravanned to Sasabe, Sonora, a major crossing point by migrants into Arizona. The delegation traveled to Sasabe with the objective of interacting with undocumented migrants before they crossed into Arizona. For the delegation this proved to be one of the most emotional of the various planned activities. Directed by a CHR representative that was familiar with the area the delegation's vehicles drove down a dirt road to the border to where the migrants would embark on the next phase of their dangerous journey. For some two hours the delegation witnessed vehicle after vehicle in ten- to fifteen-minute intervals unload their human cargo, which was up to fifteen migrants per van. *Polleros* charged them 50 pesos for transportation to the border crossing area. As they arrived the delegates earned their trust enough to have the opportunity to ask them questions. When asked why they had decided to make the perilous journey to the U.S., all responded that it was México's chronic poverty and lack of employment opportunities that had convinced them to migrate. They emphasized that they had no choice but to leave their families and travel north in search of work. Time and time again they said that their preference was to remain in México with their families. At the staging area, a couple of *polleros* were interviewed by some delegation members. When asked why they did what they did, they answered that it was a way to make a living while not having to leave México, and that they too had found no other job during the tough times.

Delegates offered water to the fifteen unloading from one van. As the twelve men and three women, ranging in age from fifteen years to mid-twenties, waited for the *coyote*, one of two brothers was interviewed by Father Guillen. He told Guillen that he had been forced to leave Michoacán because there was no work. The young man also said that the problem of immigration was due to a corrupt Mexican government that was incapable of providing a decent wage and work for its people. When asked by delegates their destinations, some replied Chicago, while others said Atlanta. Delegation members passed out information cards that explained their rights and that also included the telephone numbers to consulate offices. Before they crossed into Arizona, Guillen blessed them as a group evoking God's protection for a safe journey.[46] What was apparent was the existence of a well-organized system of migrant trafficking. The *polleros* delivered the migrants to the staging area where they were met by *coyotes* who guided them across the border into Arizona and beyond—all for a price.

The delegation next set off to Douglas for a meeting with Consul Miguel Escobar. While en route to Douglas, outside of Sasabe on the U.S. side of the border, the delegation witnessed large tracts of desert brush being set on fire. It seemed obvious that the fires were being set by the fire department and Border Patrol to make it difficult for the migrants to hide. When asked by delegates why they were setting the fires they said that they were clearing the heavy brush for

firebreak purposes. One delegate who was a Vietnam War veteran said it reminded him of the U.S.'s "scorch and burn" method used in Vietnam against the
Viet Cong and North Vietnamese.

While in Douglas, nine members of the delegation met late that afternoon
with Consul Escobar. He provided an in-depth account of the vigilante and militia activity in Cochise County. He explained that the influx of the migrant exodus had fostered a growing contagion of vigilante militia anti-immigrant activity. The consul stressed that the influx was supported by well-organized *coyote*
rings that had made transporting the human cargo into a very lucrative business.
He identified Spencer's ABP, Simcox's Civil Homeland Defense, and Foote's
Ranch Rescue as the main armed militias active in his area. He provided a profile of each of the militia groups. To him, Spencer's use of the Internet and the
drone airplane were indicators of the militias' high-tech ability to harass and intimidate crossing migrants. He reported that Roger Barnett was still active; however, Simcox's militia had been rather inactive. The Consul described Foote's
Ranch Rescue as being the most dangerous because it was heavily armed and adhered to a strong paramilitary posture.[47]

Escobar warned of a looming firestorm of conflict along the Arizona–Sonora
border, particularly in Cochise County. He used the example of several incidents
involving armed vigilantes that could have become volatile. He said migrants
were apprehended and detained. With weapons pointed at them, they were often coerced into sitting or lying down on the hot desert sand for long periods of
time. At times the migrants were threatened with being shot, were verbally
abused, and in a few instances, were actually shot at. Escobar said that migrants,
even when abused by the vigilantes or militias, were not interested in civil suits
or seeking criminal charges, thus preventing consulate officials from assisting
them in seeking remedy.[48] He said most migrants adhered to a rather pacifist attitude and avoided any entanglement with law enforcement or judicial authorities. Escobar said, "*Prefieren que los boten*" (they prefer to be deported).[49]

When asked if outside of Arizona Mexicano or Latino politicians or organizations had been in contact with him on the vigilante and militia crisis, his response was a succinct no. He said that even in Douglas, although the majority
of the population was Mexicano, no local leader or organization had yet to mobilize a countervailing effort against the vigilantes and militias. From his report,
it was evident that he felt very much alone in the struggle to fend off the rancher
vigilante and militia tide in Cochise County. Immediately after the meeting with
Escobar, a press conference was held.

With all thirty-one members lodged at the historic Gadsden Hotel, the delegation on Saturday morning held a debriefing session. The discussion concluded that the border situation was a powderkeg. After the session, the delegation drove into Agua Prieta, México, and met leaders and supporters of the

Partido de la Revolución Democrática (PRD). This stage of the delegation's schedule was coordinated by Felipe Aguirre, California state PRD chair. A bi-national press conference was held, followed by a meeting. Attended by some fifty persons, the agenda focused on the creation of a "bi-national movement" against the growing rancher vigilante and militia menace. PRD leaders spoke in solidarity, stating that they were ready to do their part. Aguirre and others of the delegation spoke of what was being done in the U.S. to deal with the problem. It was agreed that efforts would continue on both sides of the border to combat their domestic terrorist activities.

After leaving Agua Prieta, México, the delegates returned to their respective states. Those driving back to California for security reasons did so as a caravan of several vehicles. The caravan traveled to Sierra Vista in search of ABP leader Glenn Spencer; We were not able to find a physical address, only a post office box. A NAHR press release was left in his box, letting him know that the delegation had been there. The day before, Jose Angel Gutierrez sought unsuccessfully to locate him as well. The caravan planned to travel to Tombstone and confront militia leader Simcox; however, due to the tight schedule, time did not permit.

While in Douglas, a local newspaper reporter informed me that the delegation had stirred up a hornet's nest of activity and criticism by a number of local residents. While the delegation at no time encountered resistance or threats from anyone, it was anticipated that sooner or later this would happen. A few weeks after our return to California, I received a number of vitriolic and sometimes threatening e-mails and phone calls at my office at the University of California, Riverside. One e-mail said, "If you're trying to start a war you should consider the outcome." Another said, "When defending the border from invasion . . . SHOOT, SHOVEL, SHUT-UP."[50] The following are comments taken from various newspaper articles, which are cited in my report.[51]

- Jack Foote of Ranch Rescue reacted by saying, "I have been in Cochise County since Saturday morning and I have been out taking long walks in the desert with my fellow volunteers both in daylight and after dark. We have yet to bump into [anyone], so they can't be looking for us too hard."
- Chris Simcox of Civil Homeland Defense said, "They are all a bunch of blowhard troublemakers—a lot of threats and no action."
- Glenn Spencer of American Border Patrol responded, "[Navarro] is straightening up his organization under the guise of attacking us. . . . They want to be gladiators without going into the coliseum."

NAHR and I became targets of their relentless attacks via the Internet, articles, hate mail, and threatening calls.

Within a few a weeks I prepared a NAHR delegation report. The conclusion or bottomline was that the rancher vigilante and militia activities in southern Arizona were but the calm before the storm. The report made several major conclusions: (1) that there was a contagion of militia activity in Arizona, especially in Cochise County, that needed to be contained; (2) that Arizona-based CHC and Border Action Network were doing what they could to deal with the vigilante and militia crisis, and that no Mexicano or Latino organizations or politicians from outside of Arizona were involved; (3) that the rancher vigilante and militia crisis had reached a volatile and dangerous level because of their expansion and the constant arrival of other extremist hate groups and militias to the region; (4) that at the national or bi-national levels, no mass movement existed among Mexicanos and Latinos to effectively deal with these domestic terrorist activities; (5) that federal and state officials in Arizona were deliberately slow to respond to the increased vigilante and militia activities; (6) that Mexicanos and Latinos needed to take a more assertive posture in dealing with their antimigrant activities; and (7) that the militias and vigilante ranchers in southern Arizona were products of this country's failed immigration policies, especially the militarization of the U.S.–México border.[52]

The report's most important conclusion was that the migrant exodus from México and Latin America to the U.S. would not end. In order for the migration to end these countries' capitalist economies needed to be transformed to where they had the capacity to produce jobs with livable wages and other economic opportunities. On the U.S. side, its capitalist economy needed reform to where it would not be dependent and/or addicted to the migrant exodus to fill its pool of cheap labor. The report stressed that the migrant exodus was a product of the "globalization of capital" and that it stimulated the "push" factors of poverty and inequality and on the "pull" side the U.S. economy's reliance on exploitable cheap labor.[53] The report also accentuated strategically on the need to create a bi-national response and insisted that consideration be given to taking the issue before the United Nations and/or the Organization of American States, that the Mexican government pressure the Bush administration to act on the issue, and lastly, that a bi-national summit be held in Douglas within three months of the release of this report to develop a strategic plan of action for the implementation of the previous recommendations.[54]

NAHR Border 2003 Summit

On June 9, 2003, the report was released at a press conference held at Riverside, California. The report, along with a letter sent to Congressman Ciro D. Rodriguez, chair of CHC, again requesting congressional hearings on the growing vigilante and militia crisis were released to the media. The letter reiterated to Congressman Rodriguez that Congressman Raul Grijalva of Arizona and Joe Baca of California had endorsed the call for hearings. The letter read, "This is an extremely important issue of life and death to our people. Already some 2,355 migrants have died since 1995. Add the danger of the armed militias and rancher vigilantes to the mix and the crisis, especially in Arizona, becomes explosive."[55] As occurred in 2000 with the first request, CHC initiated no action. In fact, there was no official reply. Congressman Baca did however tell me that while CHC was working on the request, internal politics within CHC was preventing the push for hearings.

On August 29–31, 2003, a Bi-National Conference on Migrant and Worker's Rights was held in México City. It was organized by the PRD. Jose "Pepe" Jacques Medina, representing PRD's *La Comision Permanente Binacional para los Derechos Plenos de los Trabajadores Migratorios*, was the event's chief organizer. NAHR sent a small delegation to participate in the conference. Present as well were other delegations of Mexicanos representing labor, political, and civil and immigrant rights organizations from California, Texas, Illinois, Washington, Ohio, Arizona, North Carolina, Massachusetts, and Florida. Prior to departing to México City, NAHR held a press conference to make known the purposes of the binational conference, which was to promote Mexicanos' political rights in the United States, binational labor concerns, and human rights as they related to the continued militarization of the Cactus Curtain. Attended by some 200 persons, the conference started at 4:00 p.m. on August 29 at the México City Museum.[56] At the plenary session various speakers addressed a number of conference themes. During my presentation I addressed the growing rancher vigilante and militia border crisis and stressed the need to struggle against them using a bi-national approach. During the course of the two-day conference, several workshops were held that focused on the impact of NAFTA, the ramifications of the proposed Free Trade Agreement of the Americas (FTAA), and on the prospects for immigration reform in the U.S. NAHR's call for a U.S.–México border summit to be held on the Arizona–México border area was approved. The closing conference ceremony was held in the Senate chambers.

On November 20–22, NAHR convoked in Douglas, Arizona, the Bi-National U.S./Mexico Border Crisis Summit. The dates selected were important because November 20 is celebrated as the start of México's Revolution of 1910. During the three-day Summit, several events were organized both in Sonora, Mexico and in Douglas, Arizona. NAHR assumed responsibility for activities organized on the U.S. side while on México's side the effort was coordinated by Jacques Medina, representing PRD's *La Comision Permanente Binacional para los Derechos Plenos de los Trabajadores Migratorios* (CPBDPTM). Summit participation was by invitation only and those invited included pro-migrant rights organizational representatives, activists, and there were even Mexican congresspersons, and union leaders.

On Thursday, November 20, in Cananea, Sonora, a major symposium commemorating México's *Dia de la Revolucion Méxicana* (Day of the Mexican Revolution) was sponsored by CPBDPTM in collaboration with the *Sindicato de Mineros*. NAHR's twenty-person delegation attended along with some 100 from México. The evening's program included an official welcome by the *Sindicato de Mineros'* Secretary General Napoleon Gomez Urrutia, who spoke on the theme of México's Revolution of 1910 and on the need to continue the struggle for workers' rights both in México and in the U.S. Jacques Medina addressed the significance of the scheduled events and in particular the border summit. I spoke on the need to develop a bi-national movement in defense of the Mexicano migrants in the U.S. Other speakers addressed a number of themes related to labor and immigration issues.[57]

On Friday, November 21, the bi-national delegation comprised of some thirty persons traveled to Altar, located near the Sonora–Arizona border. A nine-member delegation of Mexican congresspersons that represented *La Comision de Poblacion Fronteras y Asuntos Migratorios* joined the ranks of the delegation. Altar was an important community for it was a key stopping place for migrants who were headed north to the U.S. It was there that they secured transportation, supplies, and hired a *pollero* or a *coyote*. The delegation was officially welcomed at the city hall by Altar's mayor. The delegation then met with Reverend Rene Castañeda, who directed a local refugee center that provided assistance to migrants, specifically food, lodging, clothing, and spiritual support. The priest said that he struggled from day to day to secure sufficient resources to operate the center's various programs. The congresspersons took a lot of notes, asked questions, and promised to look into what they could do to help his center.[58]

After the delegation's visit to Altar, they next traveled on a dirt road to Sasabe, Sonora. For NAHR this was the second visit to this border town used as a main crossing point by migrants.[59] Just prior to our arriving to Sasabe, the caravan was stopped by Mexican border patrolmen and Beta officials, who inquired as to the nature of the delegation's travel to Sasabe. While in route, the delegation encountered scores of large vans packed with migrants traveling to Sasabe. At one point our caravan stopped to observe the constant stream of vehicles. The presence of the Mexican congresspersons created an ambience of cordiality, cooperation, and constructive dialogue. In fact, as van after van was stopped for inspection by Beta, the delegation was granted the opportunity to dialogue with several of the migrants. The delegation split into three groups to get to as many migrants as possible to ask them very basic questions, for example, "Where are you coming from?" "What is your destination?" "Why did you undertake such a dangerous journey?" and "What problems have you encountered in your migrant exodus to the U.S.?" The vans kept arriving every ten to fifteen minutes, which verified the vast numbers of migrants who on a daily basis crossed from Sasabe into the hot and dangerous Sonoran desert of Southern Arizona.[60]

The responses of the sixty or so migrants interviewed were similar. Overwhelmingly, most said that they were from Michoacán, Oaxaca, Puebla, and Chiapas, and as to their desired destination in the United States, most said they were headed to the Midwest, for example, Chicago, and southern states such as Georgia and Alabama. Almost unanimously they said that the absence of jobs and lack of economic opportunities in their respective states was why they were going to the U.S. Many of the males who were interviewed said that they were married with children and that their inability to feed their families was the major reason for their leaving their homeland in search of work. Several of the migrants were vociferously hypercritical of the Fox administration as being responsible for México's impoverished status and migrant exodus.

In one of the exchanges Father Guillen asked a young mother, who could have been no older than eighteen years of age and who was accompanied by her two children, one of them two and the other four years old, why was she making the dangerous trip? She answered that life was economically intolerable in Oaxaca and that she and her two children were going to Chicago to join her husband who worked in construction. None made reference to any abuse, but instead focused on the economic hardships, that is, financial costs, of their journey and on not knowing what to expect in their journey north. As the vans regrouped, with tears in his eyes, Father Guillen blessed them, asking that God bless them and keep them safe in their journey to their destination. Prior to the migrants' departure, delegation members passed out printed information cards that contained information as to the dos and don'ts of crossing and the names of agencies to contact in different parts of the country. Each migrant was also given several bottles of water.

The delegation continued on its way to Sasabe México, where it met with city officials. Delegates spoke to people in the streets, businesses, and restaurants, asking questions pertinent to the issue of the migrant exodus. Late that afternoon, the delegation returned to Douglas, where a debriefing meeting was held at the Gadsden Hotel to review the day's activities and finalize the planning and agenda for the border summit, which would be held at the same hotel the next day. There was total consensus that the experiences in both Altar and Sasabe were invaluable since as participant observers we had succeeded in interacting with a number of migrants just before they crossed into Arizona.

Next day the U.S.–México Bi-national Border Summit was held in Douglas at the Gadsden Hotel. It was attended by seventy persons from both countries, including five of the nine congresspersons from México, and representatives from Tucson's CHC. The Summit's agenda focused on the delegation's Altar and Sasabe experiences. The agenda also addressed the general topic of the immigration crisis, specifically the militarization of the U.S.–México border, the vigilante and militia crisis, the increased migrant deaths crossing the border, and the need for immigration reform, especially legalization. The summit's purpose was to initiate a process of bi-national dialogue and ultimately action on these and other related border crisis issues.[61]

During the three-hour Summit, México's congresspersons blasted the U.S. government for its militarization of the Cactus Curtain by way of, for example, Operation Gatekeeper. Jacques Medina, Summit co-coordinator, addressed the disparity of U.S. border enforcement that existed between the U.S–Canadian and U.S.–México borders. He cited that out of the total 11,700 Border Patrol agents, 9,700 were stationed along México's 2,000-mile border and only 700 along Canada's 4,000-mile border. As the other Summit co-coordinator, I warned about the incessant intensification of the rancher vigilante and militia groups and activities, and again stressed the need of a more assertive bi-national response. The Summit concluded with agreement that more bi-national events should be held and the need for bi-national congressional hearings, which meant each country respectively would hold their own.

The culmination of the three-day Arizona–Sonora border activities entailed three protest press conferences. Coordinated by me, they were held at Roger Barnett's ranch, Jack Foote's Ranch Rescue's border compound, and the local U.S. Border Patrol facilities. The caravan of some fifteen vehicles, mostly vans, was accompanied by embedded newspaper and television reporters and two film groups doing documentaries on the militias and vigilantes. In all three instances, neither Barnett nor Foote showed their face or were available for comment. An interesting incident occurred: as the caravan left the front of the Ranch Rescue compound, reporter Stephen Wall of the *San Bernardino County Sun*, who traveled in the same van I was in, received a call on his cell phone from Jack Foote. Not knowing he was in our van, Foote informed him that his residence in the compound was under attack by a bunch of rock-throwing Mexicans. He said this to the reporter at a time when the caravan had already left the compound. Our reaction to Foote's allegation was one of laughter and disbelief—no such action ever occurred.

The delegation concluded with a protest press conference held at the U.S. Border Patrol facilities. The speakers vehemently addressed the alleged complicity of the Border Patrol with Burnett, Foote, Glenn Spencer's American Border Patrol, and Chris Simcox's Civil Homeland Defense. Mexican Congresswoman Rosa Maria Avilez, standing in front of the station said, "The U.S. government is responsible for all the deaths of Mexican migrants that have occurred since the 1990s. Migrants have been forced to cross the desert through inhospitable terrain and harsh weather because of the build-up of manpower and equipment."[62] I stated that the vigilantes and militias were "domestic terrorists" and that the migrant's only crime was fleeing from the tribulations of poverty and misery.[63] CFR's Isabel Garcia, spoke of the increasing deaths of migrants crossing the Arizona–Sonora border. And Jacques Medina promised that more bi-national activities were planned to deal with the growing border crisis.

Second Bi-National Border Meeting/Hearing

During December 2003, steps were initiated to hold the Second Bi-national Border Summit. NAHR assisted in its organization on the U.S. side and on México's side this time it was facilitated by the Chamber of Deputies *Comision de Poblacion y Asuntos Fronterizos*, hereafter referred to as *Comision*. This time, instead of calling it a summit, it was organized as a combination meeting and hearing on border issues. The meeting part was held on Friday, March 19, from 7:00 to 10:00 p.m., at the Gadsden Hotel in Douglas, Arizona. With an attendance of some fifty persons representing a number of organizations from mainly California, Arizona, Illinois, and México, the meeting's agenda included reports and focused on troubleshooting the next day's hearing schedule, which was programmed to run from 9:00 to 1:00 p.m.

The hearing drew some seventy-five persons. México's *Comision* secured the participation of nine congresspersons representing various political parties; on the U.S. side, however, while initially expressing great interest in participating, neither Congressman Joe Baca or Congressman Raul Grijalva attended. Those in attendance presented testimony on various aspects of issues exacerbating the border crisis. My report focused on the topic of Arizona's militias, rancher vigilantes, and violence on the U.S.–México border and human rights. Frank Martin Del Campo, representing LCLAA (Labor Council for Latin American Advancement) reported on the proposed Bush immigration plan. Angie Luna, representing the local Douglas LULAC (League of United Latin American Citizens) council reported on the violence against women in Juarez. Congresswoman Rosa Avilez from México reported to the attendees that the *Comisión* was engaged in developing a joint bi-national commission to monitor the diverse issues impacting the border crisis.

The absence of U.S. Latino congresspersons became an issue. NAHR had sent letters of invitation and calls had been made to CHC requestors of representation of the bi-national border summit, particularly the hearing. Congressman Raul Grijalva agreed to send a staff member[64] but no one else from CHC responded. While the caravan was in route to Douglas, *San Bernardino County Sun* reporter Stephen Wall, who traveled in the vehicle with me, wrote in his article that I said, "if [CHC] don't show up, it's a slap at the face of the Mexican delegation. It's an act of disrespect." In another related article on the matter, he reported that I said, "He [Baca] and the rest of the Congressional Hispanic Caucus need to take action not make excuses." Congressman Baca responded to my comments by stating "Armando is full of hot air. He does not realize that a lot of things that need to be done cannot be done overnight. We can have hearings, but we need legislation."[65] Baca also said that it was hard for his office to send staff, since the meeting was hundreds of miles away from San Bernardino. For the next three months or so relations between Baca and NAHR were strained.

For NAHR it became extremely difficult to maintain the momentum of trying to build a bi-national movement. After all, all of us in NAHR had full-time jobs; and what activities we organized were on our own time using our own resources. The success of our efforts created more demands for more work and activities, especially for me. I was teaching and writing a book at the time, which made my coordinator leadership role difficult and problematic. NAHR's increasingly bi-national posture and visibility had thus been a product of volunteers. Its success became increasingly overwhelming and more demanding. Adding to the difficulties was the pressure of the rancher vigilante and militia crisis; it escalated and grew and NAHR was not prepared. Adding to NAHR's pressures was the fact that it was overextended. While organizing bi-national border events it concomitantly was engaged in organizing anti-Iraq War activities; and kept the pressure on California State University, San Bernardino, to develop and implement its agreed-upon Chicano Studies Department.

Thus, during much of 2004, while NAHR as a network continued to monitor the vigilante and militia crisis, but it did not initiate any major border actions. NAHR next became involved in putting a halt to U.S. Border Patrol raids conducted in various parts of the inland empire (i.e., San Bernardino/Riverside Counties).

CHAPTER 10

NAHR's Struggle Against the Raids and Minuteman Project (2004–2005)

The immigration crisis intensified during 2004 to 2005. The country's political climate during these two years became even more xenophobic and nativist. The demographic effects of the re-Mexicanization of Aztlán and Latinoization or "browning" of the United States (U.S.) continued to feed the omnipresence of the anti-immigrant White Anglo-Saxon Protestant (WASP) ethos. Evidence of its effects was illustrated by the heightened number of raids conducted by the U.S. Border Patrol in California, the state with the largest number of Latinos, some 13 million. The U.S. Border Patrol raids fostered a rapid and well-organized response by Mexicano and Latino pro-migrant rights organizations and activists. The National Alliance for Human Rights (NAHR) was one of several entities that responded with effective and organized power. The pervasive anti-immigrant climate was also illustrated by the intensification of rancher vigilante and nativist militia activity, and particularly by the rise of the Minuteman Project (MP) in early 2005.

Using a case study format, this chapter examines NAHR's struggle against both the U.S. Border Patrol raids in California and the rise of MP and the national anti-immigrant movement (NAMM). Only when necessary is the first person used, since I was an active participant-observer in dealing with the events examined.

Summer 2004 Border Patrol Raids in the Inland Empire

BORDER PATROL RAIDS

During June and July of 2004, San Bernardino and Riverside counties were hit by a number of raids conducted by the U.S. Border Patrol. The twelve Border

Patrol agents from the Temecula station conducted raids on June 4 and 5 in the cities of Ontario and Corona. They led to the apprehension and deportation of some 154 undocumented migrants of which 94 percent were from México and the remaining 6 percent were from El Salvador and Guatemala. Gloria Chavez, a spokesperson for the U.S. Bureau of Customs and Border Protection, said the arrests were part of roving patrols conducted by the Mobile Patrol Group.[1] Local pro–migrant rights activists alleged that Ontario and Corona police departments assisted U.S. Border Patrol agents in carrying out the raids. A few days later, on June 9 in the city of Temecula, U.S. Border Patrol agents conducted another roving patrol raid that resulted in the arrest and deportation of some fifty-nine undocumented migrants.[2] As the issue unfolded, in order to dispel the impression that it was a White versus Mexicano/Latino issue, the Bureau strategically fronted Mexicanos and/or Latinos as official media spokespersons.

The sweeps targeted homes, parking lots, swap meets, and supermarkets in the two cities. Panic and fear permeated the areas where the undocumented lived, worked, and shopped. Some undocumented migrants and families refused to leave their homes, not even to buy food. Many refused to go to work or send their children to school. Literally they felt they were under a state siege as a community. Throughout the two counties, numerous Latino businesses reported a reduction of up to 60 percent in retail sales. Some businesses closed early while others for days failed to open.[3] Local Spanish radio stations broadcast information of U.S. Border Patrol sightings and other related information of the raids. *Hermandad Méxicana Nacional* (HMN), a local pro–immigrant rights agency on June 5 received some 300 calls from frightened individuals requesting information or assistance.[4]

Several local groups met on June 6 to form a "united front" to deal with the escalating raids.[5] Throughout the next few days, local and regional newspapers— from the *Inland Counties Daily Bulletin* and *The Press Enterprise* to the *Los Angeles Times* and *La Opinion*—coupled with radio and television coverage, intensified the migrants' awareness of the growing issue. On June 10, the newly formed united front that did not have a name per se, held a press conference in Ontario, which was attended by several of its leaders, including Congressman Joe Baca, whose district includes Ontario. Baca denounced the raids and sent a letter of complaint to the Department of Homeland Security, the parent department of the U.S. Border Patrol. Emilio Amaya, director of the San Bernardino–based Community Service Center, alleged that U.S. citizens and legal residents had also been detained and questioned.[6] Jose Calderon, a professor at Pitzer College, vociferously accused it of racial profiling and said, "This is an attack against all Latinos."[7]

NAHR Response to Raids

On June 13, in response to the raids, the united front held a protest rally and march. Organized in little over a week, the rally was held in the afternoon, with all assembling at Kiosk, located in downtown Ontario. Numerous local leaders, such as Emilio Amaya, Reverend Luis Angel Nieto, Jose Calderon, and Congresswoman Hilda Solis, repudiated the U.S. Border Patrol raids. With the people's anger clearly manifested, México's Consul Carlos I. Gibralt-Cabrales in San Bernardino exhorted that people remain calm.[8] The rally started out with only some 500 people, but in a matter of one hour it grew to some 2000 people. The rally culminated with a seven-mile long march from Ontario to Pomona's city hall. While it began with the participation of some 2,000 people, by the time it reached Pomona, it had grown dramatically to some 10,000 people. As the march moved on the sidewalk toward Pomona, thousands of people parked their vehicles and joined in as marchers waved placards and Mexican and U.S. flags. The march was never sanctioned by either the city of Ontario or the city of Pomona, which meant that no parade permits were obtained.[9] It was an unprecedented event in that never before in the history of the Ontario/Pomona Valley had there been such a huge mobilization. What stimulated this great success was a combination of the people's anger and frustration, the united front's organizing efforts, and the media's coverage, especially from Spanish-speaking radio.

NAHR did not directly mobilize on the issue until after the march. The reasons were four: (1) the initial organizing emanated from Ontario's local groups; (2) NAHR supported the march by disseminating information via the Internet and phone calls to help mobilize the region's Latino communities; (3) with the absence of similar organizing efforts in Corona and Escondido, NAHR would begin to work to create a similar type of unified effort throughout the inland empire and southern California; and (4) NAHR worked to consolidate the various groups, including the Ontario/Pomona united front, to develop a well-organized strategic response to the raids.

On June 15, NAHR began the process of coordinating a southern California countervailing response to the U.S. Border Patrol raids. Assisted by Father Patricio Guillen's *Libreria del Pueblo*, NAHR convoked a regional Latino leadership meeting to coalesce the Mexicano/Latino leadership and to strategically produce a plan of action designed to halt the raids. In a NAHR press release I explained the purpose of the meeting:

> The [raid] situation has reached a crisis. What the Border Patrol is doing is reminiscent of what Hitler's storm troopers did in Germany during the 1930s. Whereas for purposes of identification the Jewish people were persecuted and compelled to wear the Star of David;

Mexicanos and other Latinos today are also being persecuted—the difference being is that our brown color of skin is our identification badge.[10]

A number of organizational leaders and activists addressed the more than 100 people in attendance. Father Guillen described the raids as a "war on the poor."[11] Mexican Consul Gibralt-Cabrales reported that his government had issued a formal complaint to the Department of Homeland Security protesting the U.S. Border Patrol raids. Christian Ramirez of San Diego's American Friends Service Committee reported on the U.S. Border Patrol's raids in the San Diego area. He said, "Welcome to the nightmare of border life. This is what it's like for us every day." From the floor, Congressman Joe Baca and State Senator Nell Soto's field representatives reported that both were supportive of NAHR's efforts to unify the groups and put a stop to the raids.[12] It was also reported that throughout southern California numerous Spanish-language radio stations were providing community alerts, and informing the public as to the locations of the Border Patrol and raids in progress. In response to the aforementioned, it was reported that White nativist radio hosts, such as John and Ken from KFI, encouraged their listeners to call and complain to the Federal Communications Commission (FCC) that Spanish-language radio stations were telling their listeners how to avoid getting picked up and what to do if they were apprehended by the U.S. Border Patrol.[13]

At the meeting NAHR presented a proposed plan of action to deal with the raids. It included such actions as mounting an immigrants' rights information campaign, forming local/regional coalitions, initiating protests and marches against the U.S. Border Patrol, lobbying U.S. politicians for their intervention, securing support from México's Fox government to pressure the Bush administration into halting the raids, and, if need be, initiating litigation. The plan stressed the importance of galvanizing a massive statewide and national Mexicano/Latino response to the raids.[14] After much discussion and debate, with few if any amendments, it was adopted.

Within the next two weeks, various aspects of the NAHR plan were implemented. Ontario, San Bernardino, and Riverside regional coalitions were formed and began meeting on a regular basis. Plans were formulated for possible protests and counteractions against the U.S. Border Patrol and contingency plans were developed should the raids and sweeps continue, which included organized civil disobedience. By late June, the U.S. Border Patrol reported having apprehended in the counties of San Bernardino and Riverside a total of 450 undocumented migrants.[15] Congressman Baca and Congresswoman Solis pressured Homeland Security officials to cease their raids. Baca wrote a letter to Robert Bonner, commissioner of U.S. Customs and Border Protection. In the letter, he expressed concern over the apparent expansion of their jurisdiction to engage in disruptive enforcement in crowded residential and workplace communities.[16] A congressional delegation that included Solis, Javier Becerra, Lucille Roybal-Allard, and Baca met with Asa Hutchinson, Undersecretary of Homeland Security, to review the legality of the Temecula Border Patrol mobile operations.[17]

A major victory for the pro-immigrant rights side was scored when Hutchinson publicly admitted that the U.S. Border Patrol agents had broken department policy. Mario Villareal, a spokesperson for Customs and Border Protection, an agency of Homeland Security, said, "While the Border Patrol activities in Temecula were within their statutory authority, there was not an appropriate . . . headquarters review and approval prior to the beginning of the operation." Solis reported that even though Hutchinson had agreed to keep a close eye on such operations in the future, he did not, however, discount the possibilities of conducting similar operations in the coming months.[18]

In response to Hutchinson's statement and the death of an undocumented migrant while detained in a holding cell at the Temecula Border Patrol Station, on July 5 NAHR, flanked by some forty organizational representatives and activists carrying U.S. and Mexican flags, held a protest press conference in front of the Temecula facility. Dozens of U.S. Border Patrol agents dressed for riot control lined up shoulder to shoulder in front of the facility, while others were positioned on rooftops as snipers, and a large contingent was held in reserve at the back of the building. Barricades were set up in front of the facilities. A helicopter flew constantly over the Temecula station. And about twenty White counterprotestors, in support of the U.S. Border Patrol, with U.S. flags and placards with anti-immigrant slogans, demonstrated, and using their bullhorns vociferously protested NAHR's protest. Tensions were high so the two protesting groups were separated by Riverside County Sheriff deputies.

NAHR speaker after speaker homed in on the "rogue raids" that were conducted in a Gestapo-like manner by the mobile patrol units and on the pervasive climate of fear created that was reminiscent of Nazi Germany during the 1930s.[19] NAHR's cardinal objective was to pressure U.S. Border Patrol officials into stopping the raids and/or sweeps. Furthermore, they were warned that if they did not, there would be severe consequences. In my press comments, I warned that the forty protestors present would quickly grow to hundreds and if necessary to thousands. Right after the press conference, I met briefly with U.S. Border Patrol officials on both the issue of the raids and the undocumented migrant's death; however, they refused to discuss either issue in any detail. Nonetheless, they did let me know that an autopsy had been ordered for the dead migrant.

The Temecula protest proved to be a great media victory for NAHR. Print and electronic media coverage was extensive, which was an intrinsic aspect of NAHR's protest strategy. The idea was to generate major media coverage and then use it to pressure the U.S. Border Patrol into stopping the raids; and two, the media coverage would help in organizing subsequent NAHR actions. It also helped that television, radio, and newspaper accounts dramatized the presence of large number of U.S. Border Patrol agents and Riverside County Sheriff personnel, which numbered nearly 100. Also reported was their overall paramilitary posture that projected a "state of war climate." When asked by the press to comment, I said that NAHR's protestors had walked into a "war zone" where we were designated as the enemy and "they were ready to do battle with us, but our battle plan was non-violent."[20]

During July, NAHR increased the political pressure directed at U.S. Border Patrol officials. It coordinated a number of concurrent activities: (1) newly formed local coalitions held community meetings; (2) Spanish-speaking media, especially radio stations, continued to inform the public; (3) congressional leaders Solis and Baca continued to communicate with Homeland Security officials; and (4) the scope of NAHR's networking outreach efforts to other pro-migrant entities and activists were expanded to a southern California regional basis as well as statewide in order to forge a more powerful pressure response. By the end of June, NAHR's mobilization efforts had produced scores of entities and activists prepared to take on the U.S. Border Patrol should more sweeps be initiated. Luckily, due to the growing pressure applied, the raids stopped.

For the various groups and activists that participated in the mobilization this was a great victory; however, for the U.S. Border Patrol agents in Temecula, it was not so great. *North County Times* reporter William Finn Bennett reported that "frustration is growing at the Temecula Border Patrol station, following a management decision to cut back on illegal immigrant sweeps." He cited Ron Zermeno, shop steward for the National Border Patrol Council at the Temecula station, who said, "We don't know which way to turn—for once, we were doing our job, what the government pays us to do."[21]

While there was a stop put to the raids, NAHR believed that they could again start up. Therefore, NAHR convoked a planning summit in Ontario on July 9 at Our Lady of Guadalupe Parish Hall. Attended by some seventy-five leaders from throughout southern and central California, the summit's agenda focused on fine-tuning NAHR's existent mobilization strategy for preventing future U.S. Border Patrol raids and sweeps.[22] As organizer of the summit, my message was that we continue to be vigilant and not become complacent and that we needed to continue the buildup of our organizational capability to advocate and mobilize. At the Ontario summit, a call was made for a statewide meeting on immigration to be held in Los Angeles.[23]

Later that month, NAHR, in conjunction with a delegation from the Central American Resource Center led by Angela Sanbrano, met with Corona Police Department officials on the matter of the Honduran migrant's death at the U.S. Border Patrol station in Temecula. The NAHR investigation on the matter revealed that initially Ecar Paz Moradel had been arrested by the Corona Police

Department for vandalism and being under the influence of drugs. He was released to U.S. Border Patrol agents and was taken to the Temecula station where he died mysteriously in a holding cell. It had been reported to the public that Moradel had hung himself in his cell. On the table for discussion was the Corona Police Department's relationship with the U.S. Border Patrol and specifically the allegation that they had assisted them in the raid conducted in Corona. Police Chief Richard Gonzales unequivocally denied that his police officers had participated in the raid. I was able to secure an assurance from him that the Corona Police Department's role was not to enforce immigration law.[24]

The statewide meeting was held in Los Angeles on August 7. It was facilitated by Community Service Center under the leadership of Carlos Montez. The some 100 persons in attendance focused on strengthening efforts statewide to respond to any future U.S. Border Patrol raids or sweeps. In my address, I stressed the importance of not becoming overconfident or complacent and that we must develop a statewide mobilization plan. I reminded them that stopping the Border Patrol raids came about because of effective organization, leadership, and power demonstrated by our communities. I also reminded them of the growing vigilante and militia crisis in southern Arizona.[25] The meeting ended in conflict, however, over divisions that existed within the Los Angeles-based groups; therefore, there was no statewide plan of action.

During the rest of 2004, NAHR shifted its organizing efforts from immigration to protesting the Iraq War and occupation. In October it organized a multiethnic anti-Bush protest rally in San Bernardino that drew some 300 people. The effort was organized for the purpose of discouraging voters from voting for the reelection of President Bush. NAHR also participated in a statewide march and rally that called for equal rights for immigrants, held in Los Angeles on October 16. Organized by the newly formed Coalition for Immigrant Rights and Against the Raids, under the leadership of Carlos Montes, both events drew some 1,000 people, mostly from Los Angeles.

NAHR Confronts the Minuteman Project

By January 2005 the press began to report on the incipient organizing efforts of James Gilchrist, a retired accountant from California, and Chris Simcox, founder and leader of the Civil Homeland Defense (CHD) to launch a new nativist militia—the Minuteman Project (MP). By February the press was carrying frequent articles on MP's border surveillance activities scheduled for the month of April 2005 along the Douglas area Arizona–Sonora border.

In January 2005 NAHR began to prepare for a response. Several regional bimonthly meetings were held and increasingly discussions focused on MP's developments and implications. Calls were made to various NAHR contacts in Arizona, including CHR's leadership. Maria Anna Gonzales, a research analyst with the University of California, Riverside, Ernesto Galarza Applied Research Center, conducted research on MP and its leaders Gilchrist and Simcox, and I did the same. The research helped NAHR prepare for the countervailing opposition to MP in April. NAHR held several community meetings in Riverside and in San Bernardino, with the principal agenda item being MP.

By early March NAHR's research on MP had revealed that Arizona's pro–migrants rights organizations were planning some actions for April 1; however, it seemed to NAHR that their response lacked assertiveness and was largely symbolic at best. After much deliberation, the decision was made to organize a delegation of activists from California that would travel to Arizona and carry out a number of actions during the early days of the MP's month-long border activities. By way of the telephone and the Internet NAHR disseminated information statewide on its delegation to Arizona.

Some of Arizona's pro–migrant rights organizations upon learning of NAHR's intervention were not supportive of its proposed plans to take an aggressive posture toward MP, yet NAHR continued to seek their support, in particular that of CHR. Around the Douglas area, NAHR succeeded in securing support from some local Latino activists. CHR's leadership, however, turned a rather cold shoulder and made it clear that NAHR's intervention in Arizona was not welcome. NAHR's response was that the rise of MP as a militia was a serious escalation of the ongoing rancher vigilante and militia border surveillance patrols and that it needed to be stopped in its tracks. Furthermore, that it needed to be addressed at a regional to national level.

In an effort to garner support and minimize the fallout of not having the major pro–immigrant rights groups in Arizona on board, on March 18, NAHR convoked a press conference in San Bernardino to formally announce its "binational action strategy" designed to counteract the domestic terrorist and militia-driven MP. Activists representing a number of organizations spoke out against what they perceived as MP's malevolent players and proposed border surveillance activities. NAHR announced that its volunteers would be present on both sides of the Arizona–Sonora border to protest and initiate its bi-national strategy against MP. In the NAHR press release, I explained, "We intend to create in the ensuing weeks beginning on March 31 a countervailing mobilization both in the United States and México that will demonstrate with action that as Mexicanos and Latinos we will not allow these domestic terrorists to intimidate, harass, injure, or violate the human rights of undocumented migrants. The various speakers reinforced NAHR's message that the delegation going to Arizona was committed to nonviolence and the prevention of a border conflict from occurring as a result of the MP border patrols.[26] When asked by the press to elucidate on its planned activities, I said, "We will adjust to the situation, and obviously some of us have experience in the military . . . so there will be maybe some elements of surprises in terms of activities, and that is a warning to the militias."[27] During the press conference CHC was also criticized for its silence and unwillingness to address the growing rancher vigilante and nativist militia issue or MP's rise in southern Arizona. On this point I reiterated what I had said in 2000 with the rise of armed rancher vigilantes, "If this issue was impacting African-Americans you would have Jessie Jackson and every [Black] organization calling for a national mobilization against these forces'" and emphasized that the time had come for Mexicanos and Latinos to close ranks in order to meet "this incredible threat that represents itself in the form of the Minutemen Project."[28]

The response was so overwhelming that prior to the delegation's departure to Arizona, I personally did numerous radio, television, and newspaper interviews. In no time, NAHR became an intrinsic part of the MP media hype nationwide. Concomitantly, NAHR secured extensive coverage by nativists on anti-immigrant websites, talk radio shows, and television news reports.

Sensationalism pervaded the anticipated MP April events, especially of the possibilities of a confrontation or violence between MP and protesting anti-MP groups. For instance, the media report that the infamous Latino gang *Mara Salvatruchas* had threatened MP served to exacerbate the growing tensions and the media hype. Regardless that no conclusive evidence was ever produced, the FBI in February arrested 130 *Mara Salvatrucha* gang members nationwide in an effort to minimize threats to MP volunteers.[29] When asked by the press if he was worried by the threat, MP leader Gilchrist said, "We're not worried because half of our recruits are retired trained combat soldiers. And these guys are just a bunch of punks."[30]

Prior to the NAHR delegation's departure on March 30, the press got wind that some of the pro-migrant groups in Arizona were not pleased with our efforts, which included, if need be, confrontational efforts. In response to fears of a confrontation occurring, Jesus Romo, an attorney for Border Action Network, said in reference to the NAHR delegation, "We tried to dissuade them because we don't think it would be a good idea to focus on that kind of behavior. And simply creating a confrontation would be counter-productive for everyone."[31] His statements and the actions of others only helped ensure that NAHR was put into a leading anti-MP Mexicano protagonist position. For me in particular, as was the case in 2003, the threatening phone calls and e-mails dramatically increased, as did the death threats.[32]

On March 30, in advance of the delegation's arrival, a ten-person team left Riverside for the *Agua Prieta*, Sonora, Hotel plaza. NAHR event organizers felt it necessary to set up operations in *Agua Prieta* instead of Douglas for two major reasons: (1) it was important that we establish a bi-national presence; and (2) simply put, we were outnumbered—they anticipated 1,300 MP volunteers. Our plan was to conduct anti-MP activities on the Arizona side of the border during daylight hours and for security reasons hold our regrouping, planning, and sleeping on the Mexican side of the border. The advance team's arrival stimulated a considerable number of newspaper, radio, and television interviews. Local PRD leaders facilitated the media exposure with the Spanish-language media. Others from the advance team met with *Agua Prieta's* mayor, city officials, church, and civic and business leaders, in an effort to gain their support.

That evening the rest of the NAHR delegation arrived. The thirty delegates came from Riverside, San Bernardino, Orange, Los Angeles, and San Diego counties. In addition to NAHR members/leaders the delegation also included PRD State Chair Felipe Aguirre, Comité Pro Uno's Jose Jacques Medina, Mexican Political Association State Coordinator Raul Wilson, La Unión del Barrio's Christian Ramirez, and Los Amigos of Orange County's Arturo Guevarra.[33] That evening, the delegation held a meeting at the hotel in preparation for the next three days' activities. The delegation was divided into several teams to cover all the major aspects of NAHR anti-MP organizing protest efforts scheduled for the Douglas/Tombstone/Naco area as well as on the México side of the border.

Because the number of NAHR delegates was much lower than anticipated, the delegation plans were to be highly mobile and quick in protest approach. NAHR delegation members were not permitted to carry weapons and were advised to avoid making physical threats and to avoid altercations. Yet the principle of self-defense was adhered to. Its strategy was grounded on three objectives: (1) project an image of first-rate organization and commitment to nonviolent protesting, all the while showing courage; (2) disrupt the James Gilchrist, Chris Simcox, and MP scheduled activities; and (3) use the anti-MP protests to promote the image that MP volunteers were badly organized, racist, and nativist "domestic terrorists."

The four-day stay at Agua Prieta produced numerous activities on both sides of the border. Maria Anna Gonzales, from March 30 until April 2, participated with an American Civil Liberties Union (ACLU) contingent of legal observers led by Ray Ybarra, which monitored MP's border vigilance activities, which included monitoring MP's convention at Tombstone. Throughout its twenty-one-day duration, Ybarra and his volunteers monitored MP's activities to ensure that no human rights violations occurred. Ybarra's anti-MP posture was well known by MP's leadership. He described the presence of the Minuteman volunteers at the border as constituting "unlawful imprisonment" of undocumented migrants."[34] Maria Anna's firsthand observations provided us with invaluable intelligence on the strengths and weaknesses of MP.

On March 31, as part of the ACLU observer team, Gonzales and other legal observers were present for the opening event and ceremonies of MP held in Tombstone. She took copious notes and that evening in the debriefing session, reported that only a handful of MP volunteers (i.e., no more than fifty) had shown up, far short from the 1,300 or so that Gilchrist and Simcox had publicized. She said there were more reporters and television crews totaling over 100 than there were MP volunteers. Also, as part of the anti-MP protests, a group of Azteca dancers with drums chanted and danced outside the opening MP ceremony, which upset both Gilchrist and Simcox. When interviewed by the press on her role, she said, as legal observers "we are prepared to document any violations perpetrated by the Minutemen against Mexicano migrants."[35]

While in *Agua Prieta*, another NAHR team organized a joint bi-national press conference held on March 31 at *Plaza Azueta* in *Agua Prieta*. Local Agua Prieta PRD leaders Luis Guajardo and Roberto Castro contacted the bi-national media, produced and distributed flyers, and conducted newspaper, radio, and television interviews for the purpose of promoting the NAHR's bi-national activities. Joined by local PRD leaders, several delegates addressed a number of NAHR themes and its anti-MP strategy. A cardinal point stressed by local PRD leaders was that if the NAHR delegation came under attack by MP zealots across the border an immediate blockade of the *Agua Prieta*/Douglas border crossing would occur.[36]

The next morning on Saturday, April 1, the NAHR delegation caravanned to the Douglas/Naco area and began its rapid deployment, protesting various MP activities. In the absence of any other Mexicano group, NAHR's delegation became the countering protest group to the MP. Equipped with its own portable sound system, NAHR played Mexicano music loudly. Tactically, the intent was to disrupt MP's activities, infuriating its volunteers and leaders. The music selections included protest songs, *corridos*, and polkas all for the purpose of creating an ambiance of activism for the NAHR demonstrators and also to disrupt the MP supporters' speeches. At each event there were numerous Mexican flags, standards, and placards. Tensions were high between the two sides and the media was eating it up, since they were just looking for a violent incident to occur.

Throughout the day, Gonzales, using her cell phone, kept the delegation abreast of the MP's activities, especially as to their whereabouts, especially Gilchrist and Simcox. Armed with picket signs and bullhorns, the NAHR delegation initiated some five anti-MP protests and held press conferences after each, which drew extensive media coverage. The NAHR delegation deliberately sought to locate and confront directly either one of the two MP leaders or both. But MP volunteers, never numbering more than 200 and cognizant of NAHR's presence, reported its activities to both Gilchrist and Simcox, keeping them a jump ahead of us. On one specific occasion, near the Border Patrol stations close to Naco, the delegation missed Gilchrist by just a few minutes. At another anti-MP protest the situation became tense and precarious. Reporters Sharon McNary and Chris Richards of the *Press Enterprise* describe the encounter:

> Yards away, across the narrow asphalt street that leads to the Border
> Patrol Headquarters, UC Riverside Professor Armando Navarro and

another 20 demonstrators gathered to protest the Minutemen Project. They held up a Mexican flag and a banner saying in Spanish, "It
is my country, it is my struggle." Navarro's group turned on the music—Spanish hip-hop, then Mexican polka. In Spanish they chanted,
too: "the force united will never be defeated."[37]

A near confrontation occurred between the NAHR delegation and some
seventy-five or so MP volunteers, when MP volunteer Jerry Doehr of Green Valley, Arizona, angered over NAHR's disrupting loudness, crossed the street. Suddenly scores of reporters converged on both Doehr and me, pushing in with
cameras and microphones. I took the initiative and denigrated MP's nativist and
racist politics. I said to him, "This is a warning for you . . . I don't think you want
to be associated with these paramilitaries and vigilantes." Doehr responded by
offering me a cold drink, which I accepted.[38] He then walked back to his camper
truck across the street. It displayed to the media NAHR's nonviolent posture; yet
its fearless resolve, even when outnumbered by three to one, to confront the MP
zealots; and its ability to control the message. After the thirty-minute protest, the
NAHR delegation left to another protest in search of Gilchrist, but again we had
just missed him.

That afternoon the NAHR delegation returned to *Agua Prieta* for its scheduled anti-MP rally. Organized by a combination of NAHR delegation members
and local groups headed by the PRD, it attracted some 400 people, far short of
the 1,000 that had been anticipated. Both the mayors of *Agua Prieta* and *Calexico*, local *Agua Prieta* leaders, and delegation members addressed the small enthusiastic crowd and media event.[39] NAHR delegation members and local *Agua
Prieta* leaders provided details on what had been agreed earlier, which was to
hold a one-day "closure" of the *Agua Prieta*/Douglas border on May 1 and "boycott" of Douglas's businesses. Its purpose was to apply bi-national political pressure at the local, state, and federal levels to get authorities to publicly condemn
the MP and take steps to proactively impede its organizing activities in southern
Arizona. Local *Agua Prieta* leaders also issued a call for local people to boycott
U.S. goods during a specified time that was announced later. The mayors of
Agua Prieta and Douglas, while initially supportive, after the rally expressed their
disapproval of the planned two events stating that they would negatively impact
their respective community's economies.

On Sunday, April 3, the NAHR delegation returned to California. During
the three-week duration of MP's border surveillance activities, some anti-MP
Mexicano and Latino activists traveled and protested the anti-immigrant efforts;
however, no "organized" Mexicano group replaced NAHR's delegation as a
countervailing voice to MP. NAHR's strategy was to return to Arizona but due
to its own internal weaknesses, that is, lack of resources, staff, and the volunteer
status of delegates, it did not go back.

As for other activities corresponding with NAHR's four-day stay in Arizona, it would suffice to say that they were minimal at best. Considering that MP had set up camp in their own backyard, the pro-immigrant rights activists of Arizona failed to respond massively to it. Not one day was there a significant number of protesters at any of the MP's events. On April 1, in symbolic fashion, a group of Latino Arizona state legislators, led by State Representative Ben Miranda, came into the Douglas area to convey to the public their opposition to the MP.[40] During the next three days, outside of a few CHR members, most Mexicanos, Latinos, and Whites present at the NAHR activities were there as individuals. The other protests were organized chiefly by CHR, which is comprised of both Whites and Mexicanos. One such event was a thirty-minute vigil of silence by the "Women in Black," in which NAHR too participated.

NAHR's post-delegation and anti-MP strategy was predicated on it being a precipitating "catalyst" for further protests by others. Strategically, the intent was to create a "multiplier effect," where other Mexicano and Latino groups from throughout Aztlán and elsewhere in the country would come to the Douglas area and pick up where NAHR left off. The hope was that each protest would be larger and stronger than the last, culminating with a massive "mobilization" on a given weekend. NAHR's plan, however, never materialized. On the other hand, during the last Saturday of the third week of MP's border surveillance activities, CHR held a march that drew a couple of hundred anti-MP activists.

During the rest of April NAHR monitored MP's daily developments, maintained communication with supporters in the Douglas area, held community meetings, disseminated information via the Internet to other groups, and encouraged others to travel to southern Arizona to protest. I spent most of my time organizing for the May 1 shutdown of the *Agua Prieta* border crossing and the Douglas economic boycott. On México's *Agua Prieta* side the idea was to mobilize thousands who would march from the downtown area and proceed to the border crossing area, where a protest rally would be held, shutting down the border for eight or so hours. On the U.S. side the preceding would be duplicated also involving large numbers of protestors. The concurrent protests would come together at the border and become one massive bi-national mobilization. The economic boycott of Douglas's businesses would go into effect.

In a surprise move, at the end of MP's third week of border surveillance Gilchrist and Simcox abruptly ended its activities. Thus, with the exception of ACLU legal monitoring efforts and NAHR's anti-MP protest activities and those of CHR, there was little to no Mexicano or Latino countervailing activity. In essence, Latinos failed to show their presence in great numbers to the rising MP menace.

In late April, Gilchrist and Simcox wasted no time in announcing their plans to expand MP nationwide. NAHR reacted by initiating in southern

California a series of meetings in preparation for MP border operations planned for June. The meetings were also utilized by NAHR to organize for the planned May 1st *Agua Prieta* border closing and boycott. As a precursor to the May 1 events, a weekend boycott of Douglas's businesses was organized by *Agua Prieta's* local PRD leadership in mid-April. According to reports, there was a small decrease in the number of Mexicanos crossing from *Agua Prieta* into Douglas.

While the numbers were low, they were enough to warrant an angry intervention by *Agua Prieta* Mayor Figueroa and Douglas Mayor Borane, and other city officials and business leaders, who angrily called for a halt on the planning of both events.

In an interview with *Los Angeles Times* reporters, Borane, using strong words, derided the NAHR proposed blockade: "They're prostituting our city like the Minutemen, for personal gain. We don't want them here. They're not needed, invited, or welcomed." He further commented, "With his [Navarro's] attention-seeking actions, he's going to impact us worse than the Minuteman Project because he can hurt us economically by shutting the border down."[41] The political and economic pressure became so great that local Agua Prieta PRD leadership was pressured into abandoning the effort. Without local organizing support on the México side, NAHR was compelled to cancel the border blockade.[42]

Nevertheless, during May and June, NAHR monitored MP's activities and expansion. For NAHR, the demands on it were such that as its coordinator I was in over my head in commitments and work. I was teaching full time at UCR, writing my fourth book, conducting research on my fifth book (on the immigration crisis), and trying to coordinate NAHR's organizing activities. The pressure exerted by the media for interviews and television appearances were overwhelming. It was apparent that NAHR's anti-MP organizing efforts in southern Arizona had catapulted it onto national/international levels of media attention. For me, this was reflective of the major organizational and leadership void that existed among Mexicanos and Latinos on the controversial issue of MP.

Adding to the caldron of problems, NAHR as a network did not possess the requisite organization, membership, resources, staff, office, and so forth, to keep up with the demands created by our successful anti-MP intervention. None of the organizations and/or activist leaders within NAHR's network was capable of assuming a national to international leadership role. For that reason I encouraged other groups and leaders within and outside of NAHR to take the leadership in the struggle against MP.

Gilchrist, Simcox, and other militia leaders, such as Spencer and Foote, and groups like Save Our State (SOS) in California orchestrated a concerted attack on NAHR and me. Their principal weapon of attack was the Internet. Their Internet sites listed me as being a separatist and seditionist, and they gave me other labels. Numerous threats and hate calls were made to my university office as well as to my personal cell phone. UCR police set up a system to monitor my office telephone and trace threat calls. Anti-immigrant forces also worked, unsuccessfully, to pressure UCR Chancellor France Cordova and the UC president to have me fired. They sent letters, e-mailed, called, and held a protest of three to five persons at UCR and distributed flyers. There were also the local and national nativist radio and television commentators who attacked me and NAHR's anti-MP organizing efforts.

Another problem facing NAHR's organizing activities was the developing schisms among emergent activist forces in California. This was evident in late April when there was debate among some activists in California over my leadership role in the struggle against MP and on the planned May 1st closing of the Agua Prieta border crossing. It was somewhat disheartening for me to know that some of the activists were hypercritical of my leadership on the issue of MP. Equally frustrating was that for the last five years, NAHR had carried the ball in California against the rise of the armed rancher vigilantes, nativist militias, and now MP in southern Arizona, yet now, all of a sudden, these persons, neophyte activists, if you will, began to maneuver to capture the so-called leadership of the Mexicano anti-MP movement. Indicative of the debate surrounding my leadership role was an article written by Professor Rodolfo Acuña sent via the Internet entitled, "A Pretext to Do Nothing":

> Dwelling on personality or organizations is the easiest way to avoid doing anything on an issue. On that score, over the years, people have asked me why I went to Cuba with Armando Navarro or marched with him at the border . . . My answer is simple: Armando has a history and is generally more right on the issues than he is wrong. Moreover, he is doing something . . . Right now he is the only voice from California who is saying something about the thugs on the Arizona border.[43]

In a response to the Acuña article, Nativo Lopez, president of the Mexican American Political Association (MAPA) wrote:

> I agree with Rudy, Armando has taken the lead on this issue and we are required, to the degree that life permits us, to join the initiative . . . An acknowledged leader of our people has taken the lead and deserves our support. It's not about Armando, it's about the injustice heaped at our people and the need to articulate a political and practical response . . . I also encourage people to join and unite with the National Alliance for Human Rights and other organizations who have demonstrated the "cajones" . . . to respond to the racist challenge—both on the line and in the media.[44]

In May, I decided that the time had come for me to disengage from my anti-MP organizing leadership role because of personal reasons previously explained and NAHR's limited resource capacity to effectively address the day-to-day organizing demands of acting as a countervailing force to MP. However, my disengagement proved to be gradual, since in the ensuing months NAHR began to assist other groups in preparing for planned MP activities in California. NAHR's organizing role became one of disseminating information on MP activities, holding planning and community meetings, and activating other activists and groups in California to take the leadership mantle.

Meanwhile, in California, as early as April, SOS leader Joseph Turner accelerated his attacks on *jornaleros* (day workers) at various Home Depot centers. The rise of MP and other anti-immigrant groups fomented the rise of pro-migrant rights coalitions. Joined by progressive Left groups they responded with counterdemonstrations against the numerous SOS protests. NAHR was supportive of the anti-SOS protests but due to its overwhelmingly heavy task-oriented anti-MP agenda did little to no organizing around the issue.

On May 28 an anti-MP organizing conference was held at UCR-led and organized by Jessie Diaz, a sociology graduate student, and MEChA undergraduate students, with some 100 people in attendance, discussions focused on developing a strategy to counter the planned MP border surveillance activities along the California–México border, scheduled to start in the upcoming summer weeks.[45] Their efforts produced an opportunity to expand NAHR's anti-MP organizing efforts in California.

On June 18, in El Centro, California, NAHR, in conjunction with the Institute for Socio-Economic and Progressive Community Development, led by Eric Reyes, and District 1 Imperial County Supervisor Victor Carrillo of Calexico, held a strategic planning session at the Women's Improvement Club on the expected start of the MP surveillance of the Méxicali–El Centro border area on September 16. Attended by some fifty persons, including local Mexicano elected officials and activists, NAHR assisted in the development of an anti-MP strategy for the area. At a press conference held right after the meeting near the border fence separating both countries, I reminded the crowd and press that this was a very historical moment for us as well as the people of California and the people of México. We were witnessing the unification of two communities that are divided by this imaginary "wall" (as I tapped on the border fence). Reyes enunciated that it was an honor to work with NAHR in developing "the confidence to be able to work with one another on the issues of human rights no matter where one lives or where they were born."[46] A consequence of the media coverage was a flood of slanderous attacks on me by MP sympathizers. They became so intense that the local politicians and activists who welcomed NAHR's participation now ran for cover, distancing themselves from me and NAHR. To their credit, however, they did organize against MP's actions.

Throughout the remaining months of 2005, nationwide several Mexicano and Latino groups hastily formed coalitions to combat the spread of MP. Nowhere in the country was it as intensive and explosive as it was in California. When interviewed on this matter, I explained, "This is not Arizona. Here [in California] you have numerous groups throughout the state that are pro-immigration rights, and some of them are willing to go much further than some of us. The situation could be very explosive."[47]

The Cactus Curtain, especially around the Campo area of the San Diego–Tijuana border, became a political battleground of anti-MP resistance by a number of Mexicano/Latino/Left groups and activists. One such entity was the newly formed *Gente Unida* Coalition (GUC) led by Enrique Morones from San Diego. Several GUC volunteers camped in the Campo area for weeks keeping tabs on MP activities. During the month of July and again from September to December two NAHR members, Vicente Rodriguez from San Diego and Danny Morales from Riverside, camped with others and monitored and at times disrupted MP's border surveillance efforts.

From their perspective, it was a war zone. Both Rodriguez and Morales kept me abreast of the volatile and precarious developments of the Campo border area. Their reports often alluded to the escalating tensions for open conflict between MP domestic terrorists and their human rights adversaries, all of which was corroborated by heavy media coverage. During their stay at the border, they reported on several incidents that occurred, where shots had been fired and of near-physical confrontations between the two opposing forces. GUC leader Morones, who also headed Border Angels, a San Diego group that for years had provided water and food to undocumented migrants as they crossed, when interviewed on the growing tensions said, "They have guns and are acting like G.I Joe on the border."[48]

Jessie Diaz on almost every weekend mobilized both Mexicano and Left groups from Los Angeles and southern California to the Campo area in support of GUC, and in an assertive manner confronted MP volunteers. As a result, MP in the Campo area that reached Méxicali was put into a defensive posture. Consistently, they were outnumbered and outorganized. Along with various other groups, GUC also supported several protests against SOS protests, such as the one in Baldwin Park in mid-June when SOS alleged anti-American inscriptions on a city's arch. Whereas anti-SOS/MP protestors numbered some 500, SOS supported by MP could only produce forty protestors.[49]

By midsummer a plethora of groups and activists took up the mantle of leadership in California in countering the expansion of the Nativist Anti-Migrant Movement (NAMM) into the state as well as aggressively challenging

SOS. An incident at the Campo border area occurred that compelled me to join the border efforts when Mark Belgen, a district representative for State Senator Bill Morrow, Republican from Carlsbad, who with the state senator had been at Campo in support of the Jim Chase's California Minutemen, alleged that I had kicked him in the shin. A police report by Belgen described the incident: "Navarro did not say anything, but did kick dirt on him. Belgen said he was between the cars. He noticed Navarro looking around and then Navarro suddenly kicked him once in left shin. Navarro immediately returned to the group of protestors, but continued glaring at Belgen." The report stated that he wanted me to be prosecuted on a charge of "battery."[50]

On July 18, James Gilchrist put out a nationwide call for MP reinforcements to support Jim Chase's California Minutemen. The bulletin he issued read: "We witnessed the literal siege of VFW Post #2080 by about 60 belligerent, death-threatening anti-Americans twice during that day [July 16]," which he claimed were repelled by San Diego County Sheriff Department officers.[51] In the nationally circulated MP bulletin, Gilchrist targeted me as being behind the "rampage":

> The rampage was orchestrated by Armando Navarro, a known anti-American racist, who holds a comfortable, taxpayer funded, tenured position as a professor (of hate and blood-letting), at the University of California–Riverside, Ca., and who has devoted his life to promoting the conquest of the seven southwestern US states. He calls for the conquest to be carried by force, if necessary. Navarro and his minions whose combined IQ [is] that of a dead house plant, all appeared to be under the influence of drugs.

In his call for reinforcements, Gilchrist stated that MP volunteers were prepared to initiate a protest at UCR "demanding the ouster of Navarro from his department at a state funded institution, which Navarro has selfishly turned into a department of *tyranny*."[52] For days thereafter, numerous other nativist websites and links carried Gilchrist's call for reinforcement bulletin. On July 19, three days after the alleged incident, Belgen issued a press release on his allegation.

Apparently, I was the victim of mistaken identity. But because the media failed to do their homework they didn't realize that I wasn't even there that day. For days the media and pro-Minutemen radio talk hosts around the country, such as San Diego's Rick Roberts, focused in on the incident. The *North County Times* reported that "Navarro said Monday that the charge was a serious matter and that he had no comment on the incident."[53] I figured that I would allow Gilchrist, Belgen, and the MP network to publicly hang themselves—perhaps even initiate a suit against them for slander. I secured an attorney, Mosies Vasquez, and on July 29, in front of the UCR Administration Building, joined by some fifty supporters, I convoked a press conference and in a brief statement

I unequivocally denied that I had assaulted Mr. Belgen, and that I could prove it since I had yet to travel to the Campo border area. Vasquez, who did most of the talking, while acknowledging that I had not been present, said that MP's attacks on me were "part of the rough and tumble of politics" and that "the defamatory statements accusing [me] of a crime went too far."[54] Vasquez concluded the press conference by saying that if an apology was not forthcoming by Belgen, Gilchrist, Chase, and radio host Roberts then I was poised to sue for defamation.[55]

North County Times reporter Deirdre Newman, who covered the press conference, reported that several concurrent apologies had been made. Both Gilchrist and Chase said on July 29 that they apologized. The reporter wrote, "Mr. Gilchrist extends his apology if, in fact, Navarro was wrongly identified." Chase said that he had been told by Belgen that I had assaulted him and believed him because he trusted him. Prior to the press conference, when pressured by the media Belgen said he was not sure if I was the person who assaulted him. But when contacted by the press to comment on the demanded apology, he refused to comment. Roberts did not respond to the reporters' calls. Gilchrist, using MP's website, disseminated information which explained that I had not been the one who assaulted Belgen. Newman also reported that the San Diego Sheriff's Department had filed no charges against me.[56] This meant that those leaders of MP who had made the false allegations against me had been embarrassed publicly. I am not sure exactly why it happened, but the intensity and frequency of MP hate mail and death threats were reduced to a trickle. Equally important was that I did not have to engage in a time-consuming and expensive slander suit.

During the remaining months of 2005, the Mexicano/Latino response to NAMM increased in California. MP's border patrolling of the Campo area continued to create resistance by a number of pro-migrant rights groups, such as GUC. In September, as MP-affiliated groups sought to expand their border surveillance efforts to the El Centro–Méxicali area, GUC and other pro-migrant rights groups held an anti-MP protest that culminated with a march on the border, drawing some 200 protestors which NAHR supported. As MP's border activities across the Cactus Curtain increased so did resistance against them. Increasingly, the debate in Congress for immigration reform intensified. For many groups and leaders it created a political and media shift from MP to the politics of immigration reform. With the passage of the Sensenbrenner legislation, HR4437 in December, the political stage was set for the emergence in 2006 of the greatest immigration reform movement led by Mexicanos and Latinos ever recorded in this country's history.

CHAPTER 11

The Restrictionist Nativist Legislative Surge (2004–2007)

The country's immigration crisis intensified during 2004 to 2007. The growth and activities of the armed rancher vigilantes, nativist militias, and particularly the rise of the Minuteman Project (MP) and nativist anti-immigrant movement (NAMM) coupled with the acceleration of the re-Mexicanization of Aztlán and, nationwide, the Latinoization or "browning" of the United States (U.S.) contributed to its intensification. The country's anti-immigrant White Anglo-Saxon Protestant (WASP) ethos in the context of recent U.S. history reached an unprecedented high. Integral to NAMM's "nativist bandwagon" were the politicians. Their involvement engrained even more the country's nativist WASP ethos that permeated its political culture and climate. During the next three years a nativist legislative surge developed at all levels of government—from local city councils and state houses, to the halls of Congress and the presidency itself—that sought to pass a plethora of xenophobic, nativist, and racist restrictionist-oriented anti-immigrant reform laws, ordinances, and initiatives.

This chapter provides an in depth examination of the nativist legislative surge that occurred at all three levels of government from 2004 to 2007. Furthermore, the impact of the Bush administration's war on terrorism and migrant exodus are also dealt with.

Politicians Enter the Anti-Immigrant Movement

RISE OF THE LEGISLATIVE SURGE

Throughout this country's immigration experience, as documented extensively in the previous chapters, politicians, from a policy perspective, have played a pivotal leadership role. Anti-immigrant politics has included leadership from a number of sectors that have included organizations, unions, churches, media, and so forth. Yet the most important has been the politician who proposes, passes, and executes the country's immigration laws. During the first five years of the 21st century, the nativist leadership came mainly from rancher vigilantes, militias, anti-immigrant organizations, media, and some intellectuals. But from 2004 to 2007, it was the nativist politicians who legislatively drove NAMM. Their weapons of choice were xenophobic rhetoric, ordinances, initiatives, and legislation.

At the core of the politician's nativism were fear and desperation. At the core of their concerns was the Latino demographic transformation that was pervading the country. Their fear was due chiefly to their xenophobic political posture on the myriad political, cultural, economic, and social consequences inherent to the migrant influx. With a Latino population that numbered some 44 million in 2005 and a reported undocumented migrant population of 11 million, nativist politicians began to pay attention to MP leader James Gilchrist's estimation that the number was more like 30 million.[1] They were acutely aware that within the next thirty years or so, if not sooner, Whites relegated throughout much of Aztlán would become the "new minority" and Mexicanos and Latinos be the "new majority." The ramifications of such a demographic change meant that Whites could inevitably lose their political and economic power. Hence, with a sense of urgency, politicians joined nativist "domestic terrorist" rancher vigilantes, militias, and other anti-immigrant organizations as participants of NAMM in their efforts to stop the influx of undocumented migrants. It was the attack of September 11, 2001, however, that gave them the needed wind in their nativist anti-immigrant sail.

9/11'S IMPACT ON IMMIGRATION REFORM

The historical roots to the nativist legislative surge that began in 2004 could be traced back to the election of Republican George Bush as president in 2000. His administration in 2001 appeared to be prepared to make immigration reform a domestic priority issue. Likewise, in México the election of *Partido Acción Nació-nal* candidate Vicente Fox as México's new president prioritized the issue. Both administrations signaled that the time was propitious for immigration reform. By late 2001 a consensus was reached as the result of a number of bilateral meetings. Both governments anticipated that a historic accord on immigration reform would be reached. On September 11, 2001, the bombing of the Twin Towers in New York and the Pentagon in Washington, D.C., reversed both countries' anticipated immigration accord. September 11 fostered a resurgence of nativism. Supported by both Republican and Democratic politicians, the Bush administration seized the moment to create a "policy nexus" between immigration reform and the war on terrorism. For most in Congress the two issues became intertwined if not inseparable.

Nativist politicians directed their attention to border security, specifically the Cactus Curtain. They did not target the U.S.–Canadian border, in spite of the fact that the 9/11 terrorists did not enter the U.S. via its southern border. They alleged that the next terrorist attack on the U.S. would come from "Al Qaida terrorists" who would slip through what they considered the country's most porous border (namely the Cactus Curtain). The double standard became evident, considering that the Canadian 4,000-mile border for all intents and purposes was an "open border" in comparison to México's 2,000-mile border, which was going to be further militarized. On the impact of 9/11 on the discourse of immigration, Justin Ankers Chacon and Mike Davis wrote:

> In a micro-flash, the tragedy of September 11 allowed the right-wing forces to regain the initiative against an advancing immigrant's rights agenda. The policy of immigrant containment dovetailed with the domestic component of the protean "War on Terrorism," which has unabashedly singled-out, restricted, and/or criminalized the presence of Arabs, Arab-Americans, Muslims, and others profiled as "potential terrorists." The omnipresent phantom of domestic terrorism, refracted through the border-phobic imagery of "invading hordes," created an opportunistic wedding between pro-war hawks and anti-immigrant restrictionists.[2]

Another scholar, Jonathan Xavier Inda, who wrote on 9/11's impact, stated that "subsequent to the 9/11 attacks, terrorism has generally come to be regarded as the greatest threat facing the nation. And since . . . the hijackers were foreigners who somehow managed to get into the United States, the movement of people in and out of the country has become indissociable from this threat."[3]

As a supposed consequence of 9/11, the Bush administration in 2002 created the Department of Homeland Security (DHS), headed by Secretary Thomas Ridge. Its domestic responsibility was the protection of the country from another terrorist attack and also overseeing the enforcement of the country's immigration laws. The Immigration and Naturalization Service (INS) was restructured, became part of DHS, and was redesignated ICE (Immigration, Customs, and Enforcement). The U.S. Border Patrol now also came under DHS, which continued to have the responsibility of border security and enforcement. The linking of immigration to terrorism was articulated in an article in the *Providence Journal*, authored by Mark Krikorian, executive director of the Center for Immigration Studies out of Washington, D.C., who wrote, "Of the DHS's many responsibilities, immigration control is central."[4]

The Bush administration's war on terrorism created a nationwide culture of paranoia and fear. During the ensuing four years, many of the country's citizenry, frightened and politically gullible, bought into the administration's pandering to scare tactics. In a Machiavellian manner their borderline hysteria was manipulated into feeling a sense of uncertainty and fatalism. These emotions fed into the country's existent WASP ethos, which combined fostered ill feelings if not fear and hatred of both foreigners and immigrants. This was manifested in 2001 with the passage of the commonly called USA Patriot Act, perceived by progressives as being quasi-fascistic because its provisions violated the privacy rights of the country's citizenry. The federal government's law enforcement agencies' authority was also expanded for the stated purpose of fighting terrorism in the U.S. and abroad.[5] In 2005 some of its most egregious provisions were modified by Congress because of challenges to their constitutionality. In foreign policy, the Bush administration used 9/11 to justify in great part its "neo-Manifest" imperialist-driven "preemption" doctrine. Both 9/11 and the war on terrorism were vital to the administration's justification (although fraudulent) for the U.S.'s invasion of Iraq in 2003 and its occupation.

Both 9/11 and the Patriot Act redefined the immigration debate. Immigrants, who were already considered so-called foreigners, especially from México, became suspected of terrorism. The Bush administration exploited the so-called immigration crisis in an effort to deflect criticism from its domestic and foreign policy failures, especially the Iraq War and occupation fiasco. For immigrants, as scholars Chacon and Davis stated, "the Bush Administration has also used the post 9/11 climate of paranoia to terrorize immigrants in the workplace." They allude to how DHS set up fake Occupational Safety and Health Administration meetings in the workplace to supposedly instruct the workers on their workers' rights; however, the meetings were actually for herding up undocumented migrants for deportation.[6] Regardless of the hostile nativist political climate, the migrant exodus intensified.

INCESSANT MIGRANT EXODUS

The INS in 1999 reported that 1,579,010 migrants had been apprehended, and in 2000 the number reached an all-time high of 1,643,679.[7] With greater frequency nativist anti-immigrant forces and xenophobic politicians vociferously promulgated to the general public that the U.S.–México border was "out of control" and the country was being invaded. By 2003, nativist politicians had accelerated their calls for restrictionist immigration reform, which called for border enforcement—further militarization of the Cactus Curtain—but rebuked "amnesty" unequivocally.

In 2001, most likely due to 9/11, according to DHS the number of undocumented migrants apprehended and deported dropped to 1,235,718, in 2002 the number dropped even further to 929,809, and in 2003 to 905,065.[8] Yet by 2004 a significant reversal occurred: DHS reported that the number had increased to 1.1 million.[9] By 2005, the number increased to 1,241,089, of which some 92 percent were natives of México.[10] Nativist politicians, such as Colorado's Congressman Tom Tancredo, in demagogue fashion, connected the issue of 9/11 and the war on terrorism to the issue of immigration. "More than 76,000," he said, "were non-Mexicans from countries with terrorist cells such as the Philippines, Indonesia, Iran, Syria, Pakistan, and Iraq."[11]

The number of undocumented immigrants was exaggerated by divergent nativist sectors, including numerous receptive media outlets. MP leaders alleged in 2005 that about 75,000 undocumented crossed the border each week and that some 4 to 5 million entered the U.S. each year.[12] Conversely, the Census Bureau and several mainstream think tank estimates were about 350,000 and 500,000 per year. The Pew Hispanic Center's figure of "unauthorized migrants" that successfully crossed into the U.S. since 2000 was 500,000 per year.[13] Of the previous figure, 69 percent of those who crossed in 2000 were from México. As to the total size of the undocumented migrant population, the estimates also varied. INS in January 2000 estimated the number to be about 7 million. The Urban Institute's estimate in March 2002 was 9.3 million. These were dramatic increases, understanding that the INS in October 1992 had reported the number to be 3.4 million.[14] In 2005 nativist militia leaders, politicians, journalists, and scholars estimated the number to be about 20 million. A year later, MP's leadership argued that the figure was more like 30 million. The Pew Hispanic Center in 2005 released a report that concluded that after years of steady growth, the number of undocumented residents in March 2004 had reached an estimated high of 10.3 million, with Mexicanos numbering 5.9 million or 57 percent of the total. As of March 2005, the estimated number was 11.1 million, including some 6 million Mexicanos.[15]

The figures for legal immigration into the U.S. for the post-9/11 years also got the attention of both nativist and nonnativist politicians. The high number of legal migrants coming from México served to buttress the nativists' attack on México and Mexicanos. In 2005 there were some 36 million foreign born legally living in the U.S. Legal immigration on a decade by decade basis had increased dramatically since the 1950s. According to the U.S. Census, in the 1950s the number was 2.5 million; 1970s, 4.5 million; 1980s, 7.3 million; 1990s, 10 million; and from 2000 to 2005 it averaged 1 million per year.

Nativist Legislation Surges (2004–2007)

ARIZONA'S PROPOSITION 200

At the state level, the legislative surge was kicked off in Arizona with the passage of Proposition 200 in 2004. Congress's inability to push through comprehensive immigration reform legislation opened the door for Arizona to initiate its own anti-immigration reform. As a state, Arizona historically was fertile political ground for nativist-inspired legislation. After California in 1986 successfully passed Proposition 61, the English-only initiative, Arizona in 1988 followed with the passage of the country's most restrictionist English-only law. Called Proposition 106, it mandated that all government functions be carried out in English. This included public officials' conversations with constituents and city employee dealings with residents. It remained on the books until 1998 when the State Supreme Court overturned it.[16]

Arizona in 2000 passed the nativist-inspired initiative Proposition 203. It was modeled after California's 1998 Proposition 227, which dismantled bilingual education. It required that students who had not mastered the English language be placed in English "immersion" classes, with only classes and material provided in English and no other language.[17] In 2003 many of Arizona's estimated 500,000 undocumented migrants became the target of Arizona's nativists. From October 1, 2003, to September 30, 2004, the Border Patrol reported the apprehension in the Tucson sector of some 490,000 undocumented migrants. It also reported that for every one arrested, three to five made it successfully across.[18] In 2004, among all the nation's states, Arizona was the heaviest border corridor for the migrant exodus.

With the migrant exodus at its highest in southern Arizona, the state's political climate was hypernativist, as illustrated by the passage of Proposition 200, a draconian initiative similar to California's Proposition 187. In explaining the conditions that proved favorable for its passage, Margot Veranes and Adriana Navarro wrote, "Residents were . . . frustrated with low paying jobs, poor health care, and funding being directed at schools and public benefits programs." Nativists joined in with a handful of fringe local groups to promote the "hateful agenda of blaming immigrants for the state's woes."[19] The leading protagonist was a citizens' group called Project Arizona Now (PAN). As described by Daniel Sheehy, PAN "took matters into their own hands to help save their state from the illegal invasion."[20] In 2003, PAN launched a successful anti-immigrant state initiative campaign to get Proposition 200 on the ballot. It required the collection of some 122,612 valid signatures. Like California's Proposition 187, Proposition 200 required that all applicants for nonfederal public funds had to prove their eligibility. In order to qualify for access to services they had to provide proof of their U.S. citizenship via a passport or birth certificate. Furthermore, all local and state government employees were required to report undocumented migrants to federal authorities or face criminal charges. Lastly, it mandated proof of citizenship before a person could register to vote and presentation of a valid photo ID when voting.[21]

On November 2, 2004, Proposition 200 passed overwhelmingly, garnering some 56 percent of the vote. According to exit polls, support for it was strongest among Whites, but surprisingly 47 percent of the Mexicano/Latinos voted for it as well.[22] Also supporting it were 70 percent of Republicans, 42 percent of Democrats, and 51 percent of Independents.[23] It won in spite of the fact that it was opposed by a number of major political figures: Democratic Governor Janet Napolitano, Republican U.S. Senators John McCain and Jon Kyl, both Republican and Democratic presidential and vice presidential candidates, Arizona's Chamber of Commerce, and México's President Vicente Fox.[24] Integral to PAN's success in passing Proposition 200 was the organizational and financial support it garnered from Washington-based FAIR (Federation for American Immigration Reform), which contributed some $500,000.

Also helping ensure the passage of Proposition 200 were the research studies that pandered to the fears and racism of Arizona's White majority electorate. One study concluded that undocumented migrants cost Arizona taxpayers $1.3 billion. Another study reported that Arizona's taxpayers were spending $810 million a year to educate the children of undocumented migrants.[25] Anti-Proposition 200 proponents, on the other hand, argued that both documented and undocumented migrants contributed significantly to Arizona's economy. A number of studies clearly demonstrated that they paid $300 million more annually than they received in services, that they paid $1.5 billion in mortgages and rents, that other financial institutions in the state received $57 million in transaction costs and fees from remittances sent to México, and lastly, that Mexicano purchasing power in Arizona was estimated at $3.9 billion in 2001.[26] These facts, however, were overshadowed by the depth and scope of Arizona's pervasive nativism.

Proposition 200, unlike California's Proposition 187, overcame several court challenges. In May 2005 the Mexican American Legal Defense and Educational Fund (MALDEF), American Civil Liberties Union (ACLU), and the Mexican government challenged the basis for the proposition as being erroneous. However, all their supportive arguments were dismissed by the U.S. Court of Appeals for the Ninth Circuit. In 2006 several civil rights and voter registration groups filed suit in *Gonzalez v. Arizona*. Its voter registration and identification provisions, such as that of requiring photo identification, were also challenged. On August of 2006, the motion was denied. Its provision as to whether Arizona can require proof of U.S. citizenship in order to vote in its state elections also survived several legal challenges. In October 5, 2006, the Ninth Circuit enjoined application of Proposition 200. The U.S. Supreme Court on October 20 vacated the decision and remanded the case for further proceedings. In the latest legal challenge to Proposition 200, the Ninth Circuit on April 20, 2007, denied a plaintiff's motions for preliminary injunction and the case was remanded to the District of Arizona.[27] In responding to the "Yes on Proposition 200" legal challenges, Dan Stein, president of FAIR, said in a press release:

> We worked closely with local groups in Arizona because we believe what they have done there can be a model for citizen action all across the country. The Ninth Circuit's decision will undoubtedly be a tremendous boost to that effort as Americans use the political process to force government to control illegal immigration and to protect their interests and resources.[28]

In 2006 Arizona's anti-immigrant legislative surge continued with the passage of four anti-immigrant propositions. The nativist campaign to make English the state's official language under the aegis of Proposition 103 passed. Interestingly, the issue dispelled Latino community voting stereotypes. Exit polls indicated that between 40 percent and 50 percent of Mexicanos and Latinos voted for all four propositions. The Pew Hispanic Center found that about 48 percent of Mexicano/Latino voters backed the measure, and that 41 percent voted to reelect Republican Senator Jon Kyl, who had made immigration a central campaign issue. Another measure, Proposition 300, sought to expand the scope of services denied to undocumented migrants.[29] It restricted access to adult literacy services, adult education, state-funded child care, and in-state tuition for undocumented migrants.[30] It passed with 40 percent of Mexicanos/Latinos voting for it.[31] Unlike Proposition 200, it required a report on the "number of persons" denied services based on their legal immigration status. There were two other anti-immigrant initiatives passed in 2006: one measure denied bail to undocumented migrants and the other prohibited undocumented migrants from collecting punitive damages.

A cardinal reason that Arizona was so successful at passing nativist legislation was the absence of a unified Mexicano/Latino community committed to working on the behalf of the undocumented migrants. The high percentage of Mexicanos and Latinos who politically supported Arizona's proposed nativist laws clearly illustrated the prevalence of disunity and "Brown nativism." It was apparent that many in the Mexicano/Latino community were either a citizen or permanent resident and that they had bought into the nativists' egregious argument that undocumented migrants needed to be deported because they took jobs, depressed wages, and did not contribute to improving their quality of life. The results also clearly suggested two other points: (1) the Mexicano/Latino vote in Arizona was not homogeneous or unified and there were serious divisions on the issue of undocumented migration; and (2) there were leadership and organizational weaknesses within the Mexicano/Latino community, so much so that the pro-migrant factions were incapable of responding in a unified and effective manner to defeat the anti-immigrant measures. Bruce Merrill, a pollster at Arizona State University illustrated the preceding when he stated that "the misconception with Hispanics is that they are a homogenous political group like African Americans. There are as many VFW, flag waving Hispanics with pick-ups with guns in their racks as there are Cesar Chavez Chicanos."[32]

STATE LEGISLATIVE SURGE EXPANDS

Arizona's passage of Proposition 200 during 2005 became a powerful catalyst for generating similar initiatives and laws in several other states. It literally had a legislative "multiplier effect." The state legislatures of Virginia, Colorado, and Georgia in 2005 passed legislation that restricted access to services for immigrants. In California, on January 13 Democratic State Senator Gil Cedillo reintroduced SB60, which would allow undocumented workers to secure a driver's license; however, in October Governor Schwarzenegger, after a bitter legislative fight with Democrats, again vetoed the contentious bill. Cedillo argued that his driver's license bill would reinforce "national security" as stipulated by the guidelines of the Real ID Act, yet he failed to secure the required votes needed to override the governor's veto.[33] In explaining his veto, Schwarzenegger said that SB60 "could undermine national security efforts to identify individuals who posed enormous risk to the safety of Californians."[34] In December 2005 Republican Assemblyman Ray Haynes spearheaded a ballot measure that would create a California border police that would enforce immigration laws, but it failed to secure the required number of signatures to get on the ballot.[35]

During 2005, at the state level, New México Democratic Governor Bill Richardson in August exacerbated the Cactus Curtain crisis by declaring a state of emergency in four border counties due to what he said was growing crime due to migration. In a prepared statement, he said, "Violence directed at law enforcement, damage to property and livestock, increased evidence of drug smuggling and an increase in the number of undocumented immigrants" led to his decision to declare the emergency. He declared that there were "potentially catastrophic conditions."[36] The Mexican government was quick to criticize Richardson's decision. A few days later, Arizona Democratic Governor Janet Napolitano likewise declared a state of emergency along the four Arizona counties bordering México. Their motivation to take such action was also because they could have access to state and federal emergency monies that could be used for border enforcement purposes: New México's was $750,000 and Arizona's was $1.5 million.[37] California Governor Schwarzenegger said that California would not declare a state of emergency, but would leave the door open.

In 2005 the Arizona state legislature considered more than twenty anti-immigrant bills that sought to expand Proposition 200's application. That same year, however, Governor Napolitano in May vetoed legislation, SB1167, that would have made English the state's official language. According to Kari Lydersen, "The vetoed bill asserted that the 'official language of the state of Arizona is English,' and proposed to 'preserve, protect, and enhance the role of English' by protecting the rights of persons in the state who use English, and avoiding any official actions that ignore, harm or diminish the role of English as the language of the government and encouraging greater opportunities for individuals to learn English."[38] She argued that people should be encouraged to speak English, but the proposed bill would not have done that. Nationwide, the effects of the nativist legislative surge were evident in that twenty-seven states by 2005 had already declared English as the official language.[39]

Further indicative of the nativist surge was Republican gubernatorial candidate Don Goldwater, who in 2006 proposed unsuccessfully the construction near the border of detention or concentration camps for undocumented migrants. He also proposed that undocumented migrants be used to construct a wall between Arizona and México.[40] Arizona in 2006 by its example fed into the expansion of nativist legislation in other states.

Numerous states introduced anti-immigrant legislation similar to Arizona's Proposition 200. They included Hawaii, Colorado, California, Utah, Georgia, Washington, Idaho, Wisconsin, Kansas, Nebraska, Missouri, Oklahoma, Virginia, Arkansas, Alabama, Tennessee, Ohio, North Carolina, and Maryland.[41] In California, despite six failed attempts, in January 2006 State Senator Cedillo reintroduced SB60 under the new title of SB1160. It would allow undocumented migrants to apply for a driver's license; once more, Governor Schwarzenegger vetoed it. In 2006, twelve other states passed nativist-inspired legislation. Louisiana, for instance, approved a law that stiffened penalties for businesses that hired undocumented migrants. Missouri passed legislation that denied unemployment benefits to undocumented migrants. Wyoming prohibited undocumented students from receiving grants. Pennsylvania and Maryland passed benefit cuts to undocumented migrants, patterned on those in Colorado and Georgia.[42] Colorado passed legislation that created the State Patrol's Immigration Enforcement Unit, which went into effect in July of 2007. Lastly, New Jersey and Connecticut passed laws that allowed officers to assume an immigration enforcement role.

Luckily, not all proposed anti-immigration legislation introduced in 2005 and 2006 passed. A number of states were successful in defeating a number of nativist-inspired laws. According to Tanya Broder,

> The overwhelming majority of the bills proposing to restrict immigrants' access to services considered by state legislatures in 2006 died in legislative committees, failed to pass, or were vetoed. After hearing testimony about the potential harm to public health, safety, and the local economy, and after concluding that state and local measures restricting services do not alter federal immigration policy, state legislatures rejected the vast majority of these bills. The most extreme measures suffered resounding defeats.[43]

The legislatures of California and Kansas in 2005 successfully defended legislation granting in-state tuition to students, regardless of citizenship or legal immigration status.[44] Initiative drives in California and Washington that were essentially copies of Proposition 200 that sought to deny a range of services to undocumented migrants failed to qualify for the ballot due to insufficient signatures. The Indiana state legislature in 2006 overwhelmingly rejected HB1383, which mimicked most of California's Proposition 187. In 2006 a measure similar to Arizona's Proposition 200 was soundly defeated in Oklahoma. The Nebraska legislature in 2006 overrode the governor's veto of a measure to provide access to in-state tuition for undocumented students.

Congress's failure to pass immigration reform legislation in 2007 further energized the nativist legislative contagion at the state level. Tamar Jacoby, a senior fellow at the Manhattan Institute, explained that "the battle is definitely shifting to the state and local level. The public doesn't like illegality, and local politicians sense that. Because the federal government did not do something, that impulse is even stronger."[45] Governor Napolitano signed the draconian Fair and Legal Employment Act, which mandated effective January 1, 2008, that all Arizona employers be compelled to run new hires through the Basic Pilot program that entailed an electronic employment verification system that cross-checked names with Social Security numbers. It harshly punishes businesses that knowingly hire undocumented workers. It is a two-strike employer sanction law that on the first offense suspends an employer's business license and on the second revokes it.[46]

Several other states in 2007 embraced the nativist path of the legislative surge. In the first eleven months of 2007, as reported by *The Nation* in January 2008, "forty-six state legislatures passed nearly 250 immigration laws—some 1,560 were introduced, nearly triple the same number for the same period in 2006." Nativist politicians, especially Republicans, in 2007 scapegoated the undocumented by resorting to extremist anti-immigrant nativist laws, which were "ethnic cleansing" oriented. One such state was Oklahoma: undocumented migrants comprised around 5 percent of Oklahoma's population of 3.6 million. In March 2007 the state House of Representatives passed 88 to 9 the Oklahoma Taxpayer and Citizens Protection Act, also referred to as House Bill 1804.[47] Authored by Republican State Representative Randy Terrell, it went into effect on November 1, 2007, and was the country's strictest anti-immigrant state legislation. Its measures included: (1) transporting, concealing, harboring, or sheltering undocumented migrants was a felony; (2) undocumented migrants were not eligible for driver's licenses and other official government identification; (3) required government agencies and private businesses with government contracts to check new hires against a federal database; (4) denied some public benefits, such as rental assistance and fuel subsidies, to undocumented migrants; (5) prohibited local governments from adopting "sanctuary" policies that precluded law enforcement and other agencies from cooperating with ICE officials; and (6) allowed state and local police to enforce immigration law and legal workers to sue employers who fired them and kept undocumented workers on the payroll.[48]

Its "ethnic cleansing" of Mexicanos and Central Americans became evident in September of 2007 when the Tulsa area schools reported that 25,000 Latino students had left the state as it went into effect.[49] Their destinations were chiefly Arkansas and Texas, and it was reported that some had returned to México. Overall, by the end of December, the undocumented migrant "reverse exodus" from Oklahoma had intensified. Representative Terrill, as a follow-up, was preparing to introduce in 2008 a bill that he calls "Son of 1804," which would make English the state's official language and allow police to seize property of those who violate HR1804, including landlords.[50]

In the state of New York, Democratic Governor Eliot Spitzer in late 2007 sought unsuccessfully to pass legislation that would give undocumented migrants and immigrants access to securing a driver's license. He was effectively pressured by nativists, such as CNN's Lou Dobbs, to backpedal on his effort. Dobbs ripped into Governor Spitzer, depicting him as arrogant, spineless, and "a spoiled rich kid brat" as well as an "idiot."[51] Even Democratic presidential candidate Senator Hillary Clinton, while participating in a Democratic presidential debate, when asked if she supported Spitzer's proposal, in a matter of minutes went from saying yes to saying no.[52]

LEGISLATIVE SURGE AT THE LOCAL LEVEL

Local governments from 2004 to 2007 were not exempt from the nativist legislative surge. In fact, anti-immigration politics for many nativists remained local. According to Sheri Steisel, immigration specialist with the National Conference of State Legislatures, "There is a tremendous amount of frustration at the local level now that the federal government has abrogated its responsibility."[53] The Mexicano and Latino diaspora, "Brown migrants" looking for jobs, during the first seven years of the twenty-first century continued to settle in the southern states. They settled in local predominantly White/Black communities that previously had few if any Latinos. Broder elucidates: "Rather than heading to states with traditionally large foreign-born populations, the new arrivals tended to migrate to a diverse array of new destinations where job opportunities were more abundant and where housing and other living costs were lower."[54] Their arrival fostered among both Whites and Blacks a xenophobic if not racist reaction. Some Whites, never really exposed to Browns, felt especially threatened culturally, socially, and economically by their presence. The locus of their racism, prejudice, and bigotry shifted from Blacks to Browns. Some Blacks also reacted in a nativist fashion. However, their main cause for resistance and alarm was much more economic, that is, competition for jobs, and second, culturally.

In some southern states there were Whites and Blacks who were not prepared to receive or accept the demographic changes as a result of the influx of Browns into their cities and neighborhoods. Using their majority political power status, nativist Whites particularly resorted to the use of the political process as a means by which to halt the Brown insertion into their communities and in some cases were extreme in proposing a form of "Brown cleansing." The proposed legislation would "limit immigrants' ability to obtain jobs, find housing, get a driver's licenses, and receive government services." Regardless of how they worded it, the policy outcome was still the same, the depopulation of Browns in their communities.

In late 2005 in the city of San Bernardino, Joseph Turner, nativist leader and founder of the anti-immigrant group Save Our State (SOS) in California, filed on October 10 an initiative entitled "City of San Bernardino Illegal Immigration Relief Act Ordinance."[55] This initiative would have meant the "institutionalization" at the local level of "ethnic cleansing." The ordinance contained seven anti-immigrant provisions: (1) barred the city of San Bernardino from operating, constructing, maintaining or funding any day laborer centers; (2) prohibited any day laborer center in the city from helping undocumented workers find jobs and held the entity operating the center strictly liable for violations; (3) established new administrative requirements regulating day laborer centers and imposed minimum fines of $1,000 for each violation; (4) criminalized anyone who used a vehicle to transport day laborers to a job site, which meant the vehicle was subject to seizure and impoundment by the city; (5) denied for five years city businesses permits, contracts, and grants to any for-profit business found to be "aiding and abetting" undocumented workers; (6) prohibited undocumented workers from renting or leasing property in the city and held the property owner liable, with violations imposing a minimum fine of $1,000; and (7) required that, to the extent possible, under current state and federal law, all official city business be conducted or written in English only.[56] In explaining the SOS initiative, Turner stated:

> Local politicians state over and over that there's nothing they can do about [undocumented] immigration. . . . They say it's a state and federal issue, so they'll ignore it. What I'm saying is there are things you can do at the local level to mitigate the harmful effects of illegal immigration.[57]

The city raised several legal issues, but regardless, a federal court decision allowed Turner's petition to be accepted by the city clerk. SOS was required to secure 2,216 valid signatures from registered voters in San Bernardino in order for it to be placed on the ballot in a special election or for the November 2006 elections.[58] On April 24, 2006, Turner submitted between 3,124 and 3,150 signatures for verification; on May 4, 2006, the city clerk verified that a sufficient number of valid signatures had been gathered and submitted the measure to the city council for approval or rejection.[59] Resistance to the proposed SOS nativist measure came from different sectors of the community. The National Alliance for Human Rights (NAHR), leaders, local politicians, and a myriad of civil rights, community, and religious groups closed ranks to work for its defeat. On May 15, 2006 the majority of the City Council, led by Mayor Patrick Morris, in a 4 to 3 vote rejected the proposed ordinance, which meant that the city's voters were to decide its fate by holding a special election sometime within a 90 to 135 day period.[60] Mayor Morris criticized the proposed ordinance, arguing that if passed, it would cost the city more than $1 million in enforcement and lost business.[61]

During the ensuing two months, city officials moved aggressively to avoid holding a special election by resorting to the courts. Supported by NAHR, ACLU, MALDEF, and the National Lawyers Guild, Mayor Morris secured the legal intervention of attorney Florentino Garza, who in turn secured private attorneys from the legal firm Reed & Davidson, who successfully argued that City Clerk Rachel Clark should have issued a certificate of insufficiency when the signatures were turned in to her by Turner.[62] On June 26, 2006, Superior Court Judge A. Rex Victor ruled that Turner's SOS needed to secure additional signatures in order to qualify for the ballot. He ruled that the city of San Bernardino had used a flawed formula when it came to determining the number of signatures the petitions required. He further instructed Turner that he had only ten days to secure an additional 2,500 signatures. At the crux of the judge's decision was that the city charter stipulated that for an initiative to get on the ballot, it required that the number of petition signatures must equal 30 percent of the ballots cast in the last city election at which a mayor was elected.

Turner's 3,100 signatures were based upon the 2001 election results; however, instead they should have been based on the February 2006 mayoral race, which had a much higher voter turnout. Turner needed to produce an additional 2,500 signatures for a total of 4,771 signatures in ten days. Turner's reaction to the defeat was that he would start from scratch and try to qualify an anti-immigration measure far "more draconian" than the first.[63] While Judge Victor's decision was a great victory for NAHR and all the other organizations and individuals that took on the fight to put an end to SOS's sponsored local initiative, Turner's efforts ignited a similar effort in Hazleton, Pennsylvania.

Hazleton, Pennsylvania, was the next city to jump onto the nativist legislative bandwagon. Modeled after San Bernardino's initiative, the city council on a 4 to 1 vote in June 2006 approved a similar ordinance that penalized landlords who rented to undocumented migrants as well as those who hired the undocumented. Speaking in support of the ordinance, Hazleton's mayor, Lou Barletta, said that "it's something that cities can do on their own as the federal government tries to protect the borders of our country. This is a toll cities can use to protect the border of their city."[64] The ACLU, the Puerto Rican Legal Defense and Education Fund (PRLDEF), the Community Justice Project, the law firm of Cozen O'Connor, Rudy Espinal, and the president of Hazleton's Hispanic Business Association responded with a lawsuit, *Lozano v. Hazelton*, in federal court. They argued the ordinance infringed on the civil rights of the undocumented migrants, violated federal law, and was racist and divisive. A federal judge in 2006 blocked the enforcement of the ordinance.[65]

A small city of 30,000, Hazleton experienced the demographic infusion of "Brown" migrants, fostering a nativist reaction by Whites that alleged that Latinos were destroying the city. The Latino population in 2006 had reached 10,000, a third of the city's population. Nativists argued that the dramatic increase in the immigrant population caused a serious increase in demand for city services, city schools became overcrowded, immigrants drove without driver's licenses, and they were involved in vandalism, graffiti, and playing loud music. City officials, however, capitalized on the issue of two undocumented migrants who were charged in a fatal shooting. They used it as an organizing issue to fan the fires of nativism in their push for a xenophobic ordinance. Hazleton received national media coverage, helping it propagate the nativist legislative surge to other cities nationwide.

On July 26, 2007, however, in a landmark decision in *Lozano v. Hazelton*, U.S. District Judge James M. Munley ruled that the Hazleton ordinance was unconstitutional. In his 206-page decision, Judge Munley blocked the Hazleton measure from taking effect and concluded that local officials lacked the authority to supersede federal immigration law and impose penalties on businesses for hiring undocumented migrants. The judge ruled that "federal law prohibited Hazleton from enforcing any of the provisions of its ordinances."[66] The permanent injunction issued by the court against the Hazelton ordinance affected its following provisions: (1) imposition of a $1,000 per day fine on landlords who rented to undocumented migrants; (2) revocation of the business license of any employer who hired undocumented migrants; (3) declaration of English as the town's official language; and (4) prohibition of city employees from translating documents into another language without approval.[67] He further added, "Allowing states or local governments to legislate with regard to the employment of unauthorized aliens would interfere with congressional objectives to control immigration policy." The judge also noted, "We cannot say clearly enough that persons who enter this country without legal authorization are not stripped immediately of all their rights because of this single illegal act." Furthermore, the Constitution, under the Fourteenth Amendment, provides that no person may be deprived of "due process of law," including undocumented migrants, and the judge said that they had a right to challenge discriminatory ordinances.[68]

Mayor Barletta's reaction to the court's decision was that "Hazelton [wasn't] going to back-down . . . I will do everything I can to make Hazelton the toughest city in America for illegal immigrants. I will not sit back because the federal government has refused to do its job."[69] Along with the mayor, city officials threatened, if necessary, to appeal the decision to the Third U.S. Circuit Court and to the U.S. Supreme Court. City Attorney Kris Kobach called the judge's decision a "paradigm of judicial activism" and said the case was "ripe for appeal."[70]

The long-awaited decision dealt a major blow to the local nativist legislative surge efforts nationwide. ACLU Legal Director Vic Walczack reacted to the decision by explaining that the Hazelton decision was extremely important since numerous communities were waiting for its legal outcome, especially because it was the first to be subjected to a full trial in federal court. Foster Maer, an attorney for PRLDEF, said, "This [decision] deals a body blow to efforts by localities to try to regulate immigration."[71] The city of Escondido, California, in October of 2006 passed a Hazelton copycat ordinance, which too was challenged by ACLU and was abandoned because of exorbitant legal fees. City official's reaction to the Hazelton decision was split, but seemed to preclude for the moment another attempt.[72] Angelo Paparelli, president of the Academy of Business Immigration Lawyers, said, "I think the cities and states will be given a handy justification for not taking action and I hope the pressure will be redirected back at Congress, where it belongs."[73]

In a matter of a week Hazelton's legal defense fund successfully raised some $360,000 for its appeal of the decision from private sources around the country. The city, however, had yet to pay a dime of taxpayer's money for defending the ordinance.[74] The ability of city officials to raise such large amounts of money in such a short period of time was an indicator of the nativism that pervaded the country. Although the ordinance was never enforced because of a legal moratorium, a "Brown exodus" occurred that created serious economic consequences on Hazelton's already wrecked economy. The city's overall Latino population in 2007 decreased by almost two-thirds.

By late 2007 the nativist outcry against undocumented migration was much louder. Journalist Dave Montgomery wrote that at the local and state levels, "scores of organizations are marshalling forces in what former House speaker Newt Gingrich calls 'a war at home' against illegal immigration."[75] In Morristown, New Jersey, in July 2007, a rally that attracted hundreds of demonstrators for and against stricter immigration law enforcement ended in conflict. Five people were arrested and two needed medical attention.[76] Efforts to create "ethnic cleansing" legislation were heaviest in a number of county and local cities in the "old South." In Virginia, the county of Prince William in October 2007 voted to crack down on undocumented migrants by allowing police to enforce immigration law and created a Criminal Alien Unit, denying virtually all services, including substance abuse counseling to them.[77] Not all local politicians in Virginia, however, were supportive of Prince William County's nativist resolution. Fairfax County Chairman Gerald Connolly vehemently criticized Prince William County officials' handling of the immigration issues. He said its decision to have local law enforcement officers check the status of undocumented migrants was tantamount to "racial profiling."[78] In Panama City Beach, Florida, the Sheriff's Department was actively involved in the apprehension of the undocumented at construction sites.[79]

In other parts of the country, local nativist anti-immigrant organizing efforts also increased. In Arizona, Maricopa County Sheriff Joe Arpaio, after apprehending undocumented migrants, would have them wear a particular color clothing, including socks that identified them as being undocumented. Arizona pro-migrant rights activist Elias Bermudez circulated a doctored picture of Arpaio dressed as a Ku Klux Klan member holding a noose with a Latino man in the background. Arpaio responded that he was upset over the photo, but told the press that the more they attacked him, the more he was "going to lock up illegals."[80] In California, SOS, MP, and other nativist groups, although more sporadically, continued their protests against *jornaleros* (day workers) at Home Depots. In Costa Mesa, California, local law enforcement was still performing its controversial role of enforcing immigration laws. In Simi Valley, California, in September, pro-migrant rights forces clashed with SOS counter-protestors over the issue of an undocumented mother and her son being given sanctuary by the United Church of Christ.[81] Thus, at the close of 2007 scores of cities and counties nationwide enacted hundreds of anti-immigrant ordinances, laws, and initiatives that illustrated the dynamic increase in the local nativist legislative surge.

Federal Legislative Surge Begins

At the federal congressional level, the nativist legislative surge did not materialize with any great intensity until 2005. The main reasons were two: (1) politicians' preoccupation with 9/11's war on terror; and (2) the Iraq War occupation
and insurgency. Immigration reform did not become a public policy priority until three years later, when politicians accelerated their calls for restrictionist immigration reform. Their lexicon accentuated "border security," not "amnesty" or
"guest worker" programs. In particular, "amnesty" was considered a pejorative
term, which denoted rewarding persons who had violated the country's immigration laws. As early as 2003, the Agricultural Job Opportunity, Benefits, and
Security Act, known as the AgJOBS Bill, was proposed. The bill, which called
for a massive increase in the number of undocumented guest workers, was not
voted on due to strong nativist political opposition. Again in the ensuing year,
nativist political forces scored another victory in Congress by preventing a vote
on the Save Our Summer Act of 2004. Basically the bill sought to increase the
number of H-2B visas for temporary skilled and unskilled foreign workers from
66,000 to 106,000.[82] In 2004 President Bush intensified his call for a "guest
worker" immigration reform proposal, but failed to push it.

Congress in 2005 passed the Real ID Act. It enabled DHS to establish standards for a national identification system by 2008 by consolidating all state driver's license data into a federal database. It not only pressured states into passing
legislation that denies the issuance of a driver's license to undocumented migrants; but it also gave DHS free rein in the further construction of an "iron curtain" along the U.S.–México border. Indicative of the rising nativist legislative
surge, Congress in June 2005 debated the CLEAR (Clear Law Enforcement for
Criminal Alien Removal) Act. Introduced by Georgia Republican Congressman
Charlie Norwood and Alabama Republican U.S. Senator Jeff Sessions, it proposed that the country's 660,000 law enforcement officers act as immigration
enforcement agents, meaning they would be allowed to arrest and detain suspected undocumented migrants. It sought to elevate unauthorized immigration
from a civil to criminal offense, which was punishable by jail terms and steep
fines; cracked down on groups or entities that provided sanctuary; and would
have funded construction of twenty-one new detention centers to house undocumented migrants.[83] Although it failed to pass, it was adopted as a floor amendment to Congressman Sensenbrenner's HR4437 later that year.[84]

Influenced by the pressures created by growing NAMM, Congress's Republican and Democratic leadership by late spring of 2005 moved the legislative
agenda of immigration reform to the front burner. The debate in Congress on
immigration reform, especially in the House, reached an unprecedented high.
Both political parties began to put forth various proposed immigration legisla-

tive proposals or acts. The following two proposed bills became the locus of debate that started in the summer of 2005.

MCCAIN-KENNEDY BILL

On May 12, 2005, Senators John McCain (R-AZ) and Ted Kennedy (D-MA) and Representatives Jim Kolbe (R-AZ), Jeff Flake (R-AZ), and Luis Gutierrez (D-IL) put forth concurrently the Secure America and Orderly Immigration Act (SAOIA) of 2005, otherwise known as the McCain-Kennedy Bill. In summary form, SAOIA's cardinal nine provisions included: (1) an earned legalization program; (2) a temporary worker program; (3) an electronic employment verification system; (4) amendments to the antidiscrimination provisions of the Immigration and Naturalization Act; (5) an improved family reunification system; (6) measures to increase border enforcement; (7) restrictions on who could provide legal representation to beneficiaries of SAOIA; (8) civics integration-related proposals; and (9) access to health care.[85] To nativists in both houses, it was a liberal and pro-immigrant legislative reform proposal that they could not support.

CORNYN-KYL BILL

On July 20, 2005, Senators John Cornyn (R-TX) and Jon Kyl (R-AZ) introduced the Comprehensive Enforcement and Immigration Reform Act (CEIR) of 2005. Unlike SAOIA, CEIR did not provide a path for permanent resident status for undocumented migrants already living and working in the U.S. It did little to relieve the backlog that plagued family reunification. Instead, it created a temporary worker program for non-U.S. citizen workers. After five years, it required them to return to their country of origin. It established a separate new temporary worker program. Once their temporary period was completed they were required to return to their respective countries. In the area of enforcement, it imposed new immigration restrictions and established a national ID system based upon new Social Security cards and mandatory federally regulated state IDs and driver's licenses. The bill did not have any formal provision for "legalization," but it did allow those who were unlawfully in the U.S. to apply for a "deferred mandatory status." It meant that if they had been in the U.S. and employed prior to July 20, 2004, they were allowed to stay and work for a period of five years as temporary workers. They were ineligible for most assistance benefits or programs. It authorized state and local enforcement agencies to perform immigration enforcement functions and called for stronger border enforcement measures.[86]

The intensity of the nativist legislative surge produced a number of conflicting proposals. Two such immigration proposals were: (1) the Save America Comprehensive Immigration Act (SACI) of 2005, authored by Congresswoman Jackson Lee (D-TX); and (2) the Rewarding Employers that Abide by the Law and Guaranteeing Uniform Enforcement to Stop Terrorism Act (REAL GUEST), introduced by Congressman Tom Tancredo (R-CO). Briefly, the former provided a broad legalization program, which required five years of residence. It provided for no new temporary worker program, but augmented family reunification. In addition, it included various provisions that sought to restore fairness to the circumstances in which immigrants were subject to removal and eliminated section 287(g), the provision that allowed the DHS to enter into an agreement that allowed law enforcement entities to engage in immigration enforcement. The latter was extensively restrictionist in nature. Its provisions included increased border enforcement, further militarization of the border, criminalization of immigration status violations, increased governmental control, database tracking of all persons in the country, authorization for state and local enforcement agencies to enforce federal immigration laws, provision for stronger employer sanctions, and elimination of all current temporary worker programs and replacement with a single program.[87] Tancredo spent the ensuing months of 2005 traveling extensively nationwide, giving speeches on his draconian anti-immigrant proposal, which helped fuel the nativist legislative surge. In the House he led a nativist conservative anti-immigrant caucus comprised of some eighty-eight members.

By September 2005, immigration reform became a priority issue for the Republican-controlled Congress. In October, admittedly influenced by the MP's patrols of the border and the rise of NAMM, Texas Republican Senator Kay Hutchison submitted her own proposal that called for giving local police the power to arrest undocumented migrants and for the creation of a "border marshal" program that would allow local peace officers to patrol the border.[88] It was one of a spiraling slew of anti-immigrant proposals for border enforcement that sought to politically demonize immigrants. By November, inundated by a number of immigration proposals, the House and Senate Republican Judiciary Committee leaders were prepared to take on immigration reform proposals. In September, Texas Republican Congressman Henry Bonilla wrote a letter to President Bush in which he exhorted immediate action to cope with a "state of emergency" along the border.

On November 28, President Bush, in a speech delivered at Davis-Monthan Air Force Base near Tucson, gave the go-ahead to the Republican-controlled Congress for repressive border enforcement measures and a guest-worker program. With the exception of his guest-worker proposal, on the issue of border security, he sided with the most extreme nativist forces of the Republican Party.[89] Within a week, Republican Congressman James Sensenbrenner, chair of the House Judiciary Committee, put forth his draconian HR4437.[90] After bitter debate both among Republicans and Democrats, the House of Representatives on December 16 on a vote of 239 to 182 passed the 163-page HR4437, a stringent "border security/enforcement" bill.

One controversial amendment to the bill, authored by Georgia Republican Congressman Nathan Deal, called for ending "birthright citizenship" for children born in the U.S. to undocumented migrants; however, it was defeated. Opposition to it came chiefly from Democrats and a few Republicans who wanted a guest-worker program or tougher border control measures. Indicative of major differences among Republicans, the bill ignored President Bush's repeated calls for a guest-worker program that would temporarily legalize millions of undocumented workers.[91] The most controversial provision of the bill called for the "criminalization" of 12 million undocumented migrants in the country, which basically meant that they would be treated as felons. Furthermore, anyone harboring or assisting the undocumented migrants would also be subject to a felony charge. Other provisions of HR4437 included:

- A further militarization of the U.S.–México border by providing funding for the construction of a two-layered 700-mile-long border fence and installation and use of military high-tech electronic equipment, including sensors, radar, satellites and unmanned drones to patrol the border with México;
- The intervention of state and local law enforcement agencies in the enforcement of federal immigration law, which meant that especially the twenty-nine counties contiguous to the border would be reimbursed; and
- Stronger employer sanctions that required employers to verify the legal status of all employees by checking with the Social Security Administration and DHS by phone or computer and would increase employer fines from a minimum of $200 to a minimum of $5,000 and as much as $25,000 per violation.

HR4437 did not have a "legalization" provision. It would end the "catch and release" policy for the undocumented, which allowed them immigration hearings before they could be deported. It made having multiple drunken-driving convictions a deportable offense. The bill also increased the penalties for smuggling people across the border. In sum, HR4437 sought to bolster border security, fight terrorism, and curb the migrant exodus into the U.S.[92] According to Sensenbrenner, it would "help restore the integrity of our nation's borders and re-establish respect for our laws by holding violators accountable."[93]

NATIVIST CONGRESSIONAL LEGISLATIVE
SURGE INTENSIFIES (2006)

From the time of the passage of HR4437 in December 2005 to the summer of 2006, the nativist legislative surge intensified. Congress during this time failed to enact immigration reform as a result of extreme polarization and divisions within it. So severe was the chasm that the nativist legislative surge was transformed into the legislative quagmire, which meant that no consensus could be reached by Congress on immigration reform. While various legislative proposals were introduced in both the House of Representatives and Senate no one proposal prevailed. Neither Democrats nor Republicans could muster the votes necessary to push through a proposal due to the gridlock. Most Republicans prioritized border security and in most cases rebuked legalization or a guest-worker program. Most Democrats followed a less restrictionist legislative perspective that often included legalization, a guest-worker program, and border security.

A rather dialectical legislative process occurred: some proposals died in committee, while others in 2005 such as McCain-Kennedy and HR4437 lost traction. Both became platforms by which other proposals were subsequently developed. During the first six months of 2006 political support for HR4437 dwindled. Two major reasons explain why. One was the rise of the massive pro-migrant mobilizations produced by the *Movimiento Pro-Migrante* (MPM) that vociferously opposed it. The opposition and attacks against it were furious and acrimonious, so much so that it became its "battle cry." Most Democrats and Republicans in the Senate realized that HR4437 was a liability rather than an asset. Some die-hard House Republican nativist zealots, however refused to give it up, but by the summer of 2006 it died in the Senate mainly due to the intransigent rift within the Republican Party. While House Republicans supported it, most Senate Republicans as well as President Bush did not. By January the differences had turned into an open rift between mainly House ultranativist zealots and the Senate moderate nativist pragmatists. While both espoused and adhered to the anti-immigrant WASP ethos, the former were hyperxenophobic zealots, led by Sensenbrenner, who unequivocally rebuked legalization and a guest-worker program and embraced border security. Their provisions bordered on paranoia, fascism, and were isolationist.

The latter were moderate and less extreme in their nativism and were generally supportive of President Bush's immigration proposal that called for a guest-worker program, employer sanctions, border security, and like Senator McCain supported some form of legalization. They were pragmatists in that they wanted to ensure that the country's capitalist interests had continued access to cheap migrant labor. They did not support HR4437 for fear that it would negatively impact the economy by creating an acute labor shortage. Their moderation was also grounded on the fear that its enactment because of its harshness would create a political backlash, especially among Latino voters, who were deemed important for the upcoming November congressional elections. The Republican National Committee in January took a moderate nativist pragmatist stand and called for a guest-worker program.[94] Also, New México Republican Senator Pete Domenici in February introduced a legislative proposal that called for a temporary-worker program that allowed undocumented workers in the U.S to apply for temporary worker status for up to three consecutive three-year periods (nine years total). After six years, they would be eligible to apply for permanent residency without having to leave the country.[95] Due to existent divisions among Republicans it did not prevail.

Further indicative of the moderate nativist pragmatists was President Bush's proposal in February to increase the budget of the Border Patrol to $3 billion, a 29 percent increase over the previous year. It provided additional money to hire 1,500 new agents and allocated $274 million to fund a guest-worker program. This strengthened the legislative position of the moderate nativist pragmatists.[96] Yet President Bush's proposal then and throughout the ensuing months, while accentuating a guest-worker program, never developed political traction.

Senate Judiciary Committee Chair Arlen Specter did not promote HR4437. Instead, in late February, he introduced his own moderate nativist proposal, which was soundly derided by his colleagues. It included a guest-worker program that would allow from 8 to 9 million undocumented migrants who entered the country before January 4, 2004 and were employed, to apply for temporary legal status. Qualified applicants could apply for a three-year work visa and one three-year extension before being required to return to their home countries. It called for an increase in the number of green cards granted to workers annually from 140,000 to 290,000. His plan also included tough employer sanctions measures, border enforcement, and border security, such as a "virtual" wall instead of the 700-mile iron curtain. Although Specter combined some aspects of the McCain-Kennedy proposal, it was introduced as an alternative to it.[97] Specter's proposal was attacked by all sides. From a pro-immigrant rights perspective, it was flawed since it did not allow guest workers to ever be eligible for citizenship.[98]

Congress's legislative quagmire was exacerbated over the debate in the Senate of the McCain-Kennedy bill. On March 27, the Judiciary Committee voted 12 (8 Democrats and 4 Republicans) to 6 (all Republicans) in support of the McCain-Kennedy bill's legalization provision, which as explained previously, allowed the country's estimated 12 million undocumented migrants to become citizens without leaving the country and provided for a guest-worker program, with provisions that would lead to permanent residency and citizenship.[99] It met stiff resistance, especially from Republican ultranativist zealots, over the legalization provision. In early April, Republican Majority Leader Senator Bill Frist and Minority Leader Senator Harry Reid intervened and endorsed a compromise measure submitted by Republican Senators Chuck Hagel and Mel Martinez, which became known as the Hagel-Martinez Compromise (S2454). It incorporated several provisions of Senator Specter's amendment and Senator Hagel's earlier-introduced legislation of late 2005 and amended the McCain-Kennedy proposed legislation approved earlier by the Judiciary Committee. As a legislative metamorphosis, it included the following provisions:

- *Permanent residency/citizenship provisions:* allowed undocumented migrants five years or more to remain and continue working as legal temporary workers. After working an additional six years, payment of at least a $2,000 fine, and payment of back taxes, learning English, and clearing a background check, it allowed them to apply for permanent residency. After an additional five years of being a permanent resident they would be eligible for citizenship. While holding legal temporary worker status, they would have three years to gather required materials for a change in their status. They would be required to go to a border port of entry and reenter as legal temporary workers, and by the fifth year they would be eligible to apply for permanent residency. Those with less than two years in the U.S. would have to leave the country and could apply for temporary worker visas or legal residency from their home country.
- *Guest-worker provision:* it created a guest-worker program for an estimated 1.5 million migrant farm workers, who would also be eligible for legal permanent residency. Those migrant farm workers who had worked seasonally in agriculture in the U.S. for three years could apply, as could foreign workers who had never worked in the U.S. It provided for 325,000 temporary visas for future workers and increased the number of employer-based green cards from 290,000 to 450,000 per year.
- *Border security/enforcement provision:* it added 14,000 new border patrol agents by 2011 to the current force of 11,300 to a potential total of 25,300. It also provided for additional sophisticated monitoring electronic equipment and vehicles to monitor the U.S.–México border and allowed for the construction of additional detention centers for apprehended undocumented migrants.
- *Approval of the DREAM Act provision:* allowed states to charge in-state tuition to undocumented college students with high school diplomas or GEDs and no criminal record.[100] The political reaction to it was mixed. In the Senate, Senator Specter told reporters, "While it admittedly is not perfect, the choice we have to make is whether it is better than no bill, and the choice is decisive." On the House side, ultranativist zealots such as Congressman Tancredo and others viewed it as being quasi-treasonous.[101]

On April 7, the Associated Press reported that the landmark Hagel-Martinez bill fell victim to internal disputes in both parties. The Senate vote produced only thirty-eight votes (all Democrats—twenty-two short of the sixty needed) in favor of it. Its demise was a product of competing irreconcilable amendments, filibustering, and partisan wrangling. President Bush blamed Minority Leader Senator Reid who refused to permit votes on more than three Republican amendments. Senator Reid fired back and said, "It was President Bush and Republicans in Congress who lacked the backbone to stand up to the extreme right wing of their party, filibustered reform twice in two days, and put partisan politics ahead of border security and immigration reform." "Politics got ahead of policy on this," lamented Senator Kennedy. As the Senate left for a two-week break, the Hagel-Martinez Compromise was gridlocked,[102] an illustration of how divided the Republican Party was on the issue of immigration reform.[103]

During a visit to Irvine, California, in late April 2006 President Bush sought to jump-start the congressional debate on immigration. He reiterated his support for the immigration reform proposal for border security and a guest-worker program. He said, "Massive deportations of the people here is unrealistic."[104] Within the House, especially the Republican nativist zealots of HR4437 were not all supportive of the president's call for a guest-worker program, whereas House Democrats were open to the call. The Senate voted 59 to 39 to divert $1.9 billion from President Bush's $106.5 billion proposed budget request for the Iraq War to be used for border security, specifically to pay for aircraft, patrol boats, and other vehicles, as well as border check points, and a fence along the San Ysidro–Tijuana border.[105]

During the rest of April, even with the Senate divided, efforts were made, especially by Democrats, to revive the Hagel-Martinez Compromise. Finally on May 11, 2006, an accord was reached and passed the Senate. Brokered by Senator Reid and Majority Leader Frist it appeared to have broken the legislative stalemate.[106] What ensued, however, was not the case. Ultranativist zealots fought it with the introduction of nearly two dozen amendments, which watered it down. One such amendment was introduced by Senators Feinstein and Kyl on May 11 that sought to crack down on border tunnel builders. The measure imposed prison sentences of up to twenty years and up to ten years for anyone that knew and did not report it.[107] On May 17 the Republican ultranativist zealots successfully pushed through with bipartisan support an amendment for the construction of a 370-mile-long wall and 500-miles of vehicle barriers along specific areas of the border.[108] On May 18 the Senate voted 63 to 34 on the amendment to declare English the country's official language. In the same ultranativist zealot spirit, earlier in May in an effort to symbolize national unity, the Senate passed a resolution that required that the "Star-Spangled Banner" and the "Pledge of

Allegiance," the oath recited by immigrants when becoming citizens, be sung or spoken in English.[109]

While the Senate was caught up in a heated debate, President Bush on May 15 repromulgated his expanded immigration reform proposal. It called for 6,000 National Guard personnel to act as backup to the U.S. Border Patrol as part of the $1.95 billion plan to enhance border security. They were to provide surveillance and support until 6,000 additional border patrol agents could be hired and trained. The duration of their deployment was to be for two years. He reiterated his call for a guest-worker program and for the first time supported the construction of 370 miles of fences along the border. The Bush plan also included a provision for tamper-proof employment cards, stricter scrutinizing, and much more stringent enforcement of employer sanctions. It also called for more local and state law enforcement to provide support along the border. From the Oval Office, President Bush said, "We do not yet have control of the border, and I am determined to change that." His intent was to reverse the thinning public support for immigration reform and encourage the Congress to reach a consensus on the issue. With tensions rising between the two countries, due to some 200 alleged Mexican army incursions into U.S. territory, President Bush called México's President Fox and assured him that his intentions were not to militarize the border, but to provide additional support for the U.S. Border Patrol.[110]

The Bush plan sought the middle ground in securing support from Congress,[111] but politically the reaction to it was mixed. From media critiques to politicians, such as California Governor Arnold Schwarzenegger, were all hypercritical. Issues arose that the National Guard was not trained for border surveillance duty. Others argued about the issue of militarization and about the National Guard being overextended with significant numbers already deployed to Iraq. Its role at the border was also questioned, since it was prohibited from detaining or apprehending undocumented migrants or directly patrolling the border. Its deployment was scheduled to begin in June 2006.[112]

On May 25, after a bruising fight with the ultranativist zealots, the Senate by a 63 to 36 vote passed the Hagel-Martinez Compromise. Many of its provisions survived the grueling legislative process. Some minor amendments were adopted, such as the fines and fees for application for temporary status, which increased from $2,000 to $3,250.[113] The Senate also agreed for the construction of at least 350 miles of triple-layer fencing along the U.S.–México border. The legalization provision stipulated that those that were in the country for more than five years would be given temporary resident status and eventually permanent residency and citizenship. Those with less than five years in the country, but more than two years, had to leave the country and go to a port of entry and apply for temporary residency; those with less than two years had to leave the country.[114]

In June it too, however, became a casualty of the legislative quagmire. Congress was plagued by irreconcilable differences between the Senate's Hagel-Martinez Compromise and the House's HR4437, which precluded a joint Conference Committee from acting on the matter. At the core of the problem was that the two measures were diametrically opposed. The House's HR4437 was totally border security and enforcement-oriented, while the Senate's Hagel-Martinez Compromise was multifaceted and comprehensive and included both legalization and guest-worker provisions.

By mid-June, House Republican leaders with their "border enforcement only" posture intransigently continued their support of HR4437.[115] They succeeded in derailing any meaningful compromise between the House and Senate. Using a delaying tactic, the House Republicans enunciated that prior to any compromise with the Senate the House would conduct hearings during the summer in various cities nationwide in order to get the people's input on the immigration reform impasse. Republican House Speaker Dennis Hastert commented, "We are going to listen to the American people, and we are going to get a bill that is right." Democrats in the Senate were critical of the legislative maneuver. Senator Ted Kennedy accused the House Republicans of a "cynical effort to delay or kill a comprehensive immigration bill." Senator Reid accused Republicans of stalling and called on President Bush to prod House members of his party. He told the press that President Bush had "complete domination over his Republican Congress. Let him tell us how much he really wants a bill."[116]

In July and August 2006, public hearings were held by both the House and Senate. The House hearings in particular became symbolic shows orchestrated by ultranativist zealots as "delaying tactics" to derail the Hagel-Martinez Compromise and to advance their border security/enforcement agenda. Some pro-immigrant rights activists and groups sought to testify, but soon realized the hearings were staged political shows that did not allow much access. Pro-immigrant rights groups decried the lack of voice and input and protested.[117] On the Senate side, Republican Senator Specter responded to the House hearings by calling for the Senate to also hold hearings.[118] By the end of summer, the House and Senate public hearings sealed the casket of immigration reform for the 109th Congress. Congress failed to reconvene and take up the matter of the Hagel-Martinez Compromise.

THE SURGE IN QUAGMIRE

From September to November of 2006 the issue of immigration reform was superseded by the November 7 congressional elections. The nativist federal legislative surge nonetheless continued in September with a number of submitted individual immigration proposals. One such piece of legislation emphasized border security. It was taken up by Congress and passed in late September. It provided for the allocation of $1.2 billion for the construction of a 700-mile-long fence along the border, the hiring of an additional 1,500 agents, and the purchase of an additional 6,700 more beds for DHS's detention centers. Republicans in control of both the House and Senate in vying for its passage garnered support from Democrats. The House in mid-September passed it, 283 to 138. In the Senate, the bill was supported by fifty-four Republicans and twenty-six Democrats. Prior to its passage, México's President Vicente Fox condemned the legislative action as not being illustrative of friendship between México, Latin America, and the U.S. and followed up with a formal protest.[119] México's newly elected *Partido Acción Nacional* President Felipe Calderon in December 2006 as well vehemently criticized the construction of the 700-mile-long wall. In January 2007, the Congressional Research Service estimated the cost over twenty-five years of building and maintaining a 700-mile-fence would be as high as $49 billion.[120]

In the November 7 congressional elections the Democrats won control of both the House and Senate. Democrats in the House gained thirty-one seats, enough to take control from the Republicans after they had controlled it for twelve years. Of the 435 seats, Democrats controlled 233 to the Republican's 202.[121] With thirty-three seats up for reelection, Democrats won control of the Senate by a razor thin majority of fifty-one to forty-nine.[122] The Iraq War and its insurgent-infested occupation became the paramount issues of the 2006 congressional elections. The political push for immigration reform was kept alive mainly by pro-migrant rights groups, coalitions, and activists.

The Democrat-controlled 110th Congress convened in January 2007 and the issue of immigration reform was deferred. It was nowhere to be found on the Democratic Party's first "100 hours" agenda. Neither House Speaker Nancy Pelosi nor Senate Majority Leader Harry Reid had made immigration reform a priority policy item for the new Congress. Nevertheless, most Democrats supported the McCain-Kennedy Bill, which included a form of legalization that would allow an increase of visas, allowed for family members of undocumented migrants to come to the U.S., called for a temporary guest-worker program, and created a more fraud-proof worker authorization system.[123] Politically, debate on the issue of immigration reform did not pick up momentum until March with President Bush's visit with México's President Calderon in Merida, México. It was part of President Bush's five-country tour that included visits besides México to Brazil, Uruguay, Colombia, and Guatemala. Even prior to his meeting with President Bush, Calderon took a more independent posture than his predecessor Vicente Fox. In a pronouncement to the press, he made it clear that he was not interested in being Bush's front man in the U.S.'s efforts to countervail

Venezuelan President Hugo Chavez's influence in Latin America. Calderon also reminded President Bush that México was unequivocally against the construction of a 700-mile-long wall, which he likened to the Berlin Wall, and reiterated the need for the U.S to enact immigration reform. President Bush's public response was that upon his return to the U.S., he would work hard to pass comprehensive immigration reform, and reiterated his priority for a guest-worker proposal, but never alluded to legalization.[124]

In late March, the Bush administration floated once again its immigration plan. Under his plan undocumented workers could apply for three-year work visas that were designated as "Z" visas, and could be renewed indefinitely. Their renewal would cost $3,500 each time. Z visa holders would be eligible for emergency social services and primary and secondary education. Z visa holders would not receive any special preference in applying to become citizens. They would have to pay $2,000 when they applied to become a legal permanent resident or obtained their green card and $8,000 when they were approved. To secure a green card for "permanent residency" however, they would have to return to their native country and apply at a U.S. embassy or consulate. Also, prior to their legal reentry they would have to pay a $10,000 fine. On "border security," it called for augmenting the U.S. Border Patrol to 18,300 agents, for the construction of 200 miles of vehicle barriers and 370 miles of physical fencing, and for the utilization at the border of sophisticated electronic monitoring equipment. Identification cards would be required of all job seekers, including citizens and noncitizen migrants. Border security provisions would have to be in place prior to the start of the Bush plan's guest-worker program.[125] Some of the ultranativist zealot Republicans perceived the Bush plan as amnesty in disguise. Republican Senator Charles Grassley said, "If it walks like a duck and it quacks like a duck, it's a duck."[126] Democrats too were hypercritical for it lacked a legalization provision. Senator Kennedy said Democrats could possibly agree on its border enforcement provisions, however, it failed to address unsettled important issues.

On March 22, a few days prior to President Bush releasing his immigration proposal, Democratic Congressman Luis Gutierrez and Republican Congressman Jeff Flake had introduced bipartisan immigration reform legislation, the Security Through Regularized Immigration and a Vibrant Economy (STRIVE) Act of 2007. It was a modified version of previous immigration reform legislation considered by the 109th Congress, such as that proposed by McCain-Kennedy and Hagel-Martinez. Designated HR1645, the STRIVE Act was the beginning of an acrimonious immigration reform debate that pervaded Congress for the next four months. The following is a summary of its salient provisions:

- *Border enforcement:* it stipulated that as part of its certification requirements, prior to the implementation of the legalization or guest-worker program, the border enforcement provisions had to be enacted. It provided for the expansion of border enforcement personnel to a total of 15,350 and purchase of unmanned aerial vehicles and related technological surveillance technologies for patrol of U.S. borders. It authorized DHS and the Department of Justice to reimburse law enforcement and state and local prosecutors respectively for performing border-related assistance.

- *Interior enforcement:* it provided for the construction of twenty additional detention facilities for 20,000 individuals at any one time. It increased the number of ICE agents by 1,200. It increased criminal penalties for drunk driving, smuggling, gang membership, illegal entry, and reentry, and for the unauthorized employment of undocumented workers. Reaffirmed the use of state and local law enforcement agencies in the course of immigration enforcement.

- *Employment verification:* it would ensure the availability of a system for employers to electronically, that is, biometrically, verify workers' employment authorization. It called for the establishment of criminal penalties for employers and workers who violated the employment verification system.

- *New worker program:* it would establish an H-2C worker visa program, which would be valid for three years and renewable for an additional three years. The provision would ensure that U.S. workers have the first shot at available jobs and would not be displaced or adversely affected. Under its flexible visa cap, the initial cap would be at 400,000 and would be adjusted up or down based upon market fluctuations. New workers would be eligible for citizenship, as well as their spouses and children, after working in H-2C status for five years and paying an additional fee of $500.

- *Visa reforms:* a limit of 480,000 for family-sponsored visas would be set. Employment-based immigrant visas would increase from 140,000 to 290,000 per fiscal year. There would be an increased cap on H-1B visas of 115,000, which could be increased but could not exceed 180,000. It would prioritize immigrants with advanced skills and education, who would be exempt from the visa cap.

- *Legalization:* as part of the certification requirement, prior to its activation, it would be required that border and employer enforcement provisions be in place. It would provide for temporary status and a path for permanent residency for many of the country's 12 million undocumented migrants that arrived prior to June 1, 2006. They would have to pay a fine of $2,000 and back taxes, and pass a background criminal and security check. If after six years they learned English and civics and had a clean record, and the head of household had left and reentered the U.S. legally, they would be eligible for legal permanent status. After completing the preceding, they would be eligible for citizenship, but had to go to the back of the line. Applicants would need to meet employment requirements for six years preceding the application for adjustment, pay a $1,500 fine plus application fees, pay all taxes, undergo medical examination, meet English and civic requirements, and pass criminal and security checks. Other provisions included the Development, Relief, and Education for Alien Minors (DREAM) Act of 2007 and AgJOBS Act of 2007.[127]

Criticisms levied by pro-immigrant rights advocates, especially the progressives, against the STRIVE Act were several. One, it framed immigration policy reform from a national security perspective. Its interior law enforcement, coupled with its border security and enforcement provisions, further accelerated the militarization of the border and created the criminalization of undocumented migrants—made them subject to increased racial profiling, detentions, and deportation. Two, because of its certification border security and enforcement requirement, the legalization provision would not kick in for at least two years until these were in effect. Three, it strengthened employer sanctions, which made it easier for employers to fire or discriminate against undocumented migrants. Four, under its visa H-2C, it did not increase the cap of 480,000 visas. This onerously affected the reunification of families, because with current backlogs it could take up to twenty years to reunify families. Five, its legalization program was problematic in that applicants had to first satisfy the temporary requirement of six years. Then the immigrant could apply for permanent status; however, given backlogs, the wait could take up to ten years. Permanent resident status required applicants to leave the country and reenter through a port of entry. And six, once given their legal status, they would not be eligible for citizenship for at least another five years, which translated to a total of least twenty years.[128] Thus, in the end STRIVE Act like several of its predessors became a casualty of the legislative quagmire.

Next Congress by mid-May 2007, after weeks of debate and internal negotiations, an agreement was forged for a new bill, called the Secure Borders, Economic Opportunity and Immigration Reform Act of 2007 (SBEOIR) or S1348.[129] It was an amalgamation largely based on three previously unsuccessful immigration bills: (1) the McCain-Kennedy bill; (2) the Cornyn-Kyl bill; and (3) Senator Specter's Comprehensive Immigration Reform Act of 2006, which never passed the House. The bill's sole sponsor was Majority Leader Reid, but was crafted and supported by Senators Kennedy, McCain, Kyl, and Lindsay Graham. It also received input and support from the Bush administration, namely Homeland Security Secretary Michael Chertoff and Commerce Secretary Carlos Gutierrez. Other important senators who had input in crafting the bill were the "gang of twelve," which included Senators Dianne Feinstein, Mel Martinez, Ken Salazar, and Arlen Specter. The following is a summary of S1348's main provisions:

- *Legalization:* the bill created a renewable Z visa for those undocumented migrants who were lawfully in the U.S. prior to January 1, 2007. Triggers would be in effect, meaning border security measures would have to be operational (estimated to take eighteen months). It required the Secretary of Homeland Security to certify that these triggers were in place within eighteen months of enactment before the guest-worker and Z visa could start. The exception would be probationary status for Z workers for agricultural workers. It incorporated the DREAM Act, which legalized postsecondary undocumented students and allowed states to offer undocumented students in-state tuition fees.

- *Family-based immigration:* the bill would reset the number of family-based, family-backlog, merit-based immigrants, and provided for eventual Z visa immigration green cards. An annual total of 440,000 visas would be allotted to process the backlog of family-backlog categories. The current employment-based green card system would be replaced by a merit-based point system. Eligibility would be predicated upon points awarded for occupation and job experience, education, and knowledge of English. Points would also be allocated to those with certain family relationships, that is, adult child of a legal permanent resident or U.S. citizen or sibling of a U.S. citizen, that are no longer eligible for visas under the family immigration system. Only persons who accumulated sufficient number of points would be able to secure a green card.

- *Border security:* under Title I (border enforcement) it would include "triggers" which would increase the number of border patrol agents (18,000); build 370 miles of fencing, 200 miles of vehicle barriers, and 70 ground-based radar and camera towers; deploy four unmanned aerial vehicles and support systems; construct detention camps that could handle up to 27,500 undocumented per day, and so forth.

- *Guest-worker program:* the bill created a new "Y" visa that would allow an undocumented immigrant with a job offer, who had completed a background check, had a medical exam, and paid a $500 fee to apply to enter the U.S. legally to work. Y visas were good for only two years and could be renewed for two more years, provided the worker lived outside the U.S. for one year between the two-year extensions. It provided for Y-1 visa (nonseasonal); Y-2A visa (agricultural workers, shepherds, goatherds, dairy workers); Y-2B visa (nonagricultural workers); and Y-3 visa (nonagricultural worker's spouses and minor children). The Y-1 visa program had a cap originally of 400,000 and was reduced by the Senate to 200,000 with annual adjustments based upon labor market demands. The Y-2A had no numerical limitation, while the Y-2B visas were to be initially limited to 100,000 and were subject to annual adjustments based upon market fluctuations.

- *Employer sanctions:* the bill would implement a worksite enforcement system that utilized an electronic employment verification system (EEVS), which would reduce a list of documents that had to be presented to employers in order to prove identity and legal status. Penalties would be much more stringent for unlawful hiring, employment, and record-keeping violations.[130]

On both sides of the Senate arena, Democrats and Republicans were divided on its merits. Both parties challenged it with a plethora of amendments. It incorporated a number of restrictionist provisions coupled with border security, a guest-worker program, and employer verification; it had something each senator could support, but concomitantly things they could also oppose. Majority Leader Reid's reaction to S1348 was cautionary. He said, "I have serious concerns about some aspects of this proposal. . . . We need to improve the bill as it moves through the legislative process." In the House, Democratic Congressman Xavier Becerra, who represented the Congressional Hispanic Caucus attacked it: "It's a pretty radical shift to go to an employment based visa system as opposed to family system. You will continue to have close family members separated from their loved ones because of this policy."[131] Republican nativist senators and congresspersons labeled S1348 as "amnesty," a politically lethal charge that rekindled the polarization and tensions. A plethora of trade-off amendments were introduced. Some were accepted, while others were rejected; the legislative process went forward, but the differences were exacerbated.

On June 7, three Senate votes on cloture (allows the Senate to end debate) in support of what became known as the "Grand Bargain" failed. The first cloture vote lost 33 to 63, the second lost 34 to 61, and the third also lost, 45 to 50.[132] After the first vote, Reid told reporters that if another vote on cloture failed, "the bill's over with. The bill's gone." In response to the vote, he postponed consideration of S1348 until "enough Republicans are ready to join us in moving forward on a bill to fix our broken immigration system."[133] President Bush intervened and exhorted the Senators to bring back S1348 for further discussion and debate. On June 26, a vote was taken as to whether or not to continue debate; it passed 64 to 35. A tidal wave of lobbying was exerted by conservative ultranativist zealot forces that included radio and television broadcasters and listeners, organizations, bloggers, and so forth, so much so that the Senate's Internet server and phone system crashed at times.

Mexicano and Latino and pro-immigrant rights groups, coalitions, and activists, including all progressives and some moderates, also opposed its passage. Paradoxically, the extreme nativist right joined with progressive ranks in lobbying for its defeat. Nationwide, pro-immigrant rights forces denounced it as "draconian and egregiously restrictionist." A National Alliance for Human Rights (NAHR) report that I wrote stated that "the Senate has produced an utterly nativist and restrictionist proposed immigration reform legislation that is a concoction of haphazardly put together egregious political compromises that fall extremely short on immigration reform."[134] On June 28, the Senate voted on S1348 and on a final cloture vote of 46 to 53, it lost. Supporters needed sixty votes to prevail, ending the 110th Congress's efforts to effectuate immigration reform in 2007.

The reaction was strangely one of victory for right-wing ultranativist zealots and Mexicano/Latino progressives, some moderates, and liberals in Congress. Conversely, for President Bush it was a major defeat for his administration. One journalist even prior to the vote dubbed it as "Bush's Domestic Iraq."[135] S1348's defeat was a manifestation of the profound and insurmountable divisions that permeated Congress and the country as a whole on the wedge issue of immigration reform. With its passage a failure in the Senate, the House's STRIVE Act never got the opportunity to be crafted into a "companion bill" that resembled S1348. Thus, its defeat was illustrative of the detrimental effects of the legislative quagmire.

As 2007 came to a close what transpired politically was increasing talk of resuming immigration reform efforts using a "piece by piece" approach. With legalization exempted, the priority areas were border security, a guest-worker program, the DREAM Act, and AgJOBS.[136] But in the end, immigration reform was tabled by Congress as a nonpriority policy issue. Thus, as to the overall status of the nativist legislative surge, with the exception of the federal level, at the local and state level at the end of 2007, it was politically very much alive.

CHAPTER 12

Rise of the Countervailing Movimiento Pro-Migrante (2006)

In response to the nativist legislative surge, the greatest pro-immigrant mass movement in the country's history emerged—*El Movimiento Pro-Migrante* (MPM). From January to May 1, 2006 the country experienced its rise, which was characterized by a plethora of unprecedented pro-migrant rights mobilizations. Millions of undocumented and documented migrants and pro-migrant rights advocates, impelled by a combination of discontent, fear, anger, and rising expectations, organized, marched, and protested across the country in scores of cities for the defeat of House Resolution 4437 (HR4437), which sought to criminalize the country's 12 million undocumented migrants, and further militarization of the Cactus Curtain (the U.S.–México border). Never in the history of the United States (U.S.) had such a political phenomena occurred. At the great marches and the May 1 historic boycott and mobilization, scores of massive mobilizations were held in numerous cities, large and small, across the country. The country as a whole was startled with a political awakening of millions, especially migrants, who momentarily replaced their quiescent apathy with vociferous civic participation. These events shattered the myth that undocumented migrants in particular were apathetic, apolitical, and nonparticipatory.

This chapter examines the historical preconditions that led to the rise of MPM in January 2006, the great mobilizations that ensued, and the May 1st Boycott and Mobilization that became MPM's zenith.[1] As in the previous three chapters, because of my involvement in a leadership capacity and as a participant-observer, I resort to the use of the first person.

Rise of MPM's Historic Mobilizations

MPM'S SOCIAL MOVEMENT'S THEORETICAL ASPECTS

Massive pro-migrant rights protest mobilizations shook the country from January to May 2006. They were a result of the rise of MPM, an unprecedented social movement. There are many definitions of what constitutes a social movement. Joseph Gusfield, for example, defined a social movement as "socially shared activities and beliefs directed toward the demand for change in some aspect of the social order."[1] As a form of spontaneous collective action, MPM fits sociologist's John Wilson's definition: a social movement "is a conscious, collective, organized attempt to bring about or resist large-scale change in the social order by institutionalized means."[2] The usage of conscious, collective, and large-scale change is applicable to MPM, since it was the masses of participants who sought the defeat of HR4437 and approval of a comprehensive immigration reform legislation that specifically included legalization. From a social change perspective, social movements come in two forms: reform and revolutionary. Both differ in the scope of change proposed and in their strategies to attain it. Traditionally, revolutionary movements have sought a major "violent transformation" of the social order, whereas reform movements have sought to not destroy the existent social order, but to change aspects of it, usually via nonviolence and by working within the system. MPM's relatively short longevity embodied the latter. It proved to be spontaneous, transitory, and extremely limited in its change agenda. Strategically, it worked within the reform political parameters of the system, which meant that tactically it adhered to peaceful nonviolent unconventional protest in its politics to influence the legislative immigration reform process. It lacked, however, some of the other ingredients vital to the viability of a mass movement, such as a well-defined ideology, acclaimed leaders, permanent viable mass-based organization, common strategy and tactics, and a sustained power capability.[3]

No change oriented mass-movement arises in a historical vacuum and MPM's rise was no exception. In other words, both reform and revolutionary social movements rise only when conditions within a society are "ripe" or "propitious," meaning permeated by major discontent, dislocations, and disruptions. Francis Fox Piven and Richard A. Cloward buttress the argument when they state that "whatever position one takes on the 'causes' of mass unrest, there is general agreement that extraordinary disturbances in the larger society are required to transform the poor from apathy to hope, from quiescence to indignation."[4] Therefore, the multiple "historical preconditions"[5] that occurred between 1999 and 2005 prepared the ground for its rise. As previously addressed in chapters 6 through 11, the armed rancher vigilantes in Arizona (1999–2005), the nativist militias (2001–2005), the Minuteman Project (MP; 2005–2007), the rise of hate groups, and the barrage of nativist legislation (2004–2007) ensured that no major immigration reform was produced, especially legalization. As "historical preconditions," all the previously mentioned combined were the requisite political conditions that fomented the rise of MPM.

The passage of HR4437 in December 2005, however, was the straw that broke the camel's back. Migrants and immigrants alike felt a sense of growing frustration, discontent, and fear. More and more they felt that they were under attack and that legalization was becoming less and less likely. They became frightened of losing what they had worked so hard for and their expectations for the future were looking gloomier by the day. Eric Hoffer writes about the prerequisite of discontent for the rise of a mass movement: "For [people] to plunge headlong into an undertaking of vast change, they must be intensely discontented yet not destitute, and they must have the feeling that by the possession of some potent doctrine, infallible leader, or some new technique they have access to a source of irresistible power."[6]

Theorists Francis Fox Piven and Richard A. Cloward write that "both the theorists of rising expectations and those of immiseration agree that when expectations of men and women are disappointed, they react with anger." They argue, however, that "hardship" rather than "rising expectations" is historically more important as a precondition for massive turmoil by the poor to occur.[7] For Barrington Moore, the factor that creates a revolutionary mass uprising is a sudden increase in hardship, buttressed by the presence of serious deprivation.[8] Hence, MPM's rise as a mass movement was ascribable to "relative deprivation." Ted Robert Gurr, in his classic work *Why Men Rebel*, defines it as a precondition for major social change:

> Relative deprivation is defined as a perceived discrepancy between men's value expectations and their value capabilities. Value expectations are the goods and conditions of life to which people believe they are rightfully entitled. Value capabilities are the goods and conditions they think they are capable of attaining or maintaining given the social means available to them. Societal conditions that increase the average level or intensity of expectations without increasing capabilities increase the intensity of discontent.[9]

According to Steve Breyman, "protestors are guided by emotions rather than rational calculations." Their "protest activity is abnormal because it is not rooted in institutions, and is fundamentally different from institutional activity."[10] It is based on the links between actions and/or situations fostered by social institutions and people's observation of them, thus producing action based upon their perceptions. When threatening disparity exists between what they have and what they want, frustration, aggression, anger, and ultimately discontent set in, which suggests that conditions for a mass movement are ripe.

A "deprivation effect" coupled with existent "political opportunities"[11] within the country's political marketplace produced the requisite climate of change propitious for MPM's rise. As the discrepancy or gap between migrants' value expectations and value capabilities widened, the political opportunities for change increased, and so the political preconditions ripened. Reaction to the passage of HR4437 in December 2005 became the precondition that acted as a "precipitant"[12] for MPM to emerge. Its passage created conflict, controversy, debate, and discontent. The level of discontent and anger among migrants and immigrant rights forces reached its apogee in December, when they perceived the legislation as being draconian and threatening. It literally threatened to change the migrants and immigrants' life, status, and vested interests. Among its provisions, as delineated in chapter 11, was its "criminalization" of 12 million migrants and immigrants, which meant that they would be designated as felons and faced possible incarceration and deportation. During the ensuing weeks, their reaction was one based on their perceptions of what they had versus what they wanted and what they could get.[13]

The undocumented, in particular, lived under a specter of fear of being apprehended and deported, yet they had adapted to it. They worked, sent remittances to their home countries, and remained largely apathetic, indifferent, and not politically involved. Their paramount concern was to ameliorate their quality of life and that of their families, either in this country or in their respective native countries. As hard as it sounds, for most undocumented migrants, their impoverished socioeconomic status in this country was a dramatic improvement over the one they left back in their native country. The passage of HR4437, however, threatened to change all that. At this juncture, with their rising expectations being thwarted, they felt seriously threatened. They were confronted with the reality of knowing that HR4437 was putting them in jeopardy of losing almost everything: their jobs, material well-being, and homes. Even worse, their family units stood to be disrupted and they would be relegated to felon status and subject to deportation. Psychologically, it reminded them of having to return to egregious poverty, unemployment, chronic inequality, and, in some cases, political repression and violence.

HISTORICAL RISE OF MPM

The passage of HR4437 created mixed reactions politically. At the national level, the Bush administration's reaction was generally supportive to its border security aspects, but was hypercritical of it because it did not incorporate the administration's call for a "guest-worker" program. Republicans, as examined in chapter 11, presented different political currents when it came to HR4437's provisions. One political current, comprised of ultranativist zealots, for example, Congressman Sensenbrenner (as one of many), hammered on border enforcement and security; the other side, made up of moderate nativist pragmatist Republicans such as Senator McCain and the Bush administration, saw economic value and profit in having access to migrants as a source of cheap labor for meeting the country's economic demands and prioritized a guest-worker program. As for Democrats, especially those that supported the McCain-Kennedy immigration reform proposal, they were hypercritical of its lack of comprehensiveness, argued that it was myopic in scope, and therefore vowed to defeat it. Its passage unleashed a partisan political war. Congress's inability to reach a consensus on immigration reform engendered a legislative quagmire that lasted well into 2007.

An incident that further added to the undocumented migrant's growing frustration and apprehensions was the shooting of Guillermo Martinez. On December 30 a U.S. Border Patrol agent shot and killed eighteen-year-old Martinez while he attempted to cross from Tijuana into San Ysidro. The agent alleged that the shooting was in self-defense because Martinez had thrown a large rock at him. Ten days later the U.S. Border Patrol reported two separate incidents in Texas claiming that agents were shot at from México's side of the border. American Friends Service Committee Director Christian Ramirez from the San Diego office reported that the killing of Martinez was preceded in previous months with other shooting incidents involving U.S Border Patrol agents: on October 3, 2005, an undocumented migrant was shot and killed, and on October 26 and November 13, undocumented workers also had been shot and wounded.[14] The incidents, which received national to international media attention, angered México. México's politicians, of various political parties, in a chorus of unprecedented nationalist unity expressed outrage at the fatal shooting of Martinez. They vehemently condemned the U.S. Border Patrol, and also directed their attacks to HR4437.

Adding to the deterioration in U.S.–México relations was México's vehement criticism of HR4437. México's President Vicente Fox unequivocally rebuked it as draconian in its impact, especially the "criminalization" and "iron curtain" provisions and publicly warned that his administration would work for its defeat in the U.S. Senate. Luis Ernesto Derbez, México's foreign minister, described it as "stupid and one-handed." In early January the foreign ministers of México, Colombia, the Dominican Republic, El Salvador, and Costa Rica at a conference addressed their concerns with HR4437, particularly on human rights and construction of the 700–mile-long border wall.[15]

México's media exacerbated the issue by drawing a nexus between the Martinez shooting and HR4437. One newspaper, *El Excelsor*, alleged that particularly the latter was tantamount to "ethnic cleansing."[16] From México to several other Latin American countries, bitter criticisms and denunciations of HR4437 surged. Late in January, a 2,400-foot-long tunnel was discovered in the Tijuana–Otay border crossing area, which allegedly was used by a cartel to transport drugs. Authorities found some two tons of marijuana.[17] *New York Times* reporter James C. McKinley wrote, "Whatever reasons for sneaking over the border, the shooting of Mr. Martinez, 20, has fanned the flames of anger in México over what many here see as an increasingly hard line in the United States against illegal immigrants. His death has become a rallying point for politicians of all stripes, who have condemned the shooting as a racist violation of human rights."[18]

By January 2006 the anti-immigrant political climate was such that political opportunities emerged for the undocumented to become engaged, active, and increasingly defiant. This also applied to pro-immigrant rights activists, groups, and coalitions that acted as accelerators (factors, entities, and/or events) expediting the genesis and growth of MPM. They possessed a sufficient degree of leadership, organizational experience, vision of opposition to HR4437, and some experience in mobilization protest strategies and tactics. On January 9, 2006, in Arizona, the rise of MPM was manifested with the first major anti-HR4437 mobilization by pro-immigrant rights groups. A large protest rally was held in Phoenix, Arizona, on the capitol lawn, organized by *Inmigrantes Sin Fronteras* (ISF), led by Elias Bermudez.[19] Attended by some 4,000 persons,[20] the accelerator in this case was Arizona Governor Janet Napolitano's $100 million immigration proposal that included stationing of the National Guard along the border, toughening penalties for fraudulent identification papers, and punishing businesses that employed undocumented migrants.[21] ISF's comprehensive outreach strategy included canvassing of communities by distributing flyers; utilization of Spanish-speaking radio, especially Bermudez's ninety-minute KIDR-AM talk show; and support especially from evangelical churches, labor, and several other sectors.

In a short period of time, ISF successfully tapped the Mexicano/Latino communities' fears and frustrations and sparked an unprecedented fervor among Arizona's migrants and activists that served to help ignite MPM's "mobilization contagion."[22] At the rally, Bermudez said, "The power of this movement is not the leaders. It's not the organization. It's in the people." Reporter Daniel Gonzalez of the *Arizona Republic* wrote, "By tapping into the frustrations and fears of undocumented workers over the airwaves, Bermudez managed to help organize a powerful and well-financed new coalition, ISF, that sought to impact the immigration reform debate in Arizona."[23] For ISF this was extremely important, since Arizona's eighteen-member Latino Caucus (seventeen were Latino), in spite of its opposition to many of the anti-immigrant laws passed by the ninety-member state legislature, had been unable to stop or alter the nativist legislative surge or defeat Governor Napolitano's anti-immigrant and pro-militarization legislative agenda. In reference to the aforementioned, Representative Ben Miranda said, "I don't have much prospects (for this session)."[24]

In California, in response to the passage of HR4437 on January 12, 2006, the National Alliance for Human Rights (NAHR) under my leadership convoked an emergency meeting in San Bernardino attended by some 300 Mexicano/Latino leaders and activists from throughout southern California. The crux of the agenda was explained in a NAHR press release: "The purpose of the meeting is to initiate a Latino strategy and mobilization process for 2006 in California that will produce a coordinated strategy designed to defeat the Sensenbrenner legislation."[25] Also in attendance were some twenty-five nativist leaders and followers of the MP and Save Our State (SOS). Pro-migrant rights leaders who spoke were: Congressman Joe Baca; Assemblyman Joe Baca, Jr; Herman Baca, Committee on Chicano Rights; Father Patricio Guillen, *Libreria del Pueblo*; Jose Calderon, Pomona Valley Latino Roundtable; Enrique Morones, *Gente Unida* Coalition; Nativo Lopez, Mexican American Political Association; Felipe Aguirre, mayor pro tem, city of Maywood; John Trasviña, Mexican American Legal Defense and Education Fund (MALDEF); Elva Martinez, Central American Resource Center (CARECEN); Father Luis Angel Nieto, pastor of Resurrection Catholic Church; and Hector Carreon, *La Voz de Aztlán*.[26] The presentations addressed various aspects of the immigration crisis. I drafted and submitted for approval a plan of action calling for a number of specific direct actions and mobilizations.[27]

The presence of MP and SOS leaders and supporters created a disturbance. With some eight television stations present as well as other press, the meeting was tense and the possibility existed of violence erupting any minute. Some pro-migrant rights activists demanded that the MP and SOS supporters be thrown out of the meeting. Tempers rose as verbal attacks flew. My concern was that the situation could get out of control and that it would be recorded by the television and newspapers that were present. After all the scheduled speakers spoke, I recommended to the plenary session that a summit be held on February 11 in Riverside to be facilitated by NAHR in order to effectively develop a strategic response to HR4437. Media coverage of the leadership meeting was extensive, from local to national to international, which included CNN, Univision, Telemundo, and Azteca.[28] I was publicly criticized after the meeting by a pro-migrant rights activist from Los Angeles for not having had the MP and SOS contingent expelled from our meeting.

During the next few months there were several actions that energized the toddler-like MPM. One example of this was when several Mexicano and Latino groups in central and northern California called for a "sobriety boycott," calling on pro-immigrant rights supporters to not drink alcoholic beverages during the month of February. Concomitantly, there were calls made for mobilizations by a number of groups in different parts of the country.[29] Earlier in the month, in Rancho Cucamonga and Burbank, pro-immigrant rights groups and activists battled SOS and MP protests at Home Depot against *jornaleros* (day workers). In January, led by Nativo Lopez, MAPA and Mexicano/Latinos battled Orange County officials over federal officials training sheriff's deputies and Costa Mesa police on immigration law and its enforcement. This was a policy adopted previously by the Los Angeles and San Bernardino Sheriff's Departments among others nationwide.[30] Costa Mesa adopted the policy to have its police department act as an immigration enforcement agency. Nationwide, the political split within the Republican Party over immigration reform by January had widened even further. At a meeting of the Republican National Committee, ultranativist zealots openly battled the more moderate nativist pragmatists.[31] At the state level, Democratic New México Governor Bill Richardson offered to allocate an additional $2 million to combat drug and undocumented migrant trafficking.[32]

By February, MPM continued to manifest signs of its rise. One such event was the *Gente Unida* Coalition, led by Enrique Morones from San Diego, initiation of a pro-migrant rights caravan from San Diego to Washington, D.C., in an effort to pressure members of Congress into voting down HR4437. Two of the key organizers were NAHR members Vicente Rodriquez from San Diego and Danny Morales from Riverside. In mid-January, Morones announced at a press conference that the caravan would stop in several communities from California to Washington, D.C., and hold rallies or special events in order to network and secure media coverage. Their major objective was to foster an awareness of the dangers of HR4437 and call for its defeat. A second objective was to educate people on the tragedy of some 463 migrants who had died crossing the dangerous Cactus Curtain the previous year, and of the 4,000 that had died since Operation Gatekeeper went into effect in 1994.[33] *La Opinion* on January 12 reported that a migrant died every sixteen hours crossing the dangerous border. Also integral to the caravan's activities was to plant crosses in numerous cities as a sign of respect for those who had died crossing the border.

The caravan began on February 2, the 158-year anniversary of the signing of the Treaty of Guadalupe Hidalgo, at the site where Guillermo Martinez had been killed. For the next three weeks the caravan stopped in communities, networked with local groups, and exhorted the people to create the political momentum to stop HR4437. The caravan participants, meaning those who went to Washington, D.C., and back never numbered more than fifteen. In Holtville in Imperial County, accompanied by local community members, they planted some 400 crosses at a local cemetery honoring the mostly unnamed undocumented migrants who were buried there. Prior to arriving in Washington, D.C., the caravan stopped in Atlanta, in order to protest CNN's Lou Dobbs for what they considered to be his racist, nativist, and anti-immigrant reporting. On February 15 upon arriving in Washington, D.C., the caravaneers held a rally/press conference in front of the country's capital building. On February 21 the caravan headed back to California, replicating its activities.[34]

On February 11, NAHR held a Mexicano/Latino Leadership Summit at the Riverside Convention Center. It too became an important accelerator to MPM's rise. Without any resources, the NAHR volunteer staff of Mary Ann "Maria Anna" Gonzales and a few others, under my direction, within less than four weeks raised the requisite money, held organizing meetings, secured the facilities, and moved expeditiously to contact directly by telephone and Internet hundreds of pro-immigrant rights leaders, activists, coalitions and organizations from throughout the West and Midwest states for the purpose of inviting them to attend. During NAHR's outreach efforts, recruiters encouraged the various factions to continue, or begin for that matter, their own mobilization efforts in their respective areas. A press conference was held on January 30 in Riverside to promote the upcoming Summit. Understanding the importance of timing and framing of the message the press conference was kicked off with the following statement:

> Understanding the horrific anti-immigrant political climate rampant throughout the country and the severity of the consequences of the racist Sensenbrenner legislation . . . Méxicanos and Latinos in this country are under a state of siege reminiscent of the McCarthy Era. The difference being that the Bush Administration and nativist Republicans are targeting not communists, but "us" as their targets of persecution. Hence, this largely is motivated not by the "Red Scare" but by demographic "Brown Scare."[35]

Attended by organizational and coalitional representatives, the various speakers addressed the importance of the Summit. Its cardinal two interrelated objectives were explained: (1) to develop a bi-national strategic plan of action for the defeat of HR4437; and (2) to create a pro-immigrant rights bi-national or transnational movement that would call for comprehensive immigration reform. Related to the Summit's two objectives was the message that "2006 needs to be a year of massive mobilizations, activism, and political participation at all levels to countervail the heinous, racist and nativist crusade. The political climate is ripe, meaning the conditions are present, and the requisite forces exist for such a historical undertaking."[36]

On Saturday, February 11, the Bi-National Summit at the Riverside Convention Center was attended by some 550 pro-migrant rights leaders and activists from various parts of the South, West, and Midwest, and also from México.

The Summit's agenda was light on speakers and heavy on work sessions. The program featured a mission statement by me followed by a taped statement by California Speaker of the Assembly Fabian Nunez, and a report by México's *Partido Revolucionario Democrático* (PRD) Senator Reymundo Cardenas. Jose Jacques Medina from México, who headed the delegation of Mexican union leaders, argued for the building of a bi-national movement with México.[37]

Congressman Joe Baca, who was scheduled to speak, never showed. Five work sessions were lead by: (1) conventional lobbying: Felipe Aguirre, Maywood mayor pro tem, and Angela Sanbrano, executive director of CARECEN; (2) direct action strategy: Herman Baca, Committee on Chicano Rights; (3) organization: Juan Jose Peña, New México Hispanic Roundtable, and Carlos Montes, Service Employees International Union (SEIU) organizer; (4) finances: Dr. Manuela Sosa, NAHR, and Gilberto Esquivel, NAHR; and (5) in plenary session was the approval of plan of action: Russell Juarequi, NAHR legal coordinator. The following is a summary of the approved NAHR strategic plan of action:

- *International:* send a delegation to México City, March 15–18, 2006, to meet with Mexican government and party officials, including President Vicente Fox, and Latin American ambassadors, as well as leaders from unions, human rights groups, church, and press in order to push for open bi-national support for the defeat of HR4437.
- *National:* in coordination with national organizations based in Washington, D.C., and groups back East, on February 28, 2006, kick off an aggressive lobbying and direct action campaign to pressure the Senate to defeat HR4437 and promote legalization. A second action was to hold a national Mexicano/Latino day of protest (i.e., marches) on March 10, 2006, calling for the defeat of HR4437 and for legalization. A third action was a call for massive mobilizations nationwide.
- *State:* at the state level three actions were recommended: (1) in California, conduct a march and rally on February 25, 2006, in Costa Mesa; (2) hold a massive mobilization in Los Angeles on March 25, 2006; and (3) set up meetings with U.S. senators in their respective states prior to February 27, 2006.
- *Local:* starting in the month of February, participating activists and groups should form local and regional coalitions in order to provide the needed "base of power" to accelerate massive mobilizations.[38]

The plan of action was adopted overwhelmingly, with only minor changes. Two events were added that extended the schedule from a two-month to a three-month period: (1) hold a major bi-national mobilization for May 5; and (2) hold another summit sometime in April to fine-tune the aforementioned events and also to plan for the next phase of the mobilizations.[39]

During the month of February a number of other events and activities nurtured MPM's growth. In Southern California, *Comité Latino*, led by Mario Liascano of the Coachella Valley and a participant of the Summit, initiated a number of protest demonstrations that mobilized hundreds of people against HR4437.[40] Nativo Lopez, president of *Hermandad Méxicana Latinoamericana*, and several hundred protestors demonstrated at the Costa Mesa City Hall, condemning the city's controversial anti-immigrant policies. Nativist city officials who were in the majority had since 2005 shut down a job center that had helped immigrants secure work, disbanded the human relations committee that investigated acts of discrimination, and allowed local police to assume the role of immigration enforcement agents. Lopez and others called for an economic boycott of those businesses in Costa Mesa that supported Mayor Allan Mansoor, who had been designated an honorary member of MP, and was a chief protagonist of the city's anti-immigrant policies. The targeted businesses were given two months to openly repudiate the policies or else become targets of the boycott. The media described the city's political situation as tense to where fear and anger among undocumented migrants was pervasive.[41]

Also in the month of February the Los Angeles City Council passed two resolutions: one condemned MP and like groups and the other was against HR4437. The former prohibited MP from holding activities within city limits and the latter rebuked HR4437 and instead praised the manifold contributions that immigrants have made to the city. Angelica Salas, director of Coalition for Humane Immigrant Rights Los Angeles (CHIRLA), and Angela Sanbrano, director of CARECEN, presented to the city council a petition of 10,000 signatures that were collected in ten days calling for HR4437's defeat.[42] Pro-migrant rights groups in Vista, California, held a counterdemonstration against Gilchrist's MP rally.[43] In Orange, California, police arrested eight *jornaleros* in a Home Depot parking lot, stating that they had violated the city's ordinance that prohibited "soliciting for work." They were turned over by the police to the U.S. Border Patrol, which precipitated protests by Nativo Lopez.[44]

Meanwhile, in Arizona the pro-immigrant rights groups increased their vigor against the growing nativist legislative surge. Some 200 persons representing various pro-immigrant rights coalitions and organizations met in Phoenix to strategically develop ways of putting the brakes on the forty-nine anti-immigrant legislative measures that were being considered by the state legislature. At the forum held in February, several Mexicano/Latino state legislators spoke about the measures. Tony Herrera, president of the *Coalicion Unidos en Arizona*, asserted that the attacks were not just on the immigrant communities, but that they were on the entire Latino community.[45] By the end of the month, Governor Napolitano's proposal to station the National Guard along the border had momentum.

Likewise, in California, Republican Tom Harman introduced anti-immigrant legislation that would prohibit businesses that employed undocumented migrants from deducting their pay as a business expense, cut legal aid funding from agencies that provided legal services to undocumented migrants, and provided funding for local and state enforcement agencies to enforce immigration laws.[46] Numerous pro-immigrant rights groups from up and down the state publicly attacked the proposed measures. All three measures were ultimately defeated by a Democrat-controlled legislature, especially the Assembly, which was under the leadership of Speaker Fabian Nuñez, a long-time pro-immigrant activist turned politician.

In late February, in Las Vegas, a coalition of pro-immigrant rights and labor groups under the leadership of labor leader Miguel Barrientos, who had attended the NAHR Summit, on February 18 held an anti-HR4437 and pro-immigration reform march that drew some 5,000 people. On February 23 pro-immigrant rights groups in Houston, organized *"La Marcha por la Dignidad y el Respeto"* that drew tens of thousands.[47] On February 28, the AFL-CIO openly came out against HR4437 and called for legalization and in particular, spoke out against President Bush's proposed guest-worker program.[48] After traveling across the county for twenty-seven days visiting forty cities and holding press conferences and protests, the San Diego-based *Gente Unida* coalition's nationwide caravan arrived in Washington, D.C. It held a rally at the capitol building attended by hundreds of pro-migrant rights supporters.[49] A week later, coordinated by the Los Angeles-based National Day Laborer Organizing Network, led by Pablo Alvarado, a dozen *jornaleros* (day workers) began a three-month nationwide run that passed through twenty-five states and over fifty cities. The run, which started in California and ended in Washington, D.C., sought to bring attention to the exploitation and discrimination faced by migrant workers.[50]

Congress increasingly focused on the immigration reform agenda as there was growing resistance to HR4437 by Democrats. Democrats in both House and Senate increasingly showed their support for the McCain-Kennedy proposal that included legalization. Meanwhile, the Bush administration and moderate Republican Senator Pete Domenici proposed legislation that included a guest-worker program and legalization.[51] México in February sent a congressional delegation comprised of senators and deputies to Washington, D.C., to push for the realization of an immigration reform accord that was not as restrictionist as HR4437.[52] On the international level, the foreign ministers of eleven Latin American countries who had met in Colombia openly repudiated HR4437 and its draconian provisions. Mexican Foreign Secretary Ernesto Derbez said after the February 13 meeting that "the point we have made is that (the border wall) doesn't seem to us to be a solution." The governments of other Central American countries also joined the eleven in their opposition to HR4437.[53] Concurrently, some nativist Republican congresspersons and members of the Committee on Homeland Security participated in a fact-finding mission and held a hearing on the alleged Mexican military intrusions into the U.S.[54]

MPM INTENSIFIES

During March and April, MPM produced a plethora of accelerators, meaning massive marches. Mexicano and Latino pro-immigrant rights groups and activists nationwide made political history when millions of people, the majority being migrants, became engaged in numerous gigantic mobilizations. Never before in the history of the country's immigration experience had an ethnic/racial group ever displayed such massive power. The stereotypes or myths of Mexicanos and Latinos as being apathetic, complacent, unorganized, and/or politically backward were quickly rebuked. In a relatively short period of time, they proved nationwide that they were capable of creating a critical mass, a power capability. Undocumented migrants put aside their fears and political inhibitions and joined others in forging MPM.

On March 7, thousands rallied outside the nation's capitol, hearing from local and federal officials, for example, the Congressional Hispanic Caucus (CHC), calling on the Senate to not support HR4437 and to support legalization.[55] In Trenton, New Jersey, a march that same day drew thousands of people as well. Three days later, on March 10, honoring the call for massive mobilizations for this date as agreed to at the February Riverside Summit, Emma Lozano and Julie Santos, among a few others from Chicago, of *Coalición Sin Fronteras*, made political history. In four weeks, using a media-hype technique and a strong grassroots campaign, they produced the first of MPM's great marches, which numbered between 250,000 and half a million persons.[56] The mobilization got extensive national and international media coverage. Its impact was incredibly important for it engendered a multiplier effect.[57] Pro-migrant rights activists and groups across the country saw it as an indicator of the timing being just right for the rise of a mass movement. In Sacramento, also on March 10, the Chicano Consortium, under the leadership of Elfren Gutierrez, who too had attended the NAHR Summit, held a rally/protest at Southside Park that was attended by a few hundred protestors.[58] Indicative of the growing mobilization contagion on March 23 in the city of Milwaukee thousands marched and demanded immigration reform.[59]

With MPM's momentum growing nationwide, NAHR sought to make it international in scope. Adhering to what was agreed upon at the Summit, on March 15 through March 19, a NAHR bi-national delegation comprised of twenty-seven members traveled to México City. The delegation consisted of several activists and leaders, such as Emma Lozano and Julie Santos from Chicago Elias Bermudez and others from Phoenix; Alfredo Lopez Duran from Texas; eleven others from California; and eight from México. The participation of Bermudez and Lozano and Santos was important for the delegation, since they had been instrumental as accelerators in giving life to MPM with their massive marches respectively in Arizona and Illinois. Jose Jacques Medina, sub-secretary of the PRD's Migrant Secretariat and coordinator of Red Migrante, while in México City arranged for the delegates to meet with members of México's Congress, political parties, unions, press, church officials, and several embassy representatives.

A day prior to the delegation's departure to México, a press conference was held in Riverside. As coordinator of the NAHR delegation, I explained that the delegation's three main objectives were to: (1) secure support against HR4437 from México's Congress, political parties, unions, Catholic Church, and various Latin American ambassadors; (2) garner their support for immigration reform that included legalization; and (3) promote the rise of a hemispheric transnational or at minimum a bi-national movement for the realization of the two preceding objectives. On the latter objective, the delegates hoped to convince those in México to concurrently become engaged in "solidarity mobilizations" that would convert MPM into a "transnational movement" in support of both previous objectives. Delegate member Reverend Luis Angel Nieto from Los Angeles explained to the press that the delegation's major challenge was to sensitize México's leaders to the critical nature of discrimination that Mexicano migrants faced in the U.S.[60]

A meeting was requested with President Vicente Fox, but it never materialized. The delegates met, however, with México's congressional leaders, specifically those from the PRD and *Partido Acción Nacional* (PAN). The meetings with the leadership of both the Senate and the Chamber of Deputies were conducted in a roundtable format. Various aspects of the U.S.'s immigration crisis were discussed, specifically NAHR's three objectives. They assured the delegates that México's government was diplomatically doing everything possible to pressure the Bush administration and U.S. Congress into not supporting HR4437. The delegation also met with México's political party leadership, for example, PRD, PAN, and PRI, among others, which proved to be highly productive. As a discussion point the delegates at each meeting solicited them to organize and participate in direct actions against HR4437 and support legalization. They agreed to work to defeat HR4437, to support immigration reform, and to consider the direct action request. Officials of México's National Commission on Human Rights and top union leaders likewise concurred to publicly denounce it and in the case of unions, organize against it in the ensuing weeks.[61] Some members of the NAHR delegation met with fifty or so leading journalists that represented México City's various newspapers, who also agreed to pressure their respective newspapers to prioritize the defeat of HR4437 and call for legalization. A small contingent of delegates met with Cuba's ambassador and Venezuela's consul, and both agents confirmed that their governments were supportive of the delegation's mission.

While most of the delegation returned to the U.S., a few members remained in México. Led by Pepe Jacques Medina they met with the ambassadors of Brazil, Argentina, and Bolivia. They too committed to encourage their governments to diplomatically do as much as possible to pressure the Bush administration into not supporting HR4437. The meeting with Catholic Cardinal Norberto Rivera was also productive. While he said that the Catholic Church could not organize direct actions, he committed to publicly speaking out against the egregious impact HR4437 would have should it become law.[62]

Delegation members while in México also utilized the time to analyze the effects of the emergent MPM. The delegates agreed that upon their return to the U.S. they would make a collective call for multinational mobilizations on May 1, the International Day of the Worker. Initially, at the February NAHR Summit in Riverside, it had been agreed that May 5, Cinco de Mayo, would be used for a series of massive mobilizations. Cinco de Mayo was too limited since it was a Mexican holiday and not one celebrated by other countries in Latin America, whereas May 1 is celebrated worldwide. It was decided that May 1 would be a day of mobilization and boycott.

Specifically, May 1 efforts would consist of concurrent massive political mobilizations that included marches, school walkouts, and a one-day work stoppage and boycott of businesses. The rationale for the economic boycott was grounded on the reality that this country's capitalist bustling financial system is overwhelmingly dependent on cheap migrant labor, and that if well organized, it could literally paralyze the country's wealth for one day. It was agreed that such an effort would be even more effective if it were implemented on a transnational basis. The delegates believed that if done correctly, May 1 could send a powerful message to President Bush, Congress, and the country's capitalist plutocratic elites that were working to ensure the enactment of HR4437.

From mid-March to April, Pepe Jacques Medina in México City continued to act as an envoy for NAHR. He and others met with ambassadors of various Latin American countries. He also acted as a liaison with the divergent sectors of México's governmental entities, political parties, unions, media, and church leadership. The idea was to get them all to sign off on the "NO! on HR4437" effort and to have them commit to the May 1 boycott and mobilization.

Several Latin American governments became increasingly hypercritical of HR4437 and related immigration reform matters. During the rest of March and well into April, México's Congress and political parties intensified their criticism of HR4437 and called for reform, unions initiated marches in México City and a boycott of certain U.S. products, and the media accelerated its coverage of MPM mobilizations. NAHR's delegation effort in México City acted as an accelerator, for it helped secure support for MPM at both a bi-national and transnational level.

Upon its return, the NAHR delegates went back to their respective areas to organize for May 1. On March 23, led by Elias Bermudez, Alfredo Gutierrez, and State Representative Ben Miranda, 20,000 marched in Phoenix, and with clamors of "Si Se Puede" ("yes, it can be done") and placards that read, "We are not Criminals," they protested against Senator Jon Kyl. Similar demonstrations occurred in Tucson, Atlanta, Milwaukee, and elsewhere.[63] On March 24, tens of thousands marched in Denver, filling Civic Center Park.[64] In the South, with a growing migrant population, in unprecedented fashion, numerous coalitions held pro-immigrant rights protests and marches. In Charlotte, North Carolina, a march drew 5,000; Nashville, Tennessee, drew several thousand; and Birmingham, Alabama, drew a modest 150. Marches were also held in South Carolina and Georgia.[65]

On March 25, 2006, in Los Angeles, however, MPM produced the mother of all migrant mobilizations, the "Great March." It was organized by the March 25th Coalition, led by activist leaders Javier Rodriguez, Jessie Diaz, Russell Jaurequi, Maria Durazo, Reverend Jose Luis Nieto, Juan Jose Gutierrez, Reverend Richard Estrada, and Nativo Lopez, and scores of other activists, coalitions, unions, and church groups from throughout southern California. The political support and participation of numerous Latino notables (such as Los Angeles Mayor Antonio Villaraigosa) at the rally and organizational and funding support from labor unions (such as SEIU and Local 660), religious and pro-immigrant rights organizations, and other coalitions combined made the event a success. The march also attracted the participation of non-Latinos. Progressive organizations, such as Act Now to Stop War and End Racism (ANSWER), closed ranks in solidarity. Support also came from the Korean Resource Center of Los Angeles.[66]

Estimates of the march's size ranged from a low of 500,000 to a high of 1 million.[67] The Great March was embellished by an ocean of humanity carrying flags from the U.S., México, and several Latin American countries and placards with diverse messages.[68] The most prominent, however, was "No to HR4437" and "Yes on legalization." The historic mega march stretched for more than twenty blocks down Spring Street, Broadway, and Main Street to City Hall. At City Hall hundreds of thousands gathered with fervor, clamoring and chanting, and Azteca dancers blessed the four winds. Speaker after speaker vociferously addressed two common themes: "No to HR4437" and "Yes to legalization." While the event itself had a multiethnic message of solidarity with all immigrants, the rally concluded with a powerful sense of Latino power and there was the thunderous roar of *"Aqui estamos y No nos vamos"* ("we are here and we will not leave").

NAHR too participated in the march. When proposed on February 11 at the Riverside Summit, the expectation was that at best the number could reach somewhere between 100,000 to 200,000 people. No one ever expected the magnificent turnout. The 1 million in attendance surpassed all the marches held during the turbulent sixties and seventies, the era of the civil rights, Black, Chicano, and antiwar movements, or in recent history.

Its unprecedented success was ascribable to a combination of factors, which included the effect of the rise of the MPM; propitious political timing; great organizing by the March 25th Coalition; support of labor, countless pro-migrant rights coalitions, groups, activists, priests, and politicians; and a media barrage that included radio, television, and press. The power of the airwaves convinced, reassured, and raised the migrants' level of expectations and consciousness to where the great multitude of Latinos responded with fervor in massive numbers.

Several radio celebrities in the Los Angeles area—Renan "El Cucuy"Almendarez Coello, Humberto Luna, and Eddie "Piolin" Sotelo, among others—utilized their high-rated programs to promote the march. They, along with other media outlets, such as television and press, succeeded in giving migrants a sense of purpose, motivation, and inspiration. Migrants were convinced that they should put aside their fear and direct their frustration, discontent, and hope instead into participating in the march. Referring to the catalytic power of the Latino media, Mike Garcia, SEIU president of Local 1877 said, "They were the key to getting so many people out." Agreeing with Garcia was Felix Gutierrez, professor of journalism at USC's Annenberg School of Journalism, who explained that the DJs' message was directed to appeal to the migrants' vested interest, meaning they focused on how HR4437 was going to adversely affect them. "They were much closer to their audience, in terms of the direct effect," said Gutierrez.[69]

Religious leaders also helped assure undocumented migrants that the time had come for them to participate in the struggle for immigration reform. Catholic Cardinal Roger Mahoney's pronouncements against HR4437 and call for a just immigration reform added to the march's organizing mobilization contagion. Catholic Bishop Gerald Barnes of the Dioceses of San Bernardino, who headed the migration committee for the U.S. Conference of Bishops with his spiritual pronouncements, also helped to encourage migrant participation.[70] In explaining the active involvement of the Catholic Church, Barnes said, "This is not about politics from our point of view; this is about how we treat other human beings."[71] With the Catholic Church advocating for the migrants' interests and the participation of several priests, the migrant communities felt comfortable and safe in participating. Considering its size and the diversity of groups that participated, the Great March was peaceful, festive, and amazingly it ended with no arrests or incidents, not to mention that they left the site virtually spotless.

The victory of the march was due to the fact that so many people worked to make it a success. However, it was the overwhelming number of migrants that turned out on March 25 and demonstrated their solidarity, collective power, and participation in an extraordinarily unparalleled manner that made this march a success. The march was not only a victory for migrants but it was also a triumph for all people, groups, and coalitions who came together in solidarity calling for the defeat of HR4437 and for humane immigration reform. Los Angeles's Great March clearly demonstrated to the nation and world that Mexicanos, Latinos, and pro-migrant rights forces had forged in a very short period of time a powerful mass movement, MPM.

On March 25, thousands also marched in San Francisco, as well as in numerous other cities in California. The next day, Sunday, March 26, the United Farm Workers (UFW), supported by a number of organizations (e.g., CHIRLA, CARECEN, and SEIU local 660), held its annual Cesar Chavez March in Los Angeles. Some 4000 people marched in East Los Angeles against HR4437 and for "humane immigration reform," specifically for AgJOBS.[72] During the two or so weeks prior to both marches, there was reported conflict over what was perceived as competing marches, which created MPM's first public cleavage in California. On March 26, in Dallas, led by State Representative Roberto Alonzo, some 2,500 people marched and rallied at City Hall.[73]

MPM's mobilization contagion was also evident among high school students. Across the country, from California to Texas to Washington, D.C., high school students mobilized for the march in the days that followed.[74] On Monday, March 27, some 100,000 students throughout California participated in walkouts. In southern California the total was estimated at over 40,000 and in Riverside and San Bernardino Counties the number reached 6,000.[75] Students in Los Angeles succeeded in briefly closing down Freeway 101, causing L.A. Mayor Villaraigosa to intervene in an attempt to persuade them to return to their schools. The next day, some 12,000 students from throughout southern California, waving mainly México's flag, again walked out. One march that involved hundreds of students in Los Angeles disrupted transportation on the San Diego Freeway in Van Nuys. At another march, hundreds of students ran up the 6th Street off-ramp in Long Beach toward the Long Beach Freeway. In yet another march, student protestors tried to stymie the flow of traffic at the Vincent Thomas Bridge in San Pedro.[76] While most walkouts occurred in California, there were a few in other states. In Texas, for example, some 1,500 students walked out in Dallas, in Houston there were 150 who walked out, and numerous other student protests were reported throughout the state.[77]

By the end of March, in Los Angeles County the student walkouts for the time being came to an end. They dwindled largely due to stringent enforcement of truancy laws by school district officials, which included suspension and detention. Law enforcement agencies too were used by school districts to quell the walkouts. For school districts, the walkouts were a financial disaster, since the absence of each student meant a loss of $28.60 in state funding, which for some districts mathematically translated to losses of hundreds of thousands of dollars per day.[78] In other parts of California, however, students continued to nurture MPM's mobilization contagion with walkouts and protests.[79] In Kern County, on March 29 some 3,000 students walked out in a peaceful protest. In Bakersfield alone some 1,800 students took to the streets. The walkouts produced a few scuffles with police; however, for the most part they were nonviolent and ended with only a few arrests.

In early April there was a primarily White nativist backlash by moderate to ultranativist zealots who made MPM efforts a political issue. They vilified the marches as radical mobilizations. They were hypercritical and infuriated with the pervasive use of México's flag in the mobilizations, suggesting that the flying of any flag other than the U.S. flag was unpatriotic. In reaction to Denver's earlier mobilization, Republican State Representative Dave Schulthesis called the use of Mexican flags at the demonstrations "disrespectful to our country." He elucidated: "It angers me and it makes me resolved to fight this issue. I don't like in your face rebellion. We're not México and we don't fly Mexican flags in this country. We fly American flags." Increasingly, pro-migrant rights organizers, cognizant of the criticism, sought to limit, if not prohibit, the carrying of especially México's green, white, and red flag.[80] Even Latino Republican Congressman Henry Bonilla on "Meet the Press" said the carrying of México's flag was an "insult" to the country.[81] Yet when interviewed by the press, those carrying the Mexican flag said that they did so to demonstrate their pride in their heritage, culture, history, and as Mexicanos, who they were as a people.

It was not just the flag issue per se that fueled the nativists' anger, but also the masses of "Brown humanity," especially migrants that had displayed such great power. Nativists understood that Whites were quickly becoming a minority in Aztlán and inevitably nationwide. To extremist nativists, the huge mobilizations were tantamount to a "rebellion," a reminder of the "re-Conquista." Adding to their anger, frustration, and growing fear was that at no point during MPM's brief history, had White nativist forces ever come close to showing or demonstrating an equal power capability. Their best protest figures involved only a few hundred.

During April, MPM's nationwide mobilization contagion intensified, unleashing the migrants' power capability. They were not deterred by the intensification of attacks or backlash by nativist forces. Several major White-owned newspapers like the *Los Angeles Times* reported that MPM had enlisted the participation of "few Blacks." In the article, Black activist Najee Ali summarized: "Once I saw the half million, I felt fear, in a sense, that [Blacks] might be marginalized in the future when it comes to jobs and political empowerment."[82] Was it righteous impartial reporting or was it motivated to create further divisions between Mexicanos/Latinos and Blacks? Regardless of the justification, it was evident that the country's immigration crisis was acutely polarizing the country along ethnic and racial lines.

In collaboration with *Inmigrantes Sin Fronteras* (ISF) from Arizona, the Second Bi-National Mexicano/Latino Leadership Summit was held on April 8, in Phoenix. Unlike the first Summit held in Riverside, this Summit was plagued early on by infighting between MSF's leader Elias Bermudez and the faction that organized the second Summit. Whereas the first Summit convoked some 550 or so persons this one only attracted around 150. The summit's cardinal purpose was to formulate MPM's second national strategic mobilization phase, which was to be in the months of May to July. NAHR disseminated the invitation information regionally and MSF was responsible for the Summit's logistics, media, and securing participation from others in Arizona. As a result of MSF's internal power struggles, the Summit meeting site initially selected and publicized was canceled the day before the Summit by some MSF members associated with Bermudez. The faction that attended the Summit secured a new meeting place the morning of the Summit. As a result, the delegation from México that included PRD Senator Reymundo Cardenas, Jose Jacques Medina (sub-secretary of PRD's Migrant Affairs), and others from several states (that is, California, Illinois, Nevada, and New México) were lost for some three hours, which meant the Summit started incredibly late.[83]

Unlike the first Summit held in Riverside, where a drafted plan of action was submitted for approval by the attendees, because I received criticism by some that I had manipulated the Summit's results, I chose not to prepare one this time. Instead I presented verbally a number of recommendations on how to prolong and strengthen MPM's efforts for securing legalization: (1) support for the May 1 boycott and mobilization; (2) MPM nationwide mobilization in Washington, D.C., for sometime in May and a lobbying effort for legalization; (3) call for multiple nationwide mobilizations for July 4, 2006; and (4) call for a structural consolidation of all coalitions, groups, and organizations into a permanent immigration reform-oriented federation.

The infighting pervaded the debate to where none of my or others' recommendations were seriously dealt with. The MSF faction that chaired the plenary session, preoccupied with their internal divisions, did not present a plan of action or any viable ideas. After some opposition on their part, the May 1 mobilization passed by a slim vote. The MSF faction adamantly opposed the rest of my recommendations, particularly the July 4 mobilizations. They voted it down on the grounds that it would further alienate the White community because they would perceive the protests to be unpatriotic. The failure to formulate a strategy for post-May 1 and the fractures that surfaced were indicative of MPM's developing rifts.[84]

The failures of the Phoenix Summit did not affect the planned MPM mobilizations for April. In Brooklyn, on April 1 thousands of pro-migrant rights supporters marched. The huge march was a mosaic of immigrants and migrants from various countries that numbered in the thousands. The march began at the Brooklyn Bridge and ended with a rally at the Federal Building Plaza in Manhattan. Various speakers, instead of accentuating on HR4437, focused on legalization.[85] On April 9, hundreds of thousands of demonstrators marched in numerous cities nationwide exhorting Congress to pass immigration reform with a comprehensive legalization provision. In Dallas, some 500,000 persons dressed in white marched, waving thousands of mostly U.S. flags, and demanded legalization. In California that same day, some twenty cities held marches and/or various other types of protests that involved literally hundreds of thousands.[86] In San Diego, some 100,000 protestors took to the streets. They carried a combination of U.S. and Mexican flags, and their placards read "We march today, we vote tomorrow." Several other marches were held in other states, such as Illinois, Alabama, and Minnesota.[87] In California's San Bernardino and Riverside Counties, NAHR encouraged groups to continue to protest, but it concentrated its organizing efforts toward the May 1 boycott and mobilization. In Los Angeles, the March 25th Coalition and MAPA/Hermandad *Méxicana Latinoamericana* in late March did the same.[88]

On Monday, April 10, the country was shaken by the massive number of marches held in some 100 cities. Dubbed as National Day of Action for Immigrant Justice, it was reported to be the largest national mobilization of immigrants in this country's history.[89] Maura Reynolds and Faye Fiore in their front-page lead story, headlined, "Across the U.S., 'We Are America'" wrote, "The demonstrations across the nation were a culmination of a growing immigrant rights movement that began last month in response to House legislation passed in December."[90] Throughout Aztlán, cities like Los Angeles, San Jose, San Francisco, Fresno, Bakersfield, Sacramento, Las Vegas, Salt Lake City, Phoenix, Albuquerque, Denver, El Paso, Dallas, San Antonio, and Houston mobilized hundreds of thousands of pro-migrant rights supporters. The numbers participating in the marches ranged from 10,000 to 100,000. In Phoenix, the seventy organizations that convoked the march using the theme, "*Somos America*" ("we are America"), produced the largest mobilization in the region with over 250,000. The faction that had boycotted the Summit earlier managed to close ranks and scored a major victory. Not since the anti-Vietnam War mobilizations had the country been rocked by such a massive number of marches.

Pro-migrant rights mobilizations also occurred from the Pacific Northwest in Washington and Oregon; to the Midwest in Omaha, Milwaukee, and Chicago; to the East in Philadelphia, Boston, and New York; to the South in Atlanta; and in numerous smaller cities across the country as well. In Washington, D.C., a mobilization held at the National Mall was attended by nearly 500,000, which became the capitol's fourth largest march of its history. The Million Man March in 1995 drew some 875,000; the March for Women's Rights in 2004 galvanized some 700,000; the anti-Vietnam War mobilization of 1969 produced 600,000. The media alluded to the mobilization as the "Immigrant Rights Movement" or the "Immigrant Civil Rights Movement." It surpassed by 100 percent the famous Civil Rights March on Washington led by Dr. Martin Luther King in 1963.[91] In reference to the mobilizations New York Times reporter Randal A. Archibold wrote, "The idea we [Mexicanos] were a sleeping giant, sitting under a cactus saying mañana is gone. This is a community showing conviction and power. It is not a passive community."[92]

In numerous papers, the mobilizations received front page coverage. On television and radio news broadcasts, the mobilizations were the lead story. On the negative side, however, a Zogby poll taken from March 31 to April 3 found that 61 percent of likely voters felt less sympathetic to the plight of undocumented migrants after seeing the first round of major mobilizations, including the one on March 25 in Los Angeles. Of the 8,000 surveyed 32 percent said the protests made them more sympathetic. On the positive side, two polls taken in late April said the opposite.[93] The Washington Post conducted a poll, which revealed that 63 percent of those interviewed indicated that they favored legalization. In California, in another poll conducted by Field and cited in an editorial in La Opinion, it was reported that some 75 percent of the state's voters supported legalization. The editorial concluded that "in reference to the undocumented what seems to be happening is an increase in the acceptance of their presence in general."[94]

As for the undocumented migrants who participated in the marches, some employers said that they should be fired. In response, a number of pro-migrant rights groups and officials from México's consulates called for investigations of such employers by the Equal Employment Opportunity Commission (EEOC). The number who lost their jobs is unknown, but the newspaper La Opinion cited several instances where migrants lost their jobs.[95] While MPM succeeded in mobilizing millions, it never developed the capability to protect participants from either losing their jobs or putting a halt to the Immigration, Customs, and Enforcement (ICE) operations that began to occur.

Federal, state, and local governmental entities' reaction to MPM's mobilizations were ostensibly negative. At the federal level, DHS reacted in two ways. One, it reported that the Cactus Curtain was a "bordering danger," meaning it was becoming increasingly violent and precarious, and warned the public of a possible "catastrophic attack" by terrorists. It argued that immigration and national security were intertwined.[96] Two, it initiated via ICE nationwide operations (raids) at several wood products plants, apprehending some 1,187 undocumented workers. Nativist conservative Republicans hailed the nationwide raids and stressed the importance of employer sanctions and border security as themes for immigration reform.[97] As a result of tightened border controls and stringent enforcement, fewer undocumented in April sought to return to their native country. Prior to Operation Gatekeeper, Mexican studies showed that 20 percent of undocumented males returned home after six months in 1992, compared with 7 percent in 2000.[98] In support of HR4437, several nativist groups, MP and FAIR, among others nationwide, reacted at the federal level by accelerating their demands for its passage and supported the nativist legislative surge at both the state and local levels.

In California, ten bills were introduced by various Republicans with most seeking to deny social services to undocumented migrants and/or creating a state border patrol or authorizing police to enforce immigration laws. Because both state chambers were controlled by Democrats the proposed legislation died in committee.[99] At the local level the nativist legislative surge also grew. In Riverside, the County Board of Supervisors voted unanimously to crack down on undocumented migrants by allowing the sheriff's deputies to ascertain a person's immigration status. If they were found to be undocumented, upon completing their sentence, the undocumented were turned over to ICE officials for deportation. The policy was also adopted by San Bernardino County in January and Los Angeles County in February 2006. Other law enforcement entities in Arizona, Alabama, Florida, and North Carolina followed suit.[100]

Nativist politicians and groups intensified their attacks on MPM efforts because of the issue of Mexican flags in its mobilizations. Nativist press, television, and radio hosts and DJs cast aspersions on those who waved the Mexican flags, saying that they were not loyal to the U.S. In some cities, some White nativist groups protested the April 10 mobilizations. In Tucson, an MP group of no more than 100 publicly burned Mexican flags.[101] Typical of the xenophobic nativist anti-immigrant ethos and particularly the Mexicano bashing, *Washington Times* reporter Valerie Richardson, in her article entitled, "Mexican Aliens Seek to Retake 'Stolen' Land" wrote, "*La reconquista*, a radical movement calling for Mexico to 'reconquer' America's Southwest, has stepped out of the shadows at recent immigration-reform protests nationwide as marchers held signs saying, 'Uncle Sam Stole Our Land,' and waved México's flags."[102] As was the case in March, many Mexicanos disregarded the criticisms and brought their flags anyway to the marches as a statement of pride.

México's reaction to MPM was one of general support. President Fox exhorted Mexicanos in the U.S. to continue to participate, providing that they respected the country's laws. He asked the U.S. Congress and President Bush to produce comprehensive immigration reform legislation. Andres Manuel Lopes Obrador, PRD's presidential candidate, spoke out in support of the MPM mobilizations and was hypercritical of President Fox's failure to pressure the U.S. to pass a successful immigration reform accord.[103] For NAHR's delegation that traveled to México City in March, the strong endorsement for the marches by Obrador and PRD in particular was a triumph of its lobbying efforts.

LEAD-UP TO THE HISTORIC MAY 1 BOYCOTT

MPM experienced a relative calm before the cascade of the historic May 1 events. Although protests continued, the organizing priority for NAHR, among others, became May 1. From late March to April, NAHR organized a number of community town-hall meetings in both San Bernardino and Riverside Counties for the purposes of educating, preparing, and organizing the people for the numerous marches that were being planned for the two counties on May 1. In Los Angeles, as was alluded to previously, by late March, Javier Rodriguez and Jessie Diaz and others from the March 25th Coalition, MAPA State President Nativo Lopez, and (by April 10) a plethora of other groups were on board preparing for the May 1 event.

Throughout the rest of April in some parts of the country there were sporadic pro-migrant rights protests being carried out, such as in San Francisco, where some 2,000 pro-migrant rights protestors took to the streets and demanded the defeat of HR4437 and called for immigration reform.[104] There were also a few walkouts by high school students in various parts of the country. The one walkout that captured national media attention was in Denver on April 18. Waving both Mexican and U.S. flags, some 2,000 students from fourteen high schools secured a parade permit and peacefully marched through downtown Denver. They held a rally at the capitol building and demanded legalization and repudiated HR4437.[105]

The suicide of Anthony Soltero, age fourteen, a student at De Anza Middle School, on March 30 in Ontario, California, also received national media coverage. R. Samuel Paz, a civil rights attorney based in Culver City, at a press conference explained that Soltero committed suicide after he was called into the vice principal's office on March 30 for having participated in a walkout. The vice principal threatened him with jail for his involvement. Paz also reported that the school administrator allegedly also threatened the young boy's mother with a $250 fine in addition to barring him from graduation activities. When his mother arrived home she discovered that Soltero had shot himself. He was taken to the hospital where he died the next day. Montezuma Esparza, executive producer of the HBO movie *Walkout*, and other activists attended a press conference in support of the family. A few days later, Paz announced that a lawsuit was pending against the Ontario-Montclair School District on grounds that school officials had violated Soltero's civil rights, and for abuse of power.[106] The circumstances that led to his death were indicative of the excessive punishment some students received from school officials for exercising their civil rights.

During April MPM organizers began to publicly air their divisions. The Associated Press reported on MPM in an article entitled, "Divisions Emerge over May 1 Boycott and Mobilization." The lead paragraph read, "Organizers of the movement that led hundreds of thousands of immigrants onto the nation's streets are split over whether to press ahead with the next big protest—a May 1 national work stoppage and student boycott."[107] Divisions among activists over who was responsible for being the leader or leaders of certain marches began to surface.[108] MPM also became plagued by schisms over strategic differences for the May 1 economic boycott. The two tactical schools of thought clashed: (1) the progressives; and (2) the moderates.

The "progressives" were comprised essentially of leftist groups and activists that ideologically were anticapitalist and prosocialist or nationalist in their politics and were strategically more militant. They propounded a one-day work stoppage or boycott: workers were not supposed to go to work; parents were not supposed to send their children to school; and parents and students were to participate in major mobilizations. The "moderates," on the other hand, were more eclectic and less doctrinaire. They adhered to neoliberalism and were less assertive. Moderates were comprised of religious, labor, and social service entities, leaders, and activists that did not support the perceived radical approach of the May 1 boycott. Instead, they professed holding mobilizations after work hours, were against holding school walkouts, and vehemently opposed the economic boycott, fearing it would create a backlash, especially from the White community. In a statement to the press I said, "Our credibility as a community is on the line. We've shown our power politically, but if we can't show it economically we are going to lose it." As a moderate, Cardinal Mahoney said, "Go to work. Go to school. And then join thousands of us at a major rally afterward."[109]

In California, progressives included NAHR, March 25th Coalition, *Hermandad Mexicana Latinoamericana*, MAPA, Committee on Chicano Rights, Mexican Political Association (MPA), Hermandad Méxicana Transnacional, *Comite Pro Uno*, and *Movimiento Estudiantil Chicanos de Aztlán* (MEChA), among several other groups and coalitions, and a few local and state politicians. The California State Senate endorsed the progressive position by passing a resolution, 24 to 13, that split along party lines. It stressed the "tremendous contribution immigrants make on a daily basis to our society and economy." Democratic Senate Majority Leader Gloria Romero added, "It's one day . . . for immigrants to tell the country peacefully, 'We matter . . . [we're] not invisible.'"[110] Numerous coalitions and activists from San Diego to San Francisco also endorsed it. Some progressives alleged that the reason some moderates opposed the May 1 mobilization and boycott was because they feared losing funding. From immigrant social service provider agencies to the Catholic Church itself, they were afraid such perceived radical actions would alienate their funding sources or their White and business supporters.

The ranks of moderates was basically the We Are America Coalition, which included such notables as Cardinal Mahoney, Dolores Huerta, El Cucuy, Piolin, Mayor Antonio Villaraigosa, Supervisor Gloria Molina, and some 125 church, labor, and immigrant rights groups, such as CARECEN and CHIRLA.[111] The fracture spread nationwide. Several national Latino organizations adhered to the moderate position: National Council of La Raza (NCLR), LULAC, MALDEF, and CHC, among others. NCLR in late April, instead of supporting the economic boycott, announced a voter registration initiative called Leap to Action.[112] MALDEF Vice President John Trasviña publicly warned that "there are legal risks in leaving the jobs without authorization."[113] Fearing the impact of an economic boycott on their collective bargaining contracts, unions such as the UFW and SEIU also adhered to the moderate position. Other labor leaders felt the boycott was premature. Differences also surfaced between the two pro-migrant rights forces, such as on a guest-worker program, which moderates seemed to support and progressives unequivocally rejected.[114]

Contributing to the rising schism was lack of a unified posture on immigration reform. From its rise in January to April, it was impelled by a common call to defeat HR4437, followed by its call for immigration reform, which meant legalization. Progressives propounded complete legalization for the country's 12 million undocumented migrants, opposed a guest-worker program, and were hypercritical of ultranativist zealots' preoccupation with stringent "border security measures." They were not willing to compromise. Moderates essentially shared the same views; however, where they differed was in their pragmatism. They focused on legalization and equivocated on the guest-worker program and border security issues. As long as Congress produced a legalization program, they were not adamant in their opposition to other nativist-inspired measures. They felt that something was better than nothing. The Senate's passage of the Hagel-Martinez Compromise illustrates the preceding. The progressives rebuked it unequivocally and the moderates by and large embraced it.

It came as a surprise when Dolores Huerta joined Mahoney in echoing opposition to the May 1 mobilization and boycott. She spoke out against the economic boycott and school walkouts. In *La Opinión* on April 18, she said, "The idea of a boycott is good, but always when they are directed against companies that support anti-immigrant movements."[115] She disagreed that it was a good idea for workers to risk losing their jobs, which could affect their families. On the issue of the school boycott, she opposed to it on grounds that students had already sent their message with previous walkouts. Instead, she suggested that especially documented immigrants participate in voter registration drives, which would have a greater impact politically.

MPM's divisions over strategy and tactics became national in scope and cut across various sectors. The media that had been instrumental in uplifting hopes and encouraging immigrants to become involved in the MPM mobilizations of March too was divided. Radio personalities, such as Piolin and El Cucuy, among others, did not support the progressives' call for an economic boycott. El Cucuy in particular feared that the May 1 economic boycott would create a backlash and would fuel an anti-undocumented movement.[116] Access by progressives to radio and television became extremely limited. Univision, as a media conglomerate comprised of numerous television and radio stations, openly opposed the progressives and was the most blatant in its opposition to the May 1 mobilization and boycott. It provided biased news coverage that supported the moderate posture. Numerous news reports were slanted to instill fear, raising concerns about the detrimental economic and educational impact a boycott and school walkouts would have.

In mid-April, NAHR held a press conference in Riverside and threatened to call for a national boycott against Univision. It released a secret memo sent by a Univision top executive to the news departments of its radio and television stations calling on its employees to not support the May 1 boycott-related events. It read: "Let us unite, so we can ask not to participate in this wrongful protest of the National Boycott. . . . We will not be influenced by groups of extremists, agitators or union leaders." The memo also read, "We need to be very sure the boycott doesn't bring with it harsh consequences, like increasing the hate of our own race."[117] Competing networks, such as Telemundo and Azteca, were encouraged to move aggressively to provide comprehensive coverage of the upcoming May 1 progressive events, and they did. I received an angry, threatening call from Univision's Los Angeles news director. NAHR encouraged the public, especially progressive entities, to call or e-mail Univision's channel 34 general manager and news director. NAHR's pressure on Univision worked. By late April, without actually calling for the boycott, Univision joined the other Latino television networks in providing coverage of preparations for the May 1 mobilizations and boycott.

MAY 1 MOBILIZATION AND BOYCOTT

On May 1, over 2 million mostly Mexicano and Latino migrants nationwide participated in the unprecedented protest/boycott events. Influenced by the film *A Day without a Mexican*, NAHR opted to call its boycott and mobilization in the San Bernardino and Riverside Counties "A Day without a Mexican/Latino Boycott and Mobilization." NAHR, from a political marketing perspective, believed that both events should involve the "total" Mexicano/Latino community and not just migrants. It felt that MPM needed to broaden its support and participation base, particularly because the nativist attacks had escalated and were directed specifically at the whole of both communities. Other progressives in different areas and cities called it "A Day without an Immigrant."

Never in U.S. political history had the country experienced such massive mobilizations as on May 1, the International Day of the Worker. Associated with the international struggle of workers, May 1 had produced, especially during the era of the Soviet Union, worldwide gigantic mobilizations. But with the hegemony of global capitalism, few countries since the 1980s had demonstrated such a fervent commitment to what was perceived by capitalist adherents as a socialist or Marxist day of mobilization. On May 1, 2006, MPM produced an unprecedented 150 marches. The roars of festive protestors waving U.S., México, and other countries' flags, placards demanding the defeat of HR4437, and the chants for immigration reform, especially legalization, were recorded by an overwhelmed media. In Los Angeles, because of the divisions between the progressives and the moderates each had separate mobilizations at different times; the former around noon, the latter late afternoon. The progressive march organized in great part by the March 25th Coalition drew some 250,000 people, whereas the moderate march garnered some 400,000. It should be noted, however, that thousands who participated in the former also participated in the latter.[118]

The impact of the historic mobilization and boycott on California's schools was major. In Los Angeles County alone some 71,942 student absences were recorded. In the city of Pomona school district officials reported a 23 percent student absence rate. In the inland empire, which includes large chunks of both San Bernardino and Riverside Counties, the number of student absences varied from district to district. San Bernardino District schools reported up to 40 percent student absences; Chaffey Union High School District, 20 percent; Chino Valley Unified School District, 10 percent; and Coachella Valley officials reported absences as high as 64 percent. Statewide, hundreds of thousands of students did not go to school and instead participated in the street mobilizations. Throughout California, in a plethora of cities, MPM's peaceful mobilization contagion was apparent. In Riverside and San Bernardino Counties, NAHR supported marches drew 6,000 in Riverside, 3,000 in the Coachella Valley, 3,000 in

San Bernardino, 1,000 in Moreno Valley, 300 in Pomona, 300 in Claremont, 1,000 in Ontario, 1,000 in Perris, and 1,000 in Corona. Marches were recorded in some twenty-eight cities in California. An estimated 50,000 marched in Sacramento, 50,000 in San Francisco, 30,000 in San Jose, 13,000 in San Diego, 10,000 in Santa Ana, 8,000 in Huntington Park, and tens of thousands more in smaller cities. In San Ysidro at the U.S.–México border about 1,000 people from both sides of the border blocked the lanes into the U.S. for about one hour.[119] The preceding numbers do not include those who stayed home or did not go to school, which were also in the thousands. Workers and students boycotted their work and schools, did not purchase goods, and hundreds of businesses closed.

MPM's power capability (i.e., capacity to create a critical mass) was evident in numerous parts of the country. The estimated total nationwide who participated in the marches was over 2 million. This translated to 2 million persons who boycotted work and school. The preceding estimate is realistic taking into account as previously stated that in California alone the total number was at least 1 million. According to the Associated Press, according to police estimates in two dozen cities, the total number was 1.1 million. The fact was that mobilizations were held as stated previously in some 150 cities, not just 24. Chicago alone produced a march of at least 400,000; New York, 100,000; Denver, 75,000; Houston, 30,000; Orlando, 20,000; Miami, 10,000; Portland, 9,000; Salem, 8,000; Tampa, 5,000; Atlanta, 4,500; New Orleans, 3,000; Phoenix, 2,500; and Detroit 1,000.[120] In over 137 smaller cities, people in the hundreds also took to the streets in support of the historic efforts.

As to just how effective the boycott was, the answer is debatable and problematic and largely depends on the person's stance on immigration reform. From an antimigrant posture, the results were negative. For some the "White backlash" against MPM was exacerbated. White-led nativist forces were hypercritical and expressed their criticisms in various forms. In a few cities, small numbers of MP types sought to demonstrate against them, but failed miserably, in that nowhere did they produce massive numbers. Anti-immigrant groups like MP and SOS, including politicians such as Colorado Congressman Tom Tancredo, reacted as if México had invaded the U.S. Several radio talk hosts, such as KFI's Jon and Ken, encouraged their audiences to go and spend money and drive because of the lack of traffic.[121] For the nativists, it energized their efforts to attack MPM.

The pro-immigrant rights forces claimed that the May 1 mobilization and boycott was a major victory. Nationwide, hundreds of thousands of businesses honored the spirit of the call by closing for one day. *La Opinion* on May 3 in extensive front-page articles provided a partial assessment of the day's results. It reported that nationwide a total of some 5 million people had participated in some fashion or another. Doing a content analysis of newspapers reporting on the marches, at the very minimum, at least 3 million people participated in the

150-plus massive mobilizations. In California alone over 1 million participated. As to the boycott itself, 90 percent of the businesses closed in the city of Huntington Park. The ports of Los Angeles and Long Beach experienced an 80 percent reduction of truck traffic. In reference to school boycotts in Los Angeles County some 158,125 students did not attend classes. Numerous newspapers reported on the closing of hundreds of local businesses. In San Bernardino and Riverside Counties, the local newspapers reported that scores of businesses closed; restaurants had difficulty staying open; and construction, landscaping companies, and factories were left without sufficient workers.[122] Nationwide, Associated Press reporter Gillian Flaccus on May 2 reported that hundreds of thousands of mostly [Latino] immigrants missed work and took to the streets Monday, flexing their economic muscle in a nationwide boycott that succeeded in slowing or shutting down many farms, factories, markets, and restaurants.[123]

Internationally, especially throughout Latin America, May 1 received ardent support. Organized by unions and supporters of the Zapatistas, thousands took to the streets of México City in support of migrants in the U.S.[124] They called it "A Day Without Gringos" and boycotted U.S.-owned supermarkets, fast food restaurants, and U.S.-made goods.[125] Thousands also marched in solidarity in Central America, Cuba, Venezuela, and other South American countries. The response from Latin America was a triumph for MPM, but particularly for NAHR since via its delegation's visit to México in March had garnered transnational support for MPM.

Thus, while the May 1 historic boycott and mobilization did not paralyze the country's economy, it did demonstrate the Mexicano and Latino communities' capacity to wield political and economic power.

CHAPTER 13

Decline of the Movimiento Pro-Migrante and its Mobilizations (2006–2007)

As abruptly as the *Movimiento Pro-Migrante* (MPM) emerged in January 2006 it disappeared five months later. The great mobilizations that produced the millions of people in the streets throughout the nation in the struggle to defeat HR4437 and promote legalization abruptly became moribund. The great masses of undocumented and documented migrants that had energized and impelled MPM suddenly stopped participating and supporting efforts to keep it alive. The "climate of change" that had fostered among them a sense of hope, optimism, and rising expectations for a just and humane immigration reform was replaced by an acute and profound sense of hopelessness, chronic cynicism, and pervasive alienation characterized by their withdrawal from activism, a resurgent nativist driven "climate of fear," which pervaded the country. Congress's failure to produce immigration reform in 2006 and again in 2007 added to the migrants' growing alienation and the country's xenophobic, nativist, and racist political climate. Attempts by proimmigrant rights activists to reignite MPM by holding more marches failed. Its decline was also ascribable to its inherent social movement contradictions.[1]

Using my social movement paradigm, this chapter examines MPM's decline. The salient de-accelerators that contributed to its decline and demise are analyzed within its framework of a climate of change, leadership, organization, ideology, strategy and tactics, and power capability.

MPM's Inherent Social Movement Contradictions

VITAL INGREDIENTS OF A SOCIAL MOVEMENT

As a mass movement[2] MPM was theoretically plagued by several inherent contradictions that acted as de-accelerators, contributing to its collapse. In order to understand the role they played, they are examined within the context of my own paradigm on social movements,[3] which postulates that integral to the rise and sustenance of any social change-oriented mass movement, be it reform- or revolutionary-oriented, there are six requisite interdependent variables or ingredients: (1) climate of change; (2) leadership; (3) organization; (4) ideology; (5) strategy and tactics; and (6) power capability. The incipient stage of a mass movement, its growth, and ultimately its success hinges upon the presence and balance of interaction of all six variables.

While each ingredient is vital and indispensable to a mass movement's rise, maintenance, and growth, the presence of a "climate of change" is by far the most important. This signifies that political conditions must be such that frustration and discontent are rampant in society. People must be upset and frustrated enough for them to be willing to break from their sense of apathy, complacency, and/or indifference. "Leaders" are indispensable to any social movement, for they direct, lead, inspire, and manipulate the people's frustration, aggression, and discontent. Likewise "organization(s)" is/are a requisite for any social movement, for it structures the people's participation. "Ideology" provides it with a set of beliefs, ideas, direction, and/or vision. "Strategy and tactics" are required to realize its ends or ideology. And a "power capability" equips it with sufficient numbers of organized people and finances, both required to produce a critical mass.

A mass movement can emerge without the presence of all six variables. But if several or even one are missing, it is argued that it becomes difficult for a mass movement to sustain itself over time. Ideally, a mass movement's maintenance, growth, and longevity are dependent on a concomitant balance of interaction of all six ingredients. Thus, MPM's decline is examined using the above social movement paradigm.

MPM'S CLIMATE OF CHANGE TURNS INTO A CLIMATE OF FEAR

As examined in chapter 12, for both immigrants and migrants the political climate, which began to change from a "climate of fear" that preceded the passage of HR4437 in December 2005 to a "climate of change" that began in January 2006, reached its zenith by the May 1 mobilization and boycott. The anger, frustration, discontent, rising expectations, and hope that characterized the climate of change were replaced again by the climate of fear's cynicism, resignation, apathy, and mistrust. What ensued was that the country's political climate, impelled by the WASP ethos became repressively more anti-immigrant, especially anti-Mexicano migrant. This induced pronounced fear among immigrants, which precipitously led to their withdrawal from participating in MPM. The change in the political climate contributed significantly to MPM's decline and was precipitated by four salient de-accelerators (i.e., events or situations): (1) Immigration, Customs, and Enforcement (ICE) operations; (2) Congress and President Bush's failure to produce immigration reform; (3) the anti-immigrant WASP ethos intensified; and (4) police attacks on migrants.

The leading de-accelerator was the numerous ICE operations against businesses from April 2006 to 2007. The Department of Homeland Security's (DHS) promulgation of a comprehensive immigration enforcement strategy for the country's interior, called the Secure Border Initiative (SBI), which sought to "secure America's borders and reduce illegal migration." Its first phase "focused on gaining operational control of the nation's borders through additional personnel and technology; while also re-engineering the detention and removal system to ensure illegal aliens [were] removed from this country quickly and efficiently." DHS Secretary Michael Chertoff said, "This department will counter the unscrupulous tactics of employers with intelligence-driven worksite enforcement actions and combat exploitation by dangerous smuggling organizations with the full force of the law."[4]

DHS's pronouncement of SBI was followed by an acceleration of ICE's operations nationwide. Throughout 2006 ICE operations were well publicized and expanded dramatically. One day prior to Chertoff's announcement ICE initiated a nationwide big sweep on IFCO Systems, a Dutch-based wood products company, targeting forty plants located in twenty-six states, set a record for federal enforcement arrests in a single day. About 1,187 workers were arrested on suspicion of being undocumented and seven IFCO mangers were charged with immigration-related crimes. ICE officials alleged that IFCO's managers systematically recruited undocumented workers and assisted them in obtaining false identification, provided them with transportation beyond the border, and advised them on how to avoid trouble with the police.[5] *La Opinion* on April 21 in an article entitled *"La Redada enardece los animos"* reported on the rise in fear among the undocumented. ICE's well-publicized operations propagated fear. ICE's operations became increasingly frequent during 2006 and by the end of the year 221,664 undocumented migrants had been deported, an increase of some 37,000 or about 20 percent over the previous year.[6]

Throughout 2007 ICE continued its fear producing, relentless operations. In January it conducted another nationwide operation that netted the arrest and deportation of 761 undocumented from some fourteen countries.[7] That same month in Tucson and San Francisco combined, over 300 undocumented were apprehended and deported. In southern California's five counties some 761 were arrested and deported. In February, in another nationwide sweep, ICE initiated operations in some seventeen states and the District of Colombia. Its agents descended on popular eateries like House of Blues, Hard Rock Café, Planet

Hollywood, ESPN Zone, and China Grill. A total of sixty-three businesses were hit, producing 195 arrests in one evening. Janitorial/cleaning services provided by Nevada-based Rosenbaum-Cunningham International Inc. were also targeted. ICE agents filed criminal charges against the company's top three executives.[8] In Chicago, pro-migrant rights activists in February and weeks after battled the detrimental effects of ICE's operations, namely the breakup of immigrant families. Demanding an immediate moratorium, Julie Santos, one of the leaders, argued, "On a daily basis in the USA we must bear witness to the destruction of families." For months thereafter, they held press conferences, protested, met with politicians, and lobbied congressional leaders to put a halt to what they called the "ICE raids."[9] In August, some 300 ICE agents surrounded a chicken processing plant operated by Koch Food near Cincinnati that netted 160 arrests.[10]

However, in September, a U.S. District Court judge in California issued a temporary restraining order. It required that DHS send out notices from the Social Security Administration to suspected employers informing them of non-matching records between an employee's name and Social Security number. Employers were compelled to resolve any discrepancy within ninety days and dismiss the employee if not in compliance or the employer faced up to $10,000 in fines for knowingly hiring an undocumented person. The suit, initiated by the American Federation of Labor and Congress of Industrial Organizations (AFL-CIO), American Civil Liberties Union (ACLU), and the National Immigration Law Center, alleged that DHS exceeded its authority in making such a policy.[11] In September the United Food and Commercial Workers International Union sought court intervention to protect the Fourth Amendment rights of its workers regardless of legal status. The suit named DHS and ICE as defendants. Filed in the U.S. District Court of the Northern District of Texas it sought to enjoin the government from illegally apprehending and detaining workers while at their workplace. The basis of the suit was that in December of 2006, more than 12,000 meatpacking workers, including citizens, legal residents, and immigrants in the process of legalization, were apprehended because of ICE raids.[12]

That month, a two-week ICE operation in Los Angeles and San Bernardino Counties, touted as the largest of its kind, apprehended 1,300 undocumented.[13] The crackdown was part of a national effort by ICE to target some 597,000 undocumented migrants who had ignored judicial orders to leave the country. ICE officials emphasized that its operations only targeted those undocumented who were perceived to be a safety threat, particularly criminal elements, such as gang members, sex offenders, and drug traffickers. Of the total 2,667 arrested during the year ending September 30, only 576 had criminal records. ICE justified its actions in California because it said that the number of undocumented migrants in the state was estimated to be 2.4 million.[14] Antonio Branabe, an organizer for the Coalition for Humane Immigrant Rights of Los Angeles said, "The raids are supposed to be targeting the criminals, but they are breaking up families, they are affecting the economy, they are affecting the communities. We are desperate to find a way to stop these raids."[15]

To undocumented migrants, ICE's operations meant deportation, which translated to being uprooted from their families, homes, and communities, and losing their jobs, cars, material possessions, and their hope for a better life. As a result of ICE's operations, scores of families were separated. With husbands, or at times wives, being deported, children were sometimes left behind alone and unsupervised for extended periods of time. In other situations, both parents were deported, leaving children alone to fend for themselves with no economic means by which to survive.[16] Being deported forced them to return to their respective countries that were plagued by poverty, unemployment, low wages, inequality, chronic social problems, violence, and in some cases, political repression. Finally, it meant a loss of their financial capacity via remittances to support their nuclear or extended families in their respective home countries, which for Mexicanos alone in 2007 was nearly $25 billion.

A second de-accelerator was Congress and President Bush's failure to generate immigration reform. By May 1, 2006, it had become rather evident that HR4437 was no longer a threat per se, but the undocumented migrants' expectations had risen for legalization. The failure of Congress in June 2006 to approve the Hagel-Martinez Compromise and during July 2007 the Border Security and Immigration Act of 2007 was a clear signal to them that hard and difficult times lay ahead. Their sense of fear was increased with the federal government's further militarization of the Cactus Curtain, that is, passage of legislation to build a 700-mile-long iron curtain.

The failure of the federal government to produce immigration reform contributed substantially to the nativist legislative surge's intensification at the state and local levels. Through their anti-immigrant laws, ordinances, and initiatives, they instilled fear within the undocumented communities. They became targets of ethnic cleansing measures by being denied services, employment, and housing, and they were subjected to repression.[17] The Hazelton, Pennsylvania, contagion spread nativism, xenophobia, and racism to numerous other local communities. Indicative of this way of thinking, Beardstown, Illinois Mayor Bob Walters said when interviewed by *Time* magazine, "If I got up and said I'm going to run each and every Mexican out of town on a donkey, the voters here would cheer me on."[18] Beyond ICE operations, local law enforcement operations too fostered fear in the vulnerable undocumented. In late June 2007, in Panama City Beach, Florida, acting as immigration enforcement officers, police pulled up to a construction site, watching to see who would run, then gave chase and arrested them on charges such as trespassing, for cutting through somebody's yard, or loitering, for hiding in someone's yard, or reckless driving, for speeding off in a car.[19] The ACLU questioned the constitutionality of the police action. During a three-month period, the police apprehended some 500 undocumented migrants and turned them over to ICE. As a result of the police actions many migrants left towns, becoming increasingly mobile, moving from one community to another or from one state to another.

The immigrants' fears were further intensified by the legislative surge at the state level in Arizona, Oklahoma, and Georgia, to name a few states passed heinous nativist anti-immigrant ethnic cleansing laws (see chapter 12). This precarious political reality caused a "spiraling-down" of expectations among the undocumented, which translated to a pronounced sense of alienation. In other words, the immigrants' political adrenaline fostered by MPM simply could not hold up against the country's heightened anti-immigrant political climate that ensued.

A third de-accelerator that contributed to the climate of fear was the intensification of the country's anti-immigrant WASP ethos. MPM mobilizations fostered a backlash especially of White nativists, who ironically were themselves products of the emerging climate of fear but for different reasons. Nationwide, the millions of mostly Latino migrants who marched and demanded the defeat of HR4437 and called for legalization served to exacerbate the anti-immigrant attitudes of nativism and even racism. The Great March of Los Angeles and the numerous mobilizations that followed reminded White nativists of the consequences of the "browning" of the U.S., particularly of Aztlán. The immigration crisis in its totality for them heightened fear that the Latino was becoming a threat to the country's White cultural hegemony, especially in Aztlán.

This reverse fear can be described as a "national psychosis."[20] The U.S. between 2006 and 2007 was increasingly pervaded by a nativism that turned racist[21] in nature. It did not denote just a fear of foreigners, but in particular perceived Mexicanos and Latinos to be a threat culturally to the country's WASP ethos. The "collective psyche" of a great many White people and even some Blacks was permeated with attitudes of xenophobia,[22] nativism, and racism. A hostility toward Mexicanos and Latinos existed that their physical characteristics, culture, and language were considered by some a serious threat to the dominant WASP ethos. The numerous pronouncements by vigilante and militia leaders like Barnett, Spencer, Foote, Simcox, and Gilchrist, to politicians like Sensenbrenner, Tancredo, and Hunter, to media personalities such as Dobbs, O'Reilly, and Putman resonated with racism and bigotry directed at Mexicanos and Latinos.

They among others produced fear and uncertainty that the undocumented were taking jobs away from domestic U.S. workers. Increasingly, they were depicted them as being an economic burden on the country's taxpayers; of intensifying the country's myriad of social problems, especially crime and drugs; and of being demographically a threat to Whites' numerical hegemony, especially in Aztlán. From a national security perspective, some ultra-nativists alleged that the country's border with México was out of control and that U.S. sovereignty was threatened by a migrant invasion being orchestrated by México. Combined, these nativist sentiments contributed to the acrimonious practices of scapegoating and immigrant bashing. By the end of 2007 the WASP ethos had evolved to where it became intolerantly hyper-Anglocentric.

In 2007, the immigration crisis divided and polarized the country's politics and ethos. For the undocumented, the results of these polls served to reinforce their apprehensions and fears. Although the results of polls were subject to manipulation as to how the questions were worded and asked, using a content analysis of several polls that focused on questions pertinent to immigration, the responses of most reflected the presence of an anti-immigrant ethos. A *New York Times*/CBS poll conducted from May 18–23, 2007, of 1,125 adults found that 82 percent believed that the U.S. could be doing more to keep the undocumented migrants from crossing the border, 81 percent felt that undocumented immigration was either a very serious (61 percent) or somewhat serious (30 percent) issue, and 69 percent felt that undocumented immigrants should be prosecuted for being in the U.S. illegally.[23] A Rasmussen Report poll conducted August 15–16 of 800 voters found that 71 percent thought that the government was not doing enough in the arena of immigration and 68 percent believed it was "very important" to improve border enforcement and reduce undocumented immigration.[24] A nationwide UPI Zogby poll conducted June 15–18, with a population sample of 8,300 adults, when asked which of three immigration issues was most important, 42 percent chose enforcement of existing laws. Border security was the second most important with 29 percent, and the least favored option with 23 percent was a guest-worker program and legalization. Immigrants living and working in the U.S were seen as a burden by 46 percent while only 17 percent saw them as a benefit.[25]

By and large, the polls suggest that the country's Democratic and Republican parties on the issue of immigration reform were not exempt from the anti-immigrant national psychosis. Most of the polls indicated that Republicans were vociferously and adamantly more anti-immigrant than were Democrats or Independents. The UPI Zogby poll cited above found that 59 percent of Democrats supported legalization, whereas for Republicans the number was much lower, 30 percent, and for Independents 39 percent. Sixty-five percent of Republicans considered undocumented migrants to be a burden, 52 percent of Independents saw undocumented migrants as a burden, and Democrats were more inclined to see them as either a benefit, 36 percent, or neither a benefit nor a burden, 38 percent.

Among Democrats, enforcement tied with reform at 37 percent. Among Republicans it tied with border security at 44 percent. Among Independents enforcement was at 47 percent, border security at 30 percent, and reform at 20 percent.[26] A Rasmussen poll revealed that 80 percent of Republicans believed border enforcement was very important and needed improvement and that undocumented immigration needed to be reduced, compared to 64 percent for Democrats, and 64 percent for Independents.[27]

Last but not least, the fourth de-accelerator that contributed to the migrants' climate of fear was the Los Angeles police attack on migrants that occurred on May 1, 2007 after a march held in Los Angeles commemorating the 2006 historic May 1st mobilization and boycott. Attended by some 6,000 to 10,000, depending on which source is used, an incident occurred at MacArthur Park that turned violent. Los Angeles Police officers used excessive force against a peaceful crowd that did nothing to provoke or warrant the violence directed at them. There was calm until a few individuals at the park threw empty water bottles at a couple of officers. Instead of isolating those few responsible, police clad in riot gear used batons and rubber bullets to clear the park. Forty-two persons were injured, which included nine media employees and seven police officers. Ninety-four persons filed complaints alleging that they were mistreated by police. City officials including Mayor Antonio Villaraigosa and Police Chief William J. Bratton called the actions of the officers "disturbing" and pledged a full investigation.[28]

The investigation concluded that the police melee was quite simply "a command and control breakdown."[29] The police actions were the only violence recorded during the scores of marches held since the rise of MPM in January 2006. On March 17, 2007, about 2,000 marchers waving mostly U.S. flags and shouting "No to deportation" returned to the streets and marched to MacArthur Park. A rally was held again to call for the legalization of the country's 12 million undocumented migrants. Among political and religious dignitaries present were Mayor Villaraigosa, Assembly Speaker Fabian Nuñez, and Auxiliary Bishop Gabino Zavala. The march ended without incident, but its low numbers suggested that the undocumented were not willing to risk being beaten, arrested, and deported. Thus, the egregious effects of the climate of fear were omnipresent.

ABSENCE OF NATIONAL/STATE
LEADERSHIP ADDS TO MPM'S DECLINE

Leadership is an intrinsic and requisite ingredient for the formation of a mass movement. MPM's failure to produce a well-defined leadership at both the national and state levels hastened its decline. Leadership is an indispensable ingredient to any change-oriented social movement. Leaders influence the behavior of followers toward the realization of a common agenda or objective. They serve in a myriad of political roles: they inspire and motivate people to get involved and into action; they mobilize resources; they are strategic architects of ideas and strategies; they frame demands; they are conciliators of unity; they are the mechanics of organizational development; and lastly, they are the articulators of ideas and visionaries who pilot or navigate or do both for a mass movement. Both "collective behavior" and "resource mobilization" theorists concur on the importance of leadership to mobilization. From their perspective, leaders create the impetus for movements by: (1) creating and directing action; (2) defining problems and proposing solutions[30]; and (3) by helping create other conditions in the value-added process of collective behavior.[31] Leaders as political entrepreneurs mobilize resources and form organizations as a response to incentives, risks, and opportunities.[32] Eric Hoffer[33] and Saul Alinsky, among others, acknowledge that a climate of change must exist, but they point out that if no leader or leaders are present to manipulate the people's sores of discontent, frustration, and expectations, no mass movement will arise.[34] Equally important, a mass movement's viability and longevity is greatly determined by the breadth and effectiveness of its leadership.

MPM's leadership was essentially local, plural, and decentralized. Few if any states had leaders with a statewide constituency. MPM at no time had even a semblance of national leaders. That is not to say that in the minds of some pro-migrant rights activists they perceived themselves as such. No local or regional MPM leader became its Cesar Chavez, Martin Luther King, or Malcolm X. None of the leadership of the existent so-called national Latino organizations rose to major prominence within MPM. Furthermore, none of the Latino politicians at either the federal or state levels of government reached a national leadership status.

There was a major disconnect between the national and state organizational and political leadership and those MPM leaders at the local level. The core of MPM's leadership was local, meaning city or county based. They came from the ranks of a plethora of coalitions and local organizations. At times some local MPM activists assumed temporarily some state or national leadership recognition and prominence. Article after article during MPM's brief longevity addressed this political leadership reality. The fact was that the people's participation in mass numbers was due to the political conditions rather than on the prowess of the leaders who made up the MPM's ranks. No national or state leader emerged that was able to reconcile the growing differences among MPM's pluralistic leadership. The result was that by March 2006, after the great marches of Chicago and Los Angeles, MPM succumbed to the "politics of self-destruction," which similarly had contributed to the demise of the Chicano movement.

As differences surfaced among MPM's local leadership, increasingly immigrants became disillusioned over the overt clashes of leadership agendas. Blatant were the verbal disagreements after the Great March of Los Angeles, when clashing egos collided over who was the main leader that had produced the event. These leadership squabbles also occurred in Chicago, Phoenix, and elsewhere. Growing internecine conflicts obviated a closing of MPM's leadership ranks and the building of a unified mass movement. The clashing of egos also inhibited MPM from strengthening its organizational structures; adopting a common legislative vision for immigration reform; developing a commonly supported strategic plan; and lastly, building MPM into a viable and sustainable mass movement. This leadership competition often was plagued by fostered distrust, envy, and jealousy among the event organizers to where it impacted MPM's capacity to show power at the state or national level.

The leadership squabbles in some areas produced a splintering of coalitions and in some cases the decline or end of others. The presence of "parochialism" also contributed to MPM being beset by the politics of self-destruction. At times, the local leadership was plagued by a stultifying geographical myopism, which was characterized by a blinded sense of localism or territorial influence. This precluded coordination at a regional, state, and/or national level. Some of MPM's leadership from large cities that had produced large marches perceived themselves as being far more important and powerful than those who were from smaller communities who had produced smaller marches. While some excellent and capable leaders did emerge, there were also those who were mediocre at best. Too many of the latter were, for example, inexperienced in organizing; in the leadership dynamics of keeping working together; in working the media; and developing resources. Differences in class—some were lower class, while others were middle class—and differences in education were all factors that also contributed to MPM's leadership problems. The masses never anointed one or several leaders at either the state or national level as MPM's *lideres maximos*. Thus, MPM's leadership was ostensibly local, but the absence at both the state and national level of recognized, visible, and viable leadership also contributed to MPM's decline and ultimate demise.

Fleeting Organization

Organization is an adjunct to leadership. The leader uses the power of organization to impel a mass movement. Organization denotes defined goals and objectives, structure, hierarchy, by-laws, membership, and/or constituency. While spontaneity is a salient characteristic of a mass movement, some level of organization must exist to provide its structural foundation. No one organization can be the mass movement. The reality is that movements are comprised of a multiplicity of organizations, coalitions, and individuals; consequently, they are heterogeneous and pluralistic. According to Jo Freeman and Victoria Johnson, a mass movement "has one or more core organizations in a penumbra of people who engage in spontaneous supportive behavior that the core organizations can often mobilize but less control."[35] Revolutionary Bolshevik Lenin believed that organization is the most powerful weapon in the arsenal of the proletariat.[36] Reformer Saul Alinsky, who perceived organization to be a weapon for change, wrote, "Change comes from power and power comes from organization."[37] Samuel Huntington, writing about social change, states, "Organization is the road to political power." He further elucidates: "In the modernizing world [as elsewhere] he controls the future who organizes its politics."[38] Theorist Herbert Blumer defines social movements as developing by "acquiring organization and form."[39] History is replete with examples of how organization was essential to reform movements, such as, NAACP and Southern Christian Leadership Conference and to revolutionary movements, Russia's Bolsheviks, Cuba's July 26 Movement as examples.

As a mass movement, MPM was comprised of a myriad of coalitions, interest groups, and ad hoc activist groups. What became problematic was that it was sustained foremost by a plethora of recently formed local coalitions. Coalitions by their very nature are temporary arrangements of groups and individuals that come together in the pursuit of a common objective. They tend to be transitory or fleeting, which negates any sense of permanency. In most cases, once the objective has been realized or failure occurs, the coalition disintegrates, and shortly after vanishes. Coalitions have certain inherent characteristics that differentiate them from interest groups: (1) they are not incorporated; (2) they lack in most cases a well-defined structure; (3) they do not possess hierarchical leadership roles; (4) they do not have a paid membership base; and (5) in most cases, they do not have a designated budget, full-time staff, or office. What they do have in common with interest groups is their desire to influence public policy. Their longevity is dependent upon the leadership's acumen to adhere to practices of building trust, developing relationships, negotiating areas of agreement and disagreement, and of overcoming internal tension and possible schisms.[40] Coalitions that form part of a mass movement can be called "pre-interest" groups. Some mass movements and the entities that comprise them can evolve into political interest groups.[41]

Too many of MPM's coalitions were spontaneously formed, loosely structured, collective arrangements of a few zealous pro-immigrant rights activists who understood that the time was propitious to mobilize on a pro-immigrant policy agenda. Pressed for time and driven by MPM's mobilization contagion, they expeditiously pulled together enough people to form a core group, which then called themselves a coalition and started organizing. There was no time to go through the laborious process of incorporating, writing by-laws, and so forth. Further, without a membership base, too many of the coalitions were comprised of only a few activists. This became evident when many of them put out their flyers or literature. They would list scores of organizations, unions, ad hoc groups, and other coalitions, creating the impression there were scores of people behind the proposed mobilization or action. With few exceptions, most listed had few people behind them. The exceptions were pressure groups, such as unions, that did possess a credible membership constituency. Yet with some exceptions, even the unions seldom produced great numbers.

In reality most coalitions were paper tigers, meaning they lacked a mass base of support. Their leadership appeared before the press as generals commanding armies. In other words, they were oligarchic, led by the few in the name of the many. None were organized to where they could systematically reach out and build a grassroots base of support. As a result, immigrants caught up in MPM's contagion never developed a sense of loyalty and membership to the respective coalitions organizing in their areas. Some coalitions would splinter and out of the parts new coalitions would emerge. Most coalitions were local, although a few claimed to be regional, state, or national in scope. Yet after May 1, 2006, a great number of them became nonexistent. One such case was *Gente Unida* Coalition based out of San Diego, led by Enrique Morones, which after its second car caravan of the Southwest held in February 2007 disappeared.

By the end of 2007 only a handful of the coalitions that had contributed to MPM's rise were still functional. One of the most persistent coalitions to have survived the dry political mobilization period of May 1, 2006, to November 2007 was the March 25th Coalition. Since its inception in March 2006, it consistently sought to organize marches and other direct actions in support of immigration reform. Although at times torn by internal strife and by mobilizations that produced low numbers, its principal leader Javier Rodriguez kept it together and as of late 2007 was still operational. As a coalition it was instrumental in forming a new national coalition, that is, the National May 1st Movement for Worker and Immigrant Rights. Another coalition, the We Are America Coalition, along with the March 25 Coalition in 2007 forged a new coalition, the We Are All Elvira and Saulito Unity Coalition. Its leadership describes itself as the "bedrock of the immigrant movement."[42] It was the major driving force in California organizing the "National Day of Action" held on September 12, 2007, a one-day nationwide consumer boycott.

The new coalition embraced sanctuary activist Elvira Arelanno and her son, Saul, as its new unity symbols for reviving MPM. It sought to put a halt to the ICE raids and to protest for immigration reform. *Comité Latino* of the Coachella Valley, led by Mario Lascano, during 2007 consistently organized direct actions, that is, pickets and rallies. As a coalition, it maintained an office and small staff and, unlike most other existent coalitions, had a grassroots capacity for its mobilizations. NAHR, which is not a coalition but rather a network, in September 2007 began to hold "Know Your Rights" community forums in anticipation of ICE operations. Efforts were also in motion to organize pro-immigrant rights self-defense committees. In northern California, the *Frente de Mexicanos en el Exterior* (Front of Mexicans Living Abroad) led by Al Rojas was active prior to the rise of MPM and remained active after its demise. Its actions included mobilizations in support of immigration reform and political actions involving México's politics.

As 2007 came to a close a few coalitions outside California continued to organize some pro-migrant rights activities. In Phoenix, the coalition *Inmigrantes Sin Fronteras* held on September 3–9 an economic boycott. Boycott organizers, such as Elias Bermudez, underscored the importance of the action: "The city of Phoenix has become the avant-garde of the battle for Latinos in the United States. We are in the country's hottest trench of battle . . . [Because] of the attacks today we are at the edge of the precipice."[43] The results of the boycott were mixed: boycott organizers claimed it was effective, while others claimed it was more symbolic. In Tucson, led by Isabel Garcia, also around for years, the Coalition for Human Rights consistently dealt with a number of pro-migrant rights issues. Yet in other parts of Aztlán and the country few of the MPM coalitions were still around and active.

Integral to MPM's organizational ranks were a number of Latino pressure groups. Their chief function was to influence public policy vis-à-vis immigration reform. While they played an important pressure role during MPM, at no time did they command an exceptional organizational national or state leadership role. Ideologically, most were moderate in their politics and adhered to a neoliberal perspective and rebuked militant unconventional protest politics. None possessed a "progressive" posture, a *barrio* power base and a *barrio* mobilization capacity. At no time did they demonstrate any presence or nexus with the undocumented masses; nor did they systematically put forth an organizing effort to recruit them as members into the ranks of their structures, chapters, or lodges. In great part this was ascribable to class differences in orientation and membership as well as strategic divergences, especially with progressive-oriented coalitions that adhered to unconventional protest strategies, which obviated such efforts. Their primordial concern was to not project an image of militancy or radicalism for fear of losing possible funding or alienating members or political and economic elites.

The above analysis was applicable to the following so-called national Latino organizations: National Council of La Raza (NCLR), League of United Latin American Citizens (LULAC), and National Association of Latino Elected Officials (NALEO). All three essentially took on a lobbying posture and disseminator of information role. At times, especially NCLR and LULAC did make attempts to interact and coordinate with scores of local and regional coalitions. The Mexican American Legal Defense and Education Fund (MALDEF) also monitored and put out reports on the nativist legislative surge at all levels. NALEO and the Congressional Hispanic Caucus (CHC), both comprised of politicians, lobbied Congress, but at times were in conflict with local coalitions over specifics of proposed immigration reform legislation.

At the state level, as an interest group, the California-based *Hermandad Mexicana Nacional Latinoamericana* was an exception to the aforementioned analysis. Led by Nativo Lopez, who simultaneously was national/state chair of the Mexican American Political Association (MAPA), *Hermandad Mexicana Nacional Latinoamericana* embodied a progressive direct action politics. It had offices, staff, and membership, and was proactive and involved in organizing several marches, protests, and conferences both in California and in other states. After May 2006 through 2007 none of the national or state entities mentioned did much of anything to arrest MPM's decline or demise or to revive it.

In California, immigrants' rights social service providers CARECEN (Central American Resource Center) and CHIRLA (Coalition for Humane Immigrant Rights of Los Angeles) were influential MPM moderate-oriented entities. Both nonprofit corporations formed in 1986, had offices, staff, and budgets, and provided a number of immigration-related services and functioned concomitantly as advocates, especially on immigration reform. CHIRLA in particular was the driving organizing force for the creation of the We Are America coalition, whose motto was "Today We Act, Tomorrow We Vote." In Chicago, *Centro Sin Fronteras* was led by Emma Lozano, who as a progressive played a key leadership role in organizing the great Chicago march of March 10, 2006, among others, took several delegations to lobby Congress in Washington, D.C., and was the main organizer behind the Elvira Arellano deportation issue. Yet for all the fine work done, it was not enough to halt MPM's decline. Thus, at the close of 2007, with Latinos being nearly 47 million and Mexicanos numbering some 30 million, at all levels, they suffered from an acute organizational leadership void.

MPM's Absence of an Ideology

MPM's absence of a cohesive ideology or common vision also contributed to its demise. Change-oriented mass movements are generally guided by a common sense of purpose, objectives, or set of beliefs that help agglutinate the diversity that embodies it. Philip Selznick draws the nexus between organization and ideology. He writes that "although ideology, to be translated into power requires organization, effective organization also requires ideology."[44] Most theorists of mass movements that seek change concur on the importance of ideology to their development and sustenance. As normative judgments, ideology creates a new mythology that inspires, motivates, and energizes people to challenge other existent ideologies and mythologies by positing their own. An ideology offers an explanation of the past, an interpretation of the present, and a vision of the future. It becomes the belief system that "specifies discontents, prescribes solutions, justifies a change from the status quo, and may also identify the agents of social change and the strategy and tactics they are to use."[45] It performs a number of social-psychological functions, which arouse the emotions, anger, frustration, and rising expectations and ultimately the participation of its targeted population. Also, ideology provides the political beliefs, values, and orientations that guide the people's political behavior and buttresses the dominant system's political culture. It further articulates political, social, economic, or cultural ills and denounces existent laws, political structures, or beliefs, which are embodied in a program of goals and new beliefs via action and mass mobilization. According to Reo M. Christenson et al., a "political ideology is a belief system that explains and justifies a preferred political order for society, either existing or proposed and offers a strategy [processes, institutions, programs] for its attainment."[46] In sum, it provides direction, purpose, and cohesion and rationalizes a people's grievances and demands.

MPM, as a reform-oriented movement, was spontaneous, reactive, heterogeneous, and too narrowly committed to two key objectives: (1) defeat of HR4437; and (2) to a nebulous and undefined call for immigration reform, especially legalization. At no time did MPM develop a macro, common, and comprehensive vision. Its change agenda was specific and myopic. The divergent forces within MPM never reached an accord as to its common immigration reform vision. Efforts to create a consensus failed. A few progressives, such as attorney Peter Shay and Nativo Lopez, among others, produced immigration reform proposals. While adopted by some groups, such as *Hermandad Mexicana Nacional Latinoamericana* and MAPA, among others, none became MPM's immigration reform vision. The cardinal reason was that the proposal was never adopted by the totality of the groups that comprised it.

MPM never developed a defined belief system that challenged or justified the present political order. As a mass movement, it was not driven by ideas of transforming society. Instead most activists and groups emphasized making "micro" reforms to the country's immigration laws. It never went beyond a call for piecemeal change and it did not develop its own vision or ideology to address the real systemic forces behind the immigration crisis.

Contributing to MPM's decline were the differences between progressives and moderates. As examined previously, most progressives understood that capitalist economies produce the inherent conditions or contradictions, that is, poverty, unemployment, inequality, and political repression, pushing desperate migrant workers north to the U.S. The propounded view was that the immigration crisis was symptomatically a product of neoliberalism and the globalization of capital. On the other hand, moderates much more neoliberal in their ideological inclinations focused on the micro aspects of the immigration crisis rather than on its source—neoliberalism. Their preoccupation was legalization, from the perspective of pragmatically finding a legislative remedy to legalizing the country's 12 million undocumented migrants. Their slogan in Spanish, "*Ya marchamos y ahora votamos*" ("we marched and today we vote"), was indicative of the strategic change. Thus, the multiplicity of coalitions, groups, and activists that comprised MPM did not possess a common ideology and failed to develop a consensus and definition for comprehensive immigration reform. The failure to go beyond the call for HR4337's defeat and legalization impacted MPM's decline.

MPM'S ABSENCE OF A STRATEGIC TACTICAL PLAN

In order for any mass movement to succeed in its ideological attainment, it needs to be driven by strategy. As a political variable, strategy connects a climate of change, leadership, and organization to ideology. No leader can manipulate the conditions or direct organizational activity that is guided by an ideology that lacks a strategy, which is requisite to the pursuit for social change. The word strategy in its original Greek translation means "the art of the general," which has a military context. Clausewitz defined strategy as "the art of the employment of battles as a means to gain the object of war. In other words, strategy forms the plan of the war, maps out the proposed course of the different campaigns which compose the war, and regulates the battles to be fought in each."[47] Strategy denotes a "course of action" or "plan of action" that delineates how to achieve a common goal or goals. "Strategies are the master plans for managing and directing the flow of influence from change agent to targets."[48] Theorist Mostafa Rejai explains that strategy refers "in essence to the skill, commitment, and resourcefulness of the [leaders] to fashion all necessary tools and undertake all necessary activity toward the realization of their objectives." He goes on to say that strategy "entails the manipulation of conditions"[49]; while they have a cause and effect, the two are analytically distinct. Integral to any strategy are tactics, meaning the methods used to achieve its goals or objectives. To Saul Alinsky, there could be no strategy without tactics. For him, strategy entailed "ends" and tactics were the "means" by which ends are realized.[50]

MPM was never guided by a comprehensive strategic plan of action. At best there was a semblance of one adopted in February at the NAHR Riverside Summit. The word "semblance" is apropos since it was only developed for a three-month period and the Summit was not nationwide but regional. At no time did MPM have a common strategy approved or supported by the numerous leaders, organizations, and coalitions. NAHR's attempts to produce a second phase to the initial strategic plan failed at the Phoenix summit in April. During July 2006 another national summit was called in Chicago that included the participation of the March 25th Coalition; however, it too failed to produce a new strategy. In September 2006 and 2007, the Southwest Voter Registration and Education Project held what was billed as a Latino Congresso (congress) in Los Angeles, which was attended by several hundred people. There too the issue of immigration was addressed, but again no strategy was developed. From the summer of 2006 to late 2007 numerous meetings, summits, and conferences were held by both moderate and progressive entities, but none produced a strategy to revive MPM.

Moderates and some progressives after the 2006 May 1 tactically adopted a more conventional pressure lobbying approach. While the latter also continued to push for massive mobilizations, the former pushed for voter registration and citizenship training programs in preparation for the November 2006 congressional elections. Eliseo Medina, executive vice president of the SEIU, warned, "The Democrats can't take for granted that the Latino vote will stay with them if they don't do anything."[51] In preparation for the November elections, various groups within NAHR conducted voter registration, political education, and "get out the vote" activities targeting the Mexicano/Latino communities. In the process, two of its leaders, Victoria Baca and Gil Navarro, were elected to school boards, both after ten years of trying. The former was elected to the Moreno Unified School District and the latter to the San Bernardino County School Board.

Lobbying for legalization became a priority for both moderates and progressives. This entailed direct lobbying of politicians in Congress, letter writing, e-mails, phone calls, press conferences, conducting radio and television interviews, and so forth. The NCLR assumed a major leadership role in coordinating lobbying efforts in Washington, D.C. Activists prioritized meetings with key members of Congress, such as now Majority Leader Senator Harry Reid and Speaker of the House Nancy Pelosi. Lobbying efforts, however, produced few direct meetings with Congress's key leadership. Vicente Rodriquez, on behalf of NAHR and *Gente Unida* Coalition, acted as a liaison to other coalitions. He reported that after spending weeks in Washington, D.C., lobbying, he and others never succeeded in meeting directly with either Reid or Pelosi. Angela Sanbrano, executive director of the Central American Resource Center, commented, "We are not going to impact the political process with marches alone."[52]

In November 2006, NAHR put forth a strategy for holding a bi-national summit in January 2007 in Washington, D.C. The intent was to regroup and solidify MPM's leaders in order to revive it in preparation for the oncoming immigration struggle for the 2007 congressional session.[53] Numerous coalitions signed off on the effort, but due to the lack of support by the Congressional Hispanic Caucus (CHS), which reneged on its commitment to convoke the summit, it never took place. Even worse, a delegation of Mexicano congresspersons and senators scheduled to attend the Summit, led by Congressman Jose Jacques Medina, visited Washington, D.C., in February and was slighted by CHC Chair Joe Baca. According to Medina, Baca did little to promote the importance and significance of their visit. This occurred at the same time as the CHC was plagued by internal cleavages between Chair Baca and Congresswoman Loretta Sanchez, among others, over allegations of Baca's insensitivity to his female colleagues.[54]

Radio DJ Piolin in May 2006 met with President Bush and a year later participated in a national petition drive that secured hundreds of thousands of signatures calling for legalization that were delivered to the Senate. During the rest of 2007, both progressive and moderate activists lobbied Congress. Numerous coalitions and groups were in and out of Washington, D.C., desperately trying to influence policy makers in both houses to incorporate legalization into their proposed immigration reform legislation. None of these moderate activities received much media attention, indicative of the absence of MPM. With the defeat of the Senate proposal in late June 2007, disillusionment and skepticism pervaded the few moderate coalitions and groups.

After May 1, 2006, progressives appeared to be intransigently set on a one-dimensional strategic approach of just "marching." They did not take into account that to have successful and powerful mobilizations, there must be a combination of other ingredients, such as propitious conditions, that is, climate of change, experienced and competent leadership, organization to direct, a vision to inspire, and a strategy and tactics based upon having a power capability—the very ingredients that are being used to examine the decline of MPM.

Moderates and progressives alike after May 1 failed to initiate efforts to organize the migrant masses. No coalition or leader harnessed the people-power that had been unleashed in 2006. They failed to comprehend that organizing people is a difficult, tedious, and complex process that requires great skill and patience. By late 2007 the few progressive and moderate coalitions that were still active were weak, and none had developed a strategic plan designed to rekindle MPM or to create a new movement. There was no effort being made to convert the few loose coalitions into a functional, permanent, and powerful *barrio*-based grassroots advocacy organization, that is, interest group. While some pro-immigrant rights activists talked about preparing for the anticipated wave of ICE raids, massive deportations, and possible repatriations, nothing was really put into place to deal with such a looming crisis. Moreover, strategically there was no major organized effort to systematically initiate a political education, consciousness building, and leadership training process for the migrant communities; worst, the *barrios* nationwide in 2007 were defenseless against the ICE operations.

In August 2007 there were some reconciliatory efforts initiated by both moderates and progressives. "It took the sacrifice of that brave woman (Arellano) to break our myopic visions," said Xavier Rodriguez of the March 25 Coalition.[55] In Los Angeles, several of the pro-immigrant rights coalitions and groups momentarily put aside some of their differences and coalesced under the aegis of a new coalition, *Todos Somos Elvira Arellano y Saulito*, and held a solidarity march. Their coalescing, however, did not help ensure that the National Day of Action was a success.

The National Day of Action proved to be a strategic disappointment. The march failed to attract large numbers; only a few hundred people showed. Nativo Lopez, president of MAPA, was hypercritical of it and attributed the low numbers to a lack of good planning and that it was organized precipitously due to Arellano's deportation and alleged that its lack of participation was due to the divisions of its leaders and the lack of organization.[56] After the march, Arellano was apprehended by ICE agents outside Los Angeles's Our Lady Queen of Angels Catholic Church and then deported to Tijuana. She traveled to México City, where PRD Congressman Jose Jacques Medina facilitated numerous meetings with Mexican government officials and with President Felipe Calderon. She requested diplomatic status, which would have allowed her to travel to the U.S.; nonetheless, she was denied. On the México side of the San Ysidro–San Diego border crossing, a rally was held where Arellano called for an end to U.S. immigration policies that lead to the separation of U.S.-born children from their undocumented parents. In Washington, D.C., Saul Arellano, along with some 150 persons, lobbied Congress to restart efforts for immigration reform. Arellano supporters got into a scuffle with police after a press conference, which resulted in the arrest of two for disorderly conduct.[57]

During 2006 to 2007, the "sanctuary movement" emerged as a form of defense and protection against raids and deportations for immigrants. Led by Felipe Aguirre, mayor pro tem of Maywood, California, the pro-immigrant city council voted to become a sanctuary city. A city where 96 percent of the residents were either Mexicano or Latino, it received national media coverage and was vehemently criticized by nativists. A sanctuary designation overtly discouraged a city to collaborate, especially its police, with federal immigration officials in conducting raids or operations.[58] ICE, however, did not need local authorization to make immigration arrests. As a result, Aguirre became the target of death threats by City Clerk Hector Duarte, who was charged with soliciting murder, jailed for eight months, and given two years probation. Shortly after, Coachella, a city where Mexicanos comprised 97 percent of the population, under the leadership of Mayor Eduardo Garcia also declared itself a sanctuary city. Other sanctuary cities in California that did likewise included Bell Gardens, Huntington Park, Los Angeles, San Francisco, and El Centro. Across the country as of late August 2007 there were a total of thirty-two cities. New York, Chicago, and Seattle were also declared sanctuary cities.[59] Thus, strategically and tactically MPM, as a mass movement, was a creation of great mobilizations. When they stopped producing gargantuan numbers it rapidly declined.

Lack of Power Capability

MPM succumbed to a profound absence of a "power capability." "Power" denotes having the requisite resources, people, and money to achieve a certain end. According to Saul Alinsky, "Power is the very essence, the dynamo of life . . . It is the power of active citizen participation pulsing upward, providing the unified strength for a common purpose. Power is an essential life force always in operation, either changing the world or opposing change."[60] Two resources constitute power: (1) organized people; and (2) money. "Capability" entails the presence of a climate of change, leadership, organization, ideology, and strategy and tactics to utilize these two power resources; as already examined, MPM fell short in all the preceding requisites. MPM lost its power capability after May 1 and what contributed to its decline and demise was "power deflation," meaning the incapacity to demonstrate power to create a critical mass, that is, massive mobilizations.

From May 2006 to December 2007, Mexicanos and Latinos failed to demonstrate a power capability. The omnipresence of the climate of fear among migrants and the myriad of de-accelerators previously examined obviated massive mobilizations for immigration reform. Coalition after coalition sought unsuccessfully to reignite the embers of MPM's "mobilization contagion." Even those activists who had claimed to be the great architects of the massive marches in Los Angeles, Phoenix, and Chicago, among other cities in 2006, failed to recapture MPM's power. A major indicator of the presence of a climate of fear was a march held in Chicago in July that only drew 10,000, whereas on March 10, 2006, at minimum some 300,000 persons had been mobilized. By late July, various coalitions promulgated calls for Labor Day mobilizations. March 25th Coalition spokesperson Javier Rodriguez in late July said, "People are out there waiting, they want to march."[61] He and others who had predicted mega marches were wrong. On September 4, Labor Day pro-immigrant marches were held in

Los Angeles, Phoenix, and Washington, D.C., among other cities, but only small numbers were produced. The Los Angeles march produced less than 2,000. One newspaper reported, "Buoyed by the huge immigrant protests in April and May, some organizers had predicted that a million people would take to the streets around Labor Day . . . But this time, only a few thousand people protested."[62]

After the Labor Day weekend, fewer and fewer mobilizations were held nationwide, which was a clear indication that MPM had really declined. When interviewed by the *New York Times*, on why MPM had lost momentum, I explained that "the movement sputtered once it was clear that the harshest legislation, HR4437, would not pass. . . . Divisions set in over strategy. . . . There was no consensus on what to do next. We lost an opportunity to create a transition to a new rhythm."[63] Roberto Suro, director of the Pew Hispanic Center said, "There was effort to resurrect that collective outpouring of the spring, and it clearly didn't succeed. The question is what do they do next? If it's going to be a movement, it's definitely struggling, not just for legs, but probably for air right now." Some march/rally organizers disagreed and said MPM was alive and well, but merely going through growing pains.[64]

Throughout 2007 several marches were held in different parts of the country. They produced, however, small numbers. In California, NAHR organized the first mobilization of 2007 that consisted of a march/rally in San Bernardino on March 17. Cognizant of the declining numbers participating in pro-migrant rights marches, it broadened its call to include three issues: immigration reform, withdrawal of U.S. forces from Iraq, and peace in communities between Blacks and Latinos.[65] There were some 1,000 in attendance, with a counter-protest across the street of some 100 MP and SOS anti-immigrant protestors. Their presence validated the people's climate of fear. Of the initial number that participated in the march, only about 500 remained for the rally due to a fear of possible violence.

In organizing the events, NAHR followed all the mandates as prescribed by the city. A controversy, however, ensued over its decision to bill NAHR via me for $17,500 for security provided by police. In spite of the fact that NAHR had a permit and liability insurance, and worked cooperatively with city and police officials, which none of the 100 MP and SOS protestors had done, City Attorney John Penman decided to charge me personally for the said amount. After securing support from ACLU, MALDEF, and the National Lawyers Guild, NAHR threatened the city with a lawsuit based on a violation of First Amendment rights. At a press conference held in May at the footsteps of City Hall, surrounded by some seventy-five supporters and a lot of media, Penman succumbed to pressure and announced that the city would not compel us to pay the fees.[66]

For weeks after several groups and coalitions throughout the country tried to repeat the May 1 historic activism, but as described by *New York Times* reporter Randal C. Archibold, "tens of thousands of people pressing for immigrants' rights demonstrated on Tuesday in dozens of cities. But with advocates splintered over tactics, the crowds paled in comparison with the turnout last year."[67] Whereas last year over 1 million participated, the combined rallies/marches drew a total estimated at 300,000 people. In comparison to the rallies/marches of 2006, those of 2007 were smaller and fewer. The following provides the cities and participation estimates: Chicago, 150,000; Milwaukee, 80,000; Los Angeles, 25,000; New York, 25,000; Phoenix, 15,000; Denver, 10,000; Detroit, 10,000; Tucson, 10,000; San Francisco, 10,000; Dallas, 5,000; Oakland, 2,000. Numerous other cities held similar rally/march events that drew several hundred each.[68] Unlike the 2006 May 1 historic mobilization and boycott's cardinal objective which was to impact the economy, these mobilizations were largely politically motivated. They lacked the economic weapon of the boycott.

At the height of the Senate debate on immigration reform, on June 24 in Los Angeles a march for immigrants' rights was held by Act Now to Stop War and End Racism (ANSWER) and a host of other organizations, drawing only a few thousand. On August 18, a march was organized in downtown Los Angeles by various groups, attracting only a few hundred people. On August 25, with the theme of "Solidarity with Elvira," a march was held in Los Angeles protesting the deportation of Elvira Arellano. Organizers of the We Are All Elvira and Saulito Coalition, comprised of the March 25 Coalition and the We Are America Coalition, claimed the participation of some 2,000 people,[69] while police said it was closer to 600.[70] The National Day of Unity march/rally and boycott held on September 12 in Los Angeles that focused on Elvira's deportation, according to the newspaper *La Opinion*, drew a mere 100 and nationwide it too failed to produce major mobilizations and boycotts. An informal survey taken of various Latino businesses and people in the streets of Los Angeles suggested the consumer boycott had failed. The border rally held in Tijuana at the border crossing, led by Arellano, produced no more than twenty people. Thus, by late 2007 the few promigrant rights mobilizations that were held since the May 1st mobilization and boycott of 2006 lacked a power capability. It was apparent that without it, MPM as a mass movement was moribund and its reincarnation to a new movement was nowhere in sight.

The Immigration Crisis: What Now?

Immigration Crisis: A Compendium

As has been discussed throughout this book, the United States (U.S.) today is in the midst of an unprecedented immigration crisis. Migrants have come to the U.S. for a number of reasons: some because of religious persecution, others for economic reasons (that is, their country's grinding poverty, unemployment, and overall economic hardship), while still others due to political repression. Regardless of their motivation, all immigrants and migrants share a profound desire for new and better opportunities.

The U.S.'s immigration experience is characterized by a myriad of historical events that were and continue to be shaped by dislocations within the country's capitalist economy and driven by a multiplicity of "push" and "pull" forces. These forces have fostered a nativism that has permeated the country's immigration experience from its incipience. Its ominous presence has been evident in the proposal and passage of the array of restrictionist laws, particularly during the nineteenth and early twentieth centuries. Undeniably, U.S. immigration mythology is imbued and driven by the notion that this country is a "nation of nations," a "nation of immigrants." Today as a nation-state it is comprised of peoples from all 192 nations represented in the United Nations and that in the context of the twenty-first century it is the world's largest ethnic/racial salad bowl.

As examined throughout this book, the U.S. has experienced several immigration crises, all of which have been the result of the country's capitalist economy's unrelenting demand for cheap labor, regardless of where it came from. For Mexicanos, today's immigration crisis is traced back to the late 1890s, which eventually led to the genesis of the current re-Mexicanization of Aztlán and by the 1980s, because of the influx of immigrants from Cuba and Central America, led to the Latinoization and "browning" of the U.S.

Globalization Capital: Purveyor of Immigration Crises

In order to fully understand the current immigration crisis, it is important to revisit its etiology. As elucidated in this work's introduction, what truly makes the current immigration crisis different from past crises is the acuteness at a macro level of the economic crises that pervades due to the globalization of capital, particularly as it is affecting the U.S. and Europe today. As was argued earlier, contemporary immigration is impelled by global capitalism's inherent contradictions, that is, a myriad of "push" factors, namely associated with impoverished and social problem-ridden economies of the developing and underdeveloped countries. The consequential result is the exodus of millions who simultaneously are being "pulled" into the developed capitalist economies of the First World, especially those of the U.S. and Europe, who are being uprooted and driven to migrate.

Today some 3 billion people live under the specter of global poverty. In 2008 its prevalence is precipitating a growing global food crisis. From Latin America to Africa to Asia people are either starving or dying because of hunger. Countries like Egypt, Haiti, and Bangladesh are experiencing serious food riots. World Bank officials have reported that in developing countries poor people spend up to 75 percent of their income on food.[1] The nightmare of Darfur, Sudan, is a vivid example of an underdeveloped country today experiencing massive hunger and starvation, soaring malnutrition, and genocide. It is an indication of the acute and evident shortcomings of global capitalism. In the global capitalist context, developing and underdeveloped countries are unable and often powerless to deal with the growing globalization of poverty and scarcity of food.

Global capitalism has created a cause and effect, to where a number of regions and countries of the world are concurrently experiencing their own immigration crises. In the early months of 2008 it was estimated that about 150 million migrant workers worldwide labor outside their respective home countries and send some $240 billion in remittances to their respective native countries (all dollar amounts are in U.S. currency).[2] The Western Hemisphere, particularly the U.S., México, Central America, and the rest of Latin America, is plagued by capitalism's induced economic crises to where it too suffers from the global immigration crises. The World Bank in 2008 reported that 45 million people of México's population of 104 million live in poverty. Central America's population of 43 million too suffers from poverty that ranges from 50 to 60 percent. The interconnectedness of global capitalism to these two mass populations was evident in their remittances, which reached a high in 2007 of nearly $24 billion for México and, according to the Inter-American Development Bank, grew to $12.1 billion for Central America. Yet by 2008 due to the U.S.'s recessionary crisis the aforementioned amounts were decreasing dramatically.

The empirical systemic aspects of the globalization of capital are clearly evident in 2008 with the "global recessionary crisis." Increasingly, the global capital economies, according to the International Monetary Fund (IMF), are in a state of crisis. Japan's economy is expected to expand by a mere 1.4 percent in 2008 and 1.5 percent in 2009; Germany is slowing down in 2008 to a trickle of 1.4 percent and 1 percent in 2009; and Canada will slow down in 2008 to 1.3 percent and have a slight pickup to 1.9 percent economic growth in 2009.[3] According to Associated Press reporter Jeannine Aversa, "The IMF now sees a 25 percent chance that global growth will drop to 3 percent or less in 2008 and 2009—equivalent to a global recession . . . with the U.S. sliding into a deep recession amid housing, credit, and financial slumps. IMF predicts the projected growth of the U.S. economy will be a feeble 0.5 percent in 2008 and 0.6 percent in 2009."[4]

Moreover, the global recessionary crisis is inextricably linked to the globalization of capital's induced economic crises, which in part is the result of corporate plunder. In the U.S. a number of recent events buttress the preceding supposition. Billed as the biggest money crisis since the Depression, a Wall Street investment bank, Bear Stearns, in March 2008 in five days tumbled into a crisis that forced the Federal Reserve to intervene with a $30 billion loan in order to avoid a sudden collapse that might have caused a full-market panic.[5] Its seriousness was further evident with the subprime mortgage crisis that, according to *Time* magazine writer James Fox, erupted during the summer of 2007 "and evolved into something bigger and more ominous—possibly the greatest challenge to the American way of financial capitalism since the Depression."[6] Its gravity is such that some 2 to 3 million families in 2008 and 2009 are expected to lose their homes. Another indicator is unemployment in April that increased to 5.1 percent. With company after company laying off workers, the unemployment figures are expected to climb even higher in 2008.

For the last few years, the five biggest oil companies, that is, ExxonMobil, Chevron, Conoco Phillips, Shell, and BP, collected huge profits. In 2005 they raked in a net profit of $100 billion.[7] In 2008 the price of gasoline in the U.S. increased to an exorbitant record of $4.00 per gallon, dramatically hurting the poor and middle class; in spite of this, all five oil companies posted gargantuan profits of $123 billion in 2007.[8] ExxonMobil recorded the highest net profit of $40.6 billion, more than ever made by a public U.S. company.[9] Paradoxically, that same month, oil company top executives requested congressional subsidies in the amount of $18 billion.[10]

A related aspect of the immigration crisis as underscored throughout this analysis is the economic and labor dependence on and addiction of the U.S. economy to foreign cheap labor. Without the availability of a large pool of cheap exploitable migrant labor, this country's economy would be severely damaged to where a paralysis of certain sectors would occur, such as agriculture, service industries, light manufacturing, meat processing, and so forth. Already states and cities that have enacted brutal anti-immigrant and ethnic-cleansing laws and ordinances, such as Arizona, Oklahoma, and Colorado, and cities like Hazelton, Pennsylvania, are being impacted economically negatively, that is, businesses closing, labor shortages, and so forth. Farmers in Arizona in 2008 were not planting their fields for fear that they would not have enough workers to harvest the crops.[11] In Colorado in 2007 farmers reported labor shortages, leaving farmers to turn to Colorado's inmate population as replacements.[12] Oklahoma in 2008, with its passage of severe nativist legislation, was experiencing a similar "reverse exodus" of migrant labor.

Another ill effect of global capitalism is the U.S.'s "outsourcing" of jobs at the expense of U.S. workers. A total of 3.2 million jobs, one in six factory jobs, since the start of 2000 have gone overseas to developing and underdeveloped countries. The U.S. continues its transition from being an industrial and manufacturing economy to becoming a predominantly service one. According to Associated Press journalist Martin Crutsinger, "Eighty-four percent of Americans in the labor force are employed in service jobs, up from 81 percent in 2000. The sector has added 8.78 million jobs since the beginning of 2000."[13] Even some service jobs are in jeopardy, as illustrated by the establishment of telephone caller centers in India and the Philippines. Especially China's exploding capitalist economy is sucking dry manufacturing jobs from forty-eight of the country's fifty states, which in 2008 were in recession. Its severity is a matter of fact: the U.S. economy in 2006 experienced a trade deficit of $765.3 billion, which meant that it imported $765 billion more in goods and services than it exported. The economic prognosis for the future of the U.S. economy is ominous at best: Princeton economist Alan Blinder predicts that the number of jobs at risk of being shipped out of the country could reach 40 million over the next ten to twenty years.[14]

The outsourcing of jobs is driven by unbridled corporate greed. Incited by a relentless worship of capital accumulation, transnational corporations today plunder, exploit, and are creating havoc with the world's markets, resources, and people's welfare. Case in point, México, a recipient of U.S. outsourcing during 2001 to 2008, suffered when those jobs were taken to other Second and Third World economies. Hundreds of *maquiladoras* closed and more than 200,000 jobs were lost. The major beneficiary of the globalization of outsourcing was China. Most people in the U.S, particularly nativists in their myopia are oblivious to the fact that the Bush administration incarnates the political-economic alliance of global capital and the country's elite plutocracy. Few realize that today's representative democratic system is evolving into a "corpocracy," which denotes "rule by a fusion of government and the new sovereigns—multinational corporations." In metaphoric terms, their new world republic is the globalization of capital. Their symbol of unity is not the eagle, or the red, white, and blue, or the cross, but rather their almighty God profit, and their altar is the planet that economically must be exploited of its resources, especially oil. The country's two-party system is ideologically a capitalist one-party dictatorship controlled by a plutocratic corporate cabal of special interests.[15] Historically, both political parties have sought to foster on a global scale and domestically a propitious investment climate for corporations. Indisputably, the country's trade and economic policies abroad in particular have been designed to advance the interests of U.S. transnational corporations. Domestically, U.S. trade policy has also been linked to immigration, satisfying the capitalist economy's profound addiction to and dependency on cheap labor, which migrant and immigrant labor provides. Thus, it is the power of capital, not the people so far, that drives the engine of the Republic's politics.

Elections at the national and state levels are lucrative economic enterprises that cost tens of millions of dollars, largely controlled by the influence of a corporate capital. Up to 2007, national elections were tantamount to symbolic exercises of directed representative democracy controlled chiefly by capital interests. The 2008 presidential elections, for some people and activists, offered hope for change should Democratic presidential candidate Barack Obama win. Others, however, especially on the Left doubted that little could be done to alter capital's inextricable influence over the country's politics and superstructure.

The country's political transition to a "corpocracy" is further buttressed by the empirical fact that a U.S. Government Accounting Office (GAO) study in 2004 reported that 61 percent of U.S. corporations, including 39 percent of large corporations, paid no corporate taxes between 1996 and 2000. In 2007 they shouldered a mere 14.4 percent of the total U.S tax burden, compared with about 50 percent in 1940.[16]

Based upon the above globalization of capital analysis and its etiological relation to the immigration crisis, a number of other conclusions are derived and are therefore presented. One such related conclusion is that not enough people in the U.S. are willing to accept its validity. Few accept or comprehend the nexus between the present immigration crisis and the globalization of capital and to capitalism's inherent contradictions. With few exceptions, most nativists, politicians, scholars, media, and even pro-migrant rights activists do not deal with the complexity of immigration reform from a macroeconomic systemic perspective. Instead the answers provided by congressional politicians and the Bush administration during 2005 and 2007 were myopic, micro-oriented, and short-term remedies that lacked resolution to the said crisis. Their emphasis was on border security and enforcement, severe employer sanctions, restrictionist immigration laws, militarization of the country's borders, and the passage of nativist and racist state and local laws. At this juncture, most reject legalization and even guest-worker programs.

While short-term perspective micro-oriented immigration reforms that accentuate legalization are desirable and must be sought as was postulated in the work's introduction, they will not halt the migrant exodus. This is buttressed by the historical fact that the Immigration Reform and Control Act in 1986 was enacted with the paramount objective of stopping it, but failed miserably to do so. While some 3 million undocumented migrants became permanent residents, from the late 1980s to the present the migrant exodus has been incessant and today continues to grow. This is empirically validated by the migration since 1986 of millions of undocumented to the U.S., chiefly from México and Central America. The country's total immigration population in 2008 numbered at least 38 million. Legal immigration in 2006 was 1,266,000 and undocumented immigration by the end of 2008 is expected to reach around 2 million. According to the Census Bureau, by 2007 it had increased to somewhere between 700,000 to 850,000 per year. In the Tucson, Arizona, sector alone in 2007 some 380,000 were apprehended by the U.S. Border Patrol and 237 migrants died crossing.[17] Understanding the growing precariousness of México and Central America's impoverished economies, the influx of the migrant exodus is expected to continue but at a decreased level due to the current recessionary crisis in the U.S. economy, which in 2008 is characterized by increasing unemployment, housing foreclosures, inflation, and increasing gas and food prices. The country's inhospitable nativist political climate further is impacting the momentary decrease in migrant exodus. Yet any upturn in the U.S. economy will undoubtedly, once again intensify it, since the globalization of capital crisis in México and the rest of Latin America regardless will continue without major changes occurring in their capitalist economies.

In response to the above, both political parties, Republican and Democratic, have no viable policy answers to stopping the incessant influx of the migrant exodus. This is rather evident in their utter failure to enact immigration reform during the past three years. Even in dealing with micro-oriented reforms, Congress so far has been unable to realize a consensus on immigration reform due to their immersion in their self-generated legislative quagmire or morass. From a policy perspective both Congress and the country's two corporate political parties are intellectually myopic, limited, and not erudite on the policy aspects of the issue of immigration. They consequently lack viable answers to its resolution. Even worse are nativist politicians, who are just plain ignorant, mentally deficient, and/or are blinded by their xenophobia, nativism, and racism. In general, it is evident that politicians of both political parties fail to grasp the cause and effect of the inextricable correlation between the globalization of capital, its induced economic crises, migrant exodus, and immigration crisis. Rather than place blame where it belongs, on the capitalist system, they instead, especially nativists, pander to the fears of the White masses by attacking and scapegoating poor, defenseless, and vulnerable immigrants and migrants.

Since 1986 the Republican Party has embraced a conservative and ultrazealot nativist avant-garde party leadership role. At all levels of government, Republican politicians have embraced a zealous anti-immigrant posture that is nativist and xenophobic. Since 2004 to the present, Republicans have been at the forefront of what is described in this work as the "nativist legislative surge"—the passage of anti-immigrant laws. The passage by the House of Representatives in December 2005 of Republican Sensenbrenner's HR4437 and attempts to pass numerous other restrictionist border security measures since then is indicative of the ultrazealot nativism that has pervaded it as a political party. It's nativist politics bordered on being racist and panders to its essentially xenophobic White constituency. Nativist Republicans have sought to promote the criminalization of immigrants, especially migrants from México and Latin America. The result has been the polarization of the country. While Democrats are not free from the cancerous growth of nativism, as a political party, it has unsuccessfully struggled for some sort of comprehensive immigration reform that includes legalization.

Their nativism and xenophobia is driven by a combination of fear, hatred, and racism, which since 1986 has been directed specifically toward Mexicanos. It is driven in great part by two interdependent variables: historic and demographic. As was examined, the former as a matter of historical fact unpleasantly reminds them that the Southwest or Aztlán was stolen forcibly by the U.S. from México in 1848. Outside of the native peoples no other ethnic/racial group in the U.S. can make this historical claim. For nativist Whites the effects of the re-Mexicanization of Aztlán means that demographically they will soon constitute the region's new minority; therefore, they are resolute in their struggle to reverse the threat of the migrant exodus.

Most nativists do not fully understand the consequences of passing draconian anti-immigrant restrictionist border security and enforcement legislation, that consequently in all probability, in México and Central America there would be absolute social upheaval. The migrant exodus of nearly 1 million that enter annually into the U.S., coupled with the annual remittances amounting in 2007 to $66.5 billion, especially those sent to México and Central America, have significantly precluded their economies from collapse or even worse, revolution. A political and economic fact is that immigration/migration act like a safety valve. An unstable México could lead to the realization of a U.S. military scenario developed by former President Reagan's Secretary of Defense Caspar Weinberger and his coauthor Peter Schweizer, who in their work *The Next War* predict a war and invasion of México in the twenty-first century.[18]

Intellectually, nativists do not draw the correlation between immigration/migration and two interconnected facts: (1) the country's capitalist plutocrats are driven by avarice, materialism, and the pursuit of profit; and (2) transnational corporations control the world's economies and nation's wealth. For instance, nativist Patrick Buchanan at times is critical of the Bush administration's "neo-Manifest Destiny" foreign policy, yet he fails to link the country's immigration crisis to the global capitalist crises.[19] Since 9/11, President Bush and his administration have violated the Constitution's separation of powers doctrine and the checks and balances system. By way of executive orders, the Bush administration has effectively pandered to the fears of the people using the scare tactic of an imminent second terrorist attack. A seemingly leaderless and powerless Congress has acquiesced to his "cowboy" foreign policy that is predicated on the doctrine of preemptive war. It is with a global scope a reincarnation of the Monroe Doctrine and Manifest Destiny, meaning it ideologically propagates capital's gospel of free trade, illusionary democracy, and U.S. global hegemony.

Another intrinsic aspect to today's immigration crisis which seldom is acknowledged by nativists and non-nativists alike is that U.S. foreign policy is predicated on ensuring the global expansion and preservation of capital and its markets as illustrated by its superpower military role of being the international policeman of capital. As an empire with some 750 military bases located worldwide and an estimated military budget in 2007 of $572 billion, the sun never sets for Pax Americana. The U.S.'s militarism is illustrated by the fact that in 2008 worldwide U.S. military expenditures are 48 percent of the worldwide total, whereas the combined military budgets of the rest of the 192 nation-states amounted to 52 percent of the total $1,473 trillion.[20]

The U.S. markets itself to the world as being the beacon of democracy. Yet under its guise, including that of freedom, the Bush administration has engaged this nation in blatant imperialist wars in Iraq and Afghanistan. It misled this country and the world into believing its allegations that Iraq possessed weapons of mass destruction and that there was a nexus between Saddam Hussein and Al-Qaida; therefore Iraq was invaded. In fact, the real reason for the Iraq War was the Bush administration's hegemonic efforts to control the oil of the Middle East, especially that of Iraq. In military, political, and economic terms, the war was a violation of the United Nations Charter because Iraq did absolutely nothing to warrant the U.S.-led aggression against it.

To date, the Bush administration has spent some $522 billion on the Iraq War and occupation. Another $80 billion[21] was added. And in 2008, the U.S. was spending some $14 billion every month, with no end in sight. Joseph E. Stiglitz, a Nobel Prize-winning economist and critic of the war, projects that the long-term costs of the Iraq War and occupation will be more than $4 trillion. The Congressional Budget Office, among others, predicts the costs will total some $1 trillion to $2 trillion, depending on the length of the occupation and number of military and nonmilitary personnel deployed. As of April 2008, the price in military casualties has been 4,000 U.S. soldiers killed and some 30,000 wounded and maimed,[22] and a low estimate of some 650,000 Iraqis killed since 2003. In April the so-called surge did not work, so once again Iraq was on the verge of being engulfed by an outright civil war. Bush's response of course was to maintain the status quo and let the next president deal with the debacle that his administration created. Bush in 2008 continued to rattle the sword of U.S. militarism against Iran. This is in spite of the fact that the CIA in December of 2007 reported that Iran had suspended its nuclear arms program in 2003. Nonetheless, the Bush administration appeared to be positioning itself for an attack on Iran, perhaps in collaboration with Israel, sometime before the November presidential elections.

In 2008 there are numerous indicators that suggest Pax Americana is in decline. As a superpower, the U.S. is militarily overextended, exhausted, and not loved or respected politically by many of the peoples of the world. Moreover, on the horizon is the imminent emergence of China as a rival superpower with a population of 1.3 billion people and the highest economic growth rate among the economic global powers: 9.3 percent in 2008 and 9.5 percent projected for 2009.[23] There is also Russia, which is quickly reemerging as a superpower; a European Community of great economic power; the competitive regional powers of Japan, India, Brazil, and Iran; and the Socialist states of Cuba, Venezuela, Ecuador, Bolivia, Paraguay, and Nicaragua, which are offering alternative developmental models to neoliberalism.

On the domestic front, as a result of the increasing economic crisis in 2008, life as we know it is quickly becoming a nightmare not only for immigrants and migrants, but also for the country's middle and lower classes. The country as a whole faced the ominous possibility that the growing global recessionary crisis could turn into a depression. Millions of families today live from paycheck to paycheck; consequently, many are precariously one check away from becoming homeless. Inequality is rampant and growing to where the "wealth gap" is wider than ever. The country's capitalist economy is generating a host of other multiplying social problems that include poverty, outsourcing of jobs, unemployment, the foreclosure housing crisis, lack of affordable housing, absence of universal health care, inferior primary and secondary education, inaccessibility to a college and postgraduate education, crime, drug addiction, and overcrowded prisons, and if the preceding were not enough, a growing prevalence of nativism, racism, segregation, and deteriorating ethnic/race relations. Equally evident and extremely urgent is that in spite of the international advocacy efforts by former

Democratic Vice President Al Gore, neither political party, the Bush administration, or Congress as of early 2008 has aggressively responded to his doomsday global warming challenge.

As has been examined in this work, during times of recession and depression a resurgence of dangerous ultrazealot nativism occurs. As México and Latin America's existent economic crises exacerbate, so will the present immigration crisis in the U.S. intensify due to the ensuing migrant exodus. The interconnectedness and interdependency of these neoliberal economies means that in the case of México, metaphorically speaking, when the U.S. catches a bad cold, financially México sneezes. As previously accentuated, for México NAFTA has failed to halt the migrant exodus and in fact has further intensified it; for the U.S., it has enhanced the outsourcing of jobs. In 2008 the U.S. is faced with a dual capitalist economy: one for the plutocratic rich, characterized by chronic inequality, another for the marginalized poor relegated to Third World conditions.

While proposed immigration reform legalization and guest-worker programs could temporarily relieve the migrant exodus, extreme border security and enforcement measures would have egregious effects. If in the next few years the complete militarization of the Cactus Curtain went into effect, it would engender a diplomatic nightmare for the U.S. and México, as well as the rest of Latin America. Without addressing the detrimental effects inherent to the capitalist mode producing the myriad of "push" and "pull" forces endemic to the global economic crises, the global immigration crises will increase in intensity and continue changing the country's demographic profile.

Re-Mexicanization in the Twenty-First Century

The Western Hemisphere's immigration crisis, from the U.S. to México to the rest of Latin America, has affected substantially the rapidly changing demographics, and nativists are cognizant of the implications. Throughout the twenty-year duration of the current immigration crisis, via their politics, legislative, and organizing efforts nativists have sought to put the brakes on the country's changing demographics. Their xenophobic, nativist, and racist politics, as examined, are fostering a volatile ethnic/racial polarizing situation.

Demographically, three factors have impacted the current immigration crisis. First, never in the history of the country's immigration experience have Whites been so threatened by the prospects of being relegated to a minority status by the influx of non-White immigrants, in this case from Latin America. Second, from a political-cultural perspective, never has the country's WASP ethos hegemony been so seriously threatened as it is today by the Latino demographic transformation. And third, the migrant exodus of this said immigration crisis is not coming from White Europe, it is coming from "Brown" México, and second from "Brown/Black" Central America, the Caribbean, and South America.

Most nativists are cognizant, even terrified, of the aforementioned prospects and are determined to prevent it. If the present Latino demographic trends hold for the next forty-two years or even if the Latino population growth decreases during this time to an average of 40 percent per decade, the effect of the "re-Mexicanization of Aztlán" will be indisputably evident throughout the region's several states. Overall in Aztlán as a region, Mexicanos and Latinos will constitute its "new majority" population by no later than 2048 and possibly as early as 2040. This means the territories of Aztlán that México lost to the U.S. via military aggression will be re-occupied peacefully, thanks in great part to the globalization of capital. Migration and legal immigration from México and Latin America, high Mexicano/Latino birth rates, and White flight will continue to be its driving forces.

Nationwide the effects of the "Latinoization and Browning" of the U.S. will likewise foster in the 21st century a dramatic demographic transformation. Again based upon the demographic trends of the last fifty-two years and providing they continue, Whites in the U.S. will constitute a minority and "people of new color," the new majority by no later than 2040. This hypothesis again is based upon continued heavy Mexicano/Latino migration, legal immigration, high birth rates among Latinos, and particularly low and falling birth rates among Whites. Based upon the preceding demographic factors, it can be argued that the Latino population will reach 50 million in 2010 and by 2050 a low of 100 million to a high of 125 million. This translates to that by 2050 Latinos could well make-up at least 30-35 percent of the country's total population. Patrick Buchanan projects that if the current trends continue, "the White inevitable minority" scenario is credible, especially since he predicts that by 2050 both Latino and black populations "will have almost doubled from today's 85 million to 160 million."[24] His prediction that the Latino population will number some 100 million by 2050 is too conservative.

Even more dramatic is the country's demographic projection into the 22nd Century. If the aforementioned demographic trends remain into the next century, a logical prognostication can be made that if the "Latinoization and "Browning" of the U.S. continues at its present pace of growth, Latinos will surely compromise the country's new majority and White will become the country's new minority by as early as 2110. Thus, nativists driven by the above demographic realities, undoubtedly in growing desperation, relentlessly will continue their struggle in the 21st Century to put a halt to the "Browning" of the U.S. and maintain the hegemony of its WASP ethos-based culture, further exacerbating the country's immigration crisis.

Hence, the implications of the country's changing demographics are such that the nation will become increasingly a more multicultural, multiethnic, and multilingual society. The present WASP ethos will lose its domination; thus, figuratively speaking, the "melting pot" with its accentuation on assimilation into a White Anglo Saxon oriented society will be replaced by a more culturally pluralistic society or "salad bowl." As for Mexicanos and Latinos, as their numbers increase and become more concentrated, they will maintain more of their native countries' cultures and language. This, however, does not mean that they will be exempt from acculturation or the increasing globalization of culture. Spanish will rival English as the country's semi-official language and truly, in the prophetic words of Samuel Huntington, the U.S. will become a "bifurcated country" dominated by both English and Spanish.[25]

Theoretically, in the same way that the Mexicano/Latino population increases so will its level of political representation. The country's politics will be profoundly impacted: from the local city councils, school boards, special districts, and county board of supervisors to state legislatures, governorships, and courts and to the federal level of the House of Representatives, Senate, federal courts, and U.S. Supreme Court, and even the presidency itself. Mexicanos/Latinos could very well become the nation's most powerful political ethnic bloc. They could exercise great power and political influence, becoming a balance of power and swing vote, particularly in state/congressional/presidential elections. The White House will be within reach of becoming the "Brown House." Should neither the Democrats or Republicans or a third party represent their interests, Mexicanos/Latinos will have the numbers and capacity to forge their own political party. Implicit in the preceding is that Latinos will have broken the oppressive chains of internal colonialism's external administration and powerlessness. If organized and conscienticized, this could translate to Latinos having the requisite influence and power to impact and determine public policy at all levels, particularly at the federal domestic and foreign policy levels. In the end, however, this may not transpire due to powerful capital special interests that could economically control much of the political agenda of Mexicano/Latino politicians.

As the Latino population multiplies, socially and economically they will become increasingly segregated, stratified, and plagued by innumerable social problems. This suggests that while some socioeconomic progress will be made by some, the majority in the *barrios* (enclaves) will increasingly be subjected to a "poverty syndrome" of egregious multiple social problems that stem from internal colonialism. The likelihood is that while the number of new businesses will increase, including an array of Latino national and multinational corporations, White capital will continue to dominate. As the Mexicano/Latino population increases so will the country's immigration crisis, specifically its ethnic/racial polarization and nativism. If the country's current nativist political climate continues to intensify, ethnic/racial tensions and conflict could well be exacerbated to a dangerous level where violent eruptions occur, which if not mitigated could ultimately precipitate the country's balkanization, as well as the rise of ethnic struggles for self-determination.

Nativist Mythology of Immigration Rebuked

Today a multiplicity of nativist forces—from the armed rancher vigilantes, militias, organizations, and hate groups to politicians, media personalities, journalists, and academicians, among others—have contributed to the country's immigration crisis by their concerted efforts to persecute and character-assassinate immigrants and migrants, namely Mexicanos. In a rather concerted manner, they have been vilified, disparagingly stereotyped, and gratuitously scapegoated by nativists. Nativists from various sectors have sought to demonize them as being responsible for many of the country's socioeconomic ills. They have done so by spinning a spurious mythology, distorted data, misinformation, and lastly, subjective nativist conclusions.

It suffices to say that the list of authors is long, but there is one in particular that stands out in 2008, that is, populist nativist Patrick Buchanan. In his current work, *The Day of Reckoning*, he argues, "America is indeed coming apart, decomposing, and the likelihood of her survival as one nation through the mid-century is improbable—and impossible if America continues on her current course." He concludes, "For we are on a path of suicide."[26] On television and talk radio, innumerable nativists use the airwaves to fuel the country's nativist anti-immigrant political climate with misinformation and erroneous misconceptions, stereotypes, and myths about immigrants. They acrimoniously allege that immigrants are a burden on U.S. taxpayers and a drain on the economy; they take jobs away from domestic workers; they don't pay taxes; they overload the country's health, educational, and social service systems; they are major contributors to crime and fill the country's jails and prisons; they are a serious threat to the hegemony of the country's WASP ethos and culture; and much, much more.

Along with numerous other scholars, activists, and politicians, I ardently contend that documented and undocumented immigrants are invaluable and vital to the country's economy and progress. Today there are a number of studies that buttress the argument that they are an asset and not a liability. One such work is Aviva Chomsky's *"They Take Our Jobs!" and 20 Other Myths about Immigration*, which effectively challenges the manifold assumptions that underlie what she has identified as the twenty-one prevailing myths about immigration.[27] While it is not within the scope of this work to get into a comprehensive discussion on immigration's benefits and liabilities, it is important to tersely present, challenge, and clarify what I consider to be the five most debatable immigration fallacies.

FALLACY NUMBER ONE: IMMIGRANTS ARE A DRAIN ON THE ECONOMY

The truth is that numerous studies conducted during the last few years clearly document that immigrants are invaluable contributors to the country's economy. A report on immigration's economic impact released on June 20, 2007, by the Council of Economic Advisors concluded that "on average, United States natives benefit from immigration. Immigrants tend to complement (not substitute for) natives, raising natives' productivity and income." It further stated that "careful studies of the long-run fiscal effects of immigration conclude that it is likely to have a modest, positive influence."[28] What is more, in an open letter 500 economists, including five Nobel Laureates, stated that "immigration is a gain for America and its citizens and the greatest anti-poverty program ever devised."[29]

A report produced by the National Academy of Sciences in 2005 found that immigrants contribute more than $10 billion annually to the economy. Other estimates range as high as $80 billion. The Center for American Progress wrote, "Even conservative estimates show that undocumented immigrants play a substantial role in supporting the U.S. economy and boosting its potential."[30] In 2006 Texas state revenues collected from undocumented immigrants exceeded what the state spent on them vis-à-vis public services, such as education and health care, by $424.7 million. A study conducted by the California newspaper *Desert Sun* in late 2006 focused on ascertaining immigration's economic impact on Riverside County. It took national studies on the undocumented and then applied their findings to the estimated number of undocumented migrants living in Riverside County. The findings concluded that "extrapolated from the research of prominent social scientists, the findings—a roughly $1.5 billion economic boost and a nearly $220 million cost—surprised community leaders and immigration advocates alike. They assumed undocumented workers benefit the local community, but they did not expect such a large windfall."[31]

Undocumented workers pay the same taxes as U.S.-born residents, that is, income, sales, property, and business taxes, and in actuality received fewer tax breaks. The words of *San Diego Union-Tribune* journalist Phil Kerpen, in an article printed October 15, 2005, summarizes the contributions undocumented workers make to the economy: "Immigrants have revitalized urban economies throughout the United States and particularly improved important sectors such as small businesses, import/export, finance, construction and manufacturing."[32]

FALLACY NUMBER TWO: IMMIGRANTS CREATE UNEMPLOYMENT AND TAKE JOBS AWAY FROM DOMESTIC WORKERS

The truth is that on the issue of unemployment a myriad of immigration studies point out that the largest wave of immigration to the U.S. since the 1900s coincided with the country's lowest national unemployment rate and fastest economic growth. In 2007, while nativists allege the presence of 12 to 30 million undocumented workers, the country's unemployment rate was at a low 4.6 percent. According to the White House's Council of Economic Advisors, "foreign-born workers have accounted for about half of the labor force growth in the past decade, fueling overall economic output, creating jobs and increasing earnings for native workers by as much as $80 billion a year."[33] Furthermore, according to the Immigration Forum, many studies demonstrate that even among low-paid domestic and minority workers, undocumented workers do not cause unemployment. One such study by the Public Policy Institute of California released in February 2007 found that immigrants who arrived in the state between the years 1990 and 2004 increased wages for domestic workers by an average of 4 percent.[34]

Moreover, the Cato Institute in a recent report concluded that undocumented workers created new jobs, particularly with their purchasing power and the new businesses they start. In 2006 the combined purchasing power of the Latino community totaled $798 billion and was projected to increase by 2011 to $1.2 trillion. Another recent study conducted by the University of Arizona concluded that if all undocumented workers were removed from Arizona's workforce, the state's economic output would drop annually by at least $29 billion, or 8.2 percent. It was also reported that Arizona's undocumented worker population contributed $6.56 billion in construction output, $3.77 billion in manufacturing, $2.48 billion in service sectors, and $600.9 million in agriculture.[35]

The Pew Hispanic Center in August 2006 released a report that concluded that the arrival of millions of undocumented workers to the U.S. since the 1990s did not translate to any losses of jobs for domestic workers. A House of Representatives Committee on Small Business in May 2007 reported that undocumented workers filled the existent labor void, created small successful businesses, and that numerous industries today and in the future would not be able to operate without their labor. Another report by the Center for American Progress, on the issue of removing 2.5 million undocumented workers from the country's workforce, concluded that "only 105,000 natives could appropriately replace the 2.5 million immigrants in very low skill jobs, leaving 2.4 million positions unfilled."[36]

FALLACY NUMBER THREE: IMMIGRANTS OVERBURDEN
THE COUNTRY'S HEALTH AND PUBLIC SERVICES

Numerous studies on this lie conclude that immigrants are less likely than natives to use public services and those who do tend to be refugee groups, such as
Cubans, Russians, and Indochinese. The National Research Council in a report
on the fiscal impact of immigration, argues that too often studies overstate the
cost of immigration by measuring costs before adults reach working age. The report stated that "in fact, most immigrants tend to arrive at young working ages,
which partly explains why the net fiscal impact of immigration is positive under
most scenarios."[37] According to Justice for Immigrants, a former federal reserve
chairman pointed out that because 70 percent of immigrants arrived to the U.S.
in prime working age, it meant the country spent nothing on education, yet it
was projected that they will contribute $500 billion toward maintaining the liq-
uidity of the country's Social Security system over the next twenty years or so.[38]
Furthermore, the Social Security Administration estimates that workers without
valid Social Security cards contribute some $7 billion in Social Security tax rev-
enues and approximately $1.5 billion in Medicare taxes every year. Meanwhile,
elderly undocumented immigrants rarely qualify for Medicare or long-term services provided through Medicaid.[39]

On the issue of immigrants' impact on the health care system, the fact is it
is insignificant. According to Center for American Progress, 21 percent of total
medical costs were paid through public sources for the native population,
whereas for immigrants it was 16 percent. The National Research Council in a
report concluded that immigrants will pay an average of $80,000 per capita
more in taxes than they will use in government services during their lifetimes.
The related myth that immigrants come to the U.S. for a "free ride" on the country's health care services is utterly erroneous. The fact is that immigrants in most
jobs are not provided with health insurance.

FALLACY NUMBER FOUR: MOST IMMIGRANTS DO
NOT PAY TAXES AND DRAIN THE GOVERNMENT

The Executive Office of the President's Council of Economic Advisors report titled "Immigration's Economic Impact" dated June 20, 2007, presented three key
findings: (1) on the average, U.S. natives benefit from immigration. Immigrants
tend to complement, not 'substitute for' natives, raising natives' productivity and
income; (2) careful studies of the long-run fiscal effects of immigration conclude
that it likely to have a modest, positive influence; and (3) skilled immigrants are
likely to be especially beneficial to natives. Furthermore, it verified that the im-

pact of immigrants is likely to be positive in that they and their descendants would contribute around $80,000 more in taxes (in 1996 dollars) than they would receive in public service.[40] Another source, *The Washington Post*, as cited in the *Immigrant's List's*, "The Immigration Debate: Myths versus Facts in 2007" also supported and made this same argument.

Furthermore, the National Research Council in 1997 reported that the "undocumented pay into the Social Security system as much as $7 billion a year and contribute to Medicare in payroll taxes; yet they are unable to collect on the benefits . . . Starting in the late 1980s, the Social Security Administration received a flood of W-2 earnings reports with fake social security numbers. It stashed them in what it calls the 'earnings suspense file' in the hope that someday it would figure out whom they belonged to . . . $189 billion worth of wages ended up in the suspense file over the 1990s."[41] Another source, Justice for Immigrants, in their report "Learn the Issues" claimed that when it comes to a comparison between the amount of public benefits that immigrants use and the amount of taxes that they pay, it equals a positive financial gain for the country. One estimate cited that while immigrants earned about $240 billion a year and paid about $90 billion a year in taxes they only used $5 billion in public benefits. The Immigration Policy Center in a report stated that "unlike most Americans, who will receive some form of a public pension in retirement and will be eligible for Medicare as soon as they turn 65, [undocumented] immigrants are not entitled to benefits. Legal permanent residents must pay into the Social Security and Medicare systems for approximately 10 years before they are eligible to receive benefits when they retire."[42]

The reality is that undocumented workers contribute significantly to keeping the Social Security and Medicare systems viable and fiscally afloat in particular at a time when the country's aging White population is increasing. They pay income, sales, property, and business taxes, which numerous studies conclude are a positive asset to supporting the country's health and public services.

FALLACY NUMBER FIVE: UNDOCUMENTED IMMIGRANTS ARE DANGEROUS CRIMINALS

Numerous studies on immigration report that immigrants are less likely to commit crimes and/or be incarcerated than are the native born. This is true for the country and most large U.S. cities. In addition, they conclude that since the 1990s while the immigrant population has increased to historic new heights, the rates for violent crimes and property crime have declined sharply over the same period. A study released in February 2007 by the Washington, D.C.-based Immigration Policy Center showed that immigrant men from the ages of eighteen to thirty-nine had an incarceration rate five times lower than U.S. citizens in every group examined. It reported that among Mexicano men, for example, 0.7 percent of those foreign born were incarcerated compared to 5.9 percent of native born. University of California, Irvine sociologist Ruben G. Rumbaut, coauthor of the study, said that despite the data, many people today continue to perpetuate images or stereotypes of crime-prone immigrants. He added, "The problem of crime in American society is overwhelmingly a problem of natives, not immigrants."[43] The fact is that overwhelmingly most immigrants come to the U.S. to work and better themselves and their families. The lie about immigrants being criminals is being told by nativists in efforts to instill fear, especially in the insecure White citizenry.

Thus, as the above facts have argued against the five nativist concocted lies, immigrants—both documented and undocumented—have proven themselves to be assets to the country's capitalist economy. Without access to a source of migrant labor that is willing to work hard for low wages and no benefits, U.S. capital will not be not be able to compete globally and make its huge profits.

What Now for Mexicanos and Latinos?

In 2008 the Latino population is nearing 50 million and as has been argued relatively soon it will become the majority population in Aztlán. The question is "What next?", which also happens to be the focus of my next work, which is at this time entitled *What Need to be Done: The Building of a New Movement*. Using the Charles Dickens literary saying the "best of times, worst of times" as a framework for analysis, taken from his classic work *A Tale of Two Cities*, the fact is the Latino community finds itself today in a critical juncture. Undeniably, overall Mexicanos and Latinos since World War II have made some progress in this country. This, however, should not lead us to conclude that the majority of Mexicanos and Latinos in the U.S. are experiencing the "best of times" reality. Today in the twenty-first century it is the egregious effect of the "worst of times" scenario and that Mexicanos and Latinos are experiencing. They find themselves as argued in this work under a state of crisis and siege, especially within the immigration reform arena. The vitriolic anti-immigrant attacks by nativists during the last seven years have dominated the struggle for immigration reform.

Nativists declared "political war" against Mexicano and Latino migrants, and in early 2008 it was intensified. The Southern Poverty Law Center in early 2008 in an article said that the number of hate groups had increased to 888, an increase from 844 in 2006 compared to 602 in 2000.[44] The most prominent anti-immigrant group to be added is the Federation for American Immigration Reform (FAIR). The report also revealed a significant rise in hate crimes related to immigration against Latinos. The FBI reported that in 2006 they had totaled 819, compared to 595 in 2003.[45]

The "worst of times" political reality was enhanced by the detrimental effects of the continued nativist legislative surge. At the congressional level, Senate Republicans continued in early 2008 to put forth a smorgasbord of eleven nativist restrictionist-oriented bills, which could grow to fourteen. One bill would require jail time for undocumented migrants caught crossing the Cactus Curtain, make it harder for them to open bank accounts, and compel them to communicate in English when dealing with federal agencies. Another bill would pressure states into not granting the undocumented drivers a license by reducing 10 percent of highway funding from states that do so. Other bills sought to: (1) extend the presence of the National Guard on the border; (2) end language assistance at federal agencies and at the voting booth for people with limited English ability; (3) impose a maximum prison sentence of two years for those caught supposedly crossing illegally the border for a second time; (4) block federal funding of cities that prevent their police from enforcing immigration law; (5) authorize DHS to use information from the Social Security Administration to target undocumented migrants; (6) require construction completion of the 700-mile-long iron curtain, not including vehicle barriers; (7) impose sanctions on countries that refuse to repatriate their citizens; (8) deport any immigrant, legal or undocumented, for one drunk driving conviction; and (9) empower local and state police to enforce federal immigration laws.[46] Some House Democrats in 2007 and 2008 also began to embrace a tougher stand on immigration. Several of them endorsed Republican Heath Shuler's SAVE (Secure America through Verification and Enforcement) Act, which specifically would bolster border security and require employers to verify their workers' legal status with an electronic verification system.[47]

At the state and local levels of government, the "worst of times" scenario was also vividly evident. In 2008, Oklahoma officials and the media continued to report on the egregious effects of its ethnic cleansing-oriented state legislation, which fostered a reverse exodus of migrants to other states or their return to home countries. Likewise, Arizona in 2008 enacted one of the country's toughest laws to punish employers who hired the undocumented. Also, anti-immigrant Sheriff Joe Arpaio of Maricopa County continued to enforce federal immigration laws by initiating roundup raids of undocumented migrants. The climate of fear that pervaded Arizona fostered a reverse migrant exodus, which impacted a slowdown in the state's economy. *New York Times* reporter Randal C. Archibold on February 17, 2008, wrote, "The signs of flight among Latino immigrants here are multiple: families moving out of apartment complexes, schools reporting enrollment drops, business owners complaining about fewer clients."[48] Preliminary reports suggest that the persistent decline in the migrant population will damage Arizona's overall economy.

Mexicanos in the U.S., especially throughout Aztlán, have to deal with the detrimental effects of their internal colonized and occupied status. The millions of undocumented migrants who have arrived from México via the migrant exodus in most cases are absorbed into the *barrio*'s internal colonial-produced poverty syndrome, exemplified by growing unemployment; chronic inequality; de facto segregation; inaccessible health care; inferior primary and secondary education; lack of access to higher education; increasing crime, drugs, and alcohol abuse; and particularly, and as mentioned above, xenophobia, nativism, and racism.

Moreover, Mexicanos and Latinos in the *barrios*, because of their internal colonial status, are still underrepresented and therefore are essentially disenfranchised. The few politicians that they do have, for the most part are ineffective as leadership agents for change when it comes to confronting the innumerable issues that plague them. Their role is essentially that of being a "buffer,"[49] perpetuating the maintenance of the status quo. Most are not zealous in promoting their respective ethnic communities' interests and welfare, for they owe their political souls to special White interests. Compounding this reality is the lack of national and state leadership; lack of organizational power resulting from weak existent organizations; unorganized communities; political divisions; lack of a strategic agenda; generational differences; divisions among activists and coalitions; a climate of fear among migrants; and a pervasiveness of apathy, indifference, and complacency across the board. Overall, particularly for Mexicanos and especially migrants, in 2008 they find themselves with few political allies and supporters.

Yet in spite of the aforementioned, during the country's Democratic Party presidential primaries and caucuses up to March 2008, the Latino voter turnout was high. Clinton received the lion's share of the Latino Democratic primary vote, 65 percent to Obama's 35 percent. Nationally, however, there was no organized effort by Latinos to set the stage for the November presidential elections. This was in spite of the fact that Latinos possess the potential of becoming "swing vote" or "balance of power" in electing the next Democratic Party president; thus ultimately enhancing the possibilities for Democrats to push for immigration reform in 2009. The question that remained unanswered in 2008: Will Latinos close ranks and get organized to deliver their nearly 12 million that are registered to vote?

The answer largely depends on the results of the 2008 presidential elections. Up to the early months of 2008, the issue of immigration reform was essentially sidestepped by both Democratic Party presidential candidates Barack Obama and Hillary Clinton. During the contentious primaries both sought to stay clear of the issue for fear it could detrimentally impact their campaigns.[50] In the case of Republican Party nominee John McCain, nativist conservative forces within the party by 2008 had pressured him into retreating from his earlier maverick call in 2006 for legalization. In his quest to solidify his conservative base, he expediently shifted to an emphasis on border security and enforcement.

Depending on who wins the presidency there are basically two possible immigration reform scenarios for 2009. The first scenario is if either Clinton or Obama win, efforts in 2009 could unfold to pass immigration reform that includes the legalization of the more than 12 million undocumented migrants. This statement is buttressed by the fact that both Democratic Party candidates voiced in the primaries support for comprehensive immigration reform. Yet, both in 2006 voted for the Secure Fence Act, which authorized the construction of a 700-mile-long wall on the U.S.–México border.[51] Both have advocated legalization, while Obama's support leaned heavily toward a form of guest-worker program, Clinton's emphasis was on family unification. Thus, of the two, based upon an examination of their overall positions, the prospects for realizing immigration reform in 2009 are better enhanced if Obama were to secure victory over McCain in November.

The second scenario is if Republican presidential nominee John McCain wins the presidency, which is within the realm of possibility considering the fractious status of the Democratic Party during the early primary months of 2008, legalization will not materialize in 2009. While McCain was the coauthor of the McCain-Kennedy Bill in 2006, existent ultranativist zealot conservative forces within the Republican Party will struggle hard to prevent a repeat in 2009. For him to press for legalization, while it would gain him votes among Latinos, it would concomitantly hurt him dearly with White conservatives. Because of the pervasiveness of the WASP ethos anti-immigrant political climate, it would translate to political suicide.

The above two immigration scenarios will obviously also be impacted by what political party controls Congress after the November elections. If Democrats maintain control of both the House and Senate and increase their present thin majorities, the possibility of immigration reform becoming a policy priority in 2009 for the new Democratic administration and 111th Congress are excellent. Should Republicans manage to win control of Congress or even one of the two chambers, the nativist legislative quagmire that has obviated immigration reform will continue. Should McCain win the presidency and Democrats maintain control of both houses, some form of immigration reform will remain possible. The question is, will it be primarily restrictionist border security and enforcement-oriented immigration reform or will it be more comprehensive and include legalization? Should Democrats not control Congress the immigration crisis will intensify to an unprecedented dangerous conflict level.

Based upon the country's existent nativist political climate, a McCain win will impel nativists to push even harder for even more stringent anti-immigrant measures. In what could be a worst-case scenario, the Department of Homeland

Security could be pressured to further intensify ICE and U.S. Border Patrol repressive operations and raids in the country's cities and along the border. These actions could be reminiscent of what the old INS did in 1954 to 1956 with Operation Wetback. Depending on the future status of the U.S. economy if wrecked by recession, or worse, depression, it is almost inevitable to expect a push by nativists for repatriation/deportations. This time, however, it could affect millions instead of half a million Mexicanos, as was done by the Democratic Franklin D. Roosevelt administration during the 1930s. In addition, should the McCain scenario prevail, the country's existent ethnic/racial polarization will reach a dangerously volatile level. Relations with México and other countries of Latin America could well deteriorate even more. Consequently, this would likely unleash circumstances or forces that could destabilize particularly México and Central America, producing an international and diplomatic nightmare for the U.S. and the region.

Especially within the Republican Party, ultranativist zealot forces could well demand an acceleration of the militarization of the Cactus Curtain. Present efforts to construct a 700-mile Berlin-type iron curtain, while plagued by construction problems, would likely expand to 2,000 miles in length. The wall will be equipped with the latest electronic, virtual, and infrared equipment, and be heavily patrolled. This will entail a substantial increase in the numbers of U.S. Border Patrol agents, perhaps deployment of the National Guard, and some may actually call for a further militarization of the Cactus Curtain to where it will be completely sealed.

Thus, regardless which political party wins the presidency in 2008, the immigration crisis will continue. Regardless of the circumstances, at best, if comprehensive immigration reform is realized in 2009 or after, it will resemble more than likely the legislation proposed in Congress in 2006 by the McCain-Kennedy bill and the Hagel-Martinez Compromise. While immigration reform is desirable and must be supported, as argued earlier it will not bring resolution, but a mere transition interlude to the immigration crisis.

The Building of a New Movement

Mexicanos and Latinos must be prepared to answer the question, what now? The answer strategically is twofold: (1) on a short-term basis, Latinos must be prepared to initiate a massive mobilization effort for 2009 similar to what was done in 2006 for immigration reform; and (2) on a long-term basis, efforts must coincide to build a New Movement that is macro social change-oriented that will struggle to transform the country's liberal capitalist system into one that is egalitarian and socially democratic. Hence, based upon the current global crisis that pervades capitalism today and in particular, the country, hard and difficult times lie ahead on a number of issue fronts. For the country's middle class and poor, particularly Mexicanos and Latinos, the present crisis must be dealt with the rise of social change oriented mass movements. Crucial to the change process is the use of my paradigm on social movements, as earlier examined in this work, which includes climate of change, leadership, organization, ideology, strategy and tactics, and power capability.

For a New Movement to arise, Mexicanos and Latinos, among others, must struggle and organize to alter the current political climate of fear into one of a climate of change, where people's frustrations and discontent are driven by hope. The New Movement must be directed by a pluralism of leaders that have risen from the bottom and who are competent to lead, direct, inspire, and have the intellect and, most importantly, the support of the people. It must be based on a foundation of new grassroots *barrio*/community-based organizations, coalitions, and existent entities that have been strengthened and revitalized. It must be guided by a holistic vision for major social change of transformative ideology and one that embraces a new social-democratic egalitarianism. Strategically, it must be both national and transnational and tactically equipped to resort to both conventional and unconventional means in its pursuit of its ends and vision. Lastly, it must be impelled by a power capability that incorporates both the people's mobilization and the financial capacity to create a critical mass, and then translate both into influence and power.

In order to effectively address the many and complex dimensions of the current immigration crisis, a New Movement must rise. To do so requires that in 2009 and beyond, short term immigration reform be strategically prioritized. The new president, hopefully Obama, must be greeted on January 20, 2009, with the understanding that immigration reform is a priority for his administration. Mexicanos and Latinos in particular must expeditiously create this New Movement since as a people, we are the most affected. It will require that strategically from the onset efforts be initiated to make the incipience of the New Movement multiethnically driven. As it develops, with time it would have the capacity to address both macro-related issues, such as poverty, global warming, and inequality, and concurrently micro-related issues, such as national health care, affordable housing, jobs, and viable education for all.

All persons who fervently espouse a globalization that is peaceful, egalitarian, humane, and socially democratic must rebuke global capitalism and must unite in solidarity. Only by transforming global capitalism will its induced immigration crises pervading the planet end. For Mexicanos and Latinos in the U.S., time is of the essence, since we are the most affected. We, along with others of like mind must be prepared to get organized, take power, and create change. Our priority must be to expeditiously struggle to create a New Movement, adhering to the three "Rs": recommit, reorganize, and remobilize.

Notes

Preface

1. Maldwyn Allen Jones, *American Immigration* (Chicago: University of Chicago Press, 1992), 1.

2. Oscar Handlin, *The Uprooted: The Epic Story of the Great Migrations that made the American People,* (Boston and Toranto: Atlantic Monthly Press, 1973), 3

3. Thomas Muller, *Immigrants and the American City* (New York: New York University Press, 1993), 1.

4. Cited in Paul Smickard, *Almost All Aliens: Immigration, Race, and Colonialism in American History and Identity* (New York: Routledge, 2007), 5.

5. Samuel P. Huntington, *Who Are We? The Challenges to America's National Identity* (New York: Simon & Schuster, 2004), 221.

Introduction

1. For an examination of this theme see Jared Diamond, *Guns, Germs, and Steel* (New York: Norton, 1999).

2. Karl Marx and Friedrich Engels, "Manifesto of the Communist Party," in *Selected Works in One Volume* (New York: International, 1974), 38–39.

3. Andrew L. Barlow, *Between Fear & Hope: Globalization and Race in the United States* (Lanham, Md.: Rowman & Littlefield Publishers, Inc., 2003), 58.

4. This periodization is taken from the work of Roger Burbach, *Globalization and Post Modern Politics: From Zapatistas to High-Tech Robber Barons* (London: Pluto Press, 2001), 21. It is important to note, however, the periodization is mine and is somewhat arbitrary.

5. Barlow, *Between Fear & Hope*, 58.

6. Nikos Papastergiadis, *The Turbulence of Migration* (Malden, Mass.: Blackwell, 2000), 76.

7. Judith Gans, "Citizenship in the Context of Globalization," Udall Center for Studies in Public Policy, University of Arizona, June 2005, udallcenter.arizona.edu/programs/immigration/publications/Citizenship%20and%20Globalization.pdf.

8. Jessie Jackson, "Immigration Dignity Day Statement" (speech May 1, 2006), Operation Push, www.rainbowpush.org.

9. John Rapley, *Globalization and Inequality: Neoliberalism's Downward Spiral* (Boulder, Colo.: Lynne Rienner Publishers, 2004), 81.

10. Norman D. Livergood, "Vulture Capitalism: The Wall Street-Treasury Complex as Counterpart to the Military-Industrial Complex," www.hermes-press.com/vulture.htm.

11. Burbach, *Globalization and Post Modern Politics*, 23, 25.

12. Jeremy Brecher and Tim Costello, *Global Village or Global Pillage: Economic Reconstruction From the Bottom Up* (Boston: South End Press, 1994), 51.

13. Lance Selfa and Helen Scott, "How Capitalism Uses Immigrants," April 21, 2006, www.socialistworker.org.

14. Brecher and Costello, *Global Village or Global Pillage*, 56.

15. Burbach, *Globalization and Post Modern Politics*, 48, 49.

16. For an excellent analysis on the prevalence of this neoliberal scenario in Latin America see Naomi Klein, *The Shock Doctrine: The Rise of Disaster Capitalism* (New York: Henry Holt and Company, 2007).

17. Manuel Castells, "The Power of Identity," in *The Information Age*, vol. 2 (Cambridge, Mass.: Blackwell, 1997), 244.

18. Jackson, "Immigration Dignity Day Statement."

19. Louis DeSapio and Rodolfo O. de la Garza, *Making Americans, Remaking America: Immigration and Immigration Policy* (Boulder, Colo.: Westview Press, 1998), 4.

20. Papastergiadis, *The Turbulence of Migration*, 1.

21. For a more extensive report on each of these four theories see Stephen Castles and Mark J. Miller, *The Age of Migration* (New York: The Guilford Press, 2003), 21–30.

22. Castles and Miller, *The Age of Migration*, 22–23.

23. Castles and Miller, *The Age of Migration*, 25–26.

24. Castles and Miller, *The Age of Migration*, 26–29.

25. Aztlán refers to the Edenic place of origin of the México (the Azteca); supposedly it denotes the herons or "land of whiteness" (John R. Chavez, *The Lost Land: The Chicano Image of the Southwest* [Albuquerque: University of New México Press, 1984]). The term "Aztlán" is subject to much debate and intellectual speculation. Throughout this work, however, it is used to denote the geographical place of origin of the Azteca, which some scholars propose was located somewhere within the five southwestern states: California, Arizona, New México, Colorado, and Texas. Some say the real point of origin was near the Blyth area of Arizona/California; others argue it was somewhere in Utah or in present northern México. No one knows for sure. However, much more important to note is that Aztlán will be used to politically identify and include all land—nearly one million square miles—located in the southwest regional part of the United States, which México lost as a result of the Texas Revolt of 1836 and the imperialist War of the United States on México (1846–1848). Thus, when the term occupied is used it means all the land within the region called the "Southwest" that belonged to México prior to 1848.

26. For an extended analysis of this historical perspective, see my book *Mexicano Political Experience in Occupied Aztlán* (Walnut Creek, Calif.: Alta Mira Press, 2005), chapter 2; or Rodolfo Acuña, *Occupied America: A History of Chicanos* (New York: Longman, 2000), chapter 2.

27. Anup Shah, "Causes of Poverty," www.globalissues.org/TradeRelated/Poverty.asp.

28. William F. Jasper, "Behind the Job Loss" (June 25, 2007), www.jbs.org/node/4342.

29. Jasper, "Behind the Job Loss."

30. Sheila L. Croucher, *Globalization and Belonging: The Politics of Identity in a Changing World* (Lanham, Md.: Rowman & Littlefield Publishers, Inc., 2004), 10.

31. From this author's perspective, the "Second World" countries today are no longer those that were an integral part of the Soviet Union's economic, military, and political orbit. Today, they are comprised of countries with capitalist and socialist economies that are semi-industrialized and are developing the technological means to further propel their economy's growth and development. Countries such as México, Brazil, India, Taiwan, Venezuela, Cuba, Chile, Argentina, Egypt, Saudi Arabia, and South Korea, among others, can be described as being Second World powers. "Third World" countries are those that suffer from chronic underdevelopment characterized ideologically by primitive capitalist/feudal economies that are agrarian based and characterized by chronic poverty and social problems. They include several countries from the regions of Central America (e.g., El Salvador, Honduras, Guatemala), the Caribbean (e.g., Haiti, Dominican Republic), South America (e.g., Bolivia, Paraguay), Africa (e.g., Sudan, Congo, Somalia, Ethiopia), and Asia (e.g.. Bangladesh, Cambodia).

32. Croucher, *Globalization and Belonging*, 101.

33. Jonathan Steele, "The New Migration: Affluent, Controversial," *Guardian*, October 30, 2000.

34. London Observer Service, "British Whites To Be Minority by Year 2100," *Houston Chronicle*, October 8, 2000.

35. Patrick J. Buchanan, *The Death of the West: How Dying Populations and Immigrant Invasions Imperil Our Country and Civilization* (New York: St. Martin's Press, 2002), 100.

36. Buchanan, *The Death of the West*, 11, 12, 13, and 9.

37. Buchanan, *The Death of the West*, 101.

38. Guardian Unlimited, "37 Million Poor Hidden in the Land of Plenty," *The Observer*, February 19, 2006.

39. Guardian Unlimited, "37 Million Poor Hidden in the Land of Plenty."

40. Federal Reserve Report, "Currents and Undercurrents: Changes in the Distribution of Wealth, 1989–2004," 2006. Summary report released by *Citizens for Tax Justice*, "New Data Show Growing Wealth Inequality," May 12, 2006, www.ctj.org/pdf/wealth0506.pdf.

41. For those interested in examining in much greater detail the country's distribution of wealth see Edward N. Wolff, "Recent Trends in Household Wealth in the United States: Rising Debt and the Middle Class Squeeze," June 2007, papers.ssrn.com/sol3/papers.cfm?abstract_id=991901.

42. Matthew Miller, Editor Special Report: 'The Forbes 400," September 20, 2007 (www.forbes.com).

43. Labor Law Center, "Federal Minimum Wage Increase for 2007," November 8, 2007, www.laborlawcenter.com/federal-minimum-wage.asp.

44. Lucia Irabien, "Decrece pobreza extrema en el pais, dice Cepal," *Excelsior*, November 16, 2007.

45. E. Eduardo Castill, "Poverty Level Down, but Still Big Challenge for Mexico," Associated Press, July 28, 2004.

46. Castill, "Poverty Level Down."

47. Associated Press, "Mexican Officials Say Poverty Levels Vary Greatly by Geography," July 4, 2007.

48. Associated Press, "Mexican Youth Are More Likely to Migrate than the General Population, "August 10, 2007.

49. Castillo, "Poverty Level Down."

50. *Vamos*, "The Shocking Truth about México," www.vamos.org.mx.

51. Lisa J. Adams, "Poor Gates—He's No Longer Most Wealthy," Associated Press, July 4, 2007.

52. Eduardo Porter, "México's Plutocracy Thrives on Robber-Baron Concessions," *New York Times*, August 27, 2007.

53. Kenneth Edmond, "México, Calderon and a 3.9 Percent Wage Factor," *Herald México/El Universal*, January 8, 2007.

54. Burton Kirkwood, *The History of México* (Westport, Conn.: Greenwood Press, 2000), 207.

55. Lynn V. Foster, *A Brief History of México* (New York: Checkmark Books, 2004), 230.

56. The reason for the question mark is that many in México, including myself, do not consider him to be México's legitimate president, since in 2006 the election was stolen from PRD's Andres Manuel Lopez Obrador. Understanding México's current political, economic, and social crisis, it is doubtful that he will successfully complete his six-year term.

57. Leonardo Martinez-Diaz, "México's Economic Challenges," *The Brookings Institute*, September 5, 2007.

58. Jeremy Schwartz, "México's Job Promises Unfulfilled," *Miami Herald*, November 19, 2007.

59. *The Economist Intelligence Unit Views Wire*, "México's Economy," June 5, 2007, www.economist.com.

60. Leonardo Martinez-Diaz, "México's Economic Challenges."

61. *IMF Survey*, "Central America Aims for Stronger Growth," International Monetary Fund, August 2, 2007.

62. *Economic Commission for Latin America & the Caribbean Data Base*, December 2006, www.eclac.cl.

63. Ines Benites, "Central America: Poverty and Violence in Times of Peace," Inter Press Service, December 13, 2007.

64. Luis Alberto Cordero, "Central America: The Big Challenge Is the Distribution of Wealth," Inter Press Service, December 13, 2007.

65. Associated Press, "UN: Economic Growth Leading to Lower Poverty Rates in Latin America," November 15, 2007.

66. *Global Envision*, "What Latin America Thinks about Globalization," January 16, 2007, www.globalenvision.org.

67. For a comprehensive examination of the Latino demographics see my book *Mexicano Political Experience in Occupied Aztlán* (Walnut Creek, Calif.: Alta Mira Press, 2003), chapters 4–8.

Chapter 1

1. For a comprehensive examination of the history of the indigenous populations of Mesoamerica see Robert M. Carmack, Janine Gasco, and Gary H. Gossen, *The Legacy of Mesoamerica: History and Culture of a Native American Civilization* (Upper Saddle River, N.J.: Prentice Hall, 1996); and Michael Coe, *México: From Olmecs to Aztecs* (New York: Thames and Hudson, Inc., 1994).

2. It is important to note that the major source for this section is taken from my book *Mexicano Political Experience in Occupied Aztlán* (Walnut Creek, Calif.: Alta Mira Press, 2005), 31–44.

3. Burton Kirkwood, *The History of México* (Westport, Conn.: Greenwood Press, 2000), 14–15.

4. Lynn V. Foster, *A Brief History of México* (New York: Checkmark Books, 2004), 6–7.

5. James Diego Vigil, *From Indians to Chicanos: The Dynamics of Mexican-American Culture* (Prospect Heights, Ill.: Waveland Press, Inc., 1998), 14.

6. Geographical area that includes the central and southern parts of México and stretches into parts of Central America, specifically Belize, Guatemala, El Salvador, Honduras, and Nicaragua.

7. For a historical overview of each period see my book *Mexicano Political Experience in Occupied Aztlán*, 31–43.

8. For further reference to Mesoamerica's various civilizations see Carmack, Gasco, and Gossen, *The Legacy of Meso-America*; Vigil, *From Indians to Chicanos*; and Michael D. Coe, *America's First Civilization* (New York: American Heritage Publishing Co., 1968).

9. For a comprehensive examination of the Inca civilization see John A. Crow, *The Epic of Latin America* (Berkeley: University of California Press, 1992); and William H. Prescott, *History of the Conquest of México & History of the Conquest of Peru* (New York: Cooper Square Press, 2000).

10. Navarro, *Mexicano Political Experience in Occupied Aztlán*, 51–55.

11. The *encomienda* was a system of labor used by the Spanish crown to reward its conquistadores. Land was allocated to Spanish conquistadores and Amerindian villages located within the land grants allocated were compelled by Spanish law to contribute compulsory labor of all its inhabitants to the Spanish landowner. The landowners also received taxes from all the families living within their landowner's property.

12. Lynn V. Foster, *A Brief History of México* (New York: Checkmark Books, 2004), 74.

13. Cited in Leslie V. Tischauser, *The Changing Nature of Racial and Ethnic Conflict in United States History* (Lanham, Md.: University Press of America, Inc., 2002), 17.

14. For a more comprehensive historical examination of this whole section see my book *Mexicano Political Experience in Occupied Aztlán*, chapter 1.

15. For an examination of Manifest Destiny and the United States War against México please see my book *Mexicano Political Experience in Occupied Aztlán*, 65–83.

16. For a historical overview to the conditions that fostered English colonialism to the New World see James West Davidson et al., *Nation of Nations: A Concise Narrative of the American Republic* (Boston: McGraw-Hill, 2002), 4–32.

17. Dexter Perkins and Glyndon G. Van Deusen, *The American Democracy: Its Rise To Power* (New York: The Macmillan Co., 1962), 5.

18. For a contemporary analysis on the trials and tribulations encountered by the early settlers of Jamestown see Richard Brookhiser, ed., "Inventing America: The 400th anniversary of Jamestown," *Time*, May 7, 2007, 47–68; Lewis Lord, ed., "The Birth of America," *U.S. News & World Report*, January 29–February 5, 2007, 46–82.

19. For an excellent overview of the myriad of conditions that contributed to the English exodus see Thomas K. Grose, "A World of Change," *U.S. News & World Report*, January 29–February 5, 2007.

20. Lord, "The Birth of America," 56.

21. Charles M. Andrew, *The Colonial Period: American History* (New York: Charles Scribner's Sons, 1932), 34.

22. Marcus W. Jernegan, *The American Colonies: 1492–1700* (New York: Longmans, Green and Company, 1956), 21–22.

23. For a biographical overview of John Smith see Bob Deans, "Captain John Smith," *Time*, May 7, 2007; and Lewis Lord, "Not Just Another Smith," *U.S. News & World Report*, January 29–February 5, 2007.

24. Lord, "The Birth of America," 48–49.

25. Lord, "The Birth of America," 54–55.

26. Lord, "The Birth of America," 54–55.

27. Brookhiser, "Inventing America," 51.

28. The Mayflower Compact provided the basis for setting up their governing structure and system. Simply, it provided for a governor and several assistants to advise him, all to be elected annually by Plymouth's adult males (Davidson, et al., *Nation of Nations*, 68).

29. Cited in Wikipedia, "Pilgrims." Patricia Scott Deetz and James F. Deetz. Passengers on the *Mayflower*: Ages & Occupations, Origins & Connections. *The Plymouth Colony Archive Project*. Retrieved on May 28, 2006.

30. "Plymouth: Its History and People," pilgrims.net.

31. Lord, "The Birth of America."

32. L. Edward Purcell, *Immigration: Social Issues in American History Series* (Phoenix, Ariz.: Oryx Press, 1995), 4–5.

33. Maldwyn Allen Jones, *American Immigration* (Chicago: University of Chicago Press: 1992), 13.

34. Purcell, *Immigration*, 4. In his quote he cites Mary Beth Norton et al, *A People & Nation* (Boston: Houghton Mifflin, 1990), 32.

35. Purcell, *Immigration*, 4.

36. Perkins and Van Deusen, *The American Democracy*, 7.

37. Samuel P. Huntington, "Reconsidering Immigration: Is México a Special Case?", *Center for Immigration Studies*, November 2000.

38. L. Edward Purcell, *Social Issues in American History: Immigration*. (Phoenix, Ariz.: The Oryx Press, 1995), 5.

39. Samuel Huntington, *Who Are We? The Challenges to America's National Identity* (New York: Simon & Schuster, 2004), xv–xvi.

40. Louis DeSipio and Rodolfo O. de la Garza, *Making Americans, Remaking America: Immigration and Immigrant Policy* (Boulder, Colo.: Westview Press, 1998), 22.

41. DeSipio and de la Garza, *Making Americans*, 7–10.

42. Muller, *Immigrants and the American City*, 17.

43. Davidson et al., *Nation of Nations*, 38.

44. For an overview of the wretched conditions they faced see Howard Zinn, *A People's History of the United States: 1492–Present* (New York: Harper Perennial, 1995), 43.

45. Jones, *American Immigration*, 8, 11; and Thomas Muller, *Immigrants and the American City* (New York: New York University Press, 1993), 17.

46. Zinn, *A People's History of the United States*, 44.

47. The concept of "ethnic cleansing" is used in the work to denote a process of depopulation of a given ethnic or racial group of a given geographical space by another ethnic or racial group for the purpose of political and economic control and social/cultural hegemony.

48. For an extensive analysis of the concept of internal colonialism, see my book: *Mexicano Political Experience in Occupied Aztlán* (Walnut Creek, Calif.: AltaMira Press, 2005), 1-12.

49. Lord, "The Birth of America," 56.

50. Davidson et al., *Nation of Nations*, 44.

51. I use the word "involuntary" because that was exactly what it was. They had no say but were physically forced into becoming victims of slavery, which is subsequently defined.

52. Slavery denotes, according to the 1926 International Slavery Convention, "the status or condition of a person over whom any or all of the powers attaching to the right of ownership are exercised" (Tischauser, *The Changing Nature of Racial and Ethnic Conflict in United States History*, 36–37). More appropriately in the case of Blacks, it meant the condition of a whole racial group that was treated by Whites as their own private property, to be used and exploited for unpaid labor, and that was absolutely denied civil or human rights.

53. Tim Hashew, "The First Black Americans," *U.S. News & World Report*, January 29–February 5, 2007; and Jones, *American Immigration*, 11.

54. Zinn, *A People's History of the United States*, 23.

55. Orlando Patterson, "The Root of the Problem," *Time*, May 7, 2007.

56. Tischauser, *The Changing Nature of Racial and Ethnic Conflict In United States History*, 40–41.

57. Tischauser, *The Changing Nature of Racial and Ethnic Conflict In United States History*, 40–41.

58. Mercantilism, according to the *Oxford Concise Dictionary of Politics* was the "system of relations between state and economy prevailing throughout Western Europe and its dependencies up to the nineteenth century, under which those trades and industries were most encouraged that secured the accumulation of bullion, a national fleet and trained mariners, secure sources of strategic materials, and strong armaments production." Source: Iain McLean and Alistair McMillan, (Oxford: Oxford University Press, 2003), 345.

59. Perkins and Van Deusen, *The American Democracy*, 10.

60. Jones, *American Immigration*, 18.

61. Tischauser, *The Changing Nature of Racial and Ethnic Conflict In United States History*, 59.

62. Perkins and Van Deusen, *The American Democracy*, 11.

63. Tischauser, *The Changing Nature of Racial and Ethnic Conflict in United States History*, 52.

64. Patrick J. Buchanan, *State of Emergency: The Third World Invasion and Conquest of America* (New York: Thomas Dunn Books, 2006), 226.

65. See Jones, *American Immigration*, 39–41; and DeSipio and O. de la Garza, *Making Americans, Remaking America*, 22.

66. DeSipio and O. de la Garza, *Making Americans, Remaking America*, 22.

67. Purcell, *Immigration*, 8

68. DeSipio and O. de la Garza, *Making Americans, Remaking America*, 25.

69. Bureau of the Census, *Statistical Abstract of the Country*, 1995; cited in Tischauser's book *The Changing Nature Of Racial And Ethnic Conflict In United States History*, 58.

70. Murray L. Wax, *Indian Americans* (Englewood Cliffs, N.J.: Prentice-Hall, 1971), 32.

71. Davidson et al., *Nation of Nations*, 263.

72. Jones, *American Immigration*, 54.

73. Thomas Muller, *Immigrants and the American City* (New York: New York University Press, 1993), 19.

74. Muller, *Immigrants and the American City*, 20.

75. Zinn, *A People's History of the United States*, 89.

76. Roger Daniels, *Guarding the Golden Door: American Immigration Policy and Immigrants Since 1882* (New York: Hill and Wang, 2004), 7.

77. Mae M. Hgai, *Impossible Subjects: Illegal Aliens and the Making of Modern America* (Princeton, N.J.: Princeton University Press, 2004), 58.

78. Purcell, *Immigration*, 20–21.

79. *Wikipedia*, "Alien and Sedition Acts," en.wikipedia.org/wiki/Alien_and_Sedition_Acts.

80. Jones, *American Immigration*, 73.

81. Daniels, *Guarding the Golden Door*, 7.

82. Davidson et al., *Nation of Nations*, 263.

83. Davidson et al., *Nation of Nations*, 397.

84. The ensuing ethnographic immigration statistics are derived from the United States Bureau of the Census, 1993a, tables 1 and 2, which are cited in DeSipio and O. de la Garza, *Making Americans, Remaking America*, 18–21.

85. Murray L. Wax, *Indian Americans: Unity and Diversity* (Englewood Cliffs, N.J.: Prentice-Hall, 1971), 32.

86. Purcell, *Immigration*, 24.

87. Michael C. LeMay, *From Open Door to Dutch Door: An Analysis of U.S. Immigration Policy Since 1820* (New York: Praeger, 1987), 25.

88. Tischauser, *The Changing Nature of Racial and Ethnic Conflict in United States History*, 99.

89. Muller, *Immigrants and the American City*, 25.

90. For an excellent examination of nativism during these years see Muller, *Immigrants and the American City*, 127.

91. Jones, *American Immigration*, 128.

92. Muller, *Immigrants and the American City*, 24.

93. For more information on the San Patricio Battalion, see my book *Mexicano Political Experience in Occupied Aztlán*, 76–77.

94. Perkins and Van Deusen, *The American Democracy*, 255.

95. Peter Brimelow, *Alien Nation: Common Sense about America's Immigration Disaster* (New York: Random House, 1995), 12–13.

96. Peter N. Carroll and David W. Noble, *The Free And The Unfree* (New York: Penguin Books, 1988), 225.

97. Perkins and Van Deusen, *The American Democracy*, 255.

98. DeSipio and O. De la Garza, *Making Americans, Remaking America*, 31.

99. Davidson et al., *Nation of Nations*, 402.

100. LeMay, *From Open Door to Dutch Door*, 30.

101. DeSipio and O. de La Garza, *Making Americans, Remaking America*, 32.

102. U.S Immigration and Naturalization Service, 1993, tables 1 and 2. Cited in DeSipio and O. de la Garza, *Making Americans, Remaking America*, 20.

103. Ellis Island was opened in 1892. It is important to note that between 1892 and 1953 some 12 million immigrants were processed at this facility. For immigrants coming chiefly from Europe, it was their first encounter with their new homeland—the United States of America.

104. DeSipio and O. de la Garza, *Making Americans, Remaking America,* 18.

105. DeSipio and O. de la Garza, *Making Americans, Remaking America*, 19-20.

106. Otis L. Graham, *Unguarded Gates: A History of America's Immigration Crisis* (Lanham, Md.: Rowman & Littlefield Publishers, Inc., 2004), 7.

107. DeSipio and O. de La Garza, *Making Americans, Remaking America*, 20–21.

108. U.S Immigration and Naturalization Service.

109. Graham, *Unguarded Gates*, 7.

110. The exact number of Chinese immigrants arriving to the United States is open to debate. Scholar L. Edward Purcell, in *Immigrants*, uses a figure of 300,000; while Roger Daniels, *Guarding the Golden Door*, 16, uses a figure of 105,000, which is the figure I am using.

111. Purcell, *Immigration*, 40.

112. LeMay, *From Open Door to Dutch Door*, 62.

113. DeSipio and O. de la Garza, *Making Americans, Remaking America*, 36–37.

114. Purcell, *Immigration*, 38.

115. Daniels, *Guarding the Golden Door*, 17.

116. Brimelow, *Alien Nation*, xii.

117. U.S. Congress, Senate, *Report of the Joint Committee to Investigate Chinese Immigration*, Report 689 (Washington, D.C.: GPO, 1877). Quotations at iii–viii. Cited in Daniels, *Guarding the Golden Door*, 18.

118. Daniels, *Guarding the Golden Door*, 18–19.

119. Tischauser, *The Changing Nature of Racial and Ethnic Conflict in United States History*, 93–94.

120. Jones, *American Immigration*, 214–15.

121. LeMay, *From Open Door to Dutch Door*, 54–55.

122. Daniels, *Guarding the Golden Door*, 28.

123. LeMay, *From Open Door to Dutch Door*, 56.

124. Graham, *Unguarded Gates*, 16–17.

125. Graham, *Unguarded Gates*, 16–17.

126. Cited in Davidson et al., *Nation of Nations*, 570.

127. DeSipio and O. de la Garza, *Making Americans, Remaking America*, 26.

128. Roger Daniels, *Not Like Us: Immigrants and Minorities in America, 1890–1924* (Chicago: Ivan R. Dee, 1997), 74–75.

129. Graham, *Unguarded Gates*, 39.

130. Daniels, *Not Like Us*, 90–91.

131. Muller, *Immigrants and the American City*, 214.

132. Daniels, *Guarding the Golden Door*, 45.

133. Daniels, *Guarding the Golden Door*, 61–62.

134. Lisa Magaña, *Straddling the Border: Immigration Policy and the INS* (Austin: University of Texas Press, 2003), 15.

135. LeMay, *From Open Door to Dutch Door*, 74.

136. Graham, *Unguarded Gates*, 47.

137. Graham, *Unguarded Gates*, 47.

138. The Johnson-Reed Act is known concurrently as the Immigration Act of 1924 as well as the National Origins Act.

139. Purcell, *Immigration*, 84.

140. Matt S. Meier and Feliciano Ribera, *Mexican Americans/American Mexicans: From Conquistadores to Chicanos* (New York: Hill and Wang, 1993), 126.

141. Lawrence A. Cardoso, *Mexican Emigration to the United States 1897–1931* (Tucson: University of Arizona Press, 1980), 84.

142. Daniels, *Guarding the Golden Door*, 56.

143. Graham, *Unguarded Gates*, 48.

144. Graham, *Unguarded Gates*, 50.

145. Graham, *Unguarded Gates*, 53.

146. Daniels, *Guarding the Golden Door*, 55.

147. S. J. Makielski, Jr., *Beleaguered Minorities: Cultural Politics in America* (San Francisco: W.H. Freeman and Company, 1973), 53.

148. David E. Wilkins, *American Indian Politics and the American Political System* (Lanham, Md.: Rowman & Littlefield Publishers, Inc., 2007), xxv.

149. S. J. Makielski, Jr., *Beleaguered Minorities*, 53.

150. Quoted in Graham, *Unguarded Gates*, 19.

151. DeSipio and O. de la Garza, *Making Americans, Remaking America*, 20.

152. Daniels, *Not Like Us*, 140–41.

153. LeMay, *From Open Door to Dutch Door*, 92.

154. Jones, *American Immigration*, 240.

155. Cited in Daniels *Guarding the Golden Door*, 59-60; U.S. Department of Commerce, *Historical Statistics of the U.S. Series C88-144*, Washington, D.C.: GPO, 1957.

156. Purcell, *Immigration*, 86.

157. Purcell, *Immigration*, 86.

Chapter 2

1. Cary McWilliams, *North from Mexico: The Spanish-Speaking People of the United States* (New York: Greenwood Press, 1968), 52.

2. Oscar J. Martinez, "On the Size of the Chicano Population: New Estimates, 1850–1900," *Aztlan* 6 (Spring 1975): 50–60.

3. David G. Gutierrez, *Walls and Mirrors: Mexican Americans, Mexican Immigrant and the Politics of Ethnicity* (Berkeley, University of California Press, 1995), 19.

4. Gutierrez, *Walls and Mirrors*, 39.

5. For a comparative analysis on the demographic aspects of the occupation in California see Richard Griswold del Castillo, *The Los Angeles Barrio, 1850–1890: A Social History* (Berkeley: University of California Press, 1979), 62–63; and Albert M. Carrillo, *Chicanos in a Changing Society: From Mexican Pueblos to American Barrios in Santa Barbara and Southern California, 1848–1930* (Cambridge, Mass.: Harvard University Press, 1979), 47, 58, 116–17.

6. Robert Blauner, *Racial Oppression in America* (New York: Haryoce Associates, 1964), 83.

7. Rodolfo Acuña, *Occupied American: The Chicano's Struggle Toward Liberation*, (San Francisco: Canfield Press, 1972).

8. Armando Navarro, *Mexicano Political Experience in Occupied Aztlán* (Walnut Creek, Calif.: Alta Mira Press, 2005), 5–10.

9. Cited in Navarro, *Mexicano Political Experience in Occupied Aztlán*, 2–3

10. Gutierrez, *Walls and Mirrors*, 13.

11. Manuel G. Gonzales, *Mexicanos: A History of Mexicans in the United States* (Bloomington: Indiana University Press, 2000), 82.

12. For a comprehensive historical examination of the epoch of armed and political resistance see my book *Mexicano Political Experience in Occupied Aztlán*, chapter 2.

13. Gutierrez, *Walls and Mirrors*, 24. For a comprehensive analysis on the political disenfranchisement of the Méxicano see my book *Mexicano Political Experience in Occupied Aztlán*, chapter 2.

14. Lynn V. Foster, *A Brief History of Mexico* (New York: Checkmark Books, 2004), 132.

15. Decreed November 22, 1855, the Ley Juarez abolished merchant's courts and the church and military *fueros*, therefore creating a judicial system where all Mexicanos were subject to the same judicial proceedings.

16. Decreed on June 25, 1856, the *Ley Lerdo* put an end to communal landholdings, whether of the Catholic Church or the Amerindian communities, which negatively impacted its *ejido* system.

17. Burton Kirkwood, *The History of Mexico* (Westport, Conn.: Greenwood Press, 2000), 104–8.

18. Matt S. Meier and Feliciano Ribera, *Méxican Americans/American Méxicans: From Conquistadores to Chicanos* (New York: Hill and Wang, 1993), 104.

19. Ernest Gruening, *México and Its Heritage* (New York: Appleton-Century, 1928), 301–2.

20. Cited in John Ross, *The Annexation of Mexico: From the Aztecs To the I.M.F.* (Monroe, Maine: Common Courage Press, 1998), 52.

21. Frank R. Brandenburg, *The Making of Modern México* (Englewood Cliffs, N.J.: Prentice-Hall, 1964), 37–42.

22. James D. Cockcroft, *Mexico's Hope: An Encounter with Politics and History* (New York: Monthly Review Press, 1998), 84.

23. Meier and Ribera, *Méxican Americans/American Méxicans*, 104.

24. Julian Samora and Patricia Vandel Simon, *A History of the Méxican American People* (Notre Dame, Ind.: University of Notre Dame Press, 1977), 121–22.

25. Brandenburg, *The Making of Modern México*, 37–42.

26. Ross, *The Annexation of México*, 52.

27. Meier and Ribera, *Méxican Americans/American Méxicans*, 104.

28. For an excellent analysis on the blatant exploitation of México by foreign capitalist powers that occurred during the Porfiriato see Ross, *The Annexation of México*, 49–55.

29. Brandenburg, *The Making of Modern México*, 37–42.

30. Kenneth Johnson, *Méxican Democracy: A Critical View* (Boston: Allyn and Bacon, Inc., 1971), 18.

31. Johnson, *Méxican Democracy*, 18–19.

32. In the context of México's Revolution, "historical antagonisms" are events or circumstances that had a catalytic effect in the destabilization of the Porfiriato.

33. Robert E. Quirk, *México* (Englewood Cliffs, N.J.: Prentice-Hall, 1971), 79–80.

34. Ross, *The Annexation of Mexico*, 57.

35. Johnson, *Méxican Democracy*, 19–21.

36. Hector Aguilar Camín and Lorenzo Meyer, *In the Shadow of the Mexican Revolution: Contemporary Mexican History 1910–1989* (Austin: University of Texas Press, 1993), 6.

37. Alexander Monto, *The Roots of Mexican Labor Migration* (Westport, Conn.: Praeger, 1994), 28.

38. Ross, *The Annexation of Mexico*, 56.

39. Ross, *The Annexation of Mexico*, 56.

40. Edwin Lieuwen, *Méxican Militarism: The Political Rise and Fall of the Revolutionary Army, 1910–1940* (Albuquerque: University of New Mexico Press, 1968), 9.

41. Johnson, *Méxican Democracy*, 20–21.

42. Samora and Simon, *A History of the Méxican American People*, 124.

43. Jonathan Kendall, *La Capital* (New York: Random House, 1988), 404.

44. William Johnson, *Heroic México* (New York: Doubleday, 1968), 73.

45. Lieuwen, *Méxican Militarism*, 17.

46. For an examination on the etiology of the Méxican Revolution from a Méxicano intellectual perspective see Luis Cabrera, "The Méxican Revolution—Its Causes, Purposes, and Results," *The Annals of the American Academy of Political and Social Science*, Supplement to LXIX (January 1917), 1–17.

47. Johnson, *Heroic México*, 101.

48. Charles Cumberland, *México: The Struggle for Modernity* (New York: Oxford University Press, 1968), 241.

49. Johnson, *Méxican Democracy*, 25.

50. Lyle C. Brown, "The Politics of Armed Struggle in The Méxican Revolution, 1913–1915," in *Revolution In México: Years of Upheaval, 1910–1940*, ed. James W. Wilkie and Albert L. Michaels (Tucson: University of Arizona Press, 1984), 62.

51. Ross, *The Annexation of México*, 70.

52. Lieuwen, *Méxican Militarism,* 24.

53. Camín and Meyer, *In the Shadow of the Méxican Revolution*, 48–49.

54. Camín and Meyer, *In the Shadow of the Méxican Revolution*, 60.

55. Ross, *The Annexation of México*, 73.

56. Samora and Simon, *A History of the Méxican American People*, 128.

57. Ross, *The Annexation of México*, 78.

58. For details on the Plan de San Diego refer to my book *Mexicano Political Experience in Occupied Aztlán*, 100, 137.

59. Lieuwen, *Méxican Militarism*, 42.

60. Quirk, *México*, 94.

61. Quirk, *México*, 93–94.

62. Camín and Meyer, *In the Shadow of the Méxican Revolution*, 65.

63. Camín and Meyer, *In the Shadow of the Méxican Revolution*, 65.

64. Ross, *The Annexation of México*, 80.

65. Lieuwen, *Méxican Militarism*, 78.

66. See Quirk, *México,* 94–102.

67. Camín and Meyer, *In the Shadow of the Méxican Revolution*, 86.

68. Quirk, *México*, 101.

69. James D. Cockcroft, *Outlaws in the Promised Land: Mexican Immigrant Workers and America's Future* (New York: Grove Press, 1986), 36.

70. Mario Garcia, *Méxican Americans: Leadership, Ideology & Identity* (New Haven, Conn.: Yale University Press, 1989), 14.

71. For major works on the migrant exodus see Manuel Gamio, *Mexican Immigration to the United States* (Chicago: University of Chicago Press, 1930); and Lawrence A.

Cardoso, *Mexican Emigration to the United States* (Tucson: University of Arizona Press, 1980).

72. Ricardo Romo, "The Urbanization of Southwestern Chicanos in the Early Twentieth Century," in *New Directions in Chicano Scholarship*, ed. Ricardo Romo and Raymund A. Paredes (La Jolla: University of California, San Diego, 1978), 194.

73. Julian Samora, *Los Mojados: The Wetback Story* (Notre Dame, Ind.: University of Notre Dame Press, 1971), 17–18.

74. Leo Grebler, Joan W. Moore, and Ralph C. Guzman, *The Mexican American People: The Nation's Second Largest Minority* (New York: The Free Press, 1970), 63; and Grebler, *Mexican Immigration to the United States: The Record and Its Implications* (Los Angeles: Mexican American Study Project; Advance Report no. 2, University of California, Los Angeles, 1965), 19.

75. For a further examination of the Porfiriato's economic and demographic development of México's northern states, see Cardoso, *Mexican Emigration to the United States*, 1–17.

76. Cardoso, *Mexican Emigration to the United States*, 9, 10.

77. For an excellent examination of the economic developmental conditions that induced the migration exodus see Gutierrez, *Walls and Mirrors*, chapter 2.

78. Cardoso, *Mexican Emigration to the United States*, 18.

79. Cardoso, *Mexican Emigration to the United States*, 22.

80. David Weber, ed., *Foreigners in Their Native Land: Historical Roots of the Mexican Americans* (Albuquerque: University of New Mexico Press, 1973), 222.

81. See Cockcroft, *Outlaws in the Promised Land*, 49. See also Martinez, "On the Size of the Chicano Population," 43–67.

82. Camille Guerin-Gonzales, *Mexican Workers & American Dreams: Immigration, Repatriation, and California Farm Labor, 1900–1939* (New Brunswick, N.J.: Rutgers University Press, 1994), 30.

83. Juan Gómez-Quiñonez, *Roots of Chicano Politics, 1600–1940* (Albuquerque; University of New México Press, 1994), 297. It is important to note that prior to 1900, no precise numbers exist as to the number of Méxicanos who migrated into the U.S. from México.

84. Cited in Francisco E. Balderrama and Raymond Rodríguez, *Decade of Betrayal: Méxican Repatriation in the 1930s* (Albuquerque: University of New México Press, 1995), 6.

85. Samora, *Los Mojados*, 18.

86. For a thorough analysis on Méxican immigration into the United States from 1897 to 1931 see Cardoso, *Méxican Immigration to the United States*, 52–53.

87. David E. Lorey, *The U.S.-Méxican Border in the Twentieth Century* (Wilmington, Del.: A Scholarly Resources, Inc., 1999), 69.

88. Leo Grebler, et al., *The Mexican American People*, 64.

89. Oscar Martinez, *Méxican-Origin People in the United States: A Topical History* (Tucson: University of Arizona Press, 2001), 28.

90. Cardoso, *Méxican Immigration to the United States*, 52.

91. Arthur F. Corwin, ed., *Immigrants—and Immigrants: Perspectives on Méxican Labor Migration to the United States* (Westport, Conn.: Greenwood Press, 1978), 110, 116.

92. Lorey, *The U.S.-Méxican Border in the Twentieth Century*, 67–68.

93. Corwin, *Immigrants—and Immigrants*, 110, 116.

94. For an excellent comprehensive examination via a statistical analysis of the migrant exodus see Manuel Gamio, *El Inmigrante Mexicano: la historia de su vida* (Mexico City: Universidad Nacional Autónoma de México, 1969), 34.

95. Meier and Ribera, *Méxican Americans/American Méxicans*, 120.

96. Meier and Ribera, *Méxican Americans/American Méxicans*, 128.

97. Cardoso, *Méxican Immigration to the United States*, 103.

98. For an explanation of the particulars of both immigration acts see previous chapter, section dealing with nativist restrictive legislation.

99. For an extensive examination on each one of the immigration acts cited see Maldwyn Allen Jones, *American Immigration* (Chicago: University of Chicago Press, 1992), 231, 237, 240, 249.

100. Joan Moore and Harry Pachon, *Hispanics in the United States* (Englewood Cliffs, N.J.: Prentice-Hall, 1985), 135.

101. Leonard Dinnerstein et al. *Natives and Strangers: Blacks, Indians, and Immigrants in America*, 2nd Ed. (New York: Oxford University Press, 1990), 248.

102. Gamio, *El Inmigrate Mexicano*, 20; Emory S. Bogardus, *The Mexican in the United States* (Los Angeles: University of Southern California Press, 1934), 13–16.

103. Richard Griswold Del Castillo and Arnoldo de León, *North to Aztlán: A History of Mexian Americans in the United States* (New York: Twayne Publishers, 1997), 60.

104. Balderrama and Rodríguez, *Decade of Betrayal*, 7.

105. A major problem existed in that it was impossible to know in accurate terms the size of the Méxicano population during the first half of the twentieth century either on a regional or national basis simply because the U.S. Census Bureau collected and published very limited data pertaining to Méxicanos. Martinez, *Méxican-Origin People in the United States*, 11.

106. Martinez, *Méxican-Origin People in the United States*, 13.

107. Corwin, *Immigrants—and Immigrants*, 110, 116.

108. Corwin, *Immigrants—and Immigrants*, 11–13.

109. Rodolfo Acuña, *Occupied America: A History of Chicanos*, 4th ed. (New York: Addison Wesley Longman, Inc., 2000), 187.

110. Ricardo Romo, "The Urbanization of Southwestern Chicanos in the Early Twentieth Century," in *En Aquel Entonces: Readings in Méxican American History*, ed. Manuel G. Gonzales and Cynthia Gonzales (Bloomington: Indiana University Press, 2000), 130.

111. Leo Grebler, *Méxican Immigration to the United States: The Record and its Implications* (University of California Los Angeles: Méxican American Study Project, 1966), 16.

112. Martinez, *Méxican-Origin People in the United States*, 26.

113. Quiñones, *Roots of Chicano Politics*, 207.

114. Acuña, *Occupied America*, 165.

115. Juan Gonzales, *Harvest of Empire: A History of Latinos in America* (New York: Penguin Books, 2000), 102.

116. David Montejano, *Anglos and Méxicans in the Making of Texas, 1836–1986* (Austin: University of Texas Press, 1994), 109–10.

117. Emilio Zamora, *The World of the Méxican Worker in Texas* (College Station: Texas A&M Press, 1993), 12.

118. Martinez, *Méxican-Origin People in the United States*, 9.

119. Martinez, *Méxican-Origin People in the United States*, 11

120. Meier and Ribera, *Méxican Americans/American Méxicans*, 120.

121. Martinez, *Méxican-Origin People in the United States*, 9.

122. Gonzales, *Méxicanos*, 126.

123. Del Castillo and de León, *North to Aztlán*, 60.

124. Del Castillo and de León, *North to Aztlán*, 60.

125. Gonzales, *Méxicanos*, 121.

126. Samuel Bryan, "Méxican Immigrants in the United States," *Survey* 28 (September 7, 1912): 730.

127. Mark Reisler, "Always the Laborer, Never the Citizen: Anglo Perceptions of the Méxican Immigrant during the 1920s," *Pacific Historical Review* 45, no. 2 (1976): 243.

128. Martinez, *Méxican-Origin People in the United States*, 27.

129. Balderrama and Rodríguez, *Decade of Betrayal*, 17.

130. Grebler et al., *The Mexican American People*, 66.

131. Bogardus, *The Mexican in the United States*, 14.

132. For an excellent study on the repatriation and deportation efforts directed at Méxicanos see Abraham Hoffman *Unwanted Méxican Americans in the Great Depression: Repatriation Pressures, 1929–1939* (Tucson: University of Arizona Press, 1974), ix; and Balderrama and Rodríguez, *Decade of Betrayal*. For a study on the impact of repatriation on California see Guerin-Gonzales, *Méxican Workers & American Dreams*.

133. The concept of "repatriation" denotes a voluntary, but pressured effort to return targeted peoples to the country of origin whereas "deportation" connotes an involuntary and forced process to accomplish the same.

134. Cited in Guerin-Gonzales, *Méxican Workers & American Dreams*, 77.

135. Samora and Simon, *A History of the Méxican American People*, 36.

136. Mario Barrera, *Race and Class in the Southwest: A Theory of Inequality* (Notre Dame, Ind.: University of Notre Dame Press, 1979), 104.

137. Meier and Ribera, *Méxican Americans/American Méxicans*, 147.

138. For an examination of economic dislocations created by the Great Depression see Barrera, *Race and Class in the Southwest*, chapter 5.

139. Leobardo F. Estrada, F. Chris Garcia, Reynaldo Flores Macias, and Leonel Maldonado, *Chicanos in the United States: A History of Exploitation and Resistance*, ed. by F. Chris Garcia, *Latinos and the Political System,* (Notre Dame, Ind.: University of Notre Dame Press, 1988), 46.

140. Dinnerstein et al., *Natives and Strangers*, 249.

141. Francisco E. Balderrama, *In Defense of La Raza: The Los Angeles Méxican Consulate and the Méxican Community, 1929 to 1936* (Tucson: University of Arizona Press, 1982), 2

142. Estrada et al., "Chicanos in the United States," 46.

143. Balderrama, *In Defense of La Raza*, 2.

144. For a comprehensive examination of Mexicano repatriation in the 1930s see their book *Decade of Betrayal*

145. Robert Divine, *American Immigration Policy, 1924–1952* (New Haven, Conn.: Yale University Press, 1957), 77–84

146. Abraham Hoffman, *Unwanted Méxican Americans in the Great Depression: Repatriation Pressures, 1929–1939* (Tucson: University of Arizona Press, 1974), 166.

147. Balderrama and Rodríguez, *Decade of Betrayal*, 50.

148. For an excellent study on both the repatriation and deportation movements against Méxicanos during the Depression years see Hoffman, *Unwanted Méxican Americans in the Great Depression*, 166.

149. Barrera, *Race and Class in the Southwest*, 105–6.

150. Cited in Balderrama and Rodríguez, *Decade of Betrayal*, 53.

151. Balderrama and Rodríguez, *Decade of Betrayal*, 57–58.

152. Balderrama and Rodríguez, *Decade of Betrayal*, 57–58.

153. For an in-depth examination of the involvement of México's consulates around the Los Angeles area, see Balderrama, *In Defense of La Raza*.

154. Record Group 59, 811.111 México Reports/59, 80, 99, 122, and 141, 142, national Archives, Washington, D.C. The Méxican Migration Service collected these figures. Cited in Hoffman, *Unwanted Méxican Americans in the Great Depression*, 174–75.

155. For an excellent work on the political history of the massive Méxicano repatriations and deportations see Hoffman, *Unwanted Mexican Americans in The Great Depression*.

156. Balderrama and Rodríguez, *Decade of Betrayal*, 74.

157. Balderrama and Rodríguez, *Decade of Betrayal*, 2.

158. Estrada et al., "Chicanos in the United States," 46.

159. Balderrama and Rodriguez, *Decade of Betrayal*, 101.

160. Del Castillo and de León, *North to Aztlán*, 85.

161. Acuña, *Occupied America*, 263.

162. Joan Moore and Alfredo Cuellar, *Méxican Americans* (Englewood Cliffs, N.J.: Prentice-Hall, 1970), 28.

163. Gutierrez, *Walls and Mirrors*, 122.

164. Meier and Ribera, *Mexican Americans/American Méxicans*, 153.

165. Del Castillo and de León, *North to Aztlán*, 85.

Chapter 3

1. Rodolfo Acuña, *Occupied America: A History of Chicanos*, 4th ed. (New York: Addison Wesley Longman, Inc., 2000), 263.

2. Leslie V. Tischauser, *The Changing Nature of Racial and Ethnic Conflict in United States History: 1492 to the Present* (Lanham, Md.: University Press of America, 2002), 153–55.

3. The term "concentration camps" is more apropos, since the camps were isolated, enclosed with barbed wire, and patrolled by armed guards. Internees were treated as suspected Japanese war sympathizers. The camps were operated by a civilian agency, the War Relocation Authority.

4. Roger Daniels, *Guarding The Golden Door: American Immigration Policy and Immigrants since 1882* (New York: Hill and Wang, 2004), 88.

5. Daniels, *Guarding The Golden Door*, 88.

6. Daniels, *Guarding The Golden Door*, 90–92.

7. Robin Fitzgerald Scott, *The Mexican American in the Los Angeles Area, 1920–1950: From Acquiescence to Activity* (Ph.D. dissertation, University of Southern California, 1971), 156, 195, 256, and 261.

8. Matt S. Meier and Feliciano Ribera, *Méxican Americans/American Méxicans: From Conquistadores to Chicanos* (New York: Hill and Wang, 1993),159–60.

9. Cited in Armando Navarro *Mexicano Political Experience in Occupied Aztlán* (Walnut Creek, Calif.: AltaMira Press), 191-192.

10. Carlos G. Vélez-Ibáñez, *Border Visions: Méxican Cultures of the Southwest United States* (Tucson: University of Arizona Press, 1996), 200.

11. Meier and Ribera, *Méxican Americans/American Méxicans*, 160.

12. Richard Griswold Del Castillo and Arnoldo de León, *North to Aztlán: A History of Mexican Americans in the United States* (New York: Twayne Publishers, 1997), 102.

13. For a more comprehensive examination of this argument and on double-standard reality faced by Méxicanos in the United States during World War II see my book *Mexicano Political Experience in Occupied Aztlán* (Walnut Creek, Calif.: Alta Mira Press, 2005), 188–94.

14. Navarro, *Mexicano Political Experience in Occupied Aztlán*, 88.

15. Navarro, *Mexicano Political Experience in Occupied Aztlán*, 192–95.

16. For an extended examination on the particulars of this incident see Cary McWilliams, *North from Mexico: The Spanish-Speaking People of the United States* (New York: Greenwood Press, 1968), 228–33.

17. Arnoldo Carlos Vento, *Mestizo: The History, Culture and Politics of the Méxican and Chicano* (Lanham, Md.: University Press of America, 1998), 185–86.

18. David G. Gutierrez, *Walls and Mirrors: Mexican Americans, Mexican Immigrants and the Politics of Ethnicity* (Berkeley, University of California Press, 1995), 124.

19. Vento, *Mestizo*, 185.

20. Luis Valdez's well-known play and film *Zoot Suit* was a tribute to the Sleepy Lagoon incident.

21. Meier and Ribera, *Méxican Americans/American Méxicans*, 164.

22. A good portion of this chapter's section on the Bracero Program was taken with some revisions made from my book *Mexicano Political Experience in Occupied Aztlán*, 189–91, 236–44.

23. Juan Ramon García, *Operation Wetback: The Mass Deportation of Méxican Undocumented Workers in 1954* (Westport, Conn.: Greenwood Press, 1980), 25. For additional information on Operation Wetback, the McCarran-Walter Act of 1952, and the 1950 and 1960 Méxicano demographic and socioeconomic profile see my book *Mexicano Political Experience in Occupied Aztlán*, 244.

24. Ernesto Galarza, *Merchants of Labor* (Charlotte, N.C.: McNally & Loftin, Publishers, 1964), 61.

25. Kitty Calavita, *Inside the State: The Bracero Program, Immigration, and the I.N.S.* (New York: Routledge, 1992), 19.

26. The term *bracero* comes from the Spanish word *brazo* or literally, in English, "arm-man." Here it is used in the context of referring essentially to farm and railroad workers that participated in the Bracero Program.

27. There are a few excellent works on the history of the Bracero Program. Beyond Calavita's *Inside the State* see also Galarza, *Merchants of Labor*; Richard B. Craig, *The Bracero Program: Interest Groups and Foreign Policy* (Austin: University of Texas Press, 1974).

28. Julian Samora and Patricia Vandel Simon, *A History of the Méxican American People* (Notre Dame, Ind.: University of Notre Dame Press, 1977), 138.

29. Craig, *The Bracero Program*, 37.

30. Galarza, *Merchants of Labor*, 47–48.

31. Oscar J. Martinez, *Méxican Origin People in the United States: A Topical History* (Tucson: University of Arizona Press, 2001), 34.

32. Acuña, *Occupied America*, 286.

33. There are some disagreements among some scholars as to when and where the first contingent of *braceros* arrived in the U.S. Calavita, in her book *Inside The State*, argues that Stockton, California, was the first recipient, with some 500 *braceros* arriving on September 29, 1942. Juan Ramon García, in his book *Operation Wetback* propounds that the first contingent arrived on September 27, 1942, at El Paso, Texas.

34. Julian Samora, "Méxican Immigration," in *Méxican Americans Tomorrow*, ed. Gus Tyler (Albuquerque: University of New Mexico Press), 72.

35. Leobardo F. Estrada, F. Chris Garcia, Reynaldo Flores Macias, and Leonel Maldonado, "Chicanos in the United States: A History of Exploitation and Resistance," in *Latinos and the Political System*, ed. F. Chris Garcia (Notre Dame, Ind.: University of Notre Dame Press, 1988), 48.

36. Martinez, *Mexican Origin People in the United States*, 34.

37. Congressional Research Service, 1980a, 65. Cited in Calavita, *Inside The State*, 218.

38. Report of the President's Commission on Migratory Labor, "Migratory Labor in American Agriculture," 1951, 38–40.

39. Meier and Ribera, *Méxican Americans/American Méxicans*, 175–76.

40. Anne Lawrence, "The Formation of labor Market Boundaries: A Comparative Analysis of the Bracero Program in Agriculture and the Railroad Industry in the Southwest," unpublished paper. Cited in Mario Barrera, *Race and Class in the Southwest: A Theory of Racial Inequality* (Notre Dame, Ind.: University of Notre Dame Press, 1979), 117.

41. Meier and Ribera, *Méxican Americans/American Méxicans*, 175–76.

42. Nelson Gage Copp, *Wetbacks and Braceros: Mexican Migrant Laborers and American Immigration Policy, 1930-1960* (San Francisco, R and E Research Associates, 1971), 21.

43. Acuña, *Occupied America*, 286–87.

44. Acuña, *Occupied America*, 286–87.

45. Meier and Ribera, *Méxican Americans/American Méxicans*, 178–79.

46. John Chala Elac, *The Employment of Mexican Workers in U.S. Agriculture, 1900–1960, A Binational Economic Analysis* (Los Angeles: University of California Press, 1961), 43.

47. Calavita, *Inside the State*, 25.

48. Acuña, *Occupied America*, 287–88.

49. Samora, "Mexican Immigration," 71.

50. Craig, *The Bracero Program*, 68–69.

51. García, *Operation Wetback*, 70.

52. Calavita, *Inside the State*, 25, 27.

53. Meier and Ribera, *Méxican Americans/American Méxicans*, 179.

54. Copp, *Wetbacks and Braceros*, 30.

55. Copp, *Wetbacks and Braceros*, 30.

56. Copp, *Wetbacks and Braceros*, 181.

57. Craig, *The Bracero Program*, 71.

58. Copp, *Wetbacks and Braceros*, 30.

59. Manuel G. Gonzales, *Mexicanos: A History of Mexicans in the United States* (Bloomington: Indiana University Press, 2000), 172.

60. Meier and Ribera, *Méxican Americans/American Méxicans*, 183.

61. Samora, "Mexican Immigration," 72.

62. Subsequently in this chapter, a much more in-depth examination on the antimigrant position taken by both organizations is made. Suffice it to say that some of these more assimilationist-oriented groups perceived *braceros* and undocumented workers as impeding their integration into the system.

63. Gonzalez, *Mexicanos*, 175.

64. For a further examination of the reasons some Méxicanos opposed the Bracero Program, see Gonzales, *Mexicanos*, 175.

65. For an overview of union opposition to the Bracero Program, see Martinez, *Mexican Origin People in the United States*, 102–3.

66. Meier and Ribera, *Méxican Americans/American Méxicans*, 183.

67. Meier and Ribera, *Méxican Americans/American Méxicans*, 184.

68. Del Castillo and de León, *North to Aztlán*, 108.

69. García, *Operation Wetback*, 198.

70. Arthur F. Corwin and Johnny M. McCain, "Wetbackism since 1954" in *Immigrants—and Immigrants: Perspectives on Mexican Labor Mirgration to the United States*, ed. Arthur F. Corwin (Westport, Conn.: Greenwood Press, 1978), 72.

71. Barrera, *Race and Class in the Southwest*, 122.

72. Estrada et al., "Chicanos in the United States," 48.

73. For a brief analysis on the forces impelling the influx of Méxicano undocumented workers into the U.S. see Julian Samora, *Los Mojados: The Wetback Story* (Notre Dame Ind.: University of Notre Dame Press, 1971), 1–12.

74. Acuña, *Occupied America*, 303.

75. Meier and Ribera, *Méxican Americans/American Méxicans*, 187.

76. Meier and Ribera, *Méxican Americans/American Méxicans*, 186.

77. John Chavez, *The Lost Land: The Chicano Image in the Southwest* (Albuquerque: University of New Mexico Press, 1984), 125.

78. Estrada et al., "Chicanos in the United States," 48.

79. Interestingly, Samora and other scholars as well as politicians and organizational leaders in the Méxicano community unfortunately described undocumented migrants using the lexicon in vogue with nativists at the time. Samora, *Los Mojados*, 9.

80. Samora and Simon, *A History of the Mexican American People*, 143

81. While "wetback" denotes an undocumented worker that got wet crossing into the U.S., *alambre* means "wire" in English. Both "wetback" and *alambre* in most cases conjured up negative connotations. Persons or groups that were supportive of Méxicanos that allegedly were illegally in the U.S. preferred not to use either of the two terms. For a further elaboration on their usage see Samora, *Los Mojados*, 6–11.

82. Meier and Ribera, *Méxican Americans/American Méxicans*, 187.

83. Samora and Simon, *A History of the Mexican American People*, 187.

84. Joan W. Moore and Alfredo Cuéllar, *Mexican Americans* (Englewood Cliffs, N.J.: Prentice-Hall, 1970), 43.

85. Acuña, *Occupied America*, 304.

86. Acuña, *Occupied America*, 304.

87. Samora, "Mexican Immigration," 71.

88. Craig, *The Bracero Program*, 125.

89. Cited in Samora, "Mexican Immigration," 70.

90. Leo Grebler, Joan W. Moore, and Ralph C. Guzman, *The Mexican American People: The Nation's Second Largest Minority* (New York: The Free Press, 1970), 68–69.

91. Acuña, *Occupied America*, 300.

92. García, *Operation Wetback*, 231.

93. Acuña, *Occupied America*, 301.

94. Gutierrez, *Walls and Mirrors*, 161.

95. For a brief examination of the impact of the McCarran-Walter Act on Méxicanos in the U.S. see Gutierrez, *Walls and Mirrors*, 172–78; and Acuña, *Occupied America*, 300–303.

96. Gutierrez, *Walls and Mirrors*, 172–78.

97. Martinez, *Mexican-Origin People In the United States*, 152–53.

98. Acuña, *Occupied America*, 301.

99. Acuña, *Occupied America*, 301.

100. For an extensive and comprehensive case study on Operation Wetback see García, *Operation Wetback*, all.

101. Cited in Calavita, *Inside the State*, 47.

102. *New York Times* service broadcast, May 9, 1953, quoted in John Myers, *The Border Wardens* (Englewood Cliffs, N.J.: Prentice-Hall, 1971), 79–80.

103. American G. I. Forum of Texas and Texas State Federation of Labor (AFL), *What Price Wetbacks*, Austin, Texas, 1954.

104. Gutierrez, *Walls and Mirrors*, 142–43.

105. Reorganization of the Immigration and Naturalization Service, Hearings before the Subcommittee on Legal and Monetary Affairs of the Committee on Government Operations, House, 84th Congress, first session, March 9 and 17, 1955, 3.

106. Acuña, *Occupied America*, 304.

107. Alejandro Portes and Robert L. Bach, *Latin Journey: Cuban and Mexican Immigrants in the United States* (Berkeley: University of California Press, 1985), 63; Stanley Ross, ed., *Views Across the Border: The United States and Mexico* (Albuquerque: University of New Mexico Press, 1978), 166.

108. Acuña, *Occupied America*, 304.

109. Meier and Ribera, *Méxican Americans/American Méxicans*, 189.

110. Moore and Cuéllar, *Mexican Americans*, 43.
111. Moore and Cuéllar, *Mexican Americans*, 43.
112. Portes and Bach, *Latin Journey*, 63; and Ross, *Views Across the Border*, 166.
113. Samora, *Los Mojados*, 46.
114. Moore and Cuéllar, *Mexican Americans*, 43.
115. García, *Operation Wetback*, 235.
116. García, *Operation Wetback*, 522–23.
117. Del Castillo and ee León, *North to Aztlán*, 114.
118. Moore and Cuéllar, *Mexican Americans*, 57.
119. Grebler et al., *The Mexican American People*, 126.
120. Moore and Cuéllar, *Mexican Americans*, 57.
121. Moore and Cuéllar, *Mexican Americans*, 57.
122. Louis DeSipio and Rodolfo O. de la Garza, *Making Americans, Remaking America: Immigration and Immigrant Policy* (Boulder, Colo.: Westview Press, 1998), 20–21.
123. Grebler et al., *The Mexican American People*, 67, 76.

Chapter 4

1. The term of "irrendentism" comes from the Italian word *irrendenta*, which denotes "unredeemed." According to Iain McLean and Alistair McMillan "the term has been extended to any movement or aspiration to recover territory claimed back for ethnic or linguistic reasons." Source: *Oxford Concise Dictionary of Politics* (Oxford: Oxford University Press, 2003), 275. *Webster's Ninth New Collegiate Dictionary* defines "irredenta" as "a territory historically or ethnically related to one political unit but under the political control of another."

2. James G. Gimpel and James R. Edwards, Jr., *The Congressional Politics of Immigration Reform* (Boston: Allyn and Bacon, 1999), 61.

3. Peter C. Meilaender, *Toward a Theory of Immigration* (New York: Palgrave, 2001), 107.

4. Thomas Muller, *Immigrants and the American City* (New York: New York University Press, 1993), 47.

5. Mae M. Ngai, *Impossible Subjects: Illegal Aliens and the Making of Modern America* (Princeton, N.J.: Princeton University Press, 2004), 259.

6. L. Edward Purcell, *Immigration* (Phoenix, Ariz.: Oryx Press, 1995), 93–94.

7. Purcell, *Immigration*, 94.

8. For a more comprehensive examination and analysis on the Hart-Celler Act see Carolyn Wong, *Lobbying for Inclusion: Rights Politics and the Making of Immigration Policy* (Stanford, Calif.: Stanford University Press, 2006), 44–63.

9. Maldwyn Allen Jones, *American Immigration* (Chicago: University of Chicago Press, 1992), 266–67.

10. The term is used to describe persons whose ethnic and cultural roots and linkages were with countries from México, Latin America, and Spain. In this chapter, I use Latino, which I feel is more appropriate as an umbrella term because it is more inclusive and his-

torically and culturally appropriate. Hispanic accentuates linkages to the Iberian Peninsula, that is, Spain and Portugal, and negates the strong Amerindian and mestizo/mulatto roots of the historical experiences of the Americas. Only when the analysis warrants will Hispanic be used.

11. Juan Andrade, ed., *The Almanac of Latino Politics* (Chicago: The United States Hispanic Leadership Institute, 2006), 2.

12. U.S. Department of Commerce, Bureau of the Census, "Persons of Spanish Origin in the United States: March 1973," *Current Population Reports*, Series P-20, no. 259, January 1974.

13. U.S. Department of Commerce, "Persons of Spanish Origin," 54–58.

14. U.S. Department of Commerce, "Persons of Spanish Origin," 52–58.

15. U.S. Department of Commerce, "Persons of Spanish Origin," 62.

16. Moore and Pachon, *Hispanics in the United States,* 51–52.

17. Because it conjures up strong biases toward Spain while minimizing the Amerindian and Mestizo aspects of Latin America the term Latino includes them; consequently, making it more applicable to describe peoples whose origin and culture are rooted in Latin America.

18. Joan Moore and Harry Pachon, *Hispanics in the United States* (Englewood Cliffs, N.J.: Prentice Hall, 1985), 52.

19. Moore and Pachon, *Hispanics in the United States*, 52.

20. Moore and Pachon, *Hispanics in the United States*, 56.

21. Rogelio Saenz and Clyde S. Greenlees, "The Demography of Chicanos," in *Chicanas and Chicanos in Contemporary Society*, ed. Roberto M. De Anda (Boston: Allyn and Bacon, 1995), 9–23.

22. U.S. Bureau of the Census, General Population Characteristics; Armando Navarro, *The Mexicano Political Experience in Occupied Aztlán* (Walnut Creek, Calif.: Alta Mira Press, 2005) 426.

23. Cited in Maurilio E. Vigil, *Hispanics In American Politics: The Search for Political Power* (Lanham, Md.: University Press of America, 1987), 5.

24. Moore and Pachon, *Hispanics in the United States*, 56.

25. Moore and Pachon, *Hispanics in the United States*, 53.

26. The phrase alludes to both the demographic change brought about by the re-Méxicanization of Aztlán and the Latinoization or "browning" of the U.S.

27. Purcell, *Immigration*, 97.

28. Meilaender, *Toward A Theory of Immigration*, 107.

29. Louis DeSipio and Rodolfo O. de la Garza, *Making Americans, Remaking America* (Boulder, Colo.: Westview Press, 1998), 50.

30. Otis L. Graham, Jr., *Unguarded Gates: A History of America's Immigration Crisis* (Lanham, Md.: Rowman & Littlefield Publishers, Inc., 2004), 99.

31. Ngai, *Impossible Subjects*, 273.

32. Gimpel and Edwards, *The Congressional Politics of Immigration Reform*, 7–8.

33. Héctor Aguilar Camín and Lorenzo Meyer, *In the Shadow of the Mexican Revolution: Contemporary Mexican History, 1910–1989* (Austin: University of Texas Press, 1993), 227–28.

34. INS data, also cited in Roger Daniels, *Guarding The Golden Door* (New York: Hill and Wang, 2004), 181.

35. Purcell, *Immigration*, 103.

36. Purcell, *Immigration*, 97.

37. Michael C. LeMay, *From Open Door to Dutch Door: An Analysis of U.S. Immigration Policy Since 1820* (New York: Praeger, 1987), 114.

38. John Powell, *Encyclopedia of North American Immigration*, (New York: Facts on File, 2005), 359

39. Daniels, *Guarding the Golden Door*, 203.

40. Graham, *Unguarded Gates*, 197.

41. Moore and Pachon, *Hispanics in the United States*, 36.

42. Lisandro Perez, "The End of Exile? A New Era in U.S. Immigration Policy toward Cuba," in *Free Markets, Open Societies, Closed Borders: Trends in International Migration and Immigration Policy in the Americas*, ed. Max J. Castro (Miami, Fla.: North South Center Press, 1999), 198.

43. LeMay, *From Open Door to Dutch Door*, 114.

44. For a comprehensive account of the Cuban exodus to the United States see P. Gallager, *The Cuban Exile* (New York: Academic Press, 1980); José Llanes, *Cuban Americans* (Cambridge, Mass.: ABT, 1982).

45. Purcell, *Immigration*, 98–99.

46. Perez, "The End of Exile?", 198–99.

47. Purcell, *Immigration*, 98.

48. Purcell, *Immigration*, 266.

49. Oscar Martinez, *Mexican–Origin People in the United States* (Tucson: University of Arizona Press, 2001), 39.

50. Ngai, *Impossible Subjects*, 274.

51. Andrade, *The Almanac of Latino Politics*, 45.

52. For an excellent historical overview on the immigration issue see Rodolfo Acuña, *Occupied America: A History of Chicanos*, 4th ed. (New York: Addison Wesley Longman, Inc., 2000), 402–7.

53. Acuña, *Occupied America*, 406.

54. Acuña, *Occupied America*, 406.

55. Acuña, *Occupied America*, 403.

56. Acuña, *Occupied America*, 405.

57. Richard Griswold del Castillo and Arnoldo de Leon, *North to Aztlán: A History of Mexican Americans in the United States* (New York: Twayne Publishers, 1997), 162.

58. Lisa Magaña, *Straddling the Border: Immigration Policy and the INS* (Austin: University of Texas Press, 2003), 37–38.

59. Matt S. Meier and Feliciano Ribera, *Méxican Americans/American Méxicans: From Conquistadores to Chicanos* (New York: Hill and Wang, 1993), 285.

60. Arthur F. Corwin and Johnny M. McCain, "Wetbackism Since 1954," in *Immigrants—and Immigrants: Perspectives on Mexican Labor Migration to the United States*, ed. Arthur F. Corwin (Westport, Conn.: Greenwood Press, 1978), 73.

61. Gimpel and Edwards, *The Congressional Politics of Immigration Reform*, 135.

62. Magaña, *Straddling the Fence*, 38.

63. Meier and Ribera, *Méxican Americans/American Méxicans*, 266.

64. Carl Rowan, *Cincinnati Enquirer*, June 21, 1986.

65. Alan Simpson, *Washington Post*, April 28, 1981.

66. Cited in Daniels, *Guarding the Golden Door*, 222.

67. Del Castillo and de Leon, *North to Aztlán*, 162.

68. Gimple and Edwards, *The Congressional Poltics of Immigration Reform*, 141.

69. For a comprehensive and excellent account of the politics of the Simpson-Mazzoli legislation within both the House of Representatives and Senate see Gimpel and Edwards, *The Congressional Politics of Immigration Reform*, 136–69.

70. Jones, *American Immigration*, 287.

71. Jones, *American Immigration*, 287.

72. Jones, *American Immigration*, 287.

73. Ngai, *Impossible Subjects*, 266.

74. Jones, *American Immigration*, 287.

75. Muller, *Immigrants and the American City*, 58.

76. Muller, *Immigrants and the American City*, 59.

77. For an extensive analysis on the politics and various amendments considered by both chambers and an analysis on how Republicans and Democrats voted see Gimpel and Edwards, *The Congressional Politics of Immigration Reform*, 169–80.

78. Acuña, *Occupied America*, 424.

79. Daniels, *Guarding the Golden Door*, 225.

80. Michael S. Teitelbaum and Myron Weiner, eds., *Threatened Peoples, Threatened Borders: World Migration & U.S. Policy* (New York: Norton, 1995), 171.

81. Without getting into a historical or political analysis of its origins in the context of this work, "Chicano" denotes a Méxicano born in the United States. For a broader analysis of the term see my book *Mexicano Political Experience in Occupied Aztlán* (Walnut Creek, Calif.: Alta Mira Press, 2005), 314–15, 338–40, 406–8.

82. For an extensive examination of the Chicano movement see my books *Mexicano Political Experience in Occupied Aztlán*; *Mexican American Youth Organization: Avant-Garde of the Chicano Movement in Texas* (Austin: University of Texas Press, 1995); *The Cristal Experiment: A Chicano Struggle for Community Control* (Madison: University of Wisconsin Press, 1998); and *La Raza Unida Party: A Chicano Challenge to the U.S. Two-Party Dictatorship* (Philadelphia: Temple University Press, 2000).

83. Interview, Herman Baca, May 10, 2002.

84. For a more comprehensive examination of the myriad of conflicts that plagued the Forum see my books *Mexicano Political Experience in Occupied Aztlán*, 441; and *La Raza Unida Party*, 249.

85. Navarro, *La Raza Unida Party*, 249.

86. Gutierrez's letter was published in its entirety in *The Militant*, "A Call for Action," June 10, 1977.

87. Del Castillo and de León, *North to Aztlán*, 162.

88. Del Castillo and de León, *North to Aztlán*, 135.

89. Navarro, *La Raza Unida Party*, 251–52.

90. Navarro, *La Raza Unida Party*, 251–52.

91. Navarro, *La Raza Unida Party*, 251–52.

92. In the subsequent chapter in the section dealing with organizational development a more extensive examination of these organizations is provided.

93. For more details on the politics of the organizations and activities initiated to defeat the Simpson-Mazzoli bill see my book *Mexicano Political Experience in Occupied Aztlán*, chapter 6.

94. Navarro, *Mexicano Political Experience in Occupied Aztlán*, chapter 6.

95. Navarro, *Mexicano Political Experience in Occupied Aztlán*, chapter 6.

96. Jean Stefancic, "Funding the Nativist Agenda," in *Immigrants Out! The New Nativism and Anti-Immigrant Impulse in the United States*, ed. Juan F. Parea (New York: New York University Press, 1997), 120–21.

97. Del Castillo and de Leon, *North to Aztlán*, 161.

98. Acuña, *Occupied America*, 425.

99. Navarro, *Mexicano Political Experience in Occupied Aztlán*, 556.

Chapter 5

1. Much of this section on demographics is taken from my book *Mexicano Political Experience in Occupied Aztlán* (Walnut Creek, Calif.: Alta Mira Press, 2005), 428–30.

2. Juan Andrade, ed., *The Almanac of Latino Politics*, 4th ed. (Chicago: The United States Hispanic Leadership Institute, 2006), 2.

3. Rogelio Saenz and Clyde Greenlees, "The Demography of Chicanos," in *Chicanas and Chicanos in Contemporary Society*, ed. Roberto M. De Anda (Boston: Allyn and Bacon, 1996), 13.

4. Saenz and Greenlees, "The Demography of Chicanos," 9.

5. National Council of La Raza, "State of Hispanic America 1991: An Overview," Washington, D.C., August 2001.

6. Randolph E. Schmidt, "Hispanics Get New Census Profile," *The Press Enterprise*, July 27, 1995.

7. National Council of La Raza, "State of Hispanic America."

8. For a national breakdown of the total Méxicano population on a state basis, see U.S. Bureau of the Census, *1990 Census of Population and Housing Summary Tape 1C*.

9. Saenz and Greenlees, "The Demography of Chicanos," 13.

10. Saenz and Greenlees, "The Demography of Chicanos," 14.

11. Saenz and Greenlees, "The Demography of Chicanos," 16.

12. Saenz and Greenlees, "The Demography of Chicanos," 16–17.

13. Frank Sotomayor, "State Shows 69.2% Rise in Latino Population," *Los Angeles Times*, March 28, 1991.

14. Leonard Dinnerstein, Roger L. Nichols, and David M. Reimers, *Natives and Strangers: Blacks, Indians, and Immigrants in America*, 2nd edition (New York: Oxford University Press, 1990), 270.

15. Oscar J. Martinez, *Méxican-Origin People in the United States: A Topical History* (Tucson: University of Arizona Press, 2001), 39.

16. Arturo González, *Mexican Americans & the U.S. Economy: Quest for Buenos Días* (Tucson: University of Arizona Press, 2002), 28.

17. Ken Ellingwood, "Data on Border Arrests Raise Gatekeeper Debate," *Los Angeles Times*, October 1, 1999.

18. Patrick J.McDonnell, "1990s on Track to Set a Record for Immigration," *Los Angeles Times*, January 24, 1999.

19. Sue Schultz, "INS to Add 1,600 Agents, Inspectors," *The Press Enterprise*, February 18, 1999.

20. Cited in Martinez, *Mexican-Origin People in the United States*, 39.

21. González, *Mexican Americans & the U.S. Economy*, 25.

22. David E. Lorey, *The U.S.-Mexican Border in the Twentieth Century* (Wilmington, Del.: Scholarly Resources, Inc., 1999), 135.

23. McDonnell, "1990s on Track to Set a Record for Immigration."

24. Andrade, *The Almanac of Latino Politics*, 45, 47.

25. Robert A. Rosenblatt, "Latinos, Asians, to Lead Rise in U.S. Population," *Los Angeles Times*, March 14, 1996.

26. National Council of La Raza, "State of Hispanic America 1991."

27. Joan Moore and Harry Pachon, *Hispanics in the United States* (Englewood Cliffs, N.J.: Prentice Hall, 1985), 53 and 64.

28. Colleen Kruger, "California's Residents Are Now Outwardly Mobile," *Los Angeles Times*, October 11, 1995.

29. In chapter 7 a much more detailed examination of nativist groups is made. The intent in this chapter is merely to provide the reader with some background as to why the "political war" against immigrants was declared by nativists.

30. Richard D. Lamm and Gary Imhoff, *The Immigration Time Bomb: The Fragmenting of America* (New York: Truman Talley Books, 1985).

31. Peter Brimelow, *Alien Nation: Common Sense about America's Immigration Disaster* (New York: Random House, 1995), hardcover back cover page.

32. Thomas Muller, *Immigrants and the American City* (New York: New York University Press, 1993, 291.

33. For a more comprehensive examination of the 1990 Immigration Act see Carolyn Wong, *Lobbying for Inclusion: Rights Politics and the Making of Immigration Policy* (Stanford, Calif.: Stanford University Press, 2006), 101–7.

34. Roger Daniels, *Guarding The Golden Door: American Immigration Policy and Immigrants since 1882* (New York: Hill and Wang, 2004), 237.

35. Daniels, *Guarding the Golden Door*, 237.

36. Daniels, *Guarding the Golden Door*, 238.

37. James G. Gimpel and James R. Edwards, Jr., *The Congressional Politics of Immigration Reform* (Boston: Allyn and Bacon, 1999), 192–93.

38. Wong, *Lobbying for Inclusion*, 105–7.

39. Wong, *Lobbying for Inclusion*, 133.

40. Vernon M. Briggs, Jr., *Mass Immigration and the National Interest: Policy Directions for the New Century*, 3rd ed., (Armonk, N.Y.: M.E. Sharpe, 2003), 260–61.

41. Alma Garcia, *The Mexican Americans* (Westport, Conn.: Greenwood Press), 49.

42. Gimpel and Edwards, *The Congressional Politics of Immigration Reform*, 219.

43. Briggs, *Mass Immigration and the National Interest*, 260; and Gimpel and Edwards, *The Congressional Politics of Immigration Reform*, 225.

44. *Cuban Immigration Support*, "Cuban Immigration to the United States," usimmigrationsupport.org/cubaimmigration.html.

45. usimmigrationsupport.org/cubaimmigration.html.

46. Oscar Martinez, *Troublesome Border* (Tucson: University of Arizona Press, 2006), 134.

47. For a more extensive overview of the economic policies of de la Madrid see Lynn V. Foster, *A Brief History of Mexico* (New York: Checkmark Books, 2004), 214–21.

48. Burton Kirkwood, *The History of Mexico*, (Westport, Connecticut: Greenwood Press, 2000), 206; and Foster, *A Brief History of Mexico*, 225.

49. Mark Freeman, "México Uses $4 Billion from U.S. Bailout to Pay Investors," *Los Angeles Times*, April 5, 1995.

50. Chris Kraul, "México Says Economy Grew 8.8% in Quarter," *Los Angeles Times*, August 19, 1997.

51. John Ross, *The Annexation of Mexico: From Aztecas to the I.M.F.* (Monroe, Maine: Common Courage Press, 1998), 195.

52. James D. Cockcroft, *Mexico's Hope: An Encounter with Politics and History* (New York: Monthly Review Press, 1998), 243, 245.

53. Cockcroft, *Mexico's Hope*, 243, 245.

54. Kirkwood, *The History of Mexico*, 211–12.

55. Maria del Pilar Marrero, "Califica de 'bomba' la ley de inmigración," *La Opinion*, April 23, 1997.

56. Francisco Robles, "Cerca de 24 millones de Mexicanos se encuentran en pobreza extrema," *La Opinion*, January 16, 1997.

57. Francisco Robles, "13 millones sin trabajo en campo Mexicano," *La Opinion*, March 26, 1997.

58. Associated Press, "México workers' patience wears thin," *Press Enterprise*, January 2, 2000.

59. Associated Press, "México workers' patience wears thin."

60. The *maquiladoras*, a product of the Border Industrialization Program started in 1965, were evidence of crass economic exploitation. They consisted of hundreds of assembly plants operated chiefly by U.S., Japanese, and Korean transnational corporations along the U.S.–México border. While they created some employment, they paid their workers subsistence wages, which translated to hourly wages of 50 to 75 cents per hour.

61. For an extensive examination on NAFTA see Justin Ankers Chacon and Mike Davis, *No One Is Illegal: Fighting Racism and State Violence on the U.S./Mexico Border* (Chicago: Haymarket Books, 2006), chapter 14.

62. Iain McLean and Alistair McMillian, *Oxford Concise Dictionary of Politics* (Oxford: Oxford University Press), 359.

63. Martinez, *Troublesome Border*, 106.

64. Martinez, *Troublesome Border*, 106

65. Chacon and Davis, *No One Is Illegal*, 120.

66. Foster, *The History of Mexico*, 230.

67. For an examination of the "*maquiladora* program" see Lorey, *The U.S.-Mexican Border in the Twentieth Century*, chapter 5.

68. Foster, *The History of Mexico*, 230–31.

69. Matt S. Meier and Feliciano Ribera, *Méxican Americans/American Méxicans: From Conquistadores to Chicanos* (New York: Hill and Wang, 1993), 268–69.

70. For a further examination of the myriad of polls that showed an anti-immigrant bias see Daniels, *Guarding the Golden Door*, 232–34.

71. Elizabeth Martinez, "The U.S. Should Not Make Immigrants Scapegoats," in *Immigration Policy*, ed. Scott Barbour (San Diego: Greenview Press, Inc., 1995), 100–103.

72. Cited in Joseph Nevins, *Operation Gatekeeper: The Rise of the Illegal Alien and the Making of the U.S.-Mexico Boundary* (New York: Routledge, 2002), 86.

73. Nevins, *Operation Gatekeeper, 87.*

74. Martinez, "The U.S. Should Not Make Immigrants Scapegoats," 90.

75. For a comprehensive examination of Operation Gatekeeper see Nevins, *Operation Gatekeeper*, 11.

76. Nevins, *Operation Gatekeeper*, 11.

77. Nevins, *Operation Gatekeeper*, 11.

78. Wayne A. Cornelius, "The Structural Embeddedness of Demand for Mexican Immigrant Labor: New Evidence from California," in *Crossings: Mexican Immigration in Interdisciplinary Perspectives*, ed. Marcelo M. Suárez-Orosco (Cambridge, Mass.: Harvard University Press, 1998), 129.

79. For an interesting and in-depth analysis on the military aspects of the various border operations see José Palafox, "Militarizing the Border," *CAQ* 56 (Spring 1996).

80. Peter Andreas, "The U.S. Immigration Control Offensive: Constructing an Image of Order on the Southwest Border," in *Crossings: Mexican Immigration in Interdisciplinary Perspectives*, ed. Marcelo M. Suárez-Orosco (Cambridge, Mass.: Harvard University Press, 1998), 345.

81. Associated Press, "Legal Immigration Rate Drops to its Lowest Level in a Decade," *Press Enterprise*, August 12, 1999.

82. Sue Schultz, "INS to Add 1,600 Agents, Inspectors," *Press Enterprise*, February 18, 1999; Elsie Ackerman, "Finally, an Effective Fence," *U.S. News & World Report*, October 19, 1998; Ken Ellingwood, "Data on Border Arrests Raise Gatekeeper Debate," *Los Angeles Times*, October 1, 1999; and Michelle Mittlestadt, "INS Deports Record Number of Illegal Immigrants," *Press Enterprise*, November 13, 1999.

83. Navarro, *Mexicano Political Experience in Occupied Aztlán*, 448.

84. Leticia Garcia-Irigoyen, "Aumenta cifra de muertes en la frontera," *La Opinion*, August 5, 1999; Mark Henry, "Death Looms for Unwary Bent on Crossing Border," *Press Enterprise*, March 29, 1999.

85. La Resistencia, Summer Border Project Newsletter #1, June 30, 1997.

86. Gimpel and Edwards, *The Congressional Politics of Immigration Reform*, 225.

87. Briggs, *Mass Immigration and the National Interest*, 260–61.

88. Briggs, *Mass Immigration and the National Interest*, 260–61.

89. Gimpel and Edwards, *The Congressional Politics of Immigration Reform*, 238–39.

90. Debra L. Delaet, *U.S. Immigration Policy in an Age of Rights* (Westport, Conn.: Praeger, 2000), 126–27.

91. Delaet, *U.S. Immigration Policy in an Age of Rights*, 126–27.

92. Lisa Magaña, *Straddling the Border* (Austin: University of Texas Press, 2003), 83; and George J. Borjas, *Heaven's Door: Immigration Policy and the American Economy* (Princeton, N.J.: Princeton University Press, 1999), 119.

93. Borjas, *Heaven's Door*, 120.

94. William A.V. Clark, *Immigrants and the American Dream: Remaking the Middle Class* (New York: The Guilford Press, 2003), 54.

95. Gimple and Edwards, *The Congressional Politics of Immigration Reform*, 289–94.

96. Gimple and Edwards, *The Congressional Politics of Immigration Reform*, 289–94; and Delaet, *U.S. Immigration Policy in an Age of Rights*, 127.

97. For a specific summary of IIRIRA's provisions also see Magaña, *Straddling the Border*, 84–85.

98. Magaña, *Straddling the Border*, 53.

99. Joe R. Feagin, "Old Poison in New Bottles: The Deep Roots of Modern Nativism," in *Immigrants Out! The New Nativism and the Anti-Immigrant Impulse in the United States*, ed. Juan F. Parea (New York: New York University Press, 1997), 35.

100. For a comprehensive examination of the 1990 demographic statistics see Navarro, *Mexicano Political Experience in Occupied Aztlán*, 426–30.

101. Louis DeSipio and Rodolfo O. de la Garza, *Making Americans, Remaking America: Immigration and Immigrant Policy* (Boulder, Colo.: Westview Press, 1998), 112.

102. Jean Stefancic, "Funding the Nativist Agenda," in *Immigrants Out! The New Nativism and the Anti-Immigrant Impulse in the United States*, ed. Juan F. Parea (New York: New York University Press, 1997), 126.

103. For an abbreviated analysis on Proposition 187 see Kevin Johnson, "The New Nativism: Something Old, Something New, Something Blue," in *Immigrants Out! The New Nativism and the Anti-Immigrant Impulse in the United States*, ed. Juan F. Parea (New York: New York University Press, 1997), 177–80; Rodolfo Acuña, *Occupied America: A History of Chicanos*, 4th ed. (New York: Addison Wesley Longman, Inc., 2000), 452–53; Suarez-Orazco, *Crossings*, 97–98; Nevins, *Operation Gatekeeper*, 91–92.

104. Otis L. Graham, Jr., *Unguarded Gates: A History of America's Immigration Crisis* (Lanham, Md.: Rowman & Littlefield Publishers, Inc., 2004), 155.

105. Leo Chavez, "Immigration Reform and Nativism: The Nationalist Response to the Transnationalist Challenge," in *Immigrants Out! The New Nativism and the Anti-Immigrant Impulse in the United States*, ed. Juan F. Parea (New York: New York University Press, 1997), 63.

106. Martinez, *Mexican Origin People in the United States*, 43–44.

107. Martinez, *Mexican Origin People in the United States*, 44.

108. As a result of the great pressures produced by the civil rights movement on the issue of putting an end to discrimination in the workplace, affirmative action programs were born. They were a product of several executive orders, legislation, and government regulations. John Kennedy's Executive Orders 10925 and 11114 prohibited discrimination on the bases of race, national origin, and religion, and required affirmative action to ensure nondiscrimination by government contractors. The Johnson administration passed successfully its Civil Rights Act of 1964, which under Title VII empowered courts to order firms guilty of discrimination to take "affirmative action" in order to ensure "equal opportunity." In 1965, President Johnson signed Executive Order 11246, which rebuttressed President Kennedy's earlier Executive Orders. Paradoxically, it was Republican President Richard Nixon who was initially responsible for introducing quotas as illustrated by his adoption during the early 1970s of the "Philadelphia Plan," which called

for the direct imposition of hiring goals in the construction trade. For a comprehensive examination on the history and politics of affirmative action programs as they apply to various ethnic groups see John David Skrentny, ed., *Color Lines: Affirmative Action, Immigration, and Civil Rights Options for America* (Chicago: University of Chicago Press, 2001); and Carol M. Swain, "Affirmative Action: Legislative History, Judicial Interpretations, Public Consensus," in *America Becoming: Racial Trends and Consequences*, vol. 1, ed. Neil J. Smelser, Julian Wilson, and Faith Mitchell (Washington, D.C.: National Academy Press, 2001), 318–47.

109. Swain, "Affirmative Action," 328.

110. For an excellent examination of the effects of the Bakke decision on affirmative action programs see Susan Welch and John Gruhl, *Affirmative Action and Minority Enrollments in Medical and Law Schools* (Ann Arbor: University of Michigan Press, 1998), 107–44.

111. Skrentny, *Color Lines*, 53.

112. For an excellent overview on the issue of Proposition 209 see Acuña, *Occupied America*, 453–54.

113. Skrentny, *Color Lines*, 53.

114. Skrentny, *Color Lines*, 53.

115. Nick Anderson and Peter M. Warren, "Bid to Cut Bilingual Classes Qualifies for June '98 Ballot," *Los Angeles Times*, December 24, 1997.

116. Nick Anderson, "Debate Loud as Vote Nears on Bilingual Ban," *Los Angeles Times*, March 23, 1998.

117. Stewart M. Powell and Eun Lee Koh, "Clinton to Fight Bilingual Ban," *Press Enterprise*, April 28, 1998.

118. Cragg Hines, "Gingrich Wants End to Bilingual Education," *Press Enterprise*, January 6, 1998.

119. Jonathan Peterson, "White House to Announce Opposition to Prop. 227," *Los Angeles Times*, April 27, 1998.

120. Acuña, *Occupied America*, 455.

121. Armando Navarro, proceedings entitled "The Immigration Crisis: Latino Public Policy Response," National Summit Conference on Immigration, Ernesto Galarza Think Tank on Public Policy, University of California, Riverside, January 6, 7, and 8, 1994.

122. Frank Trejo, "Hispanic Officials, Organizers Meet to Fight Anti-Immigrant Views," *The Dallas Morning News*, January 9, 1994; Associated Press, "Hispanics Condemn Political Attacks," January 9, 1994; Mark Bryant, "Conference Puts Out Call for Latino Power," *Press Enterprise*, January 9, 1994; Jeff Dillon, "Latinos See Unity as Key to Future," *Desert Sun*, January 9, 1994.

123. Navarro, "The Immigration Crisis: Latino Public Policy Response."

124. *Los Angeles Times*, "Plan Unveiled to Counter Anti-Immigrant Sentiment," February 12, 1994; Rosalva Hernandez, "Hispanics Offer Own Immigration Reform," *Orange County Register*, February 12, 1994; George Ronney, "Anti-Immigrant Fervor Targeted by Latino Activists," *Press Enterprise*, February 12, 1994; Teresa Jimenez, "Latinos Call for Immigrant Rights," *Desert Sun*, February 12, 1994; *La Opinion*, "Líderes Latinos Lanzan el 'Plan Riverside' para Proteger a los Inmigrantes," February 12, 1994.

125. Acuña, *Occupied America*, 453.

126. Under the auspices of the National Alliance for Human Rights (NAHR), I along with numerous others from throughout Southern California participated in the said three marches. Hence, this brief account is based upon my involvement as a participant-observer. Also several from NAHR, including myself, intervened in the various school walkouts in order to ensure the safety and security of the students. In October, in San Bernardino, an anti-Proposition 187 coalition, which I assisted in forming, held a march and rally, which was attended by over 1,000 people.

127. Armando Navarro, "A Post 187 Strategy for Mobilization," second National Summit Conference on Immigration, Ernesto Galarza Public Policy and Humanities Research Institute, January 13 and 14, 1995, located in my archives.

128. Navarro, "A Post 187 Strategy for Mobilization."

129. For a further elaboration on the impact of Proposition 209 and other related issues such as the Hopwood decision, see my book *Mexicano Political Experience in Occupied Aztlán*, 450–51.

130. *Los Angeles Times*, "Let Washington Pick Up the Check," December 3, 1996.

131. Martinez, *Mexican-Origin People in the United States*, 44; and David Ogul, "1 Deputy Fired, 1 Suspended," *Press Enterprise*, June 12, 1996.

132. *Impacto 2000 Press Release*, "National Mobilization for a Rally and March along the U.S./México Border in Protest of the Republican Convention," July 26, 1996.

133. Invitation letter, Chicano Federation of San Diego County, July 27, 1996.

134. I along with other activists from California supported the march and provided some organizing assistance. A delegation of activists from San Bernardino/Riverside counties participated.

135. Document, "Puntos De Acuerdo De La Segunda Reunion De Los Signatarios Del Pacto De Californias," February 11, 1997. Navarro archives.

136. Adriana Chavira, "Latinos Plan Counter-Rally Near the Border," *Daily Bulletin*, March 2, 1997; Frank Kilmko, "Taunts Traded at Rally Marking Construction of New Border Fence," *San Diego Union-Tribune*, March 23, 1997.

137. Chavira, "Latinos Plan Counter-Rally Near the Border"; Kilmko, "Taunts Traded at Rally Marking Construction of New Border Fence."

138. Cathleen Decker, "Bilingual Education Ban Widely Supported," *Los Angeles Times*, April 13, 1998.

139. Roberto Rodriguez and Patrisia Gonzales, "A Bifurcated Approach to Bilingual Education," *Los Angeles Times*, December 14, 1997.

140. Mary Ballesteros-Coronel, "Protestan contra la 227," *La Opinion*, June 12, 1998.

141. Mary Ballesteros-Coronel and Lillian de la Torres-Jiménez, "Demandarán si la 227 es aprobada," *La Opinion*, May 30,1998.

142. Nick Anderson and Louis Sahagun, "Judge Refuses to Stand in Way of Prop. 227," *Los Angeles Times*, July 16, 1998.

143. Richard Lee Colvin and Doug Smith, "Prop. 227 Foes Vow to Block It Despite Wide Vote Margin," *Los Angeles Times*, June 4, 1998.

144. *Press Enterprise*, "Prop. 227 waiver for schools urged," September 11, 1998; and Associated Press, "New Bilingual Education Rules OK'd," *Press Enterprise*, October 9, 1998.

145. Patrick J. McDonnell, "Davis Won't Appeal Prop. 187 Ruling, Ending Court Battles," *Los Angeles Times*, July 29, 1999.

Chapter 6

1. "Vigilante" denotes a person or persons that joins and participates with a group that takes the law into their own hands to punish a crime they perceive has been perpetrated.

2. Much of the demographic data listed in this section was derived from my book *Mexicano Political Experience in Occupied Aztlán* (Walnut Creek, Calif.: Alta Mira Press, 2005), 571–80.

3. "Latino" is my term of preference that incorporates Méxicanos and all others whose historical and cultural roots are deeply imbedded in the region and part of the Western Hemisphere designated by most scholars as Latin America. However, when appropriate for purposes of placing emphasis on the Méxicano, but also involving other Latinos, Méxicano/Latino is used.

4. National Council of La Raza, *Beyond the Census: Hispanics and an American Agenda*, August 2001.

5. Genaro C. Armas, "Hispanics Now Outnumber Blacks in U.S.," Associated Press, January 22, 2003.

6. Census Bureau, "The Hispanic Population in the United States: March 2002," June 2003, www.census.gov/prod/2003pubs/p20-545.pdf.

7. Marilú Meza, "Aumenta población de Latinos," *La Opinion*, June 19, 2003.

8. *The World Almanac and Book of Facts 2005* (New York: New York Times, 2005), 8.

9. Juan Andrade, Andrew Hernandez, Laura Barberena-Medrano, *The Almanac of Latino Politics: 2002-2004* (Chicago: United States Hispanic Leadership Institute, 2002).

10. The aforementioned figures have been rounded up. For example, the exact Latino population percentage was 13.5 percent and African Americans were 12.7 percent.

11. Andrade, Hernandez, and Laura Barberena-Medrano, *The Almanac of Latino Politics 2002–2004*, 10–11.

12. The aforementioned Census Bureau demographic data was cited in the following newspaper articles: Marilú Meza, "Aumenta población de Latinos," *La Opinion*, June 19, 2003; Ricardo Alonso-Zaldivar, "Latinos Now Top Minority," *Los Angeles Times*, June 19, 2003; Stephan Wall, "Latino Growth Surges in U.S.," *Desert Sun*, June 19, 2003; Andres Viglucci and Tim Henderson, "Hispanics Pass Blacks as Largest U.S. Minority," *Miami Herald*, June 19, 2003.

13. Mark Stevenson, "Mexican Population of U.S. May Reach 18 Million by 2030," *Press Enterprise*, December 6, 2001; and Geoffrey Mohan, "Mexican Immigration Could Boom in U.S., Report Says," *Los Angeles Times*, December 6, 2001.

14. Geoffrey Mohan, "Mexican Immigration Could Boom in U.S., Report Says," *Los Angeles Times*, December 6, 2001.

15. Alonzo-Zaldivar, "Latinos Now Top Minority."

16. The aforementioned Census Bureau demographic data was cited in the following newspaper articles: Meza, "Aumenta población de Latinos"; Alonso-Zaldivar, "Latinos Now Top Minority"; Wall, "Latino Growth Surges in U.S."; Viglucci and Henderson, "Hispanics Pass Blacks as Largest U.S. Minority."

17. Ibid. The above mentioned demographics were referenced in all the above sources.

18. U.S. Census, "Hispanic Population by Type for Regions, States, and Puerto Rico: 1990 and 2000," table 2, www.census.gov/prod/2001pubs/c2kbr01-3.pdf.

19. Francisco Y. Honorio III, "New Southern Menu: Poultry and Latinos," *Hispanic Week Link Weekly Report* 19, no. 31, August 6, 2001.

20. For an excellent work on the growing tensions/conflicts between Latinos and Blacks see Nicolas C. Vaca, *The Presumed Alliance: The Unspoken Conflict Between Latinos and Blacks and What It Means for America,* (New York: Rao, 2004.

21. Stephan Simon, "Latinos Take Root in Midwest," *Los Angeles Times,* October 24, 2002.

22. Sharyn Obsatz, "Inland Area a Hub of Latino Growth," *Press Enterprise,* July 31, 2002.

23. National Council of La Raza, *Beyond the Census: Hispanics and an American Agenda,* August 2001; Richard T. Cooper, "Racial Ethnic Diversity Puts New Face on Middle America," *Los Angeles Times,* March 31, 2001.

24. Joe Donatelli, "Latinos Joining White Flight," *Press Enterprise,* November 3, 2002.

25. Brookings Center on Urban and Metropolitan Policy. Cited in Andrade et al., *The Almanac of Latino Politics 2002–2004,* 5.

26. Jennifer Mena, "7 State Cities in Diversity Top 10," *Los Angeles Times,* September 4, 2003.

27. Robin Fields and Ray Rendon, "Segregation of a New Sort Takes Shape," *Los Angeles Times,* July 5, 2001.

28. "U.S. Foreign-Born Population by Regional Origin, 1995–2005," Current Population Surveys, U.S. Census Bureau, U.S. Department of Commerce, www.census.gov/population/www/projections/ppl47.html.

29. *The World Almanac and Book of Facts 2003,* 405.

30. "Growth of U.S. Hispanics dramatic," www.quepasa.com, June 20, 2003.

31. Nicole Gaouette, "Latinos Boost U.S. Population," *Los Angeles Times,* May 10, 2006.

32. Gaouette, "Latinos Boost U.S. Population."

33. *La Opinión,* "Se Duplica la población indocumentada en los años 90," January 24, 2002.

34. *Press Enterprise,* "Fewer Border Crossers Arrested," September 17, 2002.

35. *La Opinión,* "Una Quinta parte de los 'legales' son mexicano," September 5, 2002.

36. Aaron Zitner, "Nation's Birthrate Drops to Its Lowest Level Since 1909," *Los Angeles Times,* June 26, 2003.

37. "Growth of US Hispanics Dramatic," www.quepasa.com, June 20, 2003.

38. The National Campaign to Prevent Teen Pregnancy, *Teen Sexual Activity, Pregnancy, and Childbearing Among Latinos in the United States,* Fact Sheet, October 2006, 1–2.

39. It is important to note that in order to maintain long-term population stability a country must maintain a TFR average of 2.1. For Europe at the turn of the twenty-first century the average was about 1.4.

40. Steve Miller, "Census Predicts Decline of Whites," *Washington Times,* March 18, 2004.

41. U.S. Census Bureau, "Census 2000, Summary File 1 General Profile 1: Persons by Race, Age, & Sex; Households and Families by Race and by Type," 2001, factfinder .census.gov/servlet/DatasetMainPageServlet?_program=DEC&_submenuId=&_lang=en &_ts=.

42. Cited in Navarro, *Mexicano Political Experience in Occupied Aztlán*, 577.

43. For an extensive demographic analysis, see my book *Mexicano Political Experience in Occupied Aztlán*, 571–74.

44. Lisa Richardson and Robin Fields, "Latino Majority Arrives—Among State's Babies," *Los Angeles Times*, February 6, 2003; and *Press Enterprise*, "New Majority in Births," February 6, 2003.

45. Robin Fields, "A Deepening Diversity, but a Growing Divide," *Los Angeles Times*, March 30, 2001.

46. Donatelli, "Latinos Joining White Flight."

47. Justin Pritchard, "State Stays Young," *Press Enterprise*, June 1, 2001.

48. Susannah Rosenblatt, "California Is Seen in Rearview Mirror," *Los Angeles Times*, August 6, 2003.

49. Motoko Rich and David Leonhardt, "Home Prices are Driving People from California," *New York Times News Service*, November 11, 2005.

50. Haya El Nasser, "Immigrants Emigrating from Calif. and N.Y.," *USA Today*, August 8, 2003.

51. Douglas Quan, Leslie Berkman, and Michael Fisher, "Californians Plan Exit Strategies," *Los Angeles Times*, January 22, 2006.

52. Joel Rubin, "O.C.'s Majority is White No More," *Los Angeles Times*, September 30, 2004.

53. Neil A. Hamilton, *Militias in America* (Santa Barbara, Calif.: ABC-CLIO, 1996), 2.

54. Richard Abanes, *American Militias* (Downers Grove, Ill.: InterVarsity Press, 1996), 67–68.

55. Hamilton, *Militias in America*, 4–5.

56. Stan Weeber and Daniel G. Rodeheaver, *Militias in the Millennium: A Test of Smelser's Theory of Collective Behavior* (Dallas, Tex.: University Press of America, Inc., 2004), 10.

57. Thomas J. Curran, *Xenophobia and Immigration, 1820–1930* (Boston: Twayne Publishers, 1975), 133–34; and George John and Laird Wilcox, *American Extremists: Militias, Supremacists, Klansmen, Communists, and Others* (Amherst, N.Y.: Prometheus Books, 1996).

58. Hamilton, *Militias in America*, 25–26.

59. See the following works for additional information on the particulars of the Ruby Ridge incident: Abanes, *American Militias*, 43–49; and Kenneth S. Stern, *A Force Upon the Plain: The American Militia Movement and the Politics of Hate,* (Norman: University of Oklahoma Press, 1997), 19–28.

60. Abanes, *American Militias*, 50–51.

61. Stern, *A Force Upon the Plain*, 62–63.

62. Hamilton, *Militias in America*, 20.

63. Martin Lee, *The Beast Awakens: Fascism's Resurgence from Hitler's Spymasters to Today's Neo-Nazi Groups and Right-Wing Extremists* (New York: Routledge, 2000), 351.

64. Chip Berlet and Matthew N. Lyons, *Right Wing Populism in America: Too Close For Comfort* (New York: The Guilford Press, 2000), 301.

65. Cited in Stern, *A Force Upon the Plain*, 13-14.

66. Stern, *A Force Upon the Plain*, 14.

67. Anti-Defamation League Report, "Growing Activity of U.S. Militias Shows Retooling of Movement," September 7, 2004.

68. Bob Moser, "Open Season," *Intelligence Report* 109 (Spring 2003).

69. Moser, "Open Season," 10.

70. Zoe Hammer-Tomizuka and Jennifer Allen, "Hate or Heroism: Vigilantes on the Arizona-Mexico Border" (Tucson, Ariz.: Border Action Network, 2002), 8.

71. Rudy Acuña, "Murder in Arizona . . . It's Only the Third World," June 2, 2000, article found on the Internet: www.aztlan.net/acuna4.htm.

72. Robert Greenslade, "Do States Have the Authority to Use Militias to Protect Their Borders from Intrusions by Illegal Aliens?" *Sierra Times*, May 5, 2004.

73. Anti-Defamation League, "Militia Related Activity in Arizona," July 2, 1996.

74. Tony Ortega, "Affirmative Reactionaries: Arizona's Militias Aren't the Exclusive Domain of White Supremacists—People of Color are Joining the Ranks, too," *New Times*, May 15, 2004.

75. Navarro, *The Méxicano Political Experience in Occupied Aztlán*, 574.

76. Armando Navarro, "Report on Arizona/Sonora Border Crisis," (Riverside, Calif.: Ernesto Galarza Applied Research Center, July 23, 2000), 3.

77. Navarro, "Report on Arizona/Sonora Border Crisis," 2–3.

78. John Bonné, "Huge Gaps Remain on Northern Border," July 2002, www.msnbc .msn.com/id/3070731.

79. Navarro, *The Méxicano Political Experience in Occupied Aztlán*, 591

80. Navarro, *The Méxicano Political Experience in Occupied Aztlán*, 591.

81. The term "vigilante," which is a Spanish word that dates back to around 1865, meaning "watchman or guard," is related to the word "vigilant." Jon E. Dougherty, *Illegals: The Imminent Threat Posed by Our Unsecured U.S.-Mexico Border* (Nashville, Tenn.: WND Books, 2004), 188. It is important to note that other words that describe "vigilant" are "be alert" or specifically, "watchful." Thus, the word "vigilante" itself denotes a person who joins and participates with a group that takes the law into their own hands to punish a crime they believe has been perpetrated.

82. Dougherty, *Illegals*, 188.

83. The Center for Democratic Renewal, report, "Special Spotlight: Open Season: Anti-immigrant Vigilantism," May 5, 2004, www.thecdr.org/special_spotlight.html.

84. Tomizuka and Allen, "Hate or Heroism," 1.

85. Cited in *Central America/Mexico Report*, "U.S.-Mexico Border: Armed Groups Patrol Southern Arizona," *Journal of the Religious Task Force on Central America and Mexico*, March 2003.

86. *Central America/Mexico Report*, "U.S.-Mexico Border: Armed Groups Patrol Southern Arizona," 3.

87. See chapter 8 for specifics of Barnett's vigilante incidents that got him national media coverage.

88. Navarro, "Report on Arizona/Sonora Border Crisis," 4.

89. Navarro, "Report on Arizona/Sonora Border Crisis," 4.

90. Navarro, "Report on Arizona/Sonora Border Crisis."

91. Much of the information and sources to this paragraph and overall section is taken from a report I prepared and wrote on a delegation I organized on a fact-finding effort on the escalating armed vigilante movement in southern Arizona in late May 2000.

92. Jan McGirk, "Blood and Bullets Along the Border: As Arizona's Private Posses Hunt Mexican Migrants for Sport," *The Independent UK*, May 6, 2000.

93. Tim McGirk, "Border Clash," *Time*, June 26, 2000.

94. Voices of Citizens Together news item, "Voice of Citizens Together to Support Arizona Ranchers," May 5, 2000, www.americanpatrol.com.

95. Tomizuka and Allen, "Hate or Heroism," 3–4.

96. *New York Times*, "Police Investigate Killings of Illegal Immigrants In Desert," www.nytimes.com/2002/10/23national.23BORD.html.

97. Jan McGirk, "Blood and Bullets Along the Border as Arizona's Private Posses Hunt Mexican Migrants for Sport," www.commondreams.org/healines/050600-01 .htm, The Independent UK, May 6, 2000.

98. Mark Stevenson, "Arizona Is New Point for Immigrants," Associated Press, May 29, 2004.

99. Stevenson, "Arizona Is New Point for Immigrants."

100. Tomizuka and Allen, "Hate or Heroism," 4.

101. *Border Action Network*, "Civil Lawsuits Pending against Roger, Donald and/or Barbara Barnett," www.borderaction.org.

102. *Border Action Network*, "Civil Lawsuits Pending."

103. *Border Action Network*, "Civil Lawsuits Pending." For a comprehensive account of the Morales civil suit see Susy Buchanan, "Vigilant Justice: A Momentous Confrontation Ends With A Family of U.S. Citizens Turning the Tables on America's Most Notorious Border Vigilante," *Intelligence Report*, Spring 2007.

104. Hector Carreon, "Anti-Mexican Vigilante Glenn Spencer Arrested," *La Voz de Aztlan*, August 5, 2003.

105. Much of the narrative of Spencer's anti-Méxican posture was taken from an Anti-Defamation League (ADL) report, entitled "Border Disputes: Armed Vigilantes in Arizona," 2003, www.adl.org/extremism/arizona/arizonaborder.pdf, 3.

106. ADL, "Border Disputes," 3.

107. For a rather biased but informative chapter on Spencer, see Daniel Sheehy, *Fighting Immigration Anarchy: American Patriots, Battle to Save the Nation* (Bloomington, Ind.: Rooftop Publishing, 2006), 49–94.

108. Hector Carreon, "Arizona Vigilantes Shed More Blood at the Border," *La Voz de Aztlan*, www.aztlan.net/miguel.htm.

109. Cited in Navarro, "Report on Arizona/Sonora Border Crisis," 5.

110. Bill Hess, "Group Outlines Views, Plans," *Herald Review*, September 30, 2002.

111. Moser, "Open Season," 11.

112. Found on American Border Patrol Website: www.americanpatrol.com/ _WEB2002/020729Web.html, "Paper Tasks Potshots and American Border Patrol," July 20, 2002.

113. Moser, "Open Season," 10.

114. ADL, "Border Disputes."

115. Daniel Sheehy, *Fighting Immigration Anarchy*, 93.

116. Moser, "Open Season," 7.

117. Carreon, "Anti-Mexican Vigilante Glenn Spencer Arrested."

118. Wikipedia contributors, "Glenn Spencer," *Wikipedia, The Free Encyclopedia*, wikipedia.org/wiki/Glenn_Spencer #2003_prosecution.

119. Susy Buchanan and Tom Kim, "Meet the Nativists," *Intelligence Report*, February 17, 2007.

120. Tomizuka and Allen, "Hate or Heroism,"12.

121. Tomizuka and Allen, "Hate or Heroism," 4.

122. *Terra-Noti-Mex*, "Hispanics condemn use of spy airplane to catch undocumented people May 8, 2003," found on Free Republic.com website.

123. Editorial, "American Border Patrol Rejects Militia Manifesto: Simcox Plan a Formula Disaster," Taken from ABP website: www.americanpatrol.org: http://www.americanpatrol.com/FEATURES/030320-ABP-REJECT-MILITIAIDEA/030320_Feature.html,

124. The politics and particulars of Proposition 200 will be examined in chapter 11.

125. Interview of Jack Foote, conducted by Kevin Alfred Strom, *American Dissident Voices*, broadcast December 20, 2003.

126. Cited in Border Action Report, Tomizuka and Allen, "Hate or Heroism," 2.

127. Strom Interview of Jack Foote, December 20, 2003.

128. ADL, "Border Disputes."

129. John MacCormack, "'Ranch Rescue' Billed as Racist," *San Antonio Express-News*, May 30, 2003.

130. Anti-Defamation League Press Release, "ADL Says Armed Anti-Immigration Groups in Arizona Share Ties to White Supremacists," April 2005, www.adl.org.

131. Moser, "Open Season," 13–14.

132. Moser, "Open Season," 13–14.

133. Moser, "Open Season," 13–14.

134. R. M. Arrieta, "Armed and Dangerous: Vigilantes Terrorize Migrants Crossing the Border," *In These Times*, January 27, 2003.

135. Susan Carroll, "Civilians Patrol Border—Groups put Selves, Crossers in Danger, Law Enforcement," *Tucson Citizen*, October 28, 2002.

136. Moser, "Open Season," 15–16.

137. Andrew Pollack, "2 Illegal Immigrants Win Arizona Ranch in Court," *New York Times*, August 19, 2005.

138. For an overview of the Leiva v. Ranch Rescue Case refer to the article written by Andrew Pollack "2 Illegal Immigrants Win Arizona Ranch in Court," *New York Times*, August 19, 2005.

139. MacCormack, "'Ranch Rescue' Billed As Racist."

140. Pollack, "2 Illegal Immigrants Win Arizona Ranch in Court."

141. ADL, "Border Disputes."

142. Luke Turf, "Vigilantes Targeting Mexican Military," *Tucson Citizen*, February 14, 2004.

143. Anti-Defamation League Report, "Armed Vigilante Activities In Arizona," April 21, 2005, www.adl.org.

144. Pollack, "2 Illegal Immigrants Win Arizona Ranch in Court."

145. Moser, "Open Season."

146. ADL, "Border Disputes."

147. ADL, "Border Disputes."

148. Much of the information in this paragraph was taken from an article written by Moser, "Open Season," 7.

149. Tomizuka and Allen, "Hate of Heroism," 6.

150. Moser, "Open Season," 8.

151. Chris Simcox's Open Letter to President George Bush, written in the *Tombstone Tumbleweed*, November 14, 2002.

152. Citation taken from the Tucson-based Coalition for Human Rights website: www.derechohumanosaz.net.

153. Citation taken from the Tucson-based Coalition for Human Rights website: www.derechohumanosaz.net.

154. Gabriela Rico, "Guilty Verdict in Federal Land Gun Case," *Tucson Citizen*, January 15, 2004.

155. Susy Buchanan and David Holthouse, "Minutemen Leader Troubled Past," Southern Poverty Center, www.splcenter.org/intel/news/item.jsp?aid=149&site_area=1printable=1.

156. Sheehy, *Fighting Immigration Anarchy*, 210.

157. Coalition for Human Rights website: www.derechohumanosaz.net

158. Max Blumenthal, "Vigilante Injustice," archive.salon.com/news/feature/2003/5/22vigilante/index_np.html.

159. Bobbie Hart O'Neill, "Vigilante Justice in Action," www.useless-knowledge.com/columnists/bobbieoneill/Article27.html.

160. *de Novo*, "Vigilantes in the War on Terrorism/Immigration," May 20, 2004, www.blogdenovo.org/archives/000302.html.

Chapter 7

1. Daniel Sheehy, *Fighting Immigration Anarchy: American Patriots Battle To Save The Nation* (Bloomington, Ind.: Rooftop Publishing, 2006), 249–50.

2. David Holthouse, "Arizona Showdown," www.splcenter.org.

3. Jim Gilchrist and Jerome R. Corsi, *Minutemen: The Battle to Secure America's Borders* (Los Angeles: World Ahead Publishing, 2006), 7.

4. Gilchrist and Corsi, *Minutemen*, 4–5.

5. Lara Jakes Jordan, "Minutemen to Arizona Border to Curb Illegal Immigration Crossings," *San Diego Union-Tribune*, February 21, 2005.

6. Lara Jakes Jordan, "Minutemen to Patrol Arizona Border," Found on SignOn-SanDiego.com, February 21, 2005.

7. Marc Cooper, "Lawn Chair Militias," *Los Angeles Weekly*, April 6–14, 2005.

8. Sheehy, *Fighting Immigration Anarchy*, 252–53.

9. www.WorldNetDailey.com, "Showdown at Border," March 7, 2005; Rich Connell and Robert Lopez, "Gang Sweeps Result in 103 Arrests," *Los Angeles Times*, March 15, 2005.

10. Jerry Speer, "Gang Will Target Minuteman Vigil on México Border," *Washington Times*, March 28, 2005.

11. Gentry Braswell, "Minuteman Project Begins this Week: Committed Volunteers Said to Top 1000," *Sierra Vista Herald*, March 28, 2005.

12. blatherwatch.blogs.com/talk_radio/2005/02/the company_the.html.

13. Annie Schleicher, "Civilian Militia Patrol U.S.-México Border," *Newshour Extra*, April 6, 2005.

14. Gilchrist and Corsi, *Minutemen*, 7.

15. The anti-MP activities of the NAHR and other Méxicano and Latino groups will be examined in the next chapter.

16. Bill Hess, "Volunteers in Minuteman Project to Patrol Border," *San Pedro Valley News-Sun*, January 26, 2005.

17. David Holthouse, "Arizona Showdown," SPL Center, www.splcenter.org.

18. Cooper, "Lawn Chair Militias."

19. Sheehy, *Fighting Immigration Anarchy*, 256.

20. Cooper, "Lawn Chair Militias."

21. Gilchrist and Corsi, *Minutemen*, 8–9.

22. Quoted in Justin Akers Chacon and Mike Davis, *No One Is Illegal: Fighting Racism and State Violence on the U.S.-México Border* (Chicago: Haymarket Books, 2006), 250.

23. Holthouse, "Arizona Showdown," www.splcenter.org.

24. Cooper, "Lawn Chair Militias."

25. Cooper, "Lawn Chair Militias."

26. Cooper, "Lawn Chair Militias."

27. Quoted in Sheehy, *Fighting Immigration Anarchy*, 253.

28. The ten congressional members of the Immigration Reform Caucus included caucus chair Tom Tancredo of Colorado, John D. Doolittle of California, Lamar Smith of Texas, Scott Garrett of New Jersey, J. D. Hayworth of Arizona, Phil Gingrey of Georgia, Virgil Goode of Virginia, Walter Jones of Georgia, Tom Price of Georgia, and J. Gresham Barrett of North Carolina.

29. Quoted in Sheehy, *Fighting Immigration Anarchy*, 258.

30. *Intelligence Report*, "Arizona Showdown," Summer 2005, Issue 118.

31. Greg Flakus, "Minuteman Citizen Group Angers Hispanics, Has Political Aspirations," *Voice of America*, July 4, 2005.

32. Jennifer Delson, "A Minuteman Meets His Hour of Crisis," *Los Angeles Times*, March 11, 2007.

33. Thomas Doyle, "Citizen Patrols: Volunteers or Vigilantes?" *Victoria Advocate*, July 18, 2005.

34. Sheehy, *Fighting Immigration Anarchy*, 264

35. David Kelly, "Illegal Immigration Fears Have Spread," *Los Angeles Times*, April 25, 2005.

36. Monte Alban and David Reyes, "Crowd Gets Rough and Police Swarm in after a Minuteman Event in Garden Grove," *Los Angeles Times*, May 26, 2005; and Martin Wisckol, "Immigration Event Turns Hostile," *Orange County Register*, May 25, 2005.

37. Alban and Reyes, "Crowd Gets Rough and Police Swarm in after a Minuteman Event in Garden Grove"; and Wisckol, "Immigration Event Turns Hostile."

38. Brock N. Meeks, "Minuteman Opposition Organizes Resistance," *MSNBC*, June 15, 2005.

39. *La Voz de Aztlán News Bulletin*, "Chief Anti-Mexican Bigots to Meet in Las Vegas," May 23, 2005.

40. *Orcinus*, dneiwert.blogspot.com, October 7, 2005.

41. William Finn Bennett, "Border Watch Opponents Gear Up for Fight," *North County Times*, May 23, 2005.

42. Leslie Berestein, "Minuteman Effort May Spread into S.D. Region," *San Diego Union-Tribune*, April 19, 2005.

43. Alex Meneses Miyashita, "Leaders of Minuteman Project Take Up Different Tactics, Goals," *Hispanic Link News Service*, June 22, 2005.

44. Sara Taylor, "More Minutemen to March: Patrol Group Recruits Volunteers," *Las Cruces Sun-News*, July 11, 2005.

45. Doyle, "Citizen Patrols: Volunteers or Vigilantes?"

46. Solomon Moore, "Immigration Official Praises Citizen's Patrol," *Los Angeles Times*, July 21, 2005; Jeremiah Marquez, "Homeland Security Backs Off Idea of Civilian Border Patrol," Associated Press, July 21, 2005.

47. Leslie Berestein, "Gathering also Draws Lawmen and Journalists," *San Diego Union-Tribune*, July 17, 2005

48. James Gilchrist, "Minutemen Calling for Reinforcements in Campo," communiqué, July 19, 2006, www.alipac.us/article549.html.

49. For an examination of this incident see chapter 9, which provides much more detail on it.

50. Jessie Diaz, Jr., "The Minutemen Project Has Failed Miserably in California," *Aztlánnet-News*, September 30, 2005.

51. Leslie Berestein, "Civilians Share Goals, But Disagree on Tactics," *San Diego Union-Tribune*, September 10, 2005.

52. Sharon McNary, "Border Friends, Foes to Face Off," *Press Enterprise*, September 16, 2005.

53. Jerry Seper, "Volunteers Set for California Border Vigil," *Washington Times*, September 15, 2005.

54. Seper, "Volunteers Set for California Border Vigil."

55. Anna Gorman and Richard Marosi, "Minuteman-Style Border Patrol Is Over In No Time," *Los Angeles Times*, September 18, 2005.

56. Andy Ramirez, "Unarmed Volunteers Attacked and Terrorized in San Diego, US Flag Desecrated," public letter, dated September 18, 2005.

57. Joseph Sternberg, "Minutemen Readying New York Patrol along State's Border with Canada," *New York Sun*, September 7, 2005.

58. Marty Graham, "Border Volunteers Eye San Diego," *Boston Globe*, June 24, 2005.

59. Carla Marinucci, "California Governor Defends Border Watchers," *San Francisco Chronicle*, September 22, 2005.

60. Arthur H. Rotstein, "Group Opposing Illegal Immigration Gains National Foothold," Associated Press, December 17, 2005.

61. Jerry Seper, "Minutemen Border Patrol Raises Opposition in Texas," *Washington Times*, September 23, 2005.

62. David G. Pierre, "Civilian Patrols Target Wider Circle, Though Poll Finds Opposition," *USA Today*, October 1, 2005.

63. Mark Lisheron, "Ex-Minuteman Leader Sees Danger in Texas Patrol," *Austin American-Statesman*, September 18, 2005.

64. *El Paso Times*, "Our Opinion: Minutemen Watch," October 4, 2005.

65. Sara A. Carter, "Minutemen Patrols Continue amid Criticism," *Inland Counties Daily Bulletin*, October 18, 2005.

66. Sheehy, *Fighting Immigration Anarchy*, 266.

67. Sheehy, *Fighting Immigration Anarchy*, 266.

68. Sheehy, *Fighting Immigration Anarchy*, 267–68.

69. David Haldane, "Minutemen Chief's Ballot Label May Be Blank," *Los Angeles Times*, September 3, 2005.

70. Jean O. Pasco, "Republican Tops Border Activist in O.C. Election," *Los Angeles Times*, December 12, 2005.

71. Jorge Morales Almada, "Derrota con sabor a Victoria," *La Opinion*, December 8, 2005.

72. Morales Almada, "Derrota con sabor a Victoria."

73. Mark Z. Barabak and Jean O. Pasco, "Election Good News or Bad for Illegal Migration Foes?" *Los Angeles Times*, December 8, 2005.

74. Barabak and Pasco, "Election Good News or Bad for Illegal Migration Foes?"

75. Jennifer Delson, "A Minuteman Meets His Hour of Crisis."

76. Susy Buchanan and David Holthouse, "Locked and Loaded: Chris Simcox Mainstreamed the Minutemen, Now He'd Better Watch His Back," *The Nation*, August 28/September 4, 2006, 30–31.

77. Buchanan and Holthouse, "Locked and Loaded," 30–31.

78. Sheehy, *Fighting Immigration Anarchy*, 267.

79. Buchanan and Holthouse, "Locked and Loaded."

80. Solana Larsen, "The Anti-Immigration Movement: From Shovels to Suits," *NACLA Report on the Americas* 40, no. 3 (May/June 2007): 14.

81. David Holthouse, "Minutemess," *Intelligence Report* 126 (summer 2007).

82. Susy Buchanan and David Holthouse, "The Anti-Immigration Minuteman Project Set Off an Avalanche of Imitators. Some of Them Are Downright Frightening," HispanicBusiness.com, January 30, 2007.

83. Chris Simcox, "Minuteman Project issues major planning statement," Press Advisory sent by The Minuteman Project on April 18, 2005.

84. Gilchrist and Corsi, *Minutemen*, 20.

85. Gillian Flaccus, "Proposes Revolutionary Immigration," Associated Press, cited in *La Prensa*, February 10, 2006.

86. The Movimiento Pro-Migrante and the plethora of mobilizations which created it are comprehensively examined in this work's chapter 12.

87. Steve Fetbrandt, "Bill's Fans, Foes Rally," *Press Enterprise*, March 26, 2006

88. Susy Buchanan and David Holthouse, "Extremists Advocate Murder of Immigrants, Politicians," *Southern Poverty Law Center*, March 30, 2006.

89. Martin Wisckol, "Minutemen to Patrol in 4 States," *Orange County Register*, March 30, 2006.

90. Buchanan and Holthouse, "Extremists Advocate Murder of Immigrants, Politicians."

91. Buchanan and Holthouse, "Extremists Advocate Murder of Immigrants, Politicians."

92. Buchanan and Holthouse, "Extremists Advocate Murder of Immigrants, Politicians."

93. Associated Press, "Minuteman Plans Border Return to Confront Illegal Immigration," March 21, 2006.

94. *Press Enterprise*, "Border Patrol Group Starts Third Year," April 1, 2007.

95. Melissa Ludwig, "Immigration Debate Erupts at UTSA," *San Antonio Express-News*, April 14, 2007.

96. Sebastian Montes, "Minuteman Rally Cites a Wave of Support," *The Gazette*, July 5, 2006.

97. MillerBoycott.com, "The End of Miller Time—List of Miller Brands to Boycott," September 4, 2006.

98. Sara Inés Calderon, "Border Watch Group Snubs Beermaker for Alleged 'Illegal' Backing," *Brownsville Herald*, September 23, 2006.

99. Buchanan and Holthouse, "Locked and Loaded."

100. Buchanan and Holthouse, "Locked and Loaded," 31.

101. American Border Patrol Website, "Border Fence Scam?: Simcox Fence Project Raises Doubts," www.americanpatrol.com/06-FEATURES/060620-BDR-FENCE-PROBLEM/060620_Feature.html, June 29, 2006.

102. Response from Chris Simcox to border fence controversy, "The Minuteman border Fence," MinutemanHQ.Com, July 14, 2006.

103. David Holthouse, "The Little Prince Is under Siege," *Southern Poverty Law Center*, posted in HispanicBusiness.com, January 22, 2007.

104. Associated Press, "Minutemen Finances Questioned," July 20, 2006.

105. Jerry Seper, "Minuteman Spending Outstrips Donations, Fees," *Washington Times*, November 17, 2006.

106. Holthouse, "The Little Prince Is under Siege."

107. Holthouse, "The Little Prince Is Under Siege."

108. Holthouse, "The Little Prince Is Under Seige."

109. *Intelligence Report*, "Second Minuteman Group Splits amid Accusations," *Southern Poverty Law Center* 127 (Fall 2007).

110. *La Voz de Aztlán*, "'Ethnic Cleansing' of Mexicans Begins in California City," January 4, 2006.

111. Jennifer Delson, "Laguna Beach Patriots Day Parade Is No Place for Minuteman Project, Organizers Say," *Los Angeles Times*, January 25, 2006.

112. Jennifer Delson, "Minutemen Sue O.C. City Over Parade Refusal," *Los Angeles Times*, January 26, 2006.

113. Fetbrandt, "Bill's Fans, Foes Rally."

114. Gillian Flaccus, "Minuteman Group Says It's Growing," *Associated Press*, April 27, 2006.

115. Gillian Flaccus, "Minuteman Group Launching 12-City Tour," *Associated Press*, May 3, 2006.

116. Hemmy So, "Minuteman Caravan Gets Testy Send-Off," *Los Angeles Times*, May 4, 2006.

117. So, "Minuteman Caravan Gets Testy Send-Off."

118. Agustin Duran, "Minutemen inicia campaña para militizar la frontera," *La Opinion*, May 4, 2006.

119. So, "Minuteman Caravan Gets Testy Send-Off."

120. Agustin Duran, "Ni rosas ni halagos para los 'minutemen,'" *La Opinion*, May 22, 2006.

121. Agustin Duran, "Minutemen defiende acción de la policia ante protestas," *La Opinion*, July 14, 2006.

122. Jazmin Ortega, "Schwarzenegger repite su respaldo a los Minutemen," *La Opinion*, July 12, 2006.

123. Nathan Max, "Small Protest Targets Day-Labor Site," *Press Enterprise*, August 27, 2006.

124. Jazmin Ortega, "Santuario de protestas," *La Opinion*, August 27, 2006.

125. www.immigrationwatchdog.com, "Americans Attacked at Maywood Protest," August 28, 2006.

126. Jennifer Vigil, "Proposal for Sanctuary City Sparks Rally," *San Diego Union-Tribune*, September 24, 2006.

127. Sara Ines Calderon, "Event: Texas Minuteman Hosting Fundraiser for Operation Sovereignty," *Brownsville Herald*, August 14, 2006.

128. Alexander Zaitchik, "Operation Sovereignty: A Bang, a Protest, and a Whimper," *Intelligence Report, Southern Poverty Law Center* 124 (Winter 2006): 65.

129. KXAN.com, "Minutemen Move Into Laredo," September 11, 2006.

130. Jennifer Delson, "Minuteman Leader Rousted in N.Y.," *Los Angeles Times*, October 6, 2006.

131. Delson, "A Minuteman Meets His Hour of Crisis."

132. For a more thorough examination of the power struggle see Holthouse, "Minutemess."

133. Holthouse, "Minutemess."

134. Jennifer Delson, "O.C. Judge Hears Arguments in Minutemen Project Schism," *Los Angeles Times*, March 22, 2007.

135. Holthouse, "Minutemess."

136. Martin Wisckol, "Gilchrist Denied Control," *Orange County Register*, March 23, 2007.

137. Holthouse "Minute mess."

Chapter 8

1. Hector Becerra and David Pierson, "No Counting on the Identity of the 300 Millionth Resident," *Los Angeles Times*, October 18, 2006.

2. *U.S. Bureau of the Census*, "Hispanic Americans by the Numbers," cited in Info-please, www.infoplease.com.

3. MSNBC, "Hispanics Are the Largest and Fastest Growing Ethnic Population, Census Reports," May 17, 2007, www.msnbc.msn.com.

4. Paper presented by Dan Griswold, "Mexican Migration, Legalization, and Assimilation," Cato Institute, October 5, 2005.

5. Jim Gilchrist and Jerome R. Corsi, *Minutemen: The Battle to Secure America's Borders* (Los Angeles: World Ahead Publishing, Inc., 2006), 20.

6. Department of Health and Human Services, Centers for Disease Control and Prevention, National Center for Health Statistics, "Births: Preliminary Data for 2005,"

7. Associated Press, "Hispanic Birth Rates Soars in Southeast," August 9, 2006.

8. *Arizona Indymedia*, "Jury to AZ Border Vigilante: Guilty!" November 29, 2006, arizona.indymedia.org.

9. Bob Kraft, "Editor Profession: Attorney at Law," February 12, 2007, dfwimmigration law.clarislaw.com/border-enforcement/.

10. For a comprehensive account of the Morales trespassing suit see Susy Buchanan, "Vigilante Justice," *Intelligence Report* 125 (Spring 2007).

11. Jonathan Clark, "Barnett Still Could Face Prosecution," *Daily Dispatch*, December 5, 2006.

12. Jonathan Clark, "EMTs File Complaint against Barnett," *Herald/Review*, January 5, 2007.

13. Clark, "EMTs File Complaint against Barnett."

14. The American Resistance, "Pictures of Illegal Immigration Invasion on Roger Barnett's Border Ranch in Arizona," theamericanresistance.com, no date. Text under picture indicated figure was from 2006. The 12,000 figure was also used by the *U.S. Immigration News* in a status report article on the Barnett Boys, dated December 2006, http://usimmigratiionsupport.org.

15. American Border Patrol, "Border Cam Coming Online," http://www.american-patrol.com/05-FEATURES/050919-BDR-CAM-COMING/050919_Feature.html, September 19, 2005.

16. Ted Morris, "Border Security: Government under Group's Aerial Scrutiny," *Herald/Review*, September, 9, 2007.

17. Morris, "Border Security: Government under Group's Aerial Scrutiny."

18. Blake Morlock, "Fence Tailored to Border Needs," *Tucson Citizen*, October 27, 2007.

19. Anti-Defamation League, "Border Disputes: Armed Vigilantes in Arizona," 2003, www.adl.org.

20. American Border Patrol, "Report: ABP Headquarters Fired upon Last Evening," May 23, 2007, www.americanpatrol.com.

21. Jerry Seper, "Ex-Minuteman Leaders Form New Border Group," *Washington Times*, July 6, 2007.

22. Patriots' Border Alliance, "Patriots Form Border Alliance: Minuteman and Others Re-Form The Citizens' Movement," www.patriotsborderalliance.com.

23. Gentry Braswell, "Alliance Sets Series of Ground Rules before It Starts Weekend Operation," *Herald/Review*, August 18, 2007.

24. A "hate group" has beliefs or adheres to practices that attack or malign an entire class of people, typically their immutable characteristics. Their activities include criminal acts, marches, rallies, speeches, meetings, leafleting, and publishing.

25. Southern Poverty Law Center, "Hate Groups Active in the Year 2006," *Intelligence Report* 125 (Spring 2007): 52–58.

26. Southern Poverty Law Center, "Hate Groups Active in the Year 2006."

27. Susy Buchanan and David Holthouse, "Shoot, Shovel, Shut-Up," *Intelligence Report*, (Southern Poverty Law Center) 125 (Spring 2007): 44.

28. *New York Times*, "Hate Groups Are Infiltrating the Military, Group Asserts," July 7, 2006.

29. Fox News.com, "Feds Accuse Alabama Militia of Planning Machine-Gun Attack on Mexicans," May 1, 2007, foxnews.com.

30. For an extensive examination of this militia's incident see David Holthouse and Casey Sanchez, "Armed in Alabama," *Intelligence Report* 127 (Fall 2007).

31. Southern Poverty Law Center, "Anti-Immigration Groups," *Intelligence Report*, Winter 2007.

32. Southern Poverty Law Center, "Anti-Immigration Groups," *Intelligence Report* (Spring 2001), www.splcenter.org.

33. Deepa Fernandes, *Targeted: Homeland Security and the Business of Immigration* (New York: Seven Stories Press, 2007), 214.

34. Southern Poverty Law Center, "Anti-Immigration Groups."

35. Southern Poverty Law Center, "Anti-Immigration Groups."

36. Taken from Immigration Control Foundation's Internet website: About AICF.

37. Southern Poverty Law Center, "Anti-Immigration Groups."

38. "Take Action," AICF website, www.immigrationcontrol.com.

39. Fernandes, *Targeted*, 214.

40. Southern Poverty Law Center, "Anti-Immigration Groups."

41. Right Web, "Project USA," rightweb.irc-online.org/profile/1538.

42. Southern Poverty Law Center, "Anti-Immigration Groups."

43. Information sheet, "About SaveOurState," info@saveourstate.org, August 12, 2005.

44. Found on We Can Stop the Hate.org Internet Website: www.wecanstopthehate.org/factions/save_our_state.

45. Found on We Can Stop the Hate.org Internet Website.

46. Information sheet, "About SaveOurState," info@saveourstate.org, August 12, 2005.

47. Information sheet, "The Battle for Los Angeles," info@saveourstate.org, May 19, 2005.

48. Susan Buchanan and Tom Kim, "The Nativists," *Intelligence Report* (Southern Poverty Law Center), www.splcenter.org.

49. Chris Richard, "Immigration Measure Off Ballot," *Press Enterprise*, June 26, 2006.

50. Heidi Beirich and Bob Moser, "Communing with the Council," *Intelligence Report*, no date, www.splcenter.org.

51. Media House, "The Far Right in Michigan: Council of Conservative Citizens," www.mediahouse.org, no date.

52. Media House, "The Far Right in Michigan."

53. Media House, "The Far Right in Michigan."

54. Beirich and Moser, "Communing with the Council."

55. Associated Press story found on SN News's Internet Website. www.nusd.k12 .az.us/Schools/nhs/gthomson.class/articles/duke.racist.html.

56. Associated Press story found on SN News's Internet Website.

57. Anti-Defamation League, "David Duke: In His Own Words on Immigration," www.adl.org/special.

58. Wikipedia contributors, "National Alliance (United States)," *Wikipedia, The Free Encyclopedia*, en.wikipedia.org/wiki/National_Alliance_%28United_States%29

59. Fernandes, *Targeted*, 205.

60. Website of National Alliance, www.natall.com.

61. Gilchrist and Corsi, *Minutemen*; Otis L. Graham, *Unguarded Gates* (Lanham, Md.: Rowman & Littlefield Publishers, Inc., 2004); Jon E. Dougherty, *Illegals* (Nashville, Tenn.: WND Books, 2004); and Daniel Sheehy, *Fighting Immigration Anarchy* (Bloomington, Ind.: Rooftop Publishing, 2006).

62. Samuel P. Huntington, *Who Are We? The Challenges to America's National Identity* (New York: Simon and Schuster, 2004), 221.

63. John F. McManus, "Crusading TV Anchor Lou Dobbs Targeted by Alarmists," *John Birch Society*, May 15, 2007, www.jbs.org/node/3969/print.

64. Anti-Defamation League Press Release: Report on Extremists Declare 'Open Season' on Immigrants; Hispanics Target of Incitement and Violence, April 24, 2006.

65. Karen Tumulty, "Should They Stay Or Should They Go," *Time*, April 10, 2006, 28–43.

66. For a compendium of their and others polling results see: Immigration, Polling Report, www.pollingreport.com.

Chapter 9

1. When apropos the first person is used since much of the account is based upon my research on the issue, my NAHR leadership role, and lastly, my scholarly role as a participant-observer. Under no circumstances do I suggest that this chapter documents the complete Méxicano/Latino or pro-migrant rights response to the armed rancher vigilantes and militias. As comprehensive and complete as it is its primary focus is on NAHR's countervailing organizing activities in both Arizona and California from 2000 to 2005. It is important to note that groups other then NAHR were also active. Some of their activities are examined but not comprehensively, which suggests more research needs to be done.

2. Much of the text of this section examining the Latino response in 2000 to the armed rancher vigilantes was taken from a report on the subject I authored and released at a press conference in late July 2000. The report was a research product of tape recordings, personal notes, press releases, reports, letters, newspaper and magazine articles, and my recollections as a participant-observer.

3. Letter, U.S. Attorney General Janet Reno, Coalition for Human Rights, April 25, 2000.

4. Article found on Indymedia Internet Website, "Spartacist League Says Don't Run Them Off Campus, Drive Out Racist "Minuteman" Vigilantes!" dc.indymedia.org/ newswire/display/139202, May 26, 2000.

5. Letter from Jessica Castro to Barbara Coe, May 23, 2000.

6. Letter from Armando Navarro to Congresswoman Lucille Allard-Roybal, May 28, 2000.

7. *Tucson Citizen* article posted on Southern Arizona Online Internet Website, "Teen Mother Dies in Arizona Bringing Baby from Qaxaca," May 27, 2000; *Arizona Daily Star*, June 1, 2000.

8. Navarro, Fact-finding Delegation Report, July 28, 2000.

9. Jeanette Steele, "Inland Residents to Rally Against Arizona Ranchers," *Press Enterprise*, June 1, 2000; Press release, Méxicano/Latino Fact-finding Delegation, June 1, 2000.

10. David Avila, "Protestan caceria hoy en Arizona," *La Prensa*, week of June 2–8, 2000.

11. Much of the preceding account of the delegation's trip to southern Arizona to investigate the armed rancher vigilante issue and its various activities are derived from the Delegation Report, which I authored, released, and distributed at a press conference held at the Zacatecas restaurant in Riverside, California, on July 28, 2000. The report was a research product of tape recordings, personal notes, press releases, reports, letters, and my recollections as a participant-observer. The preceding is housed in my personal archives.

12. Navarro, "Fact-finding Delegation Report," July 28, 2000.

13. Navarro, "Fact-finding Delegation Report," July 28, 2000.

14. Navarro, "Fact-finding Delegation Report," July 28, 2000.

15. Navarro, "Fact-finding Delegation Report," July 28, 2000.

16. Navarro, "Fact-finding Delegation Report," July 28, 2000.

17. Navarro, "Fact-finding Delegation Report," July 28, 2000.

18. Navarro, "Fact-finding Delegation Report," July 28, 2000.

19. Navarro, "Fact-finding Delegation Report," July 28, 2000.

20. Mary Moreno, "2 Drown in River as Many Look On," *Brownsville (Texas) Herald*, June 9, 2000.

21. Found on *La Voz de Aztlan* Internet Website, "Horrific Death of Mexican Migrant," www.aztlan.net/dragkill.htm, July 7, 2000.

22. Ignacio Ibarra, "U.S. Authorizes $5 million for State's Border Expense," *Arizona Daily Star*, July 1, 2000.

23. Much of the narrative of the section is taken from Navarro, "Fact-finding Delegation Report," July 28, 2000. When necessary other sources are included.

24. Navarro, personal notes on meeting with Congressman Baca, no date.

25. Navarro, tape recording of meeting, July 29, 2000. Also, additional sources are personal notes taken by me of the summit discussions.

26. Armando Navarro, "Proposed Plan of Action for a Latino Mass Mobilization: El Plan de Ysidro," presented at Border Summit on July 29, 2000.

27. Navarro, "Proposed Plan of Action for a Latino Mass Mobilization."

28. Roberto Hernandez, "Latino Activists Demand End to Border Violence," *Press Enterprise*, July 30, 2000.

29. Cited in article entitled, "Vigilante Violence," www.splcenter.org/intelligenceproject/ip-4y4.html.

30. It is imperative to note that no charges were filed in any of the preceding mentioned incidents. Furthermore, none of these recorded incidents were adjudicated in court. Human Rights Coalition/Indigenous Alliance without Borders Newsletter, May 2003; and Armando Navarro, "NAHR Delegation Report Southern Arizona Militia and Hate Groups, June 3, 2003.

31. Description of these incidents is derived from Mexican government documents and accounts in the *Arizona Daily Star* and *Douglas Dispatch* newspapers. Above taken from article entitled, "Vigilante Violence," www.splcenter.org/intelligenceproject/ip-4y4 .html.

32. National Alliance for Human Rights delegation member list, May 20, 2003, located in my personal archives.

33. National Alliance for Human Rights, delegation schedule for southern Arizona, May 22–25, located in my personal archives.

34. NAHR press release, "Latino Delegation Travels to Arizona to Combat Militia Activity," May 19, 2003.

35. Much of this section is based upon taped interviews, personal notes of meetings, and personal recollections of interviews and events. Interview, Ruben Beltrán, Phoenix, Arizona, May 22, 2003.

36. Interview, Ruben Beltrán.

37. Interview, Ruben Beltrán.

38. Interview, Ruben Beltrán.

39. Interview, Ruben Beltrán.

40. Interview, Ruben Beltrán.

41. Interview, Ruben Beltrán.

42. Interview, Mexico Consul Carlos Flores Visquida, Tucson, Arizona, May 22, 2003.

43. Interview, Mexico Consul Carlos Flores Visquida.

44. Patricio Guillen, report given by him at debriefing meeting on May 22, 2003.

45. Armando Navarro, tape recording of meeting, May 3, 2003, my personal notes on meeting, as well as on notes of debriefing session.

46. Armando Navarro, delegation notes of activities and debriefing notes.

47. Interview, Consul Miguel Escobar, Douglas, Arizona, May 23, 2003. Navarro meeting notes.

48. Interview, Mexico Consul Carlos Flores Visquida.

49. Interview, Mexico Consul Carlos Flores Visquida.

50. Cited in Navarro report, second delegation to Southern Arizona, 2003.

51. Navarro report, second delegation to Southern Arizona.

52. Navarro report, second delegation to Southern Arizona.

53. Navarro report, second delegation to Southern Arizona.

54. Navarro report, second delegation to Southern Arizona.

55. Letter from Armando Navarro to Congressman Ciro D. Rodriguez, June 9, 2003.

56. NAHR press release, "NAHR Delegation Travels to Mexico City for Bi-national Conference," August 26, 2003.

57. Personal written notes and tape recording of symposium, November 21, 2003, Cananea, Sonora.

58. Personal written notes and tape recording of symposium.

59. On the visit to Altar and Sasabe I took copious notes and the debriefing session on events was recorded. Hence, much of the subsequent accounts are based on preceding sources and my own recollection of events.

60. Notes on Altar and Sasabe visit.

61. Notes on Altar and Sasabe visit.

62. Stephen Wall, "Special Report: Crossing For A Dangerous American Dream," *San Bernardino County Sun*, November 30, 2003.

63. Stephen Wall, "Special Report"; NAHR Press Advisory, November 17, 2003.

64. Stephen Wall, "Supporters Want Baca to Change His Ways," *San Bernardino County Sun*, December 7, 2003.

65. Stephen Wall, "Special Report."

Chapter 10

1. Jazmin Ortega Morales, Lisa O'Neill Hill, and Sharyn Obsatz, "Arrests Spur Protest," *Press Enterprise*, June 11, 2004.

2. Janet Wilson, H. G. Reza, and Sandra Murillo, "Immigration Arrests Not Policy Shift," *Los Angeles Times*, June 11, 2004.

3. Miguel Gonzalez and Lillian de la Torre, "Negocios sufren impacto de las redadas en Inland Empire," *La Opinion*, June 14, 2004.

4. Lilian de la Torre-Jimenez, "Panico en Inland Empire por redadas de Inmigracion," *La Opinion*, June 9, 2004.

5. Lilian de la Torre-Jimenez, "Marcha contra las redadas," *La Opinion*, June 9, 2004.

6. Ortega Morales et al., "Arrests Spur Protest."

7. Wilson et al., "Immigration Arrests Not Policy Shift."

8. Lisa O'Neill Hill and Sharyn Obsatz, "Latino Arrests Spark Action," *Press-Enterprise*, June 12, 2004.

9. Miguel Angel Vega, "Migrantes reclaman Justicia," *La Opinion*, June 14, 2004.

10. NAHR press release, "Southern California Latino Leaders Meet to Put a Halt to the Border Patrol Raids," June 11, 2004.

11. Lisa Lambert, "Raids Called War on Poor," *San Bernardino County Sun*, June 16, 2004; and Jazmin Ortega Morales, "Advocates to Defend Immigrant's Rights," *Press-Enterprise*, June 16, 2004.

12. Ortega Morales, "Advocates to Defend Immigrant's Rights."

13. Maria T. Garcia and Douglas Quan, "Radio Warns of La Migra," *Press-Enterprise*, June 16, 2004.

14. NAHR plan of action, "Resistance and Mobilization," June 15, 2004.

15. William Finn Bennett, "Union Official: Frustration Grows at Temecula Border Patrol Station," *North County Times*, July 6, 2004.

16. Daniel Sheehy, "Illegal-Aliens Arrests, the Real Racists, and the 'Takeover of America,'" *Michigan News*, June 21, 2004.

17. Claire Vitucci, "Immigrant Sweep Was Not OK'd," *Press Enterprise*, June 26, 2004.

18. Solomon Moore, "Border Patrol Arrests Violated Policy, Agency Concedes," *Los Angeles Times*, June 26, 2004.

19. Michael Buchanan, "Border Patrol Raids Protested," *Californian*, June 29, 2004.

20. Katherine Steelman, "Professor Voices Outrage after Border Patrol Sweeps," *UCR Highlander*, July 6, 2004.

21. Bennett, "Union Official."

22. Mira Katz, "Latino Leaders Come Together to Organize," *San Bernardino County Sun*, July 11, 2004.

23. Tim Grenda, "Immigrant Sweeps Top Meeting Agenda," *Press Enterprise*, July 11, 2004.

24. Douglas Quan, "Activists Take Police to Task," *Press Enterprise*, July 17, 2004.

25. Lilian de la Torre-Jimenez, "Elaboran plan defensive contra redadas," *La Opinion*, August 3, 2004.

26. NAHR press release, "Mexicano and Latino Organizations to Announce Countervailing Bi-National Strategy to Minuteman Project," March 18, 2005.

27. Phxnews.com, "Mexican Right's Groups Plan to Be Confrontational with the Minutemen (Terrorists)," March 19, 2005, www.phxnews,com/fullstory.php?article=19485.

28. Sonia Melendez, "Minuteman Project Drawing Protests," Scripps Howard News Service, March 22, 2005.

29. Sara Carter, "Minutemen Set to Patrol Border," *Inland Counties Daily Bulletin*, March 31, 2005.

30. Edward Sifuentes, "Border Watch Group, Human Rights Activists Arrive for Monitoring Patrol," *North County Times*, April 1, 2005.

31. Arthur Rotstein, "Human Rights Groups Fear Border War," March 29, 2005, registerguard.com/news.

32. Mary Sanchez, "A Volatile Situation Building on U.S.-Mexico Border," *Kansas City Star*, March 31, 2005.

33. Armando Navarro, personal organizing notes, March 30, 2004, my archives.

34. Greg Strange, "Bedlam on the Border," *EtherZone.com*, www.etherzone.com.

35. Virginia de Viana y Alonso Castillo, "Emprenden acciones contra migrantes," *El Imparcial*, April 1, 2005.

36. *El Diario de Sonora*, "Bloquearian la garita en caso de aggression," April 2, 2005.

37. Sharon McNary and Chris Richard, "Patrol Meets Peaceful Resistance," *Press Enterprise,"* April 3, 2005.

38. McNary and Richard, "Patrol Meets Peaceful Resistance."

39. McNary and Richard, "Patrol Meets Peaceful Resistance."

40. Howard Fischer, "Hispanic Legislators to Monitor Monitors," *Arizona Daily Star*, March 31, 2005.

41. Susan Carroll, "Planned Border Boycott to Protest Minuteman Project," *Arizona Republic*, April 21, 2005.

42. Ashley Powers and Susannah Rosenblatt, "Group Plans to 'Close' Ariz.-Mexico border," *Los Angeles Times*, April 21, 2005.

43. Rodolfo Acuña, e-mail, "A Pretext to Do Nothing," April 22, 2005, racuna@csun.edu.

44. Nativo Lopez response letter to Acuna article, April 26, 2005, nativelopez@sbcglobal.net.

45. Sharon McNary, "Immigration Showdown Seen," *Press Enterprise*, May 29, 2005.

46. Leo Miramon, "Preparing for the Minuteman," *Imperial Valley Press*, June 19, 2005.

47. William Finn Bennett, "Volunteer Border Watch Project Raises Concerns," *The Californian*, May 29, 2005.

48. University of California, Riverside, "In the News," Media Resources, July 27, 2005.

49. David Pierson and Patricia Ward Biederman, "Protest over Art Forces Police to Draw the Line," *Los Angeles Times*, May 15, 2005; and Massiel Ladron de Guevara, "Protesta para Derrumbar un Monumento," *La Prensa*, July 1, 2005.

50. Mark Belgen incident report to San Diego Sheriff's Department, July 16, 2005, case number 05054665-D.

51. Minuteman website, "Bulletin! Reinforcement Needed in Campo, Ca," July 18, 2005, www.californiaminutemen.com.

52. James Gilchrist's Bulletin found on American Patrol Internet Website, "Minutemen Calling for Reinforcements in Campo," www.americanpatrol.com/05-FEATURES/050719-MMP-NEEDS-AID-CAMPO/MMP_UnderAttack050719.html, July 18, 2005.

53. Erin Schultz, "Allegations Fly in California Minutemen Project," *North County Times*, July 25, 2005.

54. Claudia Bustamante, "Advocate Demands Accuser Apology," *Press Enterprise*, July 30, 2005.

55. Deirdre Newman, "UC Riverside Professor Threatens to Sue over Assault Accusation," July 29, 2005.

56. Newman, "UC Riverside Professor Threatens to Sue over Assault Accusation."

Chapter 11

1. Jim Gilchrist and Jerome R. Corsi, *Minutemen: The Battle to Secure America's Borders* (Los Angeles: World Ahead Publishing, Inc., 2006), xviii.

2. Justin Ankers Chacon and Mike Davis, *No One Is Illegal: Fighting Racism and State Violence on the U.S.–Mexico Border* (Chicago: Haymarket Books, 2006), 215–16.

3. Jonathan Xavier Inda, *Targeting Immigrants: Government, Technology, and Ethics* (Malden, Mass.: Blackwell, 2006), 117.

4. Mark Krikorian, "Safety through Immigration Control," *Providence Journal*, April 24, 2004.

5. The USA Patriot Act, officially named the Uniting and Strengthening America by Providing Appropriate Tools Required to Intercept and Obstruct Terrorism Act, among its various provisions gave the federal government the power to access medical records, tax records, and information about the books a person bought or took out from a library

without "probable cause"; and the right to break into a person's home and conduct secret searches without informing the person for weeks, months, or indefinitely. On immigration, it enhanced the discretion of law enforcement and immigration authorities to detain and deport immigrants suspected of perpetrating terrorism-related acts. ACLU, "USA Patriot Act," November 14, 2003, www.aclu.org.

6. Chacon and Davis, *No One Is Illegal*, 217–18.

7. Jorge Ramos, *The Latino Wave: How Hispanics Will Elect the Next American President* (New York: HarperCollins Publishers, 2004), 50.

8. Inda, *Targeting Immigrants*, 113.

9. Chacon and Davis, *No One Is Illegal*, 210.

10. Gilchrist and Corsi, *Minutemen*, 34.

11. Daniel Sheehy, *Fighting Immigration Anarchy: American Patriots Battle to Save the Nation* (Bloomington, Ind.: Rooftop Publishing, 2006), 20.

12. Gilchrist and Corsi, *Minutemen*, 20.

13. Jeffrey S. Passel, "Report: The Size and Characteristics of the Unauthorized Migrant Population in the U.S.: Estimates Based on the March 2005 Current Population Survey," *Pew Hispanic Center*, March 7, 2006.

14. The INS and DHS reports are cited in Inda, *Targeting Immigrants*, 113–14.

15. Passel, "Report: Estimates of the Size and Characteristics of the Undocumented Population."

16. Kari Lydersen, "English Bill Vetoed in Arizona: Struggle over Rights Continues," *The New Standard*, May 13, 2005.

17. Lydersen, "English Bill Vetoed in Arizona."

18. Sheehy, *Fighting Immigration Anarchy*, 58.

19. Margot Veranes and Adriana Navarro, "Anti-Immigrant Legislation in Arizona: Leads to Calls for a State Boycott," *IRC Americas*, June 1, 2005, 1.

20. Sheehy, *Fighting Immigration Anarchy*, 87.

21. Sam Francis, "Arizona's Prop. 200 Could Signal Shift In Political Winds," *VDARE.COM*, October 11, 2004.

22. Richard Marosi, "Anti-Immigrant Initiatives Growing," *Seattle Times*, November 6, 2004.

23. Sheehy, *Fighting Immigration Anarchy*, 88–89.

24. Francis, "Arizona's Prop. 200 Could Signal Shift In Political Winds."

25. Veranes and Navarro, "Anti-Immigrant Legislation in Arizona." The authors cite as their main source "Economic Impact of the Arizona-Mexico Relationship" (2003), available online at www.thunderbird.edu/faculty-research/research-centers/econ-impact, accessed on 4/22/05.

26. Veranes and Navarro, "Anti-Immigrant Legislation in Arizona."

27. Legal cases: *Gonzalez v. Arizona*, Mountain States Legal Foundation, no date, www.mountainstateslegal.org/legal_cases.cfm?legalcaseid=141.

28. Melanie Hunter, "Appeals Court Rejects Bid: Illegal Immigrants' Bid to Challenge Prop. 200," Crosswalk.Com, no date, www.crosswalk.com/1345098/print.

29. *Yes On Proposition 200 v. Napolitano*, No. CYV2004–092999 (Maricopa County Sup. Ct., order issued March 14, 2005); Arizona Court of Appeals Div. One, CA-CV 05–0235.

30. For an excellent and comprehensive examination of various anti-immigrant state initiatives passed or proposed and local ordinances during 2005 and 2007 see Tanya Broder, "State and Local Policies on Immigration Access to Services: Promoting Integration or Isolation," *National Immigration Law Center*, May 2007, 4.

31. Sarah Lynch, "Hispanics Help Pass Laws against Illegals," *East Valley-Scottsdale-Tribune*, November 30, 2006.

32. Sarah Lynch, "Hispanics Help Pass Laws against Illegals."

33. The California driver's license issue had its roots in the late 1990s. During the ensuing years on several occasions, via the tenacious leadership of its author, State Senator Gil Cedillo, the issue was vetoed several times, first by Democratic Governor Davis and then Republican Governor Schwarzenegger on October 7.

34. Edwin Garcia, "License Proposal Re-introduced," *San Jose Mercury News*, January 11, 2006.

35. Jim Miller, "Initiative Falls Short by 100,000," *Press Enterprise*, December 10, 2005.

36. Found on The Final Phase Forum, "No Article Title," thefinalphaseforum .invisionzone.com/index.php?act=Print&client=printer&f=3&t=408, August 12, 2005.

37. Associated Press, "Mexican Government Criticizes New Mexico Emergency Declaration," August 12, 2005; John Turner Gilliland, "Illegal Alien Crisis Produces Partisan Split in Arizona," *CNSNews.com*, August 18, 2005.

38. Lydersen, "English Bill Vetoed in Arizona," 2.

39. Lydersen, "English Bill Vetoed in Arizona," 3.

40. Ana Maria Patino, letter to Paul Charlton, U.S. Attorney's Office, June 23, 2006.

41. The scope of this work precludes a specific assessment of the various legislative measures that were either proposed or passed. For a summary see Broder, "State and Local Policies on Immigration Access to Services," 1–23.

42. Nicholas Riccardi, "Immigration Hard-Liners on a High," *Los Angeles Times*, July 12, 2006.

43. Broder, "State and Local Policies on Immigration Access to Services," 4.

44. Broder, "State and Local Policies on Immigration Access to Services," 4. Broder provides several other illustrations to support her argument, which I support. Moreover, she also accentuates that the nativist legislative surge was very much politically alive in 2007.

45. Walter F. Roche, Jr., "Number of State-Level Immigration Laws is Growing," *Los Angeles Times*, August 6, 2007.

46. National Professional Employer Organization, "Arizona's Fair and Legal Employment Act," August 17, 2007, nationalpeo.com/blog; and NDN, "The New AZ Law on the Workplace and Undocumented," ndnblog.org.

47. Miguel Bustillo, "Oklahoma Bill Cracks Down on Illegal Immigrants, Employers," *Los Angeles Times*, April 3, 2007.

48. Emily Bazar, "Strict Immigration Law Rattles Okla. Businesses," *USA Today*, January 10, 2008.

49. Associated Press, "Hispanic students leaving Tulsa area schools," September 14, 2007; and Jerry Giordano, "Hispanics Moving Out of Oklahoma Before New Law Takes Effect," *KTUL, Channel 8,* August 22, 2007.

50. Bazar, "Strict immigration Law Rattles Okla. Businesses," *USA Today*, January 10, 2008.

51. Associated Press, "Dobbs Relentless with Spitzer Criticism," October 28, 2007.

52. Joe Mathews and Nicole Gaouette, "Illegal Immigrant Licenses Drive Debate," *Los Angeles Times*, November 11, 2007.

53. Roche, "Number of State-Level Immigration Laws Is Growing."

54. Broder, "State and Local Policies on Immigration Access to Services," 11. She cites as the main source of this comment Jeffrey S. Passel and Wendy Zimmerman, "Are Immigrants Leaving California? Settlement Patterns of Immigrants in the Late 1990s," *Urban Institute*, April 1, 2001.

55. MALDEF Legal and Policy Analysis: City of San Bernardino Immigration Relief Act Ordinance," www.maldef.org/publications/pdf/LEGAL%20AND%20POLICY%20ANALYSIS.pdf, no date provided.

56. Power Pac, "City of San Bernardino Illegal Immigration Relief Act Ordinance Fact Sheet," no date, PowerPac.org.

57. Stephen Wall, "Petition Targets Aiding Illegal Migrants in City," *San Bernardino County Sun*, May 5, 2006.

58. Wall, "Petition Targets Aiding Illegal Migrants in City."

59. ACLU, "Section by Section Analysis: City of San Bernardino Immigration Relief Act Ordinance."

60. Leslie Redford, "San Bernardino City Council Turns Down Racist Petition," *San Bernardino County Sun*, May 16, 2006.

61. Gillian Flaccus, "San Bernardino Council Considers Illegal Immigration Measure," Associated Press, May 15, 2006.

62. Kelly Rayburn, "Both Sides Step Outside," *San Bernardino County Sun*, June 24, 2006.

63. Ashley Powers, "Law Aiming at Migrants Faces Hurdle," *Los Angeles Times*, June 27, 2007; Kelly Rayburn, "Judge Rejects Initiative," *San Bernardino County Sun*, June 27, 2006; and Chris Richard, "Immigration Measure Off the Ballot," *Press Enterprise*, June 27, 2007.

64. Leonor Vivanco, "Pennsylvania City Mimicking San Bernardino's Proposed 'Illegal' Immigration Relief Act," *Inland Valley Daily Bulletin*, June 17, 2006.

65. John Christoffersen and Michael Rubinkam, "Two American Cities, New Haven, Conn., and Hazelton, Pa., on Immigration," www.centerdaily.com, July 24, 2007.

66. Jon Hurdle, "U.S. Court Throws Out City's Illegal Immigration Law," *Yahoo! News*, July 26, 2007.

67. Reni Gertner, "Local Immigration Ordinances Struck Down," reni.gertner@lawyersusaonline.com, August 13, 2007.

68. Editorial, "Humanity v. Hazelton," *New York Times*, July 28, 2007.

69. Statement found on Immigration Watch International Website, "Hazelton Loses First Round in Court," jonjayray.wordpress.com/2007/07/, July 27, 2007.

70. Hurdle, "U.S. Court Throws Out City's Illegal Immigration Law."

71. Hurdle, "U.S. Court Throws Out City's Illegal Immigration Law."

72. Paul Eakins, "Escondido Council Divided over Hazelton's Ruling's Effect," *North County Times*, July 27, 2007

73. David Savage and Nicole Gaouette, *Los Angeles Times*, July 27, 2007.

74. Wade Malcolm, "Hazelton Expects Legal Defense Fund to Surge Following Ruling," *Standard-Speaker*, July 28, 2007.

75. Dave Montgomery, "Groups Loudly Press for State, Local Crackdowns," *McClatchy Washington Bureau*, August 19, 2007.

76. Anthony Ramirez, "Unrest and Arrests at Immigration Rally," *New York Times*, July 29, 2007.

77. Claudia Lauer, "Ban Could Deny Illegal Immigrants Services," *Los Angeles Times*, July 14, 2007; and Peter Schrag, "Divided States," *The Nation*, January 7/14, 2008.

78. William C. Flook and Dan Genz, "Fairfax Chairman Blasts Prince William County's Controversial Immigration Plan," *The Examiner*, August 8, 2007.

79. Melissa Nelson, "Sheriff's Tactics Triggering Uproar," *Press Enterprise*, June 29, 2007; and Associated Press, "Immigrant Rights Advocate Emails Doctored Photo of Sheriff," August 16, 2007.

80. Agustin Duran, "Dictan otra medida en contra de inmigrantes," *La Opinion*, August 8, 2007.

81. Associated Press, "Groups Clash Over Immigration at Church," *Washingtonpost .com*, September 17, 2007.

82. Sheehy, *Fighting Immigration Anarchy*, 141.

83. Chacon and Davis, *No One Is Illegal*, 219–20.

84. National Immigration Forum, "Immigration Law Enforcement Act of 2006," www.immigrationforum.org/DesktopDefault.aspx?tabid=777, September 20, 2006, 1.

85. National Immigration Law Center, "Immigration Law & Policy: Comprehensive Immigration Reform (CIR)," 19, no. 4, (September 16, 2005): 4–5.

86. National Immigration Law Center, "Immigration Law & Policy," 5–13.

87. National Immigration Law Center, "Immigration Law & Policy,"14–19.

88. Todd J. Gillman, "Proposal Aims to Boost Security at the Border," *Press Enterprise*, October 6, 2005.

89. Nedra Pickler, "Bush Touts Dual Plan on Border," Associated Press, November 29, 2005.

90. CPUSA Education Commission, "2006 Immigrant Rights Club Education Guide," www.freerepublic.com/focus/f-news/1622973/posts, April 27, 2006, 4.

91. Mary Curtius, "GOP Bill Ignores Bush's Guest-Worker Plan, "*Los Angeles Times*, December 7, 2005.

92. Much of the above information on H.R 4437 was derived from the following articles: Curtius, "GOP Bill Ignores Bush's Guest-Worker Plan"; Mary Curtius, "House OKs Border Bill Without a Guest Plan," *Los Angeles Times*, December 12, 2005; Claire Vitucci and Sharon McNary, "Immigration Bill OK'd, Touted as a 'Strong Start,'" *Press Enterprise*, December 17, 2005; Maribel Hastings, "Aprobado el control migratorio," *La Opinion*, December 17, 2005; Michael A. Fletcher and Darryl Fears, "Analysts: Crackdown Won't Halt Immigration," *Washington Post*, December 18, 2005.

93. Associated Press, "Key Panel OKs Immigration Bill," December 12, 2005.

94. Peter Wallsten, "Amid Rifts, GOP Backs Guest-Worker Plan," *Los Angeles Times*, January 21, 2006.

95. Maribel Hastings, "Plan migratorio contiene via para la legalizacion," *La Opinion*, February 18, 2006.

96. Editorial, "Borderline Progress," *Press-Enterprise*, February 10, 2006.

97. Mary Curtius, "Immigration Proposal Attacked from All Sides," *Los Angeles Times*, February 25, 2006.

98. Editorial, "Bordering on Paralysis," *Los Angeles Times*, March 3, 2006.

99. Nicole Gaouette and Maura Reynolds, "Immigration Fight Heats Up," *Los Angeles Times*, March 28, 2006.

100. A compendium of the main provisions, paraphrased, taken from Associated Press, "Highlights of Tentative Senate Compromise," *Inland Valley Daily Bulletin*, April 7, 2006.

101. Editorial, "Borderline Acceptable," *Los Angeles Times*, April 7, 2006.

102. Jennifer Loven, "Bush Blames Reid for Migrant Bill Loss," Associated Press, April 9, 2006.

103. John Aloysius Farrell, "Pair of Immigration Reform Proposals Soundly Defeated," *Denver Post*, April 8, 2006.

104. James Gerstenzang, "Bush Sees Options on Immigration," *Los Angeles Times*, April 25, 2006; and Jennifer Loven, "Bush: Deportations Won't Work," Associated Press, April 25, 2006.

105. Andrew Taylor, "Senate Votes to Divert Some War Money to Tighten Borders," *Press Enterprise*, April 27, 2006.

106. Suzanne Gamboa, "Senate Deal Revives Bill on Immigration," *Press Enterprise*, May 12, 2006.

107. Michelle Mittelstadt, "Showdown Looms on Immigration," *Press Enterprise*, May 10, 2006.

108. Maribel Hastings, "Aprueban muro y vía de legalizacifin," *La Opinion*, May 10, 2006.

109. Mittelstadt, "Showdown Looms on Immigration"; and *Washington Post*, "Senate Passes English-Language Bill," May 19, 2006.

110. Sara A. Carter, "Bush Unveils Border Plan," *Inland Valley Daily Bulletin*, May 16, 2006; Robert Sallady and Nancy Vogel, "State Officials Chafe at Bush's Plan for Guard," *Los Angeles Times*, May 18, 2006; Ruben Navarrette, "Don't Put Guard On Border Patrol," *Press Enterprise*, May 18, 2006; Will Weissert, "Mexico Watches Border Moves," *Press Enterprise*, May 18, 2006; and Sylvia Moreno and Ann Scott Tyson, "Bringing in Guard Raises Concerns of Militarization," *Washington Post*, May 16, 2006.

111. Jim VandeHei and Jonathan Weisman, "On Immigration, Bush Seeks 'Middle Ground,'" *Washington Post*, May 16, 2006.

112. Carter, "Bush Unveils Border Plan"; Sallady and Vogel, "State Officials Chafe at Bush's Plan for Guard"; Navarrette, "Don't Put Guard On Border Patrol"; Weissert, "Mexico Watches Border Moves"; and Moreno and Tyson, "Bringing in Guard Raises Concerns of Militarization."

113. *Washington Post*, "Senate, House Immigration Bills," May 24, 2006.

114. Nicole Gaouette, "Senate Passes Sweeping Bill on Immigration," *Los Angeles Times*, May 26, 2006.

115. Lisa Friedman, "GOP Leaders to Stay the Course on Immigration," *San Bernardino County Sun*, June 20, 2006; and Maribel Hastings, "Audiencias en torno a la reforma migratoria," *La Opinion*, June 23, 2006.

116. Carl Hulse, "House Holds Up Overhaul," New York Times News Service, June 21, 2006.

117. Chris Ramirez, "Groups Decry Lack of Voice in Immigration Hearings," *Arizona Republic*, August 3, 2006.

118. Nicole Gaouette and Faye Fiore, "GOP Plans Competing Events on Immigration," *Los Angeles Times*, June 23, 2006.

119. Nicole Gaouette, "House Votes to Boost Border Security; Broader Immigration Issues Remain," *Los Angeles Times*, September 15, 2006; and Nicole Gaouette, "Border Barrier Approved," *Los Angeles Times*, September 30, 2006.

120. Dave Montgomery, "Border Wall Estimates Called High," *Press Enterprise*, January 13, 2007.

121. Wikipedia contributors, "United States House of Representatives Elections, 2006," *Wikipedia, The Free Encyclopedia*, en.wikipedia.org/w/index.php?title=United_States_House_of_Representatives_elections%2C_2006&oldid=217259553.

122. Wikipedia contributors, "United States House of Representatives Elections, 2006."

123. Claire Vitucci and Michelle DeArmond, "Immigration Reform Deferred," *Press Enterprise*, November 29, 2006.

124. Deb Riechmann, "Calderon Tells Bush Mexico Needs More," Associated Press, March 14, 2007.

125. Nicole Gaouette, "GOP Takes Immigration Temperature," *Los Angeles Times*, March 30, 2007; and Associated Press, "White House Floats Immigration Plan," March 30, 2007.

126. Gaouette, "GOP Takes Immigration Temperature."

127. The preceding was taken from a combination of several sources: Nicole Gaouette and Teresa Watanabe, "House Bill Offers Citizenship," *Los Angeles Times*, March 21, 2007; Xavier Rodriguez, "Corporate-Designed Immigration Reform," www.leftshift.org, April 15, 2007; National Immigration Law Center, "STRIVE ACT of 2007 Introduced," www.nilc.org, March 22, 2007.

128. For an excellent brief critique of the STRIVE ACT see Lilian Galedo, "The STRIVE ACT Is a False Promise," *New America Media*, April 14, 2007.

129. Nicole Gaouette, "Senators Craft Immigration Compromise," *Los Angeles Times*, May 18, 2007.

130. The above summary is taken from a critique I wrote on S1348 on behalf of the National Alliance for Human Rights.

131. Dave Montgomery, "New Path for 12 Million," *Press Enterprise*, May 18, 2007.

132. Michael Sandler and Jonathan Allen, "Senate Gives Up on immigration Bill," *CQ Today*, June 7, 2007.

133. Ken Strickland, "Immigration: Another Vote Likely," *MSNBC First Read*, June 7, 2007.

134. Armando Navarro, "Report: NAHR Says NO to S.1348," *National Alliance for Human Rights*, June 3, 2007. Internet. [AQ9: please complete this citation with website or journal info.]

135. Mickey Kaus, "Bush's Domestic Iraq," *Los Angeles Times*, June 4, 2007.

136. Julia Preston, "Immigration Bill Re-emerging, Piece by Piece," *New York Times News Service*, August 3, 2007.

Chapter 12

1. Joseph Gusfield, ed., *Protest, Reform, and Revolt: A Reader in Social Movements* (New York: John Wiley and Sons, 1970), 2.

2. John Wilson, *Introduction to Social Movements* (New York: Basic Books, 1973), 8.

3. In my previous works, I have argued that requisite to any reform or evolutionary social movement are six interconnected variables: (1) climate of change; (2) leadership; (3) organization; (4) ideology; (5) strategy and tactics; and (6) power capability. The longevity or success of any such movement highly depends on the presence of these six vital ingredients. The absence or weakness of any one or several will shorten and ultimately lead to a movement's demise. Armando Navarro, *Mexicano Political Experience in Occupied Aztlán* (Walnut Creek, Calif.: Alta Mira Press, 2005).

4. Frances Fox Piven and Richard A. Cloward, *Poor People's Movements: Why They Succeed, How They Fail* (New York: Vintage Books, 1979), 14.

5. I have borrowed the usage of "precondition" from Harry Eckstein's theory on the causation of revolution (Harry Eckstein, "On the Etiology of Internal Wars," in *Why Revolution: Theories and Analysis*, ed. Clifford T. Payton and Robert Blackey [Cambridge, Mass.: Schenkman Publishing Co., 1971], 124–50). He defines a "precondition" as "those circumstances which make it possible for the precipitant to bring about political violence." I insert "historical" because of the importance of understanding the significance and importance of past historical events. Antagonisms are the individual events that foster a conflict, which indubitably dialectically raises the level of political consciousness to new levels.

6. Eric Hoffer, *The True Believer* (New York: Harper & Row, 1951), 20.

7. Piven and Cloward, *Poor People's Movements*, 9.

8. Barrington Moore, "Revolution in America," *New York Review of Books*, January 30, 1969.

9. Ted Gurr, *Why Men Rebel* (Princeton, N.J.: Princeton University Press, 1970) 13.

10. Steve Breyman, *Movement Genesis: Social Movement Theory and the West German Peace Movement* (Boulder, Colo.: Westview Press, 1998), 41–42.

11. The rise of MPM can also be understood from a social movement theoretical perspective of political process and opportunity paradigm. Unlike relative deprivation, which focuses on the person's psychological aspects, it explains social movements as being primarily political rather than psychological phenomena. The political process and opportunities paradigm examines the collective structures and processes through which social movements pursue power. As to their origins, it postulates that they derive from three areas: (1) level of organization; (2) level of consciousness; and (3) the opportunity

structure. Armando Navarro, "A Compendium of Social Movement Theory," unpublished chapter, for the book *What Needs to Be Done: The Building of a New Movement.*

12. The usage of "precipitant" denotes the historical precondition that jump-starts a social movement. The concept of precipitant is used by Harry Eckstein in his work, "On the Etiology of Internal Wars," 127. He specifically defines it as "an event that which actually starts the war (occasions it), much as the turning of a flint wheel of a cigarette lighter ignites the flame."

13. James C. Davies, "The J-Curve of Rising and Declining Satisfactions as a Cause of Some Great Revolutions and a Contained Rebellion" in *The History of Violence.* Davies utilizes relative deprivation theory. It posits the argument that social movements rise, particularly revolutionary types, when an "intolerable gap" develops between what people have and want and what they get. When the gap is tolerable there is no climate of change. However, when "expected need satisfaction" rises to such a high level where it creates a huge gap with the people's "actual need satisfaction," it engenders the requisite climate of change that gives rise to a revolutionary social movement. Davies further rejects Marx's theory of degradation, meaning increasing misery and poverty is what fuels revolution; instead, he argues that revolutionary movements occur in times of "growing economic prosperity." He writes, "Revolutions are most likely to occur when a prolonged period of objective economic and social development is followed by a short period of sharp reversal." As with frustration aggression theory, Davies's J-curve theory is predicated on the existence of "chronic discontent," 90.

14. American Friends Committee press release, "End of Year Deadly Incident Involving Border Patrol Not an Isolated Incident," January 3, 2006.

15. Francisco Robles Nava, "Timido reclamo migratorio," *La Opinion*, January 10, 2006.

16. Gregory Rodriguez, "Mexico's Bluster, Mexico's Pride," *Press Enterprise*, January 15, 2006.

17. Richard Marosi, "Border Tunnel Is Called Amazing," *Los Angeles Times*, January 27, 2006.

18. James McKinley, Jr., "A Border Killing Inflames Mexican Anger at U.S. Policy," *New York Times*, January 14, 2006.

19. Daniel González, 'Radio host sparks immigrant fervor," *Arizona Republic*, Jan 17, 2006. Bermudez at the time was fifty-five and had been born in San Miguel, Sonora. He came to the U.S. during the early 1970s and later became a U.S. citizen. A Republican, he was mayor of San Luis, Arizona, from 1980 to 1982.

20. It is important to note that rally organizers estimated the attendance to be at least 10,000 people, whereas the media, as indicated by the following source, projected 4,000: Chip Scutari and Robbie Sherwood, "Napolitano Vows to Secure Border," *Arizona Republic*, January 10, 2006.

21. Nicholas Riccardi, "States Take On Border Issues," *Los Angeles Times*, January 16, 2006.

22. The concept of "mobilization contagion" is used to describe the "spreading effect" created by the said direct action, in this case the march. It suggests others in other communities and states were induced to take to the streets and do the same in their respective areas.

23. Gonzalez, "Radio Host Sparks Immigrant Fervor."

24. Yvonne Wingett, "Latino Issues Facing Battle in Legislature," *Arizona Republic*, January 14, 2006.

25. NAHR press release, "Latinos Meet to Mobilize against Nativist Immigration Legislation and Attacks," January 11, 2006.

26. NAHR, meeting printed agenda, entitled "Emergency Mexicano/Leadership Meeting," January 12, 2006.

27. Armando Navarro, "A Strategic Plan of Action," NAHR, January 12, 2008.

28. Alejandro Cano, "Junta en San Bernardino oponerse a medida antiinmigrante," *La Opinion*, January 16, 2006.

29. Jorge Morales Almada, "Anuncian plan contra la ley antiinmigante," *La Opinion*, January 14, 2006.

30. Jennifer Delson, "O.C. Officials Say No Sweeps in New Role," *Los Angeles Times*, January 19, 2008.

31. Peter Wallsten, "Immigration Rift in GOP Up for Vote," *Los Angeles Times*, January 20, 2006.

32. *La Opinion*, "Richardson propone enviar mas fondos a la frontera," January 19, 2006.

33. William Finn Bennett, "Immigrant Activists Plan March on D.C.," *North County Times*, January 16, 2006.

34. *La Opinion*, "Una Caravana por los inmigrantes," February 3, 2006; Leslie Berestein, "Immigration Protest Heads to D.C.," *San Diego Union-Tribune*, February 3, 2006; Yolanda Sansegundo, "Caravana pro Inmigrante en camino a Washington," *La Prensa*, February 19, 2006.

35. NAHR press release, "Mexicano/Latino Leadership Bi-National Summit against H.R. 4437 and Legalization," February 11, 2006.

36. NAHR press release, "Mexicano/Latino Leadership Bi-National Summit against H.R. 4437 and Legalization."

37. NAHR, "Mexicano/Latino Leadership Summit Agenda," February 11, 2006; and Armando Navarro, personal Summit notes, February 11, 2006.

38. Armando Navarro, "NAHR Proposed Legislative and Direct Actions to Defeat H.R. 4437," February 11, 2006. Found in my personal archives.

39. Navarro, personal Summit notes.

40. Sharon McNary, "Immigration Bill Spurs Protest," *Press Enterprise*, February 13, 2006.

41. Jorge Morales Almada, "Anuncian un boicot a Costa Mesa," *La Opinion*, February 3, 2006; Christopher Goffard, "Costa Mesa's Border Heat Puts a Chill in Its Latinos," *Los Angeles Times*, February 25, 2006; and Jennifer Delson, "Border Battle Is New Turf for Costa Mesa Mayor," *Los Angeles Times*, March 5, 2006.

42. Yurina Rico, "Freno a cazainmigrantes," *La Opinion*, February 4, 2006.

43. Craig Tenbroeck, "Opponents of Illegal Immigration Plan Protest in Vista," *The Californian*, February 2, 2006.

44. *La Opinion*, "Entregan jornaleros a Migracion," February 26, 2006.

45. *La Opinion*, "Hispanos salen a defenderse," February 6, 2006.

46. Aracell Martinez-Ortega, "Proponen mas leyes contr inmigrantes," *La Opinion*, no date.

47. Jose de la Isla and Alex Meneses, "Pro-Immigrant Rallies Spring throughout Entire Nation," *Hispanic Link* 24, no. 11 (March 13, 2006).

48. Roger Lindo, "AFL-CIO apoya la amnistia," *La Opinion*, March 1, 2006.

49. Jorge Morales Almada, "Regresa la caravan por los inmigrantes," *La Opinion*, March 1, 2006.

50. Martha Groves, "Day-Labor Group Starts Trek," *Los Angeles Times*, March 5, 2006.

51. Maribel Hastings, "Plan migatorio contiene via para la legalizacion," *La Opinion*, February 18, 2006.

52. *La Opinion*, "Cancillares buscan suavizar politica migratoria de EU," and "Legisladores Mexicanos viajan a Washington," February 13, 2006.

53. *Inland Valley Daily Bulletin*, "Foreign Nations Team-up to Fight U.S. Immigration Bill," February 24, 2006.

54. Sara A. Carter, "Congress Calls for Border Hearing," *Inland Valley Daily Bulletin*, February 1, 2006.

55. Alex Meneses Miyashita, "Thousands Rally Outside Nation's Capitol, Urge Senate to Legalize the Undocumented," *Hispanic Link* 24, no.11 (March 13, 2006).

56. Revolution: Voice of the Revolutionary Communist Party, USA, "Chicago Immigrants—A Defiant Show of Strength," March 19, 2006.

57. As a concept, "multiplier effect" is used to denote that it induced the holding of other marches nationwide. This meant pro-migrant rights activists in many parts of the country were influenced to organize and become integrated into the growing mobilization ranks of MPM.

58. Susan Ferriss, "Rally Fights Border Measure," *Sacramento Bee*, March 11, 2006.

59. *La Opinion*, "Un dia Sin Latinos," March 24, 2006.

60. NAHR press release, "NAHR Delegation Leaves Tuesday to Meet with Mexico's Political Leaders and Latin American Ambassadors to Push for Immigration Reform," March 13, 2006; and Eileen Truax, "Activistas migratorios viajan a Mexico D.F.," *La Opinion*, March 13, 2006.

61. Armando Navarro, "Delegation Notes and Tape Recordings," located at my archives at home.

62. Fabviola Martinez, "Defensores de migrantes de EU planean marcha en Mexico; invitan a candidates," *La Jornada*, March 18, 2006.

63. Brady McCombs, "Rallying Immigrant Advocates are Feeling a Sense of Urgency," *Arizona Daily Star*, March 24, 2006; and *Arizona Republic*, "Thousands March to Protest Immigration Legislation," March 24, 2006.

64. Richard Fausset, "Nervously, Latinos Protest in the South," *Los Angeles Times*, March 30, 2006.

65. Melissa Trujillo, "Students March on Colorado Capitol for Immigrant Rights," Associated Press, April 19, 2006.

66. Teresa Watanabe and Hector Becerra, "500,000 Cram Streets to Protest Immigration Bills," *Los Angeles Times*, March 26, 2006.

67. Watanabe and Becerra, "500,000 Cram Streets to Protest Immigration Bills"; Peter Prengaman, "Los Angeles Crowd Estimated at 500,000," Associated Press, March 26, 2006.

68. Jorge Morales Almada, "El Dia se las banderas," *La Opinion*, March 26, 2006.

69. Teresa Watanabe and Hector Becerra, "How DJs Put 500,000 Marchers In Motion," *Los Angeles Times*, March 28, 2006.

70. Teresa Watanabe, "Catholic Leaders Hope to Sway Immigration Debate," *Los Angeles Times*, March 3, 2006; Teresa Watanabe, "Immigrants Gain the Pulpit," *Los Angeles Times*, April 1, 2006; Yurina Rico, "Iglesias protegeran a indocumentados," *La Opinion*, April 2, 2006.

71. Wantanabe, "Catholic leaders Hope to Sway Immigration Debate."

72. Ruben Moreno, "Marcha por los campesinos," *La Opinion*, March 27, 2006.

73. *La Opinion*, "Critican medidas contra inmigrantes," March 27, 2006.

74. Robert Jablon, "Thousands Join Walkouts," *Press Enterprise*, March 28, 2006.

75. Cynthia H. Cho and Anna Gorman, "Massive Student Walkout Spreads across Southland," *Los Angeles Times*, March 28, 2006; Paul La Rocco, "Students Protest Legislation," *Press-Enterprise*, March 28, 2006.

76. Christopher Goffard, "Protest Reactions Reflect the Area's Deep Divisions," *Los Angeles Times*, March 29, 2006.

77. *La Opinion*, "Critican medidas contra Inmigrantes," March 27, 2006.

78. Goffard, "Protest Reactions Reflect the Area's Deep Divisions."

79. Cynthia H. Cho and Kelly-Anne Suarez, "Walkouts Dwindle at L.A. Schools but not Elsewhere," *Los Angeles Times*, March 30, 2006.

80. Mtung Oak Kim, "Foreign Flags Create Flap," *Rocky Mountain News*, March 30, 2006.

81. "Meet the Press" Transcript for Program: John Kerry, Henry Bonilla, Luis Gutierrez, J.D. Hayworth, Sun., April 9, 2006.

82. Teresa Watanabe, "Immigrant Crusade Enlists Few Blacks," *Los Angeles Times*, April 10, 2006.

83. Phoenix Summit Agenda, April 8, 2006.

84. Armando Navarro, notes on Summit and tape recordings, April 8, 2006.

85. Maria Vega, "Latinos con un mismo afan," *La Opinion*, April 2, 2006.

86. *Press Enterprise*, "Protests Building Strength," April 10, 2006.

87. Agustin Duran, "Marchas en favor de los Inmigrantes," *La Opinion*, April 19, 2006.

88. *Press Enterprise*, "Protests Building Strength"; Sharon McNary, "Area Activists Taking Time to Regroup," *Press Enterprise*, April 10, 2004; and *NewsMax.com*, "Latinos Plan Nationwide Worker Strike," March 30, 2006.

89. Greg Miller, "Immigration Activists on March Again," *Los Angeles Times*, April 10, 2006.

90. Maura Reynolds and Faye Fiore, "Across the U.S., We Are America," *Los Angeles Times*, April 11, 2006.

91. Reynolds and Fiore, "Across the U.S., We Are America"; Jorge Luis Macias, "Despierta La America Inmigrante," *La Opinion*, April 11, 2006.

92. Randal C. Archibold, "Riverside at Birth of Marches," *New York Times*, April 12, 2006.

93. Archibold, "Riverside at Birth of Marches."

94. *La Opinion*, "Se Siente impacto de las marchas," April 25, 2006.

95. Ruben Moreno, "Despiden a trabajadores por ir a las marchas," *La Opinion*, April 13, 2006.

96. Sara Carter, "Bordering on Danger," *Inland Valley Daily Bulletin*, April 9, 2006.

97. Nicole Gaouette, "Nationwide Raids Intensify Focus on Employment of Illegal Immigrants," *Los Angeles Times*, April 20, 2006.

98. Nicolas Riccardi, "Why Illegal Immigrants Fear Leaving," *Los Angeles Times*, April 12, 2006.

99. Araceli Martinez-Ortega, "Diez propuestas de ley anti-inmigrantes en Sacramento," *La Opinon*, April 13, 2006.

100. Susan Rosenblatt, "Riverside County to Screen Inmates," *Los Angeles Times*, April 12, 2006.

101. *La Opinion*, "Muestras de Repudio," April 11, 2006.

102. Valerie Richardson, "Mexican Aliens to Retake 'Stolen Land,'" *Washington Times*, April 16, 2006.

103. Francisco Robles Nava, "Fox pide un acuerdo complete," *La Opinion*, April 11, 2006.

104. Araceli Martinez-Ortega, "Protesta en San Francisco," *La Opinion*, April 24, 2006.

105. Trujillo, "High School Students March for Immigrants."

106. Jannise Johnson, "Supporters Rally around Family," *Inland Valley Daily Bulletin*, April 10, 2006; Alejandro Cano, "Possible demanda contra distrito escolar por suicidio de alumno," *La Opinion*, April 14, 2006.

107. Peter Prengaman, "Divisions Emerge Over May 1 Immigration Work and School Boycott," Associated Press, April 19, 2006.

108. In a subsequent section of this chapter the factors or issues that contributed to the MPM's decline will be examined.

109. Prengaman, "Divisions Emerge over May 1 Immigration Boycott."

110. Don Thompson, "Immigrant Boycott Endorsed," *Press Enterprise*, April 28, 2006.

111. Teresa Watanabe and Anna Gorman, "Factions Divide on Boycott," April 20, 2006.

112. Maribel Hastings, "'Salte a la Acción,' plan del Consejo Nacional de la Raza," *La Opinion*, April 27, 2006.

113. Teresa Watanabe and Anna Gorman, "Rally Organizers Differ on Boycott Issue," *Los Angeles Times,* April 20, 2006.

114. Watanabe and Gorman, "Factions Divide on Boycott."

115. Agustin Duran, "Crece obceción al boicot laboral,*"La Opinon*, April 18, 2006.

116. Duran, "Crece objecion al boicot laboral."

117. Source to memo to remain anonymous, sent to me via e-mail on April 12, 2006; Sara Carter, "Immigrant Advocates Plan Boycott of Univision," *Inland Valley Daily Bulletin*, April 14, 2006.

118. Brent Hopkins and Angie Valencia-Martinez, "Demonstrators Flood Downtown Los Angeles," *Inland Valley Daily Bulletin*, May 2, 2006; *La Opinion*, "Fuerza Inmigrante," May 4, 2006.

119. Estimates of the size of mobilizations derived from the following sources and reports to NAHR from various coalitional leaders who organized marches as part of the historic boycott. Gillian Flaccus, "From LA to NY, Immigrants Raise Peaceful, but Boisterous, Voices,"Associated Press, May 2, 2006; Sharon McNary, Michael Fisher, and Douglas E. Beeman, "Marchers Take Movement to Streets, Parks," *Press Enterprise*, May 2, 2006; George Watson, Stephen Wall, and Andrew Edwards, "A Day Without Immigrants: Protests Show Clout," *San Bernardino County Sun*, May 2, 2006; Jason Newwell, Monica Rodriguez, Caroline An, and Mark Petix, "Rallying for Rights," *Inland Valley Daily Bulletin*, May 2, 2006; Anna Gorman, Marjorie Miller, and Mitchell Landsberg, "Immigrants Demonstrate Peaceful Power," *Los Angeles Times*, May 2, 2006; Eileen Truax, "Aqui Estamos," *La Opinion*, May 2, 2006.

120. Flaccus, "From LA to NY, Immigrants Raise Peaceful, but Boisterous, Voices"; McNary, Fisher, and E. Beeman, "Marchers Take Movement to Streets, Parks"; Watson, Wall, and Edwards, "A Day without Immigrants: Protests Show Clout"; Newwell, Rodriguez, An, and Petix, "Rallying for Rights"; Gorman, Miller, and Landsberg, "Immigrants Demonstrate Peaceful Power"; Truax, "Aqui Estamos."

121. Sean Nealon and Marlene Toscano, "Clash of Views Fills the Airwaves," *Press Enterprise*, May 2, 2006.

122. Paul Herrera, "Diners, Homebuilders Have Difficulty Finding Helping Hands," *Press Enterprise*, May 2, 2006.

123. Gillian Flaccus, "Thousands skip work, school, join rallies from L.A. to NYC," *San Diego Union-Tribune*, May 2, 2006.

124. *La Opinion*, "Mas Alla De LAS," May 2, 2006.

125. *Inland Valley Daily Bulletin*, "Thousands of Workers Stage Rallies in Mexico," May 2, 2006.

Chapter 13

1. The usage of "accelerators," meaning events, situations, and circumstances, are examined in depth in chapter 13. However, as a concept it is also used as a synonym to Francis Fox Piven and Richard A. Cloward's usage of the term "dislocations" in their book *Poor People's Movements: Why They Succeed, How They Fail* (New York: Vintage Books, 1979).

2. Throughout this chapter "mass movement" is used interchangeably with "social movement," which is examined and defined in chapter 12.

3. The preceding examination of my paradigm on mass and social movements as a compendium is taken from my sixth book, which was in progress at the time of the writing of this work, entitled *What Needs To Be Done? The Building of a New Movement*.

4. Press release, "Department of Homeland Security Unveils Comprehensive Immigration Enforcement Strategy for the Nation's Interior," U.S. Immigration and Customs Enforcement, April 20, 2006.

5. Nicole Gaouette, "What Was Behind the Big Raid," *Los Angeles Times*, April 22, 2006.

6. Julia Preston, "As Pace of Deportation Rises, Illegal families Dig In," nytimes .com, May 1, 2007.

7. Sara A. Carter, "Activists Plan to Protest on Immigrants," *Whittier Daily News*, January 25, 2007.

8. Irwan Firdaus, "Arrestan mas de 100 inmigrantes en 17 estados," *La Opinion*, February 22, 2007.

9. Press release issued by Progressive Democrats of America, "Latino Leaders Protest in Front of the Most Powerful Democrat in the Nation Today: Rahm Emanuel to Request an Immediate Moratorium on the Deportations," February 26, 2007.

10. Andrea Hopkins, "U.S. Immigrants Worry as Families Face Deportation," *Yahoo News*, August 29, 2007.

11. Lou Dobbs, "Mexican President's Blatant Hypocrisy," *CNN.com*, September 5, 2007.

12. Press release from attorney Peter Schey, "Workers Will Sue to Stop Mass Arrests and Detentions by Federal Government," September 11, 2007.

13. Stacia Glenn, "Alert of ICE Mulled," *San Bernardino County Sun*, October 5, 2007.

14. Rachel Uranga, "Immigration Sweep Arrests Jump 63 Percent," *Los Angeles Daily News*, November 3, 2007.

15. Glenn, "Alert of ICE Mulled."

16. Gaouette, "What Was behind the Big Raid"; and Sam Quinones, "Deportation of Illegal Workers Leaves Families in Quandary," *Los Angeles Times*, April 22, 2006.

17. The concept of "ethnic cleansing" has various connotations. From my perspective, it connotes pressuring certain ethnic groups, in this case Méxicanos and Latinos, a minority, by the White majority. Moreover, it can be accomplished by a variety of means, some of which can be nonviolent, others violent. In this case, up to now, they have been largely nonviolent.

18. Nathan Thornburgh, "The Case for Amnesty," *Time*, June 18, 2007.

19. Melissa Nelson, "Sheriff's Tactics Triggering Uproar," Associated Press, June 29, 2007.

20. This thesis is well argued by Lorenzo Cano, in a paper he wrote, entitled "Attacks against Mexican Immigrants Have Evolved into a National Psychosis," University of Houston, June 4, 2007.

21. According to Webster's Dictionary, racism is the "belief that race is the primary determinant of human traits and capacities and that racial differences produce an inherent superiority of a particular race." *Webster's Ninth Collegiate Dictionary* (Springfield, Mass.: Merriam-Webster, Inc., 1984), 969.

22. For an examination of xenophobia see Thomas J. Curran, *Xenophobia and Immigrants: 1820–1930* (Boston: Twayne Publishers, 1971).

23. Polling Report found on PollingReport.com "CBS News/New York Times Poll," www.pollingreport.com/immigration.htm, May 18-23, 2007.

24. Poll found on Federation for American Immigration Reform, Internet Website, "Rasmussen Report Poll Conducted from Los Angeles 15-16th of 800 Likely Voters," www.fairus.org/site/PageServer?[agename=research_research74c.

25. Found on United Press International, Internet Website, "Analysis: U.S. Ambivalent on Immigration," www.upi.com/Zogby/UPI_Polls/2007/06/21/analysis_us_ambivalent_on_immigration, June 21, 2007.

26. United Press International, Internet Website, "Analysis: U.S. Ambivalent on Immigration."

27. Report found on Rasmussen Reports, Internet Website, "Public Support Strong for New Immigration Enforcement," www.rasmussenreport.com/public_Content, August 12, 2007.

28. Dan Laidman, "Chief Calls Police Actions 'Disturbing,'" *Press Enterprise*, May 3, 2007; and Patrick McGreevy and Richard Winton, "Bratton Cites Staff Failures in Melee," *Los Angeles Times*, May 30, 2007.

29. Laidman, "Chief Calls Police Actions 'Disturbing'"; and McGreevy and Winton, "Bratton Cites Staff Failures in Melee."

30. Kurt Lang and Gladys Lang, *Collective Dynamics* (New York: Crowell, 1961) 517–24.

31. Neil Smelser, *Theory of Collective Behavior* (New York: Free Press,1962).

32. John D. McCarthy and Mayor N. Zald, *The Trend of Social Movements in Ameica: Professionalization amd Resource Mobilization* (Morristown, N.J.: General Learning Press, 1973), Anthony Oberschall, *Social Conflict and Social Movements*, (Englewood Cliffs, NJ: Prentice-Hall, 1973).

33. Eric Hoffer, *The True Believer* (New York: Harper & Row, 1951), 119–37.

34. Theorists on mass movements generally concur on the critical role leadership plays in movement formation. In the study of revolutions, no one can deny the leadership contributions of a Washington, Lenin, Trotsky, Madero, Mao, Castro, or Guevara, to name a few. The same applies to reform movements, especially in the U.S., such as DuBois, King, Malcolm, Nader, and so forth. The Chicano movement (1966–1974) had a plethora of leaders, but particularly four stood out: Reies Tijerina, Rodolfo "Corky" Gonzales, Cesar Chavez, and Jose Angel Gutierrez.

35. Jo Freeman and Victoria Johnson, eds., *Waves of Protest: Social Movements since the Sixties* (Lanham, Md.: Rowman & Littlefield Publishers, Inc., 1999), 2.

36. V. I. Lenin, *What Is to Be Done?* (New York: International Publishers, 1929), 114.

37. Saul Alinsky, *Rules for Radicals* (New York: Vintage Books, 1971), 113.

38. Samuel Huntington, *Political Order in Changing Societies* (New Haven, Conn.: Yale University Press, 1968), 461.

39. Herbert Blumer, "Social Movements," in *Principles of Sociology*, ed. A. M. Lee (New York: Barnes & Noble, 1951), 199.

40. Fred Rose, *Coalitions across the Class Divide* (Ithaca, N.Y.: Cornell University Press, 2000), 129.

41. Ronald J. Hrebenar, Matthew J. Burbank, and Robert C. Benedict, *Political Parties, Interest Groups, and Political Campaigns* (Boulder, Colo.: Westview Press, 1999), 269.

42. E-mail alert, "No Spending of Immigrant Money on Wednesday, Sept 12," September 19, 2007, webmail.ucr.edu.

43. Agustin Duran, "Phoenix prepara un boicot economic," *La Opinion*, August 14, 2007.

44. Phillip Selznick, *The Organizational Weapon: A Study of Bolshevik Strategy and Tactics* (New York: McGraw-Hill, 1952), 10.

45. Freeman and Johnson, *Waves of Protest*, 3.

46. Reo M. Christenson, Allan S. Engel, Dan N. Jacobs, Mostafa Rejai, and Herbert Waltzer, *Ideologies and Modern Politics* (New York: Dodd, Mead & Company, 1975), 6.

47. Cited in Mostafa Rejai, *The Strategy of Political Revolution* (Garden City, N.Y.: Doubleday & Company, 1973), 27.

48. Rejai, *The Strategy of Political Revolution*, 23.

49. Rejai, *The Strategy of Political Revolution*, 23.

50. Gerald Zaltman, Philip Kotler, and Ira Kaufman, *Creating Social Change* (New York: Holt, Rinehart, and Winston, Inc., 1972), 267; Rejai, *The Strategy of Political Revolution*, 23; and Alinsky, *Rules for Radicals*, 24–47.

51. Peter Prengaman, "Immigrant Groups Prepare for Reform Push," Associated Press, November 16, 2006.

52. Carolina Ann, Rachael Uranga, Lisa Friedman, and Brent Hopkins, "Immigrant Rights Advocates Planning Next Step after Boycott," *Inland Valley Daily Bulletin*, May 3, 2006.

53. Armando Navarro, NAHR Washington, D.C. Mobilization Proposal, November 14, 2006.

54. Nicole Gaouette, "Latino Lawmakers Still Haven't Made Up," *Los Angeles Times*, March 7, 2007.

55. Peter Prengaman, "Immigration Reform Coalitions Rejoin, Call for Consumer Boycott," Associated Press, August 30, 2007.

56. Jorge Morales Almada, "Rotundo fracas del boicot en LA," *La Opinion*, September 13, 2006.

57. Jorge Morales Almada, "Dia Nacional de Accion, el primer paso," *La Opinion*, September 13, 2006.

58. Jennifer Delson, "Sanctuary Status is Urged for Santa Ana," *Los Angeles Times*, July 6, 2007.

59. Ester J. Cepeda, "Chicago Became a Sanctuary City in March 2006," *Chicago Sun-Times*, August 29, 2007.

60. Alinsky, *Rules for Radicals*, 51.

61. Rachel Uranga, "Organizers of L.A. March Plan More Activity," *San Bernardino County Sun*, July 29, 2006.

62. Rachel L. Swarns and Randal Archibold, "Immigrant Movement Struggles to Regain Momentum Built in Spring Marches," *New York Times*, September 11, 2006.

63. Swarns and Archibold, "Immigrant Movement Struggles to Regain Momentum Built in Spring Marches."

64. Swarns and Archibold, "Immigrant Movement Struggles to Regain Momentum Built in Spring Marches."

65. NAHR press release, "Statewide Mobilization for Peace in Iraq, Immigration Reform, and Peace among the Divergent Ethnic and Racial Communities," March 1, 2007; Alejandro Cano, "Enlazadas a favor de la paz," *La Opinion*, March 18, 2007; Charlotte Hsu, "Illegal Immigration Fires up Both Sides," *San Bernardino County Sun*, March 18, 2007; and Chris Richard, "Speaker Calls for Reform at Rally," *Press Enterprise*, March 18, 2007.

66. Jonathan Abrams, "Free Speech Has Unfair Price, Activists Say," *Los Angeles Times*, May 17, 2007; Robert Rogers, "Dissenters Protest Bill," *San Bernardino County Sun*, May 17, 2007; and Duane W. Gang, "Fee for March in San Bernardino Riles Activists," *Press Enterprise*, May 16, 2007.

67. Randal C. Archibold, "Immigrant Rights Rallies Smaller Than Last Year," *New York Times*, May 2, 2007.

68. Alex Meneses Miyashita, "Pro-immigrant Groups Rally in Cities, Towns, across the United States," *Hispanic Link* 25, no. 19 (May 7, 2007).

69. Prengaman, "Immigration Reform Coalitions Rejoin, Call for Consumer Boycott."

70. Christopher Weber, "Solidarity with Elvira," Associated Press, August 26, 2007.

Epilogue

1. Anwar Iqbal, "Food Crisis May Lead to Wars, Riots: Experts Say," April 14, 2008, www.dawn.com.

2. Tom A. Peter, "As Dollar Falls, Migrants Feel Pinch," *Christian Science Monitor*, January 29, 2008.

3. Found on Yahoo Internet News Site, Veronica Smith, "With US in Crisis, Global Economy in Peril: IMF," www.news.yahoo.com/s/afp/20080409/ts_afp/imfecononygrowthforcast_080409160213&…, April 9, 2008.

4. Found on Yahoo Internet News Site, Jeannine Aversa, "IMF Sees US Falling Into Recession," www.news.yahoo.com/s/ap/20080409/ap_on_bi_ge/world_economic_outlook&printer—;_…, April 9, 2008.

5. Justin Fox, "The Bear Trap," *Time*, March 31, 2008.

6. Fox, "The Bear Trap."

7. *People's Weekly World*, "Oil Company Profits Soar," November 11, 2005, www.pww.org.

8. David Welna, "Oil Executives Defend Profits to Congress," *NPR*, April 13, 2008, npr.org.

9. Daniel J. Weiss and Nick Kong, "Big Oil Feasts on Economic Woes," *Center for American Progress*, February 5, 2008, www.americanprogress.org.

10. Welna, "Oil Executives Defend Profits to Congress."

11. Hal Netkin, "Farmers Have no Access to Plenty of Field Hands," *Arizona Daily Star*, April 9, 2008.

12. Kirk Mitchell, "Farmers Get Help From Inmates," *Denver Post*, July 11, 2007.

13. Found on Breitbart.com Internet Website, Martin Crutsinger, "Factory Jobs: 3 Million Lost Since 2000," www.breitbart.com/print.php?id—D80KGR408&show_article—1, April 20, 2008.

14. Martin Crutsinger, "Factory Jobs: 3 Million Lost Since 2000," Associated Press, April 20, 2007.

15. See my book for an in-depth examination of this argument: Armando Navarro, *La Raza Unida Party: A Chicano Challenge to the U.S. Two Party Dictatorship* (Philadelphia: Temple University Press, 2000), chapter 1.

16. Gary Weiss, "Are You Paying for Corporate Fat Cats?" *Parade*, April 13, 2008.

17. Jorge Morales Almada and J. Emilio Flores, "Abandonados en medio del desierto," *La Opinion*, March 25, 2008.

18. Casper Weinberger & Peter Schweizer, *The Next War* (Washington, D.C.: Regnery Publishing, Inc., 1996), 163–213.

19. One major exception is Patrick Buchanan, who in his newly published book *The Day of Reckoning* (New York: St. Martin's Press, 2007), argues that the United States as a nation-state is coming apart at the seams. He writes, "Pax Americana has come to a close. Gone now is all the hubristic chatter of an American Empire. Gone is the 'unipolar world' where the United States was the undisputed hegemonic power" (13).

20. Center for Arms Control and Non-Proliferation, February 20, 2008. Cited in www.globalissues.org.

21. Robert Pollin and Heidi Garrett-Peltier, "The Wages of Peace," *The Nation*, March 31, 2008.

22. David M. Herszenhorn, "War Cost Proves Hard to Figure," *New York Times News Service*, March 19, 2008.

23. Smith, "With US in Crisis, Global Economy in Peril: IMF."

24. Buchanan, *Day of Reckoning*, 10.

25. Samuel P. Huntington, *Who Are We? The Challenges to America's National Identity* (New York: Simon & Schuster, 2004). Refer to chapter nine for comprehensive examination of this argument.

26. Buchanan, *Day of Reckoning*, 8.

27. Aviva Chomsky, *"They take Our Jobs!" and 20 Other Myths About Immigration*, (Boston: Beacon Press, 2007). See book for examination of 20 myths.

28. Executive Office of the President, Office of Economic Advisors, "Immigration's Economic Impact," June 20, 2007.

29. 500 Economists on The Independent Institute Letterhead sent, "Open Letter on Immigration to President Bush and US members of Congress, no date provided.

30. Found on Catholic Charities Internet website, "The Myths Surrounding Immigration," www.ccspm.org/myths_immigration.aspx, no date provided.

31. Nicole C. Brambila, "Economic Benefits of Valley Undocumented Outweigh Costs," *Desert Sun*, December 10, 2006.

32. Phil Kerpen, "Nativism and the Immigration Issue," *San Diego Union-Tribune*, October 17, 2005.

33. Lori Montgomery, "Immigration Lifts Wages, Report Say," *Washington Post*, June 21, 2007.

34. Giovanni Peri, "How Immigrants Affect California Employment and Wages," *Public Policy Institute of California: California Counts*, Volume 8, Number 3, February 2007, 2.

35. Found on Immigrant's List: The Immigration Debate Website, "The Immigration Debate: Myths Vs. Facts," www.immigrantlist.org/pages/myths_vs_facts.

36. Found on Center for American Progress Internet Website, "Reality Check: Debunking the Myths About Immigration that Misinform Americans," www.americanprogress.org/issues/2007/06/reality_check_immigration html/print, June 12, 2007.

37. Found on the Contemporary Perspectives on Immigration: ten Myths About Immigration, "Contemporary Perspectives on Immigration," www.lib.umn,edu/ihrc/immigration/2007/11/ten_myths_about_immigration.html.

38. Found on Immigrant Workers freedom Coalition Internet Website, stats sited from National Immigration Forum http:www.iwfr.org/fact.asp

39. Found on Center for American Progress Internet Website, "Reality Check: Debunking the Myths About Immigration that Misinform Americans."

40. Office of the President, Council of Economic Advisors report titled "Immigration's Economic Impact," June 20, 2007, 2.

41. *New York Times*, as cited in the *Immigrant's List*, "The Immigration Debate, Myths versus Facts in 2007."

42. The Immigration Policy Center as cited in the *Immigrant's List*, "The Immigration Debate, Myths versus Facts in 2007."

43. Teresa Watanabe, "Immigrants Boost Pay, Not Prison Polulations, New Studies Show, *Los Angeles Times,* February 28, 2007.

44. Susy Buchanan and David Holthouse, "Shoot, Shovel, Shut," Southern Poverty Law Center Intelligence Report, Spring 2007, Issue 126, 44-47.

45. Associated Press, "Report Links Hate Groups, Anti-immigration Activism," March 3, 2008.

46. Nicole Gaouette, "Strict Bills Ahead on Immigration," *Los Angeles Times*, March 5, 2008.

47. Gaouette, "Strict Bills Ahead on Immigration."

48. Randal C. Archibold, "Arizona Losing Immigrants," *Press Enterprise,* (New York Times News Service), February 17, 2008.

49. "Buffers" refer to those individuals or organizations that perpetuate the internal colonialism of Aztlan's *barrios* and *colonias* by not pressing for major social change. They propose rather limited and nonthreatening change or reforms to the social order and do not challenge its authority or legitimacy. They seldom resort strategically to polarizing nonconventional methods. Most adhere to identity politics when expedient. However, their cardinal political leadership role is to buffer, meaning absorb or neutralize conflict or other social change threats emanating from the colonized. From a cultural perspective, they are acculturated pluralist, and ideologically they are liberal capitalist. Navarro, *Mexicano Political Experience in Occupied Aztlán* (Walnut Creek, Calif.: Alta Mira Press, 2005), 11–12.

50. Dowell Myers and Manuel Pastor, "Don't Forget Immigration Reform," *Los Angeles Times*, March 22, 2008.

51. Bret Schulte, "A Balancing Act," *U.S. News & World Report,* March 24/31, 2008, 38–39.

Index

About the Author

Armando Navarro is a political scientist and professor of ethnic studies at the University of California, Riverside. He received his AA degree in political science from Chaffey Community College; BA in political science from Claremont McKenna College in 1970; and his Ph.D. in political science from the University of California, Riverside. His areas of teaching specialization include Mexicano/ Latino Politics, social movements, United States politics, and contemporary issues.

Professor Navarro is the author of several books that include *Mexican American Youth Organization: Avant-Garde of the Chicano Movement in Texas*, published by the University of Texas Press (1995); *The Cristal Experiment: A Chicano Struggle for Community Control*, published by the University of Wisconsin Press (1998); *La Raza Unida Party: A Chicano Challenge to the U.S. Two-Party Dictatorship*, published by Temple University Press (2000); and *Mexicano Political Experience in Occupied Aztlán: Struggles and Change*, published by Alta Mira Press (2005). He is currently working on his fifth book, tentatively entitled *What Needs To Be Done? The Building of a New Movement* scheduled for completion late 2009.

Professor Navarro has also authored numerous articles, book chapters, monographs, and reports. The topics have included Chicano/Latino politics, Chicano political history, redistricting, community organizing, immigration, education, and the Los Angeles Eruption (riots) of 1992.

Professor Navarro is the founder and former director of the Ernesto Galarza Applied Research Center at the University of California, Riverside. As an organic intellectual, he brings to academia forty years of experience of advocacy activism in dealing with a myriad of local, state, national, and international social justice, human rights, and social change issues that affect Latinos. Internationally, he has led, facilitated, and participated in numerous delegations to Latin America, specifically Cuba, Mexico, Central America, and Venezuela.

As a result of his scholarship and advocacy activism, Professor Navarro has gained widespread visibility and recognition both domestically and internationally.